Church, Faith and Culture in the Medieval West

General Editor: Brenda Bolton

About the series

In the last generation an important transformation has taken place in the study of the Medieval Church in the Latin West. This new focus has moved away from a narrow concentration on single religious themes to introduce a greater cultural awareness. Recent cross-disciplinary studies on the Church's rules on consanguinity provide a case in point while other research has benefited from theological, political or literary perspectives.

This new Ashgate series, *Church, Faith and Culture in the Medieval West* will contain some of the most innovative work from this area of current research and will be drawn not only from more established scholars but also from those who are younger. The series, therefore, will contribute much new work, approaching the subject either vertically throughout the period from c.400 to c.1500 or horizontally throughout the whole of Christendom. The series is conceived as primarily monographic but will also include some collected essays on themes of particular relevance and the significance of individuals. The aim will be to draw authors from a range of disciplinary backgrounds, but all will share a commitment to innovation, analysis and historical accuracy.

About the volume

The year 2000 witnessed the 900th anniversary of the birth of Adrian IV, the only Englishman to sit on the papal throne. His short pontificate of four and a half years, distracted by crisis and controversy and followed as it was by an 18-year schism, could be judged a low point in the history of the papacy. The studies in this book challenge the view that Adrian was little more than a cipher, the tool of powerful factions in the Curia. Relations with the Empire, the Norman kingdom and the Patrimony are all radically reassessed and the authenticity of 'Laudabiliter' reconsidered. At the same time, the spiritual, educational and devotional contexts in which he was operating are fully assessed; his activities in Catalonia and his legatine mission to Scandanavia are examined in the light of recent research, and his special relationship with St Albans is explored through his privileges to this great abbey. These studies by leading scholars in the field, together with the introductory chapter by Christopher Brooke, reveal an active and engaged pope, reacting creatively to the challenges and crises of the Church and the world. This is the first large-scale work on Adrian since 1925, and is supported by a substantial appendix of relevant sources and documents in translation.

Church, Faith and Culture in the Medieval West

General Editor: Brenda Bolton

Other titles in the series:

Adrian IV The English Pope (1154–1159)

Adrian IV grants a privilege to Abbot Leonate and the monks of S. Clemente a Casauria (Paris, Bibliothèque Nationale, MS. Lat. 5411, *Chronicon Casauriensis*, fol. 253r)

Adrian IV The English Pope (1154–1159)

Studies and Texts

Edited by

BRENDA BOLTON
University of London, UK

ANNE J. DUGGAN
King's College London, UK

ASHGATE

Published by
Ashgate Publishing Limited
Gower House
Croft Road
Aldershot
Hampshire GU11 3HR
England

Ashgate Publishing Company
Suite 420
101 Cherry Street
Burlington, VT 05401-4405
USA

BX 1225
.A27
2003

i 0754607089

Ashgate website: http://www.ashgate.com

British Library Cataloguing in Publication Data
Adrian IV, the English Pope (1154-1159) : studies and
    texts. - (Church, faith and culture in the medieval West)
    1. Adrian, IV, Pope 2. Popes - Biography 3. Church history -
    12th century - Sources
    I. Bolton, Brenda II. Duggan, Anne
    282'.092

Library of Congress Cataloging-in-Publication Data
Adrian IV, the English Pope (1154-1159) : studies and texts / edited by Brenda
Bolton and Anne J. Duggan.
        p. cm. -- (Church, faith, and culture in the Medieval West)
    Includes bibliographical references and index.
    ISBN 0-7546-0708-9 (hardback : alk. paper)
        1. Adrian IV, Pope, d. 1159. I.Bolton, Brenda. II. Duggan, Anne. III. Series.

BX1225 .A27 2002
282'.092--dc21
[B]
                                                                    2002074436

ISBN 0 7546 0708 9

Printed and bound in Great Britain by MPG Books Ltd, Bodmin, Cornwall

Contents

ii. Privileges and Charters

Preface

The nine-hundredth anniversary of the birth *c.* 1100 at Abbots Langley, Hertfordshire, of Nicholas Breakspear, who was to become Pope Adrian IV, was celebrated in a conference at St Albans on 15 July 2000, attended by some two hundred participants from the United Kingdom, the United States of America, Italy, and Norway. Its focus was the world and legacy of the only Englishman to sit on the papal throne.

Of the five papers originally presented, four are published here in a substantially extended form; and a further five have been specially written for this volume, in order to extend its range and depth. And, since this pontificate has been largely neglected in recent historical scholarship, a substantial collection of Latin sources, with English translations and scholarly apparatus, has been appended, to provide more ready access to the materials upon which a proper evaluation of Adrian's reign depends.

For the support given to the organization of the conference, the editors wish to acknowledge the contribution of the Newman Association, the St Albans' Christian Study Centre, the Ecclesiastical History Society, and the St Albans and Hertfordshire Architectural and Archaeological Society. In particular, they wish to thank the organizing committee for its untiring enthusiasm in arranging and overseeing the whole celebration. One crucially important member of the original team, Mr James Corbett, local historian and author, died in late 1999, without seeing the project come to fruition. In some ways, this volume is a tribute to him.

For the frontispiece, they thank Professor Susan Boynton of Columbia University for obtaining the transparency from which the illustration was developed, and the Bibliothèque Nationale Française (Paris) for permission to publish the image.* Finally, they gratefully acknowledge the generous grant awarded by the Isobel Thornley Bequest of the University of London.

*See Laurent Feller, 'Le cartulaire-chronique de San Clemente a Casauria', *Les cartulaires*, Actes de la Table ronde organisée par l'École nationale des chartes et le G.D.R. 121 du C.N.R.S. (Paris, 5–7 décembre 1991), ed. O. Guyotjeannin, L. Morelle et M. Parisse, Mémoires et documents de l'École des chartes, 39 (Paris, 1993), 261–77; Elizabeth Bradford Smith, 'Models for the extraordinary: Abbot Leonate and the Facade of San Clemente a Casauria', *Medioevo: i modelli*, Atti del Convegno internazionale di studi, Parma, 27 settembre–1 ottobre, 1999 (Milan, 2002), 463–76.

Contributors

Anders Bergquist: Formerly Canon Residentiary of the Cathedral and Abbey Church of St Albans and Ministerial Development Officer of the St Albans Diocese.

Brenda Bolton: formerly Senior Lecturer in History, University of London, Westfield College.

Christopher N. L. Brooke: Dixie Professor Emeritus of Ecclesiastical History, University of Cambridge and Fellow of Gonville and Caius College.

Anne J. Duggan: Professor of Medieval History, University of London, King's College.

Christoph Egger: Assistant Professor, University of Vienna and the Institut für Österreichische Geschichtsforschung.

Damian J. Smith: University of Birmingham and the Universitat Pompeu Fabra, Barcelona.

Susan E. Twyman: Lecturer, Faculty of Continuing Education, University of London, Birkbeck College.

Abbreviations

*	Sources marked with an asterisk are found in Part II
AHP	*Archivum Historiae Pontificiae*
BIHR	*Bulletin of the Institute of Historical Research* (now *Historical Research*)
BL	British Library
Boso, *Vita Adriani*	*Le Liber Pontificalis*, ed. L. Duchesne, Bibliothèque des Écoles françaises d'Athènes et de Rome, 2nd ser. 3, 2nd edn, 3 vols (Paris, 1955–7), ii, 388–97
Brixius	J. M. Brixius, *Die Mitglieder des Kardinalkollegiums von 1130–1181* (Berlin, 1912)
CCCM	*Corpus Christianorum, Continuatio Mediaevalis* (Turnhout, 1953–)
Codex	*Codex Iustinianus*
Decretum	*Decretum Gratiani; Corpus Iuris Canonici*, ed. E. Friedberg, i (Leipzig 1879)
DHGE	*Dictionnaire d'histoire et de géographie ecclésiastiques*, ed. A. Baudrillart, A. de Meyer, E. van Cauwenbergh, and R. Aubert (Paris, 1912–)
Digest	*The Digest of Justinian*, ed. Theodor Mommsen and Paul Krueger, English translation, ed. by Alan Watson, 4 vols (Philadelphia, 1985)
DNB	*Dictionary of National Biography*, ed. L. Stephen and S. Lee (66 vols, London, 1885–1901; repr. 22 vols, Oxford, 1921–2)
Duggan, *Decretals and the 'New Law'*	Charles Duggan, *Decretals and the Creation of New Law in the Twelfth Century: Judges, Judgements, Equity and Law*, Variorum (Aldershot, 1998)
EEA	*English Episcopal Acta* (Oxford, for the British Academy)
EHR	*English Historical Review*
GC	*Gallia Christiana* (nova), 16 vols (Paris, 1715–1865; repr. Farnborough, 1970)
Gesta abbatum	*Gesta abbatum monasterii Sancti Albani, a Thoma Walsingham... compilata*, 3 vols, in *Chronica monasterii S. Albani*, ed. H. T. Riley, 12 vols in 7, RS 28 (London, 1863–76), 4/i–iii (1867–9)
Giraldus Cambrensis	*Giraldi Cambrensis Opera*, i–iv, ed. J. S. Brewer; v–vii, ed. James F. Dimock; viii, ed. George F. Warner, RS 21 (London, 1861–91)
Heads of Religious Houses	*Heads of Religious Houses, England and Wales*, i, *940–1216*, ed. D. Knowles, C. N. L. Brooke and V. C. M. London (2nd edn, Cambridge, 2001)

Institutes	*Justinian's Institutes*, trans. Peter Birks and Grant McLeod (with the Latin text of Paul Krueger) (Ithaca, New York, 1987); cf. J. A. C. Thomas, *The Institutes of Justinian, Text, Translation and Commentary* (Amsterdam/Oxford, 1975)
Italia Pontificia	P. F. Kehr, *Italia Pontificia*, Regesta Romanorum pontificum, 10 vols. in 8: i–viii (Berlin, 1906–35; repr. 1961); ix, ed. W. Holtzmann (Berlin, 1962); x, ed. D. Girgensohn (Zurich,1975)
JL	P. Jaffé, *Regesta Pontificum Romanorum ad annum 1198*, ed. S. Loewenfeld, F. Kaltenbrunner, and P. W. Ewald, 2 vols (Leipzig, 1885–88)
JohnS, i, ii	*The Letters of John of Salisbury*, i: *The Early Letters*, ed. and trans. W. J. Millor and H. E. Butler, NMT (London, 1955; corr. edn, OMT, Oxford 1986); ii: *The Later Letters (1163–1180)*, ed. and trans. W. J. Millor and C. N. L. Brooke, OMT (Oxford, 1979)
Liber censuum	*Le Liber censuum de l'église romaine*, ed. L. Duchesne *et al.*, 3 vols (Paris, 1889–1952)
Liber Pontificalis	*Liber Pontificalis*, ed. L. Duchesne, Bibliothèque des Écoles françaises d'Athènes et de Rome, 2nd Ser. 3, 2nd edn., 3 vols (Paris, 1955–7)
Mansi	*Sacrorum conciliorum nova et amplissima collectio*, ed. J. D. Mansi, cont. I. B. Martin, L. Petit, 53 vols. (Florence/Venice, 1759–98; Paris, 1901–27; repr. Graz, 1960–61)
MGH	*Monumenta Germaniae Historica, inde ab anno Christi quintesimo usque ad annum millesimum et quingentesimum* (Hanover/Berlin, 1824–)
MGH Constitutiones	*Constitutiones et acta publica imperatorum et regum*, 8 vols (Hanover/Leipzig, 1893–1927) = *MGH Leges* (in 4to), Sectio IV
MGH SRG	*Scriptores rerum Germanicarum in usum scholarum ex Monumentis Germaniae historica separatim editi*, 61 vols (Hanover, *et alibi*, 1839–1935; variously re-edited and reprinted)
MGH SRG, NS	*Scriptores rerum Germanicarum*, New Series (Berlin, 1922–)
MGH SRM	*Scriptores Rerum Merovingicarum* (Hanover, 1885–)
MGH SS	*Scriptores* (in folio), 32 vols in 34 (Hanover, 1826–1934).
Muratori, *Rer. Ital. SS*	*Rerum Italicarum Scriptores*, ed. L. A. Muratori, 25 vols (Milan, 1723-51)
NCE	*New Catholic Encyclopedia*, 2nd edn (New York, 2002).
NMT	Nelson's Medieval Texts
Ohnsorge, *Legaten Alexanders III.*	W. Ohnsorge, *Die Legaten Alexanders III. im ersten Jahrzehnt seines Pontifikats (1159–1169)*, Historische Studien, 175 (Berlin, 1928)

OMT	Oxford Medieval Texts
Partner, *Lands of St Peter*	Peter Partner, *The Lands of St Peter. The Papal State in the Middle Ages and Early Renaissance* (London, 1972)
PL	*Patrologiae cursus completus, series latina* (*Patrologia latina*), 221 vols, ed. J. P. Migne (Paris, 1841–64)
PUE	*Papsturkunden in England*, ed. W. Holtzmann, 3 vols, Abhandlungen...Göttingen, phil.-hist. Klasse, i, NS 25 (Berlin, 1930); ii, 3rd Ser., 14–15 (Berlin 1935–6); iii, 3rd Ser., 33 (Göttingen, 1952)
QF	*Quellen und Forschungen aus italienischen Archiven und Bibliotheken*
Roger of Wendover	Roger of Wendover, *Flores historiarum*, ed. Henry G. Hewlett, 3 vols, RS 84 (London, 1886–9)
RS	Rolls Series: *Rerum Britannicarum Medii Aevi Scriptores, Chronicles and Memorials of Great Britain and Ireland during the Middle Ages, published...under the direction of the Master of the Rolls*, 99 vols (London, 1858–96)
SCH	*Studies in Church History* (London, 1964–).
SChr.	*Sources Chrétiennes*
TRE	*Theologische Realenzyklopädie*
TRHS	*Transactions of the Royal Historical Society*
Vitae abbatum	*Vitae Viginti Trium Abbatum S. Albani* in *Matthaei Paris Monachi Albanenses Angli, Historia Major*, ed. William Wats (London, 1639, repr. 1683), 989–1074
William of Newburgh	William of Newburgh, *Historia Rerum Anglicarum, in Chronicles of the Reigns of Stephen, Henry II, and Richard I*, ed. Richard Howlett, RS 82/i–ii (1884–5)
Zenker	Barbara Zenker, *Die Mitglieder des Kardinalkollegiums von 1130 bis 1159* (Diss. Würzburg, 1964)
ZRG kan. Abt.	*Zeitschrift der Savigny-Stiftung für Rechtsgeschichte, kanonistishe Abteilung*

PART I
The Pontificate of Adrian IV

Chapter 1
Adrian IV and John of Salisbury
Christopher N. L. Brooke

Pope Adrian IV illustrates to a quite exceptional degree the cosmopolitan nature of twelfth-century religious culture. He was born in England, near the western edge of Christendom, yet passed his early maturity in Provence, as canon and abbot of Saint-Ruf at Avignon. As such he was a leading member of one of the most rapidly expanding religious orders, which expressed in a complex of fashions the religious impulses of the age throughout western Christendom. From Saint-Ruf he was called to the centre of the western church, to Rome itself, as cardinal; from there he was sent for a while to the northern frontier, to Scandinavia, on a crucial mission. Finally, in 1154, he was elected pope.

Why it was so cosmopolitan an age is one of the supreme puzzles of medieval history. For the present we are concerned only with the fact. In the late eleventh and early twelfth centuries students in search of the new learning hastened to distant schools whose fame had somehow reached them—to Liège, Laon, Orléans, Montpellier, Arles, and a dozen others; as the century advanced, more and more went to Bologna or Paris from every corner of Europe. Litigants in search of justice or injustice travelled to Rome, or wherever the papal Curia might be found. Pilgrims and crusaders journeyed to many regions, above all to the Holy Land. The love of travel—anyway for a part of humankind—was central to the culture of the age.[1] These adventures started on a remarkable scale in the eleventh century, and perhaps they have never ceased. But at the turn of the twelfth and thirteenth centuries we can discern a certain narrowing of horizons: provincial universities were founded in Oxford and Cambridge and elsewhere, so that students could study without travelling afar—and so forth.

This is not to say that the universal perspectives involved in the twelfth-century renaissance affected every contemporary attitude: far from it. The same period saw a heightening of local awareness, and the development in all manner of ways of local loyalties, as Rees Davies and others have taught us.[2] Between the longer and the shorter view, between local loyalties and the cosmopolitan culture, there were many tensions. What is significant is that they flourished together. Human nature is full of paradoxes, and paradox is close to the heart of historical understanding.

---

[1] On this theme, see C. Brooke, *Europe in the Central Middle Ages*, 3rd edn. (Harlow, 2000), ch. 9; cf. Anne Duggan, 'The New Europeans', in *The Making of Britain: The Middle Ages*, ed. Leslie M. Smith (London, 1985), 23–40.

[2] R. R. Davies, 'The peoples of Britain', I–IV, *TRHS*, 6th series, 4 (1994), 1–20; 5 (1995), 1–20; 6 (1996), 1–23; 7 (1997), 1–24.

Thus if there ever was to be an English pope, the mid-twelfth century was a likely time to encounter him.

The path to Rome

Of Adrian's early life we know very little. His father's name was recorded in Canterbury obituaries as Richard, priest and monk.[3] The only reliable early account is by Cardinal Boso in the official Roman *Liber Pontificalis*; but this is exceedingly terse on his early life—it tells us merely that he was English by birth and in adolescence left his homeland and his family in pursuit of letters, coming to Arles—where in due course he became a canon of Saint-Ruf, then near Avignon, later translated to Valence.[4] Adrian's father was a priest—we cannot be sure he was already in higher orders when his son was born, but it is likely that he was in orders incompatible with legal marriage, so that Adrian was in all probability technically illegitimate (however much his family lived in accordance with some of the accepted social norms of its time and place).[5] There may thus have been special reasons for the cardinal's reticence; but in any case it was not the practice of the authors of papal biographies to record much detail about the pope's early life: one has only to recall the rivers of ink which have flowed in speculation about who Gregory VII's parents were, and where he was a monk, to observe the force of this tradition.[6] Even of Adrian's eminent successor, Cardinal Roland, Alexander III, John Noonan in a celebrated article asked 'Who was Rolandus?' and had much ado to answer his own question.[7] Serious attempts have been made to fill out Boso's summary of Adrian's—or Nicholas Breakspear's—youth by recourse to two English sources: William of Newburgh and Matthew Paris.[8] William tells two highly improbable stories which savour of gossip rather than sober history: he tells us that the young Nicholas was abandoned by his father when he became a monk

---

[3] *JohnS*, ii, 10–11 n. 26, citing Canterbury obits, of which the earliest (in London, BL, Cotton MS Nero C. ix, fol. 5) has been edited by R. Fleming, 'Christchurch's sisters and brothers: an edition and discussion of Canterbury obituary lists', in *The Culture of Christendom: Essays in Medieval History in Commemoration of Denis L. T. Bethell*, ed. M. A. Mayer (London, 1993), 115–53; the ref. to Richard is on 133, under 8 February: 'obiit Ricardus sacerdos et monachus sancti Albani, pater Adriani papae'. I suggested in *JohnS*, ii, 10–11 n. 26, that John's reference to Adrian's mother, 'tormented by cold and hunger', could be to his human mother; but it seems most unlikely that the pope's mother was still alive in 1164, even more unlikely that she was not cared for—if so, the reference is evidently to the English church suffering persecution.

[4] See C. Egger, below, ch. 2, at nn. 9–10.

[5] Cf. C. N. L. Brooke, *The Medieval Idea of Marriage* (Oxford, 1989), ch. 3; C. Egger, below, ch. 2, at n. 16.

[6] For recent views of Gregory's parentage and early life see H. E. J. Cowdrey, *Pope Gregory VII* (Oxford, 1998), 27–9; on his monastic career, see also Brooke, *Europe in the Central Middle Ages* (edn of 2000), 323 n. 15.

[7] J. T. Noonan, 'Who was Rolandus?', in *Law, Church and Society: Essays in Honor of Stephan Kuttner*, ed. K. Pennington and R. Somerville (Philadelphia, 1977), 21–48.

[8] For the sources, see below, Part II/i, nos 3, 6a–b.

at St Albans, had to live on the monastery's daily handouts, and could not afford to go to school. After a harsh rebuke from his father for his idleness, he travelled many hundreds of miles and became a hanger-on at Saint-Ruf, eventually being received as a canon—there is no mention of the schools. Later he became abbot of Saint-Ruf but his canons quarrelled with him, and this led him to frequent visits to the papal Curia, where he became friends with Pope Eugenius III who made him a cardinal. These stories by-pass the two best authenticated features of his early life: the search for the schools of the wandering scholar and the diplomatic skill which Nicholas, as cardinal legate, was to show in reordering the churches of Scandinavia. Viewed critically, both William of Newburgh's tales seem implausible: the kind of stories which might well circulate to explain two very striking puzzles in the career of the only Englishman to become pope: why he fled from St Albans in the first place, and how the abbot of a Provençal house came to be sufficiently well known to an Italian pope to be made a cardinal. The only certain fact about his relations with St Albans are that his father became a monk there, and that Adrian as pope rained privilege after privilege upon the abbey, of which he evidently retained fond memories.[9] As for Saint-Ruf, it was evidently the case that he travelled to the Curia on the business of his house: we have Cardinal Boso's word for it.[10] It is indeed likely that he was involved in serious local problems which demanded papal support. A few years later—while he was pope—the house was moved from the outskirts of Avignon to the neighbourhood of Valence. For a young community to move from site to site was not uncommon—some early Cistercian houses moved two or three times. But for an old established monastery of the fame and prestige of Saint-Ruf to seek a new home was a very rare event. Whatever lay behind it, we can imagine that already in Abbot Nicholas' time there was frequent need to resort to Rome—and no doubt that the abbot's personality and mental and spiritual qualities appealed to the Cistercian Eugenius.[11]

Unlike William of Newburgh, Matthew Paris and the monks of St Albans evidently had access to some genuine information about the family and early life of the pope.[12] The difficulty is that Matthew regularly embroidered his information, and the only facts in his account which we can check are wrong. He tells us his father's name was Robert de Camera, whereas better sources call him Richard;[13] that he was rejected as a postulant monk at St Albans by Abbot Robert, who was elected in 1151, when Nicholas was a cardinal;[14] that he studied in Paris—a natural invention for an imaginative thirteenth-century monk called Paris—and (most excusably) that Saint-Ruf was near Valence when he became a canon there. This

---

[9] See Brenda Bolton, below, ch. 8.

[10] *Vita Adriani,* 388.

[11] See C. Egger, below, ch. 2; U. Vones–Liebenstein, *Saint-Ruf und Spanien* (2 vols, Turnhout, 1996), esp. i, 473–84.

[12] On Paris and his writings, see R. Vaughan, *Matthew Paris* (Cambridge, 1958), esp. 182–9 on the *Gesta abbatum.*

[13] See n. 3 above.

[14] *Heads of Religious Houses,* 67. The autograph MS reads simply 'R.': see ch. 2, n. 8.

trail of error does not inspire confidence in what remains; and yet, ironically, the other details are those most likely to be right. He gives his father the surname 'de Camera'—which perhaps suggests he was a clerk in the abbot's chamber[15]—tells us that his surname was 'Brekespere', and that he came from Abbots Langley, which fits well with the idea that Adrian's father was in the abbot's employment. For Matthew undoubtedly had access to good information on the period from the late eleventh century on, from the roll of Adam the Cellarer.[16] When he lacked this guidance, he made nonsense of the history of the abbey in the tenth and eleventh centuries; and even when he came to the accession of Abbot Paul in 1077, he succeeded in converting the nephew of the Lombard Archbishop Lanfranc into a Norman.[17] Thus the combination of genuine and false information is what we would expect—and find; and only on a few local details, such as Langley and the Camera, is he likely to be correct.

There is one other English witness who brings us much nearer to Adrian than William of Newburgh or Matthew Paris could do, and that is John of Salisbury. John's career, like Adrian's, is a model illustration of the cosmopolitan culture of the age. Between 1136 and 1147 he was a student in the schools of France, mainly (it seems) in Paris; between 1147 and 1161 he was in the service of Theobald,

---

[15] If it existed as early as this. The *Gesta abbatum*, i, 107, attributes the construction of 'camere abbatis' to Abbot Ralph (1146–51), much too late for 'Richard de Camera'. R. L. Poole, 'The Early Lives of Robert Pullen and Nicholas Breakspear...', repr. in Poole, *Studies in Chronology and History* (Oxford, 1934), 287–97, at 292, took 'de Camera' to refer to the king's chamber; but the links with Langley and St Albans suggest that Richard was in the abbot's rather than the king's service. By the thirteenth century the 'camera abbatis' both as a room or dwelling and as a financial institution seems to have been well established in some at least of the old Benedictine houses. A good example is Peterborough: in *The White Book of Peterborough*, ed. S. Raban, Northants Record Soc. 2001, no. 14, the 'camera abbatis' is a financial institution, in no. 15 it is a room. But I have not found, even at Peterborough, an earlier use of the phrase than the 1220s (*Carte Nativorum: A Peterborough Abbey Cartulary of the Fourteenth Century*, ed. C. N. L. Brooke and M. M. Postan, Northants Record Soc. [1960], no. 538). W. Dugdale, *Monasticon Anglicanum* (edn of 1817–30), ii, 37, has reference to four servants in the 'camera abbatis' at Evesham, apparently in the 1090s. (Professor Jane Sayers has kindly told me that this text will form an appendix in her forthcoming edition of the *Evesham Chronicle of Thomas of Marlborough* in OMT.) Nonetheless, separate financial arrangements for the abbot's side of a monastery's finance were clearly made necessary by the practice of the early Norman kings, especially William II, of keeping monasteries vacant and enjoying their revenues, and it is likely that a miniature version of the royal *camera* existed at St Albans in the early twelfth century.

Matthew's reference to (Abbot's) Langley (which may be confirmed by a garbled entry in one of the Canterbury obituaries: see *JohnS*, ii, 10–11 n.) may seem in conflict with Boso, who derives the family 'de castro' of St Albans. But it seems very likely that if the abbot had an able clerk in his chamber, he would endow him with one of the abbey's livings not far away, such as Abbots Langley.

[16] Vaughan, *Matthew Paris*, 182–5.

[17] For the abbots of St Albans, see *Heads of Religious Houses*, 64–7, 254–5. For Abbot Paul, see also *The Monastic Constitutions of Lanfranc*, 2nd edn, ed. D. Knowles and C. N. L. Brooke (OMT, 2002), xxxiii–iv and nn. 23–4.

archbishop of Canterbury—one of Theobald's chief legal advisers and in particular his representative in the papal Curia, attending Theobald at the papal council at Reims in 1148, and crossing the Alps ten times on his visits to the Curia in Italy.[18] In the course of these visits he met Adrian on several occasions and became quite intimate with him, and so we have a series of tantalizing vignettes of the English pope from the uniquely gifted pen of John of Salisbury—tantalizing, because he failed to leave a full-length sketch of his friend for us to enjoy; all the more tantalizing, because it is highly probable that he intended to make Adrian the central character of his reminiscences of the papal court, his *Historia pontificalis*, which breaks off (in the only surviving manuscript) in the early 1150s without any mention of Cardinal Nicholas, still less of Pope Adrian.[19] John and Nicholas may have met at Reims in 1148;[20] they were probably at the Curia together at the turn of 1149 and 1150, when Nicholas became cardinal bishop of Albano, and again in the summer of 1150, when John visited the Curia in Apulia.[21] At the turn of 1150 and 1151, they undoubtedly met at Ferentino, and from then on we may map their friendship in a series of texts from John's letters.

1. 'I continually recall with joy and exultation', John wrote to Adrian in the mid- or late 1150s, 'the words which proceeded from your lips, when at Ferentino you gave me your own ring and belt as a pledge of things to come'.[22] Thus we may securely date the intimacy between Nicholas and John to the turn of 1150 and 1151, at Ferentino. As for the 'things to come', they may have implied the hope for promotion from the pope which all his clerical friends doubtless harboured, John not least; but he can hardly have foreseen at Ferentino that Adrian would shortly be pope: the embassy to Scandinavia and the pontificate of Anastasius IV had to intervene.

2. At the turn of 1155 and 1156 John spent three months at the Curia in Benevento. He tells us this much in the *Policraticus*; and in the *Metalogicon*, in describing what must have been the same visit, he tells us that the pope made him sit at his own table and share his own cup and dish at dinner—and that he gave him a ring to pass on to the English king in token of his grant of Ireland 'in hereditary right' to Henry II.[23] But John went north to France and England in the spring of 1156 to face a hurricane of royal anger.[24] The ground of this crisis is

---

[18] *JohnS*, i, 253–6.

[19] C. N. L. Brooke, 'Aspects of John of Salisbury's *Historia Pontificalis*', in *Intellectual Life in the Middle Ages: Essays presented to Margaret Gibson*, ed. L. Smith and B. Ward (London, 1992), 185–95, at 189.

[20] John was certainly there: for the likelihood that Nicholas was too, see below, ch. 2, at n. 50.

[21] *JohnS*, i, 253–5. Nicholas signs papal privileges from 30 January 1150 to 21 February 1152 (*JL*, ii, 20). Later in 1152 he went to Scandinavia as legate.

[22] *JohnS*, i, 90 (no. 52), 255; cf. *Policraticus*, vi.24 (ed. C. C. J. Webb, Oxford, 1909), ii, 69; *JohnS*, ii, 650–1 and n. 3 (no. 289).

[23] For Benevento, see *Policraticus*, vi.24, ed. Webb, ii, 67; *Metalogicon*, iv. 42, ed. J. B. Hall and K. S. B. Keats-Rohan, *CCCM* 98 (Turnhout, 1991), 183; *JohnS*, i, 256.

[24] *JohnS*, i, 257–8, alleged he was back in England by July 1156; this is corrected by

most fully explained by John in his letter 19 written in the autumn of 1156; most fully, but not most clearly, for the letter was addressed to his closest friend, Abbot Peter of Celle, the supreme master of allusive, elusive letter writing of the century, whose letters have at last been brought into the light of day in Julian Haseldine's fine edition.[25] Peter's letters were not intended to be understood by a modern audience, and John tended when writing to him to imitate his mannerisms. When called on to explain the intricacies of a legal case (as in many of his early letters) John can be lucidity itself: his masterly letter 131 on the marriage litigation of the Anstey case is a good example. But when playing with his friends—and especially with Abbot Peter—he can be very obscure; and Janet Martin's studies of his use of classical sources has taught us not to assume he was always truthful.[26] What seems to have happened is that his visit to the Curia coincided with the visit of envoys sent by Henry II to greet the new pope—and win concessions from him. The royal embassy comprised the bishops of Évreux, Le Mans, and Lisieux and the abbot of St Albans; and John's role is nowhere explicitly stated.[27] It seems clear that in all his visits to the Curia he went as Theobald's *alter ego*, and there is no doubt, as we shall see, that the handling of appeals from the archbishop's court to the pope was a major part of John's task in these months. But if the pope saw fit to give John the token ring, we must surely assume that John was also in some sense acting as royal envoy—or at least, that the pope chose to treat him as such. John evidently had a crucial part to play in Theobald's plans for enforcing his will on the English church and the English king. Theobald has been strangely underestimated by most historians; yet there can be no doubt of his towering achievement. Before 1154 he worked to restore unity in a divided kingdom; and so far as that affected the church, his efforts were consummated when he could witness the promotion of his own archdeacon to the archbishopric of York shortly followed by Henry II's accession in 1154.[28] As archbishop of Canterbury and legate for the whole kingdom, he promoted relations with the papacy; and John's letters written on his behalf show a steady flow of appeals to Rome passing most of the time without many hints of royal disfavour—they are the supreme surviving evidence of the critical importance of the 1150s in the growth of appeals to the Curia. But in Henry II Theobald had a mercurial, unpredictable, wilful, and exceedingly powerful royal master. The letters of John of Salisbury are a unique witness to the way in which

Anne Duggan, below, ch. 9, n. 49. In fact, he was evidently in France with Theobald in the spring of 1156, when letters 6–11 were drafted in Theobald's name. On the crisis, see esp. G. Constable, 'The alleged disgrace of John of Salisbury in 1159', *EHR*, 69 (1954), 67–76.

[25] *The Letters of Peter of Celle*, ed. and trans. J. Haseldine (OMT, Oxford, 2001).

[26] J. Martin, 'John of Salisbury as classical scholar', in *The World of John of Salisbury*, ed. M. Wilks (*Studies in Church History*, Subsidia 3, Oxford, 1984), 179–201, esp. 191–6 on his re-writing of ancient texts and manufacture of 'pseudo-antiques'.

[27] *Gesta abbatum*, i, 125–9, esp. 126.

[28] On Roger's early career, see now *EEA* 20, ed. M. Lovatt (2000), xxiii–xxviii. On Theobald's role as the preserver of unity, see esp. *JohnS*, i, no. 116, 190–2; cf. *JohnS*, i, xxv–xxvi; A. Morey and C. N. L. Brooke, *Gilbert Foliot and his Letters* (Cambridge, 1965), 88–95.

Theobald managed Henry—so that appeals flowed to Rome and at least one of Theobald's candidates was successful in the election to a bishopric.[29] Theobald attempted to manage Henry most effectively by planting his archdeacon, Thomas Becket, on him as royal chancellor: John's letters give us a vivid insight into the difficulties and ambiguities of Becket's position.[30] But there is no doubt that in the main Theobald was successful. It seems likely that he cast John for the same role in relations with the pope, especially after the election of Adrian IV, with whom John was already friendly. John was playing an ambiguous part, similar to that of some later envoys who plied between king and pope. In the 1340s William Bateman was a leading judge in the papal Curia at Avignon; but he was also prepared from time to time to act on behalf of Edward III of England—and he played the game with such finesse that when Clement VI provided him to the see of Norwich in 1344, he was welcomed by the king and able to act as a leading royal diplomat in the papal court in the years which followed.[31] John of Salisbury was less successful: his letters to Becket show that he had all the subtlety and finesse needed to understand what was expected of such a man; but it may be that he allowed himself to be too much allured by the pope's friendship, to the point that he appeared to be the pope's man, not the king's or the archbishop's—and there is no doubt that he was being spied on by an inveterate enemy. Why Arnulf, bishop of Lisieux, had his knife into John of Salisbury is quite unclear; but we need not doubt John's word that it was so. And Arnulf was also at Benevento.

'After I returned from the Church of Rome,' wrote John to Abbot Peter,[32] 'Fortune piled on me...a load of bitter troubles.... The indignation of our most serene lord, our all-powerful king...has grown hot against me in full force. If you ask the reason, perhaps I favoured him more than was just, and worked for his advancement with greater vigour than I should; for I sighed for this with all my heart's longing, namely that I might behold him whom I deemed to be kept in exile by the malice of Fortune, reigning by God's mercy on the throne of his fathers....' This at first sight seems perfectly clear: John has suffered for supporting Henry's accession to the English throne—and it has been shrewdly observed by Anne Duggan that this is a thrust at Bishop Arnulf, who had notoriously opposed the claims of Henry's mother, the Empress Matilda, to the throne.[33] But what John

---

[29] *JohnS*, i, nos 117, 120, 128–9, 133, reveal the strenuous efforts of Theobald (and John himself) which lay behind the election of Bartholomew, bishop of Exeter, in 1160–61.

[30] See esp. *JohnS*, i, 221–3 no. 128 (quoted in C. N. L. Brooke, 'John of Salisbury and his world', in *The World of John of Salisbury*, 1–20, at 16–17, repr. in Brooke, *Churches and Churchmen in Medieval Europe* [London, 1999], ch. 14, at 270–1).

[31] On William Bateman, see A. Hamilton Thompson, 'William Bateman, bishop of Norwich, 1344–1355', *Norfolk Archaeology*, 25 (1935), 102–37, esp. 104–9; cf. Brooke, *A History of Gonville and Caius College* (Woodbridge, 1985, corr. repr. 1996), esp. 5–6 and 5 n. 7.

[32] *JohnS*, i, 31–2, no. 19.

[33] Below, ch. 7, n. 176; John of Salisbury, *Historia Pontificalis*, ed. and trans. M. Chibnall (NMT, 1956, repr. OMT, 1986), 83–5; M. Chibnall, *The Empress Matilda* (Oxford, 1991), 75–6; Morey and Brooke, *Gilbert Foliot*, 119–20. For what follows, on

says is also clearly nonsense; how could he have suffered disgrace for supporting Henry's cause in 1154? It only makes sense if we feel the heavy irony of the passage, and consider how else John had supported Henry's claims; and it seems highly probable—though it cannot be certain—that we have here a disguised reference to the pope's gift of Ireland to the king. I fully accept that this was not the published, or perhaps the main, ground of John's disgrace; and I am entirely convinced by Anne Duggan's brilliant demolition of the supposed 'Canterbury plot' to encompass Ireland in the province of Canterbury, and her very subtle and satisfying reconstruction of the documentary history which lies behind the bull *Laudabiliter*. But we have John's word for it that he brought a ring back from Adrian in token of a grant of Ireland: 'On my petition he granted and gave Ireland to Henry the illustrious king of the English, to possess by hereditary right, as his letter bears witness to this day. For all the islands are said to belong to the Roman Church of ancient right, from the donation of Constantine, who founded and endowed it. He sent too a gold ring by me adorned with a splendid emerald, by which might be accomplished investiture of the right to rule over Ireland.'[34] This was based on the assumption that the offshore islands were papal property; and the form of the grant of Ireland was probably repugnant to the king—especially if Anne Duggan is right (as I believe she is) in arguing that the grant Adrian made was conditional on the consent of the Irish. What Henry sought was papal approval for adventure in Ireland; what he received involved a claim that he went there only by permission of a papal overlord. An Englishman of humble origin was claiming that the king was his vassal. The message must have been highly uncongenial, and would of itself be sufficient to explain the king's anger. To a modern observer the whole incident is repugnant: two Englishmen engaged in friendly chat in Benevento took it for granted that it would be to the advantage of the Irish to submit to the English king. The conditions were probably stringent; but they do not excuse Adrian or John, who assumed that they were playing a part in civilizing a barbarous people.[35] It is a very unhappy fact that this was a part of the legacy of the one English pope.

In his letter to Abbot Peter, John went on to give the ostensible grounds of his disgrace. 'This [supporting the king's cause] is not the fault of which I am accused, but innocent as I am, I am charged with a crime far beyond my power to commit.... I alone in all the realm am accused of diminishing the royal dignity. When they define the act of offence more carefully, these are the charges that they hurl upon my head. If anyone among us invokes the name of Rome, they say it is my doing. If the English Church ventures to claim even the shadow of liberty in making elections or in the trial of ecclesiastical causes, it is imputed to me, as if I were the only person to instruct the lord archbishop of Canterbury and the other

Adrian IV and Ireland and the bull *Laudabiliter*, see Anne Duggan, below, ch. 7, part iv; eadem, 'The Making of a Myth: Giraldus Cambrensis, *Laudabiliter*, and Henry II's lordship of Ireland', forthcoming.

[34] *Metalogicon*, iv. 42, ed. Hall and Keats-Rohan (above, n. 23), 183.

[35] For Theobald's view of the Welsh, see. *JohnS*, i, 135–6, no. 87.

bishops what they ought to do...' And so he planned to go into exile—to France or to the Church of Rome.

There is a strange contrast between the freedom of appeals to which John's letters bear witness, and the charges against him confirm, and the angry letter to Theobald attributed to Adrian IV and dated 23 January 1156—at the very time that John was visiting the pope—claiming that Theobald had been obstructing justice, especially to the monks of St Augustine's abbey at Canterbury, and was in the king's pocket.[36] That Theobald reckoned he had been very unfairly treated over the affair of St Augustine's is strongly confirmed by John's letters 8 and 9 written for the archbishop in France in the spring of 1156; and we are always wise to take the rhetoric of twelfth-century ecclesiastics with a pinch of salt.[37] In part, the tone of the letter may reflect John's own efforts to make clear to the English audience that neither he nor the archbishop were truly in the pope's pocket. But the tone of the letter is excessively bitter, and it comes to us from the archives of St Augustine's, an abbey which had no love of archbishops and had shown little conscience about forgery; we should perhaps not rely too securely on its authenticity.[38] But even without this bull, John's letters make it abundantly clear that he and the archbishop had to sail between the Scylla of royal suspicion and the Charybdis of doubts about Theobald and his servants in the papal Curia. The papal schism which followed Adrian's death reveals some of the divisions in the Curia of his time; and John's intimacy with the pope may have made him an object of suspicion in Benevento as well as in Westminster.

3. However this may be, John's letters reveal from time to time both the archbishop's confidence that the pope was friendly to his aims and purposes, and John's assurance in their intimacy. In his letter 50 he writes on behalf of the canons of Merton, relying on the pope's favour towards the canons of his own order, and towards John himself: 'May it profit the brethren of Merton that, while you were in the church of Saint-Ruf their good odour reached even unto you, as your highness used to tell me, your servant, when we talked together'. And most telling of all, the bold (and sadly prophetic) denouement to one of his letters to Adrian: 'May you fare well for ever, father—and bear in mind what all know, but very few declare in your hearing, that "a Roman pontiff cannot long be pope"' (*Romanum pontificem non posse diu pontificari*).[39]

---

[36] Thomas of Elmham, *Historia Monasterii S. Augustini Cantuariensis*, ed. C. Hardwick, RS 8 (London, 1858), 411–13.

[37] See G. Constable, *The Reformation of the Twelfth Century* (Cambridge, 1996), 26. There is an intriguing contrast between the denunciation of the archdeacons of Suffolk and Sudbury in *JohnS*, i, nos 14–15, 46, and the cosy amity of the letters John wrote to the same archdeacons a decade or so later: ii, nos 240, 253.

[38] The classic study of St Augustine's forgeries (attributing the main collection to the late eleventh century) is W. Levison, *England and the Continent in the Eighth Century* (Oxford, 1946), Appendix I; see also S. E. Kelly, ed., *Anglo-Saxon Charters*, IV, *St Augustine's Abbey, Canterbury, and Minster-in-Thanet* (British Academy, 1995).

[39] *JohnS*, i, 76 (no. 41).

4. In a celebrated passage at the end of his *Metalogicon*, John of Salisbury lamented Adrian's death, 'an occasion for weeping for all good people, but for none more so than for me.'[40] Writing in 1167 to Walter, a fellow-Englishman whom Adrian had elevated to his own see as cardinal bishop of Albano, John spoke out. 'Me by a special bond of charity he [Pope Adrian] loved more than any of our fellow-countrymen, and reckoned the chances of my fortune as part and parcel of his own. His affection for me was known to us two and to a few others; had not the fates stolen him prematurely from our midst…it would have been known by now to the world too.'[41] It seems clear that John had expected to become a cardinal. It may have been a pipe dream; but is likely enough that Adrian harboured the idea of promoting another of his fellow-countrymen, and one personally so congenial, who would have been an adornment to the intellectual life of the Curia, and whose experience in the law courts in Canterbury and Rome would have been of considerable practical value. It seems likely that the idea flourished during John's long stay at Benevento in 1155–6. But Adrian—for all the warmth and geniality revealed by John's references to him—was an eminently practical man and a diplomat. When John felt the anger of the English king, Adrian, on uneasy terms with both the emperor and the king of Sicily, could hardly afford to alienate the most powerful of his royal supporters in northern Europe. John's promotion would have to wait for a more favourable season, which the pope's early death postponed *sine die*.

At the outset I portrayed Pope Adrian IV as a representative of a cosmopolitan age and culture. In the promotion of Cardinal Walter and the writings of John of Salisbury we can perceive that Nicholas Breakspear had not forgotten his origins: he liked to have Englishmen about him; he showered privileges on his father's abbey; he gave some encouragement to the English king to subdue Ireland to his rule. In one of the less attractive letters which John wrote for Theobald, a highly prejudiced view of the Welsh was paraded before the English pope in support of Maurice, bishop of Bangor.[42] One sentence is of particular interest: Theobald is made to charge the Welsh that 'they carry on a regular slave trade and sell Christians into foreign parts where they become the captives of the infidels'. It is not at all improbable that this was true—though if so, almost certainly the English were as much involved as the Welsh, for in the eleventh century Bristol had been a notable centre of the slave trade—and it is possible that the prosperity of Bristol and Chester in this age owed something, perhaps even much, to it.[43] But it is piquant

---

[40] *Metalogicon*, iv. 42, ed. Hall and Keats-Rohan, 183 (cf. text at n. 34).

[41] *JohnS*, ii, 434–5 and n. 3 (no. 235); cf. *JohnS*, i, 256; C. Brooke, 'John of Salisbury and his World' (see n. 30), in *The World of John of Salisbury*, ed. M. Wilks, *SCH, Subsidia* 3 (Oxford, 1984), 12; repr. in Brooke, *Churches and Churchmen*, 266.

[42] If indeed *JohnS*, i, no. 87, was addressed to Adrian, which is likely, but not certain.

[43] For Bristol, see Rosalind and Christopher Brooke, *Popular Religion in the Middle Ages* (London, 1984), 106, 164. That Chester was a centre of the slave trade is entirely conjectural; but it has been observed that Bristol and Chester both sprang into prominence as centres of trade at much the same period in the tenth and eleventh centuries.

that the accusation should have been made to the pope in the 1150s, for Adrian himself took a particular interest in the welfare of the unfree.

The question was put to him: can a slave marry? In social custom, it was unthinkable that a slave could take any significant step in life without his lord's consent. But marriage was a sacrament, and any social or legal restriction on the flow of grace was unthinkable. Adrian quite simply quoted Galatians 3: 28: 'There is neither Jew nor Greek, there is neither bond nor free, there is neither male nor female: for ye are all one in Christ Jesus.' Thus Adrian: 'Just as in Christ Jesus there is neither a free man nor a slave, who may be prevented from receiving the sacraments of the Church, so too ought not marriages between slaves to be in any way prevented.'[44] It may be significant that it was a pope from northern Europe who made this judgment—where, even in England, slaves (but not perhaps the slave trade) were very rare or extinct by this date, while the institution flourished still in the south. It may also be that the decretal had little effect in practice for some generations. But it was a noble saying; and it is still the law of the Church.

At the outset I portrayed Adrian IV as a representative figure in a cosmopolitan culture. This is not to deny Adrian IV his own personal qualities and achievements—though one has to say that our evidence about him is in many ways less ample than we should wish. Yet the timely commemoration of him represented by the essays in this volume reminds us that there is still much that concerns him which can be found and interpreted. He emerges as an exceptionally interesting pope, if a little overshadowed by his friend and successor, Roland, Pope Alexander III, who had the fortune to survive his election by over twenty years, four times as long as Adrian—and who would have been buried under the dust of the papal schism if he had only lived five years as pope. Still, Adrian's five years saw notable activity. They will always be remembered for the first breach with Frederick Barbarossa, and an ever deeper involvement in the politics of southern Italy, both of which (through no fault of Adrian's) bore much evil fruit after Adrian's death. For some of us he will be remembered first of all for his friendship with John of Salisbury. Adrian's pontificate was brief—so too was John XXIII's, at the turn of the 1960s and 1970s. We cannot attribute to Adrian the profound reorientation of the Church with which Pope John has often been credited. But Adrian was an exceedingly active pope; his hand was everywhere, even—perhaps especially—at St Albans, from which he sprang. This fine gathering of new learning and of the sources, is a very welcome and timely reminder of a remarkable man, and of his role in a cosmopolitan age.

---

[44] See below, ch. 9, at n. 15. Cf. P. Landau, 'Hadrians IV. Dekretale "Dignum est" (*X.* 4. 9. 1) und die Eheschliessung Unfreier in der Diskussion von Kanonisten und Theologen des 12. und 13. Jahrhunderts', *Studia Gratiana*, 12 (1967) = *Collectanea S. Kuttner*, ii, 511–53; C. N. L. Brooke, *The Medieval Idea of Marriage* (Oxford, 1989), 51–2, 264–5.

Chapter 2

The Canon Regular:
Saint-Ruf in context

Christoph Egger

When the papal chamberlain and cardinal Boso in his continuation of the *Liber Pontificalis* described the early life of Pope Adrian IV, he used nearly biblical language to describe young Nicholas Breakspear's progress from the Benedictine abbey of St Albans in Hertfordshire to the monastery of Augustinian canons regular of Saint-Ruf in Avignon, thus, at least to the medieval reader, suggesting a parallel between the biblical patriarch Abraham and the future pope. As Boso told it, Nicholas left his homeland to improve his education and, while he was pursuing his studies in Arles, he received the religious habit of a canon regular at Saint-Ruf.[1] Apart from the conventionally-phrased reference to his desire to advance his knowledge of 'letters', Boso provided no explanation for Nicholas's departure from England; neither did he record what he studied, or why the young Englishman chose to became an Austin canon in Provence.

To augment this tantalizingly brief summary, one must turn to the more extended treatment provided by two English chroniclers, William of Newburgh and Matthew Paris, who wrote in the late twelfth and mid-thirteenth century respectively, but they are consistent neither with one another nor with Boso.

William of Newburgh, himself an Austin canon, adds important details. He describes Nicholas as a poor young man who made his way 'from the dust' to the very apex of the ecclesiastical hierarchy.[2] His father was a clerk of slender means (*non multae facultatis*), who abandoned the world to become a monk, leaving behind his young son. Although William does not comment on the boy's economic situation, it cannot have been comfortable. There is no record of his early education; but when he reached adolescence, Nicholas was too poor to go to the schools. Instead, he received a daily dole from St Albans. Deeply embarrassed, his father piled verbal abuse upon him. Destitute and alone, and as a freeborn man ashamed 'either to dig or to beg' in England, he went to France. Since he did not prosper in

---

[1] Boso, *Vita Adriani*, 388:* 'Hic namque pubertatis sue tempore, ut in litterarum studia proficeret, egrediens de terra et de cognatione sua, pervenit Arelate, ubi dum scolis vacaret, a Domino factum est ut ad ecclesiam beati Rufi accederet et in ea religionis habitum facta canonica professione susciperet.' This account echoes Gen. 12: 1, 'Dixit autem Dominus ad Abram: egrede de terra tua et de cognatione tua et de domo patris tui...'. For Boso's continuation of the *Liber Pontificalis*, see Odilo Engels, 'Kardinal Boso als Geschichtsschreiber', in idem, *Stauferstudien. Beiträge zur Geschichte der Staufer im 12. Jahrhundert*, ed. Erich Meuthen and Stefan Weinfurter, 2nd edn (Sigmaringen, 1996), 203–24. For the full text of the *Vita*, see below, Part II/i, 'Narrative Sources', no. 1.

[2] William of Newburgh, i, 109.*

France (*cum in Francia minus prosperaretur*),[3] he went to more distant parts, crossing the Rhône to Provence. There he found the distinguished house of canons regular at Saint-Ruf, entered its service, and so commended himself to the brethren that they invited him to take the habit, and later elected him abbot. William does not say that Nicholas studied in 'France', rightly distinguishing between the kingdom of France and the county of Provence, which until the late Middle Ages was a more or less independent territory and at least formally part of the Romano-German Empire.

Writing toward the middle of the thirteenth century, the account of Matthew Paris, monk and chronicler of St Albans, is separated by about fifty years from William's and by more than a century from the early years of Adrian IV's life. This chronological distance is, however, compensated to a considerable extent by the survival at St Albans of much earlier, twelfth-century records, to which Matthew had access when he was compiling his *Gesta abbatum monasterii Sancti Albani*. Among these was the roll of Bartholomew the clerk, which is likely to have been his main source for the history of the abbey until the death of Abbot Robert de Gorron (1166). To this narrative, Matthew occasionally added further information, either incorporated into the text during the process of compilation, or later inserted in the margins of the autograph manuscript.[4]

Matthew's account of Adrian's early life as contained in the chapter describing the deeds of Abbot Robert de Gorron (1151–66),[5] begins with a chrono-logical difficulty, however. Robert presided over St Albans from 1151, when Nicholas was already cardinal bishop of Albano. A close look at the autograph manuscript reveals further interesting details. The account of Adrian's early life was inserted on an erasure in handwriting, which, though it is certainly Matthew Paris's own, is to be dated later than the handwriting of this part of the *Gesta abbatum*. Very probably the erased text was the beginning of the extensive account about St Alban's struggles for the church of Luton,[6] which Matthew added after the Adrian-account in the lower margin of the same column, by doing so securing the uninterrupted continuation of the text in the next column. The handwriting closely resembles that of another addition, containing a reference to a different part of the manuscript, which Matthew wanted to insert here.[7] It thus can be assumed

---

[3] *Ibid.*

[4] London, BL, MS Cotton Nero D. i, For the disentanglement of the several layers in Matthew's *Gesta abbatum*, see Richard Vaughan, *Matthew Paris*, Cambridge Studies in Medieval Life and Thought, NS 6 (Cambridge, 1958), 182–5.

[5] London, BL, MS Cotton Nero D.i, fols 40vb–48vb; cf. *Gesta abbatum*, i, 110–82 (*Vitae abbatum*, 1015–36). For the account of Adrian's origins, see fol. 41ra; *Gesta abbatum*, 112–13 (*Vitae abbatum*, 1016).* For abbot Robert see *Heads of Religious Houses*, 67.

[6] Cotton Nero D.i, fols 41ra–42va; *Gesta abbatum*, i, 113–24 (*Vitae abbatum*, 1016–19).

[7] Cotton Nero D.i, fol. 30vb, lower margin: 'Nota quod beatus Albanus surreptus fuit et restitutus...Cum danorum rabies et cetera. Quere in libro hoc ad signum huic correspondens [drawing of the head of a lion]. Require supra post istoriam de offa rege ante XVI folia'.

that Matthew inserted the account of Adrian's early life from a yet unknown source at some time after he wrote the original text of the *Gesta abbatum*, perhaps as late as 1255.

Another observation concerns the name of the abbot, which in both editions is given as Robert, though the manuscript has only the abbreviation R.[8] It is possible that Matthew Paris himself was not that certain about the chronological setting of Adrian's early life and therefore did not expand the abbreviation found in his source. Other St Albans' abbots, whose names began with an R., include Ralph (1146–51) and Richard (1097–1119). If the abbot who brushed off young Nicholas had indeed been Richard, this would fit much better into Adrian's biography.

The clerk Nicholas, who had been born in a nearby village, approached the abbot, seeking admission to the monastery. As an examination of the candidate produced unsatisfying results, the abbot refused, and told him to attend the schools. Nicholas therefore went to Paris, where he studied most successfully. Afterwards he became a canon of Saint-Ruf near Valence, and finally, after successfully representing his house at the Curia, was nominated cardinal. Matthew committed another inaccuracy here, because Saint-Ruf was still located at Avignon when Nicholas made his profession. The canons moved to Valence some time in Adrian's pontificate—perhaps as late as 1158, and it was he who authorized the transfer from Avignon.[9] It is therefore possible that Matthew's source for this account dates from the later twelfth or early thirteenth century, when Saint-Ruf's location at Valence had become common knowledge.[10] A few lines later Matthew gives another description of the early life of St Albans' famous son. At this point, however, following an account of the death of Anastasius IV and the accession of Adrian IV which he had taken from Robert of Torigny's *Chronicle*,[11] Matthew

Though this note has later been altered, the reference is still correct: in the left margin of fol 25va (old foliation 24va) a drawing of the back of a lion is to be found, which points to a text which begins 'Cum danorum rabies'. The script of this text (fols 25va–26vb) is similar to Matthew's later handwriting, as shown in Vaughan, Matthew Paris, plate IIIb. Cf. *Gesta abbatum*, i, 12–19. Wats, who used Cotton Nero D.i, did not insert the addition into his edition of the *Gesta abbatum*.

[8] 'Huius quoque tempore quidam clericus nomine Nicolaus...venit ad abbatem R., postulans humiliter ...': Cotton Nero D.i, fol 41ra; *Gesta abbatum*, i, 112 (*Vitae abbatum*, 1016).*

[9] See below, n. 63.

[10] See, for instance, Alberic of Troisfontaines, *Chronicon*, ed. P. Scheffer-Boichorst, *MGH SS*, 23 (Hanover, 1874), 842: 'Rome mortuo papa Anastasio fit papa Nicholaus natione Anglicus, qui dictus est Adrianus huius nominis quartus, qui primo fuit abbas canonicorum regularium Sancti Rufi de Valencia, et exinde factus cardinalis ad papam ascendit. The same mistake was made by Bernard Gui: see at n. 44 below.

[11] *Ibid.*, 'Post paucos...Sancti Ruphi in Provincia'; *Chronique de Robert de Torigni abbé du Mont-Saint-Michel suivie de divers opuscules historiques*, ed. L. Delisle, 2 vols (Paris, 1872–3), i, 288. The same source was used at this point in the Annals of Waverley, in: *Annales Monastici*, ed. H. R. Luard, 5 vols, RS 36 (London, 1864–9), ii (1865), 236. It is probably this account, to which Matthew refers when he says: 'Hic Nicolaus, de quo prelibavimus paucula...' *Gesta abbatum*, i, 124 (*Vitae abbatum*, 1019).*

names his father as a certain Robert de Camera,[12] a man of modest learning (*litteratus aliquantulum*) who, after living respectably (*honeste*) in the world, became a monk at St Albans. In contrast with William of Newburgh's version, which made the father responsible for Nicholas's ignominious departure from England, Matthew Paris says that Robert asked the abbot to receive the young man, described as clerk and scholar (*clericus et scholaris*), as monk. But when Nicholas was examined his abilities were found insufficient. Driven by shame, he went away to Provence, where he was made a canon of Saint-Ruf.[13]

Various attempts have been made to reconstruct Adrian's early life from these accounts, whose omissions, silences, and contradictions leave ample space for conjecture and speculation;[14] but a closer examination of these narratives may yet yield new insights into the precise nature of Nicholas Breakspear's relationship with St Albans, the place and character of his higher education, and the circumstances of his entry into the Augustinian abbey of Saint-Ruf.

To begin with his approach to the great Benedictine abbey. In both segments of Matthew Paris's account, emphasis is laid on the abbot's examination of the prospective monk; and in the first, he was advised to go away and study in the schools. Such advice seems strange for a candidate for the monastic life. St Albans had a distinguished school of its own, and there would have been no need for a novice to go outside the monastery to acquire the necessary learning. It might be asked whether Nicholas really wanted to become a monk, as Matthew suggests, or whether his intentions were different. William of Newburgh and Matthew Paris agree in calling Nicholas *adolescens*, an expression usually used for persons aged between approximately 12 and 28 years.[15] Matthew Paris, however, says that he was a clerk (*clericus*),[16] though not a very educated one.[17] It might well have been that what Nicholas was seeking, with his father's support, was not admission to the cloister but nomination to one of the abbey's churches. Appointment to an ecclesi-

[12] For evidence that Nicholas's father was named Richard, not Robert, and that he was both priest and monk, see *JohnS*, ii, 10, n. 26. In the autograph manuscript of the *Gesta abbatum* (Cotton Nero D.i, fol. 42va) 'de Camera' was added in the margin, probably by Matthew himself.

[13] *Gesta abbatum*, i, 125 (*Vitae abbatum*, 1019).*

[14] See, among others, Reginald L. Poole, 'The Early Lives of Robert Pullen and Nicholas Breakspear', in idem, *Studies in Chronology and History*, ed. Austin L. Poole, (Oxford, 1934), 287–97, at 291–5; Richard W. Southern, *Medieval Humanism and Other Studies* (Oxford, 1970), 234–52; Ursula Vones-Liebenstein, *Saint-Ruf und Spanien. Studien zur Verbreitung und zum Wirken der Regularkanoniker von Saint-Ruf in Avignon auf der iberischen Halbinsel (11. und 12. Jahrhundert)*, 2 vols, Bibliotheca Victorina, 6 (Turnhout, 1996), i, 239–56.

[15] William of Newburgh, i, 109:* 'adolescentiam ingressus'; *Gesta abbatum*, i, 112 (*Vitae abbatum*, 1016),* 'aetate adolescens'. See Adolf Hofmeister, 'Puer, Iuvenis, Senex. Zum Verständnis der mittelalterlichen Altersbezeichnungen', in *Papsttum und Kaisertum. Forschungen zur politischen Geschichte und Geisteskultur des Mittelalters. Paul Kehr zum 65. Geburtstag dargebracht*, ed. Albert Brackmann, (München, 1926), 287–316.

[16] *Gesta abbatum*, i, 125 (*Vitae abbatum*, 1019),* 'quidam clericus', 'ipse clericus'.

[17] *Gesta abbatum*, i, 112 (*Vitae abbatum*, 1016),* 'in arte clericali satis supinus'.

astical benefice, especially one involving the *cura animarum*, would have been a much more appropriate occasion for an examination than reception into the monastic community. Clerical celibacy was much less established in the early twelfth century than it was to become, and clerics of all ranks are found with wives or mistresses. At the same time, it was perfectly lawful for clerics in minor orders (below the grade of sub-deacon) to contract valid marriages. Often the sons of clerics embarked upon a clerical career, too. Nicholas's father had been a cleric and perhaps a priest (though he may have been ordained later in life);[18] his brother Ralph was also a cleric, who held a church from Westminster abbey, and later became a regular canon at Missenden. This same Ralph had a son N., who in the early 1170s held a fee from St Albans.[19] The Breakspear family therefore appears to have been a dynasty of clerics and young Nicholas might have wanted to follow this tradition.

According to William of Newburgh, Nicholas was too poor to attend the schools.[20] This would certainly have been the case if he had been denied a benefice by the abbot. It was as a penniless youth, then, that he went first to France (Paris?) and then on to Provence, to improve his clerkly skills, and with them his chances of preferment. It was a path which many ambitious young clerks were to tread in the twelfth century, although their beginnings may have been more auspicious than his. At any rate, Boso, William of Newburgh, and Matthew Paris agree on his poverty; and the fourteenth-century French Dominican Bernard Gui, who was well-informed about events in the south of France, describes him as 'a poor or very poor cleric (*pauper clericus sive clericus pauperculus*)'.[21]

The sources, however, do not agree about his exact destination. Boso says that Nicholas went directly from England to Arles, while William of Newburgh writes that he went first to France, and left only because 'he did not prosper sufficiently' there (*minus prosperaretur*).[22] William does not say what Nicholas did in France and why he 'did not prosper sufficiently'. Did he again fail to secure a benefice? Matthew Paris's conviction that Nicholas studied at Paris and proved to be an

---

[18] William of Newburgh, i, 109:* 'patrem habuit clericum quendam non multae facultatis'; Ralph de Diceto, *Ymagines historiarum, ad annum* 1161: 'Nicholaus natione Anglicus, ex patre presbitero, summus pontifex fuit, vocatus Adrianus papa quartus' (*Radulfi de Diceto decani Lundoniensis opera historica*, ed. W. Stubbs, 2 vols, RS 68 [London, 1876], i, 305). Innocent III later recalled (in 1200) that Nicholas's alleged priestly parentage was proposed as grounds for his deposition by Frederick I: '...et eundem Adrianum moliebatur, sed frustra, cum quibusdam deponere, opponens ei quod esset filius sacerdotis ...' (*Regestum Innocentii III papae super negotio Romani imperii*, ed. Friedrich Kempf, Miscellanea Historiae Pontificiae, 12 [Rome, 1947], 74–91 no. 29, at 85).

[19] *The Letters and Charters of Gilbert Foliot*, ed. Z. N. Brooke, Adrian Morey, C. N. L. Brooke (Cambridge, 1967), 493–495 nos 465–6.

[20] Poole ('Early Lives', 293) suggested that Nicholas like Thomas Becket studied at the Austin priory of Merton; but Vones-Liebenstein (Saint-Ruf, i, 244, n. 24) argues convincingly that this hypothesis is improbable.

[21] *Bernard Gui, Flores chronicorum seu catalogus pontificum Romanorum*, in Muratori, *Rer. Ital. SS*, 3/i, 440.* Cf. Vones-Liebenstein, *Saint-Ruf*, i, 246, n. 37.

[22] William of Newburgh, i, 109.*

excellent scholar[23] may be no more than a chronicler's attempt to fill in a gap in his knowledge. His account fits into a career pattern which from a thirteenth-century writer's point of view was obvious. But no other known medieval source confirms that Nicholas sat at the feet of masters like Peter Abelard, Hugh of Saint-Victor, Gilbert of Poitiers, or Robert Pullen. That he had really been among the many twelfth-century Englishmen[24] who studied at Paris seems highly doubtful.[25] Nor could he have met John of Salisbury there. By the time that John began his studies in 1138,[26] Nicholas was very probably a canon at Saint-Ruf. Their friendship dated from John's visits to the Curia, not from their student days.

Although Paris in the first half of the twelfth century became more and more the most important centre of learning in medieval France, the schools of other cities like Laon, Chartres, or Orléans were not without distinction. And while they, like Paris, became renowned for the teaching of the *artes* and of theology, schools in Provence became celebrated centres for the teaching of Roman law. Important works emerged from them, including three significant commentaries on Justinian's *Codex*: the *Summa Trecensis*, compiled by Master Géraud at Saint-Gilles or Arles in the late 1130s, the *Summa Codicis Tubingensis*, and the vernacular *Lo Codi*, written in Provençal.[27] Montpellier, Narbonne, and Saint-Gilles were important centres for the study and teaching of this law; so, too, was Arles. And according to

[23] *Gesta abbatum*, 112–13:* 'Parisius adiens, ubi scholaris vigilantissimus effectus, omnes socios discendo superavit.'

[24] See Astrik L. Gabriel, 'English Masters and Students in Paris during the Twelfth Century', in idem, *Garlandia. Studies in the History of the Medieval University* (Notre Dame [Ind.]/Frankfurt, 1969), 1–37.

[25] As early as the 1930s, R. L. Poole ('Early Lives', 292) raised doubts about Nicholas's Parisian studies; Vones-Liebenstein (*Saint-Ruf*, i, 245, and n. 31) comes to more positive conclusions. For the English student and later master Robert Pullen, see Poole, 'Early Lives', 287–291; F. Courtney, *Cardinal Robert Pullen. An English Theologian of the Twelfth Century*, Analecta Gregoriana, 10 (Rome, 1954).

[26] For John of Salisbury's education, see his own account in his *Metalogicon*, ii. 10 (ed. J. B. Hall, *CCCM*, 98 [Turnhout, 1991], 70–3, and the ongoing discussion about the interpretation of this text: Olga Weijers, 'The Chronology of John of Salisbury's Studies in France (Metalogicon, ii. 10)', in *The World of John of Salisbury*, ed. Michael Wilks, Studies in Church History, Subsidia 3 (Oxford, 1984), 109–16; K. S. B. Keats-Rohan, 'The Chronology of John of Salisbury's Studies in France: A Reading of *Metalogicon*, 2.10', in *Studi Medievali*, 3rd ser. 28 (1987) 193–203; Richard W. Southern, *Scholastic Humanism and the Unification of Europe*, 2 vols (Oxford, 1995–2001), i, 214–21.

[27] There is a vast bibliography. For an overview, see André Gouron, *La science du droit dans le Midi de la France au Moyen-Age*, Collected Studies Series, 196 (London, 1984); idem, *Études sur la diffusion des doctrines juridiques médiévales*, Collected Studies Series, 264 (London, 1987); Jean Pierre Poly, 'Les Maîtres de Saint-Ruf. Pratique et enseignement du droit dans la France méridionale au XIIe siècle', in *Annales de la Faculté de Droit, des Sciences Sociales et Politiques et de la Faculté des Sciences Èconomiques [Bordeaux]*, Centre d'études et de recherches d'histoire institutionelle et régionale, 2 (1978), 183–203. For Master Géraud, see also André Gouron's various studies in *Juristes et droits savants: Bologne et la France médiévale* (Aldershot, 2000), esp. VI, 488–95 and XI, 14–16.

Boso, it was there that Nicholas Breakspear *scolis vacaret*.[28] Here indeed may be the crucial clue to Adrian IV's education. Although no source expressly says so, it is highly likely that he attended the lectures of masters of Roman law at Arles.

Of even more importance for his future life was the contact with the regular canons of Saint-Ruf. Canons regular played a key role in the church reform movement of the eleventh and twelfth centuries. They emerged from communities of clerics at cathedral or other churches who tried to lead a life inspired by the ideal of the primitive church: communal life and personal poverty. Soon popes like Alexander II or Gregory VII discovered the usefulness of these communities for the promotion of ecclesiastical reform. Of utmost importance were two bulls issued in 1092 by Pope Urban II in favour of the canons regular respectively of Rottenbuch in Bavaria and Saint-Ruf in Avignon.[29] These texts have rightly been called the 'magnae cartae' of the regular canons, because for the first time the pope formally acknowledged their way of life as equal to the monastic vocation—and provided it with an ancient and venerable tradition. According to Urban, his namesake Urban I was the first proponent of the canonical profession, which was then organized by St Augustine and improved by St Jerome. It thus followed the example of the primitive church and deserved emulation and support.[30] Of equal importance were the rights conferred on the canons: they were free to elect their prior or abbot; they could ask a bishop of their choice for the administration of the sacraments, if their diocesan bishop was a heretic or schismatic; a canon wanting to transfer to another, more severe order had to seek permission from his brethren and superior; and, above all, the canons' way of life was confirmed and they were ordered to keep it.[31]

Urban II mentioned St Augustine as the organizer of the regular canons. In fact Augustine had instituted a communal way of life in his episcopal palace at

---

[28] *Vita Adriani*, 388.*

[29] JL 5459 for Rottenbuch, dated early (5?) February 1092, printed in Johannes Laudage, 'Ad exemplar primitivae ecclesiae. Kurie, Reich und Klerusreform von Urban II. bis Calixt II.', in *Reformidee und Reformpolitik im spätsalisch-frühstaufischen Reich*, ed. Stefan *Weinfurter*, Quellen und Abhandlungen zur mittelrheinischen Kirchengeschichte, 68 (Mainz, 1992), 47–73, at 71–3. The bull for Saint-Ruf is JL 5763, dated 4 July 1092, printed in *Codex diplomaticus ordinis sancti Rufi Valentiae*, ed. Ulysse Chevalier, Collection de cartulaires dauphinois, 9 (Valence, 1891), 8–9, no. 5. For the date see Vones-Liebenstein, *Saint-Ruf*, i, 465, n. 588. Urban II's significance for the history of the canons regular is described by Horst Fuhrmann, 'Papst Urban II. und der Stand der Regularkanoniker', *Sitzungsberichte der Bayerischen Akademie der Wissenschaften, phil.-hist. Kl.*, Jg. 1984, Heft 2 (Munich, 1984).

[30] 'Hanc martir et pontifex Urbanus instituit, hanc Augustinus suis regulis ordinavit, hanc Ieronimus suis epistolis informavit...Itaque non minoris estimandum est meriti hanc vitam ecclesie primitivam aspirante ac prosequente domini spiritu suscitare...': Laudage, 'Ad exemplar', 72–3; *Codex diplomaticus ordinis sancti Rufi*, 8 (slightly different).

[31] '...constituentes ne cuiquam omnino liceat hunc vestri statum ordinis commutare, cuius tantus in tot terrarum partibus fructus exuberat, ut plures ecclesie vestri saporis dulcedine condiantur': *Codex diplomaticus ordinis sancti Rufi*, 8–9; the text for Rottenbuch (ed. Laudage, 73) is slightly different.

Hippo. Several texts, organizing this communal life, either written by Augustine himself or ascribed to him, served as guidance for the regular canons of the middle ages. Besides, similar to monastic communities, the canons devised *consuetudines*—guidelines for the communal life and liturgy—which came to be the distinguishing features of the different congregations that came into being in the eleventh and twelfth century. Often based on the customs of the mother house, these sets of observances differed from each other with respect to liturgy, clothing, meals, or the attitude to pastoral care. The orders of canons regular were thus much more varied than the monastic orders, and appealed to a wide variety religious and intellectual aspirations. Important observances include those followed by the canons of Arrouaise,[32] Saint-Victor in Paris,[33] the reform movement inaugurated by Archbishop Conrad I of Salzburg in Austria and Bavaria,[34] or those of Saint-Ruf.

The origins of Saint-Ruf date back to 1039, when four canons of the cathedral chapter of Avignon decided to establish a communal life in the abandoned church of S. Ruf outside the walls of Avignon.[35] The community grew fast and its influence spread throughout Provence, southern France and, due to favourable political circumstances, as far as Catalonia. Existing ecclesiastical institutions, like cathedral chapters, were reformed (for instance the chapter of Maguelonne) and new priories founded, which were often not only spiritually but also economically dependent upon Saint-Ruf. The influence of the use of Saint-Ruf reached as far as Germany and Bavaria, as can be shown from the *consuetudines* of the houses at Marbach (Alsace) and Indersdorf (Bavaria).[36]

[32] See Ludo Milis, *L'ordre des chanoines réguliers d'Arrouaise. Son histoire et son organisation, de la fondation de l'abbaye-mère (vers 1090) à la fin des chapitres annuels (1471)* (Bruges, 1969). The Arrouaisian observance was widespread in England: see John Compton Dickinson, *The Origins of the Austin Canons and their Introduction in England* (London, 1950); idem, 'English Regular Canons and the Continent in the Twelfth Century', *TRHS*, 5th Ser., 1 (1951), 71–89.

[33] *L'abbaye parisienne de Saint-Victor au Moyen Age. Communications présentées au XIIIe Colloque d'Humanisme médiévale de Paris (1986–1988)*, ed. Jean Longère, Bibliotheca Victorina, 1 (Turnhout, 1991).

[34] Stefan Weinfurter, *Salzburger Bistumsreform und Bischofspolitik im 12. Jahrhundert. Der Erzbischof Konrad I. von Salzburg (1106–47) und die Regularkanoniker*, Kölner Historische Abhandlungen, 24 (Köln/Wien, 1975); Peter Classen, 'Gerhoch von Reichersberg und die Regularkanoniker in Bayern und Österreich', in: *La vita commune del clero nei secoli XI e XII. Atti della settimana di studio: Mendola, settembre 1959, 1: Relazioni e questionario*, Miscellanea del centro di studi medievale 3 = Pubblicazioni dell'università cattolica del sacro cuore, ser. 3, scienze storiche 2 (Milan, 1962), 304–40; repr. in idem, *Ausgewählte Aufsätze*, ed. Josef Fleckenstein, Vorträge und Forschungen, 28 (Sigmaringen, 1983), 431–60.

[35] Charles Dereine, 'Saint-Ruf et ses coutumes aux XIe et XIIe siècles', in *Revue bénédictine*, 59 (1959), 161–82; Yvette Lebrigand, 'Origines et première diffusion de l'Ordre de Saint-Ruf', in *Le monde des chanoines (XIe-XIVe s.)*, Cahiers de Fanjeaux, 24 (Toulouse, 1989), 167–79; Vones-Liebenstein, *Saint-Ruf, passim*.

[36] Josef Siegwart, *Die Consuetudines des Augustiner-Chorherrenstiftes Marbach im Elsass (12. Jahrhundert)*, Spicilegium Friburgense, 10 (Freiburg/Switzerland, 1965), 57–60.

The order of Saint-Ruf was less rigorous than other canonical congregations, however. The canons wore cowls made of linen instead of wool; they were allowed two meals a day from Easter to 13 September; and they could eat meat and drink wine.[37] Moreover, like the Victorines, they were a learned order.[38] Although the destruction of Saint-Ruf's medieval library during the wars of religion makes it difficult to establish what its particular intellectual interests were, there is some evidence that it was a centre for theological debate. Its sacristan in the mid-twelfth century, for example, Adhemar of Saint-Ruf, was a follower of Gilbert of Poitiers, whose teachings on God and the divine nature he defended in an extensive collection of *sententiae* compiled from the writings of the early Fathers; and he also wrote a treatise on the Trinity.[39] The survival of an abbreviated version of the patristic collection in the library of the Cistercian monastery of Zwettl in Lower Austria testifies to the Europe-wide connections of Saint-Ruf.[40] At the same time, their location, just outside Avignon, placed them within the region of the written law (*Lex scripta*) and close to the cities where Roman law was taught and practised. Indeed, an early *summa* on Justinian's *Institutes* has been associated with Saint-Ruf (*c.* 1130); and it might well be that the canons' network of relations across Europe served as a means to spread the teaching of these schools.[41]

These few remarks must suffice to characterize the community which young Nicholas Breakspear joined at an unknown date, probably before 1140, when

---

[37] See the letters of Abbot Poncius II of Saint-Ruf (1116–25) and Bishop Walter of Maguelonne to the bishop of Chaumouzey and his cathedral chapter, in Dereine, *Saint-Ruf*, 167–74. The letters defend the uses of Saint-Ruf against the more rigorist 'ordo novus' which was propagated by several groups of regular canons at the beginning of the twelfth century and was followed by Norbert of Xanten's newly founded Premonstratensians.

[38] Vones-Liebenstein, *Saint-Ruf*, i, 442–4.

[39] Franz Pelster, 'Die anonyme Verteidigungsschrift der Lehre Gilberts von Poitiers im Cod. Vat. 561 und ihr Verfasser Canonicus Adhemar von Saint-Ruf in Valence (um 1180)', in *Studia mediaevalia in honorem R. J. Martin* (Bruges, 1948), 113–46; Nikolaus M. Häring, 'The *Tractatus de Trinitate* of Adhemar of Saint-Ruf (Valence)', *Archives d'histoire doctrinale et littéraire du moyen-Âge*, 39 [vol. 31] (1964), 111–206; idem, 'Die Vätersammlung des Adhemar von Saint-Ruf in Valence', *Scholastik*, 38 (1963), 402–20; idem, 'In search of Adhemar's Patristic Collection', *Mediaeval Studies*, 28 (1966), 336–46.

[40] Nikolaus M. Häring, 'Eine Zwettler Abkürzung der Vätersammlung Adhemars von Saint-Ruf (Valence)', *Theologie und Philosophie*, 41 (1966), 30–53. For the background, see Peter Classen, 'Zur Geschichte der Frühscholastik in Österreich und Bayern', in idem, *Ausgewählte Aufsätze*, ed. Josef Fleckenstein, Vorträge und Forschungen, 28 (Sigmaringen, 1983), 279–306 (first in *Mitteilungen des Instituts für Österreichische Geschichtsforschung*, 67 [1959], 249–77). I hope to publish further material on this interesting connection in the near future.

[41] This has been argued by Gouron and especially Poly (above, n. 24); Winfried Stelzer, *Gelehrtes Recht in Österreich. Von den Anfängen bis zum frühen 14. Jahrhundert*, Mitteilungen des Instituts für Österreichische Geschichtsforschung, Ergänzungsband, 26 (Vienna/Cologne/Graz, 1982), 21–44 was able to demonstrate the southern French influence on the 'Grazer Rechtsbuch' and the 'Admonter Rechtsbuch' from twelfth-century Austria. Further research needs to be done.

'Nicolaus canonicus Sancti Rufi' wrote a charter for Archbishop William of Arles, then papal legate in Catalonia.[42] From a letter of Count Ramon Berenguer IV of Barcelona to Adrian IV, written in 1156, in which Oleguer, the abbot of Saint-Ruf 1111–16 who became bishop of Barcelona, is called 'once your father', it could be inferred that Nicholas had joined the order during his period of office. But the expression was probably intended to apply more generally to the whole order, not just the former canon Nicholas, since Oleguer's cult as a saint began to emerge around the middle of the twelfth century.[43]

There remains the question of how Nicholas came into touch with Saint-Ruf. Although 'we shall never know what took him there',[44] some speculations may be put forward. The expressions William of Newburgh uses to describe Nicholas's first contact with Saint-Ruf are quite remarkable: '...ad quem locum ille veniens, et subsistendi occasionem ibidem inveniens, quibus potuit obsequiis eisdem se fratribus commendare curavit.' Because he seemed to be an agreeable character, prudent, and swift to carry out instructions (*ad iniuncta impiger*), he was liked by everybody (*placuit omnibus*); therefore, 'having been asked [by the brethren] to receive the habit of canonical order', he became a canon.[45] This remarkably precise account makes it clear that Nicholas did not immediately join the order when he came to Avignon. He first worked for the canons, and only after proving himself was he invited to make his profession. What 'work' he might have done is perhaps revealed by Bernard Gui's early fourteenth-century summary of Adrian's life. In it, Bernard says that 'at first, as a poor or very poor clerk, he was maintained in the church of St James in Melgueil in the diocese of Maguelonne; then as brother, and afterwards as abbot of Saint-Ruf near Valence (*fuitque primo ut pauper clericus, sive clericus pauperculus in ecclesia beati Jacobi in Melgorio Magolonensis dyocesis enutritus; tandem sic frater et post abbas sancti Ruffi prope Valentiam*).'[46] Far from being a piece of later embroidery, this account has all the hallmarks of authenticity, for the church of St. James in Melgueil was a priory dependent on Saint-Ruf itself. Vones-Liebenstein has pointed out that the canons of the mother house did not undertake pastoral care themselves; instead, they appointed clerks to minister in their dependent churches. These chaplains were affiliated to Saint-Ruf, but they did not become canons in the strict sense.[47] For the young cleric Nicholas, such an appointment would have offered what he had been denied at St Albans—*subsistendi ibidem occasionem*—and admission to the first

---

[42] Dated 2 May 1140: *Gallia christiana novissima*, iii, ed. J.-H. Albanès and U. Chevalier (Valence, 1900), 209–10 no. 537, mentioned by Poole, 'Early Lives', 294; Vones-Liebenstein, *Saint–Ruf*, i, 247.

[43] '...de reuelatione scilicet beati Ollegarii, olim patris uestri...': Paul Kehr, *Das Papsttum und der katalanische Prinzipat*, Abhandlungen der preussischen Akademie der Wissenschaften, Jg. 1926, phil.-hist. Kl., no. 1 (Berlin, 1926), at 90–1.

[44] Southern, 'Medieval Humanism', 235.

[45] William of Newburgh, i, 110.*

[46] Bernardus Guidonis, *Flores chronicorum*, 440.*

[47] Vones-Liebenstein, *Saint-Ruf*, i, 270–5, ii, 440.

rung of the clerical ladder.[48] His diligent discharge of duties required of him commended him to the community at Saint-Ruf, and he was called to higher service in the mother house itself, as a full member of the community.

Whatever the precise circumstances, he had become a canon of Saint-Ruf by 1140 at the latest, and soon afterwards he was elected abbot. The exact date of his elevation is not known. His predecessor Fulcher is mentioned only once, in 1143; Nicholas occurs first as abbot in a papal letter in favour of Saint-Ruf issued by Eugenius III on 29 January 1147 in Vico d'Elsa near Siena,[49] and he was probably at the Curia when the letter was issued. Pope Eugenius was then on his way to France where, in March 1148, he held the important council of Reims. Although there is no record of his presence at the council, it is likely that Abbot Nicholas was among the prelates who attended, since he was not named in the list of those who were excommunicated for having disobeyed the pope's summons.[50]

One of the main papal concerns was the securing of sufficient support for the new crusade, which St Bernard was to lead. Abbot Nicholas, then, had come to the attention of Pope Eugenius in 1147, when he impetrated a privilege for Saint-Ruf; and the pope may have spotted him again at Reims in March 1148. As long ago as 1953 Giles Constable suggested that the pope sent him on a mission to Spanish crusaders 'to whom he acted perhaps as an unofficial legate'.[51]

As a matter of fact, Abbot Nicholas is known to have been in Catalonia in late spring 1148, when he was present at the siege of Tortosa,[52] and he was probably still there in February 1149, when the bishop of Barcelona gave a church to Saint-Ruf.[53] Abbot Nicholas's Catalan activities were of great significance to the order. Saint-Ruf became the most important collaborator in Count Ramon Berenguer IV's endeavours to build an ecclesiastical organization in the territories recently recovered from Saracen rule, with the result that the Saint-Rufian observance became popular with the Catalan nobility as well as the ecclesiastical hierarchy— to no small advantage of the order.[54]

Notwithstanding his success with respect to the external condition of the order, however, Abbot Nicholas soon faced increasing difficulties in the internal. According to William of Newburgh, his fellow canons, who had recently

---

[48] William of Newburgh, i, 110;* cf. Poole, 'Early Lives', 292–3.

[49] JL 8999; *Codex diplomaticus ordinis sancti Rufi*, 30–1 no. 22.

[50] Nikolaus M. Häring, 'Notes on the Council and the Consistory of Rheims (1148)', *Mediaeval Studies*, 28 (1966), 39–59, at 40–3; idem, 'Die spanischen Teilnehmer am Konzil von Reims im März 1148', *Mediaeval Studies*, 32 (1970), 159–71, at 161.

[51] Giles Constable, 'The Second Crusade as Seen by Contemporaries', *Traditio*, 9 (1953), 213–79, at 262 (repr.in idem, *Religious Life and Thought [11th and 12th Centuries]*, Collected Studies Series, 89 [London, 1979], n. 10); Vones-Liebenstein, *Saint-Ruf*, i, 253–6.

[52] 'In adquisitione Ilerdensis et Dertusensis ecclesie laborem ac sudorem nostrum partim oculis uestris uidistis, non uisa relatione percepistis': Letter of Count Raymond Berenguer IV to Pope Adrian IV, Kehr, *Das Papsttum*, 90; Vones-Liebenstein, *Saint-Ruf*, i, 254.

[53] *Ibid.*, i, 254–5; ii, 728–9 no. 2.

[54] *Ibid.*, i, 364.

unanimously elected him, soon regretted their choice and appealed against him to the pope.[55] Eugenius III managed to reconcile the two parties, but the agreement did not last for long. When further complaints were brought before him, he ordered the canons to elect a new abbot; and Nicholas was promoted cardinal bishop of Albano.[56] The background of these arguments is not known. It is possible that Nicholas wished to impose a more rigorous regime, or that there was disagreement between him and them about the organization of the order. Whatever they were, it is clear from William of Newburgh's account that the initiative for the disputes came from the canons, not from the abbot.[57]

Nicholas must have been present at the Curia in December 1149, for on the twelfth of that month he received a papal letter in favour of Saint-Ruf. This is his last recorded act as abbot.[58] His first recorded subscription to a solemn papal privilege as cardinal bishop of Albano was on 30 January 1150.[59] According to the use of the Roman church, episcopal consecrations were usually conferred during the four penitential periods of three days each, known as Ember Days. Since the December Ember Days were observed on the Wednesday, Friday, and Saturday following the third Sunday in Advent, which in 1149 fell on the 14th, 16th, and 17th of the month, it can be assumed that Nicholas was consecrated on 17 December 1149. There is no mention of disputes within the order in Boso's account. For him, Nicholas's elevation was merely just another step in the future pope's career: 'Accidit autem ut pro incumbentibus ecclesie sibi commisse negotiis ad apostolicam sedem veniret, et peractis omnibus causis pro quibus venerat, cum redire ad propria vellet, beate memorie papa Eugenius eum secum retinuit et de communi fratrum suorum consilio in Albanensem episcopum consecravit.'[60]

If William of Newburgh is right—that he left Saint-Ruf under something of a cloud, he does not seem to have harboured any ill-will towards his former brethren. Indeed, his choice of papal name may have been a tribute to Saint-Ruf,

---

[55] 'Quibus cum aliquandiu praefuisset, poenitentia ducti atque indignati quod hominem peregrinum levassent super capita sua, facti sunt ei de cetero infidi atque infesti. Odiis itaque paulatim crudescentibus, ut iam graviter aspicerent in quo sibi paulo ante tam bene complacuerat, tandem confectis et propositis contra eum capitulis ad sedem eum Apostolicam provocarunt': William of Newburgh, i, 110–11.*

[56] *Ibid.*, 111.*

[57] Vones-Liebenstein, *Saint-Ruf*, i, 249–50, whose speculations concerning disagreements about the theology of Gilbert of Poitiers are not entirely convincing.

[58] *Papsturkunden in Spanien. Vorarbeiten zur Hispania Pontificia*, i, ed. Paul Kehr, Abhandlungen der Gesellschaft der Wissenschaften zu Göttingen, philologisch-historische Klasse, N.F. 18 (Berlin, 1926), 331–2 no. 60. Because this letter is dated at St Peter's on 12 December (*Datum Rome apud sanctum Petrum ii id. decembris*), Kehr assumed that it belonged to 1152, since no (other) extant document can be shown to have been issued from St Peter's between 29 Nov. and 19 Dec. in 1149. But Eugenius was at the Lateran in December 1149 (JL 9359–63), and it is highly possible that he spent a few days at St Peter's, perhaps in connexion with the consecration of the new cardinal bishop.

[59] JL 9370; cf. Brixius, 56 no. 16; Zenker, 36–8.

[60] Boso, 388.* For his important legation to Scandinavia, see below, ch. 4.

where the cult of St Adrian was well established. A Catalan priory, Sant Adrià de Besòs, was dedicated to this saint; and when the canons had to move to another Saint-Rufian priory, they dedicated an altar in honour of Adrian there.[61]

Like his predecessor, Adrian IV issued numerous bulls in favour of the Austin canons,[62] at least ten of which are for Saint-Ruf; and in a letter issued on 17 April 1155, he explicitly acknowledged the 'special bond of affection' that tied him to Saint-Ruf, who had been 'a mother' to him, so that she should experience the favour (*beneficium*) of the father who had once been her son.[63] Even more telling is the mandate directed to the archpriest and the chapter of the cathedral of Pisa in 1156. Adrian recommends to them 'certain brethren from the church of Saint-Ruf whom we are sending to your area to cut stones and columns (*quosdam fratres ecclesie sancti Rufi, quos pro incidendis lapidibus et columnellis ad partes vestras dirigimus*)'. The chapter is asked to assist them in finding stone-cutters and to help them in every possible way to conduct their business.[64] The brethren's quest for Italian marble, perhaps from the quarries of Carrara, may have been provoked by the intended removal of the abbey of Saint-Ruf from Avignon to Valence, where the new monastery was built on an island in the Rhône (1158).[65]

The exact reasons for this transfer—very unusual indeed for a well established religious house—are not known. Probably several circumstances were responsible. Above all, Saint-Ruf's relations with the chapter of the cathedral of Avignon had been strained from the beginning, as the canons suspected their bishop, who supported Saint-Ruf, of diminishing their own and the cathedral's property and rights. They would have preferred Saint-Ruf to have been a dependency of the cathedral chapter, rather than an independent and growing religious order with an organizational structure of its own. Early in the 1150s this conflict was intensified by the chapter's refusal to confirm an exchange between Bishop Gaufred of

[61] Vones-Liebenstein, *Saint-Ruf*, i, 251. The saint in question is perhaps the legendary martyr, patron of S. Adriano in Rome, whose feast is celebrated on 4 March (*Bibliotheca Hagiographica Latina*, nos 3744–5).

[62] See Michele Maccarrone, 'I Papi del secolo XII e la vita comune e regolare del clero', in *La vita commune del clero nei secoli XI e XII, Atti della settimana di studio: Mendola, settembre 1959*, 1: Relazioni e questionario, Miscellanea del centro di studi medievale, 3 = Pubblicazioni dell'università cattolica del S. Cuore, ser. 3, scienze storiche 2 (Milano, 1962), 349–411, repr. in idem, *Romana Ecclesia – Cathedra Petri*, ed. Piero Zerbi, Raffaello Volpini, and Alessandro Galuzzi, 2 vols, Italia Sacra, 48 (Roma, 1991), ii, 757–819, at 793–7.

[63] 'Licet ex iniuncto nobis a Domino apostolatus officio debeamus omnibus ecclesiis providere, pro illis tamen precipue nos opportet esse sollicitos quibus speciali vinculo caritatis sumus astricti, quatinus et nos videamur exequi quod debemus et que nobis mater extitit honestatis et in religione studuit actencius informare patris beneficium senciat et illius qui olim filius merito vocabatur': *Codex diplomaticus ordinis sancti Rufi*, 34–5 no. 27. The other letters are 34–40 nos 26–31, 43–7 nos 33–5, 48 no. 37. This list could easily be increased if bulls in favour of the dependent priories were included.

[64] JL 10172; *Italia pontificia*, iii (Berlin, 1908), 339 no. 41; *PL*, clxxxviii, 1461 no. 95.

[65] On 14 March 1159 Adrian IV confirmed the acquisition of the island. For the possible background of the transfer, see Vones-Liebenstein, *Saint-Ruf*, i, 473–84.

Avignon (1143–76) and Saint-Ruf, which would have strengthened the bishop's position.[66] Besides, the political setting in Provence was changing. Bishop Gaufred and the brethren of Saint-Ruf both supported the count of Barcelona, who had been the hitherto unquestioned power in the area. But the increasing influence of the counts of Toulouse, the counts of Forcalquier, and the emperor Frederick I, combined with the endeavours of the citizens of Avignon to form an independent commune, resulted in a much more complicated and instable situation.[67] Bishop Odo of Valence's gift of the island of Épavière, *ad construendam ibidem sancti Rufi abbatiam,*[68] was therefore an opportunity to regain and even improve the original condition of the order. In Valence, Saint-Ruf was wholly independent from the cathedral chapter and free of all dues to the bishop; and its attachment to the counts of Barcelona became more and more relaxed. The transfer to Valence thus inaugurated a new chapter in the abbey's constitutional development, and resulted in a reorientation of the order's sphere of action.

Not only did Adrian grant privileges to and support his confrères in their quest for marble, he seems to have recruited at least one of them to the Curia. At an unknown date, he sought information from Archbishop Theobald of Canterbury about a certain Walter, now canon of Saint-Ruf. In his reply, Theobald gave a short account of Walter's parentage and his reputation in the bishopric of Chichester. Both were highly praised, and especially Walter's relationship with William de Briouze, lord of Bramber in Sussex.[69] If this is the same Walter whom Adrian consecrated as cardinal bishop of Albano in 1158, as Timothy Reuter thought,[70] then not only was there another Englishman at Saint-Ruf in the middle years of the century—this time a man with excellent connexions—but Adrian procured the admission of a fellow-countryman into the College of Cardinals. In a letter written in late 1167 to the cardinal bishop Walter, John of Salisbury called Adrian IV their common father (*utriusque nostrum pater*), suggesting a close relationship not only between himself and the former Pope, but also between Walter and Adrian.[71]

Although there remain many unresolved questions about details of Adrian's early life, the careful re-reading of Boso and Bernard Gui—the one who was closest of all to his subject, and the other with access to local knowledge in the Arelate—points to a highly plausible explanation of the Englishman's qualities. Employment by the canons of Saint-Ruf, together with training in the demanding discipline of the learned law, and his energy and comparative youth, which first attracted the attention of Eugenius III, all combined to equip him for entry into a papal Curia dominated by educated and talented personalities.

---

[66]   Vones-Liebenstein, *Saint-Ruf,* i, 479.

[67]   *Ibid.,* i, 480–482.

[68]   *Codex diplomaticus ordinis sancti Rufi,* 40–2 no. 32.

[69]   *JohnS,* i, 86 no. 49.

[70]   *JohnS,* ii, xv (*Corrigenda* to vol. i). Apart from Theobald's statements, nothing is known about Walter's earlier life: Brixius, 60 no. 12; Zenker, 39.

[71]   *JohnS,* ii, 432–8 no. 235, at 432–4.

Chapter 3

The Abbot-Crusader:
Nicholas Breakspear in Catalonia

Damian J. Smith

Contemporaries generally viewed the Second Crusade to the East as a failure and modern historiography has not substantially altered that assessment.[1] The venture, initiated in response to Zengi's capture of Edessa on 24 December 1144, by Eugenius III's crusading bull *Quantum Predecessores* of 1 December 1145, and preached by Bernard of Clairvaux, met with one setback after another. In 1147, the army of King Conrad III of Germany was depleted when hit by a flood near Constantinople, before being decimated, succumbing to a trap laid by the Turks. Already having faced a less than warm reception from the Byzantine Emperor Manuel Comnenus, the army of King Louis VII of France, after some initial success, was routed by the Turks in the Cadmus Mountains in January 1148. In July 1148, the remnants of the Christian armies failed dismally in their attempt to capture Damascus by siege.[2] In a second theatre of war, a crusade against the pagans of the Baltic in 1147, hampered by the distrust between the Danish and Saxon forces, achieved so little that it too must be counted a failure.[3] These events, most notably the Damascus debacle, not only let loose many accusations of treachery and bad faith, but also placed the very concept of crusading in question. While St Bernard sought to find reason for the defeat in the sins of the crusaders,[4] it was the papacy (and the pope, who had originally envisaged a campaign to recover

---

[1] G. Constable, 'The Second Crusade as Seen by Contemporaries', *Traditio*, 9 (1953), 213–79; *The Second Crusade: Scope and Consequences*, ed. J. Phillips and M. Hoch (Manchester, 2001); *The Second Crusade and the Cistercians*, ed. M. Gervers (New York, 1992).

[2] E. Caspar, 'Die Kreuzzugsbullen Eugens III.', *Neues Archiv der Gesellschaft für ältere deutsche Geschichtskunde*, 45 (1924), 285–305; M. Meschini, *San Bernardo e la seconda crociata* (Milan, 1998); V. Betty, 'The Second Crusade', in *A History of the Crusades*, ed. K. Setton, 6 vols, Madison 1969–89, i, 463–511; A. Forey, 'The Failure of the Siege of Damascus', *Journal of Medieval History*, 10 (1984), 13–25; C. Walker, 'Eleanor of Aquitaine and the Disaster at Cadmos Mountain on the Second Crusade', *American Historical Review*, 55 (1949–50), 857–61.

[3] H-D. Kahl, 'Wie kam es 1147 zum Wendenkreuzzug?', *Europa Slavica-Europa orientalis*, eds. K-D. Grothusen and K. Zernak (Berlin 1980), 286–340; F. Lotter, 'The Crusading Idea and the Conquest of the Region East of the Elbe', *Medieval Frontier Societies*, eds. R. Bartlett and A. Mackay (Oxford, 1989) 267–306; K. Jensen, 'Denmark and the Second Crusade: the formation of a crusader state?', in *The Second Crusade: Scope and Consequences*, 164–79.

[4] Bernard of Clairvaux, 'De consideratione ad Eugenium papam', in *Opera*, ed. J. Leclercq and H. Rochais, 8 vols (Rome, 1957–77), iii, 410–13.

Edessa), rather than the Cistercian order, which experienced most damage from the fall-out. The amount of business brought to the Curia dropped astonishingly in the years 1149–50; fewer petitioners were coming to Rome, and the reputation of the papacy was significantly diminished.[5]

The crusade in the Levant, however, was increasingly perceived by the papacy, by St Bernard and his contemporaries, and by the participants themselves, as part of a wider movement to turn back the Muslim tide. From 1114, the papacy had placed campaigns in the Iberian Peninsula on the same level as the crusades to the East and the battle against the Moors was progressively imbued with crusading ideals,[6] and here the crusade met a degree of success, which counterbalanced the losses in the East. This should not necessarily be attributed to the moral superiority of the Christians of the Peninsula, as one contemporary believed.[7] The key to their victories lay in the fact that first in North Africa and then in al-Andalus, the Almoravid Empire was being fatally undermined by the Almohad movement, which sought to return to the moral values, social norms, and politico-religious observances of Islam's beginnings, and was prepared to direct a holy war against other Muslims.[8] It is not coincidental that Christian advances followed the Almohad capture in March 1147 of the city of Marrakech. The crisis of the Almoravid regime (1143–7) did not make Christian conquests easy, but it made them possible. On 17 October 1147, Almería fell to forces led by the 'Emperor' Alfonso VII of Castile (1126–57), backed by the Genoese and Count Ramon Berenguer IV of Barcelona (1131–62). A week later, and after a four-month siege, Afonso Henriques of Portugal (1128–85), with strong international support, took Lisbon. A new campaign of Alfonso VII against Jaén in 1148 met with little success but Ramon Berenguer initiated the siege of Tortosa, which fell on 30 December. With little breathing space, the count, taking advantage of incursions into the Segrià by Count Ermengol VI of Urgell (1102–54) in the summers of 1147–8, began the siege of Lleida (Lérida), while Aragonese forces attacked Fraga and Mequinenza. Lleida and Fraga fell on 24 October 1149 and Mequinenza soon after. Almería was retaken by the Almohads in August 1157, but the other towns were never recaptured by the Moors. The captures of Lisbon, Tortosa, and Lleida (which would become

---

[5] R. Hiestand, 'The Papacy and the Second Crusade', in *The Second Crusade: Scope and Consequences*, 32–53, at 46; M. Hoch, 'The Price of Failure: the Second Crusade as a turning-point in the history of the Latin East', in *ibid.*, 180–200, at 193.

[6] R. Fletcher, 'Reconquest and Crusade in Spain', *TRHS*, 37 (1987), 31–49; J. Goñi Gaztambide, *Historia de la bula de la cruzada en España* (Vitoria, 1958); F. Sabaté, *L'expansió territorial de Catalunya (segles IX–XII): ¿conquesta o repoblació?* (Universitat de Lleida, 1996).

[7] Henry of Huntingdon, *Historia Anglorum*, ed. and trans. D. Greenway, OMT (Oxford, 1996), 752–3.

[8] M-J. Viguera Molíns, *Los Reinos de Taifas y las Invasiones Magrebíes* (Editorial Mapfre, 1992); A. Huici Miranda, *Historia política del imperio almohade*, 2 vols (Tetuán, 1956); P. Guichard, *Al-Andalus frente a la Conquista Cristiana* (Valencia, 2001), 85–112; R. Le Tourneau, *The Almohad Movement in North Africa in the Twelfth and Thirteenth Centuries* (Princeton, 1969), ch. 1.

the bridge between Aragon and Catalonia and the major seat of government of the Christian kings) were of vital importance in the Christian conquest of the Peninsula.[9] In essence, the Iberian successes at the time of the Second Crusade laid the groundwork for the Christian capture of territory far more extensive than the Latin kingdom of Jerusalem at its widest extent.

International participation was not a prerequisite for crusading, but in many of the Iberian campaigns foreign knights played a major role. In the conquests of Lisbon and Tortosa, there was considerable English participation.[10] As in a later age, the English found the maritime resorts more to their liking than the interior. While there is considerable evidence for major English settlement in Tortosa, entries in the cathedral cartulary of Lleida, the *Llivre Vert*, suggest that few ventured to that region.[11] Nicholas Breakspear, however, was involved in both campaigns. As Count Ramon Berenguer IV was later to remind the then Pope Adrian IV in 1156, the Englishman had witnessed the count's toil and sweat in the acquisition of the churches of Lleida and Tortosa.[12] Nicholas's presence at these momentous events is explained not by his 'Englishness', but by his position as tenth abbot of Saint-Ruf. The canons of Saint-Ruf had extensive interests in Catalonia, where their houses were very influential.[13] They were therefore in close contact with ecclesiastics in the region and also with the counts of Barcelona, who, in turn, held power in Provence. Adrian, as pope, retained a lively interest in Iberian affairs, despite

---

[9] 'Cafari ystoria captionis Almarie et Turtuose ann. 1147 et 1148' in *Annali Genovesi di Caffaro e de' suoi continuatori*, ed. L. Belgrano, Fonti per la storia d'Italia, 11 (Genoa, 1890), 77–91; *De expugnatione Lyxbonensi*, ed. and trans. C. David (New York, 2000); J. Williams, 'The Making of a Crusade: the Genoese Anti-Muslim Attacks on Spain, 1146–8', *Journal of Medieval History*, 23 (1997), 29–53; S. Barton, 'A Forgotten Crusade: Alfonso VII of Léon-Castile and the Campaign for Jaén (1148)', *Historical Research*, 73 (2000), 312–20; C. Hillenbrand, 'A Neglected Episode of the Reconquista: a Christian Success in the Second Crusade', *Revue des études islamiques*, 54 (1988), 163–70; R. Hiestand, 'Reconquista, Kreuzzug und heiliges Grab: Die Eroberung von Tortosa 1148 im Lichte eines neuen Zeugnisses', *Gesammelte Aufsätze zur Kulturgeschichte Spaniens*, 31 (1984), 136–57; N. Jaspert, '*Capta est Dertosa, clavis Christianorum*: Tortosa and the Crusades', in *The Second Crusade: Scope and Consequences*, 90–110; J. Salrach, *El procés de feudalització [segles III–XII]* (Barcelona, 1998), 372–7; J. Tortosa Durán, 'La conquista de la ciudad de Lérida por Ramon Berenguer IV, conde de Barcelona', *Ilerda*, 17 (1953), 27–66.

[10] S. Edgington, 'The Lisbon Letter of the Second Crusade', Historical Research, 69 (1996), 328–39; De expugnatione Lyxbonensi, passim; A. Virgili, Ad detrimentum Yspanie: La Conquesta de Tortosa i la formació de la societat feudal (1148–1200) (Valencia, 2001), 57–8.

[11] R. Miravall, *Immigració britànica a Tortosa (segle XII)* (Barcelona, 1980); Arxiu de la catedral de Lleida, *Llivre Vert*, f. 84r (1154), f. 264r (1182) refer to a 'Ramon Angles' who may possibly be an English knight at the siege.

[12] P. Kehr, *El Papat i El Principat de Catalunya fins a la unió amb Aragó* (Barcelona, 1931), 123; J. Villanueva, *Viage Literario a las iglesias de España*, 22 vols (Madrid, 1803–52), v, 263.

[13] U. Vones-Liebenstein, *Saint-Ruf und Spanien. Studien zur Verbreitung und zum Wirken der Regularkanoniker von Saint-Ruf in Avignon auf der iberischen Halbinsel (11. und 12. Jahrhundert)*, 2 vols, Bibliotheca Victorina, 6 (Turnhout, 1996).

his other preoccupations. He would later ratify the union of Aragon and Catalonia, which then constituted the 'Crown of Aragon', and, in the year of his death he was instrumental in preventing an Anglo-French invasion of Spain.

The letter of Ramon Berenguer to the pope, preserved in the cathedral archive of Tortosa and a rare survival of its kind, dealt with matters of local ecclesiastical and political importance, most notably the restoration of the Tortosan church. The Count recalled to Adrian 'the blessed Oleguer, once your father'.[14] He was aiming to strike the right note by mentioning a towering figure, influential in both their lives. Although with slightly more favourable beginnings, the rise of Oleguer was not dissimilar to that of Nicholas.[15] Oleguer was born about 1060, the son of another Oleguer, an official of Count Ramon Berenguer I of Barcelona (1035–76), and Guisla. He was given to the church of Barcelona as a child and rose through the ranks before becoming an Augustinian canon and, in 1093, prior of the community of St Adrià de Besòs, on the outskirts of Barcelona, one of the first foundations of Saint-Ruf in Catalonia. In 1110–11 he was promoted to be abbot of Saint-Ruf where he remained until 1116, when he was elected, against his wishes, as bishop of Barcelona.[16] On 21 March 1118, Gelasius II granted Oleguer the pallium as the new archbishop of Tarragona, while he retained the see of Barcelona in plurality.[17] Oleguer dedicated himself to the huge task of the restoration and resettlement of Tarragona, but he remained closely tied to the affairs of the south of France until his death in 1137. First as abbot of Saint-Ruf and then as archbishop, he exerted an enormous influence on the extension of the Order's possessions, customs, and liturgy in Catalonia, most importantly, in Tarragona itself.[18] Oleguer was, after many attempts, canonized in 1675, the information concerning his life being taken from the *Vitae sancti Ollegarii*, transmitted by two fourteenth-century Barcelonan manuscripts derived from a lost mid-twelfth-century original, probably written by his Barcelonan contemporary, Master Renall the Grammarian.[19] Thus, as Ramon Berenguer's letter suggests, Nicholas's predecessor at Saint-Ruf was already considered a saint.

Nicholas, however, not only inherited Oleguer's office as abbot of Saint-Ruf but also his commitment to the crusading movement. For Abbot Oleguer, as Jas-

---

[14] Kehr, *El Papat*, 123; Villanueva, *Viage Literario*, v, 263; cf. above, ch. 2, n. 43.

[15] G. Gonzalvo i Bou, *Sant Oleguer (1060–1137): Església i Poder a la Catalunya Naixent* (Barcelona, 1998); S. Puig i Puig, *Episcopologio de la sede barcinonse* (Barcelona, 1929), 133–53; L. McCrank, 'The Foundation of the Confraternity of Tarragona by Archbishop Oleguer Bonestruga, 1126–9', *Viator*, 9 (1979), 157–77; McCrank, 'Norman crusaders in the Catalan reconquest: Robert Burdet and the principality of Tarragona, 1129–55', *Journal of Medieval History*, 7 (1981), 67–82.

[16] JL, 6523; Vones-Liebenstein, *Saint-Ruf*, i, 214–24.

[17] JL, 6636; Kehr, *El Papat*, 78.

[18] Vones-Liebenstein, *Saint-Ruf*, i, 223; McCrank, 'Confraternity of Tarragona', 162–6.

[19] *Vitae sancti Olegarii*, in *España Sagrada*, ed. E. Flórez and M. Risco, 51 vols (Madrid, 1747–1879), xxix, 472–99; J. Rius Serra, 'Los Procesos de canonización de San Olegario', *Analecta Sacra Tarraconensia*, 31 (1958), 37–64; R. Beer, 'El maestro Renallo, escritor del siglo XII', *Boletín de la Real academia de la historia*, 10 (1887), 373–9.

pert has noted, was 'arguably the person who contributed most to extending the notion of "crusade" in Catalonia'.[20] In 1113, he had met with Pisans and Catalans to plan a crusade to the Balearics.[21] In 1118, Gelasius II (who had spent time at Saint-Ruf) granted him jurisdiction over Muslim Tortosa, anticipating its recovery.[22] In 1119, Oleguer had preached the crusade in Spain proclaimed by Calixtus II and at the Lateran council of 1123 he was appointed legate *a latere* with responsibility for the crusade in Catalonia. Oleguer supported the attacks of the count of Barcelona and non-Catalan crusaders on Tortosa and Lleida, towns not only important in themselves but essential for the stability of Tarragona and its region. Disputes between Aragonese and Catalans and a disastrous defeat at Corbins in 1124, provided serious setbacks. It appears that after Corbins, Oleguer went on a pilgrimage to the Holy Land and then returned to act as peacekeeper and fundraiser for renewed attacks against Tortosa and Lleida (1126–8).[23] It was now that Oleguer set up the confraternity of Tarragona to contribute funds for the restoration of the diocese. In 1130, named anew as legate for the crusade, he sought an international coalition to end the power of the Almoravids in the northeast of the Peninsula, but he was hampered by increasing illness,[24] and, at his death in 1137, Tarragona remained insecure, Tortosa and Lleida were still unconquered, and the archdiocese was incomplete.

A decade after Oleguer's death, it was for Nicholas Breakspear, tenth abbot of Saint-Ruf, to fulfil the dream of the fourth abbot. Saint-Ruf's Catalan interests and Oleguer's promotion of the crusade form an essential backdrop to the involvement of Nicholas in the events of 1148–9. It is not improbable that, at the Council of Reims in March 1148, Eugenius III approved Nicholas's Catalan journey.[25] The latest phase of the Christian offensive was already in train when he encountered Ramon Berenguer IV, to whom Oleguer, as archbishop of Tarragona, had been an important adviser in the early years of his rule (1131–7). The count was an enthusiastic supporter of ecclesiastical reform, being particularly generous to the Cistercians (he was the founder of Poblet), the Templars and the Hospitallers.[26] His

---

[20] Jaspert, '*Capta est Tortosa*', 94.

[21] *Liber Maiolichinus de gestis Pisanorum illustribus*, ed. C. Calisse (Rome, 1904), 48–9, 137.

[22] JL, 6636.

[23] *La documentación pontificia hasta Inocencio III (965–1216)*, ed. D. Mansilla, Rome 1955 [*MDI*], no. 62; McCrank, 'Confraternity of Tarragona', 163; Gonzalvo, *Sant Oleguer*, 26–7; Villanueva, *Viage Literario*, v, 237 (Corbins); *España Sagrada*, xxix, 498 (Holy Land).

[24] McCrank, 'Confraternity', 164–77; idem, 'Norman Crusaders', 71, 79; Gonzalvo, *Sant Oleguer*, 28–9, 44, 85–95; *España Sagrada*, xxix, 481–2, 498–9.

[25] Hiestand, 'The Papacy and the Second Crusade', 38; N. Häring, 'Notes on the Council and the Consistory of Reims (1148)', *Mediaeval Studies*, 28 (1966), 39–59; Häring, 'Die spanischen Teilnehmer am Konzil von Reims im März 1148', *Mediaeval Studies*, 32 (1970), 159–71.

[26] F. Soldevila, *Ramon Berenguer IV el Sant* (Barcelona, 1955); P. Schramm, 'Ramón Berenguer IV' in *Els primers comtes-reis: Ramon Berenguer IV, Alfons el Cast, Pere el Catòlic*, ed. E. Bagué, J. Cabestany, P. Schramm (Barcelona, 1960), 1–53; A. Altisent,

privileges to Saint-Ruf on 31 May 1136 and 15 March 1158, as well as his many donations to the house in Lleida in the 1150s and in his will of 1162, made him a figure of vital importance in the consolidation of the order.[27] The association, first of the counts of Besalú, and then those of Barcelona, with Saint-Ruf, was partly a matter of devotion and partly for practical benefits.[28] This was quite normal. The counts fought for both their spiritual and their worldly survival and when the two coincided, so much the better. They tied themselves to the reform papacy, which strongly supported the canons, and introduced to their land churchmen with discipline, devotion, administrative ability, and, as was increasingly important, a good knowledge of law.

Although Ramon Berenguer carries the sobriquet 'El Sant', his influence on the political, administrative, and legal history of Catalonia was even greater than on the history of the Church. It was during his reign that Aragon and Catalonia were united. He increasingly fostered good relations with Castile, which would become the 'policy' of his dynasty, and sought the partition of Navarre. But from the viewpoint of Nicholas's life, it was perhaps the ever-advancing power of Catalonia in Provence and the conquests from the Moors that were most important. Nicholas spent about half of his life in Provence, a region with which Catalonia had close linguistic, cultural and commercial ties. In 1112, with the agreement of the marriage of the count's father, Ramon Berenguer III (1096–1131; count of Provence, 1112–31) to Countess Dolça of Provence, the house of Barcelona had gained control of Provence, Gavaldà, Carlat and Rodez, but it found itself faced by bitter opposition from the counts of Toulouse and the lords of Baux.[29] At the very time that Nicholas was at Melgueil and then near Arles, the count's brother, Berenguer Ramon, count of Provence (1131–44), married Beatrice, the heiress to the rich domain of Melgueil. A massive coalition was formed against him, involving the count of Toulouse, the lords of Baux, many other local lords, the Genoese and the Pisans. What is particularly pertinent here is that Conrad III of Germany, the theoretical overlord of Provence, backed the pretensions of Raimon de Baux against Berenguer Ramon. In 1144, Berenguer was killed in a Genoese attack upon his lands.[30] For three years and probably at the time when Nicholas became abbot

---

Història de Poblet (Poblet, 1974); A. Forey, *The Templars in the Corona de Aragón* (London, 1973); M. Bonet, *La Orden del Hospital en la Corona de Aragón. Poder y gobierno en la castellanía de Amposta (siglos XII–XV)*, (Madrid, 1994).

[27] Vones-Liebenstein, *Saint-Ruf*, i. 281–305; ii, 546–7, 557, 667–9, 671–2.

[28] Vones-Liebenstein, *Saint-Ruf*, i. 57–84, 157–237, 281–305; J. Fried, *Der Päpstliche Schutz für Laienfürsten: Die politische Geschichte des päpstlichen Schutzprivilegs für Laien (11–13. Jh)* (Heidelberg 1980), 56–63, 87–103.

[29] *Liber Feudorum Maior*, ed. F. Miquel Rosell, (Barcelona, 1945–7), nos 875–6; M. Aurell, *Les Noces del Comte: Matrimoni i Poder a Catalunya (785–1213)*, 372–5; idem, 'L'expansion catalane en Provence au XIIe siècle', *La formació y expansió del feudalisme català. Estudi General 5–6*, ed. J. Portella (Barcelona, 1985–6), 175–7.

[30] *Histoire générale de Languedoc*, 16 vols, ed. C. Devic and J. Vaissète (Toulouse, 1872–1893), v, 522, 530, 546; J.-P. Poly, *La Provence et la société féodale (879–1166)* (Paris, 1976), 334–6; E. Smyrl, 'La famille des Baux (Xe–XIIe siècles)', *Cahiers du Centre*

at Saint-Ruf, the count of Toulouse and the lords of Baux controlled Provence. In February 1147, Ramon Berenguer IV entered Provence and reduced most of the county to obedience. The count of Toulouse departed for the Holy Land in August, the Baux were forced into exile, and attacks on Melgueil decreased. But the Baux continued to rebel for many years and in doing so they were to be encouraged by the support of the new German emperor, Frederick Barbarossa.[31] It is perhaps significant for the reading of Nicholas's later career, and his difficulties with the empire, that the place where he had started his career and the comtal house, which was the vital support in the spread of Saint-Ruf in Catalonia and Provence, suffered considerably at the hands of a coalition backed by the empire. Here, at least, were some grounds for hostility towards Conrad and Frederick. The change in the relationship between Catalonia and the empire (and a brief flirtation with the antipope Victor IV) appears to have come about only after Nicholas's death, when Riquilda of Poland, niece of Barbarossa, was married in 1161 to Ramon Berenguer III of Provence (1150–66), nephew of his namesake, the count of Barcelona.[32]

The crusade against the Moors engaged most of the energies of the count of Barcelona (Ramon Berenguer IV) from 1147 onwards. The co-ordinated land and sea attack on Tortosa began on 29 June 1148.[33] Genoese and Catalan forces, arriving by sea from Barcelona, encamped before the outer wall on the banks of the Ebro. Ramon Berenguer, the flower of Catalan knighthood, the Occitans, and some Genoese encamped before the slopes of the Banyera hill. The English, Flemish, Templars and Hospitallers held the land to the north of the town. Though the outer walls were quickly taken, the Muslim Tortosans took refuge in the *suda* (the fortress) and awaited help from Valencia, which never arrived. The counts of Barcelona and Urgell conquered the castle of Ascó, to impede help from the Segrià, and Tortosa fell on 30 December 1148, over three hundred years after Louis the Pious had first attempted its capture. The Church had responded well to Eugenius's promulgation of the crusade, and the archbishop of Tarragona, as well as the bishops of Barcelona, Girona, and Vic, were all present at the siege alongside Abbot Nicholas and other brothers of Saint-Ruf.[34] There are no reports of Nicholas Breakspear's activities during the campaign, but the excellent study of Vones-Liebenstein has shown that he was working tirelessly for his Order—attempting to settle disputes within the congregation, receiving new donations, and laying the groundwork for the establishment of the Saint-Rufian customs in the

d'Études des Sociétés Méditerranéennes, 2 (1968), 34–6; Aurell, 'L'expansion catalane', 179.

[31] Smyrl, 'La famille', 37–44, 75–104.

[32] Aurell, *Les Noces del Comte*, 376–7; Kehr, *El papat*, 87; Schramm, 'Ramón Berenguer', 31–3.

[33] Virgili, *Ad Detrimentum Yspanie*, 42–72; Constable, 'Second Crusade', 231–7; Jaspert, '*Capta est Dertosa*', 95; J. Belza, 'La conquista de Tortosa en su aspecto militar', *Revista de Historia Militar*, 5 (1961), 31–50.

[34] *Codice diplomatico della Republicca di Genova*, ed. C. Imperiale de Sant'Angelo, (Rome, 1936), i, 190; Virgili. *Ad Detrimentum Yspanie*, 45; Vones-Liebenstein, *Saint-Ruf* i, 252–4.

cathedral chapter of the newly conquered town.[35] The siege of Lleida began in March 1149, with an army mainly of Catalans led by Ramon Berenguer and the count of Urgell, while the Aragonese besieged Fraga and Mequinenza, so none could give help to the other. Ramon Berenguer conducted the Lleidatan siege from his camp at Gardeny, but it is unlikely that Nicholas was at the siege beyond the early summer, and almost certain that he was not there when the city fell in October.[36] The establishment of the house of Saint-Ruf at Lleida and the imposition of its customs on the chapter would be left to other hands. By December 1149, Nicholas was in Rome.[37] His extended absence in Catalonia may have caused problems at the motherhouse but this was surely not of prime importance to the pope.[38] The victory at Tortosa was already known and sung of and the abbot could give news of the imminent fall of another great town.[39] Nicholas had reached Eugenius III, perhaps bringing news of victory, at a time when the papacy was battered and bruised by failure. Before Christmas, he was cardinal bishop of Albano.

Meanwhile, Count Ramon Berenguer faced a serious problem concerning the union of Aragon and Catalonia. The story went back over twenty years.[40] In October 1131, Alfonso I 'the battler', king of Aragon (1104–34), had dictated a will in which, childless, he bequeathed his kingdom to the orders of the Temple, the Hospital, and the Holy Sepulchre. He confirmed the will just before his death in 1134. It may be that he intended to prevent Pope Innocent II, his overlord, from granting the kingdom to Alfonso VII of Castile. His provisions were unacceptable to many of the Aragonese nobility, who instead chose as king, Alfonso's brother Ramiro II (1134–7; d. 1157), who was a monk. Some nobles revolted and Alfonso VII of Castile invaded. Ramiro, in spite of his monastic vow, married Agnes of Poitou, and they produced an heir, Petronila, the name perhaps chosen to appease the

---

[35] Vones-Liebenstein, *Saint-Ruf*, i, 250–79.

[36] J. Lladonosa, *La conquesta de Lleida* (Barcelona, 1961); J. Tortosa Durán, 'La conquista', 59–62; X. Eritja i Ciuró, 'Cap a la conquesta feudal de Lleida', in *Lleida: de l'Islam al Feudalisme*, ed. J. Busqueta (Lleida, 1996), 85–96; J. M. Font i Rius, *La reconquista de Lérida y su proyección en el orden jurídico* (Lleida, 1949); Vones-Liebenstein, *Saint-Ruf*, i, 255. Professor Flocel Sabaté is currently writing a new study of the conquest based on all the archival sources.

[37] Vones-Liebenstein, *Saint-Ruf*, i, 346–55. *Papsturkunden in Spanien. I Katalonien*, ed. P. Kehr (Berlin, 1926), 331–2 no. 60, with the corrected date of Egger, ch. 2 above, n. 58.

[38] William of Newburgh, i, 110–11 and Egger, ch. 2 above.

[39] L. Paterson, 'Syria, Poitou and the *reconquista* (or Tales of the undead): who was the count in Marcabru's *Vers del lavador*?', in *The Second Crusade: Scope and Consequence*, 135, 145.

[40] *Liber Feudorum Maior*, no. 6 (will of Alfonso); E. Lourie, 'The Will of Alfonso I, "el batallador", King of Aragon and Navarre: A reassessment', *Speculum* 1 (1975), 635–51; Aurell, *Les Noces del Comte*, 340–51; Fried, *Päpstlicher Schutz*, 186–93; S. de Vajay, 'Ramire II le Moine, roi d'Aragon, et Agnès de Poitou dans l'histoire et dans la légende', *Mélanges R. Crozet* (Poitiers, 1966), 727–50; T. Bisson, *The Medieval Crown of Aragon* (Oxford, 1986), 16–17, 31–5.

pope.[41] But Innocent II could not accept either the elevation or the marriage of a professed monk. In August 1137, Ramiro, having found a husband for Petronila, performed public penance for the marriage which he had entered into for the sake of the dynasty, and resumed the Benedictine habit.[42] Petronila's husband was the twenty-four-year-old Ramon Berenguer, who, it was agreed, would retain Aragon, even if the one-year-old Petronila died.[43] Between 1140 and 1143, the count reached agreements with the three military orders which had been deprived of Alfonso I's bequests. He granted substantial territories to them, with promise of more through conquest, and they renounced their rights.[44] Ramon Berenguer ruled in Aragon and Catalonia and married Petronila in 1150.[45] Rome co-operated with the count in crusade and reform but it had not given 'de iure' recognition to the manner of the union because it had never recognized the kingship or marriage of Ramiro. As in Portugal, legitimization by the pope was seen as important for protecting the dynasty.[46]

It was Adrian, at Sutri, on 24 June 1158, who legitimized the 'Crown of Aragon', which subsequently conquered many lands from the Moors and became a major power in the Mediterranean world in the following centuries. Adrian simply ignored the existence of the monk-king Ramiro II. Alfonso had bequeathed his lands to the three orders and they in turn had conceded them to Ramon Berenguer, and the Pope confirmed the concession both to Ramon Berenguer and his heirs.[47] It was the straightforward solution of a practical man. Adrian valued the alliance with his old friend, the count. In 1156, Ramon Berenguer had declared himself *homo, miles, et servus* of the pope. His conquests were the *opus Dei* and *ad augmentationem sancte Romane ecclesie.*[48] Adrian reciprocated. He took the count

---

[41] Aurell, *Les Noces del Comte*, 347. Innocent called on Alfonso VII of Castile to help execute the will of Alfonso I (*Papsturkunden in Spanien*, i, no. 50)

[42] *Documentos de Ramiro II de Aragón*, ed. A. Ubieto Arteta (Zaragoza, 1988), no. 119; Aurell, *Les Noces del Comte*, 345.

[43] *Documentos de Ramiro*, nos 110, 113; *Liber Feudorum Maior*, no. 7.

[44] *Liber Feudorum Maior*, nos 10–12; *Colección de documentos inéditos del archivo general de la Corona de Aragón*, ed. P. de Bofarull et al., 42 vols (Barcelona 1847–1973), iv, 93–9 no. 43.

[45] A. Ubieto, *Los esponsales de la reina Petronila y la creación de la corona de Aragón* (Zaragoza, 1987), 70–1.

[46] Afonso I of Portugal was recognized as king by Alexander III only in 1179 (JL, 13420); Fried, *Päpstlicher Schutz*, 141–2.

[47] *Papsturkunden in Spanien*, i, 364–5 no. 81: 'Eapropter, dilecte in Domino fili Raim(unde) illustris comes, illius devotionis sinceritatem et integritatem fidei, quam erga beatum Petrum et nos ipsos habere dinosceris, attendentes, iuxta tue peticionis instantiam totam terram, quam Adefonsus quondam Aragonen(sium) rex sine herede decedens Sepulchro Domini, Hospitali et Templo pro anime sue salute reliquit, et fratres Sepulchri cum concessu patriarche, Hospitalarii et Templarii eandem terram tibi postea concessisse noscuntur, sicut ab eis nobilitati tue concessa est et scriptis propriis roborata, tam tibi quam heredibus tuis auctoritate apostolica confirmamus et presentis scripti patrocinio communimus'.

[48] Kehr, *El Papat*, 123 no. 10; Villanueva, *Viage Literario*, v, 263.

under papal protection,[49] granted him the privilege *Sacrosancta romana,* according
to which he could be excommunicated only by a legate *a latere* or by the Roman
pontiff.[50] It also confirmed the *libertas,* which Ramon Berenguer's ancestors had
enjoyed in Aragon, Barcelona, and the remainder of their lands.[51] Almost a year
later, on 13 May 1159, Adrian reminded the count of the praise which the bishop
of Huesca had showered upon him during a visit to Rome, and urged him to ever
greater deeds and devotion.[52]

The privilege of protection was related to the war against the Moors. Ramon
Berenguer faced two possible threats. The Almohads first invaded the Peninsula in
1146 but it was in the 1150s that they established their power.[53] From 1151–2, the
Almohads possessed Guadix; from 1153, Málaga; Granada from 1154–7; the West
of al-Andalus completely by 1157–8 and, also, in 1157, they took Almería. Their
extension into the Eastern Peninsula was blocked by a Muslim ruler, Ibn Mardanis
(the famous 'King Lobo' of the Christians), who ruled in Valencia and Murcia
(1147–72) and was generally allied with Castile and Barcelona.[54] But, in 1158,
perhaps conscious of Almohad successes, Lobo broke his alliance with the count
and conspired with his enemies from the kingdom of Navarre. Adrian acted to re-
solve this problem for his old friend and the wider problem of the Almohads. On
19 June 1158, in letters addressed to the archbishops of Tarragona, Narbonne, and
Auch, he redirected the Templars of the Peninsula against the multitudes of infidels in their regions, and declared that those who helped the brothers financially or
militarily would enjoy the same indulgences as crusaders to the East,[55] thus revers-
ing his earlier encouragement of Templar participation in the Holy Land.[56] On 23
June 1158, Adrian wrote again to the archbishops of Tarragona and Narbonne,
ordering them to excommunicate any Christian who supported the Saracens
against the count, and to place their lands under interdict.[57]

A few months later, the Pope gave protection against a threat from a very dif-

---

[49]   (23 June 1158) JL, 10419; *PL,* clxxxviii, 1570–1.
[50]   (December 1157?) *Papsturkunden in Spanien,* i, 365 no. 82.
[51]   (26 March 1157–9) *Papsturkunden in Spanien,* i, 366–7 no. 83.
[52]   *Papsturkunden in Spanien,* i, 367–8.no. 84: 'Veniens ad nos venerabilis frater noster
D. Oscensis episcopus de statu et conversatione tua nos plurimum exhilaravit, asserens te et
iustitie cultum diligere et ecclesias Dei honeste satis et sincera caritate tractare; quod utique
tanto maiorem nobis letitiam contulit et animo nostro maius gaudium subinduxit, quanto
personam tuam ampliori affectione diligimus et in quibus secundum Deum possumus, liben-
tius honoramus. Rogamus itaque nobilitatem tuam monemus et exhortamur in Domino, ut
animus tuus de bonis ad superiora, de superioribus semper ad maiora proficiat et ita te de
cetero in his que Dei sunt habeas, ut tam in oculis hominum quam in divine maiestatis as-
pectu pro bonis operibus debeas commendabilis apparere'.
[53]   Viguera Molíns, *Los Reinos de Taifas,* 220; idem, *Historia de España Menéndez Pi-
dal,* 8/ii, *El retroceso territorial de al-Andalus Almorávides y Almohades, siglos XI–XIII*
(Madrid, 1997), 86.
[54]   Guichard, *Al-Andalus,* 113–144.
[55]   *Papsturkunden in Spanien,* i, 363–4 no. 80.
[56]   *Papsturkunden in Spanien,* i, 362 no. 78 (17 October 1157).
[57]   JL, 10419; *PL,* clxxxviii, 1570.

ferent quarter. Castile was then in grave crisis, owing to the disturbed minority of Alfonso VIII, who had succeeded Sancho III (1157–8) in 1158, exacerbated by the separation of León under Fernando II (1157–88).[58] This was the situation in which Louis VII and Henry II, respectively of France and England, who had temporarily resolved their own differences, were planning a crusade in Spain. Although Adrian warmly welcomed the Anglo-French pact,[59] he was less than enthusiastic about their Spanish ambitions. In *Satis laudabiliter* (Lateran, 18 January 1159), addressed to Louis VII, he praised their 'good intention' to 'expand the boundaries of Christianity', but reminded the French king of the disasters (of the Second Crusade), which had overtaken him as a result of the failure to consult the princes and people of the area. With this in mind, Pope Adrian urged that no action be taken in Spain without approval from the appropriate powers in the region.[60] Henry II was a close ally of Ramon Berenguer, but the uninvited appearance of northerners in his territory was unlikely to cause him great delight.[61] The Almohads were still in the first flush of their religious fervour; King Lobo was wavering. One can only speculate about what might have happened, but it is surely not improbable that Adrian spared the Iberian Peninsula a disaster on the scale of the Second Crusade to the East.[62]

[58] The peace treaties agreed between Sancho III and Raymond Berenguer in February 1158 and between Sancho and Fernando II in May 1158 relate to the crisis. In February, Sancho and Raymond envisaged Lobo's support, which must have wavered in the following months (J. González, *El reino de Castilla en la época de Alfonso VIII*, 3 vols (Madrid, 1960), ii, nos 36, 44.)

[59] (4 November 1158) JL, 10430; *PL*, clxxxviii, 1575.

[60] JL, 10546; *PL*, clxxxviii, 1615–7: 'debet enim serenitatis tuae celsitudo recolere et ad memoriam revocare, qualiter alio tempore, cum tam Conradus bonae memoriae quondam rex Romanorum, quam tu ipse inconsulto populo terrae, Hierosolymitanum iter minus caute aggressi estis...'. For further discussion of this important letter, see Duggan, ch. 9 below, at n. 44.

[61] Soldevila, *Ramon Berenguer*, 13–4, 26; Schramm, 'Ramón Berenguer IV', 33; Aurell, 377, n. 155; For evidence of hostility towards the Northern Franks in Catalonia, see T. Bisson, 'Unheroed Pasts: History and Commemoration in South Frankland before the Albigensian Crusades', *Speculum*, 65 (1990), 281–308.

[62] For his invaluable advice on bibliography, I should like to thank most warmly Dr Martin Alvira Cabrer, Universidad Complutense de Madrid.

Chapter 4
The Papal Legate: Nicholas Breakspear's Scandinavian Mission
Anders Bergquist

One of the better documented episodes in Nicholas Breakspear's career before his election to the papacy was his mission as papal legate to Scandinavia, which took place between the spring of 1152 and the autumn of 1154. This legation is only intelligible in the context of the complex relationship between the Scandinavian church and conflicting papal and imperial interests in the Baltic basin.[1] For the early history of Christianity in those regions had been much influenced by missionary endeavour directed from Germany. The new see of Hamburg had been founded as a metropolitan church in 831 for the precise purpose of overseeing the mission to the Danes, Swedes, and Slavs, with Ansgar as its bishop; and in about 849, he had joined Hamburg to the existing see of Bremen. It was expected that dioceses founded among the newly converted peoples would be subject to his jurisdiction. Thus it was that the Scandinavian bishops remained within the jurisdiction of Hamburg-Bremen until 1100 x 1104,[2] and the emerging kingdoms were simultaneously drawn into the sphere of influence of the German empire. In the wake of the papal reform movement of the late eleventh century, however, Paschal II began the process of detaching Scandinavia from its dependence on the German metropolitan. For this purpose, Alberic, his legate, visited a number of episcopal centres in southern Scandinavia. He interviewed their bishops, and decided that Asger Svensson of Lund (now in Sweden, but then in Denmark) was the most capable of ruling the new province. Lund was therefore promoted to metropolitan

---

[1] As emerges clearly from the two fundamental studies of this episode: Arne Odd Johnsen, *Studier vedrørende Kardinal Breakspears legasjon til Norden* (Oslo, 1945), with corrections and additions in *On the Background for the establishment of the Norwegian Church Province: some new viewpoints*, Avhandlinger utgitt av det norske Videnskapsakademie i Oslo, ii. Hist.-Filosof. Klasse, no. 11 (Oslo, 1967); and Wolfgang Seegrün, *Die Papsttum und Skandinavien, bis zur Vollendung der nordischen Kirchenorganisation (1164)*, Quellen und Forschungen zur Geschichte Schleswig-Holsteins, 51 (Neumünster, 1967); C. J. A. Oppermann, *The English Missionaries in Sweden and Finland* (London, 1937), 155–98; Ian Wood, *The Missionary Life. Saints and the Evangelization of Europe, 400–1050* (Harlow, 2001), 123–41. See also Göran Inger, *Das kirchliche Visitationsinstitut im mittelalterichen Schweden*, Bibliotheca Theologiae Practicae, 11 (Uppsala, 1961), 222–8. There is a brief English account of Breakspear's embassy in Lars Österlin, *Churches of Northern Europe in Profile: a thousand years of Anglo-Nordic relations* (Norwich, 1995), 28–32.

[2] *Series episcoporum ecclesiae catholicae occidentalis ab initio usque ad annum MCXCVIII*, Series 5/ii, *Hamburg-Bremen*, ed. Stefan Weinfurter and Odilo Engels (Stuttgart, 1984), 12–16.

status, and Alberic duly conferred the *pallium* on its new archbishop. The loss of jurisdiction was greatly resented by Hamburg-Bremen, but it proved to be permanent, apart from the brief interval of papal weakness, during the Anacletan schism from 1130 to 1137. At the time of Breakspear's embassy, the archbishop of Lund was Asger's nephew Eskil Christiansen, who had been translated from Roskilde to succeed his uncle in 1137, and had been appointed apostolic vicar for Scandinavia at an important legatine synod in 1139. Eskil was a significant figure in mid-twelfth-century Danish politics, widely known as a friend of Bernard of Clairvaux, and as an energetic promoter of the Cistercians in Scandinavia. The foundation of Alvastra, a daughter-house of Clairvaux, by King Sverker in 1143 was characteristic of Eskil's interests.[3]

It was the Cistercian pope, Eugenius III, another of St Bernard's friends, who created Nicholas Breakspear cardinal bishop of Albano in 1149–50 and subsequently sent him as legate to Scandinavia in 1152. In March of that year, Nicholas left the papal court, which was then at Segni.[4] We know nothing directly of the size or composition of his legatine entourage, although it is tempting to deduce that his later biographer Boso was with him, from the absence of Boso's subscription from curial documents in the period of Breakspear's embassy.[5] His instructions have to be inferred from the course of the legation. They seem to have been as follows: to break up the existing archbishopric of Lund by carving from it two new archdioceses, one for Norway and one for Sweden, for which two *pallia* were transmitted with the mission; to arrange for payment of Peter's Pence by Norway and Sweden, following the precedent already established in England;[6] to promote clerical against lay interests in the government of local Scandinavian churches; to encourage monastic life; and to promote regular discipline among the clergy generally.

The first aim may seem perplexing. Why should the papacy have wished to break up the jurisdiction of its loyal friend Eskil? The move may have been intended as a form of insurance against any eventual increase of German imperial power in the region. In case Hamburg-Bremen was once more able to re-establish its jurisdiction over Lund, the loss would be limited to southern Scandinavia; but it is equally possible that this re-organization was in response to the needs of the

---

[3] Eskil's career is conveniently set out in *Series episcoporum ecclesiae catholicae occidentalis*, Series 6, *Britannia, Scotia et Hibernia, Scandinavia*, ii, *Archiepiscopatus Lundensis*, ed. Helmuth Kluger (Stuttgart, 1992), 20–8. Eskil is also noticed in standard dictionaries; the best summaries are by Aksel Christensen in *Dansk Biografisk Leksikon*, 3rd edn (1980), iv, 256–9, and Sigurd Kroon, in *DHGE*, 15 (1963), 884–5.

[4] He last recorded attestation of a curial document was at Segni on 1 March 1152; he resolved a quarrel between the bishop and canons of Luni on 30 March: Johnsen, *Background*, 12.

[5] *Liber Pontificalis*, ii, p. xxxix.

[6] W. E. Lunt, *Financial Relations of England with the Papacy to 1327*, 2 vols (Cambridge, Mass., 1939), i, 3–84, esp. 52; cf. Henry Loyn, 'Peter's Pence', in idem, *Society and Peoples: Studies in the History of England and Wales, c. 600–1200*, Westfield Publications in Medieval Studies, 6 (London, 1992), 241–58.

rapidly evolving Church in the North. A precedent already existed for sending a cardinal there. The provincial synod held at Lund in 1139 had been presided over by Theodwin (Dietwin), cardinal bishop of Porto and S. Rufina (1134–51).[7] The sending of the cardinal bishop of Albano, a senior curial cardinal, may simply reflect the high importance attached by Eugenius III to this embassy. It may also be that the choice of an Englishman was felt to have certain advantages in Scandinavia, given the historical links that already existed between England and the Danish and Norwegian churches. There is even an 'Alban connection': the earliest monastic foundation in Norway was dedicated to St Alban (at Selje, in the twelfth century), and there was a strong tradition that Alban's relics had been removed to Odense in Denmark in the ninth century.[8]

According to the Danish historian Saxo Grammaticus, Breakspear travelled through France to England, and then by sea to Norway.[9] Johnsen doubted whether the tensions between King Stephen and the Roman court would have allowed this route, and suggested that Breakspear may have sailed directly to Norway from the Netherlands.[10] He presumably landed at Bergen or Stavanger, but there is no direct evidence. Stavanger at least had English links. Its first bishop, Reinald (hanged by King Harald Gille in 1135),[11] came from Winchester (or, less probably, from Abingdon), and this Norwegian cathedral, too, was dedicated to St Swithun. The building, with its shrine containing relics of St Swithun, was probably completed by the time Nicholas arrived in Norway. By this time Jon Birgisson was bishop of Stavanger, and it was he whom the cardinal chose as the first metroplitan of the new Norwegian archdiocese at Nidaros (Trondheim).

In April 1152, Eskil consecrated Klængr Thorsteinsson in Lund as the new bishop for Iceland, without waiting for Breakspear's arrival. Eskil then left Lund in the late summer or early autumn of 1152 to visit his friend Bernard of Clairvaux, and did not return to Scandinavia until the spring of 1153 at the earliest.[12] These can be taken as signs either that he was unaware of the legate's impending mission, or that he greatly resented it, although it is highly unlikely that there would not have been some (unrecorded) negotiations before the legation set out. A parallel legation, under Cardinal John Paparo, presided over the organization of four provinces for the Irish Church at the Council of Kells-Mellifont in 1152.[13] There is, however, independent evidence that the legate arrived unexpectedly.

[7] Brixius, 47; Zenker, 26–8.

[8] *Selja—heilag stad i 1000 år*, ed. Magnus Rindal (Oslo, 1997); Matthew Paris gives an entertaining account of the rescue of the relics from Odense by monks from St Albans: *Gesta abbatum*, i, 12–19.

[9] *Saxonis Gesta Danorum*, iv. 11. 1, ed. J. Olrik and H. Raeder (Copenhagen, 1931), 389.

[10] Johnsen, *Background*, 14.

[11] The shock created by the hanging of Bishop Reinald is reflected in *Heimskringla*, ed. Finnur Jónsson, Samfund til udgivelse af gammal nordisk litteratur, 23/i–iii (Copenhagen, 1893–1900), iii, 328.

[12] Johnsen, *Studier*, 48.

[13] See Anne Duggan, below, ch. 9, at n. 173.

Øystein Haraldsson, one of the three Norwegian kings, was absent on a raiding expedition in the summer of 1152, and did not return until the autumn.[14] Scandinavian sources hint at strained relations between Nicholas and Sigurd, oldest of the royal brothers, who had fathered a child by his mistress Kristin Sigurdsdottir. She was his first cousin, the daughter of the Jerusalem pilgrim Sigurd Jorsalfar, and the close degree of consanguinity would have added greatly to the offence in Roman eyes.[15]

We have direct evidence for only two episodes while Nicholas was in Norway. The first was the holding of a 'great council' or Meet, to agree on the new archbishopric at Nidaros, and to issue regulations relating to the church; the second was the foundation of an Augustinian monastery at Hamar. The chronology of the Norwegian visit was worked out by Johnsen as follows:[16]

late summer 1152	issue of invitations to the Council of Nidaros
soon after Christmas 1152	Council of Nidaros
early 1153	Nicholas travels from Nidaros via Hamar to Oslo, and thence to Sweden
summer 1153	Nicholas arrives in Sweden

This reconstruction may be questioned, on the simple ground that it is hard to imagine a council being assembled in the depths of the Norwegian winter. Alberic's journeys in 1104 were completed before the creation of the archbishopric of Lund. Nicholas would also have needed a better grasp of local realities before presiding over his council; he needed in particular to make an estimate of the quality of the Norwegian bishops. We might suggest that the travelling around Norway, the monastic foundation, and his delicate personal dealings with the two royal brothers, took place in the late summer and autumn of 1152, that he wintered in some convenient place (Nidaros, or among his Augustinian brethren?), and that the council took place in the spring of 1153. He would then have sailed round to Sweden immediately after the successful conclusion of the council.

The evidence for the council is extremely fragmentary; much depends on the extent to which its decisions might have been embodied in subsequent legal texts, like King Håkon Håkonsson's law code of 1224.[17] There is little doubt, however,

---

[14] Harald Gille had been succeeded by his three sons, Sigurd, Øystein, and Inge.

[15] Johnsen, *Studier*, 52–3.

[16] *Ibid.*, ch. 4. The brief account of Breakspear's visit in *Heimskringla* (iii, 380–1) says simply that he came to Norway 'in those days', i. e. during the time of Harald's three sons. The phrase recurs in Snorri's probable sources, *Morkinskinna* (ed. Finnur Jónsson, Samfund til udgivelse af gammal nordisk litteratur, 53 [Copenhagen, 1932], 453) and *Fargskinna* (ed. Finnur Jónsson, Samfund til udgivelse af gammal nordisk litteratur, 30 [Copenhagen, 1902–3], 351). Sverre Bagge, *Society and Politics in Snorri Sturluson's* Heimskringla (Berkeley, 1991), 51, shows that the imprecision in the dating of Breakspear's visit fits a wider pattern, in which recent and vividly recalled events are not precisely dated.

[17] The evidence is carefully reviewed by Johnsen, *Studier*, ch. 6; Seegrün's summary (*Papsttum*, 150–8) is over-confident in its reconstruction.

that the meeting took place at Nidaros. The kings are never mentioned as present, but it is probable that they were there, especially as some of the business touched their interests directly. The four dioceses of Norway were each represented by twelve 'wise men', and by their bishops: Jon Birgisson of Stavanger, Sigurd of Bergen, and Viljalm of Oslo. Nidaros was vacant.[18] The council sought to reduce lay (specifically royal) influence over episcopal appointments, in favour of clerical (specifically capitular) election, and there is some evidence that chapters of canons regular were established for this purpose. The influence of lay founders over churches founded by them was to be reduced. Ecclesiastical investiture was to be received from clerics, and not from lay lords. Peter's Pence was to be collected systematically. But the decision for which the council is best known is the constitution of Nidaros as the metropolitical see of a new Norwegian church province, and the translation of Jon Birgisson to be the first Norwegian metropolitan. This process contrasts with that of Alberic, who seems to have first chosen the episcopal candidate, and subsequently raised his diocese to metropolitan status in 1104. Nicholas, on the other hand, nominated Nidaros as the metropolitan see, translating the preferred candidate to it.

The cathedral at Nidaros was already well known for the shrine of King Olav Haraldsson, killed in a dynastic conflict at the battle of Stiklestad in 1030, and immediately venerated as a martyr. The choice of Nidaros may have been influenced by the growing cult of St Olav, but the prestige of its enhanced status may have encouraged the further consolidation of the cult. The present cathedral at Trondheim, which is substantially the work of Jon Birgisson's successor Øystein in the late twelfth century, reflects the wealth and prestige of a metropolitan church which also housed the relics of Norway's premier and royal saint. It also continues the 'English connexion'. Øystein was exiled in England in the 1180s, and the architecture of the cathedral closely reflects the English idioms which he encountered at Lincoln and Canterbury. The council at Nidaros may also be regarded as the first representative national assembly or *riksmøte* in Norwegian history.

Following the elevation of Jon Birgisson, Nicholas was able to leave Norway with half his mission accomplished. We have no evidence for the route of his journey into Sweden, and only fragmentary indications of his activity there. Saxo's account of the later part of the embassy is likely to be partial, although he had access to local information, and an important point in his narrative has been corroborated by a papal letter, which came to light in the 1950s.[19] First-hand evidence is available in two overlapping letters issued by Pope Anastasius IV on 28 November 1154, immediately after Breakspear's return to Rome, one addressed to

---

[18] The list of mediaeval Norwegian bishops in Gams, *Series episcoporum ecclesiae catholicae* (Ratisbon, 1873), 333–7, is no longer reliable. Cf. O. Kolsrud, *Den norske Kirkes Erkebiskoper og Biskoper indtil Reformatione*, Diplomatarium Norvegicum, 17B (Christiania, 1913). The relevant volume of *Series episcoporum ecclesiae catholicae occidentalis*, when it appears, will fill an important gap.

[19] See below, n. 24.

the Swedish bishops and the other to King Sverker and the nobles of Sweden.[20] They urge the recipients to observe the cardinal's decrees (*quae inter vos supradictus frater noster instituit; praefati fratris nostri statuta*). Neither letter tells us where the council was held, but Swedish chroniclers locate it at Linköping.[21] In this period, Linköping was frequently the seat of the Swedish king, and its bishop Gislo was the leading figure in the Swedish church. Gislo had taken part in the Synod of Lund in 1139, and had assisted Eskil in 1145 at the consecration of the new cathedral in Lund.[22]

Like the meeting at Nidaros, the council of Linköping attempted to reduce the scope of lay influence over ecclesiastical appointments, and to introduce the payment of Peter's Pence. It promoted clerical celibacy, and defined the prohibited degrees of consanguinity for marriage. It also passed an important peace-keeping decree, *de armis non portandis*. Yet the council did not succeed in establishing a Swedish archbishopric. According to Saxo, whose account may be prejudiced by Danish bias, this was because of rivalry between Swedes and Goths. They were unable to agree, either on a location for the new archbishopric, or on a candidate for appointment. Nicholas was taken aback by the unseemly conflict, and declared that neither people deserved this highest ecclesiastical honour.[23] Modern historians have suggested that the real reason was the intrigues of Eskil of Lund. Having returned in the spring of 1153 to find that he had lost part of his jurisdiction to the new Norwegian province, he was determined not to lose any more. The two explanations can of course be combined; Eskil could have exploited the rivalry between Swedes and Goths for his own purposes.[24]

If Nicholas arrived in Sweden in the summer of 1153, and set off on his homeward journey in the summer of 1154, we have a whole year in which to locate the council of Linköping, and the legate's subsequent visit to Eskil at Lund. Saxo suggests that the meeting was not an easy one, but that Nicholas mollified Eskil with a promise that he would gain more honour than he had lost. He left Eskil the *pallium* which he had been unable to confer on a Swedish archbishop, and declared that the new Swedish metropolitan would be subject to Lund. Although this may look like a Danish perspective on the meeting, it finds corroboration in a letter sent by Nicholas, who was by then Pope Adrian IV, to Eskil on 15 January 1157.[25] According to Saxo, Nicholas also tried unsuccessfully

---

[20] *PL*, clxxxviii, 1084–7 nos 86–7.

[21] Johnsen, *Studier*, 348.

[22] Cf. *Svensk Biografisk Lexikon*, xvii, 133–4 (Herman Schuck, 1969), *s.v.* 'Gisle'.

[23] *Gesta Danorum*, iv.11.1, ed. Olrik and Raeder, 389.

[24] There were also political considerations. King Svend Grathe had taken an oath of fidelity to the emperor in 1152: see Anders Leegaard Knudsen, 'Absalon and the Holy Roman Empire', in *Archbishop Absalon and his World*, ed. Karsten Friis-Jensen and Inge Skovgaard-Petersen (Roskilde, 2000), 21–35, at 22.

[25] Vladimir J. Koudelka, 'Neu aufgefundene Papsturkunden des 12. Jahrhunderts', *Römische Historische Mitteilungen*, 3 (1960), 114–28. The letter is an 18th-century copy of a 15th-century copy of the presumed original, preserved in the Dominican archive of Santa Sabina in Rome. See also Ingvar Andersson, 'Det lundensiska primatet över Sverige: ett

to dissuade King Valdemar from mounting an armed incursion into Sweden.

There is no evidence for the date of the legate's departure from Denmark, or for the route of his journey back to the papal court. As we have seen, Anastasius issued papal letters on 28 November, recommending observance of the legate's decrees. This dating is consistent with William of Newburgh's statement that Anastasius' death (on 3 December 1154) and Nicholas's election as Adrian IV took place not many days after his return.[26] It seems plausible that the prestige of the recently returned legate helped his election. He will have been able to gloss over the partial failure of his visit to Sweden, and to represent his successes in glowing terms. Early biographers marvel at his courage in visiting these inconceivably remote and barbarous lands, and in their admiration we may catch an echo of the reaction of the papal court to his return.[27] It may also have helped his election that he had been absent from curial politics and rivalries for two and a half years.

Whatever the significance of the Scandinavian embassy for Nicholas Breakspear's personal career, it was of great importance for the shaping of mediaeval ecclesial structure in Scandinavia, and perhaps for the development of the Norwegian church's self-identity in particular. Archbishop Eskil of Lund visited Adrian in Rome at the turn of the year 1156–7, and we have seen[28] that a papal letter of 15 January 1157 confirmed him as Adrian's permanent papal legate in Scandinavia. Eskil was detained on his return journey, apparently by supporters of the Emperor; at least, Adrian reproached Frederick Barbarossa with not doing more to secure Eskil's release, and the episode marks a significant deterioration in the relations of pope and emperor in the later part of Adrian's pontificate.[29] In 1158, Barbarossa declared the primacy of the archbishopric of Hamburg-Bremen over all the Scandinavian churches. Adrian died on 1 September 1159, and it was left to his successor Alexander III to complete the restructuring of the Scandinavian church, which Adrian had so ably begun. Meanwhile, King Valdemar of Denmark and Archbishop Hartwig of Hamburg-Bremen allied themselves with Victor IV, the anti-pope elected in opposition to Pope Alexander in 1159, whom Frederick I promoted; and Eskil, now restored to freedom, was forced to remain in exile in France. Northern Scandinavia, in contrast, remained loyal to Alexander. If it had been an aim of Nicholas's mission to limit the eventual damage to the papacy if southern Scandinavia were lost to a strengthened imperial power, then he succeeded. The completion of his embassy did not, however, come until 1164. A papal mission to Scandinavia, led by Master Stephen of Orvieto in 1163–4, prepared the ground for the establishment of the Swedish archbishopric, with its seat

meddelande', *Historisk Tidskrift (Stockholm)*, 85 (1965), 324–8.

[26] William of Newburgh, i, 111.*

[27] Boso, *Vita Adriani*, 388:* 'gentem illam barbaram et rudem in lege christiana diligenter instruxit'; William of Newburgh (i, 111): Eugenius III sent Nicholas as legate 'in gentes ferocissimas Dacorum et Norrensium'. It is curious that Matthew Paris makes no reference to Breakspear's Scandinavian embassy.

[28] Above, at n. 24.

[29] See below, ch. 7, at n. 109.

at Uppsala, safely clear of imperial influence in southern Scandinavia. The political divisions in the Baltic regions made it impossible to hold the consecration in Sweden, and since the papal court was itself in exile at Sens, Alexander III consecrated Stephen, a Cistercian from Alvastra, as the first Swedish archbishop.[30] Two notable exiles attended the consecration: Eskil of Lund and Thomas Becket of Canterbury. Thus was Nicholas's Scandinavian embassy concluded, five years after his death. He left behind him, in the sagas of western Scandinavia, a warm if slightly uncertain memory of this distinguished visitor from Rome: Nicholas 'the good cardinal', who had brought with him 'a thing called a pallium', who had become pope, 'and is now considered a saint'.

[30] The political background to the consecration is explored by Ingvar Andersson, 'Uppsala ärkestift's tillkomst: till 800-årsjubileet av ärkebiskop Stefans invigning', *Historisk Tidskrift (Stockholm)*, 84 (1964), 389–410. The service itself is reconstructed by Stefan's successor Nathan Söderblom, 'Ärkebiskop Stefans invigning i katedralen i Sens år 1164', in *Svenskars Fromhet* (Stockholm, 1933), 325–52.

Chapter 5

Summus Pontifex. The Ritual
and Ceremonial of the Papal Court

Susan E. Twyman

On Saturday 4 December 1154 Nicholas Breakspear was elected pope with the name of Adrian IV. Boso, the papal biographer, records that Adrian was chosen with the unanimous consent of the clergy and the Roman people, who forced him 'against his will' into the chair of St Peter.[1] It was a convention, often observed by the authors of the papal *vitae* when describing elections, to insist that a new pontiff had been created with the consent of the Romans,[2] but on this occasion such support was clearly lacking. Rome was currently controlled by the republican commune which, since taking on institutional form in 1144, had competed with the popes in attempting to govern the city under the leadership of a Senate.[3] In December 1154 hostility to papal rule was so fierce that it was evidently deemed expedient for the election to take place outside Rome at St Peter's.[4] The Petrine basilica was located in the Leonine city to the northwest of Rome, beyond the urban boundaries[5] and thus safe from the intervention of the commune.[6] Compelled to remain in the Leonine city for the first four months of his pontificate, Adrian was unable to complete the traditional inauguration procedure. Indeed, Boso and

---

[1] Boso, *Vita Adriani*, 389. For the text, see Part II/i, 'Narrative Sources', no. 1.

[2] On this convention but with reference to an earlier period, see P. Daileader, 'One Will, One Voice and Equal Love: Papal Elections and the *Liber Pontificalis* in the Early Middle Ages', *AHP*, 31 (1993), 11–31.

[3] On the Roman commune, see R. L. Benson, 'Political *Renovatio*: Two Models from Roman Antiquity' in *Renaissance and Renewal in the Twelfth Century*, ed. R. L. Benson and G. Constable with C. D. Lanham (Oxford, 1982), 339–86. The handful of documents associated with the commune has been edited by F. Bartoloni, *Codice diplomatico del Senato dal MCXLIV al MCCCXLVII*, Fonti per la storia d'Italia, 87 (Rome, 1948).

[4] W. Ullmann's suggestion that the election took place at St Peter's because the exequies for the previous pope, Anastasius IV (1153–4), had been performed at the Lateran is unsatisfactory, see 'The Pontificate of Adrian IV', *CHJ*, 11 (1955), 233–52, at 237. There is some disagreement in the sources regarding the date of the death of Anastasius IV. According to Boso (*Vita Adriani*, 388) he died on 2 Dec. Indeed, the papal biographer is keen to stress that the traditional period of mourning prescribed in the seventh century by Boniface III (606–07) was observed (*ibid.*, 389), and for Boniface's ruling, see *Liber Pontificalis*, i, 316. But the *Annales Ceccanenses* record 3 Dec., see *Annales Ceccanenses*, a. 1154, ed. G. H. Pertz (1925), *MGH SS*, 19, 284. This date is followed by JL, ii, 102.

[5] See R. Krautheimer, *St Peter's and Medieval Rome* (Rome, 1985), 13.

[6] The construction of a palace adjacent to St Peter's during the pontificate of Eugenius III (1145–53) had made it possible for popes to dwell in relative safety in the Leonine city, see *Liber Pontificalis*, ii, 387.

the other sources are unusually taciturn on the matter of the papal accession ritual and, on the whole, we can only surmise what may have happened. It was only on Maundy Thursday (23 March) 1155, and after the Romans had finally submitted to him, that Adrian was able to enter the city for the first time as pope and make the customary progress to the Lateran, the cathedral of Rome.[7]

With such an inauspicious start to his pontificate, Adrian urgently needed a means of uniting his flock around him and establishing his authority as legitimate pontiff. Thus it was fitting that Maundy Thursday should be the day on which he made the ceremonial entry into his episcopal see. On this feast-day the papal mass was traditionally performed in the afternoon at the Lateran basilica, and Boso records how Adrian, having left the Leonine city and crossed Rome in a magnificent procession, duly celebrated the divine mysteries with great solemnity.[8] If the liturgy of the day was observed according to custom, and there is no reason to doubt that it was, then Adrian must have performed a ritual which was surely among the most dramatic of the entire Roman calendar and which demonstrated in the fullest terms the pope's spiritual status in Rome and throughout Christendom.

The Maundy Thursday ritual is described in the liturgical sources of the twelfth and early thirteenth century.[9] After the *Credo*, members of the higher clergy removed the outer structure (*mensa*) of the high altar. It was transported to the nearby chapel of S. Pancrazio where it remained until Easter Saturday. In the

---

[7] Boso, *Vita Adriani*, 389, records that Adrian had placed the entire city under an interdict after rioting had resulted in the brutal attack on Guido, cardinal priest of S. Pudenziana, while on his way to meet the pope. Faced with the prospect of spending Easter without spiritual observances, the Romans submitted to papal rule.

[8] *Ibid.*

[9] The most complete account of the Holy Thursday ritual is found in the thirteenth-century pontifical of the Curia, the first recension of which was compiled during the pontificate of Innocent III (1198–1216), see *Le Pontifical Romain du moyen-âge*, ed. M. Andrieu, 4 vols, Studi e testi, 86–88, 99 (Vatican City, 1937–41), ii, *Le Pontifical de la curie Romaine au XIIIe siècle*, xlii, 455–64. Dating from the same period is the ordinal for the daily office of the papal Curia, see S. J. P. Van Dijk and J. Hazelden Walker, *The Ordinal of the Papal Court from Innocent III to Boniface VIII and Related Documents* (Freibourg, 1975), 235–6. The twelfth-century sources are: Cencius, *Liber censuum* (c. 1192), ed. L. Duchesne *et al.*, *Liber censuum*, i, [24], 294–5; Albinus, *Digesta pauperis scolaris*, (c. 1189), c. 24 (*ibid.*, ii, 129); Canon Benedict of St Peter's, *Liber politicus* (c. 1140), c. 40 (*ibid.*, ii, 151). These authors and their work are discussed further at nn. 33–6 below. See also the mid-twelfth-century office book compiled by Bernard, prior of the Lateran basilica, *Ordo officiorum ecclesiae Lateranensis*, ed. L. Fischer, Historische Forschungen und Quellen, 2–3 (Munich/Freising, 1916), 50–1 no. 128. For a detailed discussion of the ritual, see S. de Blaauw, 'The solitary celebration of the supreme pontiff. The Lateran Basilica as the new temple in the medieval liturgy of Maundy Thursday' in *Omnes Circumadstantes. Contributions towards a history of the people in the liturgy presented to Hermann Wegman on his retirement*, ed. C. Caspars and M. Schneiders (Kampen, 1990), 120–43, and by the same author, *Cultus et Decor. Liturgia e Architettura nella Roma Tardoantica e Medievale*, 2 vols, Studi e testi, 335 (Vatican City, 1994), i, 292–7. See also C. R. Ligota, 'Petrus-Petra-Ecclesia Lateranensis. A Study in the Symbolic Aspects of Papal Authority in their Bearing on the Investiture Contest', Unpublished PhD thesis (Cambridge, 1956).

meantime the altar was covered with a cloth, sealed at each corner, and guarded when not in use. The pope, having prayed for the remission of the sins of mankind, entered the exposed altar to celebrate the Sacrifice alone.[10]

The significance of the removal of the *mensa* was connected to what lay, or was believed to lie, beneath. In the late eleventh century, Bonizo, bishop of Sutri (d. 1095) referred to the ritual when explaining why the high altar of the Lateran was exceptional in that it was constructed from wood rather than stone.[11] According to Bonizo, this was because it was the very portable altar that had been used by St Peter and his successors down to the time of Pope Silvester (314–35), at which point it was established as the permanent altar of the Lateran basilica.[12] But this tradition, emphasizing the pope's unique position as the successor of the Prince of Apostles, appears to have been forgotten during the twelfth century. It was evidently revived early in the thirteenth century when Gerald of Wales (*c.*1145–1223) and Pope Honorius III (1216–27), both apparently dependent on Bonizo, referred to the Petrine origins of the altar.[13]

During the twelfth century another tradition emerged providing an alternative explanation for the wooden altar. Towards the end of the eleventh century, an anonymous author compiled a treatise describing the merits of the Lateran and the remarkable array of *sanctuaria* housed in the basilica and in the palace.[14] Inside the altar, it was claimed, were precious relics associated with Christ and his ministry. There were loaves from the Last Supper, the cloth used to wipe the feet of the apostles, the seamless robe made by the Virgin Mary, the *Sudarium*,[15] and the

---

[10] *Liber politicus*, c. 40 (*Liber censuum*, ii, 150–1): ...sed solus pontifex intrat ad altare ad sacrificium.

[11] Bonizo of Sutri, *Liber de vita Christiana*, iv. 98, ed. E. Perels, new edn. (Hildesheim, 1998), 165. But according to Bonizo the removal of *mensa* was followed not by the solitary communion of the pope but by the consecration of oil for the sick and chrism for the catechumens, a ritual also associated with Holy Thursday. See J. Braun, *Der Christliche Altar in seiner geschichtlichen Entwicklung* (Munich, 1924), 57–61.

[12] Bonizo adds that Silvester decreed that henceforth all altars were to be constructed from stone, *Liber de vita Christiana*, iv. 98 (ed. Perels, 165).

[13] Giraldus Cambrensis, *Speculum Ecclesiae*, iv. 1 (*Giraldi Cambrensis Opera*, ed. J. S. Brewer and J. F. Dimock, 8 vols, RS 21 [London, 1861–91], iv [1873], 269); Honorius III, *Sermo in Dedicatione Ecclesie Lateranensis*, ed. J. M. Powell, 'Honorius III's *Sermo in Dedicatione Ecclesie Lateranensis* and the Historical-Liturgical Traditions of the Lateran', *AHP*, 21 (1983), 195–209, at 206.

[14] *Anonymi Descriptio Basilicae Lateranensis*, ed. D. Giorgi, *De liturgia Romani pontificis*, 3 vols (Rome, 1744), i, 542–55, Appendix xiv. The *Descriptio* was much extended in several later versions, most notably by John the Deacon who added a dedicatory address to the current pope, Alexander III (1159–81). After John, the work was frequently added to and interpolated. The twelfth-century additions are reflected in the edition of R. Valentini and G. Zucchetti, *Descriptio ecclesiae Lateranensis*, *Codice topografico della città di Roma*, Fonti per la storia d'Italia, 4 vols (Rome, 1940–53), iii, 326–73. For a discussion of the manuscript history, see C. Vogel, 'La *Descriptio ecclesiae Lateranensis* du Diacre Jean. Histoire du Texte Manuscrit' in *Mélanges en honneur de Mon. M. Andrieu* (Strasbourg, 1956), 457–76.

[15] The *Sudarium*, also known as the *Veronica*, was the cloth used to wipe the sweat from

blood and water which had flowed from the side of Christ at the Crucifixion [John 19: 34].[16] There were also certain Old Testament relics: Aaron's rod which had grown buds, the tablets of the law received from God by Moses, the rod of Moses which had created a stream when hit against a rock and the golden seven-branched candlestick from the first tabernacle of the Temple of Jerusalem. But first on the author's list of *sanctuaria* was the Ark of the Covenant, and it was this prize itself which, encased in an outer structure, formed the altar.[17]

The tradition linking the high altar of the Lateran basilica with the Ark of the Covenant continued during the twelfth century; indeed, later redactors of the *De-scriptio* went to considerable lengths to refute the objections of doubters.[18] There is no evidence to suggest that claims to house the Ark ever received official papal support: none of the *ordines* describing the Maundy Thursday liturgy refer directly to its presence. But the rubrical sources do reveal that on this feast-day the Lateran altar acquired a special mystical significance. In his office book for the Lateran chapter, Prior Bernard adds to his rubric a quotation from Hebrews, 'The high priest alone enters the second tabernacle once a year, not without blood, which he offers for his own sins and those of the people'.[19] The clear indication is that the

Christ's face on the way to Calvary. It is odd that it should be listed among the relics in the Lateran, because sources dating back to the tenth century confirm that it was housed in St Peter's, see Canon Benedict, *Liber politicus*, c. 8 (*Liber censuum*, ii, 143) and Duchesne, *Liber censuum*, ii, 160, n. 10. Perhaps in an effort to explain this, one of the twelfth-century redactors of the *Descriptio ecclesiae Lateranensis* adds that this *sudarium* was but one of five cloths that had been used to wrap the body of Christ, see *Descriptio*, c. 4 (ed. Valentini and Zucchetti, 337). On the *Veronica*, see C. Egger, 'Papst Innocenz III. und die Veronica. Geschichte, Theologie, Liturgie und Seelsorge', in *The Holy Face and the Paradox of Rep-resentation*, ed. Herbert L. Kessler, Gerhard Wolf, Villa Spellman Colloquia, 6 (Bologna, 1998), 181–203.

[16] *Anonymi Descriptio Basilicae Lateranensis*, ed. Giorgi, 547–8.

[17] *Ibid.*, 547. Evidently the author had never seen any of these relics, for he adds the words 'so they say'.

[18] One redactor of the *Descriptio* added a section, c. 5, entitled *Ratio circa eos, qui op-ponunt de absconsione tabernaculi et arcae, vel altaris incensi*, ed. Valentini and Zucchetti, 339–41. Here, and in the following chapter, the Ark was provided with a full provenance, including the claim that it had been transported to Rome by Titus with the other spoils after the sack of the Temple of Jerusalem in AD 70. A chronology of popes compiled during the pontificate of Innocent II (1130–43) pointed out that the Ark had been placed in the Lateran basilica in the fourth century by the Emperor Constantine, while at the same time adding considerably to the list of Old Testament relics housed in the Lateran, see *Liber politicus*, c. 4 (*Liber censuum*, ii, 166). The *Graphia aureae urbis Romae*, a composite work compiled c. 1155 (see H. Bloch, 'Der Autor der Graphia aureae urbis Romae', *Deutsches Archiv*, 50 [1984], 55–175), states that the Ark of the Covenant had been deposited in the Temple of Peace next to the Lateran by Vespasian and Titus. The author further expanded the list of Old Testament relics contained in the Ark, adding the vestments of Aaron the priest, see *Graphia aureae urbis Romae*, ed. Valentini and Zucchetti, *Codice topografico*, iii, 83–4, c. 20.

[19] Hebrews 9: 7. Cf. *Ordo Lateranensis*, 50 no. 128; *Le Pontifical de la curie Romaine*, xlii, c. 17, 460: ...*ut significetur quod in veteri testamento scriptum est quia solus Pontifex intrabat semel in anno in Sancta Sanctorum*; cf. *The Ordinal of the Papal Court*, 236. See

papal ritual was an enactment of the Hebrew rite performed on the Day of Atonement. In order to make a blood sacrifice for the sins of mankind, the high priest
passed beyond the second veil of the Temple and entered the Holy of Holies where
the Ark of the Covenant was kept, together with the tablets of the law and the rod
of Aaron [Hebr. 9: 4]. Thus, in twelfth-century Rome, the *Summus Pontifex* provided living proof of the triumph of Christ's new covenant over the old dispensation of the Israelites by assuming the role of high priest of the Temple. Once a year
he entered the Holy of Holies and, having performed the sacrifice upon the Ark of
the Covenant, partook alone of the sacrificial blood and body of Christ.[20]

In the second half of the twelfth century the Maundy Thursday ritual was further elaborated. The novel elements appear first in the *ordo* of Cencius (*c.* 1192)
but their introduction may well date from several decades earlier.[21] According to
Cencius, once the *mensa* of the altar had been removed, two ampoules containing
golden vessels were retrieved from within.[22] Inside the golden vessels were precious stones, and preserved in cavities within the stones were the holy relics of the
blood and the water from the side of Christ. Receiving the ampoules, the pope elevated them so that the entire congregation could witness the event and make humble veneration.[23]

The exposition of Christ's blood and water was a significant liturgical development. On a popular level, custodianship of the blood of Christ, surely the most
precious relic in Christendom, highlighted the position of the pope and his cathedral as uniquely central to the Christian cult.[24] But the relics also brought a new
directness to a theological message which, most likely, had always been intrinsic

---

also Innocent III, *Sermo XIX In Coena Domini*, *PL*, ccxvii, 399.

[20] Dr Ligota has argued that the presence of the Ark of the Covenant had eschatological
significance. According to rabbinical tradition the Ark had disappeared at the time of the
first sack of the Temple of Jerusalem in 585 BC and would not be recovered until the rebuilding of the Temple at the end of time. As the Ark was now present in the basilica, it was
to be concluded that the prophesy had been fulfilled and that the Lateran was to be understood as the New Temple of Jerusalem, see Ligota, *'Petrus-Petra-Ecclesia Lateranensis'*,
27, 300–08.

[21] Schimmelpfennig has argued that much of Cencius's *ordo* reflects earlier custom, see
B. Schimmelpfennig, 'Die Bedeutung Roms im päpstlichen Zeremoniell' in *Rom im hohen
Mittelalter. Studien zu den Romvorstellungen und zur Rompolitik vom 10. bis zum 12. Jahrhundert. Reinhard Elze zur Vollendung seines siebzigsten Lebensjahres gewidmet* (Sigmaringen, 1992), 49. Furthermore, Cencius's brief description of the ritual suggests that it was
already well known.

[22] The version followed here is that of Cencius (*Liber censuum*, [24], 296), who records
the existence of two ampoules. The thirteenth-century ordinal of the papal Curia and the
pontifical of the Curia refer to just one ampoule containing the blood of Christ, see *The
Ordinal of the Papal Court*, 236 and Andrieu, *Le Pontifical de la curie Romaine*, xlii, c. 16,
460.

[23] *Liber censuum*, [24], 296.

[24] Prior Bernard notes that people 'from all parts of the world' came to witness the
Maundy Thursday liturgy, see *Ordo Lateranensis*, 50. De Blaauw argues that the display of
the blood relic points to the intensification of the cult of the Holy Blood in the Lateran,
'Solitary celebration', 124.

to the Maundy Thursday liturgy. In Hebrew tradition the blood sacrifice, performed on the Day of Atonement, was a rite of renewal.[25] It restored the harmonious relationship between heaven and earth, and brought about new life. The first Jewish converts to Christianity were obviously familiar with the ritual and, as the passage in Hebr. 9: 1–28 indicates, found in it an appropriate expression of the meaning of Christ's death and resurrection.[26] Thus, it is hardly surprising that the Hebrew blood sacrifice should become associated with Maundy Thursday because it was at the Last Supper that Christ had brought about the new covenant by offering his blood and body to the apostles, thereby instituting the Holy Sacrament.[27] The pope's action in celebrating alone highlighted his position as supreme minister and emphasized his responsibilities as Christ's vicar on earth.

It was again as Christ's vicar on earth that the pope appeared in another solemn paschal ritual noted by Boso in his *vita* of Adrian IV. The papal biographer records that, on Easter Sunday, Adrian ate the traditional paschal meal in the Lateran palace 'with his disciples'.[28] The reference to the pope's 'disciples' is explained by the fact that this feast held in the *basilica Leoniana* (also known as the *Casa major*)[29] was a re-enactment of the Last Supper.[30] The pope took the role of Christ, and five cardinal priests and five cardinal deacons and the *primicerius* (one of the leading palace officials) the roles of the apostles. The prior of the basilica played the part of Judas.[31]

The point at which the opening of the high altar of the Lateran on Maundy Thursday and the enactment of the Last Supper on Easter Sunday became a regular part of the Roman liturgical cycle is unclear.[32] The details of many papal rituals such as these only come to light in the twelfth century as a result of the proliferation of books of ceremonial containing descriptions of both the sacramental and the non-sacramental liturgy. Of particular importance are three collections of *ordines* compiled by, in chronological order, Canon Benedict of St Peter's (*c*.1140),[33]

---

[25] For a detailed discussion, see M. Barker, *The Gate of Heaven. The History and Symbolism of the Temple in Jerusalem* (London, 1991), 62–3.

[26] *Ibid.*

[27] This is emphasized by John the Deacon or another of the twelfth-century redactors of the *Descriptio* by the addition to the list of relics of the *mensa Domini*, the table at which Christ and the apostles had eaten the last supper, see *Descriptio*, c. 4, ed. Valentini and Zucchetti, 337.

[28] Boso, *Vita Adriani*, 389.

[29] This audience chamber may well be one of the *triclinia* built by Leo III (795–816), see Duchesne, *Liber censuum*, i, 315, n. 19.

[30] See Ullmann, 'The Pontificate of Adrian IV', 238–9.

[31] *Liber politicus*, c. 48 (*Liber censuum*, ii, 153); *Liber censuum*, [35], 298.

[32] The opening of the high altar may well be hinted at in a Roman *ordo* for Maundy Thursday dating from the seventh century, see de Blaauw, 'Solitary celebration', 124. See also Braun, *Der Christliche Altar*, 59 and n. 42.

[33] The collection of *ordines* compiled by Canon Benedict forms part of a compilation of diverse material known as the *Liber politicus*, see *Liber censuum*, ii, 141–77. For a discussion of the considerable problems associated with the *Liber politicus*, see Schimmelpfennig, 'Die Bedeutung Roms' (above, n. 21), and the same author's *Die Zeremonienbücher der*

Albinus, cardinal bishop of Albano (*c.*1189),[34] and Cencius, papal chamberlain and later Pope Honorius III.[35] Cencius's collection forms part of his *Liber censuum* begun in 1192.[36] Each compilation includes rubrics for the major Roman feast-days as well as for the processions and the other ceremonial activity associated with them. The *ordines* of Albinus and Cencius provide detailed descriptions of the ritual surrounding papal accession.[37] Another vital source for the papal cere-monial is the *Liber Pontificalis*. After a period of apparent decline in the tenth and eleventh centuries when little was recorded beyond the name of each pope and the length of his pontificate, the twelfth century witnessed a revival of interest in the writing of papal *vitae*. Characteristic of most of the twelfth-century lives is the evident interest on the part of the authors in recording matters relating to the cere-monial. In particular, the description by the biographer of Paschal II (1099–1118) of the process by which a new pope was installed in the Lateran basilica,[38] and Boso's detailed accounts of Alexander III's two *adventus* ceremonies at Rome (in 1165 and 1180)[39] are suggestive of a desire to keep clear written records of these procedures.

While the tendency to codify was undoubtedly a feature of the twelfth century, the proliferation of detailed rubrics for the ceremonial may also indicate greater awareness of the importance of the non-sacramental ritual as a vehicle for the ex-pression of papal ideology. It is surely no coincidence that evidence pointing to a heightening of its ritual profile should come at a time when the papacy was seek-ing to broaden and redefine both its theological and political status. The second half of the eleventh century had witnessed vigorous efforts by the papacy to assert its supremacy in relation to the empire, a struggle which was to develop into the

römischen Kurie im Mittelalter, Bibliothek des deutschen Historischen Instituts in Rom, 40 (Tübingen, 1973), 6–16.

[34] Albinus, *Digesta*, c. 11 (*Liber censuum*, ii, 123–5). See U.-R. Blumenthal, 'Cardinal Albinus, cardinal bishop of Albano and the *Digesta pauperis scolaris Albini* MS. Ottob. Lat. 3057', *AHP*, 20 (1982), 7–49.

[35] For Cencius's career, see E. Kartusch, 'Das Kardinalskollegium in der Zeit von 1181–1227', PhD thesis, Vienna, 1948, 109–12.

[36] The *Liber censuum* contains a prologue indicating that the work was compiled in 1192, but this date may relate only to the record of taxes owed to the Holy See, which forms the greatest part of the compilation. For the formation of the *Liber censuum*, see T. Montec-chi Palazzi, 'Cencius Camerarius et la formation du *Liber censuum* de 1192', *Mélanges de l'École française de Rome*, 96 (1984), 49–93. For the manuscript witnesses for Cencius's *ordo*, see T. Schmidt, 'Die älteste Überlieferung von Cencius' *Ordo Romanus*', *QF*, 60 (1980), 511–22.

[37] Albinus, *Digesta*, 123–5; Cencius, *Liber censuum*, 311–13. Two sets of rubrics for the election, consecration, and coronation have recently been edited by B. Schimmelpfennig. The so-called Basel *ordo* may well reflect mid-twelfth-century usage, see *idem*, 'Ein bisher unbekannter Text zur Wahl, Konsekration und Krönung des Papstes im 12. Jahrhundert', *AHP*, 6 (1968), 43–70. The so-called London *ordo* appears to have been compiled during the pontificate of Adrian IV, see *idem*, 'Ein Fragment zur Wahl, Konsekration und Krönung des Papstes im 12 Jahrhundert', *ibid.*, 8 (1970), 323–30.

[38] *Liber Pontificalis*, ii, 296.

[39] *Ibid.*, 413 and 446. On papal *adventus*, see at nn. 135–75 below.

long-running conflict commonly known as the Investiture Contest.[40] The *Constitutum Constantini*, the eighth-century forgery generally known as the Donation of Constantine,[41] re-emerged after centuries of obscurity to provide the basis for papal claims to sovereignty over Italy and parts of the west, as well as for claims to the ritual and insignia of the imperial office (a policy widely termed *imitatio imperii* by historians).[42] Legends associated with Constantine and his conversion and donation were to become a key part of papal symbolism in the late eleventh and twelfth centuries. In his *Dictatus papae* written *c*.1075, Gregory VII (1073–85)[43] went beyond the claims of the *Constitutum Constantini* with statements such as 'the pope alone can be called universal' and 'the pope alone is entitled to use imperial insignia'.[44] Likewise, drawing on the *Constitutum*, Bruno, bishop of Segni (d. 1123), pointed out that 'all the insignia of the Roman Empire now belongs to the pope, so that in great processions the pontiff appears in all the magnificence which formerly belonged to the emperor'.[45]

Gregory VII, more than any of his papal predecessors, laid stress on his position as *vicarius Petri* in order to justify the jurisdictional function of the papacy.[46] The pope acted in the place of the Apostle using the power of the keys in binding and loosing which had been committed to Peter by Christ [Matt. 16: 18–19]. The notion of the power of the keys remained central to papal theory,[47] but, as the Maundy Thursday ritual illustrates, in the twelfth century a new doctrine was evolving which stressed the papacy's universal status as head of all Christendom above its parochial function as bishop of Rome.[48] The title of *vicarius Christi* was

[40] For a wide-ranging consideration of the conflict between the empire and the papacy and the so-called Investiture Contest, see U.-R. Blumenthal, *The Investiture Controversy. Church and Monarchy from the Ninth to the Twelfth Century* (Philadelphia, 1988). For papal authority in general during this period see the same author's *Papal Reform and Canon Law in the Eleventh and Twelfth Centuries* (London, 1998).

[41] The best modern edition is *Das Constitutum Constantini*, ed. H. Fuhrmann, *MGH Fontes iuris germanici antiqui in usum scholarum*, 10 (Hanover, 1968). The *Constitutum Constantini* refers to the pope as *Summus Pontifex*: c. 16 (*ibid.*, 91).

[42] The concept of *imitatio imperii* was first fully expounded by P. E. Schramm, see '*Sacerdotium* und *Regnum* im Austausch ihrer Vorrechte. Eine Skizze der Entwicklung zur Beleuchtung der "*Dictatus papae*" Gregors VII.', *Studi Gregoriani*, 2 (1947), 403–57, reprinted with additions in *Kaiser, Könige und Päpste. Gesammelte Aufsätze zur Geschichte des Mittelalters*, 4 vols in 5 (Stuttgart, 1968–71), iv/1, 57–106. In the same volume, see also 'Die *Imitatio imperii* in der Zeit des Reformspapsttums', 201–08.

[43] For Gregory VII, see H .E. J. Cowdrey, *Pope Gregory VII 1073–1088* (Oxford, 1998) and the same author's 'Pope Gregory VII', *Medieval History*, 1 (1991), 23–38.

[44] *Dictatus Papae*, c. 8: *Das Register Gregors VII.*, ii, 55a, ed. E. Caspar, 2nd edn. (Berlin, 1955), *MGH Epistolae Selectae* 2, 201–08.

[45] Bruno of Segni, *Tractatus de sacramentis ecclesiae*, *PL*, clxv, 1108.

[46] See Cowdrey, 'Pope Gregory VII', 26–7. For the concept of *Petrus vivus*, see Y. M.-J. Congar, *L'Ecclésiologie du Haut Moyen Age* (Paris, 1968), 187–90, 367–70.

[47] For an expression of the doctrine of the power of the keys in ritual terms, see below, at n. 87.

[48] For a discussion of the meaning of *universalis*, especially during the second half of the eleventh century, see H. Fuhrmann, '*Ecclesia Romana-Ecclesia Universalis*', in *Rom im*

not used officially until the beginning of the thirteenth century when Innocent III
stated that the pope acted as Christ's vicar in the manner of the Old Testament
ruler Melchisedek who was both *rex* and *sacerdos*.[49] But evidence of an understanding of the papal office as the vicariate of Christ appears much earlier. Addressing Nicholas II (1059–61), Peter Damian, cardinal bishop of Ostia, described
the pope as acting in the place of Christ (*qui Christi vice fungeris*).[50] A letter of
Eugenius III (1145–53) to the canons of St Peter's may well provide the earliest
indication that the popes themselves were adopting the title of vicar of Christ.[51]

It is no coincidence that, at the end of the eleventh century, the Lateran basilica should emerge as a major relic centre, with its *sanctuaria* now rivalling even
the shrine of the Prince of the Apostles at St Peter's.[52] The notion of universality
through the vicariate of Christ gave rise to a new emphasis on the Lateran as the
papal church *par excellence*, and thus as a site for the ritual. Built in the fourth
century by the Emperor Constantine on land confiscated from the Laterani family,
the Lateran had been singled out in the *Constitutum Constantini* as *caput et vertex
omnium ecclesiarum in universo orbe terrarum*.[53] During the twelfth century this
attribution of primacy was formally expressed in the title *caput et mater omnium
ecclesiarum*.[54] The Lateran basilica, the cathedral of Rome, was now officially the
cathedral of the world. To underline this universal status, the papacy could point to
Christ's immanence, already implied in the basilica's dedication to the Saviour,[55]

---

hohen Mittelalter, 29–39.

[49] See M. Maccarrone, *Vicarius Christi. Storia del titolo papale* (Rome, 1952), 110–16,
and for an opposing view see W. Ullmann, *A Short History of the Papacy in the Middle
Ages* (London, 1972), 223.

[50] Peter Damian, *Opusculum XVII, PL*, cxlv, 386: *Tu, domine mi, venerabilis papa, qui
Christi vice fungeris, qui summo pastori in apostolice dignitate succedis*. See Maccarrone,
Vicarius Christi, 78.

[51] Eugenius III, 10 April 1153, *PL*, clxxx, 1588–91. See Ullmann, 'The Pontificate of
Adrian IV', 238.

[52] The *Anonymi Descriptio Basilicae Lateranensis* seems to have been written with the
intention of promoting the Lateran as a relic centre. For the increasing popularity of the
Lateran among pilgrims, see D. J. Birch, *Pilgrimage to Rome in the Middle Ages* (Woodbridge, 1998), 111; for contemporary propaganda, see Ingo Herklotz, *Gli eredi di Costan-
tino. Il papato, il Laterano e la propaganda visiva nel XII secolo* (Rome, 2000).

[53] *Constitutum Constantini*, c. 13 (ed. Fuhrmann, 87).

[54] John the Deacon, *Descriptio*, c. 1 (ed. Valentini and Zucchetti, 328). See U.-R. Blumenthal, 'Rome 1059: liturgy and literature' in *Roma, Magistra Mundi. Mélanges offerts au
Père L .E. Boyle à l'occasion de son 75ᵉ anniversaire*, ed. J. Hamesse, 3 vols, Textes et
études du Moyen Age, 10/i–iii (Louvain-la-Neuve, 1998), i, 41–54 at 46–8.

[55] The Lateran was originally dedicated to the Saviour, but the designation *ecclesia Sal-
vatoris* was rarely used, appearing first in the biography of Pope Martin I (649–53), see
Liber Pontificalis, i, 336. During the fifth century Pope Hilarius (461–8) attached chapels of
St John the Baptist and St John the Evangelist to the Lateran baptistery, and by the seventh
century their names had been added to the dedication of the basilica, see P. Jounel, *Le Culte
des saints dans les basiliques du Lateran et du Vatican au douxième siècle*, Collection de
l'École française de Rome, 26 (Rome, 1977), 109; M. Armellini, *Le chiese di Roma del
Secolo IV al XIX* (Rome, 1942), 122.

but now established by the presence in the high altar of the relics of the holy blood and water.

By the time of the pontificate of Adrian IV a bitter rivalry had arisen between the clergy of the Lateran and those of St Peter's over the attributions of primacy accorded the former church.[56] Furthermore, the first half of the twelfth century had witnessed a marked change in the pattern of papal burials. For centuries, it had been customary for popes to seek interment close to the remains of the Prince of the Apostles in the Petrine basilica, but during the twelfth century the Lateran began to supersede St Peter's as the favoured site for burial.[57] Of the twelve popes who died at Rome, ten are known to have been buried in the Lateran basilica.[58] The biographer of Paschal II explained the choice of this pope by pointing out that the Lateran was 'the true and proper seat of the papacy'.[59] But perhaps most disturbing for the canons of St Peter's was the emergence of a trend giving primacy to the Lateran as a site for papal enthronement.

For centuries it had been traditional for enthronement to take place after episcopal consecration at the high altar of St Peter's. Consecration, enthronement, and, perhaps from the ninth century onwards, coronation[60] were the final acts of papal elevation and were performed on the Sunday following the election.[61] By the mid-eleventh century, enthronement had become the constitutive act of pope-making.[62] Once enthroned upon the *sedes sancti Petri* the newly-elect received his pontifical name while being acclaimed by the congregation.[63] Indeed, the act of enthrone-

[56] For the rivalry between the Lateran and St Peter's, see M. Maccarrone, 'La "*Cathedra Sancti Petri*" nel medioevo: da simbolo a reliquia', *Rivista di Storia della Chiesa in Italia*, 39 (1985), 349–447, esp. 395–432; repr. in idem, *Romana Ecclesia Cathredra Petri*, Italia Sacra, 48, 2 vols (Rome, 1991), ii, 1249–1373, esp. 1308–25.

[57] On St Peter's as the traditional site for papal interment before the twelfth century, see M. Borgolte, *Petrusnachfolge und Kaiserimitation. Die Grablegen der Päpste, ihre Genese und Traditionsbildung* (Göttingen, 1989), 151; A. Paravicini Bagliani, *Il Corpo del Papa* (Turin, 1994), 20–1.

[58] Paschal II, Calixtus II, Honorius II, Innocent II, Celestine II, Lucius II, Anastasius IV, Alexander III, Clement III, and Celestine III were all buried in the Lateran basilica. Adrian IV was buried in St Peter's, next to the tomb of Eugenius III.

[59] *Liber Pontificalis*, ii, 305.

[60] On papal coronation, see below at nn. 131, 133–4.

[61] For the various stages of the accession ritual, see F. Wasner, 'De consecratione, inthronizatione, coronatione Summi Pontificis', *Apollinaris*, 8 (1935), 86–125, 249–81, 428–39. See also S. Twyman, *Papal Ceremonial at Rome in the Twelfth Century*, Henry Bradshaw Society, Subsidia 4 (London, 2002), *passim*.

[62] Increasing emphasis was placed on enthronement because the consecration rite was not invariably performed. This was due to the growing tendency to elevate men to the see of Rome who were already in episcopal orders, see W. Goez, '*Papa qui et Episcopus*: Zum Selbstverständnis des Reformpapsttums im 11. Jahrhundert', *AHP*, 8 (1970), 27–59. This trend continued during the twelfth century; indeed, Adrian IV, cardinal bishop of Albano at the time of his election, had no need for papal consecration. On papal enthronement in general, see N. Gussone, *Thron und Inthronisation des Papstes von den Anfängen bis zum 12. Jahrhundert*, Bonner historische Forschungen, 41 (Bonn, 1978).

[63] For the enthronement of Leo IX, see *Anonymous in Vita s. Leonis*, ed. J. M. Wat-

ment was inseparable from the material *sedes Petri*. By taking possession of this chair the pope demonstrated that he had acquired the Petrine powers necessary to govern the Roman Church.[64] But the election decree issued by Nicholas II (1058–61) in 1059 began the process of loosening the previously essential ties between enthronement and the throne in St Peter's.[65] The decree ruled that in the event of tumultuous conditions at Rome it was possible for an election to take place elsewhere, and under these circumstances it was doctrinally acceptable for the elect to acquire full jurisdictional powers before enthronement.[66]

The consequences of this ruling were revolutionary as it meant that a man could act as pope and govern the Church and all its possessions before his formal enthronement in Rome. But it also had a significant impact on the procedure of papal elevation in that the sequence of the ritual began to alter. Enthronement could now occur immediately after election, and its performance was no longer restricted to the *sedes Petri* in St Peter's.[67] Indeed, by the end of the eleventh century it was evidently decided that it was now the throne in the Lateran that best epitomized the universal quality of the *sedes apostolica*.[68] On 13 August 1099 Paschal II was elected pope at the church of S. Clemente and, having been clad in the red papal mantle and the tiara, he was led on horseback the short distance to the Lateran.[69] Here he was enthroned upon the episcopal throne in the basilica before taking possession of the Lateran palace.[70] It would seem that, until the end of the twelfth century, the Lateran was widely regarded as the correct site for papal en-

---

terich, *Pontificum Romanorum Vitae*, 2 vols (Leipzig, 1862), i, vc (*sic*). Another source adds that with the act of enthronement, Leo 'received the fullness of the pontifical office', *Tabula Vaticana*, ed. Watterich, *ibid.*, i, 102.

[64] See W. Ullmann, '*Romanus Pontifex indubitanter efficitur sanctus*: *Dictatus Papae* 23 in Retrospect and Prospect', *Studi Gregoriani*, 6 (1959–61), 229–64, at 247–9, repr. in *The Church and the Law in the Early Middle Ages* (London, 1975).

[65] *Decretum electione pontificiae*, a. 1059, ed. L. Weiland (Hanover, 1893), *MGH Constitutiones*, i, 539–41 no. 382.

[66] *Ibid.*, 540, no. 382, c. 8. This ruling was repeated in even more explicit terms at the Lateran Council of 1060, see *Concilium Lateranense*, *MGH Constitutiones*, i, 551 no. 386, c. 4.

[67] On 22 April 1073, amidst tumultuous conditions at Rome, Gregory VII was elected and enthroned at S. Pietro in Vincoli. Gregory was a deacon at the time of his elevation and was not consecrated bishop until 30 June. Nevertheless, for two months he exercised full pontifical authority in governing the Church, see Cowdrey, *Gregory VII*, 71–4; Ullmann, '*Romanus Pontifex indubitanter efficitur sanctus*', 246.

[68] It is possible that the emphasis on the Lateran at the end of the eleventh century was linked to the current impulse favouring a return to early Christian practices. Evidence from the fifth century indicates that the Lateran, rather than St Peter's, was regarded as the correct site for papal ordination and thus, presumably, for enthronement. When Boniface I (418–22) and the Roman priest, Eulalius, were consecrated in opposition to one another, the former based his claim to legitimacy on the fact that he had been consecrated at the Constantinian basilica, see *Liber Pontificalis*, i, 227.

[69] *Liber Pontificalis*, ii, 296.

[70] *Ibid.* For the possession-taking of the palace, see below at nn. 77–8, 90, 97, 105–7, 113, 115.

thronement.[71] But on 22 February 1198, the Feast of St Peter's Chair in Antioch, Innocent III was enthroned in the Petrine basilica.[72] Innocent, who, significantly, issued several bulls attempting to bring an end to the rivalry between the Lateran and St Peter's,[73] may well have believed that the throne he was using was the same one that had once been occupied by the apostle himself. By the end of the twelfth century a cult had developed around a wooden chair discovered in the basilica which, it was claimed, was the authentic *sedes Petri*.[74]

If the Lateran basilica, 'the mother of all churches', symbolized the pope's function as *Summus Pontifex*, the adjacent palace was no less a symbol of papal universality. The palace, like the basilica, possessed relics of Christ—his sandals, his circumcised foreskin and his umbilical cord[75]—as well as the heads of SS. Peter and Paul. These precious objects and numerous others were housed in the chapel of S. Lorenzo,[76] known as the S*ancta Sanctorum* on account of these relics.[77] This was the pope's private chapel and where he alone officiated at the main altar. While the palace was becoming an increasingly important centre for the papal liturgy,[78] it was also the focus of governmental operations both in the pope's local capacity as Lord of Rome and his universal office of Christ's *gubernator* on earth. During the twelfth century all three functions—high priest, ruler of Rome and, above all, supreme and apostolic judge—found expression in the *introductio* or ceremonial possession-taking of the palace by a new pope. Although there is no surviving account of Adrian's *introductio*, such was the importance of the cere-

---

[71] In his *ordo* for the election and consecration Cencius describes an enthronement at the Lateran, *Liber censuum*, [77], 311. Further on, however, he indicates that enthronement at St Peter's was also possible, *ibid.*, [83], 312–13. Albinus refers only to an enthronement at the Lateran, *Digesta*, xi. 3 (p. 123). But the Basel *ordo* maintains that a new pope should be enthroned at St Peter's, stating, 'it is false, if anywhere found written, that the elect should be led to the major seat or altar of the Constantinian basilica, because first he should sit in the *cathedra sancti Petri*, consecrated and wearing the pallium', see *Digesta*, i. 12 (p. 61).

[72] *Gesta Innocentii*, c. 7, *PL*, ccxiv, col. xx: ...*fuit apud Sanctum Petrum in episcopum consecratus, et eiusdem apostoli cathedra constitutus*....

[73] See B. Bolton, 'Advertise the Message: Images in Rome at the Turn of the Twelfth Century', in *Studies in Church History*, 28 (Oxford, 1992), 117–30, at 118, repr. in eadem, *Innocent III: Studies on Papal Authority and Pastoral Care* (London, 1995).

[74] See Maccarrone, 'La "*Cathedra sancti Petri*"', 424–5.

[75] On these relics, see below at nn. 113, 115.

[76] The chapel of S. Lorenzo is mentioned for the first time in the *vita* of Stephen III (768–72), see *Liber Pontificalis*, i, 481.

[77] See *Sancta Sanctorum*, ed. C. Pietrangeli (Milan, 1995). For the relics housed there, see H. Grisar, *Die römische Kapelle Sancta Sanctorum und ihr Schatz* (Freiburg, 1908); P. Lauer, *Trésor du Sancta Sanctorum. Extrait des monuments et mémoires publiés par l'Académie des Inscriptions et Belles-Lettres*, 15 (1906), 7–140. See also L. Antonelli, *Memorie storiche delle sacre teste dei Santi Apostoli Piero e Paolo e della loro solenne ricognizione nella Basilica Lateranense*, 2nd edn (Rome, 1852).

[78] Over the course of the twelfth century, the pope's increasing tendency to celebrate here with his immediate *familia* resulted in the gradual loosening of the bonds between the pope and his cathedral. On the development of the papal chapel, see R. Elze, 'Die päpstliche Kapelle im 12. und 13. Jahrhundert', *ZRG kan. Abt.* 36 (1950), 145–204.

mony that there can be little doubt that it was performed. It was Adrian's inability to enter Rome immediately after his election at St Peter's that resulted in the unusually long delay of four months between election and *introductio*.[79]

The twelfth-century *ordines* indicate that the *introductio* involved several phases.[80] In the first phase, the action took place in public when, as the biographer of Paschal II records, the pope was led from the place of election to a stone seat located in front of the Lateran basilica, known as the *sedes stercorata* (the seat of dung).[81] While seated here he uttered the words: 'He raises the poor from the dust, he lifts the needy from the dunghill to give them a place among princes, and to assign them a seat of honour' [1 Samuel 2: 8].[82] Rising from the seat, he threw money into the crowd quoting the words attributed to Peter: 'Silver and gold are not precious to me, what I have I give to you' [Acts 3: 6]. As the pope made his way to the palace, the Romans acclaimed him as 'the Lord pope chosen by St Peter'.[83]

The new pope then entered the palace and was conducted to the chapel of S. Silvestro. At the entrance of this chapel were two stone seats, which provided the focus for the next stage of the ritual.[84] The pope sat in the seat to the right and the prior of S. Lorenzo handed him the *ferula*, an episcopal staff which, according to Cencius, was 'a symbol of guiding and correcting'.[85] He also received the keys of the basilica and the palace, symbols of 'the power of opening and closing and binding and releasing given uniquely to the Roman pontiffs through St Peter, the Prince of the Apostles'.[86] Holding the *ferula* and the keys, the pope rose and moved to the seat on the left, where he received the submission of the palace officials at his feet. The pope then returned the items to the prior. After a brief pause

[79] The Basel *ordo* (i. 19, ed. Schimmelpfennig, 62) states that if a pope has been elected outside Rome the same ritual must be performed as if he had been elected inside the city.

[80] *Liber censuum*, i, [77]–[80], 311–12; *Digesta*, xi. 3 (p. 123); Basel *ordo*, i. 4–31 (ed. Schimmelpfennig, 60–3); London *ordo*, i, 4–20 (ed. Schimmelpfennig, 326–8). The possession-taking is discussed in detail by Gussone, *Thron und Inthronisation*, 283–4 and Paravicini Bagliani, *Il corpo del Papa*, 44–9.

[81] Boso, *Vita Adriani*, 296. The seat is first found termed *sedes stercorata* in the Basel *ordo*, i. 4 (ed. Schimmelpfennig, 60).

[82] The English chronicler, William of Newburgh, quotes this passage from Samuel when recording the elevation of Adrian IV, *Historia rerum Anglicarum, Chronicles of the Reigns of Stephen, Henry II, and Richard I*, ed. R. G. Howlett, RS 82/i–ii (1884–5), i, 109.

[83] The order of events differs in the *ordines*. Cencius, assuming that the election has taken place in the Lateran basilica, has the pope move on immediately to the palace. Albinus and the Basel and London *ordines* assume that the election has taken place elsewhere, and thus describe the pope entering the basilica before moving on to the palace.

[84] The ritual involving the two stone seats is first described in the *vita* of Paschal II, see *Liber Pontificalis*, ii, 296. A comparison of the biographer's account with those of the twelfth-century *ordines* suggests that there had been significant changes since the end of the eleventh century.

[85] *Liber censuum*, ii, [79], 312. For the *ferula* see Gussone, *Thron und Inthronisation*, 283–4.

[86] *Liber censuum*, ii, [79], 312.

he was given a red silk belt from which hung a purple purse.[87] Inside the purse
were twelve precious stones and some musk. The belt was a sign of chastity, while
the purse signified the pope's duty to nourish and protect the poor of Christ.[88] In
the twelve seals the power of the twelve apostles was designated, while the scent
of the musk alludes to the words of the apostle: *Christi bonus odor sumus Deo* [2
Cor. 2: 14–16].[89]

There can be little doubt that the setting in which this ritual took place was of
the greatest significance. The two stone seats were positioned between porphyry
columns supporting an arch. Upon the arch, and thus above the seated pontiff, was
an image of Christ which had once bled when a Jew had thrown a stone at it.[90]
Like the consecrated host, which was also believed to issue blood when dese-
crated, this miraculous phenomenon attested the immanence of Christ.[91] The two
stone seats represented the authority of the apostles Peter and Paul. In the seat to
the right, the pope received the *ferula* and the keys, symbols associated with the
jurisdictional powers transmitted through the Petrine succession. The symbolism
associated with the seat on the left is more complex and appears to be a mingling
of Old and New Testament connotations. The pope was girded with the red belt
and the purse, an investiture of sorts but also a reminder of the constraints of his
office. Thus, the belt signified the prerequisites of chastity and simplicity of life,
apostolic qualities emphasized by the early Christian community described in
Acts. The purse symbolized the wealth that each pope acquired on his accession
and reminded him that he must avoid venality by putting it to the correct use. As if
to illustrate his willingness to do so, the pontiff, still seated, took silver coins from
the hands of his *camerarius* and threw them into the crowd gathered below with
the words: 'He was free in almsgiving, and gave to the poor, his justice will never
be forgotten' [2 Cor. 9: 9].[92] Contained in the purse was not money but the pope's
real 'treasure'. The musk signified doctrinal authority, and alluded specifically to

---

[87]   When Paschal II performed this ceremony in 1099 he was girded with a belt to which
was attached seven keys and seven seals. According to the pope's biographer, these objects
were signs of the seven-fold gift of the Holy Spirit 'by which the pope receives, through
God's will, the ability to govern the Church through the powers of opening and closing',
Boso, *Vita Adriani*, 296. But, by the mid-twelfth century, the symbolism of the number
seven had evidently been suppressed. Elsewhere I have argued that this referred to the seven
cardinal bishops who were responsible for electing and enthroning the new pope, and were
required to participate in the power of the keys by assisting in the government of the
Church, see Twyman, *Papal Ceremonial at Rome*, 128–31.

[88]   *Liber censuum*, ii, [79], 312.

[89]   *Ibid.*

[90]   Cf. Gerald of Wales, *The Jewel of the Church. A Translation of* Gemma Ecclesiastica
by Giraldus Cambrensis, trans. John J. Hagen (Leiden, 1979), 79–80, c. 31.

[91]   On the Jewish desecration of the host, see M. Rubin, 'Desecration of the Host: the
birth of an accusation', in *Christianity and Judaism*, Studies in Church History, 29 (1992),
169–85.

[92]   *Liber censuum*, ii, [79], 312. According to the Basel *ordo* this distribution of largesse
took place at the entrance of the chapel of S. Lorenzo at the end of the ceremony, i. 29 (ed.
Schimmelpfennig, 63).

Paul, doctor of the gentiles, whom the pope must imitate by 'spreading everywhere the word of [Christ] like a sweet smell' [2 Cor. 2: 14–16]. Also in the purse were twelve stone seals representing the merit and authority of all twelve apostles, now combined in the person of the pontiff. But here the symbolism may well have had a further layer of meaning. As a model for the twelve seals, Schimmelpfennig has proposed the stones set upon the pectoral of judgment worn by Aaron the high priest [Ex. 28: 15–30].[93] The stones 'are to bear the names of the sons of Israel and, like the names on them, are to be twelve in number. They are to be engraved like seals, each with the name of one of the twelve tribes' [Ex. 28: 21].[94] But Schimmelpfennig's observation can be taken further. For just as the Hebrew high priest was to be invested with the pectoral of judgment before entering the Holy of Holies in the Temple of Jerusalem,[95] so the Christian *Summus Pontifex* is girded with the belt and the purse containing its twelve stone seals before entering the *Sancta Sanctorum* in the final act of the possession-taking of the Lateran palace.[96] The gloss given by Cencius emphasized the dual apostolic symbolism of the two stone *lectuli*, which represented respectively the primacy of Peter, Prince of the Apostles, and the preaching of Paul, doctor of the people'. It was upon these that the pope's power rested.[97] By reclining, first in the one and then in the other seat, the elect manifested his newly-acquired status as the inheritor of Peter's authority and Paul's ministry, under the presidency of Christ.[98]

According to the author of the Basel *ordo*, the two stone seats were 'not patriarchal but imperial'.[99] Indeed, there is much that links this ritual with the papal policy of *imitatio imperii*. The arrangement of the seats beneath an arch was surely intended to resemble an imperial throne room. One of the throne rooms in the imperial palace at Constantinople contained two thrones elevated on steps and covered by a canopy.[100] Furthermore, the seats (termed *sedes porfireticae* in the

---

[93] Schimmelpfennig, 'Ein bisher unbekannter Text', 63. A parallel between the pope's liturgical vestments and the priestly robes of Aaron had already been drawn in the tenth century, see C. Vogel and R. Elze, *Le Pontifical Romano-Germanique du dixième siècle*, 2 vols, Studi e testi, 226 (Vatican City, 1963), i, *Ordo lxxxi Expositio octo vestium Aaron primi pontificiis*, 292–300, esp. 295–6.

[94] The London *ordo* is alone in stating that the seals in the purse given to the pope were engraved with the names of the apostles i. 13 (ed. Schimmelpfennig, 328).

[95] See Baker, *The Gate of Heaven*, 111–12. According to one source, the vestments of Aaron were amongst the Old Testament relics believed to be kept in the Ark of the Covenant, see above n. 18.

[96] See below at nn. 105–07, 113, 115.

[97] *Liber censuum*, ii, [79], 312, 'Qui siquidem electus illis duabus sedibus sic sedere debet, ac si videatur inter duos lectulos jacere, id est ut accumbat inter principis apostolorum Petri primatum, et Pauli doctoris gentium predicationem.'

[98] For a contemporary explanation of the significance of the pope's succession from both Peter and Paul, see the *arenga* of Eugenius III's letter to the canons of St Peter's, *PL*, clxxx, 1588–91.

[99] Basel *ordo*, i. 26 (ed. Schimmelpfennig, 62).

[100] See J. Deér, *The Dynastic Porphyry Tombs of the Norman Period in Sicily*, Dumbarton Oaks Studies, 5 (Cambridge, Mass., 1959), 143–6.

ordines) as well as the columns supporting the arch were made of, or believed to be made of, porphyry,[101] a dark red marble which was highly prized for its associations with imperial power.[102] No less significant is the fact that the ritual was associated with a chapel dedicated to Pope Silvester. According to legend it was during the pontificate of Pope Silvester I in the fourth century that the Emperor Constantine had issued his Donation to the Roman Church. Constantine, afflicted with leprosy and advised by his pagan soothsayers to bathe in the blood of babies, received a vision in which SS. Peter and Paul had offered him a miraculous cure.[103] Unaware of their identity, he consulted the pontiff who showed him pictures of the two apostles and explained their importance to the Christian faith. It was believed that these very images of Peter and Paul, according to the legend so instrumental in establishing the triumph of Christianity over paganism, now adorned the high altar of the Lateran basilica.[104]

In the final stage of the possession-taking, the pope was conducted to the *Sancta Sanctorum*. Along the way he passed through a portico and beneath two other images of the apostles Peter and Paul which, says Cencius, had miraculously arrived at Rome from across the sea.[105] With distinct echoes of the Maundy Thursday liturgy, in the final act of the ritual the pontiff took possession of his private chapel. Entering the Holy of Holies alone, he venerated the relics of Christ and other *sanctuaria* housed in the three altars there.[106]

While the pope was taking possession of the palace, the Romans waited outside in the public *campus*.[107] Whether or not they were able to witness the ritual at the chapel of S. Silvestro is unclear,[108] but the pope was almost certainly visible as he passed through the palace on his way to the *Sancta Sanctorum*. Located be-

---

[101] The *sedes porfireticae* have been identified with two stone seats, one currently housed in the Louvre and the other now in the Vatican museum. These seats are made of *rosso antico*, a red marble commonly used as a substitute for porphyry, see C. D'Onofrio, *La Papessa Giovanna. Roma e papato tra storia e leggenda* (Rome, 1979), 124; Paravicini Bagliani, *Il Corpo del Papa*, 43.

[102] Deér has argued that during the twelfth century these associations gave rise to the extensive use of the stone in liturgical furnishings, *ibid.*, 146–54.

[103] *Constitutum Constantini*, cc. 7–8 (ed. Fuhrmann, 69–74). The legend of Constantine's miraculous cure and subsequent conversion pre-dated the *Constitutum Constantini* by several centuries, first coming to light in the *Legenda sancta Silvestri* probably written in the late fifth or early sixth century, see W. Levison, 'Konstantinische Schenkung und Silvesterlegende' in *Miscellanea Francesco Ehrle*, 2 vols, Studi e testi, 38 (Rome, 1924), ii, 159–247; N. Huyghebaert, 'Une légende de fondation: le "Constitutum Constantini"', *Le Moyen Age*, 85 (1979), 177–209.

[104] See *Anonymi Descriptio Basilicae Lateranensis*, ed. Giorgi, 548.

[105] *Liber censuum*, ii, [80], 312.

[106] The Basel *ordo* is alone in listing at this point the relics housed in the *Sancta Sanctorum*, i. 28 (ed. Schimmelfennig, 63).

[107] On the Lateran *campus*, see I. Herklotz, 'Der *Campus Lateranensis* im Mittelalter', *Römisches Jahrbuch für Kunstgeschichte*, 22 (1985), 3–43.

[108] The fact that the pope dispensed money to the Romans during this ceremony indicates that a window or a balcony must have been nearby.

tween the two chapels was an audience chamber, known as the basilica of Zacharias (earlier it had been called the basilica of Theodore), where the icons of SS. Peter and Paul were displayed.[109] For centuries, the popes had used this room, opening onto the portico on the north front of the palace, for making public appearances,[110] as well as for the regular distribution of alms to the poor.[111] But it was also an important site for the papal liturgy. According to Canon Benedict, on the Feast of the Exaltation of the Holy Cross (14 September), the citizens gathered at S. Maria Maggiore before moving in procession to the Lateran *campus*.[112] Meanwhile, the pope removed from the *Sancta Sanctorum* the relics of the wood of the True Cross, and the sandals and the circumcision of Christ. The cardinal clergy carried these *sanctuaria* to the portico of the palace where they were displayed to the assembled crowd before the procession moved on to the Lateran basilica for the papal mass.[113] But the ritual had evidently changed slightly by the time that Cencius compiled his *ordo* at the end of the twelfth century.[114] From his account, it appears that the relics were displayed from the chapel of S. Silvestro—thus supporting the notion of a balcony or window in this vicinity—with reference being made only to the relics of the wood of the True Cross and the heads of SS. Peter and Paul. Innocent III later questioned the authenticity of the circumcision and the umbilicus of Christ, and it may well be the case that these relics had already been replaced in the ceremony by the heads of Peter and Paul.[115]

The same part of the *campus* also provided the starting and finishing point for many of the stational processions when the pope progressed to and from the appointed church (the *statio*)[116] with a great retinue of higher clergy and palace officials.[117] With the emphasis depending on the liturgical significance of the occasion, the pope revealed himself as high priest, provider of welfare to the Romans, and

[109] Pope Zacharias (741–52) was responsible for restoring the area in front of the basilica of Theodore, see P. Lauer, *Le Palais de Latran. Étude historique et archéologique* (Paris, 1911), 88, 91. See also Duchesne, *Liber censuum*, i, 315, n. 16.

[110] During the pontificate of Sergius I (687–89), the pope appeared here after an imperial agent had arrived in Rome with orders for his arrest. The author of his *vita* records that Sergius 'went outside to the basilica named after the lord pope Theodore; opening the doors and sitting on a seat beneath the apostles, he honourably received the common soldiers and the people who had come to see him', *Liber Pontificalis*, i, 374.

[111] See, for example, the biography of Hadrian I (772–95), *Liber Pontificalis*, i, 502.

[112] *Liber politicus*, c. 74 (*Liber censuum*, ii, 159). See also *Ordo Lateranensis*, 154.

[113] *Liber politicus*, c. 74 (*Liber censuum*, ii, 159).

[114] *Liber censuum*, ii, [74], 310–11.

[115] Innocent III, *De Sacris Altaris Mysterio*, (recte *De missarum mysteriis*), xx. 30, *PL*, cxvii, 876–7.

[116] For the Roman stational system, see J .F. Baldovin, *The Urban Character of Christian Worship. The Origins, Development and Meaning of Stational Liturgy*, Orientalia Christiana Analecta, 228 (Rome, 1987), esp. 105–66. For a description of the twelfth-century papal cortège, see Cencius, *Liber censuum*, ii, [7], 292.

[117] For a detailed account of the pope's return to the palace after the stational procession, see for example the Feast of the Nativity, *Digesta*, xi. 128.

ruler of the city.[118] On certain high feast-days—the so-called *dies coronae*—the pope wore the crown during the procession. Little is known about the origins of the *dies coronae*.[119] A crowning performed in connection with accession is known from the ninth century,[120] and it is possible that the practice of parading the crown on certain high feast days followed soon after.[121] But it seems likely that the custom truly flourished in the second half of the eleventh century as a result of the policy of *imitatio imperii*. The earliest reference to a feast-day crown-wearing concerns Gregory VII who, after celebrating mass at S. Maria Maggiore on the Feast of the Nativity, returned to the Lateran wearing the crown.[122] A list of eighteen *dies coronae* is found in Albinus's *Digesta pauperis scolaris*[123] but it is unlikely that all these processions were regularly observed during the twelfth century. Some of the lesser observances may well have fallen into desuetude as a result of the papacy's frequent and often prolonged absences from Rome.

It is hardly surprising that one crown-wearing day to retain a high profile was the Feast of SS. Peter and Paul (29 June), traditionally celebrated with a procession to St Peter's. Boso notes that in 1155, the first year of his reign, Adrian IV observed this feast with all due solemnity despite the fact that the pope was absent from Rome.[124] Indeed, on this occasion a crown-wearing, celebrated on a feast so pregnant with meaning for the papacy, may well have helped to provide Adrian with much-needed prestige. Eleven days earlier on 18 June, against the will of the Roman commune, the pope had crowned the German king, Frederick Barbarossa (king 1152, emperor 1155, died 1190), as emperor at St Peter's.[125] Pope and emperor were refused entry into the city and were compelled to retreat together to the Roman countryside. It was here, at *pons Lucanus* near Tivoli, that Adrian and Frederick celebrated the Feast of the Apostles, both wearing crowns as they went in procession to the mass.[126]

This ritual expression of concord between pope and emperor was in marked contrast with the events of three weeks earlier. On 9 June 1155, Adrian and Fre-

---

[118]   See Schimmelpfennig, 'Die Bedeutung Roms', 52–9.

[119]   See H.-W. Klewitz, 'Die Krönung des Papstes', *ZRG kan. Abt.*, 30 (1941), 96–130.

[120]   *De gradibus romanae ecclesiae, Ordo XXXVI*, c. 55, ed. M. Andrieu, *Les Ordines Romani du haut moyen-âge*, 4 vols, Studi e testi, 86–88, 99 (Vatican City, 1937–41), iii, 204.

[121]   See Schimmelpfennig, 'Die Bedeutung Roms', 58.

[122]   *Liber Pontificalis*, ii, 282.

[123]   Eighteen feasts were designated as *dies coronae*: the Four Crowned martyrs (8 November); St Martin (11 November); St Clement (23 November); the first Sunday in Advent; the second Sunday in Advent (*Populus Sion*), the third Sunday in Advent (*Gaudete*), the Nativity (25 December); St Stephen (26 December); St Silvester (31 December); Epiphany (6 January); mid-Lent Sunday (*Laetare Ierusalem*); Easter Sunday; Easter Monday; the second Sunday after Easter (*Ego sum pastor bonus*); Ascension; Pentecost; SS. Peter and Paul (29 June); the pope's own anniversary (*in anniversario suo*): see Albinus, *Digesta*, x. 90.

[124]   Boso, *Vita Adriani*, 393.

[125]   *Ibid.*, 392.

[126]   *Ibid.*, 392–3.

derick met for the first time at Sutri where the German king's army was en-camped.[127] According to Boso, Frederick refused to perform the *officium stratoris*, a ritual recorded in the Donation of Constantine,[128] which involved leading the papal horse like a groom for the distance of a stone's throw.[129] The cardinals, in-terpreting this lapse in protocol as a sign of hostility, fled in terror leaving the pope alone in the king's camp. The situation was saved when senior members of the royal entourage assured Frederick that previous kings and emperors had performed the ritual in honour of St Peter.[130]

Adrian's determination to celebrate the *dies coronae* in the face of adversity may well have been redoubled by his earlier conflict with the commune. His in-ability to enter Rome after his election had meant that he could not perform the crown-wearing procession to the Lateran, traditionally the culminating act of ac-cession. Indeed, it is possible that throughout his four-month 'exile' in the Leonine city, Adrian never received coronation, an event generally recorded by papal biog-raphers, but about which Boso remains silent. The coronation signified confirma-tion of territorial rulership, something that, as yet, the Romans were unwilling to acknowledge.[131] Nor could Adrian have worn the crown when he entered Rome for the first time as pope on 23 March 1155. The solemn character of the Maundy Thursday liturgy would have prohibited a festive crown-wearing procession. The likelihood is that Adrian's coronation was delayed until Easter Monday, a feast with a special significance in the Roman calendar.

The twelfth-century *ordines* indicate that the Easter Monday liturgy was unique amongst the stational observances.[132] On this day, as was the case for the coronation procession, the pope progressed to St Peter's and then, after celebrating mass, he traversed the city to the Lateran, wearing the crown. St Peter's was the appointed station for many other annual observances,[133] but it was only on this one day of the year that the itinerary and every aspect of the ritual detail mirrored ex-actly that performed during the coronation procession. It would seem that the rea-son for this repetition was that the feast, coming as it did immediately after the Easter liturgy with its theme of renewal, was an annual commemoration of the pope's accession.

The Easter Monday crown-wearing procession, like the coronation procession itself, had a special significance in that the pope's return to the City of Rome after his visit to St Peter's was a form of epiphany. During the accession ritual the pon-

---

[127] *Ibid.*, 391.

[128] *Constitutum Constantini*, c. 16 (ed. Fuhrmann, 92). According to the *Constitutum*, Constantine had himself performed the *officium stratoris* for Pope Silvester.

[129] Boso, *Vita Adriani*, 392.

[130] *Ibid.* See I. S. Robinson, *The Papacy 1073–1198* (Cambridge, 1990), 445–6, 463–4.

[131] In the second half of the eleventh century there had been attempts to provide the crown with a universal meaning by linking the coronation with election. But the act appears to have retained its sense of the confirmation of the pope as ruler of Rome, see Twyman, *Papal Ceremonial at Rome*, 120–2.

[132] *Liber politicus*, cc. 50–51 (*Liber censuum*, ii, 154).

[133] For a list of the stations at St Peter's see Albinus, *Digesta*, x. 2 (p. 90).

tiff made his re-entry equipped with new powers—the spiritual power derived from episcopal consecration,[134] and sovereign power over the Romans and other papal territories, confirmed by the coronation—and it seems possible that on Easter Monday these powers were symbolically renewed. On both occasions the appearance of the ruler at the gates of his seat of government was expressed in the traditional terms of the *adventus*.

The reception of the ruler, termed *adventus* in Roman antiquity, survived throughout the Middle Ages.[135] Adopted by Christian kings and emperors, its ritual framework was also readily adaptable to ecclesiastical purposes, serving for the transfer of relics from an extra-mural location into the city centre, as well as for the reception of a new bishop.[136] The earliest clear evidence for papal reception ceremonies dates from the first half of the sixth century, when three popes received formal greetings at the imperial capital of Constantinople.[137] But the first detailed account of a papal *adventus* ceremony at Rome emerges only at the end of the eighth century (in 799), when Leo III, returning from a meeting in Saxony with the Frankish king Charlemagne (king 768, emperor 800, d. 814), was received by the Romans.[138] On the vigil of the feast of the apostle Andrew (29 November) the populace, ranked according to sex and status, went out to the Milvian Bridge to greet the pope, each group carrying the ceremonial signs and banners of the city.[139] Hymns and praises were sung as Leo was led in procession to St Peter's, where he celebrated mass.[140] It is most likely that a form of *adventus*, which might be termed

[134] By the twelfth century the spiritual status of a pope was not invariably enhanced by the visit to St Peter's. During this period many of the popes, including Adrian IV, were already bishops before their elevation and received benediction rather than consecration at the Petrine basilica.

[135] For ritual reception during the Hellenistic and early Roman period, see E. Petersohn, 'Die Einholung des Kyrios', *Zeitschrift für systematische Theologie*, 7 (1930), 682–702; J. Lehnen, *Adventus Principis* (Frankfurt, 1997). For late antiquity, see S. MacCormack, 'Change and Continuity in Late Antiquity: the Ceremony of *Adventus*', *Historia*, 21 (1972), 721–52, and the same author's *Art and Ceremony in Late Antiquity* (Berkeley, CA, 1981). For papal *adventus*, see Twyman, *Papal Ceremonial at Rome, passim*, and the same author's 'Papal *Adventus* at Rome in the Twelfth Century', *Historical Research*, 69 (1996), 233–53.

[136] For the *adventus* of relics see P. Brown, 'Relics and Social Status in the Age of Gregory of Tours' in *Society and the Holy in Late Antiquity* (London, 1982), 222–50, esp. 239–40; K .G. Holum and G. Vikan, 'The Trier Ivory; *Adventus* Ceremonial and the Relics of St Stephen', *Dumbarton Oaks Papers*, 33 (1979), 113–33. For episcopal *adventus* see MacCormack, 'Change and Continuity', 746–8 and M. McCormick, *Eternal Victory: Triumphal Rulership in Late Antiquity, Byzantium and the Early Medieval West* (Cambridge, 1986), 329–31.

[137] John I (523–6), Agapitus I (535–6) and Vigilius I (537–55), see *Liber Pontificalis*, i, 275, 287, and 297–8.

[138] *Liber Pontificalis*, ii, 6.

[139] The *Constitutum Constantini* made no explicit reference to *adventus* but, according to the document, the papacy had been granted the right to the imperial banner procession, see *Constitutum Constantini*, c. 16 (ed. Fuhrmann, 92–3).

[140] *Liber Pontificalis*, ii, 6.

'intra-mural', was already an established part of the papal accession ritual by this time.[141] After the consecration at St Peter's, the pope returned to Rome and performed a processional circuit of the city before a formal reception at the Lateran residence.[142]

Since late antiquity the dominant model for the *adventus* of Christian rulers had been Christ's entry into Jerusalem on Palm Sunday, an event described in the Gospel of St John [12: 12–19] as *hypantesis*, the technical term for the reception of a Hellenistic ruler.[143] This paradigm, often made explicit through the waving of palm branches and singing of the antiphon *Benedictus qui venit* (Blessed is he who comes in the name of the Lord), articulated the ruler's function as Christ's vicar on earth, charged with the duty of guiding his people to salvation.[144] Twelfth-century accounts of papal *adventus* suggest that popes, like kings and emperors, were now consciously evoking the model of the entry into Jerusalem at their receptions in what was surely a deliberate blending of the *imitatio imperii* and the *imitatio Christi*.[145] Describing the arrival of Eugenius III at Paris in 1147, the author of the *Annales Cistercienses* terms the pope *Summus Vicarius Christi*.[146] But other commentators recording papal receptions drew on biblical imagery to make the message even more explicit.

Uodalscalcus, a German monk from Augsburg, provides an eyewitness account of the arrival of Calixtus II (1119–24) at Rome on 3 June 1120.[147] As the pope approached the city, young men and children bearing branches hurried out to greet him shouting acclamations. They closed in around him and as they were forced back, the German monk places in the mouth of Calixtus the words spoken by Christ: 'Suffer the little children to come unto me, for of such is the kingdom of Heaven' [Matt. 19: 14].[148] Uodalscalcus was also conscious of the ubiquitous connotations of imperial triumph inherent in *adventus*. He notes that at a distance of three days' journey from the city of Rome and displaying the standard of the cross, 'the trophy of victory of all consuls and emperors', the Roman militia came out to meet the pope. Indeed, so magnificent was the procession, he claims, that Caesar himself, had he been present, would have marvelled at the sight and even Tullius (Cicero) would have been impressed.[149]

Boso, the biographer of Alexander III, was no less explicit when drawing a parallel between Christ and the pontiff.[150] Describing Alexander's entry into Rome on 12 March 1178, he reports that the Roman clergy went out some distance from

---

[141] See Twyman, *Papal Ceremonial at Rome*, 57–68.

[142] *Ibid.*, 68.

[143] See Petersohn, 'Die Einholung des Kyrios', 693.

[144] See E. Kantorowicz, 'The King's Advent and the Enigmatic Panels in the Doors of Santa Sabina', *Art Bulletin*, 26 (1944), 207–31, at 211.

[145] *Ibid.*, 210.

[146] *Annales Cistercienses*, I, ed. Angelo Manrique, 4 vols (Lyons, 1642), ii, 55.

[147] *Uodalscalcus de Egino et Herimanno*, ed. P. Jaffé (1856), *MGH SS*, 12, 446.

[148] *Ibid.*

[149] *Ibid.*, 446.

[150] *Liber Pontificalis*, ii, 446.

the city to meet the pope, carrying banners and crosses. Also present were the senators and the communal magistrates, accompanied by trumpet players, and the nobles with men-at-arms in ceremonial livery. The rest of the populace came out on foot, bearing olive branches. Boso describes how the citizens thronged around the pope as he approached the city and blocked his path so that the papal mount was barely able to move forward. He states that Alexander 'saw the eyes of them all turned toward him as to Jesus Christ whose vicar on earth he was'.[151] This identification with Christ is taken further by Boso when he alludes to the Saviour's Passion in noting that the pope arrived at the Lateran gate at the ninth hour and suffering from extreme weariness.[152] It was at the ninth hour that Christ had died on the cross and the moment when the veil of the Temple had been torn in two to reveal the New Covenant [Matt. 27: 45–52 and Luke 23: 44–46].

The theme of triumph, both in a Christian eschatological sense and in the context of imperial military victory, was expressed in clear terms during intra-mural and extra-mural *adventus*. In his biography of Calixtus II, Boso reports that when the pope entered Rome on 3 June 1120, arches were prepared along the ceremonial route 'according to custom'.[153] The erection of 'honorific' arches between St Peter's and the Lateran is confirmed by Cencius in his *ordines* for the papal consecration and for Easter Monday.[154] Provided by the Roman *honorabiles* and the leading guilds and corporations, they ranged in form from the iron arch set up on the steps of the Petrine basilica to the decorative riggings made of precious metal and fabric hung from building to building across the street.[155] No matter what form they took, these structures were clearly an allusion to the triumphal arches erected to honour victorious emperors in Roman antiquity. In an *ordo* for the papal coronation compiled between 1292 and 1295, William Durandus, bishop of Mende, speaks in clear terms of the 'triumphal arches' erected from St Peter's up to the Lateran.[156]

Another feature of papal *adventus*, clearly blending the *imitatio imperii* with the *imitatio Christi*, was the ritual involving the Jewish community of Rome.[157] There was a long tradition of Hebrew participation in ruler *adventus*[158] when the

---

[151] *Ibid.*

[152] *Ibid.*

[153] *Ibid.*, 337.

[154] *Liber censuum*, ii, [82], 312; [38], 299.

[155] Albinus describes these structures as ornate riggings made from gold and silver vessels and precious vestments, *Digesta*, xi. 3 (p. 124). The individuals and organizations responsible for erecting the arches received a payment, known as the *presbyterium*. For a list of those in receipt of this payment, see *Liber censuum*, ii, [39], 299–300.

[156] M. Andrieu, Le *Pontifical romain du moyen-age*, iii, *Ordo ad coronandum summum pontificem romanum*, c.19 (p. 667).

[157] The role of the Jews in papal *adventus* is discussed in detail by Twyman, *Papal Ceremonial at Rome*, 193–208.

[158] See N. Coulet, 'De l'integration à l'exclusion: la place des juifs dans les ceremonies d'entrée solennelle au moyen âge', *Annales. Economies, sociétes, civilisations* 34 (1979), 672–81.

Jews under his rule joined together with other subject peoples to offer praises to the sovereign.[159] Hebrew *laudes* performed for a pope arriving at Rome are recorded from the mid-eleventh century. When Leo IX (1048–54) entered Rome in 1049, tri-lingual acclamations were performed in his honour by the Jews, the Greeks, and the Romans.[160] The same bodies were present and offering praises when Calixtus II arrived at his episcopal see in 1120.[161]

During the twelfth century, however, a novel ritual appears to have been introduced requiring the Jews to be present at *adventus* bearing their laws in the form of the scrolls of the Torah.[162] When Eugenius III entered Rome in December 1145, the Jews were in attendance carrying the laws of Moses.[163] Likewise, when Alexander III made his entry twenty years later in November 1165, the Jews came bearing their laws 'as was customary'.[164] An example of the Jews carrying their laws at papal *adventus* provides a clearer picture of the ritual but this took place not at Rome but in France, near the monastery of Saint-Denis. Suger, abbot of Saint-Denis, records how Innocent II (1130–38) spent Easter week of 1131 at the monastery making a magnificent procession on Holy Sunday from the church of Saint Denis de l'Estreé to Saint Denis itself.[165] At a designated site along the route the Jews presented him with the scrolls of the Torah.[166] The ritual involving the presentation of the Hebrews' laws is recorded in Cencius's *ordines* for the papal coronation procession and for Easter Monday. On both occasions the papal cortege halted on its journey from St Peter's to the Lateran at a location in the region known as Parione, near the Jewish ghetto, where the presentation took place.

The meaning of the Jewish presentation of the Torah is highly significant in the present context. When describing the ritual performed for Innocent II in 1131, Abbot Suger records that the pope, on receiving the Torah, offered a supplication on behalf of the 'blinded synagogue' that Almighty God 'will lift the veil from your hearts'.[167] This Christian conception of the Jews as unable to see the truth of their own scriptures was by no means novel. It was a symbolism used by Leo I (440–61) in his sermon on the Passion of the Lord, part of which was addressed to

---

[159] For example, Gregory of Tours records how, in 585, Gunthram, the Merovingian ruler of Burgundy, was greeted at Orléans with *laudes* sung by the Syrians, the Gallo-Romans, and the Jews, see *Decem libri historiarum*, ed. B. Krusch and W. Levison (Hanover, 1951), *MGH SRM*, 1, 370.

[160] *Anonymous in vita s. Leonis*, ed. Watterich, *Pontificum Romanorum Vitae*, i, vc (*sic*).

[161] *Uodalscalcus de Egino et Herimanno*, 446–7.

[162] See Coulet, 'De l'intégration à l'exclusion', 675–7, who argues that the ritual involving the presentation of the Torah had a much longer tradition as part of ruler *adventus*. However, there is no evidence to support this view.

[163] *Liber Pontificalis*, ii, 387.

[164] *Ibid.*, 413.

[165] Abbot Suger of St Denis, *Vita Ludovici grossi Regis*, ed. H. Waquet, *Vie de Louis IV le Gros*, Les Classiques de l'histoire de France au moyen-âge, 11 (Paris, 1929), 262–4. See L. Grant, *Abbot Suger of St-Denis* (London, 1998), 194–5.

[166] *Vita Ludovici*, 264.

[167] *Ibid.*, 264.

the Jews.[168] One of the twelfth-century redactors of the *Descriptio Lateranensis ecclesiae* borrowed from this sermon when concluding his discussion of the Ark of the Covenant with an attack on Judaism.[169] Quoting Leo, he states that the blindness of the Jews, symbolized by the veil concealing the Holy of Holies, the innermost sanctuary of the Temple, has cut them off from the path to sanctity and removed their right to true priesthood.[170] Noting the words spoken by Christ, 'if you believe in Moses, then you should believe in me' [John 5: 46], the author goes on to say that the blindness of the Jews will be punished by the condemnation of their covenants which are now empty of grace and deprived of law.[171]

At the end of the thirteenth century Cardinal Stefaneschi wrote a poem commemorating the coronation of Pope Boniface VIII (1294–1303) on 23 January 1295.[172] Stefaneschi describes how, once the pontiff had arrived at the appointed site in Parione, he was greeted by the Jews, 'singing but blind of heart'. The pope was shown the law of Moses, 'pregnant with Christ', and having venerated him who is prefigured in the law, he turned his back on the Jews and delivered a sermon on their ignoble status and their inability to recognize Christ.[173] The sense expressed by the poem is clear. The pope venerated the Hebrew laws not for their intrinsic value but because of Christ's latency in them. Here then was the Christlike *Summus Pontifex* acknowledging the importance of the Hebrew prophets as witnesses to the coming of the Redeemer but abrogating the law of Moses. This message that the law of Christ had triumphed over the old covenant was also delivered during the Maundy Thursday liturgy when the pope assumed the role of high priest of the Temple.[174] Indeed, it may well be the case that on the day of the coronation and on Easter Monday the presentation of the Torah acquired added significance because the ritual was performed while the pope was on his way to the Lateran where, it was widely believed, the Ark of the Covenant and the original tablets of the Hebrew law were housed in the high altar of the basilica.

There is no reason to doubt that Adrian IV was accorded the traditional intramural *adventus* on Easter Monday, 27 March 1155, indeed, the likelihood is that this magnificent event doubled as his coronation procession. But there is a possibility that he also experienced an extra-mural *adventus* in the following year. Adrian had not returned to Rome since the citizens' riot in June 1155, following his coronation of Frederick Barbarossa without their knowledge.[175] But, as Boso reports, in November 1156, 'he returned with due honour and glory to the City and to the Lateran consistory'.[176] It is clear that on several occasions during the twelfth

[168]   Leo I, *Sermones*, Sermo 61, *PL*, liv, 346, 348–9.
[169]   *Descriptio ecclesiae Lateranensis*, c. 6 (ed. Valentini and Zucchetti, 342).
[170]   *Ibid*.
[171]   *Ibid*.
[172]   Cardinal Stefaneschi, *De electione et coronatione S .D. Bonifacii Papae VIII*, in Muratori, *Rer. Ital. SS*, 3/i, 642–55.
[173]   *Ibid*., 652.
[174]   See above at nn. 25–7.
[175]   See above, at n. 131.
[176]   Boso, *Vita Adriani*, 395. The *consistorium* was both a physical place and the formal

century *adventus* was performed for pontiffs who were retaking possession of Rome after a dispute with the Romans had resulted in their withdrawal from the City.[177] Under these circumstances ritual reception represented a stage in the process of reconciliation between pope and citizens. And this was how it was portrayed by Boso. It cannot be without significance that he chose essentially to finish his narrative of Adrian's pontificate with an account of his triumphal return to the City.

meeting of the pope and cardinals. Boso's reference to the 'consistory' may well have been intended to emphasize that Adrian was in full possession of his papal powers after his return to Rome.

[177] See Twyman, 'Papal *Adventus* at Rome', 249–53, and the same author's *Papal Ceremonial at Rome*, 164–9.

Chapter 6
St Albans' Loyal Son
Brenda Bolton

In the twelfth century, the great Benedictine Abbey of St Albans was thrice blessed. It was blessed in its location, its previous history—the cult of Alban, saint and martyr—and, uniquely, from 4 December 1154, with its own loyal son, Nicholas Breakspear, becoming Adrian IV (1154–9), the only English pope. Rapid promotion in c. 1149–50 to the elevated rank of cardinal bishop of Albano,[1] with emotive connotations for himself, led to the eventual election of Adrian. This provided the occasion for the Abbey to exploit to the full the 'special relationship' it was to have with this son of St Albans.[2] Even the choice of papal name seemed significant, recalling, as it did, the first pope Adrian (772–95), so impressed with Alban, that he was reputed to have endowed the Abbey with its initial privileges.[3] Under these circumstances, Robert de Gorron, eighteenth abbot of St Albans (1151–66),[4] immediately grasped the opportunity to encourage Adrian IV to direct his newly found authority to the Abbey's benefit so that St Albans was poised to prosper even further in the mid-twelfth century. Consequently, Abbot Robert arranged two separate embassies to the Curia in 1156 and 1157, acquiring privileges of abbatial primacy, exemption from episcopal authority, and, perhaps most importantly, confirmation of the liberty and archdeaconry of St Albans, thus securing for his house the rank of premier abbey of all England.

The first blessing of the Abbey, its location, has often been cited as the 'central fact in the history of Alban and St Albans'.[5] Situated in the historically rich south-eastern corner of the diocese of Lincoln, astride Watling Street and just one

[1] Brixius, 56, 111; Zenker, 36–8.

[2] The invaluable source is the *Gesta abbatum monasterii Sancti Albani* compiled by Matthew Paris, for which no satisfactory modern edition exists. In the light of modern scholarship, the seventeenth-century edn by William Wats (*Vitae abbatum*) has been used in preference to the more accessible Rolls Series' *Gesta abbatum*; but, for the convenience of readers, cross-references to the Rolls edn are supplied in the following notes. For full bibliographical details, see Part II/i, no. 6b.

[3] Matthew Paris, *Vitae duorum Offarum sive Offanorum Merciorum regum coenobii Sancti Albani fundatorum*, ed. William Wats (London, 1683), 961–88, 85. 'Hadrian I' in *The Lives of the Eighth-Century Popes (Liber Pontificalis)*, trans., Raymond Davis, Translated Texts for Historians, 13 (Liverpool, 1992), 107–72 contains no such reference to St Alban and Offa.

[4] *Heads of Religious Houses*, 67; *Vitae abbatum*, 1014–36 (*Gesta abbatum*, i, 110–82).

[5] Martin Biddle, 'Alban and the Anglo-Saxon Church', in *Cathedral and City: St Albans ancient and modern*, ed. R. Runcie (London, 1977), 23–42, 23; Martin Biddle and Birthe Kjølbye-Biddle, 'England's Premier Abbey: The medieval chapter house of St Albans abbey and its excavation in 1978', *Expedition, the University Museum Magazine of Archaeology/Anthropology, University of Pennsylvania*, 22 (1980), 17–32, at 17.

day's journey from London,[6] two outstanding views of the Abbey would have helped to reinforce the spiritual impact of the church as 'one of the most striking and formidable and impressive monuments of the world of medieval religion'.[7] The first is the pilgrim's distant view northwards from the summit of a low ridge of hills separating the London Basin from the flood plain of the rivers Ver, Colne, and Gade. On a bright morning, with the sun at his back, the well-read traveller of the 1150s, seeing the becoming whiteness of the building's exterior, would have had every reason to be reminded of Rodolphus Glaber's 'white mantle of churches' covering the countryside.[8] The second and closer view, from the western slopes of the valley of the River Ver and across the open and deserted site of Roman Verulamium, looks upward to the medieval town, named for England's first martyr.[9] From this vantage point, the great church rises majestically on a hill, its impressive physical position marking the highest site above sea level of any English abbey[10] and visible for miles around in every direction.

Other forces, however, were even more effective in prosecuting the Abbey's spiritual claim to its premier position and these involved the blessing of its development as a cult centre. Once the second largest town of the province of Britannia, a small Romano-British population had probably survived within the walls of Verulamium until at least 450AD.[11] Although the archaeological evidence indicating an early and strong Christian presence is far from compelling, a persistent tradition has remained of a later *martyrium* outside the walls and somewhere in the vicinity of the medieval Abbey,[12] so that St Albans' claim to be the only known site in England where the tradition of Christian worship has continued unbroken from the Roman period and then through that of the Anglo-Saxons. In this, the proto-martyr Alban, surrounded by legend, as so many saints have been, was of vital importance to the continuity of the spiritual development of St Albans. His death, now more securely dated to the Tetrarchic period, under the staunchly pagan

---

[6] '...ut omnibus, tam pedes quam eques itinerantibus, nec minima nec magna indicetur; distet a Londiniis, ubi totius regni concursus est populorum; et illac omnium Aquilonarium, meantium et remeantium, frequens hospitatio', *Vitae abbatum*, 1020 (*Gesta abbatum*, i, 128).*

[7] Christopher Brooke, 'St Albans: the Great Abbey', in *Cathedral and City*, 43–70, at 43.

[8] Rodolphus Glaber: *Rodolphus Glaber Opera*, iii. 13, ed. John France, Neithard Bulst and Paul Reynolds, OMT (Oxford, 1989), 115–17. Compare *Vitae abbatum*, 1016 (*Gesta abbatum*, i, 112), which states that Robert had the Abbey church whitened inside and out while he was sacrist and before he became abbot, 'Hic etiam piae memoriae Abbas Robertus Ecclesiam Sancti Albani, quam, dum Secretarius fuerat, plumbo pro majori parte cooperuit, interius et exterius decenter dealbavit, et quaedam vetustate consumpta reparavit'.

[9] This would have been Breakspear's view as he travelled the four miles westward from the Abbey's demesne of Langley towards St Albans.

[10] At 103 metres above sea level. St Albans only acquired cathedral status in 1877.

[11] Rosalind Niblett, 'Why Verulamium?', in *Alban and St Albans*, 1–12, at 7–9.

[12] *Ibid.*, 7; Martin Henig, 'Religion and Art in St Alban's City', *Ibid.*, 13–29, at 25.

Constantius I Chlorus (305–6),[13] together with topographical evidence for the site of the Abbey church, confirm strikingly the substance of the earliest account of the martyrdom.[14] Alban was executed on top of a hill outside a walled place, and excavations have uncovered an extra-mural cemetery certainly in use between the late third and the fifth centuries.[15] These origins of the abbey church at St Albans are analogous to those of the 'minster' of SS. Cassius and Florentius at Bonn and the church of St Victor at Xanten, and seem likely to have derived from a fourth-century basilica erected over the grave of the martyred saint.[16] Unfortunately, neither the Romano-British basilica nor its Anglo-Saxon successor have yet been found[17] but, just as 'even at St Peter's in Rome there is a stubborn gap of about a century which only faith can cross',[18] it was in one such similar gap that the Alban legend was able to develop and flourish.

From an early date, Alban's reputation as a famous martyr was sustained by documentary evidence but none of it precisely contemporary.[19] The first reference, from the 460s or 470s, by Constantius of Lyon in his *Life* of Germanus, bishop of Auxerre (418–46),[20] mentions 429 as the date when Germanus sought out Alban's tomb, storing relics in his *capsula*, including dust from the place where the saint was killed, for his basilica in Auxerre.[21] The original version of the *Passio S. Albani*, the account of Alban's suffering and death for his faith, may also date from the mid-fifth century.[22] Bede (d. 735), completing his *History* by 731–2, incorporated details from a third version of the *Passio*,[23] including the saint's trial, his debate with the judge, the hilltop execution and the appearance of a perpetual spring, together with such dramatic elements as the moment when the martyr's head and the executioner's eyes fell to the ground together.[24] However, Bede also added some crucial information of his own:

---

[13] *Ibid.*, 24–5; M. D. Smith, 'The religion of Constantius I, *Greek, Roman and Byzantine Studies*, 38 (1997), 187–208.

[14] Wilhelm Levison, 'St. Alban and St. Albans', *Antiquity*, 15 (1941), 337–59, 347.

[15] Martin Biddle and Birthe Kjølbye-Biddle, 'The Origins of St Albans Abbey: Romano-British Cemetery and Anglo-Saxon Monastery', in *Alban and St Albans*, 45–77, at 46–65.

[16] Levison, 'St. Alban and St. Albans', 338, 358; Martin Biddle, 'Alban and the Anglo-Saxon Church', in *Cathedral and City*, 23–42, at 37–9; Biddle and Kjølbye-Biddle, 'The Origins of St Albans Abbey', 45–66.

[17] Biddle and Kjølbye-Biddle, 'The Origins of St Albans Abbey', 65, at 72–3. Future excavation on the long fall of the hill further to the south may in time reveal the site. See also Martin Biddle, 'Remembering St Alban: the Site of the Shrine and the Discovery of the Twelfth-century Purbeck marble Shrine table', in *Alban and St Albans*, 124–61.

[18] Biddle, 'Alban and the Anglo-Saxon Church', 27.

[19] Richard Sharpe, 'The late antique Passion of St Alban', in *Alban and St Albans*, 30–7.

[20] Constantius, *Vita S. Germani*, vii, 1, ed. W. Levison, *MGH SRM* (Berlin, 1919), 247–83.

[21] *Ibid.*, 253, 262, 281.

[22] Richard Sharpe, 'The late antique Passion of St Alban', 30.

[23] *Ibid.*, 29–30, 36–7.

[24] Bede: *The Ecclesiastical History of the English People*, ed. Bertram Colgrave and R. A. B. Mynors, OMT (Oxford, 1972), 28–35 no. vii.

The blessed Alban suffered death on 22 June near the city of Verulamium, which
the English now call either *Uerlamacaestir* or *Uaeclingaceastir.* Here when
peaceful Christian times returned, a church of wonderful workmanship was built,
a worthy memorial of his martyrdom. To this day, sick people are healed in this
place and the working of frequent miracles continues to bring it renown.[25]

Copies of Bede's *History*, always favourite reading matter with the Benedictines,
were to be found in most medieval monastic libraries[26] and it is his version which
underpins the later traditions of the saint's life composed at the monastery of St
Albans.[27]

One such tradition implied that, within sixty years, the pagan Saxon invaders
had destroyed Bede's 'wonderful church',[28] thus allowing Offa of Mercia (757–96)
to experience the miraculous revelation on 1 August 793 of the site of the martyr's
tomb, lying forgotten and neglected. This legend not only conflicts with Bede's
account but also with what is now known of the process of christianization. Fact
and fiction merged into this account of the foundation—or refoundation—for Offa
possibly reformed what existing monastic community there was, renovated the
church and had Alban's body translated from its earthen grave into a shrine.[29] Subsequently, St Albans' claim to possess the remains of the eponymous saint was
enormously significant, the proto-martyr's body being not only its proudest possession but also the very *raison d'être* of the great Abbey. The depth of devotion
displayed to the cult by travellers and pilgrims at the shrine brought numerous gifts
and privileges to the community. Over time, these gifts and privileges led to a series of impressive building campaigns to ensure that the saint was housed in
worthy surroundings. Over time, many powerful abbots added their own blessings,
all having the influencing touch of Alban himself.

The Abbey Church, as the resting place of the saint, was where 'St Alban himself lived in his relics…its lord in a very personal and vivid sense, under God, but
over the abbot and the monks'.[30] The abbot of St Albans was thus acutely aware of
the need to be seen as the custodian of the saint's body and to create sufficiently
worthy and magnificent surroundings in which the monastic community could not
only perform the *opus Dei* but also provide for pilgrims coming to the shrine. As
Benedictines, the rule under which the monks lived accorded a supreme role to
their abbot, the autonomy allowed to each house meaning that the abbot's character and ability was all-important.[31] This was well understood by the compilers of

[25] *Ibid.*, 35.

[26] Thomson, *Manuscripts from St Albans Abbey*, i, 23.

[27] For Bede's account of the visit of Germanus, his deposit of relics in Alban's tomb and
his collection of the heap of dust from the place of martyrdom, see Bede, *Ecclesiastical
History*, 59–61, cap. xviii.

[28] Levison, 'St. Alban and St. Albans', 351.

[29] L. F. Rushbrook Williams, *History of the Abbey of St Albans* (London, 1917), 3; Levison, 'St. Alban and St. Albans', 350–4; Biddle, 'Alban and the Anglo-Saxon Church', 30–6.

[30] Brooke, 'St Albans: the Great Abbey', 53.

[31] *The Rule of Saint Benedict*, ed. and trans. Justin McCann (London, 1952), 17–25,

the *Gesta abbatum*, the most valuable source for the lives of the abbots and for all later estimates of the Abbey's reputation for spirituality.[32]

The late eleventh and early twelfth-century abbots of St Albans did everything in their power to advance and promote the position of their house and their martyr-shrine as a centre of fervent spiritual life.[33] The first abbot after the Conquest was Paul of Caen (1077–93),[34] a former monk of Bec who, like his uncle, Lanfranc, archbishop of Canterbury (1070–89), probably originated from Lombardy.[35] Lanfranc's *Monastic Constitutions*, a rich collection of customs which incorporated the best of traditional regular observance, were clearly intended for Canterbury Cathedral 'but not for Canterbury alone'.[36] Indeed, there is evidence that Lanfranc provided a copy of the *Constitutions* for Paul who is known to have quickly applied these regulations to his own community.[37] Lanfranc continued to maintain considerable influence over St Albans through generous patronage for his nephew,[38] while Paul played his part by stabilizing the Abbey's endowments[39] and replacing the tenth-century church with another in which he used much 'architectural salvage' from the ruins of nearby Verulamium. The vast new Romanesque church built by Abbot Paul far exceeded in scale and elaboration Lanfranc's own metropolitan church of Canterbury (1070–7).[40] On a site to the north of the ancient complex of church and conventual buildings, the whole eastern arm was erected between 1077 and 1088, including the transepts, crossing and the first few

145–9, cc. 2, 3, 64.

[32] 'The *Gesta abbatum* proceeds abbacy by abbacy, reviewing each prelate's known good deeds and benefactions, balancing them against his shortcomings and concluding with a general assessment', Thomson, *Manuscripts from St Albans Abbey*, i, 3. Compare Michelle Still, *The Abbot and the Rule: St Albans Abbey in the Early Fourteenth Century* (Aldershot, 2002), 48–61.

[33] Knowles, *Monastic Order*, 186.

[34] *Heads of Religious Houses*, 66; *Vitae abbatum*, 1001–5 (*Gesta abbatum*, i, 51–64).

[35] Brooke, 'St Albans: the Great Abbey', 45–6; Margaret Gibson, *Lanfranc of Bec* (Oxford, 1978), 156.

[36] *Lanfranc: The Monastic Constitutions of Lanfranc*, ed. and trans. David Knowles, rev. edn Christopher N. L. Brooke, OMT (Oxford, 2002), xviii.

[37] Although the *Constitutions* were dedicated to Prior Henry and the monks of Canterbury, the word 'abbot' occurs more than 100 times in the text and would have made the work clumsy to use at Canterbury. There is a strong case, therefore, to be argued that Lanfranc had at least one abbey in mind, that St Albans was the obvious candidate and that Abbot Paul was crucial in the making of the book. I am most grateful to Christopher Brooke for pointing this out.

[38] Eadmer: *Historia Novorum in Anglia*, ed. Martin Rule, RS 81 (London, 1884), 15; *Monastic Constitutions*, xxxv–vi.

[39] Including land in Shephall, Potton, Leting, St Albans, Glaston, and Hendreth, which had formerly been under the patronage of Stigand. *Vitae abbatum*, 1002 (*Gesta abbatum*, i, 51–64); Gibson, *Lanfranc of Bec*, 156, n. 2.

[40] Malcolm Thurlby, 'L'abbatiale romane de St. Albans', in *L'architecture romane au Moyen Age*, ed. Maylis Bayle (Caen, 1997), 79–90; Tim Tatton-Brown, 'The Medieval Building Stones of St Albans Abbey: A Provisional Note', in *ibid.*, 118–23.

bays of the nave.[41] Paul is also credited with hanging two fine bells in the central tower.[42] A large apsidal chapter house was the crowning point of the whole campaign, presenting one of the major architectural achievements of the period and capable of accommodating a total monastic community of fifty-six.[43] Richard d'Aubigny (1097–1119),[44] Paul's successor, supervised the completion of the building campaign by which time the nave measured fully fifteen bays from end to end, with a large semi-circular apse and a chancel, possibly vaulted to emphasize the sepulchral quality of the *martyrium* church.[45] This great nave, 'the space in which the church and the world met',[46] provided the theatrical setting for processions of both clergy and laity coming to Alban's shrine, embellished with relics and elaborate liturgies as prescribed in Lanfranc's constitutions.[47]

The dedication of the completed Abbey church to St Alban the Martyr took place on 28 December 1115[48] in the midst of the celebration of several solemn religious feasts concentrated within this period.[49] Henry I and his queen, Matilda, held their Christmas court there at the Abbey's expense. Among the multitude assembled there was the archbishop of Rouen, who performed the ceremony of dedication, assisted by bishops Richard of London, Ranulf of Durham, Robert of Lincoln, Roger of Salisbury, and many other bishops and abbots, together with counts, barons, and notables. Whether feasting and rejoicing, *prandentes et gaudentes*, solemnly in the Abbey church or *in conviviis* in the *palatium* of St Albans where the court was accommodated with the greatest honour, all were continuous in their praise of Alban, protomartyr of the English.[50] This mixture of traditional entertainment and serious worship undoubtedly helped to raise the profile of St Albans as a centre of pilgrimage.[51] Significantly, those present at the

[41] Biddle and Kjølbye-Biddle, 'The Origins of St Albans Abbey', 72–3.

[42] *Vitae abbatum*, 1003 (*Gesta abbatum*, i, 60–1).

[43] Biddle and Kjølbye-Biddle, 'England's Premier Abbey', 27–31.

[44] *Heads of Religious Houses*, 67; *Vitae abbatum*, 1005–7 (*Gesta abbatum*, i, 66–72).

[45] Eileen Roberts, *The Hill of the Martyr: an Architectural History of St Albans Abbey* (Dunstable, 1993), 33–67.

[46] Brooke, 'St Albans: the Great Abbey', 53–6.

[47] *Monastic Constitutions*, 22–6; Brooke, 'St Albans: the Great Abbey', 58–9.

[48] ' ...ecclesiam beati Albani quam praedessor eius Paulus fabricaverat immediatus, magnifice fecit dedicavi, anno gratiae, M.C.X.V. ... quinto Calend. Jan. feria tertia', *Vitae abbatum*, 1006 (*Gesta abbatum*, i, 70–1); F. Wormald, 'English Benedictine Kalendars after A.D. 1100', *Henry Bradshaw Society*, 77 (1939), 31–45, 33, 45. Four manuscripts of the kalendar state that the dedication was commemorated on 28 Dec. while only one manuscript mentions 29 Dec. It should be noted that the feast of St Thomas of Canterbury, instituted in 1173, was celebrated at St Albans on 30 December to avoid the conjunction of dates, *ibid.*, 45.

[49] For the liturgical provisions from Christmas to Epiphany and the feasts of St Stephen (26 December), St John the Evangelist (27 December), the Holy Innocents (28 December), St Sylvester (31 December), the Circumcision (1 January) and Epiphany (6 January), *Monastic Constitutions*, 12–15.

[50] *Vitae abbatum*, 1006 (*Gesta abbatum*, i, 70–1).

[51] Diana Webb, *Pilgrimage in Medieval England* (London, 2000), 84.

dedication, and all who turned up later on that day to this solemnity, were granted an indulgence of an unspecified number of days' remission of penance.[52] This must be linked to another contemporary indulgence issued by Robert Bloet, bishop of Lincoln (1094–1123),[53] for penitents coming to the shrine for the feast of St Alban (1 August), offering them one day's remission of penance each week for a whole year.[54] Richard seems actively to have encouraged the intervention of the bishop of Lincoln and there is no reason to think that, at this stage, the Abbey enjoyed any formal exemption from episcopal authority.[55]

Abbot Richard not only oversaw the completion of the church in honour of St Alban but also contributed his own offering of precious ornaments and vestments. He gave two *thecae* or inner chests, the first decorated with gold figures to enclose the relics of the twelve apostles and of the many martyrs which, it was claimed, St Germanus of Auxerre had reverently deposited in Alban's tomb. A second *theca*, partly gilded, partly covered with ebony, contained the relics of other martyrs and saints. In addition to several rich vestments—albs, copes, etc.—Richard also offered the church a large pictorial wall-hanging with scenes from the *Passio* of St Alban,[56] presumably of a type not uncommon in other Benedictine abbey churches.[57] By the end of his abbacy, the church had its ornaments and its two indulgences but it was for his successor to begin the acquisition of valuable papal privileges.

Geoffrey de Gorron (1119–46),[58] Richard's successor, continued the collection of items necessary for the elaborate ritual of the *opus Dei*, his abbacy marking the high point of artistic craftsmanship and achievement at the Abbey. Geoffrey, a member of a large aristocratic family from Maine, had been invited to St Albans on account of his reputation for learning, having perhaps practised as a schoolmaster in the cathedral school at Le Mans[59] and became famous on at least two other counts—for a dramatic appreciation of the liturgy through his staging of a miracle play on Katherine of Alexandria,[60] and for his later and close friendship with

[52] *Vitae abbatum*, 1006 (*Gesta abbatum*, i, 71), 'Quibus et cunctis in posterum adventantibus ea die ad tantam solemnitatem, concessa est indulgentia multorum dierum'.

[53] *EEA*, i. *Lincoln 1067–1185*, ed. David M. Smith (London/Oxford, 1980), xxxv–vi.

[54] *Ibid.*, 11, n. *13, dated simply 1097 x 15/16 May 1119, the dates of Richard's abbacy, but likely to be 1115–9. Compare *Vitae abbatum*, 1012 (*Gesta abbatum*, i, 92).

[55] Rushbrook Williams, *Abbey of St Albans*, 47.

[56] *Ibid.*, 1006 (70), 'textum unum, et dossale unum, sive tapesium, in quo Passio Sancti Albani figuratur'. Compare E. Van Drival, *Les Tapisseries d'Arras: Étude artistique et historique* (Paris, 1878), 35, 77–8; *English Romanesque Art 1066–1200*, ed. George Zarnecki, Janet Holt and Tristram Holland (London, 1984), 490. See also Kjølbye-Biddle, 'The Alban Cross', in *Alban and St Albans*, 85–110 at 107, n. 8.

[57] For example, hangings at Abingdon depicting Job, the Nativity and the Apocalypse and of St Egwin at Evesham, *English Romanesque Art*, 490.

[58] *Heads of Religious Houses*, 66–7; *Vitae abbatum*, 1007–14 (*Gesta abbatum*, i, 72–106).

[59] Brooke, 'The Great Abbey', 59–62; Thomson, *Manuscripts from St Albans*, i, 20–3.

[60] *Vitae abbatum*, 1007 (*Gesta abbatum*, 73); Thomson, *Manuscripts from St Albans*, i, 21; Lawrence M. Clopper, '*Miracula* and *The Tretise of Miraclis Pleyinge*', *Speculum*, 65

Christina of Markyate, the local anchoress.[61] In addition to a lengthy inventory of Geoffrey's benefactions to the Abbey, which included ever richer and more numerous copes, albs, chasubles, a frontal of gold, silver and gem-stones made to fit exactly the altar of St Alban, and a silver arm reliquary containing relics of the martyrs, Bartholomew the Apostle and saints Ignatius, Laurence, and Nicasius, he also donated a further three great wall-hangings, the largest of which had woven on it the *Inventio* of St Alban on a bronze-coloured field.[62] Thus, a recognizable pictorial tradition of the Alban legend was beginning to emerge, whether in the tapestries of the *Passio* and *Inventio*, or in the *St Albans Psalter*, datable to *c*.1120 to *c*.1130[63] or, again, in the image of Alban on the walrus ivory matrix of the Great Seal of the Abbey which marked the beginning of the use of the enthroned full-length saint on such conventual seals.[64]

The culmination of Geoffrey's activity was his rebuilding of the shrine of Alban, the focal point for pilgrims coming to the great Abbey. In 1124, he had commissioned a *theca gloriosa* or magnificent chest, covered in panels of silver gilt, decorated in high relief and depicting scenes from the saint's life.[65] Before the chest was completed, these panels were stripped off and melted down as coin distributed for poor relief in a time of famine.[66] The following year, the goldsmith, Anketil, a monk of the Abbey, recommenced work on the shrine. Anketil's decoration of the *theca* must have been complete by 1129, apart from the crest, for, in that year, Geoffrey transferred Alban's relics from their former chest to the splendid new one.[67] In the presence of Alexander, bishop of Lincoln, and the abbots,

(1990), 878–905, at 879, 885.

[61] The account of Christina's *Life* does not appear in London, BL, MS Cotton, Nero D. I nor in Wat, *Vitae Viginti Trium Abbatum S. Albani*, but only in Walsingham's version, *Vitae abbatum* (*Gesta abbatum*, i, 101–5). See also, Knowles, *Monastic Order*, 189; Brooke, 'The Great Abbey', 59–61 and compare C. H. Talbot, *The Life of Christina of Markyate*, OMT, rev. edn. (Oxford, 1987), 135–71; Christopher Holdsworth, 'Christina of Markyate', in *Medieval Women*, SCH, Subsidia, I (Blackwell, 1978), 185–204 and most recently, Rachel M. Koopmans, 'The Conclusion of Christina of Markyate's *Vita*', *JEH*, 51 (2001), 663–98, which modifies any previous understanding of the anchoress's relations with St Albans and the history of the Abbey.

[62] The other two depicted the Good Samaritan and the Prodigal Son. 'Dedit quoque dossale magnum, in quo intexitur Inventio Sancti Albani, cujus campus est aereus; et aliud minus, ubi effigiatur Evangelium de sauciato qui incidit in latrones; et tertium, ubi historia de Filio Prodigo figuratur', *Vitae abbatum*, 1013 (*Gesta abbatum*, 94); *English Romanesque Art*, 490.

[63] O. Pächt, C. R. Dodwell and F. Wormald, *The St Albans Psalter (Albani Psalter)* (London, 1960), 8–9; Thomson, *Manuscripts from St Albans*, i, 25; Eileen Roberts, *Images of Alban: Saint Alban in Art from the Earliest Times to the Present* (St Albans, 1999), 17–19.

[64] T. A. Heslop in *English Romanesque Art*, 310 no. 349, +SIGILLUM.SCI.ALBANI. ANGLORU PTOMARTIRIS.

[65] 'Abbas Gaufridus Beato Albano, Patrono nostro, unam thecam gloriosam inchoavit, opere mirifico, anno praelationis suae quinto', *Vitae abbatum*, 1009 (*Gesta abbatum*, i, 80).

[66] '...laminas argenteas, sed nondum deauratas, cum quibusdam gemmis incastonatis, fecit avelli, et omnia redegit in numisma', *ibid.*, 1009 (*Gesta abbatum*, i, 82).

[67] *Ibid.*, 1010–1 (i, 85–6).

Walter of Eynsham, Robert of Thorney, Elias of Holy Trinity, Rouen, and Andrew of Nogent, the bones were displayed in order that as many people as possible could glimpse them, together with the seal of the reliquary.[68] When the prior raised aloft the saint's head, a circlet of silken ribbon was visible with 'Sanctus Albanus' written in ancient gold letters, while no less a figure than Offa himself, it was claimed, had inscribed on the skull, 'This is the head of St Alban, Proto-martyr of the English'.[69]

By 1129, both terminology and chronology had become inextricably entangled and confused.[70] Offa's miraculous discovery of Alban's relics in 793 was variously referred to as an *inventio* or a *translatio*, often without discerning between the actual discovery of the body and its removal for the first time from the earth to be put into a tomb or a shrine.[71] Until 1129, the *inventio* had been celebrated on 1 August, the day which Alban shared with the feast of St Peter ad Vincula, and which was also associated with the payment of Peter's Pence, due each year on that day from the Abbey's lands.[72] In that year, Geoffrey chose the feast of the *Inventio* as the day of the translation, but ordered that its future celebration should be moved to 2 August in order to avoid conflicting with the feast of St Peter *ad Vincula*.[73] The St Albans' calendar was henceforth recognizable by its high grading of the three feasts of Alban—the *passio* or martyrdom of 22 June, the *inventio* or *translatio* of 2 August, and the *dedicatio* of 28 December—each with their respective octave.[74]

The abbacy of Ralph Gubion (1146–51)[75] continued a trend already initiated under his predecessors, Richard and Geoffrey. St Albans' connexion with Canterbury was becoming gradually weakened at the expense of new and stronger ties with the diocesan bishopric of Lincoln. Not only had Robert Bloet played a leading role at the dedication of the church in 1115 but his successor, Alexander (1123–48), was also present in 1129 at the translation of Alban's relics into Anketil's shrine, afterwards offering a feast for three hundred of the local poor.[76] Ralph spent part of his early career in Lincoln, holding some office under Bishop Alexander in what may possibly have been an irregular, extra-claustral arrangement.[77] In Lin-

[68] *Ibid.*, 1010 (i, 85).

[69] Such means of identifying relics was quite usual at this time. Compare Geoffrey de Courlon, *Le Livre des reliques de l'abbaye de St-Pierre-le-Vif de Sens*, ed. G. Julliot and M. Prou (Sens, 1887); C. R. Cheney, 'The Letters of Pope Innocent III', *Medieval Studies and Texts* (Oxford, 1973), 16–38, at 18.

[70] *Vitae abbatum*, 1012 (*Gesta abbatum*, i, 92), 'vel Inventionis vel Translationis festivitatem',

[71] Levison, 'Alban and St Albans', 351–2.

[72] Henry Loyn, 'Peter's Pence', in idem, *Society and Peoples: Studies in the History of England and Wales, c. 600–1200*, Westfield Publications in Medieval Studies, 6 (London, 1992), 241–58, at 251.

[73] *Vitae abbatum*, 1010 (*Gesta abbatum*, i, 85); Levison, 'Alban and St Albans', 352.

[74] London, BL, MS Royal, 2A, x, fols 2–7b; Wormald, 'English Benedictine Kalendars', 33, 41.

[75] *Heads of Religious Houses*, 67.

[76] *Vitae abbatum*, 1012 (*Gesta abbatum*, i, 92).

[77] Thomson, *Manuscripts from St Albans*, i, 22–3.

coln, Ralph studied the Bible under Master Wodo, an Italian. Returning to St Albans, as *amator librorum*,[78] he was in charge of the Abbey's *scriptorium*, and as abbot, seems to have continued Geoffrey's programme of replacing the abbey's service books. During his abbacy, Lanfranc's *Constitutions* were abandoned in favour of new influences from Monte Cassino and other parts of Italy.[79] Ralph also maintained the interest shown by Geoffrey, his predecessor, in seeking papal privileges by travelling in person to Auxerre, where Pope Eugenius III then was, to intercede on behalf of the Abbey.[80]

On Ralph's resignation in 1151, Robert de Gorron (1151–66), a Norman and nephew of Abbot Geoffrey, succeeded as abbot, having been first a monk of St Albans and then its successful sacrist.[81] The numerous de Gorron family wielded considerable influence in and around the Abbey but were perhaps somewhat confusingly unimaginative in their choice of names. Robert's brother was Geoffrey, monk of St Albans,[82] while another Robert de Gorron, a monk, must have been a kinsman.[83] Robert's nephew, yet another Geoffrey, was parish priest of the church of Luton[84] while Ralph de Gorron, Robert's brother,[85] and Henry, their godfather or perhaps their uncle, lived nearby.[86] Robert certainly used his relatives to carry out sensitive missions and since they were efficient, he seems not to have been accused of favouritism. Indeed, the Abbot himself earned the title of *reformator libertatum ecclesiae Sancti Albani*[87] for his highly successful activities in augmenting the liberties of St Albans, in common with many other Benedictine houses in England.[88] Robert was also the prime mover in the Abbey's successful claims to gain papal protection and exemption from the jurisdiction of the bishop of Lincoln and it was his success in this field which made possible the subsequent substantial gains in the liberties of St Albans. The request for the confirmation of privileges came first from the Abbot; the grant from the pope then followed. It was thus of enormous assistance to Abbot Robert and to his community when the former Nicholas Breakspear ascended to Peter's Chair!

After 1154, no other abbey in England could match the signal honour and blessing conferred on St Albans by the elevation of its loyal son as pope. That the

---

[78]   *Vitae abbatum*, 1014 (*Gesta abbatum*, i, 106).

[79]   Thomson, *Manuscripts from St Albans*, i, 39.

[80]   See below, n. 115.

[81]   *Heads of Religious Houses*, 67; *Vitae abbatum*, 1015–36 (*Gesta abbatum*, i, 110–82); Thomson, *Manuscripts from St Albans*, i, 44–7.

[82]   *Twelfth-Century English Archidiaconal and Vice-Archidiaconal Acta*, ed. B. R. Kemp, *The Canterbury and York Society*, 92 (2001), 23–4, no. 31, 'Gaufrido, fratre abbatis' [? early 1163 x 23 Oct. 1166].

[83]   *Vitae abbatum*, 1021 (*Gesta abbatum*, i, 132).*

[84]   *Ibid.*, 1017 (*Gesta abbatum*, i, 116).*

[85]   *Ibid.*, 1035 (i, 181).*

[86]   *Ibid.*, 1032 (i, 168),* 'Henricus de Gorron, patrinus abbatis'; Thomson, *Manuscripts from St Albans*, i, 44, 137, n. 4, suggests that he may be identified with Henry, monk and later prior of Tynemouth.

[87]   *Ibid.*, 1015 (i, 110).

[88]   Thomson, *Manuscripts from St Albans*, i, 44.

community benefited hugely from their man's presence at the Curia could not be in doubt. If, as a young man, Adrian had indeed applied to enter the novitiate at St Albans and been rebuffed,[89] he nevertheless remained favourably disposed to the house he knew so well. Indeed, the pope's ties were more than merely sentimental, for the presence in the community of one important and long-standing member was a constant reminder to him of his connexion with the Abbey. In his retirement, Richard 'of the Chamber', the pope's father, had become a monk of St Albans and was probably still living at his son's accession.[90] As cardinal bishop of Albano, Adrian had already appreciated the association of place name and saint's name. Tradition later held that he jested with Abbot Robert at Benevento, where the two met in 1156, that the abbot should boldly ask for whatever he wanted, for it would be impossible that his 'Albano' should ever fail in his duty to the Blessed Alban.[91] The pope's delight in this simple word play appears to have rung true and the Abbey's greatest benefactor lived up to the promise made to its abbot, by showering two waves of privileges upon the community.

A detailed consideration of Abbot Robert's request for the confirmation of privileges and exemptions to St Albans should be preceded by an explanation of the developing idea that it was desirable for a monastery to commend itself to the papacy as well as to enjoy those benefits accruing to an exempt house. The special relationship thus created gave the house immediate recourse to the papacy and offered protection of its rights and privileges, requiring in return an annual tribute or *census*.[92] The supreme model for such payment for protection and exemption was, of course, the monastery of Cluny founded in 910.[93] The twelfth century saw an enormous extension of the practice of exemption and it became the inevitable custom for monasteries and other religious houses to take the initiative in seeking regular papal confirmation of their privileges, particularly on the accession of each new pope or following a definitive ruling resulting from a specific dispute. Meanwhile, the houses themselves became increasingly litigious in defending their claims; particularly so, it appears, was St Albans!

In the course of the twelfth century, several popes revealed a collective willingness to confer on St Albans and its dependencies a whole series of significant and much sought-after privileges, thus reinforcing the Abbey's pre-eminent posi-

---

[89] See ch. 2 above.

[90] Biddle and Kjølbye-Biddle, 'England's Premier Abbey', 17–32, esp. 25, 28–30. For discussion on the origin of the name 'de Camera', see Chapter 1 above.

[91] 'Abbas carissime, audacter pete quod vis: non poterit Beato Albano deesse suus Albanensis', *Vitae abbatum*, 1020 (*Gesta abbatum*, i, 127).*

[92] Charles Duggan, 'From the Conquest to the Death of John', in *The English Church and the Papacy in the Middle Ages*, ed. C. H. Lawrence (London, 1965), 65–115, at 105–6.

[93] For current orthodoxy dating the foundation to 910 see Giles Constable, 'Cluny in the Monastic World of the Tenth Century', in *Il secolo di ferro: mito e realtà del secolo x, 19–25 aprile 1990*, 2 vols, Settimane di studio del Centro italiano di studi sull'alto medioevo, 38 (Spoleto, 1991), i, 401, n. 35; Christopher Brooke, *Europe in the Central Middle Ages*, rev. edn (Harlow, 2000), 319, n. 7.

tion among the English black monk houses and uniting it firmly with Rome.[94] Texts of these privileges have been recovered from a lost cartulary, together with a variety of Anglo-Saxon and post-Conquest charters relating to the Abbey and its endowments. This cartulary, having left St Albans at some time following the Dissolution of 1539, had turned up in the library of the Bollandist scholars at Antwerp by the early seventeenth century where it became MS. 73, remaining there until the third quarter of the eighteenth century, and is now unfortunately lost.[95] In the late 1630s, more than one individual from that erudite Bollandist community, working from a variety of different original sources in order to compile a collection of texts relating to certain of the English Benedictine abbeys, had assembled a transcript of much of the material contained in MS 73,[96] which was catalogued in their library as MS 157.[97] Folios 178–216 of this transcript, now Brussels, Bibliothèque Royale, MS. 7965–73 (3723) are known only from this manuscript and Walter Holtzmann's printed edition of the third volume of *Papsturkunden in England* depended almost entirely upon it for the period 1122–81.[98] Later historians of the Abbey were able to interpolate freely since its cartulary and privileges were clearly cherished, preserved and strengthened in order to bolster its claims.

Adrian's confirmations concerning the privileges of St Albans were issued within a period of eighteen months. Two separate embassies were undertaken, the first in 1156 by Abbot Robert in person and the second, just over a year later by two relatives. Abbot Robert, appointed royal proctor by Henry II, had set out on the feast of St Denis, 9 October 1155, accompanied by three Norman bishops,[99] and arrived at Benevento in early January 1156. *Incomprehensibilis*, a major privilege, issued on 5 February,[100] followed the first privilege, dated 19 January. Then ten more privileges, letters of grace, or letters were granted on 24 February, with a final two on 26 February. When Robert arrived back in St Albans on 31 May 1156, great dissension broke out with Robert de Chesney, bishop of Lincoln (1148–66),

---

[94] Jane E. Sayers, 'Papal Privileges for St Albans Abbey and its Dependencies', in *The Study of Medieval Records. Essays in honour of Kathleen Major*, ed. D. A. Bullough and R. L. Storey (repr. in eadem, *Law and Records in Medieval England: Studies on the Medieval Papacy, Monasteries and Records*, Variorum Reprints, CS 278 (London, 1988), IX, 57–85.

[95] S. Keynes, 'A lost cartulary of St Albans Abbey', *Anglo-Saxon England*, 22 (Cambridge, 1993), 253–79, at 257–63; H. Delehaye, *The Work of the Bollandists through Three Centuries 1615–1915* (Princeton, 1922), 171–4; D. Knowles, 'The Bollandists', *Great Historical Enterprises and Problems in Monastic History* (London, 1963), 1–32; P. Peeters, *L'oeuvre des Bollandistes*, 2nd edn, Subsidia Hagiographica 24a (Brussels, 1961).

[96] Keynes, 'A lost cartulary of St Albans Abbey', 262–3; Bibliothèque des Bollandistes, Boll. 23, 68r, MS. 73 (*S. Albani donationes et privilegia*).

[97] Brussels, Bibliothèque Royale, 7965–73 (3723), formerly Bibliothèque des Bollandistes, MS. 157.

[98] *PUE*, iii, 120–3, with a summary of the complete contents of the Brussels manuscript; G R. C. Davis, *Medieval Cartularies of Great Britain* (London, 1958), 94; Keynes, 'A lost cartulary of St Albans Abbey', 257.

[99] The bishops of Le Mans, Lisieux, and Évreux, *Vitae abbatum*, 1019 (*Gesta abbatum*, i, 126).* See below, ch. 7, n. 182.

[100] *PUE*, iii, 234–8 no. 100.*

over the implementation of what had been granted.[101] Abbot Robert either chose
not, or was unable, to make a second personal journey to see Adrian, sending instead, Geoffrey and Robert de Gorron early in 1157.[102] Adrian, by this time back in
Rome from Benevento, issued a further two confirmations to St Albans on 14 May
1157, one of which was *Religiosam vitam*, a major privilege.

Through a thematic analysis of these privileges, it becomes clearer that Adrian
and Abbot Robert, working together, built on a firm foundation, already hard-won,
to extend further the Abbey's rights. Adrian's regard for the Abbey of St Albans as
the most famous and illustrious among all the churches of the kingdom of the English[103] was translated into a number of papal confirmations of outstanding quality.
These can be divided into three groups: those privileges concerned with enhancing
all aspects of the cult of Alban, including processions; secondly, those confirming
the liberty of the Abbey, its possessions and its cells; and lastly, those granting
particular exemptions which served to remove the Abbey from the authority of the
bishop of Lincoln.

In *Religione ac pietate* of 24 February 1156,[104] addressed to the archbishops of
Canterbury and York and all the English bishops, Adrian singled out the cult of
Alban and his feast day for special commemoration.[105] In this letter, he repeated
and went beyond the terms of the earliest authentic papal document for St Albans
in a similar privilege of the same title, granted by Calixtus II on 22 November
1122.[106] Following Calixtus, Adrian first made clear in general terms that wherever
the body of a martyred saint was to be found, it was to be suitably honoured with
solemn obsequies.[107] It had, however, been drawn to his attention that, in the province of Hertfordshire, at the church of the proto-martyr Alban, specially erected
in the saint's honour, the monastic community there was outstandingly serving
God through daily prayers and vigils as required by the observance of their rule.
The pope ordered the bishops officially to announce and earnestly to remind the
faithful in their charge, not only those attending episcopal churches but also those
in each parish, to come together to celebrate the feast of the martyr, telling them
that they could earn an indulgence for remission of their sins through the monks'
prayers. Out of special reverence and honour for Alban, the glorious martyr of
Christ, Adrian laid down that, on the saint's annual feast day (2 August), from the
vigil of that day to the octave of those solemnities, whomsoever should come to

---

[101] *Vitae abbatum*, 1021 (*Gesta abbatum*, i, 129–31);* Rushbrook Williams, *Abbey of St
Albans*, 72.

[102] *Vitae abbatum*, 1021 (*Gesta abbatum*, i, 131–2).*

[103] *PUE*, iii, 240–1, no. 103, 'inter cunctas Anglici regni ecclesias famosa est et illustris'.

[104] *PUE*, iii, 240, no. 102; *Vitae abbatum*, 1021 (*Gesta abbatum*, i, 130).

[105] *PUE*, iii, 240, no. 102.

[106] *Ibid.*, 130–1, no. 6.

[107] Adrian addressed another version of *Religione ac pietate* to Hugh, bishop of Durham,
to remind him that the feast of the martyred king Oswin (20 August), as celebrated by the
community at St Albans' dependent cell of Tynemouth, was to be observed in the city of
Durham and throughout the diocese with the appropriate indulgence, *PUE*, iii, 252–3, no.
111.

the Abbey church out of devotion should receive a twelve-day indulgence for re-mission of penance.[108] In *Quod fraternitas* of 26 February 1156,[109] addressed to Theobald of Canterbury, Adrian further reinforced his support for St Albans, commending it for having always been the most famous among the other monas-teries in the kingdom of England[110] and requesting that the archbishop should support and defend its monastic community, not merely by providing advice but also with positive assistance.

Another aspect of the development and promotion of the cult of Alban may be traced through the long-established institution of solemn processions to the Abbey from the parish churches of Hertfordshire which lay within the diocese of Lincoln. These processions, which were held annually on the Friday of the week of Pente-cost, had also come to be associated with the payment of dues to the Abbey from the laity and tenants of the monastery alike.[111] Such ritual processions, similar to those prescribed for Palm Sunday and the Rogation Days, were certainly held at St Albans.[112] The first, an internal claustral perambulation with a portable shrine con-taining relics and the consecrated host displayed to the community; the second, a much larger procession which moved outside the monastery, with the community organized in ranks, accompanied by the ringing of bells and the full ritual appara-tus of banners, flowers, branches, crosses, lighted tapers, thuribles, and gospel books. Laity and clergy alike venerated the reliquary in the open, before returning to the church for Mass. Such processions, including those from a number of parish churches in the 'province' of Hertfordshire, generated offerings at the shrine of Alban, in the same way as the later institution of 'quests' or *quêtes* raised money for the fabric of a church building.[113] Deep hostility, however, was aroused in Lin-coln where these dues had previously been enjoyed by the bishop and chapter without any competition.[114]

Adrian's predecessor, Eugenius III, had already addressed another problem raised by these privileges. This pope, visited by Ralph Gubion at Auxerre on the

---

[108]	Levison, 'Alban and St Albans', 351–2.

[109]	*PUE*, iii, 253, no. 112.

[110]	'Ipsum namque monasterium inter alias Anglici regni ecclesias quam famosum sem-per extiterit, quam illustre et fratres, qui in eo specialiter commorantur, quam attente, quam efficaciter obsequio inhereant conditoris et quam gratum Deo iugiter exhibeant famulatum, ad notitiam tuam satis credimus peruenisse', *ibid.*, 253.

[111]	Ada Elizabeth Levett, *Studies in Manorial History*, ed. H. M. Cam, M. Coate and L. S. Sutherland (Oxford, 1938), 56, 178–207, at 179–80, '...the determination ...with which the Abbey clung to its rights, and probably to an inequality of dues and customs which bore witness both to the antiquity of the Abbey and its failure to bring any systematic policy to bear on the newer problems it had to face. St Albans shows a strange mixture of the very archaic and the irregular or unorthodox'.

[112]	*Monastic Constitutions*, 35–41, 75–82; Brooke, 'St Albans: the Great Abbey', 58–9.

[113]	Reinhold Kaiser, 'Quêtes itinérants avec des reliques pour financer la constructions des églises (xie–xiie siècles)', *Moyen Age*, 101 (1995), 205–25.

[114]	Rushbrook Williams, *Abbey of St Albans*, 71. Compare *Cartae Episcoporum. Statutes of Lincoln Cathedral arranged by the late Henry Bradshaw*, ed. Christopher Wordsworth, 2 vols (Cambridge, 1982–97), i, 307–8.

feast day of St Alban, 2 August 1147, had heard the abbot's detailed complaint and addressed a letter, *Ex parte filii*, on his behalf to Archbishop Theobald of Canterbury and Alexander, bishop of Lincoln.[115] Ralph had, it seems, complained that those men who were accustomed to pay to the Abbey at the time of the solemn procession on the Friday after Ascension Day a half penny for each plough and, on 2 August, one penny from each plough, were either delaying or refusing outright to pay their dues. Eugenius ordered archbishops Theobald and Alexander to remind their parishioners to pay the Abbey and if, within two months, the culprits had still failed to render their dues, to punish them by canonical censure.

In a further attempt to ensure that the clergy and laity alike in the 'province' of Hertfordshire were free to observe inviolably this ancient custom of processions on the Friday after Pentecost as already laid down by his papal predecessors, Calixtus II and Eugenius III, Adrian added a final clause to *Religione ac pietate*.[116] In this, he granted the same indulgence to those penitents coming in solemn procession to the Abbey church on two other significant days, namely the Friday following Ascension and the Friday of the week of Pentecost. In another letter, *Ad hoc in eminenti* of 24 February 1156, he directly addressed Robert de Chesney, bishop of Lincoln.[117] This surprisingly stern and outspoken papal missive, clearly resulting from Abbot Robert's complaint, and very likely re-edited in St Albans to give a sharper edge to it, strictly instructed the bishop that he was not to issue a simultaneous summons to attend any synod or chapter nor, indeed, was he to compel anyone setting out on their way to St Albans to go instead in procession to Lincoln. No lay person who ought to have attended the St Albans' procession was to be prevented from doing so. Furthermore, anyone who ought to have taken part but had not done so was to be corrected by the bishop within twenty days, and were any persons to refuse to be thus admonished, the abbot of St Albans was to receive the right freely and canonically to correct them. Adrian also repeated the injunction to the tenants of the monastery that they should perform their customary ploughing services on the days of the solemn procession and stated that any who might dare to withhold them, either on that day or on 2 August, the second feast of St Alban, would be liable to receive canonical punishment from the abbot.

Adrian's second group of privileges to St Albans confirmed the liberty of the Abbey, its possessions, and its cells. He granted no fewer than eight confirmations and letters related to this matter, of which the first was the privilege *Incomprehensibilis*, issued on 5 February 1156 and addressed to Abbot Robert and his brethren. Adrian, if the most generous, was certainly not the earliest of the benefactors to St Albans. In his day, that honour still belonged to Offa of Mercia[118] whose position as founder of St Albans predated the twelfth century.[119] It was perhaps unfortunate

---

[115] *PUE*, iii, 240–1, no. 69.

[116] *Ibid.*, 240, no. 102.

[117] *Ibid.*, 240–1, no. 103.

[118] *Vitae duorum Offarum*, 85; Sayers, 'Papal Privileges for St Albans Abbey', 58.

[119] Simon Keynes, 'Changing Faces: Offa, King of Mercia', *History Today*, 40 (November 1990), 14–19; *Idem.*, 'A Lost Cartulary of St Albans Abbey', *Anglo-Saxon England*, 22

that the eagerness of thirteenth-century historians to magnify the Abbey's claims by inflating Offa's role effectively denied to the monastery what it could quite legitimately claim, that is, a continuity which surpassed that of any other house in England.[120] While the Offa charters presented to Calixtus II in 1122 were probably forgeries,[121] the texts of Adrian's privileges were clearly genuine, although they have survived only in late copies. Indeed, St Albans was fortunate at this period in not having to resort to forgery as the means by which to 'improve' the majority of its privileges at precisely the time when written evidence was becoming essential.[122]

Adrian IV reconfirmed the papal protection to St Albans granted by his predecessors, Calixtus II,[123] Celestine II,[124] Eugenius III,[125] and Anastasius IV.[126] In common with the earlier privileges, *Incomprehensibilis* incorporated a list of the Abbey's pre- and post-Conquest benefactors, from Offa himself,[127] his son, Ecgfrith, Aethelred II (978–1016),[128] William,[129] and Henry I,[130] as well as the Abbey's present and future rights and possessions. It specifically detailed the churches in the liberty of St Albans,[131] and its dependent cells of Tynemouth, Binham, Wymondham, Wallingford, Hertford, Belvoir, and Beaulieu, confirming that they were free from payment of tribute and performance of such works as bridge building. In a consecutive series of similar splendid great privileges, all dated 24 February, Adrian took the dependent cells of St Albans into papal protection. He addressed *Prudentes virgines* to Agnes, prioress of Sopwell and her sisters, con-

---

(1993), 253–79; Julia Crick, 'Offa, Aelfric and the Refoundation of St Albans', in *Alban and St Albans*, 78–84.

[120] Biddle, 'Alban and the Anglo-Saxon Church', 31.

[121] Crick, 'Offa, Aelfric and the Refoundation of St Albans', 78–9. Compare *Vitae abbatum*, 1027 (*Gesta abbatum*, i, 151–2).

[122] Brooke, 'The Great Abbey', 62; Sayers, 'Papal Privileges for St Albans Abbey', 60, n. 1. Compare Keynes, 'A lost cartulary of St Albans Abbey', 262, for the intriguing possibility that Adam the Cellarer might have been involved in compiling an early collection of the abbey's charters and privileges. In any case, no serious historical challenge has ever been mounted to challenge the authenticity of Adrian's privileges.

[123] *Ad hoc nos*, 25 November 1122, *PUE*, iii, 128–30, no. 5.

[124] *Officii nostri nos*, 19 October 1143, *ibid.*, 166–7, no. 43.

[125] *Pie postulatio*, 2 August 1147, *PUE, ibid.*, 197–9.

[126] *Quae religiosis*, 2 June 1154, *PUE, ibid.*, 227.

[127] Crick, 'Offa, Aelfric and the Refoundation of St Albans', 78, probably forgeries purporting to date from the time of foundation; Keynes, 'A lost cartulary of St Albans Abbey', 271, indicates an exemption clause similar to that found in the charters of Offa.

[128] Crick, 'Offa, Aelfric and the Refoundation of St Albans', 80.

[129] William appears uniquely in this privilege.

[130] Keynes, 'A lost cartulary of St Albans Abbey', 271 indicates a list of rights similar to that found in Henry I's charter of 1102.

[131] In St Albans, the churches of St Peter, St Stephen and Kingsbury (St Michael), Watford, Rickmansworth, Abbots Langley, Redbourn, Codicote, Walden, Hexton, Norton, Newnham, Winslow, Aston Abbots, Barnet, Bramfield, Shephall, Luton, Houghton, Hartwell, Biddlesden, and Potsgrove.

firming its lands and possessions,[132] and did likewise with *Commissa nobis* to Wymondham,[133] *Quotiens illud* to Belvoir,[134] and *Apostolici moderaminis* to Tynemouth.[135] In return for the protection granted in *Incomprehensibilis*, Adrian exacted payment of one ounce of gold every year from the Abbey for himself and his successors. This sum, reminiscent of the census paid by Cluny, had been pre-figured in Celestine II's *Officii nostri nos*,[136] the earliest document to imply a special relationship with the papacy in the use of the significant phrase, *ad indicium perceptae libertatis*, a clear sign of exemption, implying that the Abbey had been 'recommended' to the Holy See.[137]

Several grants were made in order to ensure the financial stability of the religious community. In *Ea que piis*,[138] Adrian confirmed the transfer of the church of St Peter to the infirmary of the monastery while, in *Ea que venerabilibus*, Adrian granted to St Albans the patronage of the churches of Luton and Houghton, Hartwell, Biddlesden, and Potsgrave, and their tithes, lands, and appurtenances, quit of all secular exactions.[139] The income was to assist in perpetuity the monastery's duty and function of providing hospitality. To this end, and clearly at the wish of Abbot Robert, Adrian made a specific grant of ancient dues and customs which no one was expected to dare to refuse to pay to the Abbey; consisting of one half-penny from each plough in the province of Hertfordshire on the Friday after Ascension Sunday; on that same day, the revenues from the solemn procession throughout the whole province; and on the second feast of St Alban, 2 August, a penny from each plough and a penny from each household on all the lands of the monastery.

Linked to the specific obligation of hospitality, enjoined by the Rule of St Benedict,[140] was the provision that lands and possessions should be attached to the office of the Cellarer, one of the most crucial of the obedientiaries, or monastic officials.[141] In *Iustis petentium*, Adrian confirmed to the community those lands which Adam the Cellarer had acquired,[142] namely, Bygrave, Wallingford, 'Aiselue', Holt, 'Bissopescote' (Codicote), Shephall, and 'Titeberst' (Fingest), and granted them inalienably to the monks' kitchen, *ad coquinam monachorum*. The pope also confirmed all the reasonable customs of the market at Watford, granted

---

[132] *Prudentes virgines*, *PUE*, iii, 244–6, no. 107.

[133] *Commissa nobis*, *ibid.*, 246–7, no. 108.

[134] *Quotiens illud*, *ibid.*, 248–50, no. 109.

[135] *Apostolici moderaminis*, *ibid.*, 250–2, no. 110.

[136] 19 October 1143, *ibid.*, 166–7, no. 43.

[137] 'Ad indicium autem huius a sede apostolica percepte libertatis nobis nostrisque successoribus auri unciam annis singulis persoluetis', *ibid.*, 167; Knowles, 'Growth of Exemption', 214.

[138] 19 January 1156, *PUE*, iii, 261.

[139] 24 February 1156, *ibid.*, 243–4 no. 106.

[140] *Rule of Saint Benedict*, 119–23, c. 53.

[141] *Ibid.*, 81–3, c. 31.

[142] *PUE*, iii, 238–9, no. 101; Levett, *Studies in Manorial History*, 110–3, 195.

by kings Henry and William and archbishops Anselm, Ralph and William, which no one was to infringe.

Of all the privileges which Adrian granted to St Albans, the most vigorously contested was that, granted by *Incomprehensibilis*, of exemption from the authority of the diocesan. The post-Conquest diocesan reorganization implemented by archbishop Lanfranc, and the Normans' preference for linking cathedrals with important towns or centres had profoundly affected St Albans. When the small and ancient site of Dorchester-on-Thames was suppressed sometime between 1067 and 1072, the diocesan centre was subsequently transferred to Lincoln. Situated at the far end of this enormous diocese of eight and a half shires, St Albans was in a stronger position than most monasteries to resist its diocesan bishop but, at first, seems to have continued to remain under the control of the metropolitan at Canterbury, possibly because of the close connection between Archbishop Lanfranc and his nephew, Abbot Paul of Caen. Yet, in the early years of the twelfth century, Abbot Richard d'Aubigny seems actually to have chosen to withdraw and make his profession of canonical obedience to Robert Bloet, bishop of Lincoln, in order to strengthen his own rule over his monks.[143] His successors, Geoffrey and Ralph Gubion, may also have made similar professions. Later, however, when the bishops of Lincoln vigorously challenged the Abbey's extensive rights, they were to fail when confronted by the powerful privileges obtained by St Albans from Rome between 1122 and 1157.

In a seminal article of seventy years ago,[144] David Knowles identified the problem of exemption by attempting to classify the English Benedictine monasteries into three groups, according to their relationship with their diocesan bishop. Cathedral monasteries, such as Worcester, Gloucester, or Norwich, staffed by communities of monks who performed the offices and enjoyed the rights of the capitular body, comprised an institution almost unique to England, occurring elsewhere only in isolated cases.[145] Should the bishop of a cathedral monastery be a monk—as happened frequently in the period after the Conquest—then he would exercise the position of abbot in almost every respect as the immediate superior of the community. The second and by far the largest group of 'old' Benedictine monasteries enjoyed complete internal autonomy, each of them being free to elect their own abbots according to the provisions of the Rule.[146] On election, however, the abbots were still bound to request benediction from the local bishop, and remained subject to his excommunication and interdict. St Albans belonged to a third very select group of some seven houses, including Bury St Edmund's, Battle,

---

[143] 'Ecclesiam quoque istam a subjectione Cantuariae jure extractam (quam inhumane nimis archiepiscopales pertractaverunt), Lincolniensi Ecclesiae primus, profitendo obedientiam, in subjectionem redegit; ut sic monachos suos, ut dicitur, rigidius gubernaret', *Vitae abbatum*, 1006 (*Gesta abbatum*, i, 71–2).

[144] David Knowles, 'Essays in Monastic History IV. The Growth of Exemption', *The Downside Review*, 50, NS 31 (1932), 201–31, 396–436.

[145] Knowles, *Monastic Order*, 619, n. 1, at Monreale in Sicily (1176) and at Downpatrick in Ireland (*c*.1185).

[146] McCann, *The Rule of St Benedict*, 145–9, c. 64.

Malmesbury, Evesham, St Augustine's Canterbury, and Westminster,[147] which could claim exemption and total independence from the diocesan by virtue of an express grant which brought them directly under papal jurisdiction.[148] It was just such a grant that St Albans sought and obtained.

Adrian IV's special relationship with his 'home Abbey' emerges clearly in the great privilege, *Incomprehensibilis*, which was designed to secure the Abbey's independence from its diocesan by the grant of *pontificalia*.[149] Henceforth, Abbot Robert was not obliged to request the bishop of Lincoln to conduct ordinations and consecrations but instead was empowered to invite any catholic bishop of his choice to consecrate holy oil and make chrism. The community's obligation to elect its abbot, according to the Rule of St Benedict and without episcopal interference, was restated and the pope prohibited any bishop from holding a public mass or celebrating a synod in the Abbey church unless requested to do so by the abbot. Neither the abbot nor his monks could be forced to attend a diocesan synod, nor be compelled to obey episcopal decrees, thereby theoretically removing the Abbey from sentences of excommunication and interdict. Furthermore, all the churches belonging to the church of St Alban the Martyr were to be immediately subject to the abbot and no other, while those churches over which the abbot did not have pontifical rights were to be free from all exaction, apart from the customary justice exercised by a bishop over errant clergy. All these provisions were to apply equally to the cells of St Albans.

Following the provisions of *Incomprehensibilis*, Adrian issued two short letters, both on 24 February. In *Qui locum regiminis*,[150] to the archbishop of York and the bishops of Durham, Lincoln, Ely, London, and Salisbury, he expressed concern over the correction of priests and clerics with concubines in those of their churches falling under the jurisdiction of St Albans. While the possessions of these churches were still protected, should the priests' concubines not be removed within six months, Abbot Robert was to be empowered to replace the priests with honest clerks. In *Ex relatione*,[151] to Robert, bishop of Lincoln, and his archdeacon, Adrian articulated the serious complaint made to him by Abbot Robert that, contrary to law and reason, they had presumed to exact money for chrism from the churches of St Albans. Should such a rumour ever again reach the ears of the pope, then he would be unable to overlook the seriousness of the crime. Both these letters resulted from the full airing of Robert's grievances over the indignities to which the Abbey had been subjected by the bishop of Lincoln.

One other letter, standing apart from the main privileges, is none the less of interest and was recorded with considerable satisfaction in the *Gesta abbatum*.[152] Abbot Robert and Geoffrey, bishop of Le Mans, fell foul of the abbot of St Benoît-

---

[147] Glastonbury was sometimes included in this list.
[148] Knowles, 'Growth of Exemption', 201–02; idem, *Monastic Order*, 586–91.
[149] *Vitae abbatum*, 1020 (*Gesta abbatum*, i, 128).*
[150] *PUE*, iii, 242, no. 104.
[151] *Ibid.*, 242–3, no. 105.
[152] *Vitae abbatum*, 1020 (*Gesta abbatum*, i, 128).*

sur-Loire who had had the temerity to refuse them hospitality as they travelled across France on their way to Benevento. In an excoriating letter, *Si religiose professionis*,[153] Adrian, declaring it impossible to overlook such *inhumanitas*, demanded that the abbot should refund the expenses the pair had been forced to incur in the town. Before the next octave of St Martin, he was to come to the pope, bearing letters from Robert and Geoffrey, verifying that he had done this and had learned his lesson in how to be hospitable.

Returning alone, Robert's precise itinerary has not been established, but his triumphant arrival in St Albans on 31 May 1156 has been well recorded He had obtained from Adrian an order to the bishops of England to observe devotedly in their churches the celebration of the feast of St Alban the Martyr and an order to the bishop of Lincoln to allow the great annual processions of clergy and laity to his Abbey. The strict provisions of *Religione ac pietate* and *Ad hoc in eminenti*, however, caused a tremendous outcry in Lincoln, exacerbated by Abbot Robert's own actions. At a council in London, Abbot Robert had the letters read out in the presence of the Lincoln clergy and their proctors but in the pointed absence of their bishop.[154] When Robert de Chesney heard of the privilege, he appealed the Abbot and the community to the papal audience, setting the date of the appeal as the third Sunday of Advent, 16 December 1156, on the grounds that the pope had refused to allow the parishioners of the churches of Hertfordshire to make a second procession to the city of Lincoln.[155] Hugh, bishop of Durham, acted as mediator and engineered a compromise, witnessed by Richard, bishop of London, and Gilbert Foliot of Hereford, with particular respect to processions, which was agreed in *Quod ad honorem dei*, a chirograph witnessed by both parties and bearing the abbatial seal.[156] The church of St Albans was to continue to hold its accustomed annual processions on the usual days. It was also allowed to have the processions of the churches of Chesham, Luton, and Houghton Regis (and their proceeds), provided that all three agreed to furnish a procession for the church of Lincoln.[157] Outside the times of the processions of St Albans, the church of Lincoln would be allowed to hold its processions in Hertfordshire, saving the ancient liberty of the St Albans' churches, but the parishioners were not to be forced to travel as far as Lincoln.[158]

Early in 1157, Robert despatched his brother, Geoffrey, and the other Robert de Gorron, to Rome to secure further papal support and returned with Adrian's

[153] *PUE*, iii, 254, no. 113; *Vitae abbatum*, 1020 (*Gesta abbatum*, i, 128).*

[154] Dated 31 May x 28 October 1156 in *Councils and Synods, with other Documents Relating to the English Church*, i/1–2, ed. D. Whitelock, M. Brett and C. N. L. Brooke (Oxford, 1981) i/2, 831 with *Vitae abbatum* text from London, BL MS, Nero D. i, at 83–5. Compare *Vitae abbatum*, 1020–1 (*Gesta abbatum*, i, 129–30).*

[155] *Ibid.*, 1021 (*Gesta abbatum*, i, 130);* Rushbrook Williams, *Abbey of St Albans*, 71–9.

[156] *The Registrum Antiquissimum of the Cathedral Church of Lincoln, Volume II*, ed. C.W. Foster (Lincoln, 1933), 13–15, no. 207 (322). One of the witnesses was Adam the Cellarer.

[157] *Ibid.*, 14, ll. 17–21.

[158] *Ibid.*, 14, ll. 40–6.

letter, *Ea que compositione*, of 14 May 1157.[159] This confirmed the agreement between St Albans and Lincoln, making it very clear that the pope himself had his
eye on the outcome of the affair and threatening not only the wrath of God but also
of the apostles Peter and Paul on anyone who dared to infringe the agreement. At
the same time, Adrian issued the important privilege, *Religiosam vitam*,[160] which
reconfirmed papal protection for the Abbey and its possessions, precisely defining
the area of the liberty of St Albans.[161] This was to be administered by an archdeacon on behalf of the abbot and this office was to be filled by monks of the
Abbey.[162] Monastic archdeacons, carrying out their duties of visitation and correction, were able to hold synods to supervise the clergy of the churches within the
liberty. St Albans was to be ruled at all times by its abbot and, out of respect for
the Protomartyr, since the abbot enjoyed all the pontifical rights, so too, he was to
be allowed the right of wearing some of the episcopal *pontificalia*, including mitre,
gloves, ring, and sandals. He was to profess obedience to the Roman Church alone,
to hold forever the first rank among the abbots of England and to hold the first
place within the monastery or its parish, particularly in the matter of processions.
Henceforward, the abbot's own blessing should be by a bishop of his own choice,
whereas Celestine II had stated that this should be by the diocesan, *a diocesano
suscipiatis episcopo, siquidem catholicus fuerit.*[163]

An inevitable question must concern the changes which were brought to the
Abbey by Adrian IV, that 'loyal son' of St Albans. In what ways did the Abbey, its
community, its fame and its fabric alter materially as a result of his pontificate?
The privileges granted to St Albans were so generous that they caused dissension
for many years as Adrian's successors reconfirmed them. Pope Alexander III, previously Adrian's Chancellor Roland, knew Abbot Robert de Gorron well and
continued to show favour to the Abbey with more than forty letters and privileges,
enhancing and confirming his predecessor's grants.[164] The importance attached by
St Albans to securing these immunities cannot be underestimated. The Abbey's
exemption from diocesan authority was confirmed, together with its freedom to act
independently and its monastic archdeacons, with the pope alone as the Abbey's

---

[159] *PUE*, iii, 258, no. 117.*

[160] *Ibid.*, 258–61, no. 118.

[161] St Peter, St Stephen, Kingsbury (St Michael) in St Albans, Watford, Rickmansworth,
Abbots Langley, Redbourn, Codicote, St Paul's Walden, Hexton, Norton, Newnham, Winslow, Aston Abbots, Barnet.

[162] Jane E. Sayers, 'Monastic archdeacons', in *Church and Government in the Middle
Ages. Essays presented to C. R. Cheney on his 70th birthday*, ed. C. N. L. Brooke, G. H.
Martin and D. M. Owen (Cambridge, 1976), repr. in eadem, *Law and Records in Medieval
England*, VI, 177–203, at 181–2; eadem, 'Privileges for St Albans Abbey', 62.

[163] *Officii nostri*, *PUE*, iii, 166–7, no. 43.

[164] For Alexander's special treatment of St Albans, see *Vitae abbatum*, 1023 (*Gesta
abbatum*, i, 137), 'Dilexit enim Papa Alexander Ecclesiam Sancti Albani, gratia praedeces-
soris sui, Papae Adriani, ejusdem Martyris indigenae, et amatoris indefessi. Erant autem
amici praecordiales Papa Adrianus, et ejus Cancellarius Rolandus, jam Papa Alexander;
ipsique ambo personam Domini Abbatis Roberti supra omnes Angliae Abbates—nec sine
merito—specialiter dilexerant.'

ecclesiastical overlord. This helped the Abbey to secure its position as the premier
Benedictine house of all England.

Adrian had wished to be remembered in St Albans and one way by which he
achieved this was through the expression of his devotion to the cult of the eponymous martyr. His considerable generosity was recorded in the Abbey's fourteenth-
century Book of Benefactors,[165] from which it is clear that he made particularly
appropriate gifts of relics to the monks, especially those of the more than 6000
Christians who constituted the Theban Legion.[166] The feast of these martyrs on 22
September was henceforth to be observed in the Abbey's calendar[167] with extracts
from the legend and no fewer than twelve readings.[168] Among Adrian's other gifts
were a splendid *pallium*, given to him by the Emperor, some precious sandals and
a most valuable ring, together with a chasuble which, by the fourteenth century,
was actually known as 'Adrian'.[169] Such gifts ensured that the memory of the English pope would remain forever among the pontifical vestments of the church of St
Albans.[170] Whilst Adrian's interest in St Albans was so close and demonstrably
personal, the pope was to reveal himself as both wary and considerably less generous in supporting other monasteries against their diocesan. His pontificate, in fact,
was to coincide with a profound shift in attitude from 'what had previously been
an unfettered exercise of papal prerogative into the hearing and decision of suits on
strictly legal merits'.[171]

Adrian's impact on the monastery at St Albans was dramatic. His local fame
and supranational position may well have helped to increase the size of the community from some fifty-six monks at the beginning of the twelfth century to its
maximum of almost one hundred by the death of Abbot Robert de Gorron in 1166.
The excavations carried out in 1978 on the site of the chapter house help to confirm this hypothesis. The *Gesta abbatum* records that Robert rebuilt Paul of Caen's
chapter house 'from the foundations'[172] between 1154 and 1166, but the enormous
size of the building was previously unrecognized. It was a huge rectangular structure, measuring almost 91' by 30', its floor covered by some 750 nine-inch square
relief-decorated glazed tiles, arranged in 'carpet' patterns, of which about one fifth
were found to have survived. It is now suggested that the St Albans' chapter house

---

[165] London, BM, Cotton MS. Nero D vii, fols 7–11; *Monasticon Anglicanum*, ed. W.
Dugdale (re-ed. J. Caley, H. Ellis and B. Bandinel) 6 vols (London, 1817–30) ii, 218–9.

[166] This regiment, supposedly recruited in Egypt and under the command of St Maurice
of Agaune, refused to obey imperial orders to sacrifice to the gods and was slaughtered to
the last man: *Gervase of Tilbury*, Otia Imperialia, *Recreation for an Emperor*, ed. and trans.
S. E. Banks and J. W. Binns, OMT (Oxford, 2002), 208–9, 240 n, 632–5, 638–9.

[167] Wormald, 'English Benedictine Kalendars', 42.

[168] *Vitae abbatum*, 1021 (*Gesta abbatum*, i, 132–3).*

[169] Sayers, 'Privileges for St Albans Abbey', 57.

[170] 'Dominus autem Papa, ut ipsius memoria semper haberetur in Ecclesia Beati Albani...', *Vitae abbatum*, 1021 (*Gesta abbatum*, i, 132).*

[171] Knowles, *Monastic Order*, 585.

[172] *Vitae abbatum*, 1036 (*Gesta abbatum*, i, 182), 'Sepultus est in Capitulo, quod a fundamentis decenter extruxerat'.

floor was the earliest decorated medieval tiled floor in England.[173] Traces of two bands of beaded fret were found on the inner angle of the northwest interior wall while a decorated doorway with a moulded base at its north jamb provides some indication as to just how richly decorated was Robert's chapter house.[174]

This new building would have had room for about ninety monks, some forty-five or so seated on benches down each side. In the central space were the graves of Robert's abbatial predecessors; Paul of Caen (d. 1093), lying within the apse of the first chapter house, then Richard d'Aubigny (d. 1119) and Geoffrey de Gorron (d. 1146), translated to new tombs by Robert de Gorron, and finally, Ralph Gubion (d. 1151) undisturbed in his stone coffin. One other very recent grave was also left undisturbed by Abbot Robert during this great building campaign—that of Adrian's father, Richard 'of the Chamber', buried in the chapter house 'on account of his own merits and those of his son, the Lord Pope'.[175] While the date of Richard's death is unknown, it seems likely to have occurred during his son's pontificate, and the grave is, therefore, crucial in dating the various structures. Richard's burial was probably the last in the chapter house of Paul of Caen, before the demolition and reconstruction by Abbot Robert. Richard's grave lay to the north of the central line of abbots' tombs and was subsequently concealed by the tiled floor of Robert's chapter house. It contained the body of a middle-aged man, with a decayed pewter or lead chalice lying on the right side of his chest. This grave was partly overlaid by that of Adam the Cellarer (d. 1167 x 1180), identified by a book-clasp, perhaps indicating his activities as a chronicler of the Abbey. The burial of Richard 'of the Chamber' in the chapter house, close to the tombs of the founder abbots, represented a great honour. Some of that honour, whatever Richard's personal merits, can surely be traced back to the generosity of his loyal son who had so amply fulfilled the expectations of the community of St Albans.

Adrian's grants to the Abbey of exemptions and *pontificalia* were never seriously challenged until after his death in September 1159.[176] In order to mount a defence against the claims of Lincoln, Abbot Robert subsequently sent a cleric, Master Ambrose, an Italian skilled in jurisprudence, to the Curia as proctor in residence.[177] This intelligent manoeuvre clearly paid off for Alexander III's earliest

---

[173] For this and what follows, Biddle and Kjølbye-Biddle, 'England's Premier Abbey', 25–30; M. Biddle, 'St Albans Abbey Chapter House Excavations 1978', *The Fraternity of Friends of St Albans Abbey*, Occasional Papers, i (1979), 4–23.

[174] Deborah Kahn, 'Recent discoveries of Romanesque Sculpture at St Albans', in *Studies in Medieval Sculpture*, ed. F. H. Thompson (London, 1983), 71–89, at 74.

[175] 'Unde in Capitulo, tum propriis, tum filii sui, Domini papae, meritis exigentibus, meruit sepeliri, non procul a tumulo Ricardi Abbatis quae postea tegulis pavimentalibus est coopertus', *Vitae abbatum*, 1019 (*Gesta abbatum*, i, 125).*

[176] 'Audientes, itaque Lincolnienses tantam a Papa Adriano (quem "Albanensem" nominarunt) indignabatur, minas congerentes…', *Ibid.*, 1023 (i, 135).*

[177] 'Magistrum Ambrosium, clericum suum, legis peritissimum, Italicum natione (de primis tempore, scientia et moribus, Angliae legisperitis)', *Vitae abbatum*, 1022 (*Gesta abbatum*, i, 136).* Compare Knowles, 'Growth of Exemption', 215, for a presumed date of early summer 1160. On Master Ambrose, *JohnS*, i, 269.

confirmations—given in January 1161—appeared to leave the St Albans' privileges virtually unassailable.[178] At the same time, Alexander wrote to request that Bishop Robert de Chesney of Lincoln and his chapter should not impede the customary annual Pentecost processions to St Albans, so recently the subject of the composition with Lincoln.[179] At Easter 1161, Bishop Robert, enlisting royal support, claimed the right to exercise his jurisdiction as ordinary.[180] When this was denied to him, the issue between St Albans and Lincoln was finally brought to trial at Winchester on 1 February 1162,[181] when a commission was set up by the king to establish the juridical state of St Albans in the reign of Henry I.[182] Gilbert Foliot, acting for Bishop Robert, his own kinsman, put forward prescriptive claims for Lincoln and displayed the professions of obedience of Abbot Robert and his predecessors.[183] Abbot Robert responded that his own profession had included the vital saving clause, *salvis dignitatibus ecclesiae meae*, citing Offa's charter as well as recent papal privileges, and requested time to produce witnesses.[184]

The complexities of the case caused an adjournment until Lent 1163 but at that point, Bishop Robert's advocates at the Curia suddenly produced an earlier letter from Alexander III, dated 16 March 1162, instructing Abbot Robert to make good his claims before the bishops of Chichester and Norwich. Henry II, irritated at what he assumed to be a manoeuvre on the abbot's part, ordered that the case should be heard at Westminster in March 1163.[185] Armed with the Abbey's muniments and accompanied by thirty monks as witnesses, Robert claimed that, before 1097 and the abbacy of Richard d'Albigny, the submission paid to Lincoln was a formality and, furthermore, that a whole series of ordinations and consecrations had been performed at St Albans by bishops other than the diocesan.[186] Henry II examined these documents himself, in particular, the charters of Offa and Henry I, his comments revealing his personal astuteness and a considerable mastery of detail.[187] The trump card played by St Albans may even have lain in the fact that its most cherished privileges—the right of the abbot to wear some of the *pontificalia* and the freedom of the monastery and its churches to receive the blessing of

---

[178] *Quotiens illud*, 22 January 1161 and *Religiosam vitam*, 7 February 1161, *PUE*, iii, 276–7, nos 134–5. Interestingly, *Quoniam sine vero cultu religionis*, cited in *Vitae abbatum*, 1023 (*Gesta abbatum*, i, 137); JL, 10648 and described by Rushbrook Williams, *Abbey of St Albans*, 73, as a 'complete confirmation of the privileges of the Abbey' was not printed by Holtzmann.

[179] *Miramur plurimum*, 9 February 1161, *PUE*, iii, 279–80 no. 137.

[180] *Vitae abbatum*, 1023 (*Gesta abbatum*, i, 137).

[181] *Ibid.*, 1024 (*Gesta abbatum*, i, 139).

[182] For details of this protracted case, *ibid.*, 1024–9 (*Gesta abbatum*, i, 139–58); Rushbrook Williams, *Abbey of St Albans*, 72; Knowles, 'Growth of Exemption', 215–7.

[183] *Vitae abbatum*, 1025–6 (*Gesta abbatum*, i, 140–2).

[184] Knowles, 'Growth of Exemption', 215.

[185] Robert W. Eyton, *Court, Household and Itinerary of King Henry II* (London, 1878) 58–9.

[186] *Vitae abbatum*, 1026 (*Gesta abbatum*, i, 147–9); Knowles, 'Growth of Exemption', 216.

[187] *Vitae abbatum*, 1027 (*Gesta abbatum*, i, 151–2).

chrism and holy oils from any bishop they pleased—had been confirmed by a pope 'as English as the king himself'.[188] When Bishop Robert was asked to produce his charters, he was forced to admit that Lincoln's claim was based on prescription, at which the King advised him to agree to a composition. Henry himself then gave notification on 8 March 1163 that the suit between St Albans and Lincoln was ended. Robert de Chesney was forced to renounce his claim that St Albans and its fifteen privileged churches were subject to the church of Lincoln, receiving in return the village and church of Fingest, valued at ten pounds annually.[189] On Easter Sunday, 24 March 1163, after a struggle which had lasted almost six years, Robert de Gorron was finally able to enjoy the desideratum of every great abbot in England by celebrating mass at the High Altar of the Abbey and wearing the full *pontificalia* of mitre, ring, and gloves, while, at the Easter of the following year, Robert carried Adrian's privilege to its logical conclusion by inviting Bishop Geoffrey of St Asaph, to make chrism, bless the oils, and confer orders.[190] The Abbot was also able to celebrate a synod of his own clerics from the fifteen churches of the liberty twice a year, at which they could be supervised and instructed.[191]

The culmination of Robert's triumph over Lincoln actually occurred in May–June 1163 at the Council of Tours, despite Henry II's disinclination for such disputes to be carried beyond the realm.[192] Whereas it was claimed that St Albans obtained a papal confirmation of the composition with Lincoln,[193] Alexander III sent *Sicut injusta* to Bishop Robert of Lincoln, enumerating the possessions of the church of Lincoln. The pope confirmed the bishop in a variety of traditional rights over religious houses in the diocese, but St Albans was not among them.[194] Although Abbot Robert actually lost his prime place in the seating of the Council as a result of the intrigues of Abbot Hugh of Bury St Edmund's,[195] the abbot's primacy in England was henceforth accepted, as were the jurisdictional rights of St Albans over its liberty. Abbot Robert had acted swiftly to implement the tenor of Adrian's grants, doubtless assisted by Master Ambrose, 'his man' at the Curia, but only at

[188] *Ibid.*, 1027 (*Gesta abbatum*, i, 152–3), 'Abbas...confidenter dixit; —"Domine, quae dicuntur 'cornuta' ad manum habemus Privilegia. Sed veraciter testor, quod a me vel per me non sunt impetrata; immo a Papa Adriano, indigena vestro, Ecclesiae Sancti Albani, in cujus pago ipsum fuisse natum constat, me sunt ignorante transmissa'.

[189] *The Registrum Antiquissimum of the Cathedral Church of Lincoln, Volume I*, ed. C. W. Foster (Lincoln, 1931), 64–6, no. 104: *EEA*, i (Lincoln), 146–8 no. 234.

[190] On Holy Thursday, 9 April 1164, *Vitae abbatum*, 1029 (*Gesta abbatum*, i, 158–9).

[191] *Vitae abbatum*, 1029 (*Gesta abbatum*, i, 158). Compare Sayers, 'Monastic archdeacons', 188–203.

[192] Robert Somerville, *Pope Alexander III and the Council of Tours (1163): A Study of Ecclesiastical Politics and Institutions in the Twelfth Century* (Berkeley, 1977).

[193] *Vitae abbatum*, 1035 (*Gesta abbatum*, 179); Knowles, 'Growth of Exemption', 217, n. 2.

[194] 6 June 1163, *Registrum Antiquissimum*, I, 202–4, no. 254 (882).

[195] Somerville, *Pope Alexander III*, 36, 92–3, nn. 32, 33. Compare *Vitae abbatum*, 1035 (*Gesta abbatum*, 177), 'necnon et famulum Abbatis Sancti Albani ab illo loco violenter expulit, totoque noctis illius spatio nusquam recedens, pervigil servare studuit'.

considerable cost, for by Robert's death in 1166, the process of litigation had incurred debts of more than 600 marks.

Robert, however, had spent wisely in his lifetime. In 1170, Alexander III, then at Veroli, issued to his successor, Abbot Simon (1167–83), two privileges, *Venerabilibus fratribus* of 25 May[196] and *Cum vos* of the following day,[197] proclaiming that St Albans had no other bishop than the pope himself and confirming that the house came under the jurisdiction of the apostolic see 'nullo mediante'. These privileges reconfirmed those given by Adrian IV in *Religiosam vitam* and went further in declaring a whole series of episcopal rights that the abbot might enjoy, including his rights to processional dues. Future abbots of St Albans were to be extremely wary of creating any legal precedent or of jeopardizing their hard won position. Only a bishop of Lincoln of exceptional energy would henceforth be able to reverse this state of affairs.

Walter de Constantine, briefly bishop from 1183 for a year, made just such an attempt to return St Albans to the control of Lincoln, but failed. In the autumn of 1184, he complained to the king, then present at the Abbey as a *confrater*,[198] that the exemption enjoyed by St Albans was prejudicial to his position and requested permission to reopen the matter. Henry, encouraged by Abbot Warin (1183–95), swore that he himself had been present at the settlement and refused to allow any further molestation of the Abbey.[199] Only critics on the Lincoln side could match the deep suspicion felt thereafter by the monks of St Albans. One plausible writer who had spent time in Lincoln encapsulated the long-running hostility and resentment felt over exemption and, most particularly, the perceived intrusion of monastic archdeacons, leading to his posthumous vilification of Adrian IV.

Gerald of Wales (1146–1223)[200] recognized St Albans as 'the chief and most distinguished among the English monasteries' but rebuked it for its pride and love of excessive wealth and, in particular, for its insulting treatment of Bishop Hugh of Lincoln (1186–1200).[201] Gerald, as the author of two *Lives* of Hugh, felt himself in a strong position to comment. Following Hugh's episcopal consecration in London in 1186, the saintly bishop was making his way back to Lincoln for his enthronement there when the community of St Albans took it upon themselves to refuse him the right to enter the Abbey. The monks presumed that their cherished rights of exemption would be prejudiced if the bishop of Lincoln either celebrated Mass or heard divine office in their church. Bishop Hugh's retribution was swift and to the point. Excommunicating both the monastery and the monks, he ordered that

---

[196] *PUE*, iii, 306–7, no. 169.

[197] *Ibid.*, 307–8, no. 170.

[198] *Vitae abbatum*, 1039–40 (*Gesta abbatum*, i, 197); Knowles, 'Growth of Exemption', 217, n. 3.

[199] Rushbrook Williams, *Abbey of St Albans*, 84.

[200] See Part II/i, 'Narrative Sources', nos 5a and 5b.

[201] David Smith, 'Hugh's Administration of the Diocese of Lincoln', in *St Hugh of Lincoln: Lectures delivered at Oxford and Lincoln to celebrate the eighth centenary of St Hugh's consecration as bishop of Lincoln*, ed. Henry Mayr-Harting (Oxford, 1987), 19–47, at 34–5.

their churches should be placed under interdict with the result that, throughout the whole diocese of Lincoln, the community of St Albans was unable to celebrate or hear the divine office in their churches or buy and sell food or receive hospitality on their estates. Nor was anybody to presume to communicate with them under threat of anathema. According to Gerald, the monks, it seems, hastened to prostrate themselves at the bishop's feet, expressing their repentance, confessing their faults, and eventually obtaining his pardon and mercy. What Gerald failed to mention is that this state of affairs was reversed as rapidly as possible when Popes Clement III in 1188 and Celestine III in 1193 forbade anyone to 'exercise the office of bishop' in St Albans, stating and re-stating that the house fell under the jurisdiction of no-one but the pope!

Having recounted what he regarded as this abomination of monastic pride, Gerald then launched into a scathing attack on Adrian IV from whom, as an Englishman originating from St Albans, the abbot and monks had so confidently sought confirmation of their privileges of exemption. Indeed, Gerald implied that Adrian's favour had been so motivated by feelings for his locality—'because of his place of origin'—that he not only gave the monks everything that they asked for but also granted them requests that they had not even made. As a result, St Albans had secured the exceptional privilege that it could appoint its monks as archdeacons, with the power to preside over the clergy of their estates and hold chapters and engage in lawsuits, 'although the Apostle declares that no one fighting for the Lord should involve himself in worldly affairs'. Here was the crux of Gerald's argument. The monks of St Albans were interfering in the business reserved to seculars alone—by acting as archdeacons—and it was Adrian IV who was to blame!

Gerald might well have recalled other occasions during his own career when the abbots of St Albans had invited any catholic bishop to conduct ordinations and consecrations. The sources are rich in such examples: on 22 March 1203, Ralph, bishop of Down, performed ordinations in the chapel dedicated to St Cuthbert;[202] on Holy Thursday, 22 April of the following year, Herlewin, bishop of Leighlin and former monk of Canterbury, made the chrism, blessed holy oils, and conducted other rites associated with the episcopal office at the High Altar, having previously dedicated the church of Watford on 19 April in honour of the Blessed Virgin Mary, that of Rickmansworth on 20 April, also in honour of the Virgin, and on 21 April that of Sarratt. On the feast of the Holy Trinity 1212, Abbot John de Cella (1195–1214), claiming not only the ancient privilege of *ius pontificale* granted by the Roman popes throughout the lands of St Albans but also wishing to commend the Abbey's liberty, and to pass it on intact to his successors, in a special privilege to mark his seventeenth year in office, solemnly blessed nine sisters from the cell of Sopwell. Indeed, in order to mark the ninth year of his reign, the anniversary of which fell on Christmas Day, Abbot John had earlier blessed fifteen sisters at Sopwell on the same feast day, 20 June, 1204.

---

[202] 'Annales Sancti Albani a. 1200–1214', in *Anglo-Normannische Geschichtsquellen*, ed. F. Liebermann (Strasbourg, 1879), 166–72, 167.

In 1214, following Abbot John's death, his successor, William of Trumpington was blessed as abbot *solempniter et pontificaliter* on St Andrew's day, the first Sunday of Advent, at the High Altar by Eustace, bishop of Ely. Thomas, bishop of Down, summoned to the Abbey by Abbot William, celebrated solemn ordinations at the High Altar on 20 December and also dedicated the conventual graveyard, in which the bodies of the faithful had been buried during the Interdict. Bishop Thomas also dedicated the cemetery of St Peter's in St Albans on St Stephen's Day, the cemetery of St Mary de Pré on 27 December and an altar in honour of St Leonard and All Saints at the conventual church of St Alban on 28 December.

Matthew Paris (*c.* 1200–59), the Abbey's great promoter and publicist,[203] saw the crucial role of Adrian IV, both in the commemoration of the cult of Alban and in the granting of monastic exemptions, from a more favourable and supportive perspective than did Gerald of Wales. Prejudiced and gossipy Paris may have been,[204] but he had enormous pride in and enthusiasm for St Albans. Paris drew for the early part of his *Vitae abbatum ecclesiae S. Albani* or *Lives of the Twenty Three Abbots of St Albans*[205] on a lost work, probably covering the period down to the death of Abbot Robert in 1166, together with other manuscript sources contained in the Abbey's library.[206] He made no attempt to reduce this mass of early material to a straightforward narrative and, consequently, there are many displacements and duplicated passages or 'doublets'.[207] The difficulty remains to establish what he wrote himself and what he took from Adam the Cellarer (or Bartholomew the Clerk), but nevertheless, his is the 'unhampered' personal view of a member of the community at St Albans,[208] and the extant documents tend to bear out the narrative.

Matthew Paris claimed that Adrian never forgot the Abbey and 'so loved the Church of the Blessed Alban that whatever the monks sought from him was granted without difficulty'.[209] His colourful account of Abbot Robert's journey to see Adrian in 1156 certainly seems to have benefited from hindsight and can, in all likelihood, be attributed to him rather than to Adam the Cellarer. Robert had brought gifts amounting to 140 marks, gold, silver, and precious metals, five copes, three mitres, and sandals made by Christina of Markyate. According to

---

[203] Claude Jenkins, *The Monastic Chronicler and the Early School of St Albans* (London, 1922); V. H. Galbraith, 'Roger Wendover and Matthew Paris', The David Murray Lectures, 11 (Glasgow, 1944), 5–48; Richard Vaughan, *Matthew Paris*, rev. edn (Cambridge, 1979); Antonia Gransden, *Historical Writing in England c.550–c.1307* (London, 1974), 356–79.

[204] Brooke, 'St Albans: the Great Abbey', especially 64–5.

[205] BL, Cotton MS, Nero D.i, fols 30–68v., Matthew Paris's autograph manuscript.

[206] *Ibid.*, fo. 30, 'secundum antiquum Rotulum Bartholomaei Clerici; qui cum Domino Adam Cellarario diu fuerat, serviens ei, et ipsum rotulum sibi retinuit, de scriptis suis hoc solum eligens'; *Vitae abbatum*, 990 (cf. *Gesta abbatum*, xiv); Vaughan, *Matthew Paris*, 182–4; Gransden, *Historical Writing*, 374–5.

[207] Knowles, *Monastic Order*, 310; Thomson, *Manuscripts from St Albans*, i, 3.

[208] Knowles, *Monastic Order*, 310.

[209] 'Hic in tantum Ecclesiam beati Albani dilexit, ut quicquid Ecclesiae fratres ab eo petissent, sine difficultate consequerentur', *Vitae abbatum*, 1019 (*Gesta abbatum*, i, 125).*

Paris, Adrian refused everything but the mitres, and sandals—significant symbols of *pontificalia*—saying 'I refuse to take your gifts for when I fled to your monastery and requested the monastic habit, you refused to receive me.' Abbot Robert's most diplomatic reply: 'the reason we were not able to accept you was that the will of God opposed it and His wisdom has directed your life to another path', appeared to have mollified Adrian who replied 'elegantly and politely' and invited the abbot to make his request, for, as he said, 'it is not possible for the Blessed Alban to refuse his citizens of St Albans anything'.

Fortune favoured the Abbey of St Albans in the twelfth century. As one of the foremost, if not actually one of the richest, of the pre-Conquest monasteries, it claimed and eventually achieved for itself a primacy of position, soon outstripping all other Benedictine houses in England. The quality of spiritual life at St Albans, so much associated with possession of the body of the Proto-Martyr, was enhanced by the activities of a succession of able and devoted abbots of which Robert de Gorron stood out for his dedication in seeking confirmations for the Abbey. The splendid architecture, reformed liturgical observance, famous school, and indulgences for pilgrims visiting the Martyr's ever more elaborate shrine, all combined to increase the number of recruits and the size of the monastic community. At precisely the time when papal confirmations began to be much sought after, Nicholas Breakspear, loyal son of St Albans, had become pope Adrian IV. His particular devotion to St Alban and to his birthplace resulted in a whole series of confirmations for the monastery, not only considerable in themselves, but cumulatively, of lasting significance. Henceforth, the abbots of St Albans enjoyed exceptional exemption from the authority of the diocesan bishop, placing them on more or less an equal footing with the abbots of major continental houses and giving them an independence much envied by their counterparts. Adrian it was who made possible the extension of the liberty of St Albans with its powerful archidiaconal jurisdiction exercised by monks. Had his pontificate been longer, it is likely that his generosity to St Albans above all other houses would have continued. In the event, it was left to his chancellor and successor, Pope Alexander III, to maintain in the interests of the Abbey of St Albans (mitred abbot and papal bishop and all), both Adrian's memory and his actions. St Albans' loyal son could have had no better heir.

Chapter 7
Totius christianitatis caput.
The Pope and the Princes
Anne J. Duggan

A general consensus has emerged in the last forty years that Adrian's pontificate saw a deliberate shift in papal policies from a pro-imperial to a pro-Sicilian alliance, with momentous consequences not only for Italy and Sicily, but also for the empire and the whole Latin Church. According to this interpretation, Adrian's Curia was riven by deep-seated tensions, between pro-imperialists who wanted to continue the alleged pro-imperial policies of Eugenius III (symbolized by the accord reached at Constance in March 1153),[1] and pro-Sicilians who preferred an 'alliance' with the king of Sicily, in which the balance of influence shifted from the one to the other under the leadership of the papal chancellor, Cardinal Roland—the bearer and perhaps the drafter of the Besançon letter. Although seemingly well supported, this view depends on a narrow and partisan interpretation of events: it ignores the complexity of the Italian situation during Adrian's pontificate, the serpentine diplomacy of Frederick I, and the bias of most of the contemporary sources.

The concept of a 'Sicilian party' depends principally on the assertions made in October 1159 by the five cardinals (Imar of Tusculum, Giovanni of SS. Silvestro e Martino, Guido of S. Callisto, Raymond of S. Maria in Via Lata, and Simon, cardinal deacon of S. Maria in Domnica) who wrote in support of Cardinal Octavian's election to the papacy on 7 September 1159.[2] In defence of their own actions, they alleged that they had opposed the 'friendship' established at Benevento between Pope Adrian and William of Sicily, as well as 'plots' by 'the brethren who were bound to the Sicilian' to persuade the pope to excommunicate the emperor and all his supporters;[3] and it was this same 'Sicilian faction', they said, which had plotted the election of Cardinal Roland (Alexander III) and obstructed Octavian's elevation to the papal throne. A similar allegation, that Roland was 'associated with William of Sicily in a conspiracy and plot against the

---

[1] See below, n. 28.

[2] Otto of Freising/Rahewin: *Ottonis et Rahewini Gesta Friderici I. Imperatoris*, ed. G. Waitz and B. von Simson, 3rd edn, *MGH SRG* 46 (Hanover/Leipzig, 1912), cited as *Gesta*; cf. the English translation, *The Deeds of Frederick Barbarossa by Otto of Freising and his Continuator, Rahewin*, trans. Charles Christopher Mierow (New York, 1966), cited as *Deeds*: Rahewin, iv. 62 (*Gesta*, 303–7; *Deeds*, 294–7). For selections from this and other sources (marked with an asterisk in the following notes), see Part II below. For Cardinal Simon (?Aug. 1158–Dec. 1182), abbot of Subiaco, whose existence Mierow could not trace (*Deeds*, 294, n. 218), see Zenker, 140–1, 225–6.

[3] Rahewin, iv. 62 (*Gesta*, 304–5; *Deeds*, 294–5).

Church of God and the empire', was made by Octavian/Victor himself, in a letter intended principally for the emperor and the German court, and amplified by Frederick I into the 'Anagni conspiracy', which justified the repudiation of Alexander III's election at the council of Pavia (1160).[4]

The cardinals' letter, however, is hardly an objective witness. It needs to be seen for what it is—a piece of skilful propaganda, written by a small rump of the Sacred College whose candidate had failed to secure sufficient votes. Their intention was both to curry favour with the emperor, whose support would be crucial to their success, and to justify their own opposition to Roland/Alexander III, the candidate who by any reckoning commanded at least a two-third majority, by vilifying both him and his electors. Alexander's supporters could claim, with some validity, that the discreditable faction label should more appropriately have been applied to the Victorines, that Frederick's partisanship for Octavian had been manifested since at least May–June 1159, and that the Count Palatine Otto of Wittelsbach's intervention in the election was not disinterested.[5] With only one cardinal bishop among their own number (Imar of Tusculum), and at most nine members,[6] the Victorines formed neither the *maior* nor the *sanior pars* of the electorate of twenty-eight or so cardinals.[7]

Once the idea of a 'Sicilian faction' opposed to an 'imperial faction' took hold in the historiography, however, it was easy to interpret the whole sequence of events from 1155 to 1159 as the progression of a papal plot. Adrian's oscillation, from opposing William I of Sicily to recognizing him—from the renewal of the accord of Constance (1155) to the acceptance of the accord of Benevento (1156)— is seen as the consequence either of the changing balance of power among the

---

[4] Rahewin, iv. 60 (*Gesta*, 297–9; *Deeds*, 288–9); idem, iv. 79 (*Gesta*, 329; *Deeds*, 319: '...while Pope Adrian was still alive Chancellor Roland and certain cardinals...formed a conspiracy with William of Sicily...and with other enemies of the empire—the people of Milan, of Brescia, and of Piacenza' to ensure the election of a pope sympathetic to their party after Adrian's death). The reliability of this assertion is highly dubious: Michele Maccarrone, *Papato e impero dalla elezione di Frederico I alla morte di Adriano IV* (Rome, 1959), 347–60.

[5] See n. 160 below.

[6] As alleged by the Victorines: Rahewin, iv. 62 (esp. *Gesta*, 305; *Deeds*, 295); *Burchardi praepositi Urspergensis Chronicon*, ed. Oswald Holder-Egger and Bernhard von Simson, *MGH SRG* 16 (Hanover/Leipzig, 1916), 40. Cf. I. S. Robinson, *The Papacy 1073–1198: Continuity and Innovation* (Cambridge, 1990), 473, 'but their numbers rapidly dwindled to five'. The dwindling was rapid indeed, since only five cardinals could be found to issue the letter supporting the new 'pope' by the time of his consecration (4 Oct.; above, n. 2). Of these, one, Raymond of S. Maria in Via Lata, seems to have defected soon afterwards, for he signed no privileges of 'Victor IV': see JL, ii, 418; cf. Zenker, 179–80. It is also possible that Imar had not voted for Octavian.

[7] As the party supporting 'Victor IV', waned, Alexander's waxed, from the 14 whom the Victorines claimed first opted for him (Rahewin, iv. 62: *Gesta*, 305; *Deeds*, 295) to the twenty-two (5 cardinal bishops, 9 cardinal priests, and 8 cardinal deacons) who wrote to the emperor in defence of his election: Rahewin, iv. 63 (*Gesta*, 307–8; *Deeds*, 297–9). If Cardinal Roland had voted for himself, the number of votes cast for Alexander III would have been twenty-three, adding one more cardinal priest to the list.

cardinals, as the 'imperialists' were overtaken by the 'Sicilians', or, in a variation of the theme, as the successful assertion of Adrian's own anti-imperial bias, supported by that of the chancellor Roland,[8] which led through a series of deliberate affronts to the imperial dignity to its culmination in the dual election of September 1159. Thus, virtually the whole of Adrian's pontificate is seen through the distorting lens of the crisis that followed his death.

The most succinct version of this theme in the narrative sources is the compact verse-summary by Godfrey of Viterbo. According to him, pope and emperor had engaged to support one another, and neither was to make peace with the Greeks or the Sicilians without the approval of the other (accord of Constance); but the pope, wishing to be an enemy of Caesar, broke the agreement and went down into Apulia (Benevento, November 1155–July 1156). The Roman pontiff attached himself to the enemies of the empire, making pacts with the Sicilians (accord of Benevento) as well as with the Greeks (reception of envoys from Constantinople, engagement in the Greek-led conspiracy against William of Sicily, 1155–6). The cardinals were split, Octavian and Guido of Crema leading the group which rejected such pacts and favoured retention of the imperial alliance.[9] Returning to 'his Campagna' (Anagni, June–September 1159) the pope died:

> werra pro pace relicta;
> Nam caput orribilis scismatis ipse fuit.
> (having left war in the place of peace;
> for he himself was the grizzly head of schism).[10]

Virtually the whole of Otto of Freising and Rahewin's treatment of papal-imperial relations can be read as an extended development of this theme; so, too, Burchard of Ursberg's *Chronicon* and the anonymous *Chronica regia Coloniensis*. All four writers had a purpose: to promote Frederick as the bringer of peace and justice to Italy and the empire and to denigrate all who appeared to stand in his way.[11] Thus Adrian and his alleged Sicilian-loving cardinals became scapegoats for the disharmony between the two powers and the papal schism that broke out in 1159. To this end, virtually every recorded papal act in respect of the empire was 'provocation' or 'betrayal', and Adrian's 'alliance' with 'the Sicilian' was a proximate cause of the papal schism which followed immediately on Adrian's death.

---

[8] '...both the founder and the leader of their [the Sicilian] party for years': Peter Munz, *Frederick Barbarossa. A Study in Medieval Politics* (London, 1969), 210; cf. *ibid.*, 140–4, 209–12; Robinson, *The Papacy*, 470–3. See also n. 90 below.

[9] *Gotifredi Viterbiensis Gesta Friderici I. et Heinrici VI. imperatorum metrice scripta*, ed. G. H. Pertz (from edn by G. Waitz) *MGH SRG* 30 (Hanover, 1870), 10–11, cc. 10–12, lines 268–300.* For citations marked with an asterisk, see also Part II below.

[10] Godfrey of Viterbo, lines 299–300.*

[11] Burchard of Ursberg (above, n. 6); *Chronica regia Coloniensis cum continuationibus in monasterio S. Pantaleonis scriptis aliisque Coloniensis monumentis partim ex monumentis Germaniae historicis recusa*, ed. G. Waitz, MGH SRG 18 (Hanover, 1880).

Not surprisingly, many historians have been much influenced by this simple tale, so overwhelmingly supported by imperial and Victorine sources. They have tended to see a deliberate abandonment of the empire in favour of the Normans and the Greeks—a papal treason which jettisoned collaboration for confrontation and laid the basis of the destruction of the mutual regard between the empire and the papacy which they allege was central to Frederick I's policy. Whether Adrian is seen as the spearhead or the tool, this interpretation lays all the fault for the chain of events which led to the schism at the feet of an increasingly anti-imperial Curia which allied, one by one, with all the anti-imperial forces in the Italian peninsula. Frederick I thus became the victim of a villainous plot, against which a few loyal cardinals worked in vain, and Adrian the pope whose disastrous, not to say treasonable, actions, not only split the College of Cardinals and the Latin Church, but fatally destroyed the harmonious relationship between empire and papacy.

Unquestionably there were some influential cardinals who enjoyed exceptionally good relations with the new emperor. Two can be certainly identified (Octavian himself and his relative Guido of Crema),[12] and there may have been two or three more.[13] But the existence of a (very) small band of 'imperialists'—if indeed they deserve to be so labelled—does not make the rest into either anti-imperialists or pro-Sicilians. Accepting the Victorine and imperial propaganda at its face value, however, Munz and Robinson thought that it did;[14] and Robinson attempted to corroborate this interpretation by reading into Cardinal Boso's record concepts which are wholly absent from it. Typical of this approach is his unqualified assertion that 'Cardinal Boso—himself a member of the Sicilian party—claimed that the party came into existence in order to implement Hadrian's own policy'.[15] Boso claimed nothing of the sort. He did indeed record that Adrian himself had been willing to accept the very favourable peace that William of Sicily offered in August 1155 (after Frederick's departure from the region), and that it was rejected because most of the cardinals opposed it, and all were hesitant, and he also reported that the pope sent most of the cardinals back into the Campagna in June 1156, when William's then victorious army had approached to within two miles of Benevento. But although he puts a very positive pro-papal spin on these events, he never once used the politically coloured terminology employed by

[12] Octavian (Ottaviano of Monticelli), cardinal deacon of S. Nicola in Carcere Tulliano 1138–51, cardinal priest of S. Cecilia 1151–9, anti-pope Victor IV 1159–64, came from a family long identified with pro-imperial attitudes: H. Tillmann, 'Ricerche sull'origine dei membri del collegio cardinalizio nel XII secolo, ii/1', *Rivista di storia della Chiesa in Italia*, 26 (1972), 337–43; cf. Munz, *Frederick Barbarossa*, 206–8; Robinson, *The Papacy*, 471–2; Zenker, 66–70. Guido of Crema, successively cardinal deacon of S. Maria in Porticu 1145–58, cardinal priest of S. Callisto (= S. Maria in Trastevere) 1158–64, anti-pope Paschal III 1164–68, was a relative: Brixius, 54, 107–8; Zenker, 56–9.

[13] E.g. the signatories of Octavian's election manifesto (above, at n. 2).

[14] Although at one point (*The Papacy*, 470–3) Robinson recognized the bias of what he (rightly) called 'pro-imperial' sources.

[15] Robinson, *The Papacy*, 470.

Munz, Robinson, and others; nor did he employ it in his description of the dual election.[16]

Such labels are illusory. Equally illusory are Robinson's descriptions of parties forming among the cardinals and policies being devised and pursued. Such conceptualization ignores the hot-house and dangerous conditions of the time. The cross-currents of international, regional, and communal ambitions across the whole of Italy were like the shifting sands of a desert in a sand-storm. Unlike historians, neither pope nor cardinals could see what the outcome of events would be: they had to deal with each new situation as it arose. For Munz and Robinson, however, there is a clear line of pro-Sicilian, anti-imperial policy linking the election of Alexander III in 1159 with the recognition of William I in 1156.[17] Reading backwards in this way from the disputed election does not do justice to the fluidity and uncertainty of the situation in Italy, or the extent to which Frederick's own actions and inactions added fuel to the fire.

At the moment of his election in December 1154, Adrian was confronted by four major problems. A new king of the Romans, Frederick I, was advancing towards Rome for his imperial consecration, imposing obedience on recalcitrant cities and proclaiming the resumption of imperial rights as he went; a new Sicilian ruler, William I, was seeking papal confirmation of his royal status,[18] and menacing the papal states from the south; an energetic Greek emperor, Manuel I Comnenus, was engaged in multi-pronged diplomacy with the German monarchy and dissident elements in Ancona and Apulia, directed towards the re-establishment of Byzantine influence in Italy; Rome itself was in the grip of a militant revolutionary movement seeking independence. The papacy was politically and territorially trapped between all four, was the target of diplomatic and military assaults from all four, and was hanging on by the skin of its teeth to a fragile lordship, variously defined, over the assortment of heterogeneous territories directly or indirectly subject to the lordship of St Peter. Politically speaking, the pope was not master in his own house; and even the precise definition of what constituted his own house was open to doubt and challenge.[19] The question for the papacy in 1154–1156 was how to find a way through this minefield, without undermining its own legal and territorial position as lord of the papal states, overlord of the Norman kingdom, and chief priest of the Latin Church. No fair judgment on Adrian's actions can be reached without recognizing the vulnerability of pope and Curia throughout his pontificate,[20] the unreliability of their 'allies', and the determination of those with whom they had to deal to wring whatever advantage they could from each situation. Relations between all these entities was

---

[16]   Boso, *Vita Adriani*, 394,* 395,* 397–401.

[17]   Munz, *Frederick Barbarossa*, 97, 99, 140–1, 143, 189–91, 199–200, 201–2, 208–9; for Robinson, see below, n. 90.

[18]   Salvatore Tramontana, *La monarchia normanna e sveva* (Turin, 1986), 181–95.

[19]   Partner (*Lands of St Peter*, 117) comments on 'how desperate the question of internal security was for the Reform papacy'.

[20]   Robinson, *The Papacy*, 245–6.

an endlessly changing kaleidoscope of agreements, promises, and expectations. The balance of forces within the patchwork quilt that was Italy changed from day to day; and solemn agreements, often entered into for short term goals, were quickly superseded by the turn of events. In such an environment of rapid change, where fortunes could be quickly transformed for good or ill, it is not surprising that the Boethian image of *Fortuna* should have had a considerable vogue. What shaped the political history of Adrian's short reign was the movement of external forces, not the balance between alleged factions in the Curia; 'policy', if one can legitimately apply that term to Adrian's relations with the powers of the day, was shaped by events, rather than shaping them; and the single most important event was the triumph, against the expectations of many, of William I of Sicily at Brindisi on 29 May 1156.

i. The Regno[21]

The point at which the triangular claims of the papacy and the two empires overlapped was the kingdom of Sicily. Although Norman adventurers had been in Sicily and southern Italy since the mid-eleventh century, the kingdom was a relatively recent creation. It had been established, in the teeth of papal and imperial opposition, by the great Roger II, ruler of Sicily. His inheritance of the southern Italian duchies of Apulia and Calabria from his second cousin William (d. 1127), enabled him to construct a unified domain which, despite internal conflict, was more than a match for its nearest neighbour, the papal states. Even with imperial support, the papacy had not been able to resist the expansion and consolidation of Norman rule; and the papal schism of 1130–1138 enabled Roger to extort a royal title from the anti-pope Anacletus II in 1130. His achievement—the culmination of three quarters of a century of Norman aggrandizement—created a formidable new power in the Mediterranean, welcome neither to Germany nor to Byzantium nor to Rome, although the papacy had been forced to a series of compacts which established the basis of a *modus vivendi* with the new power. In return for recognition of their various lordships, the Norman rulers did homage to the pope and paid a significant annual tribute in gold. From the German perspective this looked like treason; from the Byzantine, it looked like Latin aggression against the Greek Church in southern Italy. But such judgments ignored two facts. Successive emperors, German and Greek, had been unable to defeat or subdue the Normans; and the papacy was not the willing partner or patron of what Leo IX had called 'those accursed Normans' (*illi maledicti Normanni*), although it sometimes benefited from their military support. Each papal recognition of Norman rule had followed the defeat of papal or papally-supported opposition. The concord of

---

[21] From the time of the anti-pope Anacletus II's confirmation of Roger II's royal title in 1130, the dominions of the Norman kingdom (the island of Sicily together with Apulia, Calabria and other lordships in southern Italy) were collectively known as the 'regnum Sicilie'—the *regno*: *Pontificum romanorum qui fuerunt inde ab exeunte saeculo IX usque ad finem saeculi XIII vitae*, ed. J. M. Watterich, 2 vols (Leipzig, 1862), ii, 193–5, at 194, 'coronam regni Siciliae et Calabriae et Apuliae'.

Melfi (1059) followed the defeat of papal troops at Civitate in 1053;[22] the accord of Ceprano (with Gregory VII, in 1080) followed the Norman capture of Salerno in 1076; Innocent II's recognition of Roger II in 1139 followed that pope's defeat at Galluccio, near the river Garigliano. In all three, the papal policy was to restrict what it saw as the Norman menace to designated lands in the south so as to protect the papal patrimony, upon which its own economic and political survival depended. Thus, having failed to defeat them, and being unable to expel them, it recognized the Normans as defenders of St Peter and vassals of the Holy See,[23] to the chagrin of the western empire,[24] in an attempt to restrict their expansionist potential by accommodating their ambitions in Sicily and Apulia and binding them by ties of allegiance to the Roman church. Relations remained strained, however.[25] Roger's acquisition of the royal title had been preceded by seizure of papal territories (principally Capua and northern Abruzzo), and both Lucius II and Eugenius III hoped, with imperial help, to force the king to give them up, but they failed utterly.[26] One of Eugenius III's last political acts was to engage Frederick I, the newly elected king of the Romans, to such an enterprise, at Constance on 23 March 1153.

(a) The accord of Constance, 1153

Much has been made of this so-called 'treaty' of Constance, since it has been seen as the main diplomatic achievement of Eugenius III's pontificate, cementing an alliance with the empire, while its alleged breach by Adrian IV (at Benevento, 1156) was thought to signal a dramatic reversal of 'alliances'. The use of the term 'treaty' elevates the agreement to the status of the binding commitments made

[22] *Pontificum romanorum...vitae*, ed. Watterich, i, 233–4 no. 9. Although Partner (*Lands of St Peter*, 119) thinks that the accord of Melfi represented a deliberate change in papal policy under the new pope Nicholas II (elected without imperial intervention or approval), with the Normans 'emerging as the irreplaceable stipendiaries of the Reform papacy' (122), he fully recognizes the papacy's misgivings: below, n. 25.

[23] *Pontificum romanorum...vitae*, ed. Watterich, i, 234, 'I, Robert [Guiscard]...shall to the full extent of my power support the holy Roman Church everywhere in holding and extending the regalia and possessions of St Peter, against all men.'

[24] Guiscard formally rejected the claims of the empire to jurisdiction in the south in the promise which he made to Nicholas II in 1059: 'I...promise that from all the lands which I hold under my own sway, and which I have never conceded that anyone from beyond the mountains holds, I will pay annually for each yoke of oxen 12 denarii of the mint of Pavia to you, my lord Pope Nicholas, and to all your successors....' (*Pontificum romanorum ...vitae*, ed. Watterich, i, 233–4).

[25] Dione Clementi, 'Relations between the Papacy and the West Roman Empire in the Emergent Kingdom of Sicily and South Italy 1050–1156', *Bollettino dell'Istituto Storico Italiano per il Medio Evo*, 80 (1968) 191–212. Partner, *Lands of St Peter*, calls the enfeoffment of the Normans 'a marriage of convenience' (122), and speaks (127) of Gregory VII's 'fear and dislike of Robert Guiscard', and his failed attempt to build up their Lombard opponents. Gregory's reliance on their support against Henry IV's occupation of Rome in 1184 was more an act of desperation than a pro-Norman policy.

[26] Cf. Partner, *Lands of St Peter*, 181–7.

between states in the modern world. But it was nothing of the kind. It was an 'accord and agreement'; and, far from being the pinnacle of a policy of alignment with the empire pursued by Eugenius III,[27] it should be seen as an attempt at containment.

> The king will cause one of his *ministeriales* to swear on the king's soul (*in anima regis*), and he himself, having pledged his faith with his hand in that of the lord pope's legate, will promise that he will make neither truce nor peace with either the Romans or with Roger of Sicily without the free consent and approval of the Roman church and the lord pope Eugenius and of his successors who keep the terms of the agreement with King Frederick, written below. He will strive with all the power (*viribus*) of his realm to subject the Romans to the lord pope and the Roman church, as they were for one hundred years before. He will, as a devoted and special advocate of the Holy Roman Church, preserve and defend the honour of the papacy and the *regalia* of St Peter which it now possesses against all men to the best of his ability. What it does not possess, he will with all the power of his realm assist it to recover, and defend what is recovered. And he will not grant any land on this side of the sea to the king of the Greeks. If [the latter] should invade, the king will endeavour to the extent of his power to drive him out as soon as he is able.

For his part, Eugenius promised:

> on the faith of his apostolic authority, together with the said cardinals, in the presence of the said envoys of the lord king that he will honour the king as the most dearly beloved son of St Peter, and that when he comes for the achievement of his crown he will as far as he is able crown him as emperor without any difficulty or denial, and he will aid the king in maintaining and increasing and extending the honour of his realm, in accordance with the obligations of his office. And the lord pope, having been informed (of it), out of regard for the royal dignity, will canonically admonish any who rashly dare to overthrow or undermine the justice and honour of the realm. And if they disdain to do justice in respect of the royal right and honour they shall be struck with a sentence of excommunication. Moreover, [the pope] will not grant land on this side of the sea to the king of the Greeks. If he presumes to invade, the lord pope will endeavour to drive him out with the forces of St Peter. All these things will be observed by both parties without fraud or subterfuge (*malo ingenio*), unless they are changed by the free and mutual consent of both parties.[28]

---

[27] Which Robinson (*The Papacy*, 388–9) sees as the last triumph of the pro-imperial anti-Sicilian party, created by Calixtus II and Honorius II, which he thinks had dominated the Curia for the previous three decades.

[28] *MGH Constitutiones*, i, 201–2 no. 144; *MGH Diplomata*, 10/i (1975), 85–9 no. 51; *PL*, clxxx, 1638–9 no. 24. This 'concordia et conventio (agreement and convention)' was

Seen from the papacy's point of view, this bi-partisan agreement was the best deal that could be made with an assertive young emperor.[29] Its principal aim was to bind Frederick to help the papacy to secure its position against the Roman commune, Roger of Sicily, and the Byzantines, as well as to recover and defend the *regalia* of St Peter. Assertion of imperial rights was to be balanced by a guarantee both of papal *honor* and of the *regalia* of St Peter. This latter term comprised jurisdictional, territorial, and fiscal rights over the papal states. Moreover, while Frederick was obliged not to make a separate peace with the Sicilian king, no such obligation was imposed on the pope. This was a crucial distinction. Eugenius reserved the right of independent action in an area of vital territorial interest to himself. Rebellious, disobedient, and troublesome the Sicilian kingdom may have been, but it was a papal dependency. Eugenius wanted to clip Roger's wings, but to his advantage, not the emperor's. And if Frederick could be persuaded to suppress the Roman insurrection and restrict the ambitions of his Byzantine 'brother', all the better.

(b) The Norman crisis, 1155–6

All these questions were still unresolved in the winter of 1154–5. The Constance accord was in abeyance; Frederick I, with a German army, was marching through northern Italy on his coronation journey to Rome, reclaiming imperial rights over the northern cities as he went; and William I took the opportunity of a new papal reign to seek reconciliation. The new pope thus found himself between the devil and the deep. The prospect of William's submission was attractive, but more pressing was the need to ensure that Frederick I's approach to Rome should be peaceful. William's emissaries were rebuffed, therefore,[30] and the pope denied William the royal title, addressing him as 'lord', not 'king', of Sicily, in a letter carried by Cardinal Henry of SS. Nereo e Achilleo;[31] meanwhile, Adrian ratified Eugenius's agreement with Frederick. Robinson saw this endorsement as 'a crucial part of Hadrian's strategy',[32] involving commitment to a pro-imperial and anti-

---

confirmed by seven cardinals (Gregory of S. Maria in Trastevere, Hubald of S. Prassede, Bernard of S. Clemente, Octavian of S. Cecilia, Roland of S. Marco, Gregory of S. Angelo, Guido of S. Maria in Porticu) and Abbot Bruno of Chiaravalle. Frederick's confirmation is *MGH Constitutiones*, i, 202–3 no. 145, dated 23 March 1152 (= 1153). Among the witnesses is Godfrey of Viterbo, royal chaplain. For a full discussion of the circumstances and text of the Constance accord, see Maccarrone, *Papato e impero*, 42–81.

[29] John of Salisbury, who was with Eugenius when the 'treaty' was made, later commented on the 'shamelessness of his vast and audacious scheme': *JohnS*, i, 207.

[30] *Romualdi Salernitani Chronicon*, ed. C. A. Garufi, *Rerum Italicarum Scriptores*, Nuova ed., 7/i (Città di Castello, 1935), 237.

[31] *Ibid.*, 237–8, 'Adrianus papa Henricum cardinalem Sanctorum Nerei et Achillei ad eum misit, quem rex recipere noluit...eo quod in litteris apostolicis, quas regi portabat, papa ipsum non regem, sed W(ilhelmum) dominum Sicilie nominabat. Pro quo facto Adrianus papa et tota Romana Curia contra regem turbata est et commota.' For Henry of Pisa, see ch. 9, n. 72.

[32] Robinson, *The Papacy*, 389.

Sicilian policy, later to be spectacularly abandoned. But there is no evidence that Adrian saw the accord in such stark terms. He did not challenge William's legitimate inheritance of his territories (apart from papal lands seized by his father), having addressed him as 'lord of Sicily' in the letter carried by Cardinal Henry.[33] The papacy wanted confirmation of its lordship of the *regno*, not dismantlement of the kingdom. Its chief complaints against William were his retention of papal territory and assumption of the crown without prior papal approval, and the threat of Frederick's army might induce William to restore papal territory and confirm his fidelity to St Peter and the pope. Frederick's obligation to defend Peter's patrimony, both under the accord of Constance and as emperor, implied armed intervention against a possible Norman aggression, not imperial acquisition and domination of the southern kingdom.

William I, however, followed up his dismissal of the papal envoy with an invasion of papal territory and an attack on the city of Benevento. Only the firm resistance of the citizens (who murdered their allegedly pro-royal archbishop Peter),[34] the secession of some barons, and the eruption of a baronial rebellion in Apulia saved the city, although other less well-defended places were devastated.[35] Adrian's response was to excommunicate the Sicilian ruler.[36] Meanwhile, various Apulian elements[37] hostile to William I appealed directly to Adrian as superior lord to come to their aid. This Sicilian crisis erupted at the very moment that Frederick I was marching south through Italy. It was expected that he would impose obedience on the City and take military action against the Norman ruler. In fact, having taken about eight months proclaiming and asserting his authority in Lombardy,[38] Frederick arrived in Rome too late to do other than secure his imperial coronation, and that with difficulty.[39] The summer heat produced serious sickness among Frederick's soldiers, and campaign weariness sapped the nobles' enthusiasm for further engagement. Instead of turning the forces of his realm against the rebellious ruler of Sicily, therefore, he withdrew northwards, looting and razing Spoleto on the way, because it defaulted in the *fodrum* payments, leaving the pope dangerously exposed.[40]

---

[33]   Romuald of Salerno, *Chronicon*, 238; see above, n. 31.

[34]   Romuald of Salerno, *Chronicon*, 238, 'Ciues autem eiusdem ciuitatis eidem uiriliter restiterunt et Petrum archiepicopum, quem pro parte regis suspectum habebant, interfecerunt.'

[35]   Boso, *Vita Adriani*, 389–90.*

[36]   Boso, *Vita Adriani*, 390.*

[37]   Boso, *Vita Adriani*, 393.*

[38]   October 1154–June 1155: Otto of Freising, ii. 11–28 (*Gesta*, 112–35; *Deeds*, 124–44); cf. below, at nn. 96–102.

[39]   See below, at nn. 103–04.

[40]   Otto of Freising, ii. 34*–5 (Gesta, 142–3; *Deeds*, 152–3); Boso, *Vita Adriani*, 393–4;* Romuald of Salerno, *Chronicon*, 239. Andrew of Rupecanina is later (1157) found acting with the Greeks: *Deeds of John and Manuel Comnenus by John Kinnamos* (= Cinnamus), trans. Charles M. Brand (New York, 1976), 130–1.

But before he left Italy, Frederick received a distinguished Byzantine embassy headed by Michael Palaeologus and John Ducas outside Ancona, and he sent the trusted Wibald, abbot of Stavelot and Corvey, on a mission to Constantinople. Simultaneously, he authorized the return to the *regno* of Robert II, prince of Capua, Andrew of Rupecanina, and other Norman rebels against Roger II of Sicily, who had spent many years (1139–55) in exile in Germany at the court of Conrad III, and indeed, reinstated them in their lordships.[41] Robert and his companions entered Apulia in Wibald's company, and were, so Otto of Freising says, accepted by the local people in the expectation that Frederick would himself come to their support,[42] while the Greek envoys alleged that Frederick had assigned the coastal region to them.[43] The implications of this claim for Frederick's observance of the Constance accord are plain enough;[44] but even without it, the emperor's willingness to treat with envoys who were associated with what can be described as a Byzantine exploratory force installed in Ancona confirms the view that the Greek clause of the Constance accord had become as redundant as the Sicilian. At the date of the Ancona meeting (August 1155), there was no breach between the German and Byzantine emperors; no overt opposition on Frederick's part to Greek involvement in the proposed war against William of Sicily. Both parties were happy to take advantage of the indigenous conspiracies which had erupted in the Sicilian kingdom, to stir the pot and share the spoils. The allegiance of the rebels, however, inclined towards the sources of effective support, Greek and papal, leaving the absentee Frederick on the sidelines.[45]

Into this hornets' nest the pope was inexorably drawn. In response, both to William's invasion of papal territory and to the approach of some Apulian rebels,[46] Adrian gathered an army and proceeded into the Terra di Lavoro in late September 1155, where he received the homage of Robert of Capua, Andrew of Rupecanina, and other rebel nobles at San Germano (near Monte Cassino) in mid-October,[47] reaching Benevento, the *civitas beati Petri*,[48] where the neighbouring nobles received him as superior lord (*principalis dominus*),[49] some time in November. There he remained until mid-July 1156,[50] while the rebels, in alliance with the

[41] Otto of Freising, ii. 36–7 (*Gesta*, 144–5; *Deeds*, 154–5); Boso, *Vita Adriani*, 394;* Romuald of Salerno, *Chronicon*, 239. Andrew of Rupecanina is later (1157) found acting with the Greeks: Cinnamus, *Deeds of John and Manuel Comnenus*, 130–1.

[42] Otto of Freising, ii. 37 (*Gesta*, 144–5; *Deeds*, 154–5).

[43] See below, at n. 85.

[44] Although Munz, *Frederick Barbarossa* (64 n. 2; cf. 65 n. 1) considers the undertaking to make no territorial concessions to the Greeks was 'a minor point'.

[45] Vincenzo D'Alessandro, 'Corona e nobiltà nell'età dei due Guglielmi', in *Potere, società e popolo nell'età dei due Guglielmi*, Centro di studi normanno-svevi, Atti 4 (Bari, 1981), 63–77, at 66–7.

[46] Boso, *Vita Adriani*, 393.*

[47] *Ibid.*, 393–4.*

[48] So called by Innocent II at the First Lateran Council (1123), c. 17: *Conciliorum oecumenicorum decreta*, ed. J. Alberigo *et al.*, 3rd edn (Bologna, 1973), 194.

[49] Boso, *Vita Adriani*, 394.*

[50] JL 10097–10197.

Greeks, moved south to secure Apulia and Calabria. But what should have been a joint enterprise under Frederick's leadership had become a joint enterprise in which papal lordship of the *regno* was reaffirmed, and Greek money and naval support was attracting the loyalty of cities and nobles in the region, including William I's own cousin, Robert de 'Basunvilla', count of Conversano and Loretello, 'whom they had won over by money',[51] with Alexander of Conversano, former count of Gravina in Apulia—another of Roger II's exiles, who had carved out a career for himself at the Byzantine court—acting as intermediary between the Greeks and the Apulian rebels.[52]

At first, the coalition seemed to be carrying all before it. A number of cities and towns, including the strategically important port of Bari, declared for the rebels and their Greek allies, or were reduced and captured (Trani, Andria, Montepeloso, Gravina, Mottola, Taranto, Monopoli), and Brindisi, apart from the citadel in which William's soldiers held out, was taken in April 1156. Most of Apulia, except for Naples, Amalfi, Salerno, Troia, Melfi and other well fortified places, was at least superficially secured by them.[53] Frederick I's reaction to these events is instructive. Far from endorsing the triumphs of a coalition he had helped to create, he refused to meet the Greek envoys who came to his court at Würzburg in the company of his own ambassador (Wibald), returning from Constantinople, on the grounds that they had betrayed him by 'surreptitiously' obtaining and using letters bearing his seal—thereby disowning whatever agreement he had made the previous year—and he called on the princes and prelates of the empire to vow an immediate expedition to expel 'the foreigners' from Apulia. This undertaking had scarcely been made, however, when the news of William I's victory at Brindisi (29 May) was brought to him.[54] Using forces drawn principally from Sicily and Calabria, the Sicilian king had besieged the city by land and sea.[55] He captured the Greek flotilla and also many of the Apulian rebels, upon whom he visited swift and terrible justice. From Brindisi William moved swiftly north to Bari, which he demolished, except for the cathedral of St Nicholas, leaving the capital of Apulia in ruins, and thence up the Apulian coast, recapturing all the land that he had lost without a further blow, and then turned inland to menace Benevento,[56] where the

[51]   Otto of Freising, 157 (*Deeds*, 165–6).

[52]   Cinnamus, *Deeds of John and Manuel Comnenus*, 107.

[53]   Romuald of Salerno, *Chronicon*, 239; Cinnamus, *Deeds of John and Manuel Comnenus*, 107–24; William of Tyre, *Historia rerum in partibus transmarinis gestarum*, xviii. 7 (*Recueil des historiens des croisades, Historiens occidentaux*, 5 vols in 6 [Paris, 1844–95], 1/i–ii [1844], ii, 828–9). Cf. F. Chalandon, *Histoire de la domination normande en Italie et en Sicile*, 2 vols [Paris, 1907; repr. New York, 1969] ii, 213–14.

[54]   Otto of Freising, ii. 49 (*Gesta*, 157–9; cf. 170–1; *Deeds*, 165–7; cf. 178); cf. Cinnamus, *Deeds of John and Manuel Comnenus*, 127–9; William of Tyre, *Historia*, xviii. 8 (p. 831).

[55]   Falcandus (*Ugo Falcando: La Historia o Liber de Regno Sicilie*, ed. G. B. Siragusa, Fonti per la Storia d'Italia, 22 [Rome, 1897]), 20–2; William of Tyre, *Historia*, xviii. 8 (p. 831), 'ex universa Sicilia et Calabria militaribus copiis'.

[56]   Romuald of Salerno, *Chronicon*, 239–40, 'Rex uero W(ilhelmus) per mare et per

remnants of the rebellion had converged for papal protection,[57] fearing, with good reason, the vindictive rage of the victorious Sicilian king. Robert of Capua was betrayed by one of his own vassals, handed over to the royalists, and sent as a prisoner to Sicily;[58] Michael Palaeologus had died at Bari;[59] John Ducas and Alexius Comnenus (son of Anna Comnena) were captured at Brindisi.[60] Leaderless, defeated, and in disarray, the Apulian rebellion and the Greek 'invasion' collapsed together. Accepting the *fait accompli*, although he was later to blame Pope Adrian for doing the same, Frederick transferred his attention to the 'destruction' of Milan, summoning 'all the strength of the empire' to take part in a great expedition planned to set out in June 1158. Frederick's mandate made it crystal clear that no attack on the Sicilian kingdom was envisaged. 'Be assured that we shall compel neither you', he wrote to his uncle Otto of Freising, 'nor any of our princes to cross the Apennine range.'[61] Even Manuel Comnenus, after a brief attempt to re-ignite a few smouldering embers of rebellion, was to make peace with William and recognize his royal title, in return for the safe repatriation of Greek prisoners.[62]

(c) The accord of Benevento

This turn of events left Adrian, holed up at the papal city of Benevento, totally isolated and vulnerable. There was nothing for it but to accept the logic of the situation, as his predecessors had been forced to do in similar circumstances three times in the previous hundred years, and to negotiate with the victor, whose triumphant army surrounded the city. Three cardinal priests, led by Roland of S. Marco,[63] were sent to discuss the terms of peace. The result was the accord of

terram Brundusiam potenter obsedit, et per mare et terram uiriliter impugnando, in ore gladii debellauit, cepit Grecorum nobiles, et stolium ac pecuniam multam, et plures de baroni(bus) Ap(ulie) et hom(inibus) qui ei rebelles exstiterant, de quibus multos suspendi et excaecari fecit. Quo facto Barum uenit et eam cepit, et quia Barenses castrum regis destruxerant, rex ira commotus ciuitatem a fundamentis subuertit. De hinc per maritimam Apulie rediens omnes ciuitates maritime cepit, et totam terram quam perdiderat, sine bello recuperauit. Ipse autem recto tramite Beneuentum uenit, quo inimici et rebelles eius ad auxilium domni pape confugerant.' Cf. Falcandus, 18–19; Chalandon, *Histoire*, ii, 226–32.

[57] Robert of 'Basunvill', for example, had fled to Benevento at the first sign of the king's approach: Romuald of Salerno, *Chronicon*, 239; Cinnamus, *Deeds of John and Manuel Comnenus*, 127.

[58] Romuald of Salerno, *Chronicon*, 240.

[59] *Ibid.*, 117.

[60] *Ibid.*, 129.

[61] Otto of Freising, ii. 50 (*Gesta*, 158; *Deeds*, 166–7).

[62] Cinnamus, *Deeds of John and Manuel Comnenus*, 133–4; Romuald of Salerno, *Chronicon*, 241.

[63] With Hubald of S. Prassede and Julius of S. Marcello. Emphasizing William's 'humility' and passing over the disagreeable details of the accord, Boso (*Vita Adriani*, 395*) creates a false picture of Adrian's independence and William's compliance, although the phrase 'post mutuam diuersorum altercationem capitulorum' indicates a hard-fought negotiation. William of Tyre, however (*Historia*, xviii. 8 [p. 831]), says that negotiations

Benevento (18 June 1156), drawn up not by Adrian's but by William's representatives.[64] The terms were hard enough for the papacy to swallow. Essentially, Adrian recognized William and his heirs as kings of Sicily, conceded the territorial gains made by the Normans, and promised 'in good faith to aid (William and his successors) to hold them against all men',[65] in return for the liege homage of the king, and an annual tribute in gold. The careful designation of the pope's ecclesiastical rights in the various parts of the *regno* represented a compromise. Normal papal rights of hearing appeals and sending legates were acknowledged for Apulia and Calabria, but the Sicilian church remained securely subordinated to the monarchy, though not entirely closed to papal influence, and Roger II's seizures of papal territory in Capua and in the northern Abruzzo were confirmed.[66] There followed formal investiture *per vexillum* for each constituent of the king's dominions—the kingdom of Sicily, the duchy of Apulia, and the principality of Capua.[67] The date of this accord, 18 June 1156, may well have been chosen by King William to rub salt into the wound inflicted on Frederick, since it was one year to the day since his imperial consecration in Rome.

For Frederick and the imperial court (and many historians), this 'treaty' of Benevento was Adrian's great betrayal of the empire, which marked a dramatic change of political direction, substituting a pro-Sicilian for a pro-imperial alliance, and driving a fatal wedge between the empire and the papacy.[68] Moreover, many see it not as Adrian's capitulation to *force majeur* but the triumph of a pro-Sicilian faction among the cardinals, led by Cardinal Roland, and achieved by sending the pro-imperialists away from Benevento so that the desired settlement could be made without opposition,[69] 'there is no doubt that the Treaty of Benevento

followed a siege, 'Beneventum obsedit.' For Roland, see ch. 9, at n. 78. Hubald Allocingoli, from Lucca, was one of the most experienced diplomats of the Curia, whose career spanned more than 40 years, culminating in his election as pope (Lucius III, 1181–5), cardinal deacon of S. Adriano 1138–41, cardinal priest of S. Prassede 1141–58, cardinal bishop of Ostia 1158–81 (Brixius, 43, 90; Zenker, 22–5); Julius, cardinal priest of S. Marcello 1144–58, was also a senior cardinal, whom Adrian elevated to the episcopate as cardinal bishop of Palestrina in late 1158 (Brixius, 52, 104–5; Zenker, 42–3).

[64] The address 'To Adrian, by God's grace pope of the Holy Roman Church, his most beloved lord, and father, and to his successors, William, by the same grace king of Sicily, duke of Apulia, and prince of Capua' reflects the reality of the 'treaty'. The representatives of the Sicilian king (led by his *ammiratus ammiratorum*, Maio of Bari), not those of the pope (led by the chancellor, Cardinal Roland of S. Marco), were the dominant party in the construction of the agreement.

[65] *Pontificum romanorum... vitae*, ed. Watterich, ii, 352–4 no. 1*; *MGH Constitutiones*, i (ed. Weiland), 588. Cf. D'Alessandro, *Fidelitas normannorum*, 107–9; A. Mercati, *Raccolta di documenti in materie ecclesiastiche fra la S. Sede e le auctorità civili* (Rome, 1919), 20–2; G. B. Siragusa, *Il documento originale del concordato di Benevento del 1156 esistente nell'Archivio Segreto Vaticano*, ASLP, ser. 3, 14 (1926), 3–11.

[66] See below, at nn. 71–4.

[67] Briefly recorded by Romuald of Salerno, *Chronicon*, 240–1.

[68] Even Partner (*Lands of St Peter*, 199) thought that 'The Treaty of Benevento...was a serious violation of the agreement of Constance.'

[69] Munz, *Frederick Barbarossa*, 98 n. 1, reflecting a long tradition of German

represented the fruition of Hadrian's and Roland's intentions.'[70] This judgment relies on an extraordinary under-assessment of the danger which William and his army represented to the papacy at that moment. There was nothing to stop them marching to Rome itself. Adrian's dismissal of the bulk of the Sacred College was judicious in the circumstances, since he did not know how William would treat him and them; and his decision to face the king at Benevento was both prudent and courageous: flight would simply have drawn William's forces into papal territory, exposing it to devastation and sack. It also ignores the extent to which the territorial concessions made by the papacy constituted a loss both of land[71] and of security. Not only was William invested with the principality of Capua (which included Naples, Amalfi, and Salerno), but 'Marsia and the other places beyond Marsia which we (William) ought to have' were ceded in return for an annual census of 400 *schifati*.[72] This innocent-sounding clause confirmed Sicilian lordship over a strategically significant border region, formerly imperial territory, which comprised no fewer than eight bishoprics from the Roman province,[73] and through which passed four of the ancient Roman highways leading from Norman territories directly to the City.[74]

Adrian had indeed been inclined to make peace with King William in late 1155, after Frederick's departure from Rome, but he was probably influenced not so much by pro-Sicilian and anti-imperial feelings as by the attractiveness of the terms and a realistic assessment of the probable outcome of the war. Rebellions against the Sicilian rulers had had a poor record of success, and although the intervention of the Greeks gave the appearance of greater co-ordination and more effective leadership, Adrian may have had a better understanding of the instability of what Salvatore Tramontana described as a 'hybrid and fragile coalition'.[75] His instinct was probably sound in August 1155, but he failed to carry the cardinals with him,[76] perhaps because most of the Curia still believed that Frederick would keep his coronation oath (to say nothing of Constance), and so he sent the king's envoys away empty-handed. Six months later, when the coalition had collapsed, Adrian accepted the accord of Benevento, although its terms were much less

---

commentary, traceable to H. Simonsfeld, *Jahrbücher des deutschen Reiches unter Friedrich I.*, i (Leipzig, 1908), 453. Cf. Maccarrone, *Papato e impero*, 157. See also Boso, *Vita Adriani*, 395.*

[70] Munz, *Frederick Barbarossa*, 98–9, esp. 99. Even Tramontana (*La monarchia,* 184) sees Benevento as a pro-Sicilian choice: 'Non era comunque la prima volta che la Chiesa di Roma, costretta a scagliere fra Impero e Mezzogiorno, preferiva i normanni.'

[71] Robinson, however (*The Papacy*, 390), recognized that the 'concordat' was 'entirely to the advantage of the king of Sicily'; cf. Chalandon, *Histoire*, ii, 232–4.

[72] Each valued at one quarter of an ounce of Sicilian gold. A further 600 *schifati* were to be paid for Apulia and Calabria.

[73] Teramo, Chieti, Fondi, Forcone (Città di Bagno), Gaeta, Marsi, Penne, and Valva.

[74] Via Appia, Via Latina, Via Claudia Valeria, Via Salaria.

[75] Tramontana, *La monarchia*, 183, 'quell'ibrida e fragile coalizione'. Cf. D'Alessandro, 'Corona e nobiltà', 68–9, 72.

[76] Boso, *Vita Adriani*, 394.*

attractive than what William had originally offered, as the only available option. In the longer term, of course, although Adrian could not have known it, the consolidation of the Sicilian monarchy brought internal peace and security to the *regno* for the next forty years.

Frederick's trumpeted displeasure at the accord was not only unjust and unreasonable, it was unrealistic. The accord of Constance had not excluded an independent papal reconciliation with the southern king; despite encouraging Apulian exiles and rebels and permitting the intervention of Greek men and money, Frederick had twice washed his hands of the Sicilian business, first in late June 1155, and again in 1156. At the very moment that Adrian was making peace with 'the Sicilian', as the imperialists disparagingly called him, Frederick was publicly declaring that the next expedition into Italy would be confined to the Lombard plain. In the longer perspective, of course, the final recognition of the Sicilian monarchy worked to the advantage to Alexander III in his almost twenty-year struggle against three anti-popes supported by Frederick I. This consequence, unforeseen in 1156, gave the Beneventan accord an anti-imperial colouring and a far more significant appearance than it had when it was drawn up.

ii. The Byzantine Empire

If the Beneventan accord was seen as repudiation of Constance, Adrian's rather distant association with Byzantine patronage of the Apulian rebels was portrayed in a similar light. But, here again, the pope was responding to an existing situation, not initiating or pursuing a pro-Byzantine policy to the detriment of the Empire. Greek interest in the affairs of what had been a province of the Byzantine empire was of long standing. A considerable Greek population, with Greek churches, clerics, and monasteries still remained in Sicily and southern Italy;[77] Greeks played important roles in the administration of the Norman kingdom;[78] and the Byzantine emperors had not yet abandoned hopes of re-establishing some control over the south. Like their German 'brothers', they had not accepted the finality of the Norman conquest. Their long-term diplomacy was directed towards collaboration with the German emperors in the expulsion of the Norman usurpers. Alexis Comnenus had made common cause with Henry IV in the 1080s.[79] Sixty years later, John II Comnenus arranged the marriage of his son Manuel I Comnenus, emperor from 1143, to Conrad III's sister-in-law (1142);[80] the two rulers made an

[77] André Guillou, 'Inchiesta sulla popolazione greca della Sicilia e della Calabria nel Medio Evo', *Rivista Storica Italiana*, 75/i (1963), 53–68; and 'Grecs d'Italie du Sud et de Sicile au Moyen Age: Les moines', *Mélanges d'Archéologie et d'Histoire*, 75 (1963), 79–110, esp. 83–7: both repr. with the original numeration in idem, *Studies on Byzantine Italy*, Variorum Reprints (London, 1970), nos ix and xii.

[78] For example, George of Antioch and Maio of Bari.

[79] Partner, *Lands of St Peter*, 134.

[80] Bertha, who took the Greek name of Irene: Otto of Freising, i. 24 (*Gesta*, 37 (*Deeds*, 54)).

alliance against Roger II at Thessalonica in 1148–9,[81] when Conrad and his young nephew Frederick [I] were returning from the failed Second Crusade; Abbot Wibald of Stavelot and Corvey worked tirelessly through the 1140s and 1150s to maintain good diplomatic relations with the Greeks, while reassuring the papacy that nothing would be done to its detriment; and at the very moment that Frederick I accepted the accord of Constance in 1153 (23 March), he was simultaneously exchanging embassies with the Byzantine court and discussing a possible marriage with Manuel's daughter.[82] According to the Greek chronicler John Cinnamus, he confirmed Conrad's Thessalonica agreement to assist the Greeks in the acquisition of 'Italy'.[83] It is hard to establish what promises Frederick made, but there is no evidence that he tried to prevent Greek involvement in the Sicilian enterprise of 1155–6. On the contrary, he received Michael Palaeologus and John Ducas at Ancona,[84] and some kind of imperial authorization was obtained by Greek envoys who travelled to Apulia with his own ambassador to Constantinople. So much can be deduced from Otto of Freising's explanation of Frederick's displeasure with the same envoys at Würzburg in early June 1156. When they approached the emperor in the company of Abbot Wibald, just returned from Constantinople, Frederick refused to admit them to his presence because, 'when they had departed from him near Ancona, they had surreptitiously secured certain letters sealed with his seal and when the prince returned to the transalpine country [Germany], the Greeks entered Campania and Apulia and, displaying the imperial letters, falsely declared that the regions along the sea coast had been granted them by the prince.'[85] No doubt this was the story being put about in June 1156, but it looks suspiciously like an attempt to hide the extent to which Frederick had committed himself, or had been ready to commit himself, to a joint undertaking with the Greeks; and it is extremely unlikely that Emperor Manuel would have supported the Norman malcontents without hope of significant gain for himself. Certainly, the Greeks went forward on that expectation, committing men, money, and ships under the command of Michael Palaeologus and John Ducas. From their perspective, 1155

[81] Otto of Freising, *Deeds*, 103 n. 233. The Byzantines had been perturbed by Roger II's audacious attacks on Greek maritime cities (Corfu, Corinth, Thebes, Athens) in 1147, which included the capture of silk weavers, who were transported to Palermo to establish the silk industry there: Otto of Freising, i. 34 (*Gesta*, 53–4; *Deeds*, 69–70).

[82] Cinnamus, *Deeds of John and Manuel Comnenus*, 106. For Frederick's own letter to Emperor Manuel, and Abbot Wibald of Stavelot's (with its suggestion of a marriage alliance with a lady 'de sanguine vestro'), written in March 1153, see *Bibliotheca rerum Germanicarum*, ed. P. Jaffé, 6 vols (Berlin, 1864–73), i, 548–51 nos 410–11. Note that Frederick (*ibid.*, 548–9) accords himself the full imperial style and title: 'F(redericus) Dei gratia Romanorum imperator augustus, magnus ac pacificus, a Deo coronatus', although he was strictly speaking only King of the Romans, and he addressed the Byzantine emperor as 'dilectissimo fratri et amico suo M(anuelo), Porphirogenito, sublimi et glorioso imperatori Constantinopolitano, fraternam dilectionem et de inimicis victoriam.'

[83] Cinnamus, *Deeds of John and Manuel Comnenus*, 106.

[84] See above, at n. 43.

[85] Otto of Freising, ii. 49 (*Gesta*, 157: *Deeds*, 165). Cf. Munz, *Frederick Barbarossa*, 137 n. 3.

was the year of opportunity. The accession of the untried William I in February 1154, combined with the widespread rebellion against his rule in Sicily and Apulia, the presence of Apulian refugees at the Byzantine court,[86] and Frederick I's failure to deal with the Normans, encouraged them to take advantage of the multiple instabilities that existed in the peninsula.

In what was a mirror image of Frederick's double faceted diplomacy in 1153 and 1155, Manuel sent envoys both to Frederick and to Pope Adrian in 1155, seeking agreement for a joint military enterprise against William I, supported by the Norman rebels, with whom he established contact, whatever mercenaries could be employed, and the returned exiles. Michael Palaeologus, John Ducas, and Alexander of Conversano met Frederick at Ancona, and letters were sent to Pope Adrian offering a large sum of money for the provision of troops, with the request that the pope grant the Greek emperor lordship of three maritime cities in return for assistance in expelling William from Sicily. Manuel also promised to pay five thousand pounds of gold to the pope and Curia.[87] There is no evidence either that the cities were ceded or that any money changed hands, and it is unlikely that Adrian or the Curia would have wanted to see the establishment of Byzantine power in the *Mezzogiorno*.[88] Nevertheless, when Adrian invaded Sicilian territory (Terra di Lavoro) in September 1155, it was to join up with rebels who were simultaneously linked with Frederick I and allied with and financed by the Byzantine empire; and some of them willingly offered their homage to the pope at San Germano. Frederick later (at Bologna, 1159) accused the papacy of making peace with the Greeks in contravention of the agreement (of Constance),[89] but that accusation, like the condemnation on similar grounds of the accord of Benevento, was nothing more than a smoke-screen to divert attention from his own *volte face*. Frederick had been happy to negotiate with top-level Greek envoys at Ancona, where the Greeks had established a base of operations, as he was withdrawing his troops from Italy, and he cannot have been unaware that the Apulian rebels whom his uncle Conrad III had fostered at the German court were joining up with Greek-sponsored rebels. He certainly made no recorded move to discourage Greek participation in the conspiracy against William I, the accord of Constance notwith-

---

[86] E.g. Andrew of Conversano, former count of Gravina.

[87] Boso, *Vita Adriani*, 394;* cf. Cinnamus, *Deeds of John and Manuel Comnenus*, 114; William of Tyre, *Historia*, xviii. 2 (pp. 817–19), xviii. 7 (pp. 828–9), esp. 828, 'consentiente papa'.

[88] J. G. Rowe, 'Hadrian IV, the Byzantine Empire, and the Latin Orient', *Essays in Medieval History presented to Bertie Wilkinson*, ed. T. A. Sandquist and M. R. Powicke (Toronto, 1969), 3–16, at 10–12. Chalandon (*Histoire*, ii, 212–13) thought otherwise, in the belief that Manuel was prepared to offer a reunion of the Greek and Latin churches in return for the crown of the Western empire. Such an offer seems to have been made to Alexander III in the mid-1160s, however: J. Parker, 'The attempted Byzantine alliance with the Sicilian-Norman Kingdom (1166–7)', *Papers of the British School at Rome*, 24 (NS 11, 1956), 86–93. For papal encouragement of the pro-Latin policies of the local Norman rulers in Apulia, see D'Alessandro, 'Corona e nobiltà', 70–72.

[89] Rahewin, iv. 33 (*Gesta*, 275; *Deeds*, 269).

standing. It is possible, of course, that he thought that nothing much would come of the rebellion—Sicilian rulers had been very resilient in the past—and that he was disconcerted by the early successes of the rag-bag coalition.

iii. The Romano-German Empire

As presented by imperial propagandists, the fatal breach between empire and papacy in Adrian's reign was the result of deliberate policy pursued relentlessly by Adrian and the 'Sicilian party' from mid-1156, if not before. In this chain of events, the accord of Benevento was the first triumph of the 'Sicilian party'; the Besançon incident its second; the 'alliances' with Milan, Brescia, Piacenza, and Crema in August 1159 its third; and the election of Alexander III in September 1159 its fourth: all inspired by hostility to the empire and to Frederick I.[90] Looked at from Adrian's perspective, the whole sequence of action and counter-action from early 1155 onwards reads very differently. It was Frederick's actions, not Adrian's, that exacerbated the tensions in Sicily and Lombardy; and the pope's alignment with the emperor's enemies (William I of Sicily, 1156; Milan and her allies, 1159), was the result not of design but of desperation.

(a) First encounters

Contrary to the carefully constructed image of an enthusiastically pro-imperial Curia at the beginning of Adrian's reign, there is evidence of apprehension and distrust. The renewal of the Constance accord, which seems to have been made early in 1155, was, like the original agreement, a kind of insurance policy. Its principal aim was to bind the emperor as the 'devoted and special advocate of the Holy Roman Church', to 'preserve and defend the honour of the papacy and the *regalia* of St Peter' and 'with all the power of his realm' to 'assist it to recover' any losses, and 'defend what is recovered'.[91] In what was a high-level barter,

---

[90] Robinson, *The Papacy*, 53, 79–81, 389–91, 467–8, 470–3. Cf. 472, 'In June 1159 Hadrian withdrew from Rome to Anagni with Roland and twelve other cardinals who now comprised the Sicilian party. There the pope negotiated an alliance with the cities of Milan, Brescia, Piacenza, and Crema...By the time of Hadrian's death the Sicilian party had openly aligned itself with the emperor's enemies.' Robinson's number of twelve 'pro-Sicilian' cardinals, in addition to Roland, the Chancellor, seems to depend on nothing more substantial than a count of the cardinals who signed the two privileges issued from Anagni which are published in Migne, *PL*, clxxxviii, 1636–9 nos 255–6. The first has eight signatories; the second has nine, of whom five are common to both, producing the roll-call of the 'Sicilian party': four cardinal bishops (Hubald of Ostia, Bernard of Porto, Walter of Albano, and Gregory of Sabina); three cardinal priests (Hubald of S. Croce in Gerusalemme, Hildebrand of SS. XII Apostoli, and John of S. Anastasia); five cardinal deacons (Ardicio of S. Theodoro, Boso of SS. Cosma e Damiano, Peter of S. Eustachio, Otto of S. Giorgio in Velabro, and Otto of S. Nicola in Carcere Tulliano). The Victorines said that at the first count, 14 cardinals had voted for Alexander (above, n. 7).

[91] Above, at nn. 1 and 28. There was little new in this latter formula. It reproduced *verbatim* part of the oath which Lothar III had taken to Innocent II on 4 June 1133 (and which Frederick would take on 18 June 1155): *MGH LL* (in folio), ii (1837), 82, 'Ego

imperial consecration was intended so to reinforce Frederick's protective role in respect of papal rights and lands that he would as a matter of honour respect as well as defend the status of the papacy and the integrity of the lands of St Peter, for the territorial and jurisdictional ambitions of the empire were no less a threat to papal rights than the Norman rulers of the *regno*, the Roman commune, the Byzantine emperor, or dissident nobles. Even before their first meeting, Adrian had insisted that Frederick should take the customary oath to preserve the life and limbs of the pope and his cardinals, not to imprison them, nor to deprive them of their honour and goods, and to punish any who so injured them, and to preserve the concord already negotiated between eminent persons of the two courts.[92] This insistence on a sworn undertaking to respect the person of the pope and cardinals should be seen as evidence not of antipathy but of prudent circumspection. Whatever their protestations, emperors were not above the use of force to obtain their ends. The Curia would have been well aware of the treatment meted out to Paschal II and his cardinals by Henry V in 1111, since it was inscribed in the Roman Annals and reiterated in Boso's *Vitae pontificum*. Pope and cardinals had been imprisoned for two months, until the hapless Paschal conceded the right of investiture with ring and crozier to the king (in return for guarantees about the papal patrimony), a capitulation which would have confirmed imperial power over ecclesiastics within the empire and cancelled a key element in the reform programme pursued by the papacy since the 1050s.[93] Curial anxiety about Frederick's possible behaviour was entirely understandable. In fact, the cardinals were so afraid of the king's anger that they fled, leaving Adrian unattended, when at his first meeting with the pope (near Sutri in early June 1155) Frederick had refused to perform the purely ceremonial gesture of leading the pope's horse and holding his stirrup as he dismounted. This incident throws light on all participants. The cardinals are revealed as pusillanimous; the emperor as cunning and slippery; and Adrian as a man of dignity and courage. Adrian refused to give Frederick the kiss of peace until the protocol had been observed; Frederick made a great display of consulting the elders in his court as to precedent, and kept Adrian waiting for two whole days before he conceded the formality.[94] It was a signal that this

Lotharius rex promitto et iuro tibi domino pape Innocentio tuisque successoribus securitatem vite et membris et male captionis, et defendere papatum et honorem tuum, et regalia sancti Petri que habes manu tenere, et que non habes iuxta meum posse recuperare (I, king Lothar, promise and swear to you, lord pope Innocent and your successors, security of life, members, and wrongful imprisonment, and to defend the papacy and your honour, and to maintain the regalia of St Peter which you hold, and, to the utmost of my power, to recover what you do not hold).' For the renewal, see Maccarrone, *Papato e impero*, 107–10.

[92] Boso, *Vita Adriani*, 391.*

[93] At Ponte Mammolo: *Liber Pontificalis*, ed. Duchesne, ii, 341–3, 369; Partner, *Lands of St Peter*, 149–50. Maccarrone thinks otherwise: *Papato e impero*, 112–14.

[94] Boso (*Vita Adriani*, 391–2)* describes the embarrassing diplomatic stand-off, in which the pope was left waiting while Frederick enquired what the protocol was from older members of his entourage. For a different interpretation, see Munz, *Frederick Barbarossa*, 81–3; Maccarrone, *Papato e impero*, 119–20 (who thought that the cardinals would not

emperor would insist on every jot of what he considered to be his *regalia*. Otto of Freising, understandably, suppressed this embarrassing episode, and recorded only the last stage in what was an ominous stand-off between pope and emperor-elect: 'Thither came the Roman pope, Hadrian, with his cardinals, and was received with the honour due to his office.'[95] He was indeed, but it could not have been more grudging.

It was not only the strong-arm tactics of a previous ruler that raised the cardinals' fears. By that point in Frederick's progress to Rome there had been ample demonstration of the emperor-elect's treatment of those upon whom his displeasure fell. Although Otto of Freising and the emperor himself tried to portray the progress through northern Italy as the restoration of imperial peace and justice to a lawless and troubled region, it had been anything but, and Frederick's treatment of cities that defied him, or did not obey his instructions, was a salutary demonstration of what might happen to others who did not respond quickly enough to his assumption of authority. Asti and Chieri, for example, suffered sack and total demolition for disobedience, even though their citizens had offered no resistance, having fled at his approach.[96] Tortona was subjected to a two-month siege (from *c.* 10 February to 10–16 April 1155) and then razed,[97] partly because it refused to abandon its alliance with Milan, but largely to appease its old enemy Pavia, which duly welcomed Frederick with royal honours and the iron crown of Lombardy.[98] Otto describes all this with the *sangfroid* of an observer of normal events. For him, this was the natural consequences of 'insolence', 'disobedience', 'rebellion', and 'treason'.[99] But the recipients and observers of the king's chastisement might have seen things differently. It soon became clear that his 'justice' was not even-handed. He was prepared to use German arms to settle the scores of Milan's enemies (e.g. Cremona, Pavia, Como, Lodi, Novara, Bergamo) while demonstrating inveterate hostility to her allies (e.g. Brescia, Tortona, Piacenza, and Crema), a policy of partisanship which was to characterize his relations with the northern cities until the late 1170s.[100] The Alpine passes had been so denuded of supplies that Frederick had had to make reparation to the churches which his army had violated in its quest for provisions;[101] and intermittent looting had marred his progress through Lombardy.[102]

have abandoned Adrian in the manner described by Boso).

[95] Otto of Freising, ii. 28* (*Gesta*, 132, *Deeds*, 142).

[96] Idem, ii. 19 (*Gesta*, 121; *Deeds*, 132).

[97] Idem, ii. 20–26 (*Gesta*, 122–32; *Deeds*, 132–42).

[98] Idem, ii. 27 (*Gesta*, 132; *Deeds*, 142).

[99] Idem, ii. 20–26 (*Gesta*, 122–32; *Deeds*, 132–42). The same emphasis is in the *Chronica regia Coloniensis*, 91–2, and Burchard of Ursberg, 25–6.

[100] In Sept. 1155, Frederick granted Cremona the minting rights which he had taken away from Milan: *MGH Diplomata*, 10/i (1975), 202–04 no. 120. Cf. Daniel Waley, *The Italian City Republics*, 2nd edn (London and New York, 1978), 72–3; Munz, *Frederick Barbarossa*, 89, 157–60.

[101] Otto of Freising, *Gesta*, 113; *Deeds*, 125.

[102] See his own account of this progress, addressed to his uncle, Bishop Otto of Freising,

(b) Rome and the coronation

Even in Rome, he could secure consecration and coronation only by a stratagem master-minded by the pope, which allowed a thousand of Frederick's knights to enter the Leonine city and occupy St Peter's itself at dawn on the morning of the day on which the ceremonies were to take place, and he had to fight his way out against a Roman mob.[103] It must have been some consolation that his soldiers were more than a match for the citizens, but he could not push home the 'magnificent triumph', as Otto of Freising calls it, because of lack of provisions and the sickness brought on by the summer heat and the malarial-bearing marshes around Rome.[104] The chastisement of Tortona, together with the leisurely progress through Lombardy, had cost him three valuable months.[105] Without that diversion, he would have reached Rome around 17 March instead of 17 June, before the summer heat, and well in time to confront William of Sicily; although whether he could have defeated him is an open question. His displeasure with Pope Adrian at Besançon may well have been tinged with embarrassment at his own failings in Italy, and it suited his self-image to make the papacy a scapegoat both for his own miscalculations and for what was also a change of policy in regard to the papacy and the Greeks.[106] As his propaganda had it,[107] it was Adrian who had broken the Constance accord and betrayed the empire, but the sequence of events that led inexorably to Benevento began with the emperor's own withdrawal from the fray.

(c) From the accord of Benevento to the Besançon incident

There is no doubt that Frederick I was enraged by the accord of Benevento. The injury to the empire lay not in the alleged breach of the accord of Constance but in the fact that the recognition of the Sicilian king denied Frederick the territorial

---

Gesta, 1–5, esp. 2–3; *Deeds*, 17–20, esp. 18–19: 'we...entered Lombardy in force...and destroyed almost all its strongholds by the just and righteous anger not of our knights but of the lower ranks...we caused to be taken and destroyed by fire their [Milan's] finest fortress, Rosate...Next we destroyed Chieri, a very large and well-fortified town. The city of Asti we laid waste by fire. Then we besieged Tortona, a city excellently fortified by nature and by art....Finally, after many assaults and much bloodshed...the city did capitulate...When the city of Tortona had been destroyed...'; see above, at nn. 96–7.

[103] According to Walter Ullmann, 'The Pontificate of Adrian IV', *Cambridge Historical Journal*, 11 (1953–5), 233–52, at 240–3, the ceremonial was not only marred by surreption and haste, it was significantly adjusted to separate the imperial consecration (which was carried out at a side altar by a group of senior cardinals) from the Mass, during which the pope, at the High altar, conferred the imperial insignia—sword, sceptre, and crown—upon the newly-consecrated emperor; and there was no enthronement: Walter Ullmann, 'The Pontificate of Adrian IV', *Cambridge Historical Journal*, 11 (1953–5), 233–52, at 240–3; but cf. Maccarrone, *Papato e impero*, 124–6.

[104] Otto of Freising, ii. 31,* 33–4* (*Gesta*, 139–40, 141–3; *Deeds*, 149, 151–3); cf. ii. 37 (*Gesta*, 145; *Deeds*, 154–5).

[105] Idem, ii. 20–6 (*Gesta*, 122–32; *Deeds*, 132–42).

[106] See below, at. n. 140.

[107] See below, at n. 150.

aggrandizement he might have hoped to enjoy at some later date in his reign, once the matter of Lombardy had been satisfactorily settled. He had not been able to pursue the Sicilian business in 1155 or 1156, but he was understandably perturbed by the sudden reversal of fortunes and the re-establishment of papal lordship, independently of him, over the whole of an enlarged *regno*. If William kept his part of the bargain, then the papacy would be less vulnerable to imperial pressure, and much better able to defend its position as patriarch of the Latin Church and lord of the papal states. Although there is no evidence that Frederick considered himself bound by the Constance accord, once he had secured his crown, he was able to use it against the papacy, and brand Adrian's independent peace with the king of Sicily as breach of an undertaking which he himself had had no intention of fulfilling. Indeed, it is significant that Otto of Freising did not even mention the accord in his part of the *Gesta Frederici*, perhaps because he knew well enough that no part of it had been implemented by his nephew.

Far from the Beneventan accord marking a deliberate breach with the empire, however, Adrian made strenuous efforts to maintain good relations with Frederick after Benevento, as even Robinson recognizes, when he tried to engage Abbot Wibald of Stavelot to counter hostile influences at the imperial court in January 1157.[108] This unsuccessful attempt to keep open the channels of communication with Frederick should be remembered in the context of an event which has been seen as evidence either of the pope's bad faith or of the making of outrageous claims of the feudal subordination of the empire to the papacy.

(d) The Besançon incident

In September 1157, Adrian sent a mild rebuke to the emperor for his failure to secure the release of Archbishop Eskil of Lund, who had been seized and held to ransom by a robber baron in Burgundy as he was returning to the North from an *ad limina* visit to Rome, in which Eskil's position as primate of Denmark and Sweden had been confirmed. Frederick's inaction may have been politically motivated (as Eskil's own letter suggested), since the elevation of the archbishopric of Lund had effectively detached the region from the ecclesiastical jurisdiction of Hamburg-Bremen, and accentuated the independence of the northern Baltic from imperial authority.[109] How far Frederick had been implicated in Eskil's seizure is

---

[108] *PL*, clxxxviii, 1492–3 no. 123 (19 January 1167); cf. Robinson, *The Papacy*, 466.

[109] Eskil's capture and the emperor's 'dissimulation' are recorded in the Chronicle of St Blasien, *s.a.* 1156: *Ottonis de Sancto Blasio Chronica*, ed. A. Hofmeister, *MGH SRG* 47 (Hanover/Leipzig, 1912), 9; cf. *Series episcoporum ecclesiae catholicae occidentalis ab initio usque ad annum MCXCVIII*, Series 6, *Britannia, Scotia et Hibernia, Scandinavia*, ii: *Archiepiscopatus Lundensis*, ed. Helmuth Kluger (Stuttgart, 1992), 20–28, at 23–4. For Eskil's own letter, addressed to the kings, princes, bishops, abbots, clergy, and people of Denmark, see Maccarrone, *Papato e impero*, 168–9, n. 19, where its authenticity is discussed and defended, *ibid.*, 169–71. Eskil links his imprisonment with allegations made against him by the emperor: 'Dominus imperator Romanus nos apud eum graviter peccasse imponit, et nos sui regni et sue corone diminutionem fecisse causatur.' These ecclesiastical policies were complicated by the intermittent recognition of imperial overlordship by

debateable, but he could have secured the same end by letting it be known that the Danish archbishop no longer had his grace. No doubt to emphasize the importance which he attached to the issue, Adrian entrusted this second mission to two of the foremost members of the Curia, the chancellor, Roland, cardinal priest of S. Marco and Bernard of Lucca, cardinal priest. of S. Clemente.[110] The emperor was found at Besançon (in October), where he was establishing himself as ruler of Burgundy in the right of his new wife Beatrix. The principal source for the interview is Rahewin's continuation of Otto of Freising's *Gesta Frederici I. imperatoris*. Rahewin depicted the Besançon incident as the turning-point in papal-imperial relations, for which reason he gives a verbatim copy of *Imperatorie maiestati*, the letter borne by the papal envoys,[111] and the ensuing correspondence.[112] The letter has been much debated, but the crucial passage reads,

> For, most glorious son, you should recall before the eyes of your mind, how favourably and gladly your mother, the Holy Roman Church, received you the other year, with what affection of heart she treated you, what plenitude of dignity and honour she bestowed on you, and how, very willingly conferring upon you the emblem of the imperial crown, she strove to cherish your eminence's highness[113] in her most generous bosom, doing nothing at all that she knew was in the least opposed to the royal will. Nor do we regret that we fulfilled the desires of your heart in everything, but if your excellency had received greater favours (*beneficia*) at our hand, had it been possible, we should have been delighted, considering what gain and advantage might come to the Church of God and to us through you.'[114]

One word in particular was fastened on for furious denunciation. When put into German by the emperor's chancellor, Rainald of Dassel, *beneficia* was translated in such a way as to imply that the imperial crown was a fief of the papacy, and the response was uproar, and the ignominious dismissal of the two cardinals, who were told to go straight back to Rome as quickly as they could.[115] In the *Chronica regia Coloniensis*, the letter was made to say, 'We have conferred the benefice

Danish kings in the first half of the twelfth century, which resulted in King Valdemar's acknowlegement of 'Victor IV': Anders Leegaard Knudsen, 'Absalon and the Holy Roman Empire', in *Archbishop Absalon and his World*, ed. Karsten Friis-Jensen and Inge Skovgaard-Petersen (Roskilde, 2000), 21–35, at 21–3.

[110] For Roland, see ch. 9, at n. 78. Master Bernard of Lucca, a Canon Regular, cardinal priest of S. Clemente 1145–58, cardinal bishop of Porto and S. Rufina 1158–76 (Brixius, 53, 105, 135, 136; Zenker, 29–32). He was Adrian's choice as successor: see Maccarrone, *Papato e impero*, 342–4.

[111] Rahewin, iii. 9* (*Gesta*, 174–6; *Deeds*, 181–3); *PL*, clxxxviii, 1525–7 no. 143, 20 Sept. 1157.

[112] Rahewin, iii. 11,* 16–17* (*Gesta*, 178–9, 185–9 (*Deeds*, 184–6, 191–4)).

[113] 'tuae sublimitatis apicem'.

[114] Rahewin, iii. 9* (*Gesta*, 175; *Deeds*, 182); *PL*, clxxxviii, 1526.

[115] Rahewin, iii. 10* (*Gesta*, 176–7; *Deeds*, 183–4).

(*beneficium*) of the crown upon you, nor would we have regretted if your excellency had received greater benefices (*beneficia*) from us.'[116]

Following the outrage of the imperial sources, the broad historical consensus has been to see the Besançon letter as another manifestation of the anti-imperial policy adopted by the Curia in the wake of the accord of Benevento. The use of the term *beneficium* in relation to the imperial crown was at best a diplomatic error—a *faux pas*—which suggests carelessness on the part of the drafter (thought to have been Cardinal Roland); at the worst it was a deliberate affront to the imperial dignity, either asserting an unacceptable papal supremacy over the emperor and empire or, even more sinister, the operation of a deliberate plot to enrage the emperor. This latter view was promoted by Marcel Pacaut and Peter Munz. They argued that the whole episode was engineered by Adrian and Cardinal Roland to justify the Sicilian peace to the imperialists in the Curia, by provoking a diplomatic incident which would demonstrate the emperor's hostility to papal interests.[117] Such an interpretation is scarcely credible. Even with the Beneventan accord, Adrian was hardly more politically secure in 1157 than he had been in 1155, and he knew that Frederick was committed to a major military offensive against Milan, planned for the following summer.[118] It is inconceivable that he would have wanted to inflame relations with the emperor while imperial armies were being prepared for what was intended to be the subjugation of Lombardy.

Less extreme is the view favoured by Robinson and others, that the term was intended to imply a 'feudal' dependency of the empire on the papacy.[119] The fundamental difficulty, of course, is that many words have multiple meanings. *Beneficium* was used in at least three senses in the period 800–1200. In its primary sense of 'favour' or 'benefit', derived from classical Latin, it was in common use in ecclesiastical discourse. In the powerful reprimand which Adrian delivered to Archbishop Theobald in early 1156, for example, the term is used twice: charging Theobald with having forgotten the many favours bestowed on him and being ungrateful for the great favours bestowed on him by the pope: *quod in oblivione tot beneficiorum usque adeo devenisti...dum te ingratum nobis invenire pro impensis beneficiis*.[120] The principal *beneficium* which Adrian had in mind was the grant of the office of papal legate to the English kingdom. No one has ever suggested that such an appointment was in any way 'feudal'. In his own letter to Cardinal Roland, the papal chancellor who delivered the letter to Besançon,

---

[116] *Chronica regia Coloniensis*, 94.

[117] Munz, *Frederick Barbarossa*, 140, 186; Pacaut, *Frederick Barbarossa*, 79–80. Cf. W. Heinemeyer, 'Beneficium—non feodum sed bonum factum. Der Streit auf dem Reichstag zu Besançon 1157', *Archiv für Diplomatik*, 15 (1969), 155–236. Maccarrone, *Papato e impero*, 173–95, esp. 179–80.

[118] Decided upon in June 1156 and planned for June 1158: above, at n. 61.

[119] Robinson, The *Papacy*, 469–70. Maccarrone (*Papato e impero*, 173–95, esp. 179–80) points to the similarity between Adrian's language in this letter and the phrases employed by the imperial chancery itself.

[120] *Historia monasterii S. Augustini Cantuariensis by Thomas of Elmham*, ed. C. Hardwick, RS 8 (London 1858), 411–12 no. 42. Dated Benevento, 23 January (1156).

Theobald thanked Roland 'for the honour and *favours* which you have always conferred on me and mine (*pro honore et beneficiis michi et meis a uobis semper exhibitis)*'.[121] A very long string of citations could be adduced to establish this usage in the learned Latin circles of the mid-twelfth century. But *beneficium* also meant 'benefice', in the sense of ecclesiastical office; and also, especially in Carolingian times and in German lands, it meant a territorial endowment, sometimes 'feudal', sometimes not. This latter use occurs a number of times in Eugenius III's letters, but it is usually attached to the owner's name, as in 'Godo's estate (*beneficium Godonis*)';[122] or with a specifically feudal attachment, as in the clauses *in beneficium et feudum* or *ut feudum sive beneficium*.[123] A similar usage is found in a letter of Adrian's immediate predecessor Anastasius IV, *vel in feudum, censum, ceu beneficium*;[124] and Adrian himself used the phrase *in beneficium* in a territorial or feudal sense more than once in his own letters.[125] The context, surely, determines the meaning. Even Robinson allows that the word for 'fief' in England and France was *feudum*, whereas *beneficium* was generally used in its older sense of 'benefit', 'favour', 'gift', 'good deed'. This was the meaning attached to it by Adrian in the letter of explanation presented at Augsburg in the following June: 'For although this word *beneficium* is by some interpreted in a different significance than it has by derivation, it should nevertheless have been understood in the meaning which we ourselves put upon it, and which it is known to have possessed from the beginning. For this word is formed of *bonus* (good) and *factum* (deed), and among us *beneficium* does not mean a fief but a good deed....'[126] This letter itself is dismissed as a humiliating withdrawal by the Curia from its deliberately provocative anti-imperial stance, but if there was no deliberate provocation, then there was no withdrawal from that provocation. What the explanatory letter shows is Adrian's desire, in late 1157–early 1158, to re-establish good relations with the emperor, although the attitude of the imperial court was anything but conciliatory.[127]

Examined without any *arrière pensée*, the Besançon letter reads like a pained reproof. 'I've done all I can for you, but your failure to act against the brigands

---

[121] *JohnS*, i, 15

[122] *PL*, clxxx, 1074; cf. 1125, 1621.

[123] *PL*, clxxx, 1339, 1389.

[124] *PL*, clxxxviii, 1072.

[125] *PL*, clxxxviii, 1389 (three times), 1428, 1449, 1467. See also its use in documents relating to the lands of Odo di Poli, below, Part II/ii, 'Privileges and Charters', nos 4 and 5.

[126] Rahewin, iii. 23* (*Gesta*, 195–7; *Deeds*, 199–200); JL 10386 (assigned to late January 1158). The bearers were two of the most experienced diplomats in the Curia, Henry, cardinal priest of SS. Nereo e Achilleo (ch. 9, n. 72) and Hyacinth Bobo, cardinal deacon of S. Maria in Cosmedin (ch. 9, n. 76). Their journey to Augsburg had been seriously delayed, for two Tyrolean counts, relying on the enmity between the emperor and the 'Romans', had seized, robbed, and imprisoned them and the bishop of Trento for some considerable time (Rahewin, iii. 21*: *Gesta*, 194–5; *Deeds*, 197–8). This interpretation was supported by Ullmann, 'Pontificate of Adrian IV', 244.

[127] See below, at nn. 226–8.

who have seized and maltreated an eminent prelate travelling back from the Apostolic See looks like deliberate contempt in response to our rapprochement with the Sicilian king. We hope this isn't true, since we have gladly conferred on you the crown, and would willingly have done more, to cement the goodwill between the empire and the church.' Far from being a deliberate papal provocation, the Besançon incident can be seen as a crisis largely stage-managed by Rainald of Dassel, to whom fell the task of translating the papal letter into German, and by the emperor himself, looking for a pretext to hit back at Adrian for his agreement with the Sicilian king, and also, perhaps, an excuse to prevent the two cardinals from discharging a mission to the German Church. Indeed, the *Chronica regia Coloniensis*, which reflects the outlook of the circle of Rainald of Dassel, confirmed that the offensive emphasis was given by Rainald: 'The emperor's interpreter translated this word as fief.'[128] If ever there was a manufactured dispute, this was it.

At the same time, of course, it is not unlikely that some German princes were highly sensitive to possible slurs on the elevated status of their emperor; and even without translation, the word *beneficium* could have been distinguished from the rest of the Latin of the letter. Disconnected from the context, which was conciliatory though mildly critical, the word would have fallen heavily upon German ears, attuned to discerning slights to their honour.

Quite independently of any actions or words of Adrian, the emperor was said by Rahewin to have been so affronted by the description of a fresco in the Lateran palace, depicting his predecessor Lothar III and Pope Innocent II (in 1133), that he had demanded its immediate destruction when he was on his way to Rome for his coronation. Above the image was the inscription:

Rex venit ante fores, iurans prius Urbis honores,
Post homo fit papae, sumit quo dante coronam.
(The king comes before the doors, swearing first (to maintain) the City's
privileges; afterwards he becomes the man of the pope, by whose grant he
assumes the crown.)[129]

The form and content of the fresco is known only from a sixteenth-century sketch by Panvinio, supplemented by a seventeenth-century engraving by Rasponi. Together they provide a sequence of four related events: (1) Lothar's arrival at the entrance to the Lateran basilica (transmitted by Rasponi), (2) his oath to preserve the rights of the City; (3) either his reception of the pope's kiss of peace or, more likely, his papal investiture for life *per anulum* with the lands of the Countess

---

[128] *Chronica regia Coloniensis*, 94: 'Hoc verbum pro feodo interpres cesari interpretatus est.'

[129] Rahewin, iii. 10* (*Gesta*, 177, *Deeds*, 184). Maccarrone argued, rightly, that knowledge of the fresco was more likely to have been obtained after the imperial coronation, rather than before it: *Papato e impero*, 132–3.

Matilda of Tuscany;[130] and finally (4) the papal bestowal of the imperial crown.[131] De-contextualized and misinterpreted it was political dynamite. The *Chronica regia Coloniensis* describes how it was (inaccurately) viewed at court: 'For the late Pope Innocent had caused himself to be painted on a wall at Rome, seated as it were on the papal throne, the Emperor Lothar, bowing before him with joined hands, receiving the imperial crown.'[132] Knowledge of this was in the minds of the German court at Besançon, according to Rahewin,[133] and it was cited as a cause of continuing imperial anger by the German bishops who afterwards reported the emperor's response to their admonitions to Adrian. According to them, Frederick had declared, 'It began with a picture, the picture became an inscription, the inscription seeks to become an authoritative utterance. We shall not endure it, we shall not submit to it; we shall lay down the crown before we consent to have the imperial crown and ourself thus degraded. Let the pictures be destroyed, let the inscriptions be withdrawn, that they may not remain as eternal memorials of enmity between *regnum* and *sacerdotium*.'[134]

But there was a wider context to the furious response of Frederick and his court to the papal letter, for it was not only the unfortunate papal emissaries who felt the cold wind of imperial displeasure in 1157. Against the background of the

---

[130] *MGH Constitutiones*, i (ed. L. Weiland, 1893), 169–70 no.117, papal letter (dated at the Lateran, 8 June) recording Innocent II's grant of the Matildine lands to Lothar III for life, in return for an annual tribute of £100 silver, but with reversion to the 'ius et dominium sancte Romane ecclesie...absque diminutione'. In Maccarrone's interpretation, it is this investiture, 'per anulum', which is depicted in second element in Panvinio's sketch, and he dates the event to 4 June 1133, during the coronation ceremony (Maccarrone, *Papato e impero*, 136–7, and plate 1.

[131] Vatican City, Biblioteca Apostolica Vaticana, MS Vat. lat. 2738, fo 104v–105r; C. Rasponi, *De basilica...Lateranensi* (Rome, 1646), 296–7. See Maccarrone, *Papato e impero*, 132–7, and plate 1; cf. Gerhart B. Ladner, 'I mosaici e gli affreschi ecclesiastico-politici nell'antico palazzo lateranense', repr. in *Images and Ideas in the Middle Ages. Selected Studies in History and Art*, i, Studi e Testi, 155 (Rome, 1983), 347–66 at 347, 356–6; Mary Stroll, *Symbols as Power. The Papacy following the Investiture Contest* (Leiden/New York, etc., 1991), 188–92, 206–7, and Plate 43. There was in fact nothing either new or shocking in such pictures. In fact, at least one earlier German source had depicted Henry V receiving imperial insignia (orb and sceptre) from Paschal II in 1111; and although the pope is not enthroned, the emperor is visibly inclining his head before an upright pope (Chronicle of Frutolf of Michelsberg, Cambridge, Corpus Christi College, MS 373, fo. 83r: reproduced as the cover illustration of Robinson's *The Papacy*). The Lateran frescos were painted to celebrate the enhanced role of the Lateran, since Lothar's coronation had taken place there, and not in St Peter's (which was held by the anti-pope Anacletus II), the traditional location for imperial coronations.

[132] *Chronica regia Coloniensis*, 93–4: 'Nam papa quondam Innocentius Romae in mure pingi fecerat se quasi in throno pontificali sedentem, imperatorem vero Lotharium complicatis manubus coram se inclinatum coronam imperii suscipentem.'

[133] Rahewin, iii. 10* (*Gesta*, 177; *Deeds*, 183–4).

[134] Idem, iii. 17* (*Gesta*, 188–9; *Deeds*, 193). Although frequently translated as 'empire and papacy', the phrase *regnum et sacerdotium* admits of no easy translation. Frederick was thinking of the royal/imperial and papal office.

less than triumphant descent upon Italy in 1155, the defiance of some Italian cities, particularly Milan, and the pope's recent rapprochement with the Normans, the young emperor and his court were easily persuaded that Adrian's letter—and the demeanour of the cardinals, who addressed the emperor as 'brother'—constituted a serious affront to the imperial dignity. But Frederick was easily affronted. The Besançon incident occurred only about a month after an incident at Würzburg, to which western historians have given little attention. When ambassadors from the Byzantine emperor Manuel Comnenus (whom Rahewin calls Alexius)[135] approached the great court held at Würzburg in September 1157, they were curtly dismissed for failure to show sufficient obsequiousness in their approach to 'the ruler over the City and the world'—'because their words in certain respects appeared to smack of royal pride and (in their over-ornate speech) of the arrogance of the Greeks, the emperor scorned them.... Appeased by their many entreaties and tears, however, the emperor granted them his forgiveness for these offences, having received their pledge that henceforth, abjuring bombast, they would bring him in their salutations only such reverence as befits a Roman prince and the ruler over the City and the world'.[136] The Würzburg court was a splendid demonstration of Frederick's imperial position. The embarrassments and failures of the first Italian campaign had been somewhat compensated by victory over the Poles (22 August 1157), which had resulted in the formal submission of King Boleslav IV at Würzburg.[137] Ambassadors from Denmark, Pannonia, Italy, and Burgundy were vying with one another to honour the emperor;[138] and the recently-installed Henry II of England had sent a very flattering letter, accompanied by rich gifts.[139] It is not known what the Byzantine emperor's emissaries said on behalf of their imperial master; but neither they nor their mission were welcome. They had come, too late as it happened,[140] to propose a marriage alliance between the two emperors (something that had been under discussion since 1153),[141] but Frederick's recent

---

[135] Perhaps through confusion with the Emperor Alexis Comnenus with whom Henry IV had allied against the Normans in the 1080s (Partner, *Lands of St Peter*, 134),

[136] Rahewin, iii. 6* (*Gesta*, 170–1; *Deeds*, 178).

[137] See Frederick's own account of the Polish expedition, sent to Wibald, abbot of Stavelot and Corvey (Sept. 1157), *Bibliotheca rerum Germanicarum*, i, 601–2 no. 470, which formed the basis of Rahewin's account in Rahewin, iii. 3–4 (*Gesta*, 168–70; *Deeds*, 176–8).

[138] Idem, iii. 8* (*Gesta*, 173; *Deeds*, 180).

[139] Idem, iii. 7* (*Gesta*, 172; *Deeds*, 179–80): 'We lay before you our kingdom and whatever is anywhere subject to our sway, and entrust it to your power, that all things may be administered in accordance with your nod, and that in all respects your imperial will may be done.' The purpose of the mission, in fact, was to reject the emperor's request for the return of the hand of St James, the famous relic taken by the Empress Matilda from the imperial chapel after the death of her husband Henry V in 1125, which Henry I had bestowed on Reading Abbey in 1133: see Karl Leyser, 'Frederick Barbarossa, Henry II and the Hand of St. James', *EHR*, 90 (1975), 481–506, esp. 489–99.

[140] Frederick had married Beatrix, heiress of Burgundy in June 1156, having had his marriage to Adelheid of Vohburg annulled in 1153.

[141] See above, n. 82.

marriage to Beatrix of Burgundy and the Greek coalition's defeat by William I in the previous year made them doubly *personae non gratae*. There was no longer any reason to court the Greek emperor, at least for the moment, and the humiliation of his unfortunate ambassadors provided a gratifying demonstration of Frederick's power and status. Equally, the papal envoys were *personae non gratae*. Fresh from teaching manners to the Byzantines and basking in the adulation of emissaries from many lands, Frederick was in no mood to accept either criticism from the papal Curia or a reminder of his obligations to the pope. His attitude, shared by his triumphalist court, can be read as understandable concern for the honour of the empire, but in the light of his contemptuous treatment of the Greek envoys, it looks more like a calculated insult. In both instances, the emperor turned the interviews to the discredit of the envoys, by accusing them of present or past discourtesy or dishonesty, so that his own change of policy towards their masters should appear to be the result of righteous indignation.

(e) After Besançon

Supporters of the 'Sicilian plot' paint a picture of continuous 'provocation' by Adrian in the wake of Benevento and Besançon, creating an entirely false picture of the pope's deliberate thwarting of just imperial policies, alliance with his enemies, and the raising of ever more outrageous claims, to which the emperor was forced to reply forcefully in defence of his honour. But, as argued above the 'Sicilian party' was an imperialist myth;[142] the proposition that Adrian, secure in the protection of William of Sicily, went out of his way to inflame relations with the emperor, not only ignores the evidence of how dangerous the situation was for him, but misinterprets his actions, and misrepresents the attempts by the Curia to re-establish good relations with Frederick.[143]

Three actions in particular are singled out as evidence of Adrian's enmity in the last year of his life. The first was his refusal to confirm Frederick's appointment of Guido of Biandrate as archbishop of Ravenna in early 1159, which the emperor took so amiss, Rahewin says, that he ordered the abandonment of the diplomatic protocol whereby the pope's name preceded his own in imperial letters, as well as the practice of addressing the pope in the respectful plural form. The Ravenna dispute can be seen as another proof of Adrian's anti-imperial policy, but viewed in the light of Frederick's attempt to restore and in many cases re-invent

---

[142] See above, at nn. 3–4, 8–11. The image of the Sicilian bogey in league with the papacy against the empire had an older root, however. When the Roman insurgents appealed to Conrad III for assistance against Eugenius III in 1148, they spoke of 'the pope, the Frangipani, and the sons of Pierleone, who are adherents and friends of the Sicilian...as they have planned with the pope and the Sicilian to do...agreement between the Sicilian and the pope....' (Otto of Freising, i. 29 [*Gesta*, 46–7; *Deeds*, 62–3]).

[143] See at nn. 108, 126, 148.

the most wide-ranging list of imperial rights, both the pope's refusal and the emperor's rage are understandable.[144]

The second was his protest, presented at Bologna (April 1159), against the imposition of the imperial rights announced at Roncaglia on 12–13 November 1158,[145] not only in papal territories but on ecclesiastical lands and corporations throughout Italy (apart from the *regno*). Imperial agents were active not only throughout Lombardy, but in regions belonging to or claimed by the papal patrimony—Tuscany, the Campagna, and the Matildine lands (entrusted to Welf VI, Henry the Lion's uncle)—collecting regalian taxes and supervising the election of two *podestà* in every city, to replace independently elected consuls; and agents were sent even to Sardinia and Corsica, although their efforts were frustrated by the Genoese; and the oath imposed on all public officials indicates how comprehensive was Frederick's assumption of effective power. Its crucial clause read:

> and I shall aid him to retain the crown of the empire and all its *honour* in Italy, namely and specifically the city of N. and whatever jurisdiction he ought to have in it' (*or* 'in all his power over the county or bishopric of N.'). 'I shall not deprive him of his *regalia* here or elsewhere, and if they have been taken away from him I shall in good faith help him to recover and retain them....[146]

In the (probably forlorn) hope that some accommodation could be reached without abandoning the whole Italian church to the emperor's interpretation of his *regalia* (which even Archbishop Eberhard of Bamberg recognized as novel),[147]

---

[144] Rahewin, iv. 21–2* (*Gesta*, 260–2; *Deeds*, 255–7). Cf. Partner, *Lands of St Peter*, 197–9. Guido nevertheless held the archbishopric until his death on 9 July 1169: see Karl Borchardt, 'Archbishop Gerard of Ravenna and Bishop John of Faenza', in *Proceedings of the Eighth International Congress of Medieval Canon Law*, ed. Stanley Chodorow, Monumenta iuris canonici, Series C: Subsidia, 9 (Città del Vaticano, 1992), 573–92, at 575–7.

[145] *MGH Constitutiones*, i, no. 174; *MGH Diplomata*, 10/ii (1979), 29–36 nos 238–42. Cf. Rahewin, iv. 7–9 (*Gesta*, 240–1; *Deeds*, 238–9); Godfrey of Viterbo, cc. 17–18, lines 364–93; Burchard of Ursberg, 30–2, esp. 31: 'Super quo contra novas institutiones imperatoris murmurare ceperunt Lombardi.' Cf. Munz, *Frederick Barbarossa*, 168–70.

[146] Rahewin, iv. 12–13, 23 (*Gesta*, 247–8, 266–7; *Deeds*, 244–5, 260–1). The oath is idem, iii. 20* (*Gesta*, 190–4 at 191; *Deeds*, 195–7 at 195–6). Cf. *MGH Diplomata*, 10/ii (1979), 30 no. 238, 'Omnis iurisdictio et omnis districtus apud principem est et omnes iudices a principe administrationem accipere debent et iusiurandum prestare, quale a lege constitutum est.' For an excellent discussion of Frederick's concept of imperial renewal (*renovatio imperii*) and the meaning of *regalia*, see Robert L. Benson, 'Political *Renovatio*: two models from Roman antiquity', in *Renaissance and Renewal in the Twelfth Century*, ed. Robert L. Benson and Giles Constable (Oxford, 1982), 339–86, esp. 360–9.

[147] Broadly, a extensive range of jurisdictional and fiscal rights attached to the imperial crown. With the backing of the Roman lawyers at Bologna, these were given a wide interpretation at Roncaglia, and virtually all civil administration was deemed to be derived from, and thus subject to, imperial authority. Eberhard of Bamberg's comment, addressed to Henry, one of the cardinals who presented Adrian's protest, is instructive. 'Annales

Adrian sent the four cardinals most likely to receive a favourable hearing to present the church's case.[148] As rehearsed in a regretful letter from Bishop Eberhard of Bamberg to Archbishop Eberhard of Salzburg, transmitted by Rahewin, Adrian's 'demands' were that the emperor must not send envoys to Rome without the pope's knowledge, since the Roman magistrates and *regalia* are subject to St Peter; that the *fodrum* should be collected from papal lands only when the emperor travelled through them for his coronation; that Italian bishops should swear fealty but not pay homage to the emperor; that imperial envoys were not to treat episcopal palaces as part of the imperial fisc; and that the land belonging to the Church of Rome (the Matildine lands, Ferrara, Massa, Ficarolo, Tivoli, the territory from Aquapendente to Rome, the duchy of Spoleto, the islands of Sardinia and Corsica) should be restored.[149] They received short shrift, and their offer to make a new papal-imperial accord was contemptuously refused, on the grounds that Adrian had broken the first one by making peace with 'the Sicilian'.[150] Rahewin presented the pope's complaint as deliberate trouble-making, even to the extent of alleging that the letter was carried by a single disreputable messenger.[151] Perhaps influenced by Rahewin, Munz thought that the incident was another example of the Sicilian party's duplicity, in that Adrian demanded what he knew the emperor would refuse! This is an astonishing interpretation of the event. The balance of effective power in Italy was at that point very clearly in favour of the emperor: the legal experts at Bologna had formally confirmed his policy of imperial recuperation; he had an army in northern Italy large enough to divide into three or more task forces; the annihilation of Milan and its allies was already in train. That Adrian would have wanted deliberately to widen the breach with the emperor is inconceivable, outside the realms of conspiracy theory. On the other hand, no mid-twelfth-century pope could have watched with equanimity as the whole Roncaglian programme rolled out across Italy and the lands of St Peter, nor could he have agreed to the stage-managed arbitration offered by Frederick.

---

quandoque revolvuntur, apices imperiales recitantur forte in ea forma, quae illi aetati et tam bonitati quam simplicitati temporum illorum competebat (And when the annals are unrolled, the imperial honours are perhaps read out in the form which suited that age and the goodness as well as the simplicity of those times...)': Rahewin, iv. 22 (*Gesta*, 263, *Deeds*, 257]). Even Munz (*Frederick Barbarossa*, 170) is critical: 'Frederick soon found himself in a position in which he appeared as the protagonist of the narrowest and most tyrannical interpretation of the Roncaglia decrees.' See also at nn. 226–8 below.

[148] Octavian of S. Cecilia, Henry of SS. Nereo e Achilleo, William of S. Pietro in Vincoli, and Guido of Crema (see next n.). Octavian and Guido were known imperial supporters; Henry (see n. 126 above) and William were *personae gratae*.

[149] Rahewin, iv. 34* (*Gesta*, 275–6; *Deeds*, 268–9). Cf. Partner, *Lands of St Peter*, 198–9. For the *fodrum* (hospitality tax), see *ibid.*, 199 n. 3, challenging C. Brühl, *Fodrum, Gistum, Servitium Regis* (Cologne/Graz, 1968), i, 672–4. Partner rightly argues that Frederick's claims to a general right of *fodrum* on papal lands was not supported by precedent. Cf. Maccarrone, *Papato e impero*, 313–19.

[150] Rahewin, *Gesta*, 279; *Deeds*, 271.

[151] Rahewin, iv. 18* (*Gesta*, 257; *Deeds*, 252), 'indignus et vilis nuntius'.

The third alleged provocation was his withdrawal to Anagni in mid-June 1159 with the 'Sicilian cardinals', where he 'negotiated a treaty' with the anti-imperial cities, Milan, Brescia, Piacenza, and Crema.[152] But there was nothing sinister about moving the papal court to one of its southern 'hill-stations' to escape the summer heat, and Anagni was well within the papal Campagna. It was scarcely a flight to William of Sicily's protection, as residence in Benevento might have been. And although imperialist chroniclers depict Adrian, through Cardinal Roland, fomenting disaffection among the Milanese,[153] it is clear, even from Rahewin, that the rebellion of Milan and its allies was provoked by the manner in which the Roncaglian decrees had been imposed, and especially by the way in which Milan's allies had been singled out for vindictive treatment. It was the actions of imperial agents which re-ignited opposition in Lombardy, not the plottings of Adrian's cardinals. When Rainald of Dassel and Counts Otto of Wittelsbach and Gozwin of Heinsberg came to apply the Roncaglian decrees in Milan and ordered the appointment of two *podestà*, there was a riot, and the imperial commissioners had to flee the city for their lives.[154] From the Roman lawyers of Bologna Frederick duly secured a formal judgment against Milan (April 1159), which was put under the ban of the empire: the city was to be looted and its citizens enslaved.[155] Not surprisingly, the old alliance of Milan, Brescia, Piacenza, and Crema re-formed, and, as the Milanese chronicle recorded, it was after the beginning of the brutal siege of Crema in June 1159[156] that the four cities made their approach to Pope Adrian, who made common cause with them.[157] That 'alliance', however, occurred

---

[152] Cf. n. 157.

[153] Rahewin, iv. 21* (*Gesta*, 261; *Deeds*, 255): papal letters urging the Milanese and other cities to revolt 'were *said* to have been discovered'.

[154] Rahewin, iv. 23 (*Gesta*, 266–7; *Deeds*, 260–1).

[155] Rahewin, iv. 33 (*Gesta*, 275; *Deeds*, 268). Cf. *Gesta Federici in Lombardia*, 28–30.

[156] Instigated by Cremona, the siege lasted until late January 1160: Rahewin, iv. 47–8, 54–8, 67–72 (*Gesta*, 287–8, 292–96; 312–18; *Deeds*, 279–80, 283–7, 302–307); Burchard of Ursberg, 34–9.

[157] *Gesta Federici I. imperatoris in Lombardia aucta cive mediolanensi (Annales mediolanenses maiores)*, ed. O. Holder-Egger, *MGH SRG* 27 (Hanover, 1892), 38–9, 'Dum insideretur Crema, Mediolanenses iuraverunt cum Brixiensibus et Placentinis et miserunt legatos ad Adrianum papam, qui erat in Anagnia, et concordiam fecerunt iste tres civitates cum eo, quod exinde non paciscerentur vel aliquam concordiam facerent cum Federico imperatore absque licentia Adriani pape vel eius catholici successoris; et ita iuraverunt Cremenses. Papa quoque e converso idem convenit cum eis, et convenit, quod ab illa die usque ad XL dies excommunicaret imperatorem; qui tamen non iuravit. Accidit autem, ut infra statutam diem papa moraretur.' A much more exaggerated version is transmitted by Burchard of Ursberg (*Chronicon*, 37), who attributes the story to a written account by John, a priest from Cremona, who wrote that he had heard from trustworthy men from Milan and Brescia that they were present when the conspiracy was launched, but even he places the 'conspiracy' after the beginning of the siege of Crema, not before it, as a consequence, not a cause of the Milanese rebellion: 'In qua conspiratione se astrinxerunt maxima pars cardinalium sedis apostolice, Wilelmus quoque rex Sicilie et pene universe civitates Italie cum multis baronibus et viris potentibus; dataque est immensa pecunia domino Adriano pape, ut ipse imperatorem excommunicaret.'

three or four months after Frederick's rejection of the peace overtures presented at Bologna in April. From Adrian's perspective, that rejection was ominous indeed, for it left the papacy and the papal states virtually at the mercy of a hostile emperor whose armies were already engaged in the subjugation of Lombardy.[158] In imperial circles, Adrian had become an object of contempt, and there was no further diplomatic recourse available to him, apart from capitulation to the emperor's version of imperial rights. At the same time, perhaps in the knowledge that Adrian was ill,[159] Frederick took two steps which indicate that he was already thinking of a successor. In late May–early June, he granted the Umbrian city and county of Terni, with all its *regalia*, as an imperial fief to 'his very dear and faithful friends', Cardinal Octavian and his three brothers, Otto, Godfrey, and Solimano, and then took the canons of St Peter's in Rome into his imperial protection (*sub nostram imperialem tutelam*). By granting Terni to Octavian and his family, Frederick not only rewarded a loyal clan, as his privilege expressly stated, 'As we reward the services of those loyal to the empire with appropriate favours... (*Dum fidelium imperii obsequia dignis beneficiis compensamus...*)', but significantly advanced Octavian's chances of succession, by placing in his hands an estate which controlled access from the north to two ancient Roman highways, the Flaminia and the Salaria, which led to Rome. And the privilege conferred on the canons of St Peter's may have been directed to the same end.[160]

iv. Ireland and *Laudabiliter*

If anything, Adrian's alleged 'grant' of Ireland to Henry II, generally thought to have been conveyed in the 'privilege' *Laudabiliter* in late 1155–early 1156,[161] is even more controversial than his relations with other political powers, for that action has been seen as the poisoned seed from which burgeoned the whole painful history of English/Anglo-Norman domination of Ireland. As early as 1317, Domnall O'Neill, king of Tir Eoghain, wrote that Adrian IV 'deserved to be called Anti-Christ rather than true pope (*dici meruit potius antichristus quam iustus*

---

[158] The war ended in March 1162 with the total destruction of Milan—an act of barbarism in which its old enemies (Pavia, Como, Lodi, Novara) gleefully participated, under the eyes of the emperor.

[159] Godfrey of Viterbo's description of his death would be consistent with angina or quinsy.

[160] *MGH Diplomata*, 10/ii (1979), 83–6 nos 174–5. Alexander III's claim that Frederick had wanted Octavian to succeed (*PL*, cc, 88) seems supported by this and other actions. As early as 11 May 1158, Octavian's nephew Otto, together with emissaries from the city of Rome, had made 'proposals regarding the honour of the empire' to Rainald of Dassel and Otto of Wittelsbach (*Pontificum romanorum...vitae*, ed. Watterich, ii, 365, n. 1); and it was the armed intervention of Otto of Wittelsbach and a crowd of Roman citizens, that secured Octavian's acclamation as pope.

[161] For the text, see below, Part II/i, 'Narrative Sources', no. 5b. A fuller treatment of this question is in preparation. The most detailed defence of its authenticity is in J. F. O'Doherty, 'Rome and the Anglo-Norman Invasion of Ireland', *Irish Ecclesiastical Record*, 42 (1933), 131–45, at 131–40.

pontifex)', because of it;[162] and less than a year later, in early 1318, he and other Irish princes complained bitterly to John XXII about Adrian's betrayal of Irish rights, which he attributed to his English sympathies.[163] From then on, *Laudabiliter* was cited, on both sides of the political divide, as the 'title-deed' of the English crown's authority over Ireland; yet, apart from the dubious narrative of Giraldus Cambrensis, there is no evidence that it was ever used by Henry himself; no later pope confirmed it; and there is considerable doubt about its status and authenticity. Moreover, even if *Laudabiliter* contains the essence of Adrian's letter, it does not support the interpretation generally placed upon it. Nevertheless, generations of scholars have accepted the broad outlines of the story, and many have shown great ingenuity in advancing an interpretation of Anglo-Irish affairs between 1155–6 and 1172–3 which links Henry II's assumption of authority in 1171–2 with the 'privilege' obtained from Adrian IV in 1156. As recently reiterated in a detailed study of Anglo-Norman-Hibernian relations in the twelfth century,[164] Adrian's grant in *Laudabiliter* was the result of a clerico-papal plot, hatched at Canterbury and enthusiastically supported by the English pope, to lure the young Henry into a conquest of Ireland to restore the (actually non-existent) primatial rights of Canterbury in the island, and Henry II's seizure of Ireland was a delayed consequence of that plot. But whatever Adrian granted, and he did grant something, there is no reliable evidence about the nature of the grant or proof that Henry acted on it. It was Giraldus Cambrensis, writing in the late 1180s as a propagandist defender of the deeds of his own close relatives (the Geraldines), who constructed the myth of a papally-approved Cambro-Norman-Angevin conquest of the Irish, by associating *Laudabiliter* with Henry II's triumphant assumption of authority in 1171–3 in such a way that readers would assume that the king's actions were somehow based on, or at least legitimized by, the English pope's 'privilege'. As he told it, in 1172, that is *after* the conquest had taken place, Henry 'sought from Pope Alexander III a privilege (*Quoniam ea*) empowering him, with the pope's full authority and consent, to rule over the Irish people and, as it was very ignorant of the rudiments of the faith, to instruct it in the laws and disciplines of the Church according to the usage of the church in England.' This privilege was conveyed to Ireland by William FitzAldelin (the king's deputy in

---

[162] In a letter to Fineem MacCarthy, see H. Wood, 'Letter from Domnall O'Neill to Fineem MacCarthy, 1317', *Proceedings of the Royal Irish Academy*, 37 C [1926], 141–8; cf. J. A. Watt, '*Laudabiliter* in Medieval Diplomacy and Propaganda', *Irish Ecclesiastical Record*, 87 (1957), 427.

[163] *Scotichronicon by Walter Bower: in Latin and English*, ed. D. E. R. Watt, *et al.*, 9 vols (Aberdeen, 1987–98), vi (1991), 386–7 (with English translation): 'Adrianus papa, predecessor vester, non tantum origine, quantum affectione et condicione, Anglicus...dominium regni nostri...de facto contulit indebite, ordine juris omisso omnino, Anglicana affectione, proth! dolor, excecante.' Cf. J. A. Watt, *The Church and the Two Nations in Medieval Ireland* (Cambridge, 1970), 186–8.

[164] Marie Therese Flanagan, *Irish Society, Anglo-Norman Settlers, Angevin Kingship. Interactions in Ireland in the late twelfth century* (Oxford, 1989), 7–55, esp. 7–8, 51–5, 277–8.

Ireland from mid-1173) and Master Nicholas, the king's chaplain, then prior of the St Albans' dependency of Wallingford, and published at an episcopal council convened for the purpose at Waterford,[165] where 'They also read the other privilege (*Laudabiliter*) which had been conveyed by the aforesaid, and which the king had formally procured from Alexander's predecessor Adrian through the offices of John of Salisbury, afterwards bishop of Chartres, who had been sent to Rome for this purpose. By John's hand the aforesaid Pope Adrian also sent the king of England the present of a gold ring as a sign of his investiture, and this had been immediately deposited with the privilege in the archives at Winchester.'[166] Both texts are then given in full, though oddly, considering the importance attached to them, they both lack their dates[167] So compelling and circumstantial is this account by an author who knew Ireland well, and who was closely related to the Cambro-Normans who led the 'invasion', that historians have been mesmerized by it, and have sought to explain away what close inspection reveals to be an amalgam of accurate reporting and tendentious manipulation of the truth.

All the factual details of names and places are accurate. Henry did send emissaries to Alexander III with letters from the Irish bishops; Alexander did approve what had been done; and the Alexandrine letters were conveyed to Ireland. But the two texts which Giraldus provides are highly suspect. *Laudabiliter* does not grant Ireland to the English king, and there is no independent evidence that it was used or cited in 1171–2; *Quoniam ea* is a crude fake, constructed to link the king's actions with Adrian's 'privilege' and to imply an unambiguous grant of dominion over Ireland: 'we confirm and ratify his [Adrian's] concession regarding the granting to you of dominion over the kingdom of Ireland...'. So crudely was this letter devised, however, that Giraldus was forced to omit it from his last works, including the revised *Expugnatio*, having admitted *c*. 1216 that 'others denied that it had ever been obtained (*ab aliis autem unquam impetratum fuisse negatur*)'.[168] What were published at Waterford were three quite different letters from Alexander III, issued in response to the embassy from Henry II, which transmitted letters from the Irish bishops.[169] The total silence of these unquestionably authentic papal letters about any antecedent papal grant raises serious doubts about the reliability of Giraldus's version of events and therefore about the extent of Adrian's responsibility for what happened.

---

[165] Giraldus Cambrensis, *Expugnatio Hibernica. The Conquest of Ireland by Giraldus Cambrensis*, ii. 5, ed. and trans. A. B. Scott and F. X. Martin, Irish Medieval Texts, 1 (Dublin, 1978), 142–3. For FitzAldelin, see *ibid.*, 317 n. 189, 330–1 n. 294.

[166] *Ibid.*, 144–5: see Part II/i, 'Narrative Sources', no. 5b. This account is very close to John's, except that John does not mention Rome (he had been at Benevento), nor does he say where the letter (as distinct from the ring) was lodged.

[167] *Expugnatio* (ed. Scott and Martin), 143–7.

[168] *De principis instructione*, ii. 19 (*Opera*, viii, 197); cf. *Expugnatio*, ed. Scott and Martin, lx–lxi; *De rebus a se gestis*, ii. 11 (*Opera*, i, 62–3). Among recent writers, only Ullmann ('Alexander III and the Conquest of Ireland', 372) has argued (unconvincingly) for the authenticity of *Quoniam ea*.

[169] See below, at n. 221.

The most direct evidence for Adrian's actions comes from John of Salisbury. Writing just after he had heard of the pope's death in late 1159, he said that it was at his request that Adrian had 'granted and given Ireland to the illustrious Henry II king of the English to be held by hereditary right (*iure hereditario possidendam*), as his letters testify to this day', since 'All islands are said to belong to the Roman Church by ancient right from the donation of Constantine, who established and endowed it'; and also by his agency that the pope had sent Henry a 'golden ring set with a fine emerald by which investiture of the right to rule Ireland should be made; and this ring was ordered to be kept in the public treasury [then in Winchester] until now.'[170] This statement seems explicit enough, but there is nothing about hereditary right in *Laudabiliter*, which Giraldus identified as the letter obtained by John, nor can that letter properly be seen as a 'grant'.[171] Moreover, John fails to explain when or why the grant was made. Thus decontextualized, the way was open for historians to speculate upon the event and its consequences. Broadly, scholars have concluded, following the lead of J. F. O'Doherty,[172] that the impetration of papal approval for the conquest of Ireland was part of a Canterbury plot to re-establish its claims to supremacy over the Irish Church, which had been terminated by the council of Kells-Mellifont in 1152,[173] in which Eugenius III's legate, John Paparo, cardinal priest of S. Lorenzo in Damaso, had supervised the recognition of four metropolitan sees for the island. According to this widely held theory, John of Salisbury was the clever agent of a clerical contrivance to lure the young king into a conquest which would see the archbishop of Canterbury established as primate over a subordinate Irish church. The plan went sour, however, because the king could not accept the tenor of *Laudabiliter*, with its papal claims to jurisdiction over islands and the promise of Peter's Pence. Such an affront to the royal dignity, it was thought, rendered the letter useless and its impetrator *persona non grata*, resulting in John of Salisbury's disgrace in mid-

---

[170] *Ioannis Saresberiensis. Metalogicon*, iv. 42, ed. J. B. Hall and K. S. B. Keats-Rohan, *CCCM* 98 (1991), 183, 'Ad preces meas illustri regi Anglorum, Henrico secundo, concessit et dedit Hiberniam iure hereditario possidendam, sicut litterae ipsius testantur in hodiernam diem. Nam omnes insulae de iure antiquo ex donatione Constantini, qui eam fundauit et dotauit, dicuntur ad Romanam Ecclesiam pertinere. Anulum quoque per me transmisit aureum, smaragdo optimo decoratum, quo fieret inuestitura iuris in regenda Hibernia, idemque adhuc anulus in cimiliarchio publico iussus est custodiri'; cf. the translation (from the earlier edn by Webb) by Daniel D. McGarry, *The Metalogicon of John of Salisbury: a twelfth-century defense of the verbal and logical arts of the trivium* (Berkeley/Los Angeles, 1955; repr. 1962), 274–5.

[171] See below, at n. 213.

[172] Though he thought that the 'Canterbury plot' merely paralleled and provided honourable cover for the king's secular ambitions: 'Rome and the Anglo-Norman Invasion', 140–1; idem, 'St. Laurence O'Toole and the Anglo-Norman Invasion', *Irish Ecclesiastical Record*, 50 (1937) 449–77, 600–25, esp. 459, 601, 609–10. Cf. W. L. Warren, *Henry II* (London, 1973), 195–6; Michael Richter, 'Giraldiana', *Irish Historical Studies*, 21 (1979), 422–37, esp. 430–1; Flanagan, *Irish Society*, 7–55, esp. 7–8, 51–5, 277–8.

[173] Watt, *Church and Two Nations*, 28 and n. 3.

1156.[174] But there is nothing in John's own statement, or in the letter supposedly obtained, or in the subsequent history of Anglo-Irish relations to support the theory of a Canterbury-inspired plot. Whether or not *Laudabiliter* is the indult obtained from Adrian IV, it says nothing at all about Canterbury; and it was only by leaving out crucial clauses about the rights of the local churches and the payment of Peter's Pence to Rome that Warren could turn it into such a document.[175]

Equally, there is no concrete evidence that John's disgrace was related to the letter he obtained and the ring which he had brought back triumphantly to the king. In the first place, John's own self-regarding comment in *Metalogicon* would have rung rather hollow if everyone knew that he had been disgraced because of his trumpeted success at Benevento. In the second, there was a much more explicit reason for his disfavour. In a confidential letter written at the time (in 1156), John explained to his close friend, Peter of Celle, then abbot of Montier-la-Celle near Troyes, what the reason for the king's displeasure was that 'I alone in all the realm am accused of diminishing the royal dignity. When they define the act of offence more carefully, these are the charges that they hurl at my head. If any among us invokes the name of Rome, they say it is my doing. If the English Church ventures to claim even the shadow of liberty in making elections or in the trial of ecclesiastical causes, it is imputed to me, as if I were the only person to instruct the lord of Canterbury and the other bishops what they ought to do.'[176] There is not a hint of the Irish business in any of the letters written in 1156, although his ironic statement that his disgrace was 'perhaps because I have favoured him more than was just, and worked for his advancement with greater vigour than I should; for I sighed for this with all my heart's longing, namely that I might behold him whom I deemed to be kept in exile by the malice of Fortune, reigning by God's mercy on the throne of his fathers, and giving laws to peoples and nations'[177] has been read, not unreasonably, as a veiled reference to the Irish grant;[178] but it alludes more probably to John's support for the Angevin succession,[179] and is, in any case

---

[174] Giles Constable, 'The Alleged Disgrace of John of Salisbury in 1159', *EHR*, 69 (1954), 67–76. Constable (correctly) assigned to 1156 the disgrace which earlier scholars had dated to 1159, and linked it with *Laudabiliter*, cf. Klaus Guth, *Johannes von Salisbury (1115/20–1180). Studien zur Kirchen-, Kultur- und Sozialgeschichte Westeuropas im 12. Jahrhundert* (St. Ottilien, 1978), 132–5.

[175] *Henry II*, 195–6.

[176] *JohnS*, i, 31–2. The key Latin reads, 'Solus in regno regiam dicor minuere maiestatem...Quod quis nomen Romanum apud nos inuocat, michi inponunt. Quod in electionibus celebrandis, in causis ecclesiasticis examinandis uel umbram libertatis audet sibi Anglorum ecclesia uendicare, michi inputetur...'.

[177] *JohnS*, i, 31.

[178] Constable, 'Alleged Disgrace', 75.

[179] The irony was that he who had worked to secure Henry II's succession had been denounced for dishonouring the king by one (Arnulf of Lisieux) who had opposed it, even to the extent of challenging the legitimacy of Matilda's marriage to Geoffrey of Anjou at the Second Lateran Council (1139): *The Correspondence of Thomas Becket, Archbishop of Canterbury 1162–1170*, ed. and trans. A. J. Duggan, 2 vols, Oxford Medieval Texts (Oxford, 2000), ii, 1364–5.

explicitly rejected as the occasion of the king's anger a sentence or so later in the same letter—'This is not the fault of which I am accused.'[180] The real reason for John's discomfiture was his known reformist and pro-papal leanings; and the *agent-provocateur* who informed against him to the king was specifically identified, in a letter to Adrian, as none other than Bishop Arnulf of Lisieux, who 'has heaped up the king's indignation against my poor self to such an extent that the king himself has denounced me both to the archbishop of Canterbury and to his chancellor [Thomas Becket] for abasing the royal dignity'.[181] Arnulf had been a member of the royal embassy sent to greet the new pope in October 1155 and to seek approval for an Irish invasion.[182] The envoys' stay with the pope at Benevento coincided almost exactly with John's three-month sojourn, when he ate at Adrian's table,[183] and they may well have been disturbed at the intimacy between the two, especially since it was not impossible that John might be brought into the Sacred College.[184] Much more galling for the king, however, was the rebuke which Adrian inserted, probably on John's instigation, into the mandate about the blessing of the abbot of St Augustine's, issued to Archbishop Theobald in January 1156. The most offensive sentence from the king's point of view declared, 'the right of

---

[180] 'Huius tamen culpae non arguor' (*JohnS*, i, 31). Professor Brooke, however (above, ch. 1, at nn. 34–5), sees *Laudabiliter* in the background of John's disgrace.

[181] *JohnS*, i, 48.

[182] Rotrou of Évreux, Guillaume de Passavant of Le Mans, Arnulf of Lisieux, and Abbot Robert of St Albans: *Gesta abbatum*, i, 125–9 (*Vitae abbatum*, 1019–20).* The *Gesta*, which were compiled in part from earlier St Albans' materials by Matthew Paris in the mid-thirteenth century (see Richard Vaughan, *Matthew Paris* [Cambridge, 1958; reiss. 1979], 182–5, esp. 183), name Robert as head of the mission and state (i, 126) that the envoys were sent 'to conduct some difficult royal business' at the Curia (*quaedam ardua negotia regalia...expedirent*), but they do not say what it was. Roger of Wendover, however, writing at St Albans before 1239, not only made the acquisition of papal approval for an invasion of Ireland the purpose of the royal mission, but presented a version of *Laudabiliter* as its principal fruit (*Flores historiarum*, i, 11–13); and that same story and text, appeared, with some additions, in Matthew Paris's *Chronica majora* (ii, 210–11) and *Historia Anglorum* (i, 304–5). Whether or not he should be credited with the impetration of *Laudabiliter*, the abbot was very busy on his own behalf. He secured a sheaf of privileges for his monastery between 5 Feb. and 24 Feb. 1156 (*PUE*, iii, 234–54 nos 100–10, 112–13); he remained at Benevento after the bishops had departed, and did not return to St Albans until the octave of the Ascension (31 May 1156). See also Brenda Bolton, ch. 6, at nn. 100–01.

[183] *Policraticus sive de nugis Curialium* (composed 1156–59), vi. 24 (ed. Clement C. J. Webb, 2 vols [Oxford, 1909], ii, 67). The reason for John's presence at the papal court is obscure. His own record (*ibid.*) speaks, somewhat vaguely, of his journey to Apulia 'to visit the lord Pope Adrian IV (*causa visitandi dominum Adrianum pontificem quartum...profectum in Apuliam*)', but he may have travelled with the royal envoys, and then assisted them in presenting the king's case.

[184] John had himself entertained some hopes, as one of his letters suggests: 'for I continually recall with joy and exultation the words which proceeded from your lips, when at Ferentino [probably winter 1150–1] you gave me your own ring and belt as a pledge of things to come' (*JohnS*, i, 90 and n. 1).

appeal is so smothered by you and the king of England that no-one dares to appeal to the apostolic see in your presence or his.'[185] Here, I think, we should find the cause of John's great disgrace, not in the favour obtained from Adrian IV.

The genesis of the Irish venture lies not in a Canterbury plot,[186] for which there is no evidence, but in an early scheme of Henry II himself to provide a suitable lordship for his youngest brother, William. Knowledge of this proposal comes principally from Robert of Torigny, the chronicler abbot of Mont-Saint-Michel in Normandy—and, it should be added, a firm supporter of Henry II. According to Robert, Henry had held a council at Winchester around Michaelmas (1155), in which he had discussed with his nobles (*cum optimatibus suis*) a proposed conquest of Ireland, which he intended to confer on his youngest brother, William, but that his mother's opposition had led to its abandonment.[187] This dating would correlate exactly with the dispatch of the embassy to Benevento, which had set out on 9 October.[188] The late Professor Warren, however, dismissed Robert's account on five grounds:[189] that no English chronicler records it, that Robert was ill-informed about English affairs, that it would have been very unlikely for Henry to have contemplated so great a promotion for his youngest brother when he has just deprived his middle brother (Geoffrey) of his hoped-for inheritance, that Henry had no particular interest in Ireland; and that the idea came from Canterbury not the king. The silence of the English chroniclers is not significant, since most have little to say about the early years of Henry's reign; Robert was in fact quite well-informed—he was close to the Empress Matilda, and he did record that Cardinal John Paparo's actions in Ireland had infringed the dignity of the church of Canterbury;[190] and Henry's denial of the three key

[185] *Historia monasterii S. Augustini Cantuariensis by Thomas of Elmham*, ed. C. Hardwick, RS 8 (London, 1858), 411–12 no. 42, at 412, '...ita apud te et apud regem Angliae appellatio sit sepulta, quod aliquis non est, qui in tua vel in illius praesentia ad sedem apostolicam audeat appellare.' See also ch. 9, at n. 50.

[186] This is not to say that there may not have been such ambitions during Lanfranc's time, with the occasional use of the formula *Britanniarum primas*, but although Marie Therese Flanagan attached much weight to the primacy question (*Irish Society*, 7–38), the evidence for active pursuit of authority over the church in Ireland is extremely slender. Any Irish bishop who sought consecration from an archbishop of Canterbury was obliged to make a profession of obedience; but there were only six such consecrations between 1074 and 1140 (four for Dublin, one each for Waterford and Limerick), and they were all at the request of the Irish themselves, and explained not by Canterbury's claims to primacy, but by special circumstances within the Irish Church: see *Canterbury Professions*, ed. M. Richter, Canterbury and York Society, 67 (Torquay, 1973), xciii–xcvi, 29, 31, 34–5, 39, nos 36, 42, 51, 54, 69, 81; Flanagan, *Irish Society*, 18–22, 30–3.

[187] *The Chronicle of Robert of Torigni*, ed. R. Howlett, *Chronicles of the Reigns of Stephen, Henry II and Richard I*, RS 82/iv (London, 1889), 186. A recent study, which appeared after this chapter was substantially written, accepted Robert of Torigny's statement, without discussion: Graeme J. White, *Restoration and Reform 1163–1165. Recovery from Civil War in England* (Cambridge, 2000), 4, 5.

[188] 'Die igitur Sancti Dionysii': *Gesta abbatum*, i, 125; cf. above, n. 182.

[189] *Henry II*, 194–5.

[190] Robert of Torigny, 166.

Angevin counties of Anjou, Maine, and Touraine should be seen as conservation of his own lordship rather than obstruction of his brother's rights. He did in fact attempt to accommodate Geoffrey's ambitions outside the heartland of his own domains by encouraging his promotion to the county of Nantes in Brittany, which would have meant an extension of Angevin lordship (but he died in 1158, and Henry had to find another way to securing the duchy of Brittany). In the same way, a lordship in Ireland for William, under his own overlordship, would have increased the 'family' holdings. Furthermore, he tried to compensate the young man by arranging his marriage to one of the most eligible heiresses in England, which would have brought him the great honour of Warenne, together with its countess, Isabella. But Thomas Becket forbade the marriage on canonical grounds,[191] and William died soon after (1164) 'of a broken heart'.[192] Henry's supposed lack of interest in Ireland, which Warren strongly argued against Orpen,[193] has been effectively challenged by the demonstration that Angevin links with Diarmait Mac Murchada, the king of Leinster, reached back to the war against Stephen in the 1140s, when Henry was a child, living under the protection of Earl Robert of Gloucester.[194] Mac Murchada's appeal in 1166 for Henry's assistance or, failing that (and it did fail), permission to recruit support from Henry's Cambro-Norman vassals, did not come out of the blue, therefore. Eleven years earlier, in 1155, Henry was a young man on the make, who had by skill and fortune already made himself king of England and lord of half of 'France', and he did not want to diminish his lordship by conferring estates within the 'Angevin empire' on his younger brothers. But that did not preclude satisfaction of their ambitions elsewhere. The provision of an Irish lordship of some kind for the young William would have killed more than one bird, if it could be managed. The possibility may have been no more than a gleam in Henry's eye, and one that quickly faded as more immediate problems pressed in on him, but he seized the opportunity afforded by the accession of a new pope to seek some kind of justification for what was, after all, a plan to invade a neighbouring Christian country. Having floated the idea at Winchester in 1155,[195] he made acquisition of

---

[191] Becket's denial of William's aspirations was remembered against him at the time of his murder in 1170, when Richard Brito struck the recumbent Becket so fiercely that his sword broke on the pavement, with the words, 'Take that, for the love of my lord William, the king's brother!' (William FitzStephen, *MTB*, iii, 142).

[192] Isabella and 'the vast honour of Warenne' were given to the king's remaining (illegitimate half-) brother, Hamelin: Warren, *Henry II*, 66, 195.

[193] G. H. Orpen, *Ireland under the Normans, 1169–1333*, 4 vols (Oxford, 1911–20), i, 81–4, *passim*.

[194] L. Hays and E. D. Jones, 'Policy on the Run: Henry II and Irish Sea diplomacy', *Journal of British Studies*, 29 (1990), 293–316, esp. 294–9; cf. Flanagan, *Irish Society*, 69–76.

[195] Independent evidence that an Irish venture was discussed at Winchester has been presented by Flanagan, *Irish Society*, 40, in a charter of Count John of Eu (British Library, Harley Charter 83 C. 25), recording a grant made 'apud Wintoniam eo anno quo verbum factum est de Hibernia conquirenda.' For the full text, see *ibid.*, 305–7.

papal approval one of the objectives of the embassy, consisting of three Norman bishops and the abbot of St Albans, which he sent immediately afterwards to present his felicitations to the only English-born man to occupy the throne of Peter.[196] By the time the envoys had returned from Benevento in spring 1156, however, the gleam had gone from Henry's eye: in January of that year he had already crossed to his Continental lands, where he was to remain until around April 1157, and the Irish venture was shelved, *sine die*.[197]

The contents of the papal indult cannot be reliably known, for the clear contradictions between John of Salisbury's assertion that Ireland had been granted 'by hereditary right' and the absence of such a clause not only from *Laudabiliter* and its supposititious confirmation (*Quoniam ea*) but also from the three genuine Alexandrine letters, make confident conclusions on the matter impossible. If John's statement is substantially true, that Ireland was granted to Henry by virtue of the papal claim to jurisdiction over islands, derived from the Donation of Constantine, to be held in hereditary right (*iure hereditario possidendam*), one must presume that Henry's petition for approval of his scheme to take charge of Ireland was supported by a statement of the right by which he claimed to act—in the same way that a religious house seeking papal confirmation of its possessions provided a written schedule of its claims, which were then duly incorporated into the papal privilege.[198] How the claim to hereditary right was substantiated cannot be known; but Walter Ullmann's suggestion that it may have been founded on Geoffrey of Monmouth's widely propagated construction of an ancient pan-British kingdom has much to commend it.[199] Geoffrey's writings later (1188–9) supplied Giraldus Cambrensis with the two ancient precedents which he included in the fivefold right by which Henry II ruled Ireland, namely, the story of Gurguit's grant of Ireland to the ancestors of the Irish (who had been expelled from Spain), and Arthur's subsequent conquest.[200] To these, Giraldus added the assertion that

[196] See above, n. 182. In addition to the hereditary claim (below, at n. 198), the envoys may have stressed the good consequences that would flow from Henry's lordship, as expressed in *Laudabiliter* (below, at n. 211).

[197] Eyton, 16–25. The Flemish continuator of Sigebert of Gembloux's *Chronicon*, writing at the monastery of Afflighem before 1189 (*sub anno* 1156), wrote that 'Henry the younger, king of England, turned against the French king the large and well-equipped army which he had prepared to lead into Ireland in order to subjugate it to his lordship and, with the advice of bishops and men of religion, to establish his brother as king for that island': *MGH SS*, vi (Hanover, 1844), 403. This cannot be entirely accurate, for Henry did not muster troops against Louis VII until 1161, but he did campaign in Poitou and Anjou in mid-1156, putting down his brother Geoffrey's rebellion.

[198] John had, in fact, supplied the *species facti* of a privilege obtained for Peter of Celle in 1153: *JohnS*, i, 255: 'quod tu ipse uidisti et partim fabricasti'.

[199] 'Alexander III and the Conquest of Ireland: a note on the background', in *Rolando Bandinelli Papa Alessandro III*, ed. F. Liotta (Siena, 1986), 371–87, at 382–5.

[200] Geoffrey of Monmouth, *Historia regum Britanniae*, iii. 12, ix. 10, 12 (ed. Acton Griscom [London, 1929]), 292, 445, 451–2; trans. Lewis Thorpe, *The History of the Kings of Britain* [London, 1966], 100–01, 221–2, 225–8, esp. 227. Cf. Giraldus, *Expugnatio*, ii. 6 (ed. Scott and Martin, 148–9). Giraldus also owed much of his own conceptualization of the

Bayonne, 'in our province of Gascony…is the chief city of the Basques from which the Irish originally came.' The gist of these stories would have been well known to John of Salisbury, and also to the king himself, for Geoffrey's *Historia regum Britanniae* had been dedicated to Robert of Gloucester, the mainstay of the Angevin cause, in the late 1130s, and Wace's popular French translation was already circulating.[201] Behind Henry II stood the legendary Arthur, whose kingdom had embraced Britain and Ireland, and whose tomb would be discovered at Glastonbury in 1191, following the advice, so Giraldus said, of King Henry himself.[202] One does not have to argue that Henry or John believed the stories, only that they could have provided a useful basis for erecting a claim, as they did for Edward I, as he tried to justify his claims to lordship over Scotland.[203] Adrian, then, did not create Henry's hereditary title (just as Alexander II had not created William the Conqueror's claim to the English throne in 1066): it was presented to him by one of the most learned men of the time as an existing fact. He did not adjudicate: he accepted the assertion of Henry's right at its face value, in much the same way that he accepted a monastery's list of rights and properties; and if it was expressly stated in writing, it is likely to have been hedged with saving phrases which placed the moral responsibility for the claim on the shoulders of those who made it, and confirmed the claims to the extent that they had been secured *iuste*

prophetic nature of the Cambro-Norman conquest of Ireland to Geoffrey's *Prophetiae* (in *Historia,* vii). For a general overview of Geoffrey's influence, see R. William Leckie, *The Passage of Dominion: Geoffrey of Monmouth and the Periodization of Insular History in the Twelfth Century* (Toronto/Buffalo, 1981).

[201] Wace's *Roman de Brut: a history of the British*, ed. Judith Weiss (Exeter, 1999). Not all contemporaries were taken in by Geoffrey's works. Writing at the end of the century, William of Newburgh (i, 11, 12) opened his own *Historia* with a condemnation of Geoffrey's *ridicula…figmenta*, which the author had sought to dignify with the name of History by using the Latin language, 'per superductum Latini sermonis colorem honesto historiae nomine palliavit'. This is followed (*ibid.*, 12–18) by a thorough-going demonstration of the falsity of much of Geoffrey's 'history'. In his brief account of the Irish conquest, William specifically rejects the myth of Arthurian rulership over the island: *ibid.*, i, 166, 'fabulosum est'.

[202] James P. Corley, *The Chronicle of Glastonbury Abbey*, trans. David Townsend (Bury St Edmunds, 1985), xlix; Giraldus, *De principis instructione*, ii. 19 (Giraldi Cambrensis, *Opera*, viii, 127–8), 'maxime tamen et evidentissime rex Angliae Henricus secundus, sicut ab historico cantore Britone audierat antiquo, totum monachis indicavit….' Ralph of Coggeshall (*Chronicon Anglicanum*, ed. Joseph Stephenson, RS 66 [London, 1875], 36) had a much more prosaic story—that the tombs of Arthur and Guinevere were found accidentally, when a new grave was dug for a monk who wished to be buried between the two pyramids.

[203] In an ingenious argument addressed to Pope Boniface VIII, he traced his claims to sovereignty over 'Britain' back through Arthur, *Rex Britonum,* who presided over a great festival at Caerleon (*civitas Legionum*), attended by subject kings, including the king of Scots, to Brutus, who lived in the time of the prophets Elias and Samuel. Rymer, *Foedera, Conventiones, Litterae et Acta Publica*, Record Commission, 3 vols in 6 (London, 1816–30), I/ii, 932–3. I am grateful to Brenda Bolton for this reference.

and *rationabiliter*.[204] Equally in accordance with normal papal practice, he would have stated the right by which he acted in the matter,[205] perhaps even citing the 'Donation of Constantine',[206] in which the first Christian emperor was said to have granted Pope Sylvester I and his successors extensive estates in Italy and elsewhere, as well as jurisdiction over 'adjacent' islands. Similar claims had been made explicitly by Urban II in respect of Lipari and Corsica in 1091,[207] and, in his later (1172) recognition of the conquest, addressed to Henry himself, Alexander III was to refer more obliquely to the 'special right' which the Roman church enjoys in an island, as distinct from a large land mass (*Romana ecclesia aliud ius habet in insula quam in terra magna et continua*).[208] Whatever was granted at John's request, it is unlikely to have been quite the *carte blanche* which he made it out to be.

The letter alleged to be the grant is *Laudabiliter*, whose earliest appearance is in Giraldus Cambrensis, where it is attached not to the invasion itself but to its

[204] See, for example, the privilege conferred on Byland abbey on 23 Nov. 1156 (*PUE*, iii, 256–8 no. 116: see below, Part II/ii, no. 2): 'Therefore, dear sons in the Lord, we compassionately approve your just petitions (*iustis petitionibus...annuimus*)...We ordain that whatever possessions or goods that church now possesses canonically and justly (*iuste et canonice*) or shall in the future...acquire through the gift of pontiffs, the generosity of kings or princes, the offering of the faithful, or by any other lawful means (*aliis iustis modis*), shall remain fixed and undiminished to you and to your successors...the place in which the abbey is situated, according to the boundaries contained in the charter of Roger de Mowbray...We confirm also by apostolic authority the liberties and immunities or royal customs reasonably (*rationabiliter*) conferred on your church by our dearest son in Christ, Henry, King of the English and confirmed by the written authority of his charter and ordain that they shall remain inviolate for all time.' In a similar way, a *privilege* for Henry II would have cited the grounds on which the petition was granted, together with some clause limiting the confirmation to what was lawful and just. Note the precision of the 'September letters', below, at n. 221.

[205] See ch. 9, at n. 56.

[206] In fact, an eighth-century forgery, but its authenticity was generally accepted until the fourteenth century, which may, nevertheless, enshrine some authentic elements. In the mid-twelfth century (*tempore* Alexander III), the event was depicted in a small mosaic in the architrave of the portico of the Lateran Palace: Christopher Walter, 'Papal Political Imagery in the Medieval Lateran Palace', Parts i–ii, *Cahiers Archéologiques fin de l'Antiquité et Moyen Age*, 20 (1970), 155–76; 21 (1971), 109–36, i (1970), 170–1 and Fig. 12; Stroll, *Symbols as Power*, 31–2 and Plate 19. Cf. the later (*c.* 1246) fresco in the church of SS. Quattro Coronati: John Mitchell, 'St Silvester and Constantine at the SS. Quattro Coronati', in *Federico II e l'Arte del Ducento Italiano*, ii, *Atti della III Settimana di Studio di Storia del'Arte Medievale dell'Università di Roma (15–20 Maggio, 1978)*, 15–32 at 18–19 and Fig. 3; Walter, 'Papal Political Imagery', ii, 123–4 and Fig. 25.

[207] JL 5448–9; *PL*, cli, 329–31 nos 50–1, esp. 329: 'Cum universae insulae secundum instituta regalis juris sint, constat profecto qui religiosi imperatoris Constantini privilegio in jus proprium B. Petro ejusque successoribus occidentales omnes insulae condonatae sunt, maxime quae circa Italiae oram habentur....' Cf. Ullmann's important discussion in 'Alexander III and the Conquest of Ireland', 376–7.

[208] *Pontificia Hibernica (i), Medieval Papal Chancery Documents concerning Ireland, 640–1261*, ed. Maurice P. Sheehy (Dublin, 1962), 21–2 no. 6, at 22.

aftermath, and linked with a wholly false letter of Alexander III.[209] This is not the place to discuss the authenticity in detail, but historical opinion has been shifting back towards the view that *Laudabiliter* is not quite what it appears to be.[210] Its odd placement in Giraldus, the inconsistencies between its text and John of Salisbury's description, its lack of dating clause, and the absence of any contemporary or near contemporary reference that is not traceable to Giraldus, all make it difficult to accept that it is an accurate copy of the 'privilege' obtained from the pope.[211] On the contary, comparison with the later *Satis laudabiliter*, which, after a similarly fulsome *arenga*,[212] withheld approval for a joint Franco-Angevin crusade in Spain in early 1159, suggests that Giraldus transmitted a falsified version of Adrian's rescript, which omitted crucial passages requiring the prior consultation and support of the Church, princes, and people of the region. Such caution would have been entirely typical of Adrian's actions, which sought conciliation and compromise. Even if Giraldus's text of *Laudabiliter* is taken at face value, it hardly deserves the importance which has been attached to it. It does not make Henry lord, still less king of Ireland: there is no mention of 'hereditary right', or indeed any other kind of 'right', which the king is to exercise in Ireland. After commending Henry's laudable aims to spread abroad the glorious name [of Christ ?] on earth…to enlarge the boundaries of the Church; to reveal the truth of the Christian faith to peoples still untaught and barbarous, and to root out the weeds of vice from the Lord's field', its declaratory clause allows Henry to enter the island for the good purposes stated, and expresses the wish (in the subjunctive voice) that 'the people of that land may receive you honourably and respect you as their lord (*et illius terre populus honorifice te recipiat et sicut dominum ueneretur*)'; and it concludes with an equally open-ended 'if' clause: 'If, then, you wish to bring to a successful conclusion the design you have thus conceived… (*Si ergo quod concepisti animo effectu duxeris prosequente complendum…*).'[213] *Laudabiliter* is certainly no title-deed. It refers to possible events in the future, and makes them contingent upon acceptance of Henry's lordship by 'the people of that land'. This emphasis is certainly very different from John of Salisbury's bald

---

[209] *Expugnatio* (ed. Scott and Martin), 142–7; see below, 'Narrative Sources', Part II/i, no. 2.

[210] Watt, '*Laudabiliter* in Medieval Diplomacy', 420–32 at 420, 432; idem, *Church and Two Nations*, 36, 40; F. X. Martin in Giraldus Cambrensis, *Expugnatio* (ed. Scott and Martin), 278–82; Aubrey Gwynn, S. J., *The Irish Church in the 11th and 12th Centuries*, ed. Gerard O'Brien (Blackrock, 1992), 293.

[211] For a full discussion of the text of *Laudabiliter* and its use in the later Middle Ages, see Anne J. Duggan, 'The Making of a Myth. Giraldus Cambrensis, *Laudabiliter*, and Henry II's Lordship of Ireland', forthcoming. For the ingenious suggestion that there were two bulls—*Laudabiliter* itself and a privilege conforming with John's description, see M. P. Sheehy, 'The bull *Laudabiliter*: a problem in medieval diplomatic and history', *Galway Archaeological and Historical Society Journal*, 29 (1961), 45–70. One should allow, however, that John of Salisbury may have been guilty of self-glorifying exaggeration; and that what he was instrumental in obtaining was considerably less than he claimed.

[212] See below, ch. 9, n. 44.

[213] See below, Part II/i, no. 5b.

assertion that Ireland was granted to Henry II to be held by hereditary right. If *Laudabiliter* is indeed the bull he obtained, then John is guilty of considerable verbal economy, which both amplified the nature of the 'concession' and suppressed the conditions attached to it. But then, the purpose of his reference to the matter of Ireland was to proclaim the extent of his own influence with the recently deceased pope.

It was not, however, concern for the welfare of the Irish that drew Henry II into Irish affairs in 1171, but a combination of risk-management (Richard FitzGilbert de Clare [= Strongbow], earl of Strigoil looked poised to carve out a possibly independent kingdom for himself in Leinster, following marriage to Diarmait Mac Murchada's daughter and defeat of the high-king, Ruaidrí Ua Conchobair outside Dublin in spring 1171), opportunity (appeal of Irish princes against Strongbow),[214] and political advantage (in the aftermath of Becket's murder, it suited him to be outside his own dominions).[215] *Laudabiliter* was neither his justification nor his warrant. There is no evidence at all that it was used in the context of Henry II's establishment of power in Ireland, apart from Giraldus Cambrensis's romantic attempt to justify a conquest in which his own closest relations had played a leading role, and to dress up opportunism in crusading garb. Thereafter, apart from the transmission of Giraldus's text through the filiation of later chroniclers who derived their material directly or indirectly from him, nothing was heard of *Laudabiliter* until the mid- or more probably late thirteenth century, where a version, ultimately derived from Giraldus, was used by Irish ecclesiastical protesters as the basis of an attack on English colonial misrule.[216] Although copies were sent to the Council of Vienne (1311) and to the papal Curia

---

[214] Recorded only by Gervase of Canterbury, *The Historical Works of Gervase of Canterbury*, ed. W. Stubbs, 2 vols, RS 73 (London, 1879–80), i, 234, but plausible, especially in the light of Henry's favourable reception by many Irish leaders, secular and ecclesiastical, after his landing at Bannow Bay, near Waterford, on 17 October 1171, and the ease of his assumption of power; cf. Flanagan, *Irish Society*, 199–203, 206–7, 221–8. Aubrey Gwynn (*The Irish Church*, 304–5) thought that Christian î Conairche, the Cistercian bishop of Lismore (1151–1179), who was papal legate for Ireland from 1152, had been forewarned of Henry's arrival, and had willingly collaborated with him. It was he who presided at the second council of Cashel (1172), which acknowledged Henry's lordship, and it was his name, as legate, that headed the list of Irish prelates who reported Ireland's recognition of Henry II to the pope (below, at n. 221). Cf. Watt, *Church and Two Nations*, 39.

[215] As Gervase said, i, 235, 'ut sententiam interdicti, si forte daretur, facilius declinaret vel occultius observaret.'

[216] Watt, '*Laudabiliter* in Medieval Diplomacy'. Ullmann ('Alexander III and the Conquest of Ireland', 376, n. 19) was misled into thinking that Peter of Blois had inserted a copy of *Laudabiliter* into one of his letter collections by its presence among Peter's letters in *PL*, ccviii (no. 276); but in fact it was not transmitted in any early transcription of the collection and occurs, uniquely, only in one very late (fifteenth-century) manuscript, Cambridge, Trinity College, MS B. I. 18, no. 97 (from among more than 200 MSS of Peter's letters): see E. S. Cohn, 'The Manuscript Evidence for the Letters of Peter of Blois', *EHR*, 41 (1926), 43–60, at 50, 55.

(1317–18), no subsequent pope accepted that it was what it was claimed to be, referring to the letter in which Adrian 'is said (*dicitur*)' to have conferred Ireland on Henry II.[217]

The possibility of an Irish venture had occurred to Henry II in 1155; Adrian IV issued some kind of approval, and an emerald ring for use in a future investiture was transmitted through John of Salisbury in 1156, but there the matter rested. The ring was stored in the treasury and the 'grant' remained a dead letter. Indeed, it is possible that its validity ceased with Adrian's death in 1159.[218] The intervention in Ireland of land-hungry Cambro-Norman nobles in 1169–70, which was followed in 1171–2 by Henry II's seizure of the lordship of the island, resulted from wholly secular events, utterly detached from Adrian's grant.[219] It was the procurement of foreign military support by Diarmait Mac Murchada, the ousted king of Leinster, which initiated the chain reaction that led to the recognition, at Waterford, Dublin, and Cashel in 1171–2, by the kings, princes, and bishops of Ireland, that Henry II was their lawful lord. Their recognition of King Henry was not made in pursuance of any papal directive, however, and may not have been intended to be any more durable than the short-term associations that characterized Irish politics at the time, or to confer direct power on the English king.[220] But Henry came from a very different political environment; and he set about giving legal shape to the traditional forms of Irish lordship. It was his agent, Archdeacon Ralph of Llandaff, who corralled the Irish bishops into announcing the fact of Henry's lordship in letters, which he transmitted to the papal Curia with his own hands, on receipt of which Pope Alexander III duly issued the three famous 'September letters'. Addressed to all three parties: the Irish bishops, the king of England, and the kings and princes of Ireland, and drawn up in the light of written submissions from the prelates and the oral testimony of Henry's own special envoy, they could not have been more explicit about the grounds upon which the pope accepted the *fait accompli* of Henry's assumption of the lordship of Ireland:

(to the prelates): ...we have been informed by your sequence of letters...understanding on the basis of your letters (...*ex vestrarum serie literarum nobis innotuit...ex vestris litteris intelligentes*);

---

[217] *Vetera monumenta Hibernorum et Scotorum historiam illustrantia quae ex Vaticani, Neappolis ac Florentiae tabulariis deprompsit...Ab Honorio PP. III usque ad Paulum PP. III. 1216–1547*, ed. Augustin Theiner (Vatican City, 1864), 201 no. 422, dated Avignon, 30 May, [1318]; *ibid.*, 201–2 no. 423; cf. Watt, '*Laudabiliter* in Medieval Diplomacy', 431–2.

[218] As Aubrey Gwynn supposed, *The Irish Church*, 298.

[219] This was the conclusion of O'Doherty, who had argued so persuasively for the authenticity of *Laudabiliter* (above, n. 161): 'St. Laurence O'Toole', 600–01, 'The assumption that Henry's crossing in 1171 could be regarded as in any way connected with the Bull issued in 1155 [1155–6] seems rather hard to justify'; cf. Watt, *Church and Two Nations*, 36, 'there is no evidence to warrant any linking of the Invasion with any plot to resurrect the primacy of Canterbury in Ireland.'

[220] Flanagan, *Irish Society*, 199–203, 206–7, 221–8.

(to the king): …as our venerable brothers Christian, bishop of Lismore, legate of the Apostolic See, the archbishops and bishops of the land have informed us by their letters, our dear son R[alph], archdeacon of Llandaff, a prudent and discreet man, particularly bound to the royal dignity by the bond of devotion…has carefully and diligently set forth by word of mouth…as we learn from the written information supplied by the archbishops and bishops and more fully and clearly aforesaid archdeacon's report to us… (…*sicut venerabiles fratres nostri Christianus Lesmoriensis episcopus apostolice sedis legatus, archiepiscopi et episcopi terre suis nobis litteris intimarunt, dilectus filius noster R[adulfus] Landavensis archidiaconus, vir prudens et discretus et regie magnitudini vinculo precipue devotionis astrictus…viva voce tam solicite quam prudenter exposuit…sicut eisdem archiepiscopis et episcopis significantibus et prefato archidiacono plenius et expressius nobis referente comperimus…*).

(to the kings and princes of Ireland): …it has become known to us by general rumour and reliable report that you have received our dearest son in Christ H[enry], illustrious king of England, as your king and lord, and that you have sworn fealty to him… (…*communi fama et certa relatione nobis innotuit quod vos karissimum in Christo filium nostrum H[enricum] regem Anglie illustrem in vestrum regem et dominum suscepistis et ei fidelitatem iurastis…*).[221]

It was these letters that constituted the formal papal acknowledgement of the English king's lordship, and they were so recognized at the time. Unlike *Laudabiliter*, which disappeared from the official record until the mid-thirteenth century at the earliest, the Alexandrine letters were publicly promulgated by royal authority at Waterford in 1173,[222] lodged in the royal archive until the early years of John's reign, and finally copied into the *Black Book of the Exchequer*, now in the Public Record Office, where they can still be read.[223] Needless to say, there is in them not a whisper of Adrian or of *Laudabiliter*, as there surely would have been, if the Irish bishops or Henry's own envoy had alluded to either in their submissions to the pope, although the phrase *quod laudabiliter incepisti* in Alexander's letter to the king may echo Adrian's bull.[224]

v. Conclusion

The man chosen in his late forties by Eugenius III and elevated to the top rank of cardinals from the position of abbot of Saint-Ruf is unlikely to have been a nonentity; moreover his discharge of the legation to Scandinavia was a remarkable

---

[221]   *Pontificia Hibernica* (i), 19–23 nos 5–7, at 20, 21, 23.

[222]   Giraldus Cambrensis, *Expugnatio*, ii. 5 (ed. Scott and Martin, 142–7) accurately described the summons of the council, but substituted *Laudabiliter* and the fake *Quoniam ea* for the three genuine letters of Alexander III.

[223]   London, Public Record Office, E. 164/12, fols 8v–9v; cf. *Liber Niger Scaccarii*, ed. Thomas Hearne, 2 vols (Oxford 1771–1774), i (1774), 42–8.

[224]   *Pontificia Hibernica (i)*, 22.

achievement: a diplomatic triumph, if nothing else. The interdict on Rome,[225] at the very beginning of his pontificate, which achieved the goal of driving a wedge between Arnold of Brescia and the general populace, was the action of a strong-minded man; his first encounter with Frederick I between Sutri and Nepi confirms the moral and physical courage which he was to display at Benevento. Adrian was an outsider in all senses of the term. An Englishman, a new-comer, unconnected to any great family, Italian or otherwise, and comparatively young for the office he was to bear. These aspects of his background gave him a refreshing independence of mind. In order to reach a fair assessment of his short pontificate, however, one must strip away the accretions of imperialist and Victorine propaganda, which cast almost the whole of his reign as a deliberate anti-imperial plot. It was Frederick, not Adrian, who had failed to maintain the Constance accord; it was Frederick who had stoked up the Apulian rebellion, and then abandoned the enterprise, leaving Adrian committed to a disastrous war, whose outcome was a humiliating accommodation with William of Sicily: the 'treaty' of Benevento was the price of defeat not the prize of anti-imperial diplomacy. The Besançon incident was Frederick's public repudiation of the Constance accord, cleverly presented as righteous defence of the honour of his imperial crown and a riposte to what his propaganda claimed was Adrian's betrayal of the emperor and the empire at Benevento. Thereafter, only abject capitulation to the emperor's will would have been acceptable. The Lombard revolt was Frederick's responsibility, not Adrian's; and the dual election of 1159 became a schism only because Frederick chose, first to support his preferred candidate, despite the small number of votes cast in his favour, and then to maintain his two successors, despite the opposition of nearly all Europe outside the empire, for a further fourteen years after his death.[226]

Just as William I's triumph at Brindisi in 1156 was an external factor over which Adrian had no control and with which he had to deal, so the reign of the most effective emperor of the century presented serious problems for a papacy struggling to preserve its hard won independence from imperial tutelage. Even if in partnership with the Romano-German empire, the papacy was not a dependency, and it had as much right to look to its own interests as the emperor had to look to his. It is here, of course, that the crux of papal-imperial relations lay. When asked not to negotiate behind the pope's back with the City of Rome in 1159, Frederick had replied, 'Since, by divine ordinance, I am emperor of Rome and am so styled, I have merely the appearance of ruling and bear an utterly empty name, lacking in meaning, if authority over the city of Rome should be torn from my grasp.'[227] What that rule might have implied for the papacy can only be guessed at; but Frederick's view of his rights in the rest of the Italian peninsula as exercised, or

---

[225] Boso, *Vita Adriani*, 389;* cf. Partner, *Lands of St Peter*, 188–9. For a learned, but perhaps romanticized view of the would-be revolutionary, and condemnation of Adrian's treatment of him, see George William Greenaway, *Arnold of Brescia* (Cambridge, 1931), esp. 149–63—though his general assessment of the English pope (149) is favourable.

[226] 'Victor IV' 1159–64; 'Paschal III' 1164–68; 'Calixtus III' 1168–78.

[227] Rahewin, iv. 35* (*Gesta*, 278; *Deeds*, 271).

rather executed, in 1154–5 and 1158–9, and proclaimed at Roncaglia in 1158, raised very serious doubts about his commitment to partnership with an independent papacy, whose territorial and jurisdictional rights he was prepared to honour and maintain.

The so-called 'alliance' with the papacy was nothing more than a useful tool to be discarded when it had served its purpose. The fact of the matter is that after he was safely crowned as emperor Frederick no longer needed anything other than a puppet pope. Any other kind—one who protested against the violation of the dignity of a travelling archbishop, who refused the nomination of an imperial place-man as archbishop of Ravenna, who resisted the collection of the Roncaglian taxes from his lands, who opposed the absorption of the Italian episcopate into his imperial system, who defended the territories of the church—was not what Frederick wanted; and the mere raising of a protest was viewed as an intolerable provocation to the honour of the empire. A little-discussed letter, sent to Frederick in early 1158 by Rainald of Dassel and Otto of Wittelsbach, who had been sent into Italy to receive the submission of cities in preparation for his coming, provides a chilling insight into imperial counsels at that time. Having reported that William of Sicily had angrily dismissed the two cardinals who had been sent to him, because he knew that two others had been sent to the emperor, and that they wished that the emperor could see the whole country (Italy) trembling (*Videretis totam terram tremere)*, the envoys stressed that he should not receive the papal envoys (Henry and Hyacinth) fully into his grace, 'because God has now placed you in such a position, that if you wish you can destroy Rome and have the pope and cardinals entirely at your pleasure.'[228] Rahewin's account of the subsequent interview is equally instructive. 'When to this they [the cardinals] made answer agreeable to the prince and in all respects satisfactory, and promised that the bishop of Rome would do nothing derogatory to the royal dignity, but would always preserve inviolate the honour and the *iusticia* of the empire, he guaranteed peace and friendship both to the supreme pontiff and to all the Roman clergy, and certified it for the absent by giving them also, through those who were present, a kiss in token of peace.'[229]

The prince's peace was dependent on subservience to the prince's will. Given the appointment of *podestà* to oversee the government of the northern cities and the appointment of German nobles and administrators to Italian territories, it might not have been long before the nomination of popes became once more an exercise of imperial *regalia*, as in the days of Otto III[230] and Henry III;[231] and, indeed, the

---

[228] *Pontificum romanorum... vitae*, ed. Watterich, ii, 365, n. 1: 'quia in tali statu Deus vos in praesenti constituit, quod si vultis et Romam destruere et de papa et cardinalibus omnem vestram voluntatem habere.'

[229] Rahewin, iv. 24* (*Gesta*, 197; *Deeds*, 261). Their mission (above, n. 126) had been to restore good relations after the Besançon incident.

[230] Otto nominated Brun of Carinthia (Gregory V, 996–9) and Gerbert (Silvester II, 999–1003).

[231] Suidger of Bamberg (Clement II, 1046–7), Boppo, bishop of Brixen (Damasus II, 1047–8), Bruno of Toul (Leo IX, 1048/9–54), Gebehard of Eichstadt (Victor II, 1054/5–7).

advice of his envoys in 1158 (just cited) and Frederick's maintenance of the papal schism for nineteen long years indicate that such an outcome was not beyond the realms of possibility. Instead of accepting the imperial construct of Adrian's 'betrayal of the empire', historians should examine Frederick's actions and motives more critically, and ask what place would have been left for the papal office in Frederick's *imperium*. Indeed, his imposition of homage as well as fealty on the prelates of his wife's kingdom of Burgundy at the Besançon court in 1157 (the archbishops of Vienne and Lyon, the bishops of Valence and Avignon), accompanied by imperial investiture with their *beneficia*,[232] augured ill for the treatment of Italian prelates, whom, as his response to Adrian's remonstrance in 1159 made plain,[233] he regarded equally as imperial office-holders. Professor Timothy Reuter recognized that even 'the governing elites of the north Italian cities', some of whom had looked to his support in the early years of his reign, came to believe that 'the costs—political and legal, not financial [of Frederick's régime]—were too high.'[234] The point at issue for them was freedom of action; so was it, eventually, for Adrian IV. Thomas Noble's judgment on the eighth-century papacy might equally be applied to Adrian's reign: 'Narrowly, but at great cost, did the popes escape becoming glorified German chaplains.'[235]

The only English pope assumed the papal office at a moment of particular danger. That he was able to maintain the dignity of his office, to make provision for the defence of the territories which he ruled on account of it,[236] and, though he probably did not know it at the time, to contribute to the development of its future policy, owed much to his own courage and pragmatism. The future of the papacy was to be determined by other men and other events, but he had played his part in guiding it securely through an extremely critical phase of its long history.

---

[232] Rahewin, iii. 12 (*Gesta*, 179–80; *Deeds*, 186–7).

[233] Rahewin, iv.35.*

[234] 'The Origins of the German *Sonderweg*? The Empire and its Rulers in the High Middle Ages', in *Kings and Kingship in Medieval Europe*, ed. Anne J. Duggan, King's College London Medieval Studies, 10 (London, 1993), 179–211, esp. 206, citing Alfred Haverkamp, *Herrschaftsformen der Frühstaufer in Reichsitalien*, Monographien zur Geschichte des Mittelalters, 1, 2 vols (Stuttgart, 1970), 37–101.

[235] Thomas F. X. Noble, *The Republic of St Peter. The Birth of the Papal State, 680–825* (Philadelphia, 1984), 335.

[236] See Brenda Bolton, ch. 8, below.

Chapter 8
Nova familia beati Petri.
Adrian IV and the Patrimony
Brenda Bolton

One surviving fragment from the missing *Register* of Pope Adrian IV dramatically highlights the determination with which the English pope set about recovering and reorganizing those lost territories within the Patrimony, which were claimed to belong by right to St Peter and the Holy Roman Church.[1] This problem he faced directly on his election. Acting on Adrian's personal instructions, an armed papal force under the command of Boso, cardinal deacon of SS. Cosma e Damiano,[2] mounted the siege of Acquapuzza, a strategic fortification or *castrum* near Sezze in Marittima.[3] Atenolfo, its lord, was in rebellion against the Church, and from his stronghold was threatening the free passage of travellers between Albano and Terracina, where the road deviated to pass above the Pontine Marshes to the west and skirted the foothills of the Monte Lepini to the east. On 27 September 1158, the end of this lengthy siege was marked when three of Adrian's men compelled the defeated Atenolfo to hoist the papal banner, the *vexillum sancti Petri*, and fly it from the top of his tower.[4] Atenolfo was then marched off to Cardinal Boso's tent where, in the presence of Peter, cardinal deacon of S. Eustachio,[5] Odo Frangipane, Geoffrey of Ceccano, and a host of knights and foot soldiers, he was obliged to concede the fortifications of Acquapuzza to the cardinals and to swear on the holy gospels that he would unreservedly place himself and his *castrum* in the custody and disposition of the pope himself.

The ritual ceremony of *receptio*, the formal handing over of the *castrum*, was resumed on the following day, 28 September, when the papal guard escorted Atenolfo to nearby Albano where Adrian IV, *residens in consistorio*, had gathered together his cardinals.[6] Bare-footed, with a halter around his neck indicating that

---

[1] *Liber censuum*, i, 427, no. 168; Paul Kehr, *Regesta Romanorum Pontificium – Italia Pontificia*, ii, *Latium* (Berlin, 1907), 130.

[2] 4 January 1157–2 August 1165, Brixius, 58; Zenker, 149–52.

[3] Pierre Toubert, *Les structures du Latium médiéval: le Latium méridional et la Sabine du ixe siècle à la fin du xiie siècle*, Bibliothèque des Écoles françaises d'Athènes et de Rome, 221, 2 vols (Rome, 1973), i, 313–5. *Castrum* was used to describe any fortified habitation in the Patrimony in the twelfth century, while *rocca castri* implied a central fortification or castle.

[4] For a similar ceremony on 10 December 1216 to raise the papal *vexillum* on the *rocca* of Fumone, near Alatri, see *Liber censuum*, i, 470, no. 218.

[5] Appointed March 1158, Brixius, 59; Zenker, 175–7.

[6] 'Prostravit se ad pedes domni pape in consistorio residenti[s]...astantibus episcopis, cardinalibus et aliis multis', *Liber censuum*, i, 427, no. 168.

his absolution as an excommunicate had taken place in accordance with the custom of the Church, Atenolfo prostrated himself at the pope's feet. In the presence of the cardinals and many others, he handed over a symbolic myrtle staff[7] in submission after defeat and consigned the *castrum* to Adrian in recognition of the pope's rights to it, *quod juris beati Petri esset*. In addition, Atenolfo offered his son as a hostage, together with sureties for eight hundred pounds *afforciatorum*, the 'strong' money of Lucca,[8] and swore liege homage and fidelity to the pope, to his successors, and to the Holy Roman Church. He further swore to observe the peace on the public highway—a significant promise, given the proximity of his *castrum* to the Via Appia. Adrian, displaying the 'accustomed benevolence' of the Holy See,[9] then invested Atenolfo with his *castrum* and returned Acquapuzza to him as a fief. Atenolfo, in turn, promised to perform fully his feudal obligations to the pope and his successors, to serve the papacy with his knights and dependants to the best of his ability, and to make peace and war only according to the papal mandate. He further agreed that should the Lord Pope at any time wish to wage war against other men of his *castrum*, he would freely allow him to do so, and willingly receive there the Roman pontiffs and their officials or legates.

The meticulously enacted ritual of the *receptio* of Acquapuzza in 1158 indicates the importance which Adrian, and indeed his predecessor, Eugenius III, attached to the recovery of such *castra*. Certain recurring elements emerge from the detail: the symbolism implicit in raising the papal banner over recovered papal territory, the high visibility of papal judgment *in consistorio*; submission by the rebel, with sworn oaths and the handing over of the staff of punishment; severe terms of imposed surety or bail; the public yet humane manifestation of papal sovereignty, with its explicit absolution; corporeal investiture of the fief; the obligation to maintain the peace of the highway, and the implementation of a device of high significance—that of returning strategic strongholds in the Patrimony to papal control without necessarily demanding their permanent restitution— referred to as the 'benevolence' of the pope towards the inhabitants of these fortifications.[10] Certainly, much behind-the-scenes negotiation would have been essential in order to maintain an equilibrium between ritual humiliation and positive gains by both parties to the agreement.[11] This *receptio* appears all the more striking when it is considered that it was not an Italian who was responsible for its implementation but one whose origins, however cosmopolitan he may have later become,[12] lay in England. Adrian IV's role in the recovery of the Patrimony of St Peter has generally been accorded scant mention.[13] Even Pierre Toubert, *maestro*

---

[7] In the Ancient World *fustis* was associated with a military death by beating.

[8] Toubert, *Structures*, i, 592–5.

[9] *Liber censuum*, i, 427, no. 168, 'Tunc domnus papa de consueta benignitate sedis apostolice investivit predictum A....'; Toubert, *Structures*, ii, 1152, n. 2.

[10] Toubert, *Structures*, ii, 1042.

[11] On ritual humiliation in context see Geoffrey Koziol, *Begging Pardon and Favour. Ritual and Political Order in Early Medieval France* (Ithaca/London, 1992).

[12] See chs. 1–4 above.

[13] Typically brief are the introductions by Daniel Waley, *Mediaeval Orvieto: The Politi-*

of studies on Latium in the eleventh and twelfth centuries, considered that it was 'inutile de reprendre pièce après pièce le dossier des succès pontificaux'.[14] Toubert was surely correct in arguing for a wide, analytical overview of the consequences of conquest and reorganization in the Patrimony from the 1050s down to the 1150s and beyond, and his magisterial study of 1500 pages is invaluable. Even so, it is hoped that a more focused, 'worm's eye' view of Adrian IV's energetic involvement in the recovery of papal rights and territories within the Patrimony—a process more usually associated with his successors, Celestine III (1191–98) and Innocent III (1198–1216)—will reveal that his pontificate merits close attention.[15]

The Patrimony of St Peter which Adrian IV was seeking to recover for the Church, was an assemblage of lands with Rome at its centre, largely based on the ancient duchies of Rome and Spoleto, over which the popes claimed various rights.[16] In 781, Pope Adrian I (772–95), having claimed the restoration of all papal lands inside these duchies, entered into an agreement with the emperor Charlemagne which eventually fixed the northern frontier at the ancient limits of suburbicarian or Roman Tuscany, that is, Tuscia Romana, as far as Radicofani and Aquapendente.[17] The region of the Sabina marked a less well-defined boundary eastwards to the Apennines. The River Liri formed the frontier between Campania, Marittima and the Regno, Ceprano being its southernmost town.[18] While it is difficult to show that Adrian IV consciously modelled himself on papal namesakes, the first Adrian's *Vita* in the *Liber Pontificalis* was lengthy and richly detailed,[19] listing his many gifts and solid achievements—including the repair of an aqueduct[20] and the creation of four new *domuscultae* or papal estates close to Rome.[21] Adrian I also established as *diaconiae* or deaconries, with special responsibilities for the

cal History of an Italian City-State, 1157–1334 (Cambridge, 1952), xv, 1–4; idem, *The Papal States in the Thirteenth Century* (London, 1951), 11–13. An excellent short analytical account is given by Peter Partner, *The Lands of St Peter: The Papal State in the Middle Ages and Early Renaissance* (London, 1972), 188–202.

[14] Toubert, *Structures*, ii, 1129.

[15] Michele Maccarrone, *Studi su Innocenzo III*, Italia Sacra. Studi e Documenti di Storia Ecclesiastica, 17 (Padua, 1972), 9–22, esp. 10, n. 1.

[16] For this whole complex period, see Thomas F. X. Noble, *The Republic of St Peter. The Birth of the Papal State, 680–825* (Philadelphia, 1984), espec. 153–83.

[17] See *Liber censuum*, i, 363–5 for the donation of 817 by Louis the Pious to Paschal I known as the *Ludovicianum*. The provisions were essentially determined by the agreement of 781.

[18] Maria Teresa Caciorgna, *Marittima medievale: Territori, società, poteri* (Rome, 1996), 3–8.

[19] *Liber Pontificalis*, I, 234–43; *The Lives of the Eighth-Century Popes* (Liber Pontificalis), trans., intro., and commentary, Raymond Davis, Translated Texts for Historians, 13 (Liverpool, 1992), 107–72.

[20] The Sabbatina aqueduct which took water to the atrium of St Peter's and the mills of the Gianicolo, *ibid.*, 152–3, 165–6.

[21] Capracorum at Santa Cornelia, south of Nepi; Galeria at Santa Rufina on the Via Aurelia; a second Galeria on the Via Portuensis; Calvisianum on the Via Ardeatina. All these estates were some 15 miles distant from Rome, *ibid.*, 147–50.

poor, the churches of SS. Cosma e Damiano and S. Adriano 'the martyr' on the Roman Forum.[22] The text of the *Vita* would have made excellent reading for a pontiff intent on enhancing the possessions of St Peter in and around Rome, a model indeed for Adrian IV and for those who advised him, to take to heart.

Adrian was already widely travelled by the time he became pope. As Nicholas Breakspear, he had taken passage from England to Avignon and, subsequently, as abbot of Saint Ruf, had crossed and re-crossed those northern parts of the Patrimony, passing through Tuscia Romana or the Sabina, on his way to Rome.[23] His legatine journey to Scandinavia as a cardinal[24] would certainly have made him aware of the depredations of former papal territory and dangers of the roads. His considerable administrative skills, so apparent to Eugenius III,[25] were demonstrated to a wider audience in his efficient yet sensitive handling of the Scandinavian mission between 1152 and 1154.[26] Nicholas's vision and ability were not only appreciated but moreover shared by two close contemporaries, Boso and Cardinal Roland, themselves men of intelligence and probity whom Eugenius had likewise singled out for special advancement. The Tuscan Boso served as a temporary official in the papal secretariat during the vacancy of 1149 to 1152,[27] but issued documents only as *scriptor*,[28] never officially holding the title of *cancellarius* or chancellor.[29] Roland, from Siena and a canon regular of Pisa,[30] whose rapid promotion to curial office (?1148) may have slightly predated that of Adrian,[31] was appointed as *cancellarius* of the Roman Church by Eugenius III

---

[22]   *Ibid.*, 165.

[23]   On 25 January 1147, he was in Vico d'Elsa between Certaldo and Poggibonsi on the Via Francigena, see Egger, ch. 2, at n. 49 above. Compare Giovanni Caselli, *La Via Romea: 'Camino di Dio'* (Florence, 1990), 131–3 and Francesco Dufour, *Le Strade Cristiane per Roma* (Milan, 1998), 114–8 for the importance of this area as a staging post. An alternative route from Montpellier to Rome was that taken in 1150 by Benjamin of Tudela. He sailed from Marseilles to Genoa, thence to Pisa and Lucca, arriving in Rome six days later, Debra Birch, *Pilgrimage to Rome in the Middle Ages* (Woodbridge, 1998), 48.

[24]   See Berquist, ch. 4 above. Compare Birch, *Pilgrimage to Rome*, 41–9, for the exactly contemporary reverse journey made in *c.*1150 from Iceland by the pilgrim, Nikolas of Munkathvera, who passed through Aquapendente, Bolsena, Viterbo, and Sutri on his way to Rome.

[25]   See Egger. ch. 2, at n. 51 above.

[26]   See Berquist, ch. 4 above.

[27]   F. Geisthardt, *Der Kämmerer Boso*, Historische Studien, 293 (Berlin, 1935), 25–40, suggests that he came either from Pisa or Lucca.

[28]   6 November 1149–3 May 1153, Brixius, 58; Zenker, 150. Cf. 10 January 1150, *PUE*, iii, 205–7, n. 75 and 1 November 1150, 207–8, n. 77.

[29]   Geisthardt, *Der Kämmerer Boso*, 80–2; I. S. Robinson, *The Papacy 1073–1198* (Cambridge, 1990), 95.

[30]   J. T. Noonan, Jr., 'Who was Rolandus?' in *Law, Church and Society: Essays in Honor of Stephan Kuttner*, ed. Kenneth Pennington and Robert Somerville (Philadephia, 1977), 21–48, esp. 35.

[31]   Brixius, 55–7, 112; Zenker, 85–8. Roland was cardinal deacon of SS. Cosma e Damiano by 23 October 1150 and cardinal priest of S. Marco by 30 March 1151.

some time before May 1153, and continued to serve Anastasius IV during his brief pontificate.

The election to the papacy of Nicholas Breakspear, friend and colleague of both Boso and Roland, provided the opportunity for all three to work closely together as a team in the most important curial positions.[32] Adrian acted immediately and positively in December 1154 to retain Roland as *cancellarius* and to appoint Boso as *camerarius* or chamberlain, at the head of the papal household, raising him to the cardinalate in January 1157. Boso's tenure of office during Adrian's pontificate was particularly crucial.[33] As *camerarius*, he acted variously as paymaster of the papal troops, as collector of the large amounts of money necessary to win over the Roman commune and papal vassals alike, and as archivist-custodian of venerable papal charters, early rent books, and titles to land. His diligent management of the financial and property records of the Holy See included the maintenance of detailed records of papal rights and revenues.[34] As chamberlain, Boso enjoyed a privileged access to ancient documents in the papal archives,[35] and he had responsibility for unearthing all the charters, confirmations, deeds, and financial transactions which would facilitate the recovery of papal lands.[36] Among many of his duties was the compilation of revised biographies of the popes from Leo IX onwards, and the composition of contemporary *vitae*, not only for Adrian IV and Roland (later Alexander III), but also for their predecessors, Eugenius III and Anastasius IV.[37] Boso was thus responsible for compiling or composing a significant proportion of the surviving source material dealing with papal recovery in the Patrimony, including Adrian's own work to this end. Boso himself was also a significant protagonist in the territorial recovery, illustrated by his leading role in the military campaign and capture of Acquapuzza. His *Vita Adriani*, although naturally written from a papal perspective, was a moderate and intelligent account of an eyewitness—a confidant of Adrian during his stay at Benevento, his companion and activist in investigative itineration around the Patrimony, and a friend 'who remained assiduously at his side until his death'.[38]

---

[32] Stefan Hirschmann, *Die päpstliche Kanzlei und ihre Urkundenproduktion (1141–1159)*, Europäische Hochschulschriften, iii/913 (Frankfurt-am-Main/Berlin/Berne, 2001).

[33] Geisthardt, *Der Kämmerer Boso*, 55–6.

[34] He was the forerunner of Cencius *Camerarius* and the *Liber censuum* of 1192. See T. Montecchi Palazzi, 'Cencius Camerarius et la formation du *Liber censuum* de 1192', *Mélanges de l'École française de Rome*, 96 (1984), 49–93.

[35] 'sicut continetur in publico eorum instrumento quod est in arcivis repositum', *Vita Adriani*, 396.*

[36] Toubert, *Structures*, ii, 1048–50 argues that Boso was the prototype of a new efficient and bureaucratic papal machinery of government, with teams of chancery clerks or papal chaplains, under the direction of a cardinal, empowered to carry out increasingly important tasks.

[37] For Boso's continuation of the *Liber Pontificalis*, see Odilo Engels, 'Kardinal Boso als Geschichtsschreiber', in *idem, Stauferstudien, Beiträge zur Geschichte der Staufer im 12. Jahrhundert*, ed. Erich Meuthen and Stefan Weinfurter, 2nd edn (Sigmaringen, 1996), 203–24.

[38] '…assidue usque ad ipsius obitum familiariter secum permansit', *Vita Adriani*, 397.*

Whilst the level of territorial recovery pursued in the Patrimony between the years 1155 and 1159 was unprecedented, the methods used were not specific to Adrian, nor did they result from his roots in 'feudal' England, as some have wished to believe.[39] Toubert has indicated that the geographical origins of most of the reforming popes of the eleventh century—Leo IX, Alexander II and Urban II— linked them to regions where feudal ideas were far more developed than in the Patrimony and has rightly pointed out that the English pope would have been able neither to import feudal elements from elsewhere nor to impose from above a new institutional system.[40] Adrian's English connections were not, therefore, significant in this sense. His activities were a clear continuation of those already vigorously pursued by Eugenius III, himself a Pisan and a Cistercian, in conformity with the actions of those reforming popes who were the predecessors of both men. Indeed, the evolution of these activities had, by the mid-twelfth century, enabled the papacy to put in place an impressive network of so-called *castra specialia SRE*, special fortified strongholds of the Holy Roman Church which, in return for their privileged status, bore certain defensive obligations.[41]

The reforming popes of the mid-eleventh century had led the way in inflicting serious damage on those noble families who had dominated the Patrimony for the previous fifty years. In spite of other pressing problems, Leo IX (1048–54) managed to reduce the power of the Tuscolani, the counts of Galeria, and the Crescenzi Ottaviani, thus clearing the way to enable his successors gradually to stabilize and consolidate their position through the acquisition of *castra*.[42] Two highly significant documents, specifically relating to the Sabina but indicative of contemporary papal methods elsewhere in the Patrimony, survive from the pontificate of Nicholas II (1058–61). In the first of these, essentially a 'model' contract or charter of *incastellamento*,[43] the pope set out the conditions on which he would agree to repopulate Roccantica, a deserted *castrum* purchased by the Church from its former lord.[44] This charter enforced a number of general obligations on the new inhabitants, in particular, provision for the rebuilding of the derelict buildings of Roccantica,[45] but it also included a number of highly original clauses, which illu-

[39] For example, K. Jordan, 'Die Entstehung der römischen Kurie', *ZRG kan. Abt.*, 28 (1939), 97–135. Compare Waley, *The Papal State*, 12–3; Partner, *Lands of St Peter*, 192–3.

[40] Toubert, *Structures*, ii, 1128 and n. 2.

[41] *Ibid.*, 1074; Robinson, *The Papacy*, 30–2.

[42] Toubert, *Structures*, ii, 1068–81 for an excellent summary on which this paragraph is based.

[43] For *incastellamento* see Giovanni Tabacco, 'Problemi di insediamento e di popolamento nell'alto Medioevo', *Rivista Storica Italiana*, 79 (1967), 67–110.

[44] 'Breve di Niccolò II Pontifice estratto dall'Archivio di Roccantica' in Francesco Paolo Sperandio, *Sabina sagra e profana, antica e moderna*, Historiae urbium et regionum Italiae variores, 16 (Rome, 1790, repr.. Bologna, 1967), 373–4, no. 37. This document survived by being inserted into a letter of Martin V, dated 1423, and was discovered by Sperandio. Compare Kehr, *Italia Pontificia*, ii, 72, n. 1; Giulio Silvestrelli, *Città, Castelli e Terre della regione Romana*, intro. P. Fedele (2nd edn, Rome, 1940), 442; Toubert, *Structures*, i, 402–3; ii, 1070–1.

[45] '...ut eam cum appendiciis ejus domibus reedificatis', Sperandio, *Sabina sagra*, 373.

minate the political motives underlying the foundation and particular features of this papal *castrum*. Each new settler was to pay annually to St Peter a graduated sum or *pensio*, according to their means, *secundum quantitatem possibilitatis suae*, at levels between twelve, eight, six and four pence.[46] They were also to be compelled to pay the *fodrum* or hearth tax and to acknowledge their subjection in all matters to the justice of the pope or his agents, *nuncii*.[47] In exchange, the pope took the *castrum* under his special protection, promising to defend Roccantica against all emperors, dukes, *marchese*, or counts.[48] The second document, a contract between Nicholas II and the inhabitants of *castrum Lori*, present-day Montasola, differs from the first in that the pope did not issue a summons to colonists to repopulate a deserted *castrum* but was concerned with an existing small rural community, which had placed itself under the special protection of the Roman Church.[49] Provisions for *castrum Lori* were similar to those at Roccantica on essential matters such as the payment of a graduated tax, *secundum ordines et conditiones*, recognition of the pope's exclusive rights in the matter of *fodrum* and *placitum*, and submission to *nuntii* and papal vicars.[50]

The contracts sanctioned by Nicholas II in his charters for Roccantica and *castrum Lori* were almost certainly not unique, but they reveal the early efforts of the papacy to exert authority by creating *castra immediate subjecta*, strongholds immediately subject to the Church, and particularly concentrated at the northern frontier of the Patrimony.[51] The military obligations might involve the erection of a fortified tower inside a *castrum*, the defence of its fortifications by *milites*, and the loss of tenure by the inhabitants of the *castrum*, should they offer their services to the pope's enemies. Although the papacy's reverses within the Patrimony were substantial during the pontificate of Urban II (1089–99), his successors were fully determined to maintain the impetus at the frontiers.

Paschal II (1099–1119) regained the *castra* of Ponza and Afile in the Tiburtina (1109) and Ninfa in Marittima (1110).[52] Calixtus II (1119–24) and Honorius II (1124–30), with the support of the Frangipane and the lords of Ceccano, were responsible for creating *castra specialia* along the southern frontier with the Regno at Montefortino,[53] Lariano, Giuliano, San Stefano, and Acquapuzza.[54] Following the Anacletan Schism (1130–8), the period of the 1140s and 1150s actually wit-

---

[46] '…majores scilicet denarios duodecim, inferiors autem retrogradu octo denarios, tertio denarios sex, quarto denarios duos', *Ibid*; Toubert, *Structures*, ii, 1070, n. 4.

[47] Sperandio, *Sabina sagra*, 373.

[48] A clause which Toubert took to refer to Spoleto or to the abbey of Farfa, Toubert, *Structures*, ii, 1071, n. 4.

[49] Vatican City, Biblioteca Apostolica Vaticana, MS Carte Borgiane, fasc. 31; Otto Vehse, *Die päpstliche Herrschaft in der Sabina bis zur Mitte des 12. Jahrhunderts* (Rome-Regensburg, 1929–30), 172–3; Toubert, *Structures*, i, 391–2; ii, 1071–3.

[50] Vehse, *Die päpstliche Herrschaft*, 173.

[51] Toubert, *Structures*, ii, 1073.

[52] *Liber censuum*, i, 407, nos 131–2; *Vita Paschalis*, *Liber Pontificalis*, ii, 303.

[53] Today Artena.

[54] Caciorgna, *Marittima medievale*, 4–5; Toubert, *Structures*, ii, 1074–6, esp. 1075, n. 6.

nessed a gradual diminution of conflict in Tuscia Romana, the Sabina and Marittima.[55] While the City of Rome was set apart from the Patrimony by the Commune, which pressed for the *Renovatio Senatus* during 1144 and 1145, the Roman revolt, far from weakening the papacy, actually helped to reinforce its ties with an important element among the local nobility of the Patrimony.[56]

In spite of his various political difficulties, it was early on in his pontificate, between 1146 and 1149, that Eugenius III appears to have resumed the policy of purchasing *castra* in order to build up a chequerboard of fortifications across the Patrimony. Not one of these was without its strategic importance. In an exchange dated 6 December 1146, Eugenius obtained from count Gerald of Vetralla the *castrum* of Petrignano, on the Via Cassia between Viterbo and Vetralla, for a pledge of 200 pounds in money of Lucca,[57] while a document dated 2 June 1149 records that Reynald, Gerald's son, handed over his *castra* of Piazzano and Mazzano near Sutri in pledge for forty-two pounds.[58] In 1151, Bernard, cardinal priest of San Clemente,[59] acted as the pope's representative in buying a half share in the town of Tuscolo, Monte Porzio and Montefortino, in exchange for the town of Trevi and a sum of money, thus establishing a strong papal presence in the heart of the Patrimony between the Alban Hills and the Monte Lepini.[60] In 1153, Eugenius returned to the scheme of strengthening the frontiers by displaying his strategic interest in Radicofani and Rocca San Stefano to the north of Tuscia Romana and Fulmone[61] or Falvaterra in the south.[62] Nearer to Rome, the pope also bought land at the Ponte Lucano on the River Aniene near Tivoli, astride the Via Tiburtina, having accumulated substantial sums of money with which to buy back the most important *castra*. Eugenius's English successor was to follow up his activities with even greater determination.

In Adrian's relatively short reign of four years, six months, and twenty-eight days, he spent almost exactly half the time outside Rome, either sheltering in the papal enclave of Benevento or in travelling around the Patrimony.[63] The *Vita Adriani* in the *Liber Pontificalis* falls short of providing every detail of Adrian's activity but it does reveal that, in the first two years of the pontificate, his itineration around the Patrimony occurred in short sharp bursts, reflecting the political situation. The earliest journeys were those he made between May and July 1155 in order to meet Frederick Barbarossa who was travelling southwards towards Rome

[55] *Ibid.*, 1127.

[56] Robert L. Benson, 'Political *Renovatio*: Two Models', in *Renaissance and Renewal in the Twelfth Century*, ed. Robert L. Benson and Giles Constable with Carol D. Lanham (Oxford, 1982), 339–85, at 340–2.

[57] 6 December 1146, *Liber censuum*, i, 384, no. 95.

[58] Today Mazzano Romano. *Liber censuum*, i, 384–5, no. 96.

[59] Bernard, cardinal priest of S. Clemente, 31 December 1145–3 October 1158, Brixius, 53, 136; Zenker, 29–32.

[60] 10 December 1151, *Liber censuum*, i, 382–3, no. 92; 29 December 1152, 383, no. 93.

[61] Kehr, *Italia Pontificia*, ii, 158; Partner, *Lands of St Peter*, 186–7.

[62] 29 May 1153, *Liber censuum*, i, 380–2, no. 91.

[63] See Adrian's itinerary, below, Appendix.

along the Via Cassia to be consecrated and crowned as emperor. Adrian left the City after 9 May, travelling north to meet the emperor, and in early June received imperial messengers at Viterbo who informed him that Frederick had already reached San Quirico d'Orcia. Adrian's clear intention was to move on to Orvieto, 'that most protected place', and make it the setting for his meeting with Frederick I, but realizing that he would be unable to get there, he turned aside to Civita Castellana.[64] From there he travelled by way of Nepi to Sutri where Frederick I was encamped, returning to Nepi where the emperor eventually performed the office of *strator*. Following the imperial coronation of 18 June 1155 at St Peter's, Adrian and Frederick left the City together, fording the River Tiber at Magliano, and entering the Sabina by way of the abbey of Farfa and the *castrum* of Poli. They then celebrated the Feast of the Apostles Peter and Paul (29 June) together at Ponte Lucano on the Via Tiburtina, outside Tivoli, before going on their different ways.

About the time of the Feast of St Michael, 29 September 1155, Adrian went to San Germano, the town lying in the valley beneath the great abbey of Montecassino, thence to the *castrum* of Mignano, arriving, in November, at Benevento in papal territory. Following the conclusion of the accord of Benevento in June 1156,[65] the pope was presented with the opportunity to assert his power in Rome and the Patrimony and this he seized.[66] Adrian stayed in Benevento from November 1155 for nearly eight months. Leaving that city in July 1156, he travelled to Montecassino and across the Abruzzo—along the boundaries of the Samnites—by Monte Marsicano to Narni (a very long and mountainous route), and turned northwards to Orvieto, which he had first intended to visit in 1155 and finally reached at the end of September 1156. From there, he arrived at the 'pleasant and populous' *castrum* of Viterbo where he spent part of October but, as winter was approaching, he returned to the Lateran by 12 November 1156.[67] Boso then ignores any further itineration by Adrian but lists the pope's few building projects in Rome[68] and his numerous acquisitions in the Patrimony in the typical formulaic style of the *Liber Pontificalis*, ending on 1 September 1159 with Adrian's death at Anagni.

Even before 1159, a visible papal presence was becoming linked to a more itinerant lifestyle within the Patrimony. The control of powerful noble families which had, in the eleventh century and even in the early twelfth, reduced the papal sphere of action to a few small and temporary refuges, began to grow weaker and, while the popes might still be subjected to periods of exile or lengthy absences from Rome, their perambulations in the wider region resembled rather those of a sovereign than an outcast.[69] Once the popes had begun to move more frequently

---

[64] *Vita* Adrian, i 390.*
[65] See Duggan, ch. 7, part i (c), above.
[66] Partner, *Lands of St Peter*, 191–202, at 191.
[67] *Vita Adriani*, 395.*
[68] *Ibid.*, 395–6.* He restored the roof of the chapel of S. Processo at St Peter's and raised the height of the walls at the chapel of S. Giovanni in Fonte. At the Lateran Palace, he had a cistern installed, and other necessary repairs, while at SS. Cosma e Damiano, he dedicated the altar.
[69] Toubert, *Structures*, ii, 1051.

around the Patrimony, more permanent resting places were required than the ephemeral shelter which tents or pavilions had provided. By 1154, a summer *palatium* had been raised at Segni, in addition to Eugenius III's new and better-fortified palace at St Peter's[70] where Adrian sheltered for the first five months of his pontificate. In March 1155, acting through an intermediary, Adrian rented for four deniers in money of Pavia a house belonging to the *episcopium* of Veroli at Monte San Giovanni near Bauco (Boville Ernica).[71] While the house at Monte San Giovanni may have been a temporary staging post, a whole series of summer palaces—Ferentino, Veroli, Alatri, Anagni, and Rieti—were springing up across the southern Patrimony and the Sabina as well as more substantial winter quarters, such at Albano, where Adrian had his headquarters in January 1158.[72]

One of Boso's duties as chamberlain, was to act as custodian of the papacy's territorial possessions,[73] the scope of this office being greatly increased during his tenure by Adrian's reorganization which helped to put in place a local administration. The officials and the bureaucracy who carried out this policy 'dont le cardinal Boson apparaît comme le prototype'[74] were effective in supporting the pope. On the ground, teams of officials, headed by one or more cardinals and supported by chancery clerks and papal chaplains, performed both judicial and military tasks. Adrian seems to have operated in the Patrimony through four leading cardinals,[75] in particular, Boso, created cardinal in 1157[76] and Roland, but, in addition, Julius, successively cardinal priest of S. Marcello and cardinal bishop of Palestrina,[77] and Hubald, cardinal priest of Santa Prassede and future Lucius III.[78] The official charged with preparing the pope's journeys around the Patrimony was the *comes*

---

[70] 'Fecit unum palatium apud Sanctum Petrum et Signie alterum', *Liber Pontificalis*, ii, 387; Anna Maria Voci, *Nord o Sud? Note per la storia del medioevale* palatium apostolicum apud Sanctum Petrum *e delle sue cappelle*, Capellae Apostolicae Sixtinaeque Collectanea Acta Monumenta, 2 (Città del Vaticano, 1992), 21–44, at 22. An approximate date is given by Toubert, *Structures*, 1052, n. 3, citing in an entry in the Chapter Archives of Veroli, n. 531, for 28 August 1152, 'Factum est hoc in presentia domini Eugenii III in civitate Signina, in palatio quod a fundamento construi fecit idem dominus, in presentia dominorum episcoporum et cardinalium…'.

[71] *Ibid.*, 1052, n. 2.

[72] *Liber censuum*, i, 427, no. 168.

[73] For example, in 1127, John, *camerarius* to Honorius II, acquired land in the papal enclave of Benevento. See Otto Vehse, 'Benevent als Territorium des Kirchenstaates bis zum Beginn der avignonesischen Epoche', *QF*, 22 (1930–1), 87–150; 23 (1931–32), 80–119, at 85.

[74] Toubert, *Structures*, ii, 1049.

[75] *Ibid.*, 1050. Roland, Julius, and Hubald were all sent to negotiate the accord of Benevento of June 1156. See *Vita Adriani*, 395* and ch. 7, part i (c), above.

[76] See n. 2, above.

[77] Brixius, 52; Zenker, 42–3. Cardinal priest of S. Marcello, 28 May 1144–3 October 1158; cardinal bishop of Palestrina, 1 January 1159–30 September 1161; apostolic vicar in Rome once Alexander III was driven into exile; d. 1165.

[78] Brixius, 43; Zenker, 22–5. Hubald, a Luccese, was cardinal priest of S. Prassede 21 June 1141–6 November 1158, cardinal bishop of Ostia, 19 December 1158–24 May 1181and elected pope as Lucius III, 1 Sept. 1181–25 Nov. 1185.

Campanie, or rector of Campania. This office of rector first appeared during the pontificate of Eugenius III when Peter of Ceprano arbitrated in an inheritance dispute between members of a local aristocratic family.[79] In November 1153, John, cardinal priest of SS. Giovanni e Paolo,[80] having been invested by Anastasius IV with the functions of rector, obtained the surrender to the Roman Church of vacant fiefs in three *castra* in Campania.[81] Adrian IV maintained John in office as rector, and as such he was entrusted with preparing the papal journey into the southern parts of the Patrimony, concluding with the bishop of Veroli a contract to rent a house at Monte San Giovanni.[82] This act is significant, for it reveals the stability of the office of rector, indispensable at this decisive period in the evolution of a coherent local territorial policy. Additionally, the rector ruled over an embryonic grouping of local personnel, the *curie Campanie*, to which was devolved the composition of administrative writings. At some undetermined date between 1155 and 1158, Adrian replaced John as rector with Simon, cardinal deacon of S. Maria in Domnica.[83]

Although Boso placed first in importance the papal acquisition of Orvieto, achieved only 'with great labour and diligence', he added to his list a string of other, lesser papal acquisitions: Corchiano, Santa Cristina, San Stefano with half of Proceno and Repesena, Poli, Radicofani, Orchia, land near Ponte Lucano and half of four *castra*, named as Castiglione Teverino, Cinigiano, Canepina, and Bulsignano. Considerable sums of money were paid and, although Boso makes clear that these were expensive outgoings, there is no specific indication as to the way in which these payments were financed.[84] It is possible that there was some interrelationship between the sales and purchases recorded in the more than twenty instruments of sale, deeds, and other documents concerning land transactions,[85]

---

[79] G. Falco, 'L'amministrazione papale nella Campagna e nella Marittima dalla caduta della dominazione bizantina al sorgere dei Comuni', *Archivio della Società Romana di storia patria*, 38 (1915), 677–707 at 694; Toubert, *Structures*, ii, 1056.

[80] John, cardinal priest of SS. Giovanni e Paolo (25 April 1151–26 September 1180), papal vicar (1164) and archpriest of St Peter's (30 April 1178), d. 4 January 1181, Brixius, 55, 109; Zenker, 137–9.

[81] F. Tonetti, 'Alcuni documenti del territorio verolano', *Archivio della Società Romana di storia patria*, 25 (1902), 236–7.

[82] Kehr, *Italia Pontificia*, ii, 171–2; G. Falco, 'Note in margine al cartario di Sant'Andrea di Veroli', *Archivio della Società Romana di storia patria*, 84 (1961), 195–227, at 216–8.

[83] Brixius, 59–60; Zenker, 140–1. A former monk of Montecassino and abbot of Subiaco, created cardinal deacon of S. Maria in Domnica (?1158–1183?). It was certainly usual by the pontificate of Innocent III for papal rectors to undertake tours of duty lasting not more than a year.

[84] Toubert, *Structures*, ii, 1061–8; P. Fabre, *Étude sur le* Liber censuum *de l'Église romaine* (Paris, 1892).

[85] *Liber censuum*, i, 385–400, 425–7, nos 98–120, 167–9; Geisthardt, *Der Kämmerer Boso*, 41–59.

Boso negotiated most of these transactions, all but two dated between January 1157 and July 1159, with Roland frequently in attendance.[86]

Having returned Orvieto to direct papal overlordship through arduous, behind-the-scenes negotiations by his curial officials, Adrian entered the city towards the end of September 1156, honouring it with his presence until mid-October.[87] According to Boso, this first visit to Orvieto by any pope within living memory was enthusiastically received by 'greater and lesser people' alike, while Adrian demonstrated his special benevolence towards all the inhabitants of the city, 'as if they were new members of the family of St Peter'.[88] His travels would already have acquainted him with Orvieto's spectacular rocky site and strong defensive position, the development of the 'città-fortezza' dating from his thwarted intention to make it the seat of his encounter with Frederick Barbarossa in the previous year.[89] Adrian remained in the city for an indeterminate period—perhaps for as few as two and as long as twelve weeks,[90] incidentally witnessing the torrential autumnal rain which caused the River Paglia to flood,[91] and meanwhile confirming the privileges and numerous possessions of the chapter of the church of S. Costanzo.

It was not until Adrian returned to Rome that an agreement, dated to February 1157,[92] was made between seven cardinal mediators on the papal side[93] and, on the other, Prior Rocco of S. Costanzo, acting during an episcopal vacancy, together with two consuls and two nobles, all representing the people of Orvieto. The consuls declared that they performed that homage and fealty, respecting temporalities and according to the custom of the pope's other cities.[94] This oath was to be renewed on every change of consul in Orvieto, but was always to be associated with a payment of ten pounds. The Prior and his companions undertook to instruct the

---

[86] Partner, *Lands of St Peter*, 193, suggests that Adrian's reorganization of the Patrimony was probably more important for its administrative methods than for its practical results.

[87] *Vita Adriani*, 395;* Michele Maccarrone, *Studi su Innocenzo III*, Italia Sacra, 17 (Padua, 1972), 22; David Foote, *The Bishopric of Orvieto: The Formation of Political and Religious Culture in a Medieval Italian Commune* (Ph.D. dissertation, University of California, Davis, 1998), at 97–110 for Adrian's visit.

[88] '...maiores et minores tamquam novam beati Petri familiam affectuose honorabat et in eorum congratulabatur aspectibus', *Vita Adriani*, 395.*

[89] Maccarrone, *Studi su Innocenzo III*, 22.

[90] Certainly between 28 September and 15 October, JL, 10205–9; Waley, *Mediaeval Orvieto*, 2–4.

[91] New York, Pierpont Morgan Library, MS 465, f. 90v; Maccarrone, *Studi su Innocenzo III*, 3–9, at 8; David Foote, 'How the Past Becomes a Rumor: The Notarialization of Historical Consciousness in Medieval Orvieto', *Speculum*, 75 (2000), 794–815, at 814–5

[92] February 1157, *Liber censuum*, i, 390–1, no. 106; A. Theiner, *Codex Diplomaticus Dominii Temporalis Sanctae Sedis* (Rome, 1861), i, 17–8, no. 23; Waley, *Mediaeval Orvieto*, 2, and Maccarrone, *Studi su Innocenzo III*, 24.

[93] Roland and Boso, with Julius, Bernard, Henry, Hyacinth and John: *Liber censuum*, 391.

[94] '...quod faciunt ei alii fideles sui de regalibus...secundum consuetudinem aliarum civitatum domni pape', *Ibid.*, 390–1, no. cvi.

citizens of Orvieto as to the nature of the oath they had taken, so that it could be firmly kept and observed—while, on every change of pope, the consuls were bound to swear the oath as they had done to the Lord Adrian.[95] Henceforth, the citizens of Orvieto promised to give military aid to the pope, whenever he should request it, within the triangle from Tintihano[96] and Tintinniano[97] to Sutri,[98] that is, across a whole swathe of vulnerable frontier territory, from north west to north east of Orvieto and well to its south. Whenever the pope might wish to visit the city, the Orvietans were to be held responsible for his safety and that of his companions, if they remained there or while returning with him. In return, when all the oaths had been sworn, Adrian promised to pay three hundred pounds in the money of Lucca and offered to mediate a pact between Orvieto and its enemy, nearby Aquapendente, not by force but at the wish of both parties.[99]

The re-establishment of peace, security, and papal control in the frontier area around Radicofani and the Val d'Orcia was one of the immediate objectives of Adrian IV. This must have been felt to be particularly necessary following the events of May–June 1155 when Arnold of Brescia,[100] fleeing Rome after the collapse of his alliance with the Commune, was captured at the *hospitium* of Le Briccole near La Scala on the Via Francigena[101] by cardinal Odo of S. Nicola in Carcere.[102] Arnold was subsequently released from his place of imprisonment by the pro-imperial counts of Campagnatico, whose lands lay close to San Quirico d'Orcia where the Emperor and the imperial army were encamped.[103]

An interesting initiative to control the lawless frontier zone of the Val d'Orcia was implemented in April 1156. Guido, cardinal priest of S. Pudenziana,[104] who had already once suffered at Arnald's hands, was involved, together with envoys of the Roman Church, 'legati ecclesie Romane', and a host of local bishops.[105] Thus, even before Adrian and the Curia returned from Benevento, the specific in-

---

[95] Waley, *Mediaeval Orvieto*, 2–3; Partner, *Lands of St Peter*, 193.

[96] Titignano, midway between Orvieto and Todi.

[97] Rocca d'Orcia, outside Castiglione d'Orcia..

[98] Waley, *Mediaeval Orvieto*, 3, believed erroneously that Tintihano and Tintinniano were one and the same place.

[99] L. Fumi, *Codice diplomatico della città di Orvieto* (Florence, 1884), 26, no. 38.

[100] Arsenio Frugoni, 'Arnaldo da Brescia' *Dizionario biografico degli italiani*, 4 (1962), 247–50; George W. Greenaway, *Arnold of Brescia* (Cambridge, 1931), 150–2. More generally on Rome in this period, Paolo Brezzi, *Roma e l'impero medioevale, 774–1252*, Storia di Roma, 10 (Bologna, 1947), 317–46.

[101] Dufour, *Le strade Cristiane*, 140–2 for the more recent name of Lo Spedaletto di S. Pelegrino.

[102] Odo, also from Brescia, cardinal deacon of S. Nicola in Carcere, 4 June 1152–17 February 1175, Brixius, 56; Zenker, 171–4.

[103] *Vita Adriani*, 390.*

[104] Cardinal priest of S. Pudenziana, 31 January 1145–57, Brixius, 51; Zenker, 112–3. He had been seriously attacked on the *Via Sacra* by supporters of Arnold of Brescia, just after Adrian's election, *Vita Adriani*, 389,* but had clearly recovered a year later.

[105] '...residente apud sanctum Quiricum in conventu cum episcopis, videlicet Senensi, Aretino atque Clusino, Suanensi, Castrensi, Massetano atque Vulterano...', *Ibid.*, 408.*

tention was to ensure extra protection for the sensitive area far to the north of Orvieto. At San Quirico d'Orcia, Paltonerius, son of the late count, Fortiguerra, at that moment without heirs, either male or female, renounced all his rights over the *castrum* of Monticchiello, with its *curtis* and appurtenances, in favour of Pope Adrian and the Church.[106] He handed over his *castrum* 'ad ius beati Petri et sancte Romane ecclesie cum integritate', promising that henceforth he would pay one gold bezant annually at the feast of the Ascension as long as he should live— although in this case it is not recorded whether Paltonerius received back his lands as a papal fief.[107]

In his concentration on the area of Tuscia Romana, Adrian followed in the footsteps of his predecessor, Eugenius III,[108] by fortifying the frontier post of Radicofani. The feudal service of *custodia turris et munitionum* was of vital importance in the case of such an important and strategic position but specific details are lacking for the work at Radicofani, save for Boso's description of the building of its round internal tower, fortified walls and deep moat.[109] Boso makes much of a related issue—the pope's resettlement of the deserted *castrum* of Orcia[110]—in order to ensure peace in the region by stabilizing what had become essentially 'a den of thieves',[111] and by defending it with a wall and towers erected at considerable expense. The towers of the fortifications were already in place by 18 July 1158,[112] when Gezo de Damiano, compelled by no authority but of his own spontaneous will, renounced for three thousand silver marks all the rights he, his wife and their heirs had over a house, situated in the *castrum* of Orcia, adjoining the tower of the Lord Pope. One of the boundaries of Gezo's house was the tower and another the bank (*ripa*) of the fortification. Gezo renounced a mill, a garden, and two vineyards, also included in this transaction, which was made in the *castrum* of Viterbo by Boso himself in the presence of five witnesses.

Near the 'pleasant and populous' city of Viterbo, which the pope had visited in October 1156,[113] Adrian bought half of the four *castra*, Castiglione in Teverina,[114] Cicignano,[115] Canepina,[116] and Bulsignano,[117] from the daughters of Raynaldo de Guardea for a sum of money of which the record does not give the amount.[118] For these sales, Boso records that the pope received a public instrument

---

[106] April 1156, *Liber censuum*, i, 408–9, no.134.
[107] Toubert, *Structures*, ii, 1129, n. 2
[108] 29 May 1153, *Liber censuum*, i, 380–2, no. 91.
[109] *Vita Adriani*, 396,* 'Hic fecit gironem in castro Radicophini, turribus munitum et alto fossato'.
[110] Silvestrelli, *Città, Castelli e Terre*, ii, 736–8.
[111] '...quod erat spelunca latronum', *Vita Adriani*, 396.*
[112] 'in castro quod vocatur Orcle, juxta turrim domni pape', *Liber censuum*, i, 395–6.
[113] *Vita Adriani*, 396.*
[114] Silvestrelli, *Città, Castelli e Terre*, ii, 754.
[115] Toubert, *Structures*, ii, 1077.
[116] Silvestrelli, *Città, Castelli e Terre*, ii, 702–3.
[117] *Ibid.*, 706.
[118] *Vita Adriani*, 396.*

and corporal investiture through Anterio, the papal marshall, from Vitale, *supra-dictum mulierum curatore*, the women's manager, and gives the list of witnesses to this joint transaction for which there are neither details nor date.

Adrian's agreement with Orvieto represented a small but significant step in gaining control of Tuscia Romana. Closely connected to this aim was to be the submission of the counts of nearby Calmaniare whose fiefs, within the dioceses of Orvieto, Soana, Todi, and Chiusi, permitted them to exercise strategic control over roads to the north of Rome. At Santa Cristina, on the north shore of the Lago di Bolsena, Adrian purchased from Aldebrandino and Bernardino, sons of the late count, Hugolino of Calmaniare, in a deed of sale dated 11 October 1157, two excellent mills in their entirety, with all their ironwork, paddles, and water channel, for one hundred and ninety pounds in the money of Lucca.[119] On the same day, the brothers, in an act of atonement 'for the many and grave offences which we have committed against you, Lord Pope, your predecessors and the Roman Curia', and 'because we discover that the aforementioned lands were clearly of the right and lordship of the blessed Peter',[120] donated to the perpetual ownership of the Roman church all their various territories. The most important of these donations was a half share in Proceno, a stronghold near Aquapendente, a similar half share in Rocca Ripesena, a hill village close to Orvieto[121] and, in its entirety, Rocca San Stefano, dominating the Via Cassia near Radicofani, for which the brothers promised one hundred pounds of gold to the papacy should they fail to defend these strongholds against all men. The lands of Aldebrandino and Bernardino, ceded to the Church on 11 October 1157, were to be restored to them as fiefs on the very same day in return for oaths of homage and fealty to the pope and his successors. At the same time at Santa Cristina, Massutius, Bernard and Rainier, described as cousins—possibly of the Calmaniare brothers—handed over to Alexius, Pope Adrian's steward and butler, half of another mill at the head of the stream entering the Lago di Bolsena with all its appurtenances, in return for twenty-two pounds in the money of Lucca.[122]

At Corchiano, to the north of Civita Castellana, Boso and Raymond, cardinal deacon of S. Maria in Via Lata, received the fortification from Gaito Boccaleone, by means of three separate documents, although none of these record any re-granting of the *castrum* as a fief. The first deed, dated 25 August 1158,[123] recorded the initial transfer and the corporal investiture of the stronghold. Boccaleone then absolved all the men of the *castrum* from his fealty, ordering that in the future they should owe fidelity to the Lord Pope Adrian. Stefania, Boccaleone's mother, and Odo *de Gardeia*, his cousin, made similar renunciations for any rights they might

---

[119] 11 October 1157, *Liber censuum*, i, 388–9, no. 103; *Vita Adriani*, 396,* 'duo quoque optima molendina posita apud Sanctam Cristinam'.

[120] 'Et quia easdem prenominatas terras de jure et dominio beati Petri aperte fuisse comperimus', *Liber censuum*, i, 389, no. 104.

[121] Waley, *Mediaeval Orvieto*, 3–4.

[122] October 1157, *Liber censuum*, i, 397, no. 115.

[123] *Ibid.*, i, 385, no. 98.

possess over the *castrum*. These oaths were enacted in the presence of a crowd of notables including Peter, prefect of Rome,[124] several papal representatives, and very many other bystanders, both soldiers and inhabitants of Corchiano and troops from Civita Castellana and Viterbo. On 27 August, in the presence of Adrian himself at the episcopal palace at Narni,[125] in recognition of a payment of one hundred and forty pounds of the money of Lucca from the Church, Boccaleone, in the public ritual of *receptio*, swore on the gospels to observe both the transaction and his renunciation of Corchiano, in the presence of seven cardinals, judges, curial officials and local nobles. Finally, on 30 August, Stefania, Boccaleone's mother, donated to Boso all her rights, and any which might have come to her through her husband, over the *castrum* of Corchiano, confirming this with a corporal oath and by a sign manual prepared for her by Alexius, archivist of the Roman Church.[126]

Similarly, the lordship of the *castrum Reiani*, possibly Riano between the Via Flaminia and the Via Tiberina, was handed over to Adrian, his successors and the Roman Church in a deed of gift of 7 April 1159,[127] by John Roncione and his young brother, Berardo, to whom he was guardian. The brothers promised to defend their stronghold against all comers, to pay two pounds of gold for any infringement of the agreement, and Berardo specifically promised to confirm the gift once he attained the age of twenty-five and reached his majority.

The attention of Adrian and his cardinals turned not only towards Tuscia Romana but was also directed eastwards to the Monte Prenestini and the borderlands of the Patrimony in the Sabina. On their uneasy post-coronation perambulation, Adrian and Frederick Barbarossa crossed the Tiber at Magliano and paused at the imperial abbey of Farfa.[128] Eugenius III, fleeing Rome in 1146, had chosen to be consecrated at Farfa,[129] and there he restated the abbey's ancient exemption from episcopal authority, declaring unequivocally that it belonged *ad ius et proprietatem beati Petri et Sancte Romane ecclesie*.[130] The emperor, however, in an attempt to reimpose imperial patronage,[131] had used his power, not only to invest an abbot but also to collect the *fodrum*, the hearth tax to pay for hospitality. Adrian, subsequently reiterated the position of his predecessor that Farfa belonged to the jurisdiction of the Roman Church. In order to underline his control of this region, on 4 May 1157, he granted all the appurtenances of Tribuco, a deserted *castrum*, to the inhabitants of Bocchignano, with the exception of the *fodrum* owed

---

[124] Louis Halphen, *Etudes sur l'Administration de Rome au Moyen Age (751–1252)* (Paris, 1907), 153–4.

[125] *Liber censuum*, i, 385–6, no. 99.

[126] *Ibid.*, i, 386–7, no. 100.

[127] *Liber censuum*, i, 396, no. 114; Kehr, *Italia Pontificia*, ii, 180–1. Compare Toubert, *Structures*, ii, 1129, n. 2 in which he doubts that *Reiani* can be identified.

[128] 18 June 1155, *Vita Adriani*, 392–3.*

[129] 18 February 1146, *Liber Pontificalis*, ii, 386.

[130] Paul F. Kehr, 'Urkunden zur Geschichte von Farfa in XII. Jahrhundert', *Quellen und Forschungen aus italienischen Archiven und Bibliotheken*, 9 (1906), 170–84, at 177–8.

[131] Mary Stroll, *The Medieval Abbey of Farfa: Target of Papal and Imperial Ambitions* (Leiden, 1997), 257–73, at 258.

to the pope, commending them to his special care and solicitude since both these territory belonged within the Patrimony.[132] Significantly, on the same day, 4 May 1157, Adrian IV confirmed the earlier charter to *castrum Lori*[133] in terms which revealed the contemporary situation. In his document, Adrian went beyond the provisions made by his predecessor in setting out precise terms for the *placitum* in which he laid down that two annual sessions, reserved for major causes, *de omicidiis et adulteriis*, were to be held by papal envoys.[134] Interestingly, the details of the *fodrum* were set out even more clearly than for Roccantica, indicating the greater need by the mid-twelfth century to provide hospitality for the pope himself, for his brothers, the cardinals, and for the reception of special envoys or messengers sent from the Curia.[135]

On the journey they took together in 1155, Adrian and the emperor made a significant detour on the way to Ponte Lucano outside Tivoli, when they crossed the Aniene valley in order to reach the *castrum* of Odo II of Poli.[136] The counts of Poli were potentially powerful allies and their fealty would be an important prize, for they possessed extensive allodial lands controlling the strategic area between Palestrina, Tivoli and the monastery of Subiaco. On 17 January 1157, Astaldo, archivist of the Roman Church, drew up two significant deeds, witnessed by Boso and Roland.[137] Odo di Poli, believing in the value of the record of history to remove 'all cloud of doubt', had it set down in writing that he was giving spontaneously and not through fear of death, his *castra* and all his lands[138] as a perpetual inheritance to God, to the Apostle Peter and to Pope Adrian and his successors, and to whomsoever the pope might wish to grant them. These lands were returned to Odo by contract as a 'recovered fief',[139] on the understanding that he would show fealty to the pope and his successors without any other fief. An elementary clause safeguarding the rights of both sides was included. Should the circumstances alter or Odo be unwilling or unable to defend his fief, then it was agreed that he or his heirs would pay as a penalty one hundred pounds of pure

---

[132] 4 May 1157, 'Hadrianus IV universis hominibus castri Bucciniani: concedit totam pertinentiam seu tenimentium diruti castri Tribuci', Kehr, *Italia Pontificia*, ii, 70. See also Toubert, *Structures*, ii, 1120, 1139.

[133] Vehse, *Die päpstliche Herrschaft*, 174–5.

[134] *Ibid.*, 174, 'salvis quidem nobis nostrisque successoribus, aut cui nos commiserimus, placitis de omicidiis et adulteries, bis in anno per nostrum nuntium'.

[135] *Ibid.*, 174, '…et salvis fodris ad opus nostrum et fratrum nostrorum cardinalium, receptione nuntiorum nostrorum de curia nostra'.

[136] Odo II of Poli (1139–59). *Vita Adriani*, 392, n. 1, 'cet itinéraire est extraordinaire'. In fact, it was a sound strategy by the pope's advisors to ensure that a significant block of territory between Tivoli and Palestrina should remain loyal to the papacy.

[137] *Liber censuum*, i, 387–8, nos 101–02.

[138] Poli, Faustignano, Anticoli (Corrado), Rocca di 'Nibli', Monte Manno, Guadagnolo, Saracinesco, Rocca di Murri and Castel Nuovo. Compare *Vita Adriani*, 396.*

[139] Toubert, *Structures*, 1170–1, nn. 3–4. For confirmation of these contracts in Innocent III's letter to his brother, Richard Conti, 9 October, 1204, see *Die Register Innocenz' III.*, 7. Band. 7. Pontifikatsjahr, 1204/1205, ed. Othmar Hageneder, Andrea Sommerlechner, Herwig Weigl, with Christoph Egger and Rainer Murauer (Vienna, 1997), 215–9, no. 131.

gold. Boso and Roland accepted that the pope and his successors would likewise be ready to pay a similar amount if unable to defend the contract on their part.

At Ponte Lucano, the strategic point where the Via Tiburtina crossed the River Aniene, Adrian had a chapel built on the bridge, endowing it with the necessary equipment for the celebration of the mass. Significantly, he bought two measures of land near the bridge: from the wife of Giovanni dei Benedicto, citizen of Tivoli, for seven pounds in money of Lucca and another six measures at the same place from Odo de Insula and his wife for twenty-four pounds.[140] On 18 April 1159, Rainaldus Senibaldi gave to Adrian, his successors and the Roman Church his lands and possessions near Farfa in perpetuity with the promise to defend them.[141] Should he or his heirs ever break the contract, they promised to pay to the pope and to his successors two pounds of gold.

The south of the Patrimony and its frontier with the Regno at the River Liri presented Adrian IV with some rather different problems from those of Tuscia Romana and the Sabina. His papal predecessors had already regained, amongst other *castra*, Ninfa in Marittima, Lariano and Giuliano in Campania,[142] while the earliest of all submissions to Adrian was that made on 8 July 1155 by Jonathas, son of Tolomeo II of Tuscolo.[143] Jonathas swore fealty, *fidelitas*, to the pope and his successors for his lifetime and promised on oath to help the Church against all men, excepting the emperor. In order to strengthen his fealty, Jonathas transferred his *castra* of Montefortino (Artena) and Faiola for two years to Raniero de Veczo and Berardo of Anagni, and received in return half of the city of Tuscolo in fee, on the understanding that it would freely revert to the Roman Church on his death.[144] The reservation of imperial rights, however, implicit in this undertaking is telling. Frederick's imperial coronation was only one month past, and pope and emperor had parted amicably at Ponte Lucano, where they had celebrated the feast of SS. Peter and Paul (29 June 1155) in some pomp.[145]

As part of his plan to increase the number and density of papal fortifications throughout the Patrimony, recorded in a series of documents all apparently dated 8 April 1157,[146] Adrian contracted with Adenolfo, Landolfo, and Lando, the sons of Pandolfo of Aquino, and Raynaldo, Pandolfo's brother, allowing them to exchange one sixth of their two *castra*, one ruined and the other intact, at Monte Libretti[147] in the Sabina for a sixth part of the *castra* of Monte San Giovanni, just north of Ceprano in Campania, at the frontier with the Regno. In return for papal assent to this exchange, all four from the Aquino family swore fealty to the pope, promising to defend the Roman Church against all men. In one of these agreements made be-

---

[140] *Vita Adriani*, 396.*

[141] Sta Maria de Canneto, Pomonte, Castel Ugo, Mollagara and Campo Maior, *Liber censuum*, i, 397–8, 116; Kehr, *Italia Pontificia*, ii, 70; Toubert, *Structures*, ii, 1076–7, 1116–7.

[142] See at nn. 52–5 above.

[143] *Liber censuum*, i, 399–400, no. 119.

[144] Toubert, *Structures*, ii, 1139; cf. Partner, *Lands of St Peter*, 196–7.

[145] *Vita Adriani*, 392–3;* see also Twyman, ch. 5, at n. 126.

[146] *Liber censuum*, i, 391–4, nos 107–11.

[147] Silvestrelli, *Città, Castelli e Terre*, ii, 402–3.

tween cardinals Roland and Hubald on the one hand and Landolfo on the other,[148] an additional clause was inserted to prevent Landolfo and his heirs from selling or in any other way alienating part of the *castrum* to any person who 'lives beyond the river of Ceprano',[149] that is, beyond the River Liri, in the *Regno*. If Landolfo were to decide to alienate his portion of the *castrum*, he would be obliged to ask permission of the pope, who was to have the first refusal to buy it for twenty pounds of papal money less than its value. Landolfo was to be allowed to sell or alienate it only to someone 'who is by merit not suspect' to the Roman Church.[150] It has been suggested that in this case Adrian IV did not strike a good bargain, for the bishop of Veroli also had a claim to Monte San Giovanni.[151] At Valmontone, at the head of the River Sacco, which joined the River Liri to the south of Ceprano, Adrian bought one and a half mills from Gregorio and Milo.[152]

Certain elements and issues recur in the detailed documents of *receptio* drawn up by Boso and his officials which shed light on Adrian IV's energetic attempts to recover the Patrimony for the Church. In all his dealings to recover lost lands in the Patrimony, the pope took the greatest care to act always in strict agreement with his cardinals. The contracts drawn up by Boso and his officials refer constantly to the *consensum fratrum*, and concern for the *voluntas, approbatio, consilium, assensus* of the cardinals and others.[153] The ceremonies of investiture took place in their presence. Even in his position as feudal lord, the pope took his decisions in common and manifested them while *residens in consistorio*.[154] It is highly significant that some cardinals were able to veto the very attractive offer made by William of Sicily in August 1155 at the beginning of the Norman rebellion. In honour of the blessed Peter and the Roman Church, the king offered the three important *castra* of Paduli, Montefusco, and Morcone, which encircled the papal stronghold of Benevento, and would have afforded an enhanced protective screen around the city. Despite his better judgment, and the fact that such acquisitions coincided with his strategic policies at that time, Adrian respected his cardinals' negative decision.[155]

Built into some of the agreements made on behalf of Adrian were provisions vital to ensure safety for travellers, pilgrims, merchants, and clerics travelling to and from Rome. As feudal tenants of the papacy, the counts of Calmaniare were obliged to maintain their service of *custodia stratarum* by ensuring the peace of the public roads crossing their territories around the Lago di Bolsena. The oath the Calmaniare brothers swore to Adrian IV on 11 October 1157 laid down particular and strict details.[156] They were exhorted to watch over the routes to Rome, at all

---

[148] *Liber censuum*, i, 392, no. 108.
[149] '...alicui persone que moretur ultra flumen Ceperani', *Liber censuum*, i, 392, no. 108.
[150] Toubert, *Structures*, ii, 1148–9, n. 4.
[151] Partner, *Lands of St Peter*, 195.
[152] *Vita Adriani*, 396.*
[153] Toubert, *Structures*, ii, 1184 and n. 1.
[154] *Liber censuum*, i, 427, no. 169.
[155] *Vita Adriani*, 394.*
[156] *Liber censuum*, i, 389–90, no. 105.

times and on behalf of all persons, particularly for pilgrims identified by their badges (*formae*), and excepting only publicly acknowledged robbers, enemies of the Roman church, and their own enemies.[157] They were to promise to observe a truce with other local lords, should their peers agree, and to accept all the strict conditions imposed on them. The *custodia* or guard of the *castrum* of Rocca San Stefano, dominating the Via Cassia near Sutri, was, with their agreement and the promise of expenses for five years, to be manned by troops named by the pope,[158] once these had promised fealty to the papacy. Should an offence committed in relation to the road remain uncorrected for eight days, the Rocca San Stefano would then be returned wholly to the right and dominion of St Peter. This confiscation was also to occur should the counts offend, either in the matter of the truce or in any involvement against Hospitallers, Templars, clerics, or monks, and unless due correction was made within fifteen days. In any proposed sale or alienation, the Roman church was to have the right of first refusal, while the counts were obliged to sell or alienate their lands, *sine malitia*, only to someone favourable to the pope, and without bearing a grudge. A further deed of 2 January 1159[159] confirmed the pledge by Aldebrandino, acting as agent for his brother, and made to Boso, on behalf of Adrian and the Roman church, of the Rocca San Stefano, half of Proceno, and half of Rocca Ripesena, for a loan of one hundred and forty eight pounds and five shillings in money of Lucca from the pope, who was also paying out sixteen shillings every month for castle guard.

The purpose of these provisions was to ensure the maintenance of peace, free movement, and the safety of the great pilgrim routes to Rome. The previous dubious record of the counts of Calmaniare as 'seigneurs routiers...abusifs',[160] which the obligation of *custodia stratarum* attempted to remedy, was not dissimilar to the situation of Adenolfo of Acquapuzza.[161] In January 1158, Adenolfo was forced publicly to swear that he likewise would observe the *custodia stratarum*.[162] The previous encroachment of the Pontine Marshes had forced the abandonment of the Via Appia Antica to the south of Velletri and the Alban Hills, and its replacement by way of a route across the southern flank of the Monte Lepini, through Cori, Norma, Sermoneta, and Sezze, rejoining the old road at Priverno.[163] The *rocca* of Acquapuzza commanded a particularly sensitive position, dominating the route

---

[157] '...et stratam omni tempore et omnibus personis servare, exceptis publicis latronibus et inimicis ecclesie Romane et vestris, ita tamen si formam peregrinorum non portaverint', *Ibid.*, i, 390.

[158] Scarlatanus of Radicofani, Orlandino, his brother, and the sons of Belizus,

[159] *Liber censuum*, i, 394–9, no. 105.

[160] Toubert, *Structures*, ii, 1146.

[161] *Liber censuum*, i, 427, no. 169.

[162] *Ibid.*, 427, 'juravit fidelitatem strate publice'.

[163] For Gregory I's suppression in 592 of the see of *Tres Tabernae* and its incorporation into the diocese of Velletri, L. Duchesne, 'Le sedi episcopali nell'antico ducato di Roma', *Archivio della Società Romana di storia patria*, 15 (1892), 475–503 at 499; Toubert, *Structures*, i, 629.

from Terracina to Rome near Sezze,[164] and Adenolfo's ability to commit an *offensio stratarum* was henceforth limited by his promise to perform his feudal duty, *per totam regaliam.*[165]

An explicit and relevant act of submission was made on 13 July 1159, at Sgurgola, a *castrum* high above the valley of the River Sacco, strategically placed between Segni and Ferentino.[166] Indeed, this, chronologically one of the last recorded acts of submission to Adrian, appears similar to an *ordo qualiter*, a model for the institutionalizing of the *receptio*, but one with a significant difference. This was an agreement between two friendly households, the *familia* of the pope and the *familia* of Gualganus, lord of Sgurgula. Boso was present, accompanied by the whole spectrum of papal officials—Peter Gaitanus, Roger, a subdeacon, Rodolfo, the pope's chaplain, Peter and Alexius, the papal butlers, Donellus and John Ritius, papal doorkeepers, Bovacannus and Gisilbertus, the marshals, Malavolta, the master constable, and many other servants from 'the domestic household of the Lord Pope'. All had come to the *castrum* of Sgurgola on the instructions of and by arrangement with Adrian and his cardinals. First Gualganus and his soldier sons, Simon and Godfreddo, *milites*, honourably entertained the papal household. Then the whole company moved into the upper part of the *castrum*,[167] where 'in a common audience of all the above mentioned', as well as many others 'standing around', Gualganus publicly addressed and questioned Boso in detail, before recognizing that the *castrum* of Sgurgola belonged to the jurisdiction of St Peter. He further accepted that the Roman pontiffs had entrusted the *castrum* to his parents and himself, and that they had held it in fealty to St Peter and the papacy. And in order to remove all doubt and 'as greater evidence' that this was indeed so, he ordered all those by name who were living with him in the *castrum* to swear fealty to the Lord Pope. And the oath was taken in this form:

I, Leo, priest and chaplain of the *castrum*; I, Nicolas Parente, reeve; I, Landucu, steward; I, Petrus Ciuncus, porter; I, Galganus Buccabella, cellarer; I, Nicolas de Pandolfo; I, Nicolas Marsicano; I, Petrus Abrusia, guards and watchmen of the fortification itself; swear by these holy gospels that from this hour for the future, I will be faithful to the Lord Pope Adrian and his catholic successors, and to the Holy Roman Church. Nor will I be in deed or counsel or conspiracy, the cause of their losing their life or limb, or being taken in hostile captivity. Any certain and serious damage to them, if I learn of it, I will check if I can; but if I cannot, then I will inform the pope, either myself, or by my messenger, or by letter. And if by chance, may it not be, my lord Gualganus or his sons ever at any time should be unwilling to recognize the *castrum* of Sgurgola through the blessed Peter and the Roman pontiffs, as has been said, and should wish to renounce their fealty to the

---

[164] Toubert, *Structures*, ii, 1147.
[165] *Liber censuum*, i, 427, no. 105.
[166] *Ibid.*, i, 400, no. 120.
[167] '...ad palatium et capellam, qui est in summitate ipsius arcis', *ibid.*

Lord Pope, then I, by fighting back to the best of my ability, will resist them, and
I will hold myself against them with the Lord Pope for the time being.

And as well as this, the same Gualganus absolved all members of his own *familia* in respect of the oath by which they were bound to him, bringing them into membership of another, even closer, *familia*, the 'new family of St Peter'!

Adrian's achievement in recovering lost territory within the Patrimony of St Peter was never less than impressive. In comparison with his predecessor, Eugenius III, and his successor, Alexander III, and in a shorter pontificate than theirs, he brought more *castra*, together with their inhabitants, into the jurisdiction and under the protection of the Holy See. Nor were the circumstances in which he achieved this success overly favourable. A considerable period of isolation in the new papal palace at St Peter's, from which he was unable to emerge for four months, was followed by an enforced stay of more than eight months in papal territory at Benevento. Yet, notwithstanding this isolation, he somehow managed to maintain an effective organization of curial officials, who worked behind the scenes to achieve his aims. Assisted enormously by Boso, Roland and the other cardinals, teams of officials travelled around, using local notaries whose knowledge and skills were placed at their disposal. Boso's depiction of Adrian IV as benevolent and kindly in his treatment of the inhabitants of the cities and *castra* of the Patrimony was certainly balanced. In Orvieto, where no pope had ever ventured before, Adrian made certain of his direct overlordship of the city and, in exchange, elevated Orvieto to the status of most important city of the papal territories to the north of Rome, at the same time favouring its territorial expansion. Boso described with enthusiasm the veneration given by the people of Orvieto to the pope and the pope's own benevolence towards all Orvietans great and small. It was similar throughout the Patrimony. All local *castra* and their inhabitants experienced papal benevolence: absolution from past sins, the benefit of papal protection, much safer roads, and firm, but impartial justice for all. In those cases which have been recorded, the balance maintained between subjugation and restitution of property and rights was always on a sound footing. The significance of Adrian's exceptional gains in the Patrimony has not been properly recognized. No pope was able to match them until the pontificate of Innocent III. For Maccarrone, Adrian IV was 'il grande e vero predecessore della politica di Innocenzo III',[168] or, to put it the other way round, only Innocent, the great Roman, realized the value to the papacy of following where Adrian, the unique Englishman, had led.

---

[168] Maccarrone, *Studi su Innocenzo III*, 22.

APPENDIX
Summary Itinerary of Pope Adrian IV

5 December 1154	Rome, St Peter's
25 March 1155	Rome, Lateran
16 May 1155	Sutri
1 June 1155	Viterbo
8 June 1155	Nepi
9 June 1155	in territorio Sutri
11 June 1155	Civita Castellana
15 June 1155	in campo Nepesino
18 June 1155	Rome, St Peter's
19 June 1155	Magliano Teverina
June 1155	Farfa in Sabina
June 1155	Poli
28–9 June 1155	Ponte Lucano
8 July 1155	in territorio Tusculano
30 September 1155	Ferentino (*c.* Michaelmas)
7 October 1155	Alatri
9 October 1155	Sora
17 October 1155	Ferentino
	San Germano
	In castro Capua (Mignano)
21 November 1155	Benevento
July/August 1156	Cassino, Marsicana
3 August 1156	Narni
12 August 1157	Viterbo?
28 September	Orvieto
October–November	Viterbo (*castrum*)
? 9 November 1156	Rome, Lateran
26 May 1157	Rome, St Peter's
28 May 1157	Rome, Lateran
8 August 1157	Segni
11 August 1157	Anagni
4 November 1157	Rome, Lateran
10 January 1158	Rome, St Peter's
10 February 1158	Rome, Lateran
12 June 1158	Sutri
12 July 1158	Vetralla
27–30 August 1158	Narni
22 September 1158	Vicovaro
27–8 September 1158	Albano
19 October 1158	Rome, Lateran
27 May 1159	Tusculum
15 June 1159	Anagni
d. 1 September 1159	Anagni

Chapter 9
Servus servorum Dei
Anne J. Duggan

With patriotic pride William Stubbs described Adrian IV as 'a great pope; that is, a great constructive pope, not a controversial one, like those who preceded and followed; a man of organizing power and missionary zeal; a reformer, and, although he did not take a wise way of showing it, a true Englishman.'[1] This is quite a claim for a pontificate of 4 years 8 months and 28 days, which was dominated by disputes with the city of Rome, the German emperor, and the Norman king of Sicily, and whose principal legacies, some would say, were the English domination of Ireland, and the fatal breach with Frederick I, which led to a nineteen-year schism and permanently damaged relations between the empire and the papacy. But although the political and territorial problems were complex and time-consuming,[2] they did not determine the course of papal relations with the rest of the Church. Most of the West only heard rumours, if it heard anything at all, about what was going on in Rome and Italy; and only if there was a prolonged schism in the papacy were there likely to be wider repercussions. What systematically built up papal primacy and maintained a sense of law and discipline were the routine contacts between Curia and local institutions maintained by legates, letters, privileges, and adjudications.

Nevertheless, the short span of his papacy does restrict the range and amount of material available. Unlike the popes before and after him, he did not preside over reforming councils. Innocent II, Eugenius III, and later Alexander III recapitulated aspects of a reform programme in series of councils spanning fifty years from 1130 to 1179. Innocent II had four councils (Clermont [1130], Reims [1131], Pisa [1135],[3] and Lateran II [1139]),[4] Eugenius III one (Reims [1148]),[5] and Alexander III two (Tours [1163] and Lateran III [1179]).[6] From these we can construct a reform profile. We can see them legislating on clerical life and

---

[1] 'Learning and Literature at the Court of Henry II', *Seventeen Lectures on the Study of Medieval History* (Oxford, 1887), 151.

[2] See above, ch. 7.

[3] R. Somerville, 'The Canons of Reims (1131)', *Bulletin of Medieval Canon Law*, NS 5 (1975), 122–30 (repr. in idem, *Papacy, Councils and Canon Law in the 11th and 12th Centuries* [Aldershot, 1990], no. XV); idem, 'The Council of Pisa, 1135: a re-examination of the evidence for the canons', *Speculum*, 45 (1970), 98–114.

[4] *Conciliorum oecumenicorum decreta*, ed. J. Alberigo et al., 3rd edn (Bologna, 1973), 197–203. For Alberigo's Latin text, with English translation, *see Decrees of the Ecumenical Councils*, ed. Norman P. Tanner, S.J., 2 vols (Georgetown, 1990), i, 197–203.

[5] Mansi, xxi, 225–8.

[6] Robert Somerville, *Pope Alexander III and the Council of Tours* (Los Angeles, 1977); *Conciliorum...decreta*, ed. Alberigo, 205–25; *Decrees...Councils*, ed. Tanner, i, 205–25.

behaviour, lay abuse of churches, episcopal elections, and similar matters. But Adrian's short pontificate, distracted by political and military crises on every side, precluded such activity. Neither do we have any sermons or treatises, or commentaries on scripture or canon law, from which to deduce his attitude to the problems of the day. So we have to look elsewhere, to the appointments he made, to the number and range of his contacts with the church at large even within that restricted time-span, and to the judgments he made as pope.

His choice of new cardinals throws important light on his conception of papal government and responsibility. Among the first to be brought into the College was Master Albert de Morra, whom he appointed cardinal deacon of S. Adriano al Foro in 1156 and elevated one further grade to cardinal priest of S. Lorenzo in Lucina in 1158. Albert was a canon regular, like Adrian, highly educated, and destined to finish his career as Pope Gregory VIII in 1187.[7] A second, highly significant elevation was that of Boso, who became his friend and biographer. This Italian was a life-long Curialist. Having started his Curial career in 1135 in the circle of Guy of Pisa, later Eugenius III's chancellor, he was *scriptor sancte Romane ecclesie* from 1149 until Adrian appointed him papal chamberlain in 1154–5 and cardinal deacon of SS. Cosma e Damiano in 1156. Throughout all that time he had remained at the heart of the Curia, with access to the accumulations of registers and official records in St John Lateran. It was he who began the collection of financial records that would be brought to completion in the *Liber Censuum* of Cardinal Cencius Savelli; and he compiled the biographies of popes from Leo IX (1048–54) to Alexander III (1159–81), with a backward glance at John XII (955–63) (*Liber Pontificalis*).[8] Steeped in the traditions of the Curia, no one knew the traditions of the papacy better than he. Boso was thus a perfect foil for the diplomatic and legal talents of Roland Bandinelli, whom Adrian retained in the critically important office of Chancellor, and who succeeded him as Pope Alexander III in 1159.

Albert, Boso, and Roland were all Italians; but two further elevations involved an Englishman (probably) and a Provençal, both of whom had been encountered in Adrian's earlier career in Arles and Avignon. About Walter, appointed cardinal

---

[7] Master Albert de Morra, Augustinian canon regular, originally from Benevento, was successively cardinal deacon of S. Adriano al Foro (1156–8), cardinal priest of S. Lorenzo in Lucina (1158–87), chancellor of the Roman Church (1178–87), and finally Pope Gregory VIII (21 Oct.–17 Dec. 1187): Brixius, 57–8, 112–3; Ohnsorge, *Legaten Alexanders III*, 59; Zenker, 125–9; G. Kleemann, *Papst Gregor VIII* (Bonn 1912); Pfaff, 167, 177–9; *JohnS*, ii, 755 n.

[8] Boso, cardinal deacon of SS. Cosma e Damiano (1156–66), cardinal priest of S. Pudenziana (1166–78): Brixius, 58, 113; Zenker, 149–52; *Lexicon des Mittelalters*, ii (Munich/Zurich, 1983), 478; F. Geisthardt, *Der Kammerer Boso* (Berlin, 1936): all correcting the view (cf. *DHGE*, 9 [1937], 1319–20) that he was a nephew of Adrian IV. Thomas Becket accounted him a friend and claimed that he had introduced Boso to the friendship circle of Archbishop Theobald (perhaps at the Council of Reims in 1148): *The Correspondence of Thomas Becket, Archbishop of Canterbury 1162–1170*, ed. and trans. Anne J. Duggan, 2 vols, Oxford Medieval Texts (Oxford, 2000), i, 720–1.

bishop of Albano some time in 1158, very little is securely known, though there are good grounds for believing that he was not·only a canon regular from Saint-Ruf, but a fellow Englishman; and he was destined to have a distinguished career at the heart of the papal Curia for the next twenty years.[9] In contrast, Master Raymond des Arènes, appointed cardinal deacon of S. Maria in Via Lata in the same year (before 24 April), was already a skilled lawyer (*jurisperitus*), whose talents had been employed by Eugenius III and by Saint-Ruf, and whose glosses on Gratian's *Decretum* became widely circulated under the *siglum C.* or *Car.* (for *Cardinalis*).[10] Taken together, these five embody a combination of experience, academic learning, and administrative and diplomatic skill, and reflect Adrian's belief that the Curia should be an efficient organ of papal government. None of his creations was either incompetent or unworthy of the title conferred on him. These men were chosen, as Adrian himself had been, for their ability to serve the Church—that is, the local administrative and judicial needs of the church in Rome and the patrimony, as well as the constantly expanding needs of the Latin Church at large. These were the choices of a man of affairs; and they reflected his own commitment to the daily drudgery that was papal government in his time.

Adrian was elected to a papacy whose role had been transformed from titular head of the Latin Church to an active engagement as judge and arbiter.[11] Prelates,

---

[9] Walter, cardinal bishop of Albano (1158–?1178): Brixius, 60, 118 no. 146; Zenker, 39; *JohnS*, ii, 432–3 and n. 1. His friendship with and support for Thomas Becket may be deduced from Becket's letter to him, written in late 1170: *Correspondence of Thomas Becket*, ii, 1282–5 no. 302.

[10] This identification was established by André Gouron, 'Le cardinal Raymond des Arènes: *Cardinalis?*', in *Revue de droit canonique*, 28 = *Mélanges Jean Gaudemet* (Strabourg, 1978), 180–192 (unknown to Zenker, 179–80); Rudolf Weigand, 'Die Glossen des Cardinalis—Raimundus de (Harenis)—zu C.16', *Recht im Dienste des Menschen: Eine Festgabe für Hugo Schwendenwein zum 60 Geburtstag*, ed. K. Lüdicke, H. Paarhammer, and D. Binder (Graz-Vienna-Cologne 1986), 267–83. Jean Pierre Poly, 'Les Maîtres de Saint-Ruf. Pratique et enseignement du droit dans la France méridionale au XIIe siècle', in *Annales de la Faculté de Droit, des Sciences Sociales et Politiques et de la Faculté des Sciences Économiques [Bordeaux]*, Centre d'études et de recherches d'histoire institutionelle et régionale, 2 (1978), 183–203, esp. 203. Cf. *Codex diplomaticus Ordinis Sancti Rufi*, ed. C. U. J. Chevalier, *Bulletin de la Société départementale d'Archéologie et de Statistique de la Drome*, 25/ii (Valence, 1891), 1–120, at 37–8 no. 30, which shows him acting on papal authority with a 'frater C.' (probably of Saint-Ruf, for Adrian's confirmation is addressed to Abbot Raymond) in granting a concession to Bishop Geoffrey of Avignon on 30 May 1157.

[11] This development was not without its critics; cf. Gerhoch of Reichersberg's criticism of the professionalization of judicial process which had already occurred at the Curia in his *Letter to Pope Hadrian about the Novelties of the Day*, ed. N. Häring (Toronto, 1974), 115: 'Aliquotiens tamen idem legiste, permissi ante ipsum [Eugenius III] strepitu clamoso et artificioso causas inuoluere, sic eas intricauerunt ut uix potuerit uel ipse uel cardinalium quisquam eas dissoluere.' It was the application of the 'new' processes of Roman jurisprudence to ecclesiastical cases that affronted Gerhoch. The popes, however, had not created the clamour for judgment, but they had to respond to it as efficiently as they could. See n. 12.

monasteries, and individuals were flooding the Curia with requests for confirmation of rights and properties, judgments, and advice and clarification on points of ecclesiastical law to such an extent that it could scarcely cope with the burden.[12] Even a cursory look at the letters and privileges calendared in the second edition of Jaffé-Loewenfeld's *Regesta Pontificum Romanorum* (1888) shows how active Adrian was. Eugenius III (1145–53) issued 1035 in 8.3 years (a rate of 124.6 per annum); Alexander III (1159–81) 3800 in 22 years (that is 172.72 per annum); Lucius III (1181–85), 994 in five years (198.8 per annum). These statistics derive from the materials compiled by Loewenfeld from printed sources then available in the mid-nineteenth century. Since the papal registers for the twelfth century are lost, and the survival among recipients is fragmentary and haphazard, these figures can be used as general indicators only. Nevertheless, Adrian IV's 653[13] letters and privileges in 4.6 years works out at 141.95 per annum, more than Eugenius, but less than Alexander III: in other words, occupying an appropriate level in the rising scale of papal responses to appeals and requests from the Western Church. Indeed, in the context of Adrian's much troubled pontificate, these statistics are even more significant than they appear at first sight. The pope's long stay at Benevento during the Norman war in 1155–6, for example, did not interrupt the activities of the Curia.[14]

Particularly striking, in the light of the high-profile dispute with Frederick I, is the relatively high proportion of privileges and letters addressed to recipients in imperial territories. Almost a quarter of the materials calendared in Jaffé-Loewenfeld were addressed to recipients in imperial lands (and there is one privilege for a church in Poland).[15] 'Germany' was thus second only to 'France' (which received more than a third of the calendared documents) in its reception of Adrian's acta ('Italy' came third). His relations with the German church were continuous, and constitute a very significant aspect of his reign as pope. We see him confirming privileges, intervening in disputes, supporting reform, supporting the Premonstratensians, responding to requests for advice, etc. It was a great pity that the very good relations being established with German and imperial ecclesiastics in the aftermath of the Investiture controversy should have been all but

---

[12] Charles Duggan, 'Papal Judges Delegate and the Making of the 'New Law' in the Twelfth Century', in *Cultures of Power: Lordship, status, and process in twelfth-century Europe*, ed. T. N. Bisson (Philadelphia, 1995), 172–99, repr. with the same pagination in Duggan, *Decretals and the 'New Law'*, no. I; I. S. Robinson, *The Papacy 1073–1198: Continuity and Innovation* (Cambridge, 1990), 178–208. See also at n. 62 below.

[13] JL 9943–10583 + an additional 12 in the Supplementum, ii, 760–1. Up to about two hundred more documents can be gathered from a range of regional sources (*Papsturkunden in England, in Frankreich, in Spanien, Italia Pontificia, Germania Pontificia*, etc.), producing a corpus of between eight and nine hundred items overall.

[14] One hundred and two of the *acta* calendared in JL (nos 10097–10197, 10166a) were dated from Benevento in the period 21 Nov. 1155–10 June 1156.

[15] JL 10031 = *PL*, clxxxviii, 1404–06 no. 34, *Officii nostri*, dated at St Peter's on 18 April (1155), placed the community of St Mary of Czerwinck under the protection of St Peter and confirmed its properties.

destroyed by the long schism which ensued on Hadrian's death in 1159. Responsibility for that, however, and for the deteriorating papal-imperial relations before his death, should be laid, not at Adrian's door, but at Frederick's.[16] Adrian's chancery was no less productive than Eugenius's; was no less in touch with the furthest recesses of Latin Christianity. It is here, in Adrian's responses to problems, that we can surely see the mind of an engaged and responsible pastor at work. It is here that we can see Adrian confronting particularly tricky problems and producing solutions which, like his recipe for the church in Scandinavia, attempted to mediate between conflicting claims, while maintaining the legitimate rights of all as far as that was possible.

Of particular and lasting importance in this context were the ten decretal letters which were recognized by contemporaries as having special significance, and so included in the collections of current canon law being assembled at the time. One allowed the bishop of Bisceglie to restore to sacerdotal functions a priest whose harsh treatment had resulted in the death of a boy, and another conferred the pallium on Hubert of Dol (in Brittany);[17] seven concerned the payment of tithes by privileged religious houses;[18] and one related to the marriage of unfree persons.[19] Neither the response to the bishop of Bisceglie nor the Dol adjudication left much mark on the law, for the Bisceglie letter survived only in the margin of a copy of the first-recension of Gratian's *Decretum*, and the Dol judgment was in the event overtaken by political developments, as the independence of Brittany was undermined by Henry II of England.[20] Adrian's clarification of the law on tithes, however, and his consultation on the marriage of the unfree found their way into Gregory IX's *Liber Extra* (1234), and thus into the permanent body of canon law.[21]

The exemption, not only of individual religious houses but of whole Orders, from the payment of tithes to the local parish or episcopal church had become a particularly thorny issue, setting the ancient rights of local clergy against the wide-ranging privileges of Cistercians and canons regular. Originally conceived as a means of assisting poor and struggling institutions in their early days, especially when the endowments were as yet undeveloped and unproductive, the success, particularly of Cistercian agrarian practices had made some of their monasteries economically very successful; moreover, with the passage of time, already inhabited and tithe-paying land was given to them and to canons regular, who then claimed exemption by virtue of their privileges. This could be seen, both as an infringement of the ancient rights of episcopal and parish churches, and as a

---

[16] See above, ch. 7.

[17] *Litteras quas pro negotio*, to Bisceglie; *Veniens ad apostolatus nostri*, to Tours: Appendix, nos 7 and 10.

[18] *Commissum nobis*, to Canterbury; *Dilecti filii nostri*, to Châlons-sur-Marne; *Dilectus filius noster*, to Sens and Auxerre; *Ex parte dilecti filii*, to Città di Castello; *Graues ante presentiam nostram*, to English recipients; *Nobis in eminenti*, to Pontida (Bergamo); *Presbiteri de Lauare*, to Vallombrosa: Appendix, nos 1, 3–5, 8–9.

[19] *Dignum est et a ratione*, to Salzburg: Appendix, no. 2.

[20] W. L. Warren, *Henry II* (London, 1973), 100–01.

[21] *Commissum nobis a Deo* (*X*, 3.30.4) and *Dignum est et a ratione* (*X*, 4.9.1).

scandal in a world where even the poorest peasant paid a tithe of his agricultural produce to his baptismal church. Adrian was sympathetic to the cries of protest which reached him from the areas most significantly affected. Recognizing the validity of the charges, especially where new grants of old land had been made to monasteries by generous patrons, or where, in the case of the Cistercians, existing tithe-paying inhabitants had been moved to make way for more economic management of the lands, he responded very favourably to those who sought restitution of lost tithes, recognizing the ancient right of local clergy to receive the tithes due from their parishioners, while at the same time confirming the exemption of religious who were indeed bringing virgin land into cultivation for the first time by their own efforts. This was the burden of his mandate, *Nobis in eminenti*, to the monks of Pontida, near Bergamo, in northern Italy, issued on 3 November 1155. On the complaint of the canons of Pontirolo, they were ordered to pay all tithes anciently due to Pontirolo, since 'We have resolved that men of religion should be granted only those tithes which are known to derive from newly cultivated lands (*Nos siquidem religiosis uiris non alias decimas nisi eas que de noualibus prouenire noscuntur, duximus indulgendas*).'[22] He then systematically modified privileges to Cistercians, canons regular, and others, in which the clause exempting the religious house from tithe payment, 'No one whatever, clerical or lay, may exact tithes from you for the lands which you cultivate with your own hands or at your own expense (*Sane laborum uestrorum, quos proprios manibus aut sumptibus colitis, siue de nutrimentis animalium, nullus omnino clericus uel laicus a uobis decimas exigere presumat*)',[23] was modified to read, 'No one whatever, whether clerical or lay, may exact tithes from you for the new lands which you cultivate with your own hands or at your own expense, or from the fodder of your animals (*Sane laborum noualium uestrorum, que propriis manibus aut sumptibus colitis, siue de nutrimentis animalium uestrorum, nullus omnino clericus uel laicus a uobis decimas exigere presumat*)', as in his privilege for Byland, one of the great Cistercian monasteries in Yorkshire.[24] By making one small verbal change in the privileges which were conferred in their hundreds on religious houses across the length and breadth of Latin Christendom he skilfully restricted the exemption to 'new land', meaning lands brought into cultivation for the first time by the labour of the monks/canons or their *conversi*.

The new policy was decided upon very early in Adrian's pontificate. The first surviving privilege with the adjusted formula was sent to Prémontré, head of the very popular order of Premonstratensian canons regular, on 5 January 1155,[25]

---

[22] Appendix, no. 8; cf. below, at n. 30.

[23] Cf. Innocent II's privilege for the Cistercian monastery of Old Warden (1130–43), *PUE*, iii, 164.

[24] *PUE*, iii, 256–8 no. 116, esp. 257: see below, Part II/ii, no. 3. The privilege was issued at the Lateran on 23 November 1156. The same distinction between the obligation to pay 'ancient' tithes and exemption for newly cultivated lands is expressed in Appendix, no. 3.

[25] *PL*, clxxxviii, 1377, JL 9972; also quoted by G. Constable, *Monastic Tithes: From their Origins to the Twelfth Century*, Cambridge Studies in Medieval Life and Thought, NS 10 (Cambridge, 1964), 279.

while that to Byland dates from November 1156. This was not an entirely new restriction,[26] but its systematic application marked a decisive change in papal policy and a clear rejection of the generosity of the Cistercian pope, Eugenius III, who had showered the new orders with privileges of this kind. The change was simultaneously reinforced in Adrian's decretals. Letters to prelates, monks, and canons in England, Italy, and France (Canterbury in England, Città di Castello, Pontida, and Astino in Italy, Châlons-sur-Marne, Sens, and Auxerre in France) laid down the principle that customary tithes were to be paid by monastic and canonical institutions on all except 'new lands' which were cultivated by their own hands. The best exposition of this new thinking is contained in the general directive *Graues apud presentiam nostram*, addressed to English recipients, which unfortunately survives without a date, although it probably represents an early articulation of the new policy, which is crystal clear in its exposition of the gravity of the problem and the simplicity of the new rule.

> Certain bishops, abbots, canons, and chaplains from Italy and France have laid serious complaints in our presence, that abbots and monks of the Cistercian order are unjustly taking their tithes from them, alleging that they are privileged by our predecessors and therefore are not required to pay tithes on their own cultivated lands; and so it happens, that as they acquire lands and properties, the churches which were supported by them from the earliest days of the infant Church might be destroyed. Considering such great damage and serious destruction, therefore, out of regard for discretion and justice we have decreed that the said Cistercians may keep tithes from the new lands which they cultivate by their own labour; but they must without any delay restore the rest to the churches in whose parish the lands and properties are known to belong. We define as new lands those of whose cultivation no memory survives.

The juridical importance of this letter was soon recognized. It was at an early date inserted into a decretal collection originating in Spain;[27] it was known to a commentator in Cologne by 1169, when it was copied into the *Summa Coloniensis* (commentary on Gratian's *Decretum*) with the comment that 'Pope Adrian settled this question in the decretal letter addressed to the English';[28] and by 1173–4 it had found its way into a little appendix to Gratian's *Decretum*, compiled at Troyes.[29] Even more widely known was *Nobis in eminenti*, issued on 3 November 1155 to the monks of Pontida (near Bergamo). Not only was it copied into monastic manuscripts as far apart as Ghent and Montecassino, it was cited by name in a

---

[26] Constable, *Monastic Tithes*, 244–5.

[27] Collectio Caesaraugustana (Zaragoza): see Appendix, no. 6.

[28] Quoted in Constable, *Monastic Tithes*, 288; cf. *Summa 'Elegantius in iure diuino' sive Coloniensis*, ed. S. Kuttner and G. Fransen, *Monumenta Iuris Canonici*, 1/i (New York, 1969), ps. 9, c. 38.

[29] Troyes, Bibl. de la Ville, MS 103, fol. 265va–b.

commentary composed in Bologna as early as 1157 x 59;[30] and it or something similar was cited by Stephen of Tournai, an important legal commentator, in his commentary on Gratian's *Decretum*, which was compiled, also at Bologna, in the mid-1160s.[31] Its insertion into copies of Gratian's *Decretum* also testifies to its importance at the time. There is no doubt that Adrian's directives caused a stir in canonical circles. But the most significant text from the point of view of the general law was the decretal *Commissum* (*Commisse*) *nobis* sent to Archbishop Theobald of Canterbury (undated, but likely to be in the first year of Adrian's pontificate). It has been located in no fewer than twenty-seven canonical manuscripts so far, including two copies of Gratian's *Decretum* and an anonymous commentary, and an abbreviated form of its mandatory clause became part of the permanent law of the Church through incorporation in the Gregorian *Decretals* of 1234:

> For these reasons we order you [archbishop of Canterbury] to compel them [monks of Boxley] to pay tithes in full to the said church for their cultivated lands, on which houses were formerly constructed before they settled there. And just as tithes were once paid from pasture, so now we wish tithes to be paid without diminution from the same lands, which have been brought into fruitful fertility.[32]

There had been a phenomenal expansion of privileged orders, Cistercians, canons regular, and others, and the outcry from injured tithe takers was reaching dangerous proportions. In grasping the nettle Adrian was addressing a very contentious issue with ramifications throughout the whole Latin church, and his clear-minded and even-handed approach was characteristic of his general response to problems. Indeed, John of Salisbury, who was at the Curia in Benevento when some of these letters were issued, commented very precisely and warmly on the judgment:

> Hence it was that the blessed Adrian when he saw these privileges being thus turned into a means of avarice, not wishing to revoke them altogether, he restricted their scope by the limitation that what such men may withhold from the fruits of their labour should be interpreted solely with reference to lands newly brought under cultivation. so that they will be able to enjoy their privileges without serious infringement of the rights of others.[33]

---

[30] See above, at n. 22 and Appendix, no. 8.

[31] *Die Summa des Stephanus über das Decretum Gratiani*, ed. F. von Schulte (Gniessen, 1891), 217–18, 222–3.

[32] As transmitted to *X*, 3.30.4, where it is assigned to Alexander III and Thomas (Becket) archbishop of Canterbury. For the full text, see Appendix, no. 1.

[33] Constable, *Monastic Tithes*, 286–7; *Policraticus sive de nugis curialium (1156–59)*, ed. Clement C. J. Webb, 2 vols (Oxford, 1909), vii. 21 (ed. Webb, ii, 197–8).

Although Adrian's ruling was reversed by Alexander III in respect of the Cistercians (though not entirely consistently),[34] his judgment ultimately prevailed. At the Fourth Lateran Council (1215) Innocent III reverted to something close to Adrian's judicious compromise in canon 55, when he ordered that all privileged orders were to pay tithes on all properties, whether cultivated by them or not, from which tithes had been paid before they acquired them.[35]

The second decision which passed into the permanent law of the Church related to the marriage of unfree persons. In the decretal *Dignum est* (also circulating with the incipit *Tua fraternitas*), Adrian replied to a question raised by Archbishop Eberhard of Salzburg relating to the validity of marriages contracted by *servi* without their lords' approval and even against their wishes (*inuitis et contradicentibus dominis*). Adrian's response was clear and unequivocal:

> Indeed, as your discretion knows, there is in Jesus Christ, according to the saying of the Apostle, 'neither freeman nor slave' [cf. Gal. 3: 28] who should be removed from the church's sacraments, so marriages between serfs (*inter seruos… matrimonia*) should not be forbidden on any account, and if they are contracted against the prohibition and against the wishes of lords they should not for this reason be dissolved by ecclesiastical law, although the service due to their lords should not be reduced on account of this.[36]

---

[34] Constable, *Monastic Tithes*, 294–303. The reversal began early in Alexander's pontificate. Rievaulx, Rutland, and Sibton all received the full 'sane laborum' privilege on 20 November 1160: see C. Duggan, 'Decretals of Alexander III to England', *in Rolando Bandinelli Papa Alessandro III* (Accademia Senese degli Intronati), ed. F. Liotta (Siena 1986), 85–151 at 120 (repr. in Duggan, *Decretals and the 'New Law'*, no. III).

[35] Constable, *Monastic Tithes*, 1–19, 279, 303–09; Pennington, 174

[36] WH 344, JL 10445: Appendix, no. 2. Cf. S. Loewenfeld, 'Papsturkunden in Paris. Ein Reisebericht nebst einem Anhang ungedructe Papstbriefe', *Neues Archiv*, 7 (1882), 143–67 at 167, no. 13 (omits the *arenga*, begins *Tua fraternitas*, and is attributed to Alexander III). On this important decision, see esp. P. Landau, 'Hadrians IV. Dekretale 'Dignum est' (*X* 4.9.1) und die Eheschliessung Unfreier in der Diskussion von Kanonisten und Theologen des 12. und 13. Jahrhunderts', *Studia Gratiana*, 12 (1967) = *Collectanea S. Kuttner*, ii, 511–53; J. Gilchrist, 'The Medieval Canon Law on Unfree Persons: Gratian and the decretist doctrines c. 1141–1234', in *Studia Gratiana*, 19 (1976) = *Mélanges Fransen*, i, 271–301. Cf. A. Sahaydachny Bocarius, 'The Marriage of Unfree Persons: twelfth-century decretals and letters', in *Studia Gratiana*, 27: *De iure canonico medii aevi: Festschrift für Rudolf Weigand* (Rome, 1996), 481–506, at 485, 489–95; P. Landau, 'Frei und Unfrei in der Kanonistik des 12. und 13. Jahrhunderts am Beispiel der Ordination der Unfreien', *in Die abendländische Freiheit vom 10. zum 14. Jahrhundert*, ed. J. Fried (Sigmaringen, 1991), 177–96 at 178; C. N. L. Brooke, *The Medieval Idea of Marriage* (Oxford, 1989), 51–2, 264–5. What got into the permanent law (*X*, 4. 9. 1) was the definitive clause, 'Sane iuxta verbum…exhibenda', but with the omission of the phrase 'ecclesiastico iure'. Friedberg, however, supplied the words 'ecclesiastico iudicio' from the earlier decretal collections, thus making the definition even more universal. The heading in the *Decretals* reads, 'Servus contradicente domino matrimonium contrahere potest, sed propter hoc non liberatur a servitiis domino debitis.'

Lying behind this simple statement was the whole question of the rights of lords over their serfs. In societies where peasants were tied to the soil, even if not technically slaves, their personal freedoms were often very much at the mercy of their lords. Marriage between serfs on a single estate would not, on the whole, cause problems for the lord, who would not lose the services of the couple (and would stand to gain in the procreation of children who would in due course succeed to their parents unfree status and the labour and other services attached to it); but what if serfs from neighbouring estates wished to marry? Here the human and Christian rights of the peasants conflicted with the jurisdictional and economic rights of the lords of the land. Adrian's declaration of the absolute rights of the unfree to contract valid marriages which could not be dissolved by the Church on the grounds of either the unfree status of the spouses or the opposition or prohibition of the lords was a significant step in the legal consolidation of the human and religious rights of the unfree. As in his determinations in relation to monastic tithe exemption, its lack of ambiguity was its greatest merit; and it concerned an issue which had wide ramifications. From Carolingian times onwards the Church had been grappling with the questions relating to the marriage of serfs, either with one another or with persons of free status, especially since different customs existed in different regions of the West. For the twelfth century, the most authoritative statement of the law (in Gratian's crucial C.29 qu.2 c.8) declared that 'the marriages of serfs may not be dissolved, even if they have different lords', but it ends with a significant limitation, 'This is to be observed in those instances where there was a lawful marriage with the lords' approval'. [37] And Gratian's own heading—'Lords may not by their own authority dissolve the lawful marriages of serfs'[38]—only added to the uncertainty, since it seemed to allow dissolution of such marriages by some other authority. Eberhard of Salzburg's question does not survive, but it was probably framed in the knowledge of Gratian's text, and asked if the Church could dissolve the unlicensed marriages of serfs. At a stroke, Adrian removed all ambiguity from the law; and the new directive found its way through decretal collections to Bologna, where it was known and cited in the late 1170s.[39] By the time that the standard commentary on the *Decretum* was composed (*Glossa ordinaria, c.* 1215, by Johannes Teutonicus), canonistic thought had hardened into an assertion of absolute freedom,[40] and as an authoritative statement of the Church's law Adrian's definition was received into the Gregorian *Decretals* of 1234,[41] and so remained in the Corpus of Canon Law until the issue of the new Code in 1917.

---

[37] 'Coniugia servorum non dirimantur, etiam si diversos dominos habeant...Et hoc in illis observandum est, ubi legalis coniunctio fuit, et per voluntatem dominorum.'

[38] 'Legitima servorum coniugia sua auctoritate domini non diriment.'

[39] Landau, 'Hadrianus IV. Dekretale', esp. 516 and 530.

[40] '...maxime, quia etiam eis invitis potest contrahi matrimonium'; cf. Gilchrist, esp. 291 n. 80.

[41] X, 4. 9. 1.

These two judgments alone would be enough to dignify Adrian with the title of reformer, but there is much more that can be said. An encyclical sent to all bishops throughout Germany, Sicily, and England forbade the consecration of anyone whose election was not free, and condemned ecclesiastics who used secular power against the Church;[42] and another condemned the practice of dividing ecclesiastical benefices, since clergy should have an honourable means of livelihood.[43]

To these strictly legal and ecclesiastical directives and judgments, one may add another, generally unremarked, but nonetheless important decision which potentially protected the Iberian peninsula from the expansionist plans of Louis VII and Henry II. In early 1159, he refused to authorize a joint crusade in Spain which had been proposed by the kings of France and England (in brief moment of friendship). Only the letter to Louis VII survives, but since the envoy named in it was a Norman, Bishop Rotrou of Évreux, one may presume that a parallel version, with the appropriate verbal changes, was sent to the English king. *Satis laudabiliter* was a masterpiece of diplomacy and caution, which contrived to flatter its recipient while refusing the principal request. After commending the kings' proposal to extend the boundaries of Christianity,[44] Adrian advised great caution:

> It would seem to be neither wise nor safe to enter a foreign land without first seeking the advice of the princes and people of the area. But, as we understand it, you are proposing to go there in haste, without consulting the Church and the princes of that land, although you ought on no account to attempt it, unless having learned of the need from the princes of the land, you are first asked by them.

It seems that Louis and Henry, who each had interests in the south, were planning a mutually advantageous crusade, which might, in the unsettled state of the Christian kingdoms of northern Spain, have resulted in the expansion of their

[42] *Epistolae Pontificum Romanorum ineditae*, ed. S. Loewenfeld (Leipzig, 1885), 123 no. 226.

[43] *Epistolae...ineditae*, ed. Loewenfeld, 129 no. 234; cf. K. Pennington, *Popes and Bishops: the papal monarchy in the twelfth and thirteenth centuries* (Philadelphia, 1984), 117.

[44] *PL*, clxxxviii, 1615–17 no. 241, dated from the Lateran, 18 February (1158); cf. JL 10546, *sub anno* 1159. JL's ascription of the letter to 1159 is the more likely, since it follows the (temporary) establishment of good relations between the two kings in 1158 (Warren, *Henry II*, 77). Its *arenga* reads (medieval spellings restored), 'Satis laudabiliter et fructuose de Christiano nomine propagando in terris et eterne beatitudinis premio tibi cumulando in celis, tua magnificencia cogitare, dum ad dilatandos terminos populi Christiani, ad paganorum barbariem debellandum, et ad gentes apostatices, et que catholice fidei refugiunt veritatem, Christianorum jugo et ditioni subdendos, simul cum charissimo filio nostro Henrico illustri Anglorum rege, in Hispaniam properare disponis.... Atque ad id conuenientius exequendum, matris tue sacrosancte Romane ecclesie consilium exigis et fauorem.' A very similar *arenga* had been used earlier, in *Laudabiliter*: see below, Part II/i, no. 5b. Adrian, of course, had personal experience of conditions in Spain: see above, ch. 3.

own lordships there. Such uninvited intervention was rejected; and the pope reminded Louis of the disasters which had accompanied an earlier, badly planned and ill-considered crusade (the Second, 1147), in which Louis and the German king, Conrad III had led forces to Jerusalem, 'without consulting the people of the area'. While not rejecting the idea outright, Adrian refused (or rather, more diplomatically, deferred) the grant of the general letters 'of admonition and exhortation addressed to the [king's] people', which Bishop Rotrou had requested, although he said that he would do so, 'when you wish to set out with the advice and at the request of the princes and people of that land, as stated above (*cum de consilio et postulatione tam principum quam populi terre illius, sicut superius dictum est, volueris iter arripere*)'. This letter throws important light, not only on Curial thinking about the Second Crusade, but also on Adrian's finesse, and on the likely conditions attached to the Irish grant.

For Walter Ullmann in his centenary lecture of 1955, 'the Englishman initiated the age of the great medieval popes. Adrian, the pope of action, ranks in importance in no wise below the popes of theory.'[45] For Southern, his reign was crucial on quite another ground. He reckoned that John of Salisbury's three months as an intimate of the English pope gave him a more sensitive understanding of the problems confronting the papacy, and an appreciation of the beneficial effects of papal power as operated by Adrian. This turned John into an enthusiastic papalist who was foremost in promoting papal jurisdiction in England on his return to Theobald of Canterbury's household in mid-1156. Neither of these judgments seems entirely valid. As argued above, Adrian was brought into the Curia because he fitted Eugenius III's profile. To suggest that he '*initiated* the age of the great medieval popes' is to imply a break with the policies and activities of his immediate predecessors that is hard to establish on the evidence available. There is little to differentiate him from Eugenius, except, perhaps, his daring stand against Arnold of Brescia and the Roman Senate.[46] There is more to be said for Southern's view; but John of Salisbury's papalism was *confirmed* not produced by his privileged access to Adrian's table. His familiarity with the inner workings of the Curia may even have pre-dated Adrian's own.[47] He had seen in the saintly Eugenius III the kind of universal pastor that a cleric of his educated and reformist turn of mind yearned for;[48] and he was gratified to find that a fellow-countryman was shaped in similar mould. Two of the dated letters relating to tithe were issued

[45] 'The Pontificate of Adrian IV', *Cambridge Historical Journal*, 11 (1953–5), 233–52, at 233.

[46] The interdict on Rome, which achieved the goal of driving a wedge between Arnold of Brescia and the general populace was the action of a strong-minded man: Boso, *Vita Adriani*, 389.*

[47] His *Historia Pontificalis* (see following n.) recorded his experiences at Eugenius's court in 1148–52.

[48] Though he was not entirely uncritical: John of Salisbury, *Historia Pontificalis*, ed. and trans. M. Chibnall, NMT (London, 1956), 51, 'he was too ready to rely on his personal opinion in imposing sentences (*in ferendis sentenciis spiritum proprium maxime sequebatur*)'.

during John's stay at Benevento; and a further two—the mandate to Theobald relating to Boxley and the general statement of the new policy—probably belong to the same period.[49] John could thus witness at close hand the way in which the papacy could respond sympathetically and constructively to problems brought before it. One may even detect John's influence in Adrian's fierce denunciation of Archbishop Theobald's alleged obstruction of appeals to Rome which was somewhat incongruously inserted at the beginning of a mandate relating to the profession of the abbot of St Augustine's abbey. The mandate was issued at Benevento on 23 January (1156), right in the middle of John's stay, and he would have been in a perfect position to suggest that the pope remind his own archbishop of the absolute right of appeal to the apostolic see. It contains an extended attack on Theobald's behaviour. Here are the two key sentences:

> It has come to our attention by common report that the right of appeal is so smothered by you and the king of England that no-one dares to appeal to the apostolic see in your presence or his..... In addition, you are in every way lukewarm and remiss in dispensing justice to those who suffer injustice, and you are said to seek the king's favour so much and succumb to fear of him that when we send letters to you on behalf of any one that he may have justice, he cannot secure his right through you, as we have heard from the complaints of many. [50]

Having been appointed to Theobald's household in 1147, John would have been in a good position to see what happened to judicial mandates addressed to Theobald. If my suspicion is correct, we have another pointer to John's already highly developed sense of the appellate jurisdiction of the papacy and his fears that it might be imperilled by a combination of Theobald's timorousness and the authoritarian régime of Henry II, just established in England. John was closer to Adrian than he had been to Eugenius, however: seeing a good man in charge of the Curial machine, John became an enthusiastic propagator of the benefits of papal government—and indeed sacrificed his career to it—and Southern was right to

---

[49] *JohnS*, i, 256, 257. Millor/Butler/Brooke say 'between November 1155 and July 1156', but he was back France by the spring of 1156, so must have left Benevento before the end of March. For the decretals, see Appendix, nos 4, 9, 1, 6. No. 8, to Pontida, had been issued a month or so earlier.

[50] 'Ad notitiam siquidem nostram, fama referente, pervenit, quam ita apud te et apud regem Angliae appellatio sit sepulta, quod aliquis non est, qui in tua vel in illius praesentia ad sedem apostolicam audeat appellare...Accedit etiam ad hoc, quod in exhibenda justitia his, qui injustitiam patiuntur, tepidus sis modis omnibus ac remissus, et in tantum parti regis diceris procurare favorem, ejusque timori succumbere, quos si quando litteras tibi pro aliquo, ut suam consequatur justitiam, destinemus, nullatenus poterit per te, sicut jam saepius ex multorum conquestione didicimus, quod suum est obtinere' (*Historia monasterii S. Augustini*, 412). For the argument that this letter brought about John's disgrace in mid-1156, see ch. 7, at n. 185, above. This is probably the letter which Theobald said that, 'out of reverence (for the pope and for his) honour' he had 'not thought fit to show to anyone' (*JohnS*, i, 15).

emphasize John's key role in keeping open the lines of communication between Canterbury and Rome for the remainder of Theobald's pontificate.

Earlier monastic historians (Schreiber, Viard, Mahn) found his tithe policy brutal and even harmful, a judgment accepted and amplified by some secular historians.[51] But Giles Constable successfully challenged these opinions, concluding that 'his policy on monastic tithes should be seen in a framework not of reactionary authoritarianism but of constructive reform.'[52] And the same could be said of his policy on the marriage of serfs and the integrity of ecclesiastical benefices. At the same time, of course, he supported the assertion of episcopal authority within the diocese, in conformity with the decrees of the first Lateran Council (1125),[53] except, as in the case of ancient monastic institutions like St Albans and Bury St Edmunds, for example, where it was modified by long-standing tradition.

For Adrian's perception of his role as pope, one must rely not only on these judgments, but upon what one may call the diplomatic propaganda of the letters issued in his name. Open any page of Adrian's *acta* in *Patrologia Latina* or *Papsturkunden in England* and one will be struck by the relentless repetition of phrases like 'The Apostolic office entrusted to us by God compels us', 'Since by the Lord's will, without any merits of our own, we occupy the chair of the Prince of the Apostles, we are bound to be concerned about the condition of every individual church and it is our duty to bring back to the right path any of their pastors whom we see wandering from the way of truth'; 'Since the Holy Roman Church is the mother and head of all the churches'.[54] His namesake Adrian I had used similar language three hundred years earlier: *summae apostolicae dignitatis apex, apostolicae pastoralis... cura, auctoritate beati Petri apostolorum principis, et nostra atque beati Petri fultus in ista sancta sede auctoritate; Auctoritate igitur beati Petri principis apostolorum...*;[55] and the papal councils of the twelfth century had been laden with it. Consider, for example, Innocent II's phrases in Lateran II (1139), *apostolica auctoritate decernimus... apostolica auctoritate interdicimus, apostolica auctoritate prohibemus, auctoritate Dei et beatorum Petri et*

---

[51]   G. Schreiber, *Kurie und Kloster im 12. Jahrhundert*, 2 vols (Stuttgart, 1910), i, 255–69; Warren, *Henry II*, 195–6, a 'high-gregorian who de-throned monasticism'; but this judgment ignores both the legislation of the First Lateran Council (1123), cc. 16 and 19, which reinforced episcopal authority over monasteries, and his defence of ancient exemptions, like those of St Albans.

[52]   Constable, *Monastic Tithes*, 286.

[53]   Lateran I, cc. 2, 4, 16, 18, 19. Cf. his confirmation of Battle Abbey's subordination to Chichester: JL 10002; *Chronicle of Battle Abbey*, ed. Eleanor Searle, OMT (Oxford, 1980), 164–5; Pennington, *Popes and Bishops*, 157.

[54]   'Ex iniuncto nobis a Deo apostolatus officium' (*PL*, clxxxviii, 1448); 'Ad hoc apostolorum Principis in cathedra, licet non suffragantibus meritis, auctiore Domino, residemus, ut de singularum statu Ecclesiarum debeamus esse solliciti, et earum pastores, quoties a via veritatis exorbitant, ad statum rectitudinis nos convenit revocare' (*ibid.*, 1451, to Archbishop John of Toledo); 'Quae mater omnium ecclesiarum et caput esse dignoscitur sacrosancta Romana ecclesia...' (*ibid.*, 1466).

[55]   *PL*, xcvi, 1211–13 nos 53–5.

Pauli... interdicimus.[56] There is nothing surprising here. Papal letters and privileges were drafted by teams of skilled *dictatores* who followed rigid rules of diplomatic, script, and format. From the days of John of Gaeta at the end of the eleventh century, the form and much of the language of papal documents was established, and one can detect little formal or linguistic difference in the products of the chancery from one papal reign to another. The evocative phrases 'by the authority of blessed Peter, prince of the apostles (*auctoritate igitur beati Petri principis apostolorum*)', 'by the authority of the apostolic see (*apostolice sedis auctoritate*)', and so on, came readily to their pens. They perfected the art of prefacing even the most mundane mandate or recapitulation of privilege with *arengae* which encapsulated the Roman see's claimed to Petrine authority and primacy over the whole catholic church. That these phrases were ancient and formulaic in nature is self-evident, but that does not mean that Adrian's chancery was endlessly repeating empty *formulae* that had no meaning. In fact, of course, they proclaimed the pope's sense of his apostolic inheritance and his apostolic responsibility as the successor of St Peter.[57]

This same theme is evident in his attempted rapprochement with the Greek Church in 1157–8. The context is unfortunately obscure, since the two letters, which alone provide evidence of the exchange between Pope Adrian and the Greek Metropolitan Basil of Ochrida, are undated. An earlier historical tradition linked the correspondence to an imagined papal-Byzantine alliance against William I of Sicily in 1155–6,[58] but a more likely context is the aftermath of the 1157 treaty between King William and Manuel I Comnenus, which stabilized relations between the two powers to the extent that the Greeks recognized Norman power in Apulia and the Norman kingdom relinquished its ambitions in the eastern Mediterranean.[59] There is some evidence that the pope played a part in the peace making.[60] It was perhaps at this time that Adrian sent two emissaries (Baldwin and Baldizio) to the emperor Manuel, accompanied by a letter of introduction to Basil of Ochrida, metropolitan of Thessalonica. urging the archbishop to work for the reunion of the churches, and to smooth the path of the papal envoys. It is as Peter's successor that Adrian speaks: having undertaken the charge of the apostolic see in

---

[56] Lat. II, cc. 9, 10, 16, 18.

[57] Not only did he see himself in this role, but Gerhoch of Reicherberg addressed him as such at the beginning of his pontificate (*Letter to Pope Hadrian*, ed. Häring, 26, 'tu, Adriane, successor Petri apostoli'), and spoke eloquently of his obligation '...confirmare fratres et infirmare hostes ut porte inferi non preualeant in diebus nostris aduersus ecclesiam Petro commissam, in petra fundatam, Petri fide roboratam' (*ibid.*, 118).

[58] F. Chalandon, *Histoire de la domination normande en Italie et en Sicile*, 2 vols [Paris, 1907; repr. New York, 1969] ii, 211–12; S. Runciman, *The Eastern Schism* (Oxford, 1955), 119.

[59] J. G. Rowe, 'Hadrian IV, the Byzantine Empire, and the Latin Orient', *Essays in Medieval History presented to Bertie Wilkinson*, ed. T. A. Sandquist and M. R. Powicke (Toronto, 1969), 3–16, at 13, n. 52.

[60] Nicetas Chroniates, *Historia: De Manuele Comneno*, ii. 8, ed. I. Bekker (Bonn, 1835), 127–8.

accordance with God's will, he was obliged to discharge Peter's ministry for all the churches on earth, although lacking nearly all his virtues (*Quamobrem et nos, qui hoc tempore apostolicae sedis curam suscepimus, ut Deo placet, pro omnibus ecclesiis quae sunt intra terrarum orbem constitutae, quamvis beati Petri virtutibus par nihil habeamus, ministerio tamen fungi cogimur*). Lamenting the separation between the see of Constantinople and the Holy Roman and Apostolic Church, and professing himself to be the servant of all God's servants, he addressed the archbishop as *frater in Christo*, and urged him 'to work to bring those who recognize themselves to be the Lord's sheep back to the flock of St Peter, who had undertaken their care at the Lord's command'.[61]

He was as conscious as any of his predecessors of the long tradition of the see of Peter; as much as they he relied on Peter's authority, on the primacy of Peter, and on the sense of the unifying and co-ordinating role of the papal office. But the authority was not that of a dictator. Running through many of his letters is a highly significant additional emphasis. In the decretal about tithes to the monks of Pontida, he wrote, 'Having been placed by the Lord's disposition in a lofty watch-tower (*in eminenti specula*), if the rights of all the churches are not preserved whole and unimpaired (*integra et illibata*), we would seem to occupy the place of St Peter Prince of the Apostles unprofitably (*inutiliter*) and to exercise the office of stewardship entrusted to us negligently'.[62] There is a profound sense of the heavy responsibility which the pope bears for the welfare of all churches. In another of the decretals cited above, he wrote, 'The duty of stewardship entrusted to us by God warns and exhorts us in various ways that we should provide profitably for all the faithful and churches of Christ, and it is our duty to preserve their rights whole and unimpaired (*Commissum nobis a Deo dispensationis officium admonet et exhortatur multipliciter ut universis Christi fidelibus et ecclesiis debeamus utiliter*

---

[61] 'ut...qui seipsos Dominicas oves confitentur, ad gregem beati Petri revertantur, qui Domini jussu eorum curam suscepit' (*PL*, clxxxviii, 1580–2, at 1581). For Basil's response, which emphasized the doctrinal orthodoxy and apostolic dignity of the 'magnam apostolicamque sedem Constantinopolitanam', to whose allegiance he belonged, see Mansi, xxi, 799–802, at 800, 802: 'Tuto autem, ac firmiter, Dei gratia, stetimus in beati Petri confessione. Et quem ille confessus et praedicavit, confitemur et praedicamus; nihil ex synodalibus sanctorum patrum decretis innovantes, nec adjicientes evangelicis et apostolicis verbis, ad unum apicem usque, vel jota unum. [...] Eademque tecum praedicamus et docemus ego, iique omnes, qui ad magnam apostolicamque sedem Constantinopolitanam pertinemus.'

[62] 'Nobis in eminenti specula, disponente Domino, constitutis, si cunctarum iura ecclesiarum integra non debent et illibata servari, locum beati Petri apostolorum principis inutiliter obtinere, et juxta commisse nobis dispensationis officium negligenter agere videremur. Sic enim Ecclesia Dei, nobis eam diuina prouidente gratia gubernantibus, recte suo cursu dirigitur, dum nos errata queque uigili prouisione corrigere et unicuique studemus ius proprium conseruare' (*PL*, clxxxviii, 1586). The letter concludes, 'Nos siquidem religiosis uiris non alias decimas nisi eas, qua de noualibus prouenire noscuntur duximus indulgendas' (*ibid.*, 1586–7): medieval spellings have been restored. I am grateful to Professor Christopher Brooke for suggesting 'in a lofty watch-tower' as the translation for *in eminenti specula*.

prouidere, atque integra iura sua nos oportet atque illibata).' Again, the emphasis on office, responsibility, usefulness, and the maintenance of the rights of those who appeal to him. His is a duty of stewardship (*dispensationis officium*). And in the third example, in the *arenga* of the ground-breaking decision on the marriage of serfs, he prefaced the decision with an assertion of the Apostolic See's responsibility to provide clear guidance in matters of doubt, so that the faithful could be assured of true teaching: 'It is right and reasonable that those things which appear to involve a measure (scruple) of uncertainty should be referred to the judgment of the Apostolic See, so that Christ's faithful may rejoice to find certitude in the place from which they are known to have received the teaching of the faith (*Dignum est et a ratione non discordat, quod ea que inter se dubietatis scrupulum videntur continere ad apostolice sedis iudicium referantur, ut inde Christi fideles in dubiis certitudinem se gaudeant inuenire, unde noscuntur magisterium fidei suscepisse*).'[63] We need not doubt the validity of the statement which John of Salisbury attributed to Adrian, 'The Lord has long since placed me between the hammer and the anvil, and now He must Himself support the burden He has placed upon me, for I cannot carry it.'[64] It is supported by Gerhoch of Reichersberg's contemporary comment that Anastasius IV and Adrian IV 'were preoccupied and disturbed by many things (*quia erant occupati et turbati erga plurima*)'.[65] Something of the weight of that burden can be appreciated when it is remembered that some of the most important decisions of his pontificate were made in the midst of political and military crisis from mid-1155 to mid-1157, when he was confronting the quadruple challenge of Roman insurrection, the invasion of the patrimony by William I of Sicily, the armed march of Frederick I to Rome, and the Norman war.

For Adrian, the title which followed his name in all letters and privileges, 'servant of God's servants', had more than a rhetorical meaning. Combined with the concepts of stewardship, duty, and usefulness it is the language of eminent service. And it was a service which numerous individuals and institutions sought, at great trouble and expense. These principles underlay the whole of his policy as pope: not a single theory, but a programme of dealing individually with the cases that came before him, and seeking order and fairness. Where centuries of historical development had produced overlapping and contentious rights, this pope sought *unicuique... ius proprium conseruare*: to preserve everyone's right—a clear echo of one of the basic principle of classical Roman law.[66] He knew as well as anybody how vulnerable was the Curia to the biased reports of one side, or the undue pressure of power and money. As in his determinations in Scandinavia, where he balanced Lund's losses in the elevation of Trondheim as primate of Norway with

[63] For the full text, see Appendix, no. 2.
[64] *Policraticus*, viii. 23.
[65] *Letter to Pope Hadrian*, ed. Häring, 10.
[66] As stated in Justinian's *Digest*, 1.1.10§1, attributed to the Roman jurist Ulpian, 'Iustitia est constans et perpetua voluntas ius suum cuique tribuendi. Iuris praecepta sunt haec: honeste vivere, alterum non laedere, suum cuique tribuere.'

confirmation of its status as the primatial see for Sweden, so he pursued a similar even-handed policy, as far as he could, in dealings with monasteries and bishoprics. He was generally sensitive to the aspirations of regional churches. Dol was emancipated from Tours;[67] and although he allowed himself to be persuaded to give some form of approval to Henry II's proposals for Ireland, he did not give a blank cheque, nor did he disturb the independent ecclesiastical structure of the *ecclesia hibernica* which had been established by papal authority at the council of Kells-Mellifont in 1152. Nor, indeed, was the Anglo-Norman conquest of 1170–2 the consequence of his action. Its origins lay in the disturbed state of twelfth-century Ireland and the active seeking of Cambro-Norman and Angevin military aid by the former king of Leinster. Adrian's grant played no part either in the conquest or in the subsequent establishment of Henry II's rule in the island. The relevant and effective papal mandates were issued by Pope Alexander III in September 1172, in response to an approach from Henry II, supported by letters from the Irish bishops.[68]

William of Newburgh wrote that 'Because [the young Nicholas Breakspear] was "handsome of body, smiling of face, prudent in words, and swift to carry out instructions, he pleased everybody"'.[69] That characterization was associated with Nicholas's invitation to become a canon at Saint-Ruf and could imply that he was ready to ingratiate himself with the powerful, to make friends and influence people by accommodation and charm. Did he do the same in Rome? He certainly made friends and influenced people, but the Roman Curia was a very different place from Saint-Ruf.

Surrounding the pope was an increasingly self conscious and independently-minded College of Cardinals—so called from Urban II's day. This was a body of between twenty and thirty advisers and coadjutors of the pope, whose rise to prominence can be traced from the election decree of 1059, which began the process which established the cardinals as the electoral college of the papacy. Since they elected the pope, usually from their own number, they came increasingly to form the council which the pope consulted on all important matters and judgments, and their elevated position was emblazoned on papal privileges, where their attestations are arrayed in three hierarchical groupings beneath the pope's own name. In councils they were seated to the right and left of the pope; as legates they took precedence of all prelates. The frequent occurrence of the phrase 'with the advice of our brethren' (*fratrum nostrorum consilio*) is further testimony to their active participation in papal decision-making; and incidental references by eyewitness, by John of Salisbury, for example, or by Cardinal Boso,[70] confirm that

---

[67] Appendix, no. 10. This ruling was later reversed.

[68] See ch. 7, at n. 221.

[69] William of Newburgh, *Historia rerum Anglicarum*, in *Chronicles of the Reigns of Stephen, Henry II, and Richard I*, ed. R. G. Howlett, RS 82/i–ii (1884–5), i, 110, 'Et quoniam erat corpore elegans, vultu jocundus, prudens in verbis, ad injuncta impiger; placuit omnibus.'

[70] *Historia Pontificalis*, 45, refers to cases being discussed 'in consistorio'; cf. Boso,

this was no mere form of words. The pope, then, was not the autocratic monarch beloved of critics. So, given that Adrian had little experience of Curial matters before his election, was he the creature or the master of the court? After all, he inherited a college of cardinals whose cumulative experience ran to some twenty years at the pinnacle of ecclesiastical power and included such forceful characters as Imar of Tusculum,[71] Henry of Pisa,[72] Bernard of Lucca,[73] John of Naples,[74] Otto of Brescia,[75] Hyacinth of S. Maria in Cosmedin,[76] Octavian of S. Cecilia, who was elected as Adrian's successor by a small minority of the cardinals on 7 September 1159 and became the anti-pope Victor IV (in opposition to Alexander III),[77] and, most important of all, the chancellor, Cardinal Roland of S. Marco. Plucked from scholarly life by Eugenius III, he had, like Adrian himself, been propelled to the highest rungs of the Curial ladder by virtue of his reputation. Indeed, Eugenius is said to have nominated him as a worthy successor just before he died.[78] This was not a college of ciphers, and it would not be surprising if Adrian, whose knowledge of the ways of the Curia was probably less than almost anyone already on the team, so to speak, would have relied on the experience and skill of men like this. But that does not mean that he was controlled by them. On the contrary: such a court was unlikely to have promoted to its highest rank a relatively unknown man who lacked wealth and connexions, unless he had other substantial compensating qualities. The place for a cipher, even a hard-working cipher, would

---

Vita Adriani, 394.

[71] Cardinal bishop of Tusculum (Frascati) 1142–62. A Cluniac by training (formerly Prior of La Charité-sur-Loire and abbot of Montierneuf), he was one of the longest-serving senior cardinals, whose support for Cardinal Octavian ('Victor IV') gave considerable credibility to his claims in 1159: Brixius, 44, 91–2; Zenker, 44–6.

[72] Cardinal priest of SS. Nereo e Achilleo (1151–66), was a major player in the Curia, both through his Cistercian connexions (he had been a monk at Clairvaux under St Bernard, and abbot of Tre Fontane in Rome, in succession to Bernard of Pisa, later Eugenius III) and his wide friendship circle, which included Arnulf of Lisieux, Rotrou of Rouen, Hugh of Champfleury, and Gerhoh of Reichersberg: Brixius, 54–5, 108; Zenker, 96–100.

[73] Above, ch. 7, n. 110.

[74] John of Naples, formerly associated with Saint-Victor in Paris, successively cardinal priest of SS. Sergio e Bacco (1150–8), cardinal priest of S. Anastasia (1158–83): Brixius, 55–6, 110–11; Zenker, 73–7; cf. Falcandus, i, 103–4; *JohnS*, ii, 117, n. 42.

[75] Master Otto of Brescia, cardinal deacon of S. Nicola in Carcere Tulliano (1153–75), prior of the cardinal deacons: Brixius, 56, 111–12; Zenker, 171–4.

[76] Hyacinth Bobo, whose family was linked with the Orsini, cardinal deacon of S. Maria in Cosmedin (1144–91), Pope Celestine III (1191–8), was another long-serving reformer and influential curialist: Brixius, 52, 104; Zenker, 161–7; Tillmann, 'Ricerche sull'origine dei membri del collegio cardinalizio nel XII secolo, II/i', *Rivista di storia della Chiesa in Italia*, xxvi (1972), 350–3.

[77] Above, ch. 7, n. 12.

[78] Roland [Bandinelli], from Siena, cardinal deacon of S. Cosma e Damiano (1150), cardinal priest of S. Marco (1151–9), chancellor of the Roman Church (1153–9), Pope Alexander III 1159–81: M. Pacaut, *Alexandre III: Étude sur la conception du pouvoir pontifical dans sa pensée et dans son oeuvre* (Paris, 1956), 79, 83; cf. Brixius, 57, 112; Zenker, 85–8.

have been in the lower echelons of the papal bureaucracy, not cardinal bishop of Albano and then pope.

Very little is accurately known about his early life, apart from his birth in a village near St Albans (? Abbots Langley) and his ambiguous association with the abbey, but Christoph Egger's careful reconstruction of his early years puts new flesh on the insubstantial bones of the tantalizingly reticent sources. The picture that emerges, of Adrian the lawyer, trained in the law schools at Arles, where he would almost certainly have studied Roman law, helps to explain much that has hitherto been puzzling about his seemingly meteoric rise from apparent obscurity to the pinnacle of the Latin Church. And another revealing part of the puzzle has been unveiled by Damian Smith, following the work of Ursula Vones-Liebenstein. His abbacy at Saint-Ruf involved him in the Spanish *reconquista* at an important turning-point. He was in Catalonia in 1148–9, where he supported the coalition of forces arrayed against Muslim strongholds in the frontier regions, and he was present at the crucial siege of Tortosa, which fell to Ramon Berenguer IV of Barcelona on 30 December 1148.[79] Even with this background, however, his achievements in the last decade of his life (1149–59) are by any reckoning spectacular. Arriving in Rome, either to defend himself against charges brought by his brethren at Saint-Ruf, as claimed by William of Newburgh or, as asserted more convincingly by Cardinal Boso, who would have been an eye-witness, to secure papal letters in their favour—a claim which is supported by the re-dating of one of Eugenius's privileges, he was enthusiastically received by Pope Eugenius III (to whom he was not unknown),[80] and, with the unanimous approval of the college of cardinals appointed cardinal bishop of Albano. From abbot of Saint-Ruf to cardinal bishop in one step was remarkable enough; but then, in 1152, he was sent as papal legate to Scandinavia, his mission to establish the local hierarchy, to detach the Scandinavians from Hamburg-Bremen, to encourage reform, and to bind the rapidly developing northern church to the Apostolic See. He found himself in the middle of a civil war between three rival claimants for the Norwegian throne and earned golden opinions from Snorri Sturleson for his role in ending the conflict that had distracted the region since the death of King Harald in 1136. Flushed with greater success than can have been anticipated,[81] he arrived back in Rome to find Anastasius IV installed as pope, and was unanimously elected pope, the third religious in a row, on Anastasius' death in December 1154.

From abbot to pope in four and three-quarter years is pretty good going for a non-Roman, a non-Italian, a non-noble who had not served a long apprenticeship in the Curia. There must have been more to Nicholas Breakspear than has been recorded. He had been selected by one of the most enthusiastically religious and

[79] Above, ch. 3, at n. 33.

[80] Above, ch. 2, at n. 58. For earlier contacts, see *ibid.*, at nn. 49–50. Giles Constable suggested (*ibid.*, n. 51) that he may have been acting as an unofficial papal legate in Catalonia in 1148–9.

[81] Although the creation of a separate Swedish archbishopric had to wait until 1164: see ch. 4.

spiritual popes of the century; head-hunted, one might say, because he shared Eugenius's own spiritual outlook. He was, moreover, trained in the disciplines of the learned law and had been imbued with the spirit of one of the reformed congregations. The fact that he was immediately inserted into the inner ring of cardinals, as cardinal bishop of Albano, without any apprenticeship as papal chaplain or even in the lower grades of the cardinalate, speaks volumes for the Cistercian pope's high regard for him. Moreover, he was almost immediately sent on a high profile and very important mission to settle the affairs of church in Scandinavian (problems which had been around since at least 1123). He was probably given the job because of his English origins, but the idea was not his. There can be little doubt that the broad strategy was worked out in advance by Eugenius and the Curia—and it is likely that one of his coadjutors was Boso, then a senior member of the chancery, whose knowledge of papal and ecclesiastical precedent was probably unrivalled.[82] But it was his authority as cardinal bishop that directed the mission, and it took great diplomatic skill and adroitness to define the new provinces without creating grievance. What we see here is a pattern of moderation and mediation; a policy of even-handedness, aimed at reconciling conflicting claims so that all sides should be content with the outcome. Crude judgment which left one party bitter and aggrieved was not the manner of this legate, nor was it the manner of this legate made pope. Here can be discerned traits of character and broad strategy which support William Stubbs's century-old conclusion that he was 'a great pope; that is, a great constructive pope, not a controversial one, like those who preceded and followed; a man of organizing power and missionary zeal; a reformer',[83] even though there were many controversial aspects of Adrian's career of which Stubbs was unaware. But he was a reformer in the context of continuation not revolution.

Cardinal Boso rounded off his account of the English pope with a summary of his building work in the City and the Patrimony. This emphasis was certainly a distant echo of the classical panegyric, which proclaimed the permanent glory which the building or restoration of public buildings and palaces conferred on the imperial patron, but it should not therefore be dismissed as meaningless rhetoric. Adrian entered into the tradition of restoring and improving the face of Rome; a longer and less distracted pontificate would no doubt have left a greater imprint on the physical structure of the city. In St Peter's patrimony, however, both his efforts at creating a strategic defence system and his systematic imposition of papal authority looked forward to the much better known achievements of Innocent III at the beginning of the thirteenth century.

---

[82] Such was the view of Duchesne, who commented on the absence of Boso's name from papal *privilegia* issued during that period: *Liber Pontificalis* (ed. Duchesne), ii, xxxix.

[83] Boso, *Vita Adriani*, 389: 'Erat enim vir valde benignus, mitis et patiens, in anglica et latina lingua peritus, in sermone facundus, in eloquentia politus, in cantilena praecipuus et praedicator egregius; ad irascendum tardus, ad ignoscendum velox, ylaris dator, in elemosinis largus et in omni morum compositione praeclarus.'

Adrian was neither a cipher, manipulated by the college of cardinals, of which Roland, his successor, was a key member, as well as being chancellor and probably the drafter of many of the letters issued by the pontiff,[84] nor a *prima donna*: but a man of discipline, who fitted in with the norms and routines already in place; a lawyer and canon regular whose natural instincts were for regularity and order; a priest who had exercized the *cura animarum* in the bustling city of Melgueil;[85] a man of affairs who had no fixed programme, but who responded judiciously to the problems brought before his court. He picked up the burden of St Peter; exhausted himself in the unremitting toil that the office imposed; and maintained and defended the claims of Peter's see at a moment of grave crisis.

[84] For the argument that he was the 'real power behind the throne' (Peter Munz, *Frederick Barbarossa. A Study in Medieval Politics* [London, 1969], 78), and shaper of a new pro-Sicilian and anti-imperial policy, see ch. 7, at nn. 4, 8, 70, 117.

[85] '...fuitque primo ut pauper clericus, sive clericus pauperculus in ecclesia beati Jacobi in Melgorio Magolonensis dyocesis enutritus' (Bernard Gui, *Flores chronicorum seu catalogus pontificum Romanorum*, in Muratori, *Rer. Ital. SS*, 3/i, 440); cf. above, ch. 2, at nn. 21 and 46.

APPENDIX

Decretals of Adrian IV transmitted in canonical sources
(listed alphabetically by incipit)

1. *Commissum nobis (al. Commisse nobis) a Deo…persolui*

Adrian IV to Theobald, archbishop of Canterbury, ordering him to compel the Cistercians of Boxley to pay tithes in full to the church of St Mary, in whose parish they live, from their cultivated lands from which tithes had once been paid, whether formerly used for dwellings or for pasture. Undated, but probably early (*c.* 1155).

Commissum nobis a Deo dispensationis officium admonet multipliciter et hortatur ut universis Christi fidelibus uel ecclesiis debeamus utiliter prouidere, atque integra iura sua nos oportet atque illibata conseruare. Peruenit quidem ad nos quod monachi de Borle *[recte* Boxelee] ecclesie sancte Marie, in cuius parochia commorantur, decimas ex integro non persoluunt, et eas ªsecundum canonesª reddere contradicunt. Eapropter, fraternitati tue per apostolica scripta precipiendo mandamus, quatinus predictos monachos ut ipsas decimas, etiam de illis cultis, in quibus olim domus constructe fuerant, prefate ecclesie cum ea integritate persoluant, qua priusquam in eadem ecclesia morarentur, solebant persolui, sine appellationis obstaculo, nostra auctoritate, omni cum districtione compellas. Sicut enim de pascuis olim soluebantur decime, ita nunc de eisdem ad frugum fertilitatem translatis, [decimas] uolumus absque diminutione persolui.

[1] This text is based on *1 Alc.*, with some better readings supplied from *Belv.* (as indicated).

a–a om. *1 Alc*; supplied from *Belv.*

JL 11660; WH 134. Printed: *PL*, cc, 613; *Materials for the History of Thomas Becket, Archbishop of Canterbury*, ed. J. C. Robertson and J. B. Sheppard, RS 67, 7 vols (London, 1875–85), v, 129 no. 66 (from *Belv.*); *App.* 13.12; *Cass.* 35.13; *1 Comp. Ag.* 3.26.18; *X*, 3.30.4 (Commissum nobis. Ea propter…persolui). For these *sigla*, see '*Sigla* of Decretal Collections and related works', below. Cf. Constable, *Monastic Tithes*, 301. This important letter was often wrongly attributed to Alexander III with Archbishop Thomas (Becket) as recipient, but Adrian was identified as the author in six decretal collections assembled in Continental Europe in the late 1170s and 1180s (*1 Berol., Cus., 2 Par., Oriel., Brug., Frcf.*): see Charles Duggan, 'St Thomas of Canterbury, and Aspects of the Becket Dispute, in the Decretal Collections', in *Mediaevalia Christiana XIe–XIIIe siécles. Hommage à Raymonde Foreville*, ed. C. E. Viola (Paris, 1989), 87–135 at 95 no. 3; repr. with the same pagination in Duggan, *Decretals and the 'New Law'*, no. II. He is also correctly identified in the appendices to Gratian in the Biberach and Innsbruck manuscripts. The mistaken attribution to Alexander III and Thomas Becket, sometimes called 'Saint' in the manuscripts, no doubt arose from a scribal error that arose from confusion between two consecutive popes with the initial A. and two consecutive archbishops of Canterbury with the initial Th., probably first made in the mid-1170s, after Becket's canonization in February 1173. Cf. above, at n. 32.

Canonical tradition. Complete. Appendices to Gratian: Biberach-an-der-Riss, Spitalarchiv, MS B 3515 (Gratian's *Decretum*, fol. 271vb: cf. Rudolf Weigand, 'Die Dekrethandschrift B 3515 des Spitalarchivs Biberach an der Riss', *BMCL*, NS 2 (1972), 76–81, at 79; Kuttner, *ibid.*, 3 (1973), 61–71 at 69; Innsbruck, Univ.-Bibl., MS 90, fols 273–7, fols 276r–v (no. 7: *[C]ommisse*) Decretal collections: (a) incip. *Commissum: 1 Alc.* 107; *App.* 13.12; *Bamb. (BACD)* 25.13; *Erl.* 25.13; *Lips.* 23.17; *Cass.CB* 35.13; *Tann.* 3.14.12; *Sang.* 4.10.13; *1 Comp.* 3.26.18. (b) incip.

Commisse: 1 Berol. 52; *Cus.* 26; *Belv.* 53; *Font.* 2.38 *Reg.* 122 *Wig.* 2.23; *Chelt.* 10.12; *Cott.* 4.21; *Pet.* 3.5 *2 Par.* 56.4; *Brug.* 17.12. Abbrev.: *Summa* 'Quoniam status ecclesiarum', Paris, BN, MS lat. 16538, fol. 39ra; *Oriel.* [13].15, *Commissum.* Peruenit ad nos...persolui; *Frcf.* 20.15; *X* 3.30.4 *Commissum.* Peruenit ad nos...persolui; Fragmentum H, fol. 222va–b [no. 122], Commissum. Peruenit ad nos...persolui.

2. *Dignum est et a ratione non discorda...exhibenda*

Adrian IV to Eberhard, archbishop of Salzburg: even without their masters' consent, serfs (serui) may contract valid marriages and such marriages may not be dissolved by ecclesiastical law. Undated: 1154–9.

Dignum est et a ratione non discordat, quod ea que inter se dubietatis scrupulum videntur continere ad apostolice sedis iudicium referantur, ut inde Christi fideles in dubiis certitudinem se gaudeant inuenire, unde noscuntur magisterium fidei suscepisse. Tua uero fraternitas de seruorum coniugiis, que inuitis et contradicentibus dominis contrahuntur, quid fieri debeat ab episcopatu uestro, sicut bene meminimus, requisiuit. Super quo talibus duximus respondendum. Sane iuxta uerbum Apostoli, prout tua discretio cognocit, in Christi Iesu neque liber est neque seruus (Gal. 3: 28) qui a sacramentis ecclesisticis sit ammouendus, ita quoque nec inter seruos debent matrimonia nullatenus prohiberi, et si dominis contradicentibus et inuitis contracta fuerint, nulla ratione propter hoc sunt ecclesiastico iure dissoluenda, debita tamen et consueta seruitia non ex hoc minus sunt propriis dominis exhibenda.

JL 10445; WH 344. Printed: Complete: Mansi, *Concilia,* xxii (Venice, 1776), 411, c. 7 (= *Appendix Concilii Laternensis,* 45. 7); S. Loewenfeld, 'Papsturkunden in Paris. Ein Reisebericht nebst einem Anhang ungedruckter Papstbriefe', *Neues Archiv,* 7 (1882), 167 no. 13 (begins *Tua fraternitas,* with attribution to Alexander III). Abbrev.: *X* 4.9.1 *Dignum est.* Sane iuxta uerbum...persolui.

Canonical tradition. Complete. *Flor.* 124; *Duac.* 59; *1 Berol.* 53; *Cus.* 140; *2 Par.* 79.1; *App.* 45.7 (*V* 45.6); *Bamb.* *(DT)* 56.12, *(O)* 57.6; *Erl..* 57.1; *Cass.CB* 65un; *Brug.* 49.8; *Frcf.* 5.3 + 5.2; *1 Comp.* 4.9.1. Abbrev.: (a) incip. *Tua fraternitas: 1 Vict.* 137 (Alex. III); *1 Par.* 97(Alex. III); *Claud.* 152 (Alex. III); *Wig.* 1.27 (Alex. III); *Claustr.* 56 (Alex. III); *Cott.* 2.80 (Alex. III); *Pet.* 1.94 (Alex. III); *Tann.* 7.13.9 (Adrian II!); *Sang.* 9.35 (Adrian. II!). (b) *Dignum est.* Sane iuxta uerbum, but with the significant omission of the phrase 'ecclesiastico iure': *X* 4.9.1. Cf. above, at nn. 36–41.

3. *Dilecti filii nostri...ratione uexari*

Adrian IV to Boso, bishop of Châlons-sur-Marne, on the complaint of his cathedral canons, ordering him to compel the leprosorium of St James (not Jacob) of Châlons to pay the anciently established tithes to the canons, but their new gardens and orchards are exempt: 'De noualibus autem ortis et arboribus eosdem infirmos exactione decimarum nolumus aliqua ratione uexari.' Undated: 1154–9.

JL —; WH 353a. Printed: *Decretales ineditae,* 20–1 no. 11. Cf. above, at nn. 18, 21–35.

Canonical tradition: only in the *Summa,* 'Quoniam status ecclesiarum', Paris, BN, MS lat. 16538, fols 38vb–39ra.

4. *Dilectus filius noster...ullatenus promulgare*

Dat. Beneuenti .xiiii. kal. Ianuarii.

Adrian IV to Hugh, archbishop of Sens and Alan, bishop of Auxerre, on the complaint of Abbot Peter of Montier-la-Celle, Troyes, ordering them to compel, respectively, the nuns of Foicy (Foissy) to pay tithes to the house of Saint-Florentin (a dependency of Montier-la-Celle), and G. Furnerius to restore land which he had sold to the abbot, or to appear before them so that justice might be done. Dated Benevento, 19 December [1155].

JL —; WH 366. Printed: *Decretales ineditae saeculi XII*, ed. Chodorow and Duggan, 7–9 no. 4; S. Kuttner, 'Collectio Francofurtana', *ZRG Kan. Abt.*, 22 (1933), 370–80 at 379–80.

It may not be without significance that the beneficiary of this letter, Peter of Celle, later abbot of S. Rémi of Reims, had been a friend and patron of John of Salisbury during their student days in Paris: it is possible that John pressed Peter's case, as indeed he had done on an earlier occasion in December 1153, when he was involved in the impetration of a papal privilege for Celle from Anastasius IV (=*JohnS*, i, 255). Cf. above, at nn. 18, 22–35.

Canonical tradition: *Flor.* 46; *Frcf.* 20.16.

5. *Ex parte dilecti filii nostri Ior(dani)...querimonia iterata*

Adrian IV to the bishop of Città di Castello, on complaint of the cathedral prior Jordan (1153–70), ordering him to forbid the prior and monks of S. Giacomo and the brethren of S. Fortunato to receive tithes from, or impose penance on, parishioners of the cathedral. Undated: 1154–9.

JL —; WH 454. Printed: *Alan.*; Holtzmann, 'Kanonistische Ergänzungen', *QF*, 37 (1957), 94–5 no. 46. Cf. above, at nn. 18, 22–35.

Canonical tradition: *Alan.*, Appendix, 90; *Fuld.* 3.20.15.

6. *Graues apud presentiam nostram...reconsignent*

Adrian IV to English recipients. General mandate restricting the tithe exemption of Cistercian monasteries to newly cultivated lands (*novales*). Undated, but likely to be early (1154–5).

Adrianus papa quartus: ut nulla ecclesia suis decimationibus privetur.

Graues apud presentiam nostram tam de Italicis quam de Gallicanis partibus quidam episcopi atque abbates, canonici et capellani querelas deposuerunt quod Cisterciensis ordinis abbates et monachi eis decimas iniuste auferrent, dicentes se nostris a predecessoribus priuilegiatos esse et ideo de propria cultura non debere decimas persoluere; sicque fiebat ut, dum ipsi terras et possessiones adquirerent, ecclesie que ab ipsis primordialibus nascentis ecclesie cunabulis fundate subsistebant destruerentur. Nos ergo tantum detrimentum tamque grauem ruinam considerantes, ex discretionis et pietatis intuitu statuimus ut predicti Cistercienses decimas de noualibus que proprio labore excoluerint sibi retineant; ceteras uero ecclesiis, ad quarum dioceses terre et possessiones pertinere noscuntur, sine ulla dilatione reconsignent. Novales autem illos appellamus quorum cultus memoria non extat.

JL —; WH 533b. Printed: *Decretales ineditae*, ed. Chodorow and Duggan, 140–1 no. 81; cf. *Summa* 'Elegantius in iure diuino' *sive Coloniensis*, ed. S. Kuttner and G. Fransen, Monumenta

Iuris Canonici, 1/i (New York, 1969), ps. 9, c. 38. For an English translation, see above, at n. 27; Constable, *Monastic Tithes*, p. 281. Cf. also at nn. 18, 22–35 above.

Canonical tradition: *Summa* 'Elegantius in iure diuino' (Bamberg, Staatsbibl. MS can. 39, fol. 98v; Vienna, Staatsbibl., MS 2125, fol. 92vb; Paris, BN, MS lat. 14997, fol. 103r–v), *om.* 'Nouales... extat'; *Collectio Caesaraugustana* (Paris, BN, MS lat. 3876, fol. 57r: added in margin; Vatican City, Biblioteca Apostolica Vaticana, MS Vat. lat. 5715, fol. 54va); Fragmentum E (*Collectio Trecensis*), fol. 265va–b.

7. *Litteras quas pro negotio S....satisfecit*

Dat. Laterani .iiii. n[on.] Ianuarii.

Adrian IV to Bishop [Amandus] of Bisceglie (1153–81), acknowledging receipt of his letter in favour of the bearer, the *pauper sacerdos* P., who had killed a boy in an excess of discipline. At the bishop's request (a copy of which preceded the decretal in the single surviving copy), Adrian allows that he may be restored to his priestly functions, since *voluntas et propositum maleficium distingu[ere] comprobatur* and *Sufficienter enim de ipso delicto, sicut nobis visum est, satisfecit.* Dated at the Lateran, 2 January (1157 x 1159).

JL —; WH 627a. Printed: Holtzmann, 'Kanonistische Ergänzungen', *QF*, 38 (1958), 148–9 no. 196. For the bishop's letter, see *ibid.*, 148.

Canonical tradition. Florence, Bibl. Nazionale Centrale, Conv. Soppr. A. 1. 402, fol. 8: inserted in margin of a First-Recension *Decretum*, at D. 50 c. 37; cf. Anders Winroth, *The Making of Gratian's* Decretum (Cambridge, 2000), 28. Significant for the localization of the MS, which belonged to the monastery of Camaldoli during the Middle Ages, is the fact that two further letters, addressed by a Cardinal John *legatus* to Archbishop Bertrand of Trani (1158–87) and the same bishop of Bisceglie, occur on fols 83v and 80r: see Holtzmann, 'Kanonistische Ergšnzungen', *QF*, 38 (1958), 145–6 nos 192–3. Holtzmann identified two cardinals John, who might have been the authors of these letters: John of Naples, cardinal priest of S. Anastasia (above, n. 74) and John of Anagni, successively cardinal deacon of S. Mari in Porticu (1158–67) and cardinal priest of S. Marco (1168–90), but inclined to the second, who travelled through Apulia *en route* to Dalmatia in 1163 x 64.

8. *Nobis in eminenti...ultionem*

Dat. Capue .iii. non. Nouembris.

Adrian IV to Prior A. and the monks of Pontida, ordering them to pay to the canons of [the collegiate church of S. Giovanni at] Pontirolo the tithes formerly paid to them, especially those from *Arcen* [= Arcone, north of Treviglio], and to restore any that have been seized, since 'We have resolved that men of religion should be granted only those tithes which are known to derive from newly cultivated lands (*Nos siquidem religiosis uiris non alias decimas nisi eas que de noualibus prouenire noscuntur, duximus indulgendas*).' Dated Capua, 3 November [1155].

JL 10444; WH 664. Printed: Mansi, *Concilia*, xxi (Venice, 1776), 830; *PL*, clxxxviii, 1586–7; *Italia Pontificia*, vi/1, 159 no. 2 (Pontirolo) and 394 no. 8 (Pontida); *1 Comp.* 3.26.15. Cf. Holtzmann, 'Kanonistische Ergänzungen', *QF*, 38 (1958), 88 no. 90, with references to its wide dissemination through monastic houses as far apart as Ghent and Montecassino; Constable, *Monastic Tithes*, 280; above, at nn. 18, 22–35. Note that this judgment was given while Adrian was marching south to Benevento in the failed war against William I of Sicily.

Canonical tradition. Appendices to Gratian: Biberach-an-der-Riss, Spitalarchiv, MS B 3515 (see no. 1 above), fol. 236vb; Durham, Cathedral Library, MS C.IV.1, fol. 124 (incip. *Dilecti filii nostri*; *om.* Quod si beati…usurpare); Graz, Univ.-Bibl., MS III.69, fols 283v–284v, fol. 284r–v (no. 8); Cambridge, Mass., Harvard Law Library, MS 64 (*olim* Phillipps, 3625 = 22066), unfoliated, last two folios, penultimate r–v (no. 6); Heiligenkreuz, MS 44, fol. 298ra–300vb, no. 1; Innsbruck, Univ.-Bibl., MS 90, fols 273–7, fol. 276r (no. 5); Madrid, Biblioteca Nacional, MS lat. 251, no. 12; Montecassino, MS 68, p. 560. *Summa* 'Quoniam status ecclesiarum', Paris, BN, MS lat. 16538, fol. 38v (Dilecti autem filii…indulgendas). Decretal collections: *Ambros.* 51; *1 Berol.* 51 (incomplete, ends: *Si vero huius nostri mandati etc.*); *Flor.* 131; *Cus.* 151, *2 Par.* 56.2; *App.* 13.10; *Oriel.* [13].16; *Bamb. (BAD) (C sine inscr.)* 25.11; *Erl.* 25.11; *Lips.* 23.15; *Cass.CB* 35.11; *Tann.* 3.14.10; *Sang.* 4.10.10; *Brug.* 19.4; *Frcf.* 20. 17 + Add. 6 *(Frcf.F)*; *1 Comp.* 3.26.15. Not in the Gregorian *Decretales*. The letter was cited by Rufinus in his *Summa Decretorum*, compiled at Bologna 1157–9, *Die Summa Decretorum des Magister Rufinus*, ed. H. Singer (Paderborn, 1902; repr. 1963), 333, 'Quod habet ex quodam decreto Adriani, quod sic incipit: Nobis in eminenti.'

9. *Presbiteri de Lauare…detinere*

Dat. Beneuemti .v. kal. Dec. (*2 Par.* only)

Adrian IV to the abbot and monks of the Vallombrosan abbey of Astino, on the complaint of the priests of 'Lavare' (near Bergamo), ordering them to pay that part of the tithe which they had withheld from the priests on the grounds of a papal decree, since the Apostolic See only relieved religious from tithes on *novales*. Dated Benevento, 27 November [1155].

JL 10459; WH 735. Printed: *1 Comp.* 3. 26.16; *Italia Pontificia*, vi/1, 387 no. 1. Cf. Holtzmann, 'Kanonistische Ergänzungen', *QF*, 38 (1958), 96 no. 109; Constable, *Monastic Tithes*, 281; above, at nn. 18, 22–35.

Canonical tradition. Appendices to Gratian: Innsbruck, Univ.-Bibl., MS 90, fols 273–7, fol. 276r (no. 6); Madrid, Biblioteca Nacional, MS lat. 251, no. 11. Decretal collections: *2 Par.* 56.3; *Oriel.* [13].8 (incip. *Roberti* (!)]; *Lips.* 23.5; *1 Comp.* 3.26.16. Not received into the Gregorian *Decretales*.

10. *Veniens ad apostolatus nostri…representes*

Adrian IV to the archbishop of Tours, announcing that after hearing the arguments of his and Archbishop Hugh of Dol's representatives, he has granted the pallium to the latter. Dated Sutri, 17 May [1155].

JL 10063. WH 1049. Printed: *Thesaurus novus Anecdotorum*, ed. E. Martène et U. Durand, 5 vols (Paris, 1717), iii, 898; Pierre Hyacinthe Morice, *Mémoires pour servir de preuves à l'Histoire ecclésiastique et civile de Bretagne*, 3 vols (Paris, 1742–46), i, 625; *Recueil des historiens des Gaules et de la France*, ed. M. Bouquet, *et al.*, 24 vols (Paris, 1738–1904), xv, 683; *PL*, clxxxviii, 1421–2 no. 49; J. H. Boehmer, *Corpus iuris canonici*, 2 vols (Halle, 1747), ii, 183–348, *Cass.*

Canonical tradition: *Bamb. (BADTO)* 48un; *Lips.* 57un; *Cass.* 56un; *Tann.* 6.8un; *Sang.* 7.145; *2 Clar.* 32.

Sigla of Decretal Collections and Related Works

Alan.   *Collectio Alani*, ed. R. von Heckel, 'Die Dekretalensammlungen des Gilbertus und Alanus', *ZRG Kan. Abt.* 29 (1940), 226–334.

1 Alc.   *Alcobacensis prima*. Lisbon, Bibl. Nacional, cod. Alcob. 144, fols 1v–39v: Holtzmann/Cheney, 8–25; Duggan, in *Studia Gratiana* 14 (1967), 51–71; idem, *Decretals of Alexander III*, 87–106.

Ambros.   *Ambrosiana*. Milan, Archivio capitolare di S. Ambrogio, MS M 57, fols 3007v–320r: Holtzmann/Cheney, 35–42.

App.   *Appendix Concilii Lateranensis*.

Cr.   *editio princeps*: *Concilia omnia tam generalia quam particularia*, ed. P. Crabbe (1551), ii, 820–944; Mansi, xxii, 248–453.

Lp.   Leipzig, Universitätsbibliothek, MS 1242, fols 73v–110v.

V   Vienna, Nationalbibliothek, MS 2172, fols 2r–52v.

Ln.   Lincoln, Cathedral Chapter Library 121, fols 1r–61r: Holtzmann/Cheney, 124–7.

Bamb.   *Bambergensis*: Deeters, *Die Bambergensisgruppe*.

B   Bamberg, Staatsbibliothek Can. 17 (P. 1.11), fols 1v–47r.

A   Amiens, Bibl. de la Ville, MS 377, fols 83–132.

C   *Compendiensis*, Paris, BN, MS lat. 17971, fols 153–84: Singer, *Neue Beiträge*, 8–67.

D   Tortosa, Bibl. de Cabildo, MS 40, fols 1–91.

T   Tortosa, Bibl. de Cabildo, MS 160, fols 1–41 (42.22–55.14 only).

O   Oxford, Oriel College 53, fols 340–49v (*olim* 240–49)

Belv.   *Belverensis*: Duggan, *Decretal Collections*, 71–73, 154–62; numerical concordance with WH, 212.

1 Berol.   *Berolinensis Prima*. J. Juncker, 'Die Collectio Berolinensis', *ZRG Kan. Abt.*, 13 (1924), 284–426.

Brug.   *Brugensis*: Friedberg, *Canones-Sammlungen*, 136–70; cf. 'Zu Entstehungs-ort und Redaktor der Collectio Brugensis', *Proceedings of the Eighth International Congress of Medieval Canon Law, San Diego, University of California at La Jolla, 21–27 August 1988*, ed. S. Chodorow, Monumenta iuris canonici, Series C: Subsidia, 9 (Città del Vaticano, 1992), 117–62.

Cass.   *Casselana* (see *C* and *B* below): J. H. Boehmer, *Corpus iuris canonici*, ii (Halle, 1747), Appendix, 181–348; cf. Deeters, *Bambergensisgruppe*, 7–9.

C   Kassel, Landesbibl., MS Jur. 15, fols 1–26.

B   Bamberg, Staatsbibliothek Can. 18 (*olim* P. III.1), fols 25r–43v.

Chelt.   *Cheltenhamensis*: London, BL, MS Egerton 2819, fols 11r–102r.

2 Clar.   *Clarevallensis Secunda*. Troyes, Bibl. de la Ville, MS 944, fols 93r–100v): Holtzmann/Cheney, 284–90.

Claud.   *Claudiana*: London, BL, MS Cotton Claudius A.iv, fols 193r–220r (*olim* 189r–216r): Holtzmann/Cheney, 132–4.

Claustr.   *Claustroneoburgensis*: Klosterneuburg, Stiftsbibliothek, MS 19, fols 36r–

	87v: Ferdinand Schönsteiner, 'Die Collectio Claustroneoburgensis', *Jahrbuch des Stiftes Klosterneuburg*, 2 (1909), 1–154.
*1–3 Comp.*Ag	*Compilatio prima, secunda, tertia*, in *Antiquae collectiones decretalium*, ed. Antonio Agustín (Lérida, 1576); reissued in *Opera omnia*, iv (Lucca, 1769).
1–5 Comp.	Friedberg, *Quinque compilationes*.
Cott.	*Cottoniana*. London, BL, MS Cotton Vitellius E.xiii, fols 204r–288r: cf. Duggan, *Decretal Collections*, 103–10.
Cus.	*Cusana*. Holtzmann/Cheney, 66–74.
Decretales ineditae, ed. Chodorow and Duggan	*Decretales ineditae saeculi XII*, ed. and rev. S. Chodorow and C. Duggan, from the papers of W. Holtzmann, MIC, 4 (Città del Vaticano, 1982).
Deeters, *Bambergensis-gruppe*	W. Deeters, *Die Bambergensisgruppe der Dekretalensammlungen des 12. Jhdts.*, Inaugural Dissertation...der philos. Fakultät der Rheinischen Friedrich Wilhelms-Universität (Bonn, 1954).
Duac.	*Duacensis*. Douai, Bibl. de la Ville, MS 590, fols 1r–2v, 247r–248v: Holtzmann/Cheney, 64–5.
Duggan, *Decretal Collections*	Charles Duggan, *Twelfth-Century Decretal Collections and their importance in English History*, University of London Historical Studies, 12 (London, 1963).
Erl.	*Erlangensis*: Erlangen, Universitätsbibliothek, MS 342, fols 291–306: Deeters, *Bambergensisgruppe*, 9–10.
Flor.	*Florianensis*. Sankt-Florian, Stiftsbibliothek, III. 5, fols 173r–183r: Holtzmann/Cheney, 43–63.
Font.	*Fontanensis*. Oxford, Bodleian Library, MS Laud Misc. 527 [S.C. 818], fols 24r–45v: Holtzmann/Cheney, 100–15.
Frcf.	*Francofortana*. Frankfurt, Stadt- und Universitätsbibliothek, MS Barth. 60, fols 2r–85r: S. Kuttner, in *ZRG Kan. Abt.*, 22 (1933), 370–80.
Fragmentum E	*Collectio Trecensis*. Troyes, Bibl. de la Ville, MS 103, fols 2, 265va–266.
Fragmentum H	Florence, Bibl. Riccardi 338, fols 215v–224v.
Friedberg, *Canones-Sammlungen*	Emil Friedberg, *Die Canones-Sammlungen zwischen Gratian und Bernhard von Pavia* (Leipzig 1897; repr. Graz 1958), 45–63.
Friedberg, *Quinque compilationes*	Emil Friedberg, *Quinque compilationes antiquae necnon collectio canonum Lipsiensis* (Leipzig, 1882; repr. Graz, 1956).
Fuld.	*Fuldensis*: Fulda, Landesbibliothek, MS D.3a, fols 1–88 (derived from the Weingarten MSS of the collections of Gilbert and Alan: see v. Heckel, in *ZRG Kan. Abt.*, 29 (1940), 165–70 and 353–9.
Gilb.	*Collectio Gilberti*, from Weingarten MSS (*W* below): ed. R. von Heckel, 'Die Dekretalensammlungen des Gilbertus und Alanus', *ZRG Kan. Abt.* 29 (1940), 180–225.

W	Fulda, Landesbibliothek, MSS D.14, fols 2–31v, and D.5, fols 84–139r: Heckel, 120–1 and 124–5.
Holtzmann, 'Kanonistische Ergänzungen'	Walther Holtzmann, 'Kanonistische Ergänzungen zur Italia Pontificia', *QF*, 37 (1957), 55–102 + *ibid.*, 38 (1958), 67–175; pulished separately (Tübingen, 1959).
Holtzmann/ Cheney	Christopher R. Cheney and Mary G. Cheney, from the papers of W. Holtzmann, *Studies in the Collections of Twelfth-Century Decretals*, MIC, 3 (Città del Vaticano, 1979).
Lips.	*Lipsiensis*: Leipzig, Univ.-Bibl. MS 975, fols 116–153: Friedberg, *Quinque compilationes*, 189–208; cf. Deeters, *Bambergensisgruppe*, 10–11.
Oriel.	*Orielensis*. Oxford, Oriel College, MS 53, fols 353r–54v (*olim* 253r–54v). Formerly *Orielensis II:* Holtzmann/Cheney, 127–31.
MIC	Monumenta Iuris Canonici, Series B: Corpus Collectionum.
1 Par.	*Parisiensis prima*. Paris, BN, MS lat. 1566, fols 11–46: Friedberg, *Canones-Sammlungen*, 45–63.
2 Par.	*Parisiensis secunda*. Paris, BN, MS lat. 1596, fols 11–46: Friedberg, *Canones-Sammlungen*, 21–45.
Pet.	*Petrihusensis*: Cambridge, Peterhouse 193, final quire; 114, first and final quires; 193,first quire; 203, final quire; 180, first and final quires: Duggan, *Decretal Collections*, 103–9, 189–90.
Reg.	*Regalis*: London, BL, MS Royal 15.B.iv, fols 107v–118v: Duggan, *Decretal Collections*, 81–4 and pl. II.
Sang.	*Sangermanensis*. Paris, BN, MS lat. 12459, fols 1–106v: Singer, *Neue Beiträge*, 68–354.
Singer, *Neue Beiträge*	H. Singer, *Neue Beiträge über die Dekretalensammlungen vor und nach Bernhard von Pavia*, Sitzungsberichte der kaiserlichen Akademie der Wissenschaften in Wien, phil.-hist. Klasse, 171/i (1913).
Tann.	*Collectio Tanneri:* Oxford, Bodleian Library, MS Tanner 8, pp. 593–712; cf. Walther Holtzmann, 'Die Dekretalensammlungen des 12. Jahrhunderts, I: Die Sammlung Tanner', *Festschrift zur Feier des 200jährigen Bestehens der Akademie der Wissenschaften in Göttingen, Phil.-Hist. Klasse* (1951), 83–145.
1 Vict.	*Victorina prima*. Paris, BN, MS lat. 14938, fols 226r–263r: Holtzmann/Cheney, 26–34.
WH	Walther Holtzmann's projected *Regesta decretalium*.
Wig.	*Wigorniensis*: London, BL, Royal 10.A.ii, fols 5r–62v: Hans-Eberhard Lohmann, 'Die Collectio Wigorniensis (Collectio Londinensis Regia): Ein Beitrag zur Quellengeschichte des kanonischen Rechts im 12. Jahrhundert', *ZRG Kan.Abt.*, 22 (1933), 35–187; cf. Duggan, *Decretal Collections*, 110–17, pll. V–VI.
X	*Decretales Gregorii IX*: Friedberg, *Corpus iuris canonici*, ii (1881).

PART II
Sources and Documents

i. Narrative Sources

1
Cardinal Boso, *Vita Adriani IV*

From *Le Liber Pontificalis*, ed. L. Duchesne, Bibliothèque des Écoles françaises d'Athènes et de Rome, 2nd ser. 3, 2nd edn, 3 vols (Paris, 1955–7), ii, 388–97.

ADRIANUS IIII, natione Anglicus, de castro sancti Albani, qui Nycholaus, Albanensis episcopus, sedit annis IIII mensibus VIII diebus VI.[1]

Hic namque pubertatis sue tempore, ut in literarum studio proficeret, egrediens de terra et de cognatione sua, pervenit Arelate, ubi dum in scolis vacaret, a Domino factum est ut ad ecclesiam beati Rufi accederet et in religionis habitum facta canonica professione susciperet. Proficiens ergo Deo auctore de bono semper in melius, prioratum in ipsa domo prius obtinuit, et postmodum ad abbatie apicem de communi fratrum voluntate conscendit.[2] Accidit autem ut pro incumbentibus ecclesie sibi commisse negotiis ad apostolicam sedem veniret, et peractis omnibus causis pro quibus venerat, cum redire ad propria vellet, beate memorie papa Eugenius[3] eum secum retinuit et de communi fratrum suorum consilio in Albanensem episcopum consecravit. Processu vero modici temporis, cognita ipsius honestate ac prudentia, de latere suo eum ad partes Norguerie legatum sedis apostolice destinavit, quatinus verbum vite in ipsa provincia predicaret et ad faciendum omnipotenti Deo animarum lucrum studeret. Ipse vero tamquam minister Christi et fidelis ac prudens dispensator misteriorum Dei, gentem illam barbaram et rudem in lege christiana diligenter instruxit et ecclesiasticis eruditionibus informavit.[4]

Divina itaque dispositione apostolatus sui diem preveniens, defuncto papa Eugenio et Anastasio[5] in loco eius ordinato, ad matrem suam sacrosanctam Romanam ecclesiam ductore Domino remeavit, relinquens pacem regnis, legem barbaris, quietem monasteriis, ecclesiis ordinem, clericis disciplinam et Deo populum acceptabilem, sectatorem bonorum operum. Transeunte autem modico temporis intervallo, obiit Anastasius papa; et in secunda die, convenientibus in unum pro eligendo sibi pastore cunctis episcopis et cardinalibus apud ecclesiam beati Petri, non sine divini dispositione consilii factum est ut in eius personam unanimiter concordarent et 'Papam Adrianum a Deo electum' tam clerici quam laici pariter conclamantes, eum invitum et renitentem in sede beati Petri Deo auctore intronizarunt, dominice Incarnationis anno MCLIIII, indictione III.[6]

---

[1] Boso is mistaken. Adrian's pontificate, from 4 Dec. 1154 to 1 Sept. 1159, lasted for four years, 8 months, and 28 or 29 days.
[2] For Adrian's early life, see above, ch. 2.
[3] Eugenius III, 1145–53.
[4] Above, ch. 4.
[5] Anastasius IV, 1153–4.
[6] Above, ch. 5, at n. 1.

1
Cardinal Boso, *Life of Adrian IV*

This Life of Adrian IV *was written by Boso, one of his closest collaborators, probably in the 1170s. Boso (d. 1178) first appeared in Curial circles in 1135, when he served Guy of Pisa, the later chancellor of Eugenius III. He was* scriptor sancte Romane ecclesie *from c. 1149 onwards, and may have accompanied Cardinal Nicholas to Scandinavia in 1152. Adrian appointed him papal chamberlain immediately after his own election, and made him cardinal deacon of SS. Cosma e Damiano in 1156. Boso was thus not only a friend of the subject of his biography (though not a relative: see above, ch. 9, at n. 8), but a leading member of his administration, engaged as* camerarius *in the day-to-day running of the Patrimony.*

Adrian IV, English by race, from the *castrum* of St Albans, formerly Nicholas, cardinal bishop of Albano, reigned for four years, eight months, and six days.[1]

In the time of his adolescence, leaving both his land and his family so that he could make progress in the study of letters, he came to Arles, where, while he was in the schools, the Lord brought it about that he should come to the church of Saint-Ruf and there receive the religious habit, after his canonical profession. Then, by God's will, advancing always from the good to the better, he first obtained the office of prior in that house, and afterwards ascended to the pinnacle of abbey by the common desire of the brethren.[2] It happened, however, that he came to the Apostolic See to conduct business for the church entrusted to his care, and when he wished to return to his own place, having completed all the cases for which he had come, Pope Eugenius of blessed memory kept him at his side,[3] and with the common consent of his brethren, consecrated him bishop of Albano. After a little time, having experienced his probity and prudence, he sent him as legate *a latere* to the regions of Norway, so that he could preach the word of life in that province and apply himself to the winning of souls for Almighty God. Indeed, as Christ's minister and a faithful and prudent dispenser of God's mysteries, he diligently instructed that barbarous and rude people in the Christian law and enlightened them with Church teachings.[4]

Anticipating by divine dispensation the day of his papacy, when Pope Eugenius had died and Anastasius[5] was appointed in his place, led by the Lord, he returned to his mother, the holy Roman Church, leaving peace to the kingdoms, law for the barbarians, tranquillity for the monasteries, order for the churches, discipline for the clergy, and a people acceptable to God, pursuing good works. Then, after a short time, Pope Anastasius died; and on the second day all the bishops and cardinals having assembled together to elect a shepherd, it happened not without divine arrangement that they agreed unanimously on him, and as the clergy and laity cried out together, 'Pope Adrian, chosen by God', they enthroned him, unwilling and resisting, in the chair of blessed Peter, in the year of the Lord's incarnation, 1154, the third indiction.[6]

Erat enim vir valde benignus, mitis et patiens, in anglica et latina lingua peritus, in sermone facundus, in eloquentia politus, in cantilena precipuus et predicator egregius; ad irascendum tardus, ad ignoscendum velox, ylaris dator, in elemosinis largus et in omni morum compositione preclarus.

In diebus illis Arnaldus Brixiensis hereticus Urbem intrare presumpserat, et erroris sui venena disseminans mentes simplicium a via veritatis subvertere conabatur. Pro cuius expulsione supradictus Eugenius et Anastasius Romani pontifices plurimum iam laboraverunt, set favore et potentia quorumdam perversorum civium et maxime senatorum, qui tunc ad regimen civitatis a populo fuerant instituti, antedictus hereticus munitus et tutus, contra prohibitionem domni Adriani pape in eadem civitate procaciter morabatur et sibi ac fratribus suis insidiari ceperat et publice atque atrociter adversari. Venerabilem namque virum magistrum G[uidonem], presbyterum cardinalem tituli sancte Pudentiane,[7] ad presentiam ipsius pontificis euntem, quidam ex ipsis hereticis ausu nefario in via Sacra invadere presumpserunt et ad interitum vulnerarunt. Quapropter pontifex ipse civitatem Romanam interdicto supposuit, et usque ad quartam feriam maioris hebdomade universa civitas a divinis cessavit officiis. Tunc vero predicti senatores, compulsi a clero et populo Romano, accesserunt ad presentiam eiusdem pontificis et ad ipsius mandatum super sacra evangelia iuraverunt quod sepe dictum hereticum et reliquos ipsius sectatores de tota urbe Romana et finibus eius mora expellerent, nisi ad mandatum et obedientiam ipsius pape redirent. Sic itaque ipsis eiectis et civitate ab interdicto absoluta repleti sunt omnes gaudio magno, laudantes pariter et benedicentes Dominum. In crastinum autem, videlicet die Cene Domini, concurrente undique de more ad annue remissionis gratiam et gloriosam festivitatem maxima populorum multitudine, idem benignus pontifex cum fratribus suis, episcopis et cardinalibus atque inmensa procerum et civium turba de civitate Leoniana, ubi a tempore ordinationis sue fuerat commoratus, cum honorificentia magna exivit; et transiens per mediam urbem, universo sibi populo congaudente, ad Lateranense patriachium cum iocunditate pervenit, ibique die ipso et sequente sexta feria divina misteria sollempniter celebravit, atque in Lateranensi palatio secundum Ecclesie antiquam consuetudinem Pascha cum discipulis suis festive comedit.[8] Celebrato itaque cum letitia festo, singuli ad propria cum gaudio redierunt.

Eodem tempore Wilhelmus rex Sicilie contra matrem et dominam sacrosanctam Romanam ecclesiam procaciter cornua erexit, et congregato exercitu terram beati Petri hostiliter fecit invadi. Beneventanam itaque civitatem aliquamdiu exercitus eius obsedit et burgos eius incendit; deinde fines Campanie violenter ingrediens, villam Ceperani et castrum Babucum atque alia inmunita loca nichilominus concremavit. Pro hiis ergo et aliis offensis predictus Adrianus papa Petri gladium exerens ipsum regem excommunicationis mucrone percussit.[9]

---

[7] Master Guido 'Puella', from Genoa, cardinal priest of S. Pudenziana 1145–57: Zenker, 112–3.

[8] Cf. above, ch. 5, at nn. 19–31.

[9] Cf. above, ch. 7, at nn. 34–6.

For he was very kind, mild, and patient; accomplished in English and Latin, fluent in speech, polished in eloquence, an outstanding singer, and an excellent preacher; slow to anger and swift to forgive; a cheerful giver, lavish in alms, distinguished in every aspect of his character.

At that time, the heretic, Arnold of Brescia had presumed to enter the City and was attempting to turn the minds of the simple from the way of truth by disseminating the poison of his error. The aforementioned Roman pontiffs, Eugenius and Anastasius, had already laboured much for his expulsion, but the aforesaid heretic, guarded and protected by the favour and power of certain perverse citizens, and especially by the senators who were then appointed by the people for the government of the City, was remaining shamelessly in the City against the prohibition of the lord pope Adrian, and began to plot against him and his brethren and to be publicly and violently opposed to them. For some of those heretics with wicked daring presumed to enter the *via Sacra* and wounded almost to death the venerable master G[uido], cardinal priest of the title S. Pudenziana,[7] as he was going to the pope's presence. For which reason, the pope imposed an interdict on the City of Rome, and the whole City ceased divine office until the Wednesday of Holy Week. Then the aforesaid senators, compelled by the clergy and people of Rome, came into the presence of the pontiff and at his command swore on the Holy Gospels that they would without delay expel the said heretic and the rest of his followers from the whole City of Rome, unless they returned to the command and obedience of the said pope. And thus, when they had been ejected and the City had been absolved from interdict, all were filled with great joy, praising and blessing the Lord. But, on the next day, namely the day of the Lord's Supper, as a great crowd of people was running together from all sides in the usual way to receive the grace of annual remission and for the glorious festival, the said kindly pontiff, with his brethren, the bishops and cardinals and an immense crowd of nobles and citizens, went forth with great honour from the Leonine City, where he had remained from the time of his appointment; and passing through the middle of the City as the whole populace rejoiced with him, he came with pleasure to the patriarchal seat of the Lateran, and there, on that day and on the following Friday, he solemnly celebrated the divine mysteries, and in the Lateran Palace, in accordance with the ancient custom of the Church, he ate the Pasch joyfully with his disciples.[8] Having delightedly celebrated this feast, each one returned to his home rejoicing.

At the same time, William, king of Sicily, raised his horn insolently against his mother and lady, the Holy Roman Church, and, gathering an army, he caused the lands of the Blessed Peter to be invaded with hostile intent. His army besieged the city of Benevento for some time and burned its suburbs; then, violently entering the confines of the Campagna, burned the town of Ceprano and the *castrum* of Bauco [Boville Ernica] and other unfortified places. For these and other offences, Pope Adrian, unsheathing the sword of Peter, struck the king with the sharp sword of excommunication.[9]

Interea Fredericus Teutonicorum rex cum magno exercitu Lombardiam intravit et civitatem Tardonam diu obsedit. Qua devicta et sibi subacta, celeriter properabat ad Urbem, in tanta festinantia ut merito credi posset magis hostis accedere quam patronus. Hoc igitur cognito, Adrianus papa qui eo tempore apud Viterbium residebat, deliberato cum fratribus suis et Petro Urbis prefecto atque Oddone Fragepane consilio, misit ei obviam I[ohannem], tituli sanctorum Iohannis et Pauli et G[uidonem], tituli sancte Pudentiane presbiteros, atque G[uidonem], diaconum sancte Marie in Porticu cardinales,[10] quibus et certa capitula dedit et modum ac formam prefixit qualiter cum ipso pro Ecclesia deberent componere. Qui accepto mandato cum festinantia profiscentes, eum apud Sanctum Quiricum invenerunt; et accendentes ad ipsum honorifice recepti sunt et in tentorium deducti. Post salutationem vero literas ei apostolicas porrexerunt et domni pape exposuerunt mandatum; in quibus continebatur inter cetera ut redderet eisdem cardinalibus Arnaldum hereticum, quem vicecomites de Campaniano abstulerant magistro O[ttone], diacono sancti Nycolai,[11] apud Briculas, ubi eum ceperat; quem tanquam prophetam in terra sua cum honore habebant. Rex vero, auditis domni pape mandatis, continuo missis apparitoribus cepit unum de vicecomitibus illis, qui valde perterritus eundem hereticum in manibus cardinalem statim restituit.

Ceterum ante adventum ipsorum cardinalium idem rex premiserat Arnoldum Coloniensem et Anselmum Ravennatem archiepiscopos ad presentiam sepedicti pontificis, ut de ipsius coronatione cum eo tractarent et de aliis insimul convenirent; ideoque responsum cardinalibus dare non poterat nisi prius archiepiscopos ipsos reciperet. Pontifex autem, qui propter nimium suspectum imperatoris adventum ad Urbevetanam civitatem transire et illuc imperatorem disposuerat expectare, pro repentino et inopinato illorum adventu in maiorem dubitationem devenit. Set cum ad locum illum tutissimum iam secure non posset transire, ad Civitatem Castellanem festinanter ascendit; ubi si de persona eius rex male cogitasset, iram illius secure declinare et iniquos cogitatus ipsius facile posset elidere. Archiepiscopi vero secuti sunt eum, exponentes bonam regis voluntatem, quam erga eum et totam Romanam ecclesiam habebat, et alia que sibi errant imposita nicholominus ostendentes. Quibus pontifex de consilio fratrum suorum dixit: 'Nisi prius recepero fratres meos cardinales quos ad regem delegavi, nullum vobis responsum dabo.' Cardinales itaque a rege et archiepiscopi a pontifice infecto negotio redeuntes obviaverunt sibi, dicentes ad invicem quod propter eorum absentiam responsum ab utraque parte dilatum fuerat. Ideoque habito inter se salubriori consilio, insimul venerunt ad presentiam regis in campo Viterbiensi ubi castra posuerat.

---

[10]   John of Sutri, cardinal priest of SS. Giovanni e Paolo 1151–81: Brixius, 55, 109; Zenker, 137–9. For Guido of S. Pudenziana and Guido (of Crema) of S. Maria in Porticu, see n. 5, above, and ch. 7, n. 12.

[11]   Master Otto of Brescia, cardinal deacon of S. Nicola in Carcere Tulliano (1153–75): above, ch. 9, n. 75.

Meanwhile, Frederick, king of the Germans, entered Lombardy with a great army and besieged the city of Tortona for a long time. Having conquered and subjugated it to himself he hastened quickly to the City, with such great speed that it could rightly be thought that he was an enemy rather than a defender. When he had learned this, Pope Adrian, who was then staying at Viterbo, having deliberated with his brethren, and on the advice of Peter, Prefect of the City and of Odo Frangipane, he sent to meet him G[iovanni], cardinal priest of SS. Giovanni e Paolo and G[uido], cardinal priest of the title of S. Pudenziana and G[uido], cardinal deacon of S. Maria in Porticu,[10] giving them specific instructions and laying down the manner and form of how they were to agree with him on behalf of the Church. Having accepted his mandate and setting out with haste, they found [the emperor] at San Quirico; and approaching him, they were honourably received and led into the pavilion. Then, after greeting him, they presented the apostolic letters to him and they disclosed the lord pope's commission, which said, among other things, that he should hand over to the cardinals the heretic Arnald, whom the counts of Campagnatico had taken from master O[tto], deacon of S. Nicola,[11] at Le Briccole [Lo Spedaletto di San Pelegrino], where he had captured him; and whom they had [regarded] with honour as a prophet in their land. But the king, having heard the lord pope's instructions, immediately sent his own officials and seized one of the counts, who, greatly frightened, immediately restored the heretic to the hands of the cardinals.

Further, before the arrival of those cardinals, the said king had sent in advance Arnold, archbishop of Cologne and Anselmo, archbishop of Ravenna, to the presence of the said pontiff, to deliberate with him concerning his coronation and agree with him about other matters; and therefore, he was not able to give a reply to the cardinals without first receiving those archbishops. But the Pontiff, who because of his great suspicion at the coming of the emperor had decided to go to the city of Orvieto and there wait for the emperor, became even more doubtful as a result of their sudden and unexpected arrival. But when he was not able to pass in safety to that most protected place, he went quickly up to Civita Castellana, where, if the king had thought badly of him, he would be able in safety to deflect his anger and easily shatter his wicked designs. But the archbishops followed him, laying forth the king's good will towards him and the whole Roman Church, and explaining other things which had been entrusted to them. To these, the pontiff replied, with the advice of his brethren, 'Unless I have first received my brothers, the cardinals, whom I have sent to the king, I shall not give you a reply.' Then, with their business incomplete, the cardinals and the archbishops returning from the king and the pontiff respectively, met together, saying to one another that because of their absence, a response from both sides had been deferred. And therefore, having taken more salutary counsel amongst themselves, they came together to the king's presence in the field at Viterbo where he had set up his camp.

Venerat autem ad eum Octavianus tituli sancte Cecilie presbiter cardinalis,[12] non missus a pontifice set dimissus, iam spirans seditionis et scismatis. Postquam vero predicti cardinales intraverunt ad regem et haberetur consilium super eorum legationem de satisfaciendo mandatis Romani pontificis, idem Octavianus quod hauserat virus evomere cepit et pacem turbare; set in brevi et ratione valida repressus est a fratribus suis cardinalibus et sicut dignus erat multa confusione respersus. Tandem adversario confutato et salubri consilio comprobato, rex omnium procerum et militum suorum curiam maximam congregavit; et presentia eorundem cardinalium allata sunt sacra pignora, crux et evangelia, super que nobilis quidam milex de ceteris electus et coniuratus atque tertio iurare iussus, in anima sua et eiusdem regis iuravit vitam et membra non auferre set conservare pape Adriano et cardinalibus eius, nec malam captionem facere, honorem et bona sua eis non auferre nec auferri permittere, set et si quis auferre vellet, omnimodis prohibere et contradicere, post illatam vero iniuriam pro posse suo et vindicari faceret et emendari, atque concordiam iam pridem per principales personas utriusque curie factam inviolatam de cetero conservare.

Hoc igitur iuramento sicut dictum est et a rege prestito et a cardinalibus ipsis cum alacritate recepto, continuo accepta licentia concito gradu cardinales reversi sunt ad summum pontificem, universa que fecerant sibi et fratribus cum diligentia referentes. Placuit ergo pontifici et eius collateralibus quod talis securitatis eis a rege data et per consilium principum suorum firmiter roborata est; ideoque omni mala suspitione sublata de medio, regie petitioni de imponenda sibi corona imperii benigne annuit, et ut ad invicem sese viderent locus congruus et dies certus ab utraque parte statutus est.

Processit igitur rex cum exercitu suo in territorum Sutrinum, et castrametatus est in Campo Grasso; pontifex autem ad civitatem Nepesinam descendit, et in secunda die, occurrentibus multis Teutonicorum principibus cum plurima clericorum et laycorum multitudine, ad presentiam sepedicti regis cum episcopis et cardinalibus suis usque ad ipsius tentorium cum iocunditate deductus est. Cum autem rex de more officium stratoris eidem pape non exhiberet, cardinales qui cum eo venerant, turbati et valde perterriti, abierunt retrorsum et in predicta Civitate Castellana se receperunt, relicte pontifice ad tentorium regis. Quocirca domnus papa nimio stupore turbatus et quid sibi foret agendum incertus, licet tristis descendit, et in preparato sibi faldistrodio sedit. Tunc rex ad eius vestigia procidit, et deosculatis pedibus ad pacis osculum accedere voluit. Cui protinus idem pontifex locutus est in hec verba: 'Quandoquidem tu illum michi consuetum et debitum honorem subtraxisti quem predecessores tui orthodoxi imperatores pro apostolorum Petri et Pauli reverentia predecessoribus meis Romanis pontificibus exhibere usque ad hec tempora consueverunt, donec michi satisfacias ego te ad pacis osculum non recipiam.' Rex autem respondit et dixit se hoc facere non debere.

---

[12]   For Octavian, cardinal priest of S. Cecilia (1151–9), and later the antipope Victor IV (1159–64), see ch. 7, n. 12 above.

Octavian, cardinal priest of the title of S. Cecilia,[12] already dreaming of sedition and schism, had come to him, not sent but sent away by the pontiff. But after the said cardinals had entered the king's presence and taken counsel concerning their legation to fulfil the instructions of the Roman pontiff, the said Octavian began to vomit forth the venom which he had swallowed and to disturb the peace; but quickly and for good reason, he was silenced by his brethren, the cardinals and, appropriately, was covered with confusion. At length, with the adversary confounded and sound counsel approved, the king called all his nobles and knights to a great court; and in the presence of the cardinals, the sacred relics, cross, and gospels were brought forward, upon which a certain noble knight, chosen from the rest, and sworn, and then ordered to swear, he swore on his own soul and that of the king not to injure the life and limbs of Pope Adrian and his cardinals, but rather to preserve them, nor to make a false imprisonment, not to take away their honour or goods, nor allow them to be so taken but, by every means, to prohibit and forbid any who might so wish; and after the infliction of injury, to the fullest extent of his power, he would cause to be avenged and restored, and for the future, to preserve inviolate the concord which had just been made by the leading persons of both courts.

When this oath had been taken by the king and received by the cardinals with alacrity, immediately having received his licence, the cardinals returned to the supreme pontiff with hurried pace, carefully relating to him and his brethren all that they had done. The pontiff and his colleagues were pleased that such security had been given to them by the king and strongly confirmed by the advice of his princes; and therefore, all bad suspicion having been removed from their midst, the pope graciously agreed to the king's petition for the imposition on him of the imperial crown, and an appropriate place and a specific day was agreed by both sides where they might see one another.

Therefore, the king advanced with his army into the region of Sutri, and fortified himself in the field of Grasso; the pontiff, however, went down to the city of Nepi, and on the second day, having been met by many German princes and a great multitude of clergy and laity, he was led joyfully, with his bishops and cardinals, to the said king's presence, at his pavilion. When, however, the king did not perform the office of *strator* for the pope in the customary manner, the cardinals who had come with him, disturbed and greatly terrified, turned their backs and took refuge in the said Civita Castellana, having left the pontiff outside the king's pavilion. Wherefore, the lord pope, disturbed and amazed and uncertain what would be done to him, although sad, dismounted, and sat in the chair specially prepared for him. Then the king cast himself down at his feet and having kissed his feet, desired to come to the kiss of peace. The said pontiff immediately addressed him in these words, 'Seeing that you have denied me that customary and due honour which your predecessors, the Catholic emperors were accustomed to show to my predecessors, the Roman pontiffs until now, out of respect for the apostles Peter and Paul, until you make satisfaction to me, I shall not receive you with the kiss of peace.' But the king replied and said that he ought not to do this. Therefore,

Eapropter remanente ibidem exercitu, totus sequens dies sub istius rei varia collatione decurrit. Tandem requisitis antiquioribus principibus, et illis precipue qui
cum rege Lotario ad Innocentium papam venerant,[13] et prisca consuetudine diligenter investigata, ex relatione illorum et veteribus munimentis iudicio principum
decretum est et communi favore totius regalis curie roboratum quod idem rex pro
beatorum Apostolorum reverentia predicto pape Adriano exhiberet stratoris officium et eius streugam teneret. Alia itaque die regis mota sunt castra et in territorio
Nepesino iuxta lacum qui dicitur Iaula fuerunt translata. Ibique sicut a principibus
fuerat ordinatum rex Fredericus precessit aliquantulum, et appropinquante domni
pape tentorio per aliam viam transiens descendit de equo, et occurrens ei quantum
iactum est lapidis, in conspectus exercitus officium stratoris cum iocunditate
implevit et streuguam fortiter tenuit. Tunc vero pontifex ad pacis osculum eundem
regem primo suscepit.[14]

Post hec autem versus Urbem insimul procedentes, pro eo quod ab eis Romanus populus discordabat, licet beati Petri munitionem in potestate sua pontifex
detineret, placuit tamen ut in manu valida civitatem Leonianam rex introiret. Posi-
tis igitur exterius castris et deliberato festinanter consilio, atque dispositis que ad
coronationem spectabant, eadem die, ante horam tertiam, rex ad gradus beati Petri
armatorum maxima multitudine stipatus accessit; ibique depositis vestibus quas
gerebat, sollempniori habitu se induit, et ad ecclesiam beati Marie in Turri in qua
eum ante altare pontifex expectabat ascendens, genua sua fixit coram eo et manus
suas inter ipsius pontificis manus imponens, consuetam professionem et plenariam
securitatem, secundum quod in Ordine continetur, publice exhibuit sibi. Relicto
autem ibidem rege, pontifex ad beati Petri altare conscendit. Cuius vestigia rex
cum processione subsequens, ante portas argenteas orationem primam ab uno episcoporum nostrorum suscepit, et secundam orationem infra ecclesiam in rota super
eundem regem alius ex episcopis nostris dedit, orationem vero tertiam et unctionem tertius episcopus ante confessionem beati Petri eidem regi nichilominus
contulit. Missa itaque incepta et graduali post epistolam decantato, rex ad pontificem coronandus accessit, et presentatis imperialibus signis, gladium et sceptrum
atque imperii coronam de manibus eiusdem pape suscepit. Statim tam vehemens et
fortis Teutonicorum conclamatio in vocem laudis et letitie concrepuit, ut horribile
tonitruum crederetur de celis subito cecidisse.

Hiis igitur ante horam nonam in pace et tranquillitate peractis, populus Romanus qui clausis portis apud castrum Crescentii residebat armatus, ignorans que
facta fuerant, sine consilio et deliberatione maiorum ad civitatem Leonianam paulatim ascendit, et eorum qui in porticu remanserunt spoliis violenter direptis, omnes quos repperit usque ad imperatoris castra persequendo fugavit. Invalescen-

---

[13]   Lothar III and Innocent II in 1133: see above, ch 7, at nn. 130–2.
[14]   Above, ch. 7, at nn. 91–102.

while the army remained there, the whole of the following day passed in various discussions about this matter. Finally, having questioned the older princes and especially those who had come with King Lothar to Pope Innocent,[13] and having diligently investigated the early custom, from their replies and from the old documents, by the judgment of the princes it was decreed and confirmed by the common approval of the whole royal court that the said king should perform the office of strator for the said Pope Adrian out of respect for the blessed Apostles and hold his stirrup. And then, on another day, the king's camp was moved and transferred to the region of Nepi near the lake which is called Laula; and there, as had been ordained by the princes, King Frederick went out a little way, and as he approached the lord pope's pavilion, crossing by another path, he dismounted from his horse, and approaching from a stone's throw away, in the sight of his army, he cheerfully fulfilled the office of strator and firmly held his stirrup. Then indeed the pontiff received the king for the first time with the kiss of peace.[14]

After this, setting out together towards the City, because the Roman populace was hostile to them, although the pope held the fortification of St Peter in his power, it was pleasing that the king should enter the Leonine City with a strong force. After placing camps outside and taken speedy counsel, and having arranged everything relating to the coronation, on the same day, before the third hour, the king came to the steps of St Peter's, surrounded by a great crowd of armed men; and there, having laid aside the clothes he was wearing, he put on a more solemn dress, and going up to the church of S. Maria in Turri in which the pontiff was waiting for him before the altar, he knelt before him and placing his hands between those of the pontiff, he publicly made to him the customary profession and full security, as contained in the *Ordo*. Having left the king there, the pontiff went up to the altar of the blessed Peter. The king, following in procession, received the first prayer from one of our bishops before the silver doors, and another of our bishops said the second prayer over the king on the *rota* inside the church, but a third bishop conferred the third prayer and the unction on the king before the *confessio* of Blessed Peter. Then, after the beginning of Mass, when the gradual had been sung after the epistle, the king approached the pontiff to be crowned, and having presented the imperial insignia, he received sword and sceptre and the crown of the empire from the hands of the pope. So loud and strong was the Germans' acclamation of praise and joy, that it was believed that a terrible thunderbolt had just fallen from the heavens.

These things having been carried out in peace and tranquillity, before the ninth hour, the Roman people who were staying armed with closed gates at the castrum Crescentii, ignorant of what had happened, without the advice and deliberation of the elders, went up little by little to the Leonine City and having violently despoiled those who had remained in the portico, and, they pursued all whom they found as far as the emperor's camp. With the clamour of the injured and the unex-

tibus autem clamoribus et undique resonante inopinate tumultu, Teutonicorum exercitus ad arma velociter convolavit, strictisque mucronibus ab utraque parte acriter dimicatur. Quid plura? Cesi sunt multi et plurimi capti. Tandem populus ipse non sine multo suorum discrimine infra portas ipsius castri seipsum recepit. Pontifex autem, sicut benignissimus pastor et pius pater, super tanto excessu valde turbatus et tristis effectus, eidem populo tanquam suo gregi debita caritate compassus est. Cuius casum relevare desiderans, pro liberatione suarum ovium apud eiusdem imperatoris clementiam diutius laboravit et affectuosas preces instanter fundere non cessavit, donec universos Urbis captivos de manibus Teutonicorum ereptos in potestate Petri Urbis prefecti restitui fecit.[15]

De cetero autem imperator simul et pontifex exeuntes de finibus Urbis per campestria iuxta Tyberim, processerunt usque ad vadum de Malliano; ibique fluvium ipsum cum toto exercitu transeuntes, intraverunt Sabinensem comitatum, et per Farfam atque castrum de Poli transitum facientes, in vigilia beati Petri pervenerunt ad pontem Lucanum, in quo nimirum loco pro tam gloriose sollempnitatis celebritate moram facere decreverunt. Et ut Ecclesia Dei et imperium ampliori decore clarescerunt, communi deliberatione statutum fuit ut ad laudem Dei et exultationem christiani populi prefatus Romanus pontifex et augustus ad missarum sollempnia in die illa pariter coronati procederent. Dignum namque satis erat ut illorum duorum principium apostolorum sollempnia duo summi orbis principes in letitia et magno gaudio celebrarent, qui suscepta potestate a Domino ligandi atque solvendi portas celi claudunt et aperiunt quibus volunt.

Tunc vero Tiburtini, tanquam perfide et contumaces, a dominio et iurisdictione beati Petri se subtrahere cupientes, postposita fidelitate quam domno pape Adriano eiusque successoribus recenter iuraverant, ad presentiam ipsius imperatoris accedere presumpserunt, et clavibus civitatis ei assignatis seipsos cum civitate Tyburtina iuri eius et dominio tradiderunt. Quod factum pontifex cum tota Romana ecclesia nimium grave et omnino intolerabile ferens, super tanta iniuria beato Petro absque rationabili causa illata eidem imperatori conquestus est, et ut civitatem ipsam que ab antiquo iuris beati Petri esse dinoscitur sibi restituerit, ipsum tanquam proprium Romane ecclesiae advocatum attentius exoravit. Augustus itaque habito cum principibus suis consilio et cognita veritate, illico civitatem ipsam ei restituit, et per litteras que inferius adnotantur eisdem Tyburtinis iniunxit quatinus eidem pape tanquam domino et patri suo fideliter obedient et servire omnimode studeant.

Fredericus Dei gratia Romanorum imperator et semper augustus universis civibus Tyburtinis gratiam suam et bonam voluntatem.

Universitatem vestram nosse volumes quod ob reverentiam beati Petri principis apostolorum dilectissimo atque in Christo reverendo patri nostro Adriano pape civitatem dimisimus Tyburtinam, salvo tantum per omnia iure imperiale. Huius rei gratia omnes et singulos cives Tyburtinos a fidelitate quam nuper nobis iurastis absolvimus, attentius vobis precipiendo mandantes quatinus eidem

---

15 Above, ch 7, at nn. 103–4.

pected tumult resounding on all sides, the German army quickly flew to arms, and both sides having drawn their swords, bitterly fought. What more need I say? Many were killed and many captured. At length, the Roman people, not without great risk to themselves, took refuge within the gates of the castle itself. The pope, however, as a very kindly pastor and pious father, greatly disturbed and saddened by such great excess, had pity with due charity for the people as for his own flock. Wishing to relieve their misfortune, he laboured for the liberation of his sheep before the clemency of the emperor and he did not cease to pour forth moving prayers until he had caused all the City's captives, taken from the hands of the Germans, to be handed over to the power of Peter, Prefect of the City.[15]

For the rest, however, the emperor and the Pontiff, going out together from the confines of the City across the countryside near the Tiber, proceeded as far as the ford at Magliano; crossing that river with the whole of the army, they entered the county of Sabina, and passing by way of Farfa and the castle of Poli, they reached Ponte Lucano on St Peter's eve, where they had decided to remain to celebrate so glorious a solemnity. And, in order that God's church and the empire might shine with greater dignity, by common agreement it was decided that the aforesaid Roman pontiff and the august emperor should together process wearing their crowns for the praise of God and the delight of the Christian people. For it was indeed proper that the two highest princes of the world should celebrate in joy and greatest delight the solemnity of those two princes of the apostles, who having received power from the Lord to bind and loose, close and open the gates of heaven to whom they will.

But then the people of Tivoli, perfidious and contumacious, desiring to withdraw themselves from the lordship and jurisdiction of blessed Peter, having set aside the fidelity which they had recently sworn to the lord pope Adrian and his successors, presumed to come to the emperor's presence, and, having assigned the keys of the city to him, they gave themselves and the city of Tivoli over to his right and lordship. As the pontiff and the whole Roman Church considered this action very grave and wholly intolerable, the pope complained to the emperor about so great an injury to blessed Peter carried out without reasonable cause, and urgently implored [the emperor], as an advocate of the Roman Church, to restore to him that city which is known to belong to the right of blessed Peter from ancient times. So, the emperor, having taken counsel with his princes and having learned the truth, immediately restored that city to him, and through the letter copied below, he ordered the people of Tivoli that they should faithfully obey the pope as their lord and father, and strive by every way to serve him.

> Frederick, by God's grace, emperor of the Romans and forever Augustus, to all the citizens of Tivoli, his grace and good will.
>
> We wish all of you to know that we have restored the city of Tivoli to our very dear and reverend father in Christ, Pope Adrian, out of respect for blessed Peter, Prince of the Apostles, saving only in all things imperial right. For this reason, we have absolved each and every citizen of Tivoli from the fidelity which they have recently sworn to us, ordering and commanding you very firmly that

venerabili patri Adriano pape fideliter assistatis, devote serviatis, atque sicut domino obedire studeatis; scientes, sicut iam dictum est, a iuramento fidelitatis quod
nuper fecistis vos absolutos, salvo in omnibus iure imperiali.

Et quoniam estivus calor iam nimis excreverat et maxima multitudo ipsius exercitus pro intemperie inconsueti aeris vel mortis periculum vel exitialem infirmitatem
incurrerat, communis voluntas et instans petitio principum fuit ut imperator ad
propria, quod et factum est, sine dilatione rediret.

Eodem tempore, supradictus rex Sicilie, postquam excommunicationis sententia percussus est, in contemptu cepit habere a suis; et cum salubria fidelium suorum consilia de satisfactione prestanda contempneret, in sua elatione ac fatuitate
fere solus remansit. Quippe maiores eius comites atque barones cum maioribus
Apulia civitatibus ubi a tanta eum perversitate revocare nullatenus potuerunt, eo
relicto nuncios suos ad domnum Adrianum papam tanquam ad principalem dominum destinarunt, rogantes ut ad partes illas dignaretur accedere et terram ipsam,
que iuris beati Petri esse dinoscitur, ac personas et eorum bona in manu et potestate sua reciperet. Tunc pontifex super hiis habito cum fratribus suis consilio, con-
gregata comitum et aliorum nobilium tam de Urbe quam de Campania et aliis
circumpositis locis decora militia, circa festum beati Michaelis descendit ad Sanctam Germanum; ibique recepta fidelitate et hominio a Roberto principe Capuano et
Andrea comite aliisque nobilium illarum partium, premisit eos ante faciem suam ut
prepararent ei viam et prava in directa facerent et aspera in vias planas. Ipse vero,
post aliquot dies, per castrum Mignani et Capuanum civitatem transitum faciens,
usque Beneventum Domino comitante processit, et omnes fere barones illarum
partium eorumque terras et circumpositas civitates ad fidelitatem beati Petri et
suam tanquam eorum principalis dominus in eadem civitate recepit.[16]

Interea imperator Grecorum maximam de thesauro pecuniam per quendam
principem suum nomine Pilialogum misit Anconam.[17] Scripsit etiam eidem pontifici, rogans et petens ab eo ut de civitatibus Apulie que site sunt in maritimis tres
eidem imperatori eo tenore concederet, ut ipse ad expugnandum predictum regem
et de tota Sicila expellendum sufficienter eidem pontifici vires tam in pecunia
quam in militibus et aliis armatorum presidiis indeficienter conferret; preterea
quinque millia libras auri eidem pape eiusque curie nichilominus dare promisit.[18]
Pro hiis ergo que contra ipsum regem quotidie tractabantur, valde perterritus est, et
erroris sui pentitentia ductus ad sinum matris sue sacrosanctae Romane ecclesie et
ad obedientiam domini et patris sui eiusdem Romani pontificis redire cum omni
humilitate disposuit. Quocirca electum Cataniensis ecclesie cum quibusdam de
maioribus aule sue ad presentiam ipsius pontificis accessuros usque Salernum
transmisit, quibus plenariam potestatem dedit ut gratiam et pacem domni pape ab
eo humiliter quererent, et satisfactionem plenariam que continetur inferius cum

---

[16]   Above, ch. 7, at nn. 46–50.
[17]   Above, ch. 7, at nn. 43, 84–5.
[18]   Above, ch. 7, at n. 87.

you should stand faithfully by our venerable father, Pope Adrian, serve him with devotion, and strive to obey him as lord; knowing, as has just been said, that you are absolved from the oath of fidelity which you have recently taken, saving imperial right in all things.

And since the heat of summer had already increased greatly and a great multitude of his army had fallen into danger of death or mortal sickness as a result of the unaccustomed inclemency of the atmosphere, it was a common desire and insistent petition of the princes that the emperor should return to his homeland without delay, and so it was done.

At this same time, after he had been struck down by the sentence of excommunication, the above mentioned king of Sicily began to be held in contempt by his own; and having rejected the salutary advice of his own faithful subjects that he should offer satisfaction, he remained all but alone in his foolish pride. When his great men, the counts and barons, along with the principal persons of the cities of Apulia, were totally unable to persuade him from this utter folly, they abandoned him and sent envoys to the lord pope Adrian as their principal lord, requesting that he deign to travel to that region and receive that land, which was recognized as belonging to the jurisdiction of the blessed Peter, and their persons and property into his hands and power. The pope then took the advice of his brothers on these issues, raised a suitable military force from the counts and other nobles both of the City and the Campagna as well as from other places round about, and then went down to San Germano around the feast of St Michael; and there, having received the fealty and homage of Prince Robert of Capua, Count Andrew, and the other nobles of those parts, he sent them ahead to prepare the way for him, 'making straight in the desert a highway and every mountain low' [Isa. 40: 3–4]. After some days he himself journeyed by way of the *castrum* of Mignano and the city of Capua, and with the Lord as his companion, advanced as far as Benevento; and in that city he received all the barons of the area, and their lands, and the surrounding towns, into the fealty of blessed Peter and himself as their principal lord.[16]

Meanwhile, the emperor of the Greeks sent one of his princes called Palaeologus to Ancona with a large sum of money from the treasury.[17] He also wrote to the pope, asking and beseeching him to grant to the emperor three cities in the coastal district of Apulia, on condition that he supply the pontiff with adequate supplies of money and a large enough force of knights and other troops to drive the said king right out of Sicily; he promised, moreover, to give not less than five thousand pounds of gold to the pope and his court.[18] The king was stricken with terror by these projects being daily set in motion against him, and repenting of his error he decided to return in all humility to the bosom of his mother, the most Holy Roman Church and to the obedience of his lord and father, this same Roman pontiff. So he sent the bishop-elect of the church of Catania [Bernard] and some others from among the great men of his court to Salerno, to go on to meet the pope, giving them full power humbly to seek the pope's grace and peace on his behalf, and to make plenary satisfaction as described below and to pledge security to him.

firma securitate sibi prestarent. In primis petebat absolvi secundum Ecclesie morem; deinde hominium et fidelitatem ipsi pontifici facere promittebat; omnes quoque terre sue ecclesias cum plenaria libertate restituet; tria castra pro illatis dampnis, Padulem videlicet, Montem Fuscum et Morconem, cum pertinentiis suis in propriam hereditatem beato Petro et ecclesie Romane nichilominus dabit; Romam preterea, que tunc adversabatur pontifici, dominio ipsius armis vel pecunia subiugabit; post recuperatam domni pape et Ecclesie gratiam tantundem pecunie quantum Greci obtulerant largietur.

Auditis itaque huiusmodi oblationibus, de communi fratrum consilio venerabilem virum Ubaldum, tunc presbiterum cardinalem tituli sancte Praxedis, nunc Hostiensem episcopum,[19] domnus papa transmisit usque Salernum, quatinus a predictis nuntiis inquireret si ea que fuerant oblata veritate certa inniterentur, et quod inveniretur sibi referret. Factum est ita; et redeunte ipso cardinali, omnia que promissa ex parte regis fuerant vera inventa sunt et ad complendum parata. Bonum igitur visum est eidem pontifici ut tam utilis concordia et cum magno honore Ecclesie compositio deberet admitti. Set quia maior pars fratrum, alta nimis et omnino incerta sentiens, consentire nullatenus voluit, disturbatum est totum quod oblatum fuerat et penitus refutatum.[20] Et quoniam, iuxta evangelicum verbum, omnis qui se exaltat humiliabitur et qui se humiliat exaltabitur, postquam ipse rex ita se humiliavit et eius satisfaction recepta non fuit, exivit cum exercitu contra Grecos et Apulos qui eius terram occupaverant, et veniens usque Brundusium ubi fuerant congregati, pugnavit in campo cum illis. Quibus tandem superatis et potenter devictis atque fugatis, plenam de ipsis victoriam et triumphum obtinuit. Unde factum est quod totam Apuliam et eius fines tantus timor et tremor repente invasit ut ei deinceps resistere nullus auderet, set universi a facie ipsius fugientes, sine armis et coactione aliqua civitates et arces munitissimas illico domino eius restituerunt.[21]

Quamobrem postquam pontifex deceptum se fore cognovit et ab omnibus qui secum firmiter stare iuraverunt penitus derelictum, premisit maiorem partem fratrum suorum in Campaniam, et ipse cum paucis apud Beneventum remansit, expectans ipsius regis adventum. Evolutis autem paucis diebus, rex ipse a superioribus Apulie partibus cum exercitu movit, et Beneventum civitati usque ad duo miliaria propinquavit. Tunc sepedictus pontifex venerabiles viros predictum U[baldum] tituli sancte Praxedis, I[iulium] tituli sancti Marcelli et R[olandum] tituli sancti Marci, sedis apostolice cancellarium, presbiteros cardinales,[22] ad eundem regem direxit, quatinus ex parte beati Petri eum attentius commonerent ut ab offensis eius omnino cessaret, de illatis dampnis satisfaceret et iura matris sue

---

[19]   For Hubald Allocingoli, cardinal priest of S. Prassede (1141–58), cardinal bishop of Ostia (1158–81), see ch. 7, n. 63 above.

[20]   Above, ch. 7, at n. 16.

[21]   Above, ch. 7, at nn. 53–60.

[22]   Hubald of S. Prassede, Julius of S. Marcello, and Roland of S. Marco: see above, ch. 7, n. 63, ch. 9, at n. 78.

First, he sought to be absolved according to the Church's custom; then he promised to do homage and fealty to the pontiff; he would restore full liberty to all the churches in his land; furthermore he would give in hereditary right to Blessed Peter and the Roman church three *castra*, Padula, Montefusco, and Morcone, in return for the harm he had caused; moreover, he would by arms or money subject Rome, then hostile to the pope, to [papal] rule; after recovering the grace of the lord pope and the Church, he will give them as much money as the Greeks had offered.

On hearing these offers, the lord pope, with the unanimous advice of his brothers, sent the venerable man Hubald, then cardinal priest of the title of S. Prassede and now bishop of Ostia,[19] to Salerno, to enquire from the said envoys if what had been offered rested on reliable fact, and to report back what he had ascertained. This the cardinal did, and on his return it was found that the terms which had been promised on the king's behalf were genuine and ready for completion. It seemed, therefore, good to the pope that so useful an agreement, and a settlement which brought great honour to the Church, should be accepted. But because the greater part of the brethren, thinking it too dangerous and uncertain, would not consent to it, all that had been offered was frustrated and entirely rejected.[20] And since, according to the words of the Gospel, 'everyone that exalteth himself shall be humbled, and he that humbleth himself shall be exalted' [Luke 18: 14], after the king had humbled himself in this way and his satisfaction had not been accepted, he marched out with his army against the Greeks and the Apulians who had occupied his land, and. coming to Brindisi where they were gathered, he fought a battle with them. After they were finally overcome, totally defeated, and in flight, and the king won a complete and triumphant victory over them. As a result, such fear and trembling quickly spread through the whole of Apulia that thereafter nobody dared to resist him, everyone fled from his presence, and its strongest cities and fortresses immediately returned to his lordship without a fight or any sort of pressure.[21]

As a result of this, after the pope learned that he had been deceived and totally abandoned by all those who had sworn to stand resolutely by him, he sent the majority of his brethren into the Campagna, while he himself remained in Benevento with a few of them, awaiting the king's arrival. A few days later, the king marched with his army from northern Apulia and approached to some two miles from the city of Benevento. Then the previously mentioned pope sent to the king the venerable cardinal priests, H[ubald] of the title of S. Prassede, G[iuliano] of the title of S. Marcello, and R[oland] of the title of S. Marco, chancellor of the Apostolic See,[22] to warn him carefully on behalf of the blessed Peter to cease from all his offences, to make satisfaction for the harm he had done, and to preserve in peace

sacrosancte Romane ecclesie sibi pacifice conservaret. Quibus benigne susceptis atque tractatis, post mutuam diversorum altercationem capitulorum, rex ipse cum eodem papa eis mediantibus concordavit; et veniens ad ecclesiam sancti Marciani, iuxta Beneventum positam, ad pedes ipsius pontificis humiliter se prostravit et ligium hominium et fidelitatem coram circumastantium maxima episcoporum, cardinalem, comitum, baronum et aliorum multitudine, Oddone Fragapane iuramentum computante, sibi fecit. Recepto itaque ipso rege ad pacis osculum et collatis magnis muneribus in auro et argento ac sericis pannis eidem pontifici eiusque fratribus et toti eius curie, ab invicem leti et cum gaudio discesserunt.[23]

Egrediens autem benignissimus papa de civitate Beneventana et de finibus Samnii, versus urbem Romam iter suum direxit. Transiens vero per Monte Cassinum et per Marsicana montana, venit ad civitatem Narniam. Et quoniam civitatem Urbevetanam que per longissima retro tempora se a iurisdictione beati Petri subtraxerat, quam cum multo studio et diligentia nuper acquisierat et dominio ecclesie Romane subiecerat, bonum sibi et fratribus suis visum est ut ad civitatem ipsam accederet et sua eam presentia honoraret. Nam usque ad eius tempora, sicut ab omnibus dicebatur, nullus umquam Romanorum pontificum eamdem civitatem intraverat vel aliquam in ea temporalem potestatem habuerat. Eapropter clerus et populus et milites illius loci maiori desiderio et ampliori veneratione ipsum pontificem receperunt et modis omnibus quibus poterant honorarunt. Ipse vero aliquamdiu ibi moram faciens, maiores et minores tamquam novam beati Petri familiam affectuose honorabat et in eorum congratulabatur aspectibus. Appropinquante igitur yemis tempore, ad amenum et populosum Viterbii castrum descendit, et exinde ad Urbem et Lateranense consistorium cum gloria et honore debito remeavit.[24]

Hic beatus pontifex in ecclesia beati Petri tectum sancti Processi quod dissipatum invenit optime resarcivit, et super oratorium sancti Johannis in Fonte murum a tribus lateribus erigens navi eiusdem ecclesie coequavit. In Lateranensi quoque palatio cisternam valde necessarium et multum copiosam studiose fieri fecit, et alia multa que pro nimia vetustate consumpta fuerant in eodem palatio resarcivit. In ecclesia sanctorum Cosme et Damiani maius altare lapide superposito illi lapide quem beatus papa Gregorius consecraverat, propriis minibus mediante Quadragesima dedicavit.

Hic beati Petri patrimonium in magnis possessionibus et edificiis plurimum augmentavit. Comparavit enim castrum Corclani a Baccaleone pro CXL libris affortiatorum. Duo quoque optima molendina posita apud Sanctam Christinam ab Ildebrando et Bernardo, filius Ugolini comitis de Calmangiare, pro CXC libris eiudem monete nichilominus comparavit. Roccam Sancti Stephani cum medietate Proceni et Repeseni ab eisdem comitibus in pignore pro CXLVIII libris affortiatorum et V solidos, eo tenore quo scriptum est in publico eorum instrumento quod

---

[23] Above, ch. 7, at nn. 63–7.
[24] Above, ch. 5, at nn. 176–7.

the rights of his mother, the most Holy Roman Church. They were well received and well-treated, and, after some arguments between them about various of the clauses, the king made peace with the pope through their mediation and, coming to the church of S. Marciano, situated near Benevento, he humbly prostrated himself at the pope's feet and did liege homage and fealty to him, in the presence of a large number of bishops, cardinals, counts, barons, and a host of other people, with Odo Frangipane drawing up the oath. Then, when the king had been admitted to the kiss of peace, after giving many presents of gold, silver, and silken cloths on the pope, his brothers, and the whole Curia, they departed from one another happy and joyful.[23]

Leaving the city of Benevento and the boundaries of the Samnites, the most generous pope directed his path towards the City of Rome. Passing by Montecassino and Monte Marsico, he came to the city of Narni. And because he had recently and with great labour and diligence acquired the city of Orvieto, which for a very long time had withdrawn itself from the jurisdiction of blessed Peter, and subjected it to the lordship of the Roman Church, it seemed good to himself and his brethren that he should go to that city and honour it with his presence. For until his time, as everyone said, no Roman pontiff had entered that city or exercised any temporal power within it. Therefore, the clergy, people, and knights of that place received the pontiff with greater desire and fuller veneration and honoured him in as many ways as they were able. He, therefore, staying there for sometime, honoured both great and small as new members of the family of St Peter, and he rejoiced in their sight. As the winter time was approaching, he went down to the pleasant and populous *castrum* of Viterbo and thence he returned with due honour and glory to the City and to the Lateran consistory.[24]

Here in the church of St Peter, the holy pontiff richly restored the roof of S. Processo which he found collapsed and raising a wall with three sides over the oratory of S. Giovanni in Fonte, he made it level with the nave of the same church. Also in the Lateran Palace he caused to be made a very necessary and extremely large cistern, and he repaired many other things in the same palace, which had been consumed with age. In the church of SS. Cosma e Damiano, he dedicated with his own hands in the middle of Lent, the great stone altar above that stone which the blessed Pope Gregory had consecrated.

He much increased the Patrimony of St Peter with great possessions and buildings. He bought the fortress of Corchiano from the Boccaleoni for 140 pounds *affortiatorum*. He also bought two excellent mills at Santa Cristina from Ildebrando and Bernardo, sons of Ugolino, count of Calmangiare for 190 pounds of the same money. He received the *rocca* of San Stefano with half of Proceno and [Rocca] Ripesena from the same counts in pledge for 148 pounds *affortiatorum* and five shillings. By their spontaneous gift, he received into the inheritance of St

est in archivis respositum, in propriam beati Petri hereditatem per ipsorum sponta-
neam donationem recepit. Eodem quoque modo et eodem tenore totam terram Oddonis de Poli in perpetuam sancti Petri hereditatem nichilominus acquisivit.

Hic fecit gironem in castro Radicophini, turribus munitum et alto fossato. De-
sertum quoque Orcle castrum, quod erat spelunca latronum, pro pace ac securitate
illius terre populavit, et muro ac turribus non sine multis expensis munivit.

In ponte Lucano capellam fieri fecit, in qua calicem VI unciarum, campanam,
libros et sacerdotalia indumenta pro missarum celebratione donavit. Emit etiam
iuxta ipsum pontem ab uxore Iohannis de Benedicto, cive Tuburtino, duos modios
terre pro VII libris affortiatorum; et unum modium et dimidium pro XXVIII solidis
affortiatorum; a Gregorio quoque et Milone de Valle Montonis unum modium et
dimidium pro XX solidos papiensis monete. Emit etiam iuxtra ipsum pontem VI
modios terre ab Oddone de Insula et uxore eius pro XXIIII libris affortiatorum;
preterea medietatem IIII castrorum, Castillionis videlicet, Cincigniani, Canapine et
Bulsigniani emit a filiabus Raynaldi de Guardeia pro [*] libris affortiarum; exinde
publicum instrumentum recepit et corporalem investuram per Anterium marescal-
cum suum a Vitale supradictarum mulierum curatore, presentibus Alexio scrinario,
pincerna ipsius pape, Pedro de Arture, militie Gallesano, Malavolte Iohannis Ferri,
et aliorum multorum.[25]

Hic fecit ordinationes duas per menses decembris et martii, diaconos VII,
presbiteros V; episcopos per diversa loca numero [*]. Defunctus est autem apud
Anagniam kl. Septemb., et vectus Romam, in ecclesia beati Petri iuxta corpus
Eugenii pape honorifice tumulatus est.

Actum Bosonis, presbiteri cardinalis tituli Pastoris, qui ab ipso pontifice ab exordio eius
camerarius constitutus et in ecclesia sanctorum Cosme et Damiani diaconus ordinatus, assi-
due usque ad ipsius obitum familiariter secum permansit.

[*] A blank space was left for the later insertion of the number.

[25]   Above, ch. 8.

Peter all the land of these same counts, in the manner contained in their public instrument deposited in the archives. In the same way and in the same sense, he acquired all the land of Odo di Poli as the perpetual inheritance of St Peter.

He built a round tower in the fortress of Radicofani, defended by turrets and a deep ditch. In order to ensure the peace and security of that land, he resettled the deserted *castrum* of Orcia, which was a den of thieves, and fortified it with a wall and towers, not without great expense.

In Ponte Lucano, he caused a chapel to be made to which he gave a chalice of six ounces, a bell, books and priestly vestments for the celebration of mass. He bought near that same bridge two measures of land from the wife of Giovanni de Benedicto, citizen of Tivoli, for seven pounds *affortiatorum*; and one measure from Rinaldo for 20 shillings *affortiatorum*; one mill and a half from Gregorio and Milo of Valmontone for 25 shillings of Pavian money. Also near the bridge, he bought six measures of land from Odo de Insula and his wife for 24 pounds *affortiatorum*; moreover, he bought half of four *castra*, Castiglione Teverino, Cinigiano, Canepina and Bulsignano, from the daughters of Raynaldo de Guardea for [*] pounds *affortiatorum*; furthermore, he received a public instrument and corporal investiture through Anterio, his marshal, from Vitale, guardian of the aforesaid women, in the presence of Alessio, archivist, the pope's steward, Pietro de Arture, knight of Gallesano, Malavolto Giovanni Ferro, and many others.[25]

He celebrated two ordinations in the months of December and March, seven deacons, five priests; bishops for different [places] number [*] He died at Anagni on 1 September, and was carried to Rome and was honourably buried in the church of blessed Peter near the body of Pope Eugenius.

Drawn up by Boso, cardinal priest of the title of Pastoris [of S. Pudenziana], made chamberlain of the same pope from the beginning of his pontificate and ordained deacon in the church of SS. Cosma e Damiano, who remained assiduously at his side until his death.

[*] A blank space was left for the later insertion of the number.

2
Otto of Freising and (from Book iii) his continuator Rahewin, *Gesta Friderici I. imperatoris*

From the Latin text of G. Waitz and B. von Simson, 3rd edn, *MGH SRG* 46 (Hanover/ Leipzig, 1912).

Otto, bishop of Freising (1137–58), son of Margrave Leopold III of Austria and Agnes, daughter of Emperor Henry I, was through his mother uncle to Frederick I. He thus belonged to the inner circle of the highest German nobility around the young emperor, and his Gesta *were written in collaboration with their subject, who provided a written sketch of his principal achievements to guide the chronicler (*Gesta, *1–5;* Deeds, *17–20). Otto's is, then, a quasi-official history; but it is written by a learned and committed cleric,[26] for whom the growing disenchantment between pope and emperor was a painful development. Had he, not Rainald of Dassel, read and translated the famous Besançon letter (below, iii. 9), the diplomatic breach might have been avoided.*

[1155]

ii. 28. Igitur rex (Fredericus) ad Urbem tendens circa Biterbium castrametatur. Quo Romanus antistes Adrianus cum cardinalibus suis veniens ex debito officii sui honorifice suscipitur gravique adversus populum suum conquestione utens reverenter auditus est. Predictus enim populus, ex quo senatorum ordinem renovare studuit, multis malis pontifices suos affligere temeritatis ausu non formidavit. Accessit ad huius seditiosi facinoris augmentum, quod Arnaldus quidam Brixiensis, de quo supra dictum est, sub typo religionis et, ut ewangelicis verbis utar, sub ovina pelle lupum gerens, Urbem ingressus, ad factionem istam rudis populi animis premolli dogmate ad animositatem accensis innumeram post se duxit, immo seduxit multitudinem. [...]

ii. 31. Porro quibusdam ex circumstantibus inquirentibus ab his qui missi fuerant, an plura dicere vellent, paulisper deliberantes in dolo responderunt se prius ea quae audierant concivibus suis referre et tunc demum ex consilio ad principem redire velle.

Sic accepto commeatu a curia egredientes ad Urbem cum festinatione revertuntur. Rex dolum presentiens consulendum super hoc negotio patrem suum Romanum pontificem decernit. Cui ille: 'Romanae plebis, fili, adhuc melius experieris versutiam. Cognosces enim in dolo eos venisse et in dolo redisse. Sed, Dei nos adiuvante clementia, dicentis: *Comprehendam sapientes in astucia sua,* prevenire eorum poterimus versutas insidias. Maturato igitur premittantur fortes et

---

[26] He had studied at Paris *c.* 1128–33, where he was much influenced by Hugh of Saint-Victor, and spent a few years in the Cistercian monastery of Morimond before receiving the bishopric of Freising in 1137. For his historical work, see *Deeds*, 3–7.

2
Otto of Freising and (from Book iii) his continuator Rahewin, *Gesta Friderici I. imperatoris*

Based on the English translation by Charles Christopher Mierow (Columbia University Press, 1953; repr. New York, 1966).

Otto of Freising died in 1158, leaving his great work on Emperor Frederick unfinished. The task was taken up by Rahewin, a cleric who lacked Otto's profound learning and aristocratic background, although he had been closely associated with the bishop as chaplain (and, perhaps, secretary), and spent most of his life in the ambit of Freising, as canon of the cathedral and provost of the collegiate church of St Vitus. His historical skills are generally judged inferior to Otto's, his work marred by what Mierow, Deeds, *8, called 'borrowed finery', and although he lived until c. 1177, he did not carry the story beyond Christmas 1169. On Rahewin, see Odilo Engels, 'Kardinal Boso als Geschichtsschreiber' in* Konzil und Papst. Historische Beiträge zur Frage der höchsten Gewalt: Festgabe für Hermann Tüchle, *ed. G. Schwaiger (Munich/Paderborn, 1975), 147–68; cf.* Deeds, *7–10.*

[1155]

ii. 28. Now on his way to the City, the king encamped near Viterbo [8 June]. To him came the Roman pope, Adrian, with his cardinals, and was received with the honour due to his office. He was given a deferential hearing as he uttered bitter complaints against his people, since their endeavour to reinstate the order of senators, in their rash daring did not shrink from inflicting many outrages on their popes. There was this additional aggravation of their seditious conduct, that a certain Arnold of Brescia, under the guise of religion and to use the words of the Gospel [Matt. 7: 15] 'Acting as a wolf in sheep's clothing', entered the City, inflamed to violence the minds of the simple people by his exceedingly seductive doctrines, and induced—nay seduced—a countless throng to espouse his cause. [...]

ii. 31. And when certain of the bystanders inquired of those who had been sent [from Rome] whether they wished to say anything more, after deliberating a little they deceitfully replied that they wished first to report to their fellow citizens the things which they had heard, and return to the prince only after taking counsel.

Thus dismissed, the emissaries departed from the court and returned in haste to the City. The king, anticipating treachery, decided that he should consult his father, the Roman pontiff, about the matter. The latter said to him, 'My son, you will learn more about the guile of the Roman rabble as time goes on. For you will discover that in treachery they came and in treachery they departed. But aided by the clemency of God, who says, "I shall take the wise in their own craftiness," [1 Cor. 3: 19] we shall be able to circumvent their shrewd schemes. Accordingly, let brave and knowing young men of the army be quickly sent ahead to seize the

gnari de exercitu iuvenes, qui aecclesiam beati Petri Leoninumque occupent castrum. In presidii equites nostri ibi sunt, qui eos cognita voluntate nostra statim ad-
mittent. Preterea Octavianum cardinalem presbiterum, qui de nobilissimo
Romanorum descendit sanguine,[27] fidelissimum tuum, eis adiungemus. Sicque
factum est. Eliguntur proxima nocte pene usque ad mille armatorum equitum lec-
tissimi iuvenes summoque diluculo Leoninam intrantes urbem, aecclesiam beati
Petri, vestibulum et gradus occupaturi, observant. Redeunt ad castra nuncii haec
laeta reportantes.

ii. 32. Sole orto, transacta iam prima hora, precedente cum cardinalibus et clericis
summo pontifice Adriano eiusque adventum in gradibus rex castra movens, armatus cum suis per declivum montis Gaudii descendens,[28] ea porta, quam Auream
vocant, Leoninam urbem, in qua beati Petri aecclesia sita noscitur, intravit.

Videres militem tam armorum splendore fulgentem, tam ordinis integritate
decenter incedentem, ut recte de illo dici posset: *Terribilis ut castrorum acies ordinata*, et illud Machabeorum: *Refulsit sol in clipeos aureos, et resplenduerunt
montes ab eis.*

Mox princeps ad gradus aecclesiae beati Petri veniens a summo pontifice honorifice susceptus ac usque ad confessionem beati Petri deductus est. Dehinc cele-
bratis ab ipso papa missarum sollempniis, armato stipatus rex milite cum
benedictione debita imperii coronam accepit, anno regni sui quarto, mense Iunio,
xiiii. Kal. Iulii, cunctis qui aderant cum magna laeticia acclamantibus Deumque
super tam glorioso facto glorificantibus.

Interim a suis pons, qui iuxta castrum Crescentii[29] ab urbe Leonina usque ad
ingressum ipsius extenditur Urbis, ne a furente populo celebritatis huius iocun-
ditas interrumpi posset, servabatur. Peractis omnibus imperator cum corona solus
equum faleratum insidens, caeteris pedes euntibus, per eandem, qua introierat,
egressus portam ad tabernacula, quae ipsis muris adherebant, revertitur Romano
pontifice in palatio quod iuxta aecclesiam habebat remanente.

ii. 33. Dum haec agerentur, Romanus populus cum senatoribus suis in Capitolio
convenerant. Audientes autem imperatorem sine sua astipulatione coronam imperii
accepisse, in furorem versi cum impetu magno Tyberim transeunt ac iuxta
aecclsiam beati Petri procurrentes quosdam ex stratoribus, qui remanserant, in ipsa
sacrosancta aecclesia necare non timuerunt Clamor attollitur. Audiens haec imperator militem ex estus magnitudine sitisque ac laboris defatigatione recreari cupien-
tem armari iubet. Festinabat eo amplius, quo timebat furentem plebem in
Romanum pontificem cardinalesque irruisse. Pugna conseritur. Ex una parte iuxta
castrum Crescentii cum Romanis, ex altero latere iuxta Piscinam cum

---

[27]   For Octavian, cardinal priest of S. Cecilia (1151–9), see ch. 7, n. 12.
[28]   Monte Mario, about five hundred feet in height, is situated on the Tiber, two miles
north of Rome.
[29]   Probably Hadrian's Tomb (Castel Sant'Angelo), which was held for a time by the
patrician Crescenti family.

church of St Peter and the Leonine stronghold. Our knights are there within the fortifications; upon learning our wishes they will straightway admit them. Besides, we shall add to their number the cardinal priest Octavian, whose lineage is of the noblest blood of the Romans,[27] a man most faithful to you.' And so it was done. The next night almost a thousand armed knights were chosen, the very pick of the young men; and entering the Leonine city at the break of day they succeeded in occupying the church of the blessed Peter, its entrance and steps. Messengers returned to camp reporting these glad tidings.

ii. 32. After the sun had risen, and at the end of the first hour, Pope Adrian led the way with the cardinals and clergy and awaited the prince's arrival on the steps; the king broke camp and fully armed descended the slope of Monte Mario with his men[28] and entered the Leonine city, in which the church of the blessed Peter is known to be situated, by the gate which they call Golden.

You should have seen the soldiery, gleaming so brightly in the splendour of their armour, marching so regularly in unbroken order that it might properly be said of them: 'Terrible as an army with banners' [Song of Songs 6: 4] and that verse of Maccabees, 'The sun shone upon the shields of gold, and the mountains blazed with them' [1 Mac. 6: 39].

Presently the prince, coming to the steps of the church of the blessed Peter, was received with all honour by the supreme pontiff and led to the confession of the blessed Peter. Then, after the solemnities of the Mass had been celebrated by the pope himself, the king, attended by his knights under arms, received the crown of the empire, with the appropriate blessing. This was in the fourth year of his reign, in the month of June, on the fourteenth day before the Kalends of July [18 June, 1155]. All who were present acclaimed him with great joy, and glorified God for so glorious a deed.

Meanwhile, the bridge near the castle of Crescentius,[29] which leads from the Leonine city to the entrance of the City itself, was being guarded by his men, that the rejoicing over this celebration might not be interrupted by the frenzied populace. When all was finished the emperor, wearing the crown and mounted upon a caparisoned steed, rode alone, all the rest going on foot. By the same gate by which he had entered he returned to the camp, which adjoined the very walls, while the Roman pontiff remained within the palace which he had near the church.

ii. 33. While this was going on, the Roman people with their senators had assembled on the Capitol. But upon hearing that the emperor had received the imperial crown without their assent, they became infuriated and crossed the Tiber in great force. Advancing to the church of the blessed Peter, they did not hesitate to kill within that sacred edifice certain of the sergeants (*stratores*) who had stayed behind. An outcry was raised. Upon hearing this, the emperor ordered the soldiers (who, parched by the great heat and exhausted by their thirst and labours, were eager to refresh themselves) to put on their armour. He made the more haste because he feared that the enraged populace had attacked the Roman pontiff and the cardinals. They joined battle: on one side, near the castle of Crescentius, with the Romans; on the other side, near the *Piscina*, with those from across the Tiber. You

Transtiberinis. Videres nunc hos istos versus castra propellere, nunc hos illos ad pontem usque repellere Adiuvabantur nostri, quod a castro Crescentii saxorum ictibus seu iaculorum non ledebantur spiculis, mulieribus etiam, quae in spectaculis stabant, suos, ut aiunt adhortantibus, ne propter inertis plebis temeritatem tam ordinatum equitum decus ab his qui in arce erant predictis modis sauciaretur. Dubia itaque sorte dum diu ab utrisque decertaretur, Romani tandem atrocitatem nostrorum non ferentes coguntur cedere. Cerneres nostros tam immaniter quam audacter Romanos cedendo sternere, sternendo cedere, acsi dicerent: 'Accipe nunc, Roma, pro auro Arabico Teutonicum ferrum. Haec est pecunia, quam tibi princeps tuus pro tua offert corona. Sic emitur Francis imperium. Talia tibi a principe tuo redduntur commertia, talia [tibi] prestantur iuramenta.'

Prelium hoc a decima pene diei hora usque ad noctem protractum est. Cesi fuerunt ibi vel in Tyberi mersi pene mille, capti ferme DC, sauciati innumeri, caeteri in fugam versi, uno tantum ex nostris, mirum dictu, occiso, uno capto. Plus enim nostros intemperies caeli estusque illo in tempore maxime circa Urbem immoderatior quam Romanorum ledere poterant arma.

ii. 34. Finito tam magnifico triumpho imperator ad castra rediit ibique, et se et suis fessa lectulis recipientibus membra, nocte illa conquievit. […] Adventabat toti aecclesiae et precipue Romanae urbis pontifici et imperatori venerabile festum apostolorum Petri et Pauli. Ea ergo die, missam papa Adriano celebrante, imperator coronatur. Tradunt Romanorum ibi pontificem inter missarum sollempnia cunctos, qui fortasse in conflictu cum Romanis habito sanguinem fuderant, absolvisse, allegationibus usum, eo quod miles proprio principi militans eiusque obedientiae astrictus [non solum] contra hostes imperii [et aecclesiae] dimicans sanguinem[que] fundens iure tam poli quam fori non homicida, sed vindex affirmetur. […] Nec dubium, quin civis ad obedientiam pontifici, ad deditionem principi suo venisset, si miles extra tantum incommodum pati potuisset. Verum innumeris hac caeli corruptione in morbos gravissimos incidentibus, princeps dolens ac nolens suisque tantum morem gerens ad vicina montana transferre cogitur tabernacula. Itaque proximum ascendens Appenninum, super Nar fluvium, de quo Lucanus:

Sulphureas Nar albus aquas,[30]

tentoria fixit, circa Tyburtum a Romano pontifice, relictis sibi captivis, divisus. Ibi per aliquot dies manens acceptoque prudentum consilio corruptum, quem biberant, aerem farmatiis propellendum, exercitum quantum poterat recreavit. […]

[30]   Otto is mistaken; the quotation comes from Vergil, *Aeneid*, vii. 517.

should have seen now the Romans driving our men toward the camp, now the latter pushing the Romans back to the bridge. It was to the advantage of our men that they could not be reached by the stones and javelins hurled from the castle of Crescentius; even the women, who were watching, urged on their men (it is said), lest by reason of the boldness of the base commoners so respectable a company of disciplined knights might be smitten in the aforesaid ways by those who were in the fortification. And so, though the struggle was continued for a long time by both sides with varying fortune, the Romans were finally compelled to retreat, unable to bear the ferocious attack of our men. You should have seen our men ruthlessly and ferociously killing and wounding, wounding and killing the Romans, as if to say, 'Take now, O Rome, Teutonic iron instead of Arabian gold. This is the price your prince offers you for your crown. Thus do the Franks purchase empire. These are the gifts given you by your prince, these the oaths sworn to you.'

This battle lasted from about the tenth hour of the day until nightfall. There were slain there or drowned in the Tiber almost a thousand, about six hundred were taken captive, the wounded were innumerable, all the remainder were put to flight; of our men, strange to say, only one was killed, one taken captive. For the unhealthy climate and the very extreme heat at that season, especially in the neighbourhood of the City, had more power to harm our men than the weapons of the enemy.

ii. 34. After the conclusion of so magnificent a triumph, the emperor returned to the camp, and there he and his men threw their weary limbs upon their beds. [...] The festival of the apostles Peter and Paul [29 June], revered by the entire Church and especially by the pontiff and emperor of the Roman city, now drew near. Accordingly, on that day the emperor wore his crown while Pope Adrian celebrated Mass. It is said that there, during the solemnity of the ceremony, the pontiff of the Romans absolved all who had chanced to spill blood in the conflict fought with the Romans on the ground that a soldier fighting for his own prince and bound to obey him (warring against enemies not only of the empire but also of the Church), though he sheds blood may be declared, by divine as well as by secular law, to be not a murderer but an avenger. [...] There is no doubt that the citizens would have become more obedient to the pope, submissive to their prince, if the army outside had been able to endure so great an inconvenience. But as countless numbers were stricken by most serious maladies in consequence of the corruption of the air, the prince, though distressed and unwilling, was obliged to move the encampment to the neighbouring mountains merely to accommodate his men. Therefore, after separating from the Roman pontiff near Tivoli and turning over the prisoners to him, he ascended the nearby Apennines and pitched his tents above the river Nera, of which Lucan writes:

White Nar's sulphurous waters.[30]

There he remained for several days and, taking the advice of prudent men, granted the army as much rest as possible, that they might counteract by medicines the corrupt air they had been breathing. [...]

Continuatio Rahewini

iii. 6. Non multo post aput Herbipolim civitatem Alexii [*sc*. Manueli] Constantinopolitani imperatoris legati coram principe cum muneribus suam peragunt legationem. Quia tamen verba eorum in quibusdam fastum regalem et Grecum in subornato sermone videbantur sapere tumorem, imperator eos despexit et nisi in melius commutata sententia commodius sibi prospexissent, si fieri poterat salvo nunciorum privilegio, dissimulationem agente principe, prope fuit, ut a quibusdam ignominiosum et erumpnosum accepissent responsum.

Placatus tamen multis eorum precibus et lacrimis imperator veniam super his donavit, accepta sponsione, quod deinceps spernentes ampullosa, nonnisi eam quam deceret Romanum principem et orbis ac Urbis dominatorem, reverentiam suis salutationibus apportarent.[31] Indulgentiam et gratiam consecuti Fridericum ducem Sueviae, filium Conradi regis, adhuc adolescentulum, in presentia sua gladio accingi et militem profiteri postulant et impetrant. Amita siquidem sua imperatrix Constantinopolitana[32] et antea et nunc multis et magnificis eundem puerum visitaverat largitionum muneribus idque legatis in mandatis dedisse traditur, ne quando nisi completo hoc negotio in Greciam reverterentur, astipulante sibi cum magno favore proprio marito ob gratiam et antiquam amiciciam cum patre pueri rege Conrado habitam.

iii. 7. Ibidem tunc affuere etiam Heinrici regis[33] Angliae missi, varia et preciosa donaria multo lepore verborum adornata presentantes. Inter quae papilionem unum, quantitate maximum, qualitate bonissimum, perspeximus. Cuius si quantitatem requiris, nonnisi machinis et instrumentorum genere et amminiculo levari poterat; si quantitatem, nec materia nec opere ipsum putem aliquando ab aliquo huiuscemodi apparatu superatum iri. Litteras quoque mellito sermone plenas pariter direxerat; quarum hic tenor fuit:

> Precordiali amico suo Friderico, Dei gratia Romanorum imperatori invictissimo, Heinricus rex Angliae, dux Normanniae et Aquitaniae et comes Andegavensis, salutem et verae [pacis et] dilectionis concordiam.
>
> Excellentiae vestrae quantas possumus referimus grates, dominantium optime, quod nos nunciis vestris visitare, salutare litteris, muneribus prevenire et, quod his carius amplectimur, pacis et amoris invicem dignatus estis federa inchoare. Exultavimus et quodammodo animum nobis crescere et in maius sensimus evehi, dum vestra promissio, in qua nobis spem dedistis in disponendis regni nostri negotiis, alacriores nos reddidit et promptiores. Exultavimus, inquam, et tota mente magnificentiae vestrae assurreximus, id vobis in sincero cordis affectu

---

[31] See above, ch. 7, at n. 136.
[32] Bertha, sister-in-law of Conrad III, who, after her marriage to Manuel, had changed her name to Irene.
[33] Henry II, 1154–89.

Rahewin's continuation

iii. 6. Not long afterwards [September, 1157], at the city of Würzburg, legates of Alexius [= Manuel], the emperor at Constantinople, set forth in the presence of the prince the purpose of their embassy, bringing gifts. But because their words in certain respects appeared to smack of royal pride and (in their over-ornate speech) of the arrogance of the Greeks, the emperor scorned them, and had they not thought better of it and safeguarded their own interests more (although the prince dissembled his personal feelings), they might well have received from some a humiliating and annoying reply, if this had been possible without violation of the rights of ambassadors.

Appeased by their many entreaties and tears, however, the emperor granted them his forgiveness for these offences, having received their pledge that henceforth, abjuring bombast, they would bring him in their salutations only such reverence as befits a Roman prince and the ruler over the City and the world.[31] After obtaining his indulgence and favour, they asked and were granted that Frederick, duke of Swabia, the son of King Conrad, who was still a youth, be girt with a sword and knighted in their presence. For his aunt, the empress of Constantinople,[32] had previously, as now, honoured this boy by the bestowal of many magnificent gifts, and is said to have charged the legates never to return to Greece unless this matter had been accomplished, in which her husband heartily supported her, on account of the good will and friendship of long standing he had enjoyed with King Conrad, the boy's father.

iii. 7. In that place there were then present also ambassadors of King Henry of England,[33] who bestowed varied and precious gifts, enhanced by much graceful language. Among these gifts we beheld a pavilion, very large in extent and of the finest quality. If you ask its size, it could not be raised except by machinery and a special sort of instrument and props; if you ask its quality, I should imagine that neither in material nor in workmanship will it ever be surpassed by any equipment of this kind. He had also sent a letter full of honeyed speech, of which the following is a copy:

> To the friend dear to his heart, Frederick, by the grace of God most invincible emperor of the Romans, Henry, king of England, duke of Normandy and Aquitaine and count of Anjou, greeting and the harmony of true peace and love.
>
> We express to your excellency the utmost thanks within our power, O best of rulers, because you have deigned to visit us through envoys, to greet us in letters, to anticipate us in bestowing gifts, and—a thing we cherish even more dearly than these—to enter into treaties of peace and love with us. We have exulted and have felt our spirit somehow grow within us and be carried to greater heights, since your promise, whereby you have given us hope in the matter of setting in order the affairs of our realm, has made us more alert and more ready. We have exulted, I say, and have with all our heart arisen before your magnificence, making you

respondentes, quod, quidquid ad honorem vestrum spectare noverimus, pro posse nostro effectui mancipare parati sumus. Regnum nostrum et quidquid ubique nostrae subicitur dicioni vobis exponimus et vestrae committimus potestati, ut ad vestrum nutum omnia disponantur et in omnibus vestri fiat voluntas imperii.

Sit igitur inter nos et populos nostros dilectionis et pacis unitas indivisa, commercia tuta, ita tamen, ut vobis, qui dignitate preminetis, imperandi cedat auctoritas, nobis non deerit voluntas obsequendi. Et sicut vestrae serenitatis memoriam vestrorum excitat in nobis munerum largitio, sic vos nostri quoque reminisci preoptamus, mittentes quae pulchriora penes nos erant et vobis magis placitura. Attendite itaque dantis affectum, non data, et eo animo quo dantur excipite. De manu beati Iacobi,[34] super qua nobis scripsistis, in ore magistri Heriberti[35] et Wilhelmi clerici nostri verbum posuimus.[36]

Teste Thoma cancellario[37] aput Northamt.

iii. 8. Aderant preterea diversarum nationum, utpote de Datia, [de] Pannonia, Italia seu de Burgundia, diversae legationes, quarum portitores se mutuo videntes atque certatim munera et supplicationes afferentes singuli singulis stuporem pariter et admirationem addidere.

Mense Octobre mediante imperator apud Bisuncium curiam celebraturus in Burgundiam iter aggreditur. Est autem Bisuncium una metropoleos eius terciae partis, in quas imperator gloriosus Karolus Magnus suum inter tres filios suos, omnes regio nomine gaudentes, divisit imperium, sita super amnem Tuba.[38] In qua civitate pene omnibus proceribus terrae illius adunatis multis quoque exterarum gentium hominibus, utpote Romanis, Apulis, Tuscis, Venetis, Italis, Francis, Anglis et Hyspanis, per legatos suos imperatoris adventum prestolantibus, festivissimo apparatu et solempni favore excipitur. Tota siquidem terra eundem fortissimum cognoscens et clementissimum, amore pariter et timore permixto, novis illum fascibus honorare, novis laudibus attollere satagebat.

At priusquam ad eius provinciae negotia seu ordinationem stilus se porrigat, de legatis Romani pontificis Adriani, ad quid venerint et quomodo recesserint, quia et auctoritas eius partis maior et causa gravior, dicendum nobis erit. Prolixitatem huius narrationis non causabitur, qui materiae pondus ac temporis, quo haec tempestas protracta est et protrahitur, diuturnitatem diligenter consideraverit. Personae nunciorum erant Rolandus tituli Sancti Marci presbiter cardinalis et cancellarius Romana aecclesia auctoritate maiores sanctae Romanae aecclesiae et Bernhardus tituli Sancti Clementis presbiter cardinalis,[39] ambo divitiis, maturitate et gravitate insignes et pene omnibus aliis in Romana aecclesia auctoritate maiores.

---

[34]   The hand of St James, lodged in Reading abbey. See above, ch. 7, n. 139.
[35]   Herbert of Bosham, secretary and biographer of Thomas Becket.
[36]   Not certainly identified: possibly William de Vere.
[37]   Thomas Becket, archbishop of Canterbury (1162–70), canonized in 1173.
[38]   After the death of Charlemagne and his son Louis the Pious, the empire was divided between the latter's three sons. Besançon fell to the portion of Lothar.
[39]   Roland Bandinelli and Bernard: see ch. 9, n. 78 and ch. 7, n. 110.

this answer with sincere and heartfelt affection, that we are prepared to bring to pass according to our ability whatever we know tends toward your glorification. We lay before you our kingdom and whatever is anywhere subject to our sway, and entrust it to your power, that all things may be administered in accordance with your nod, and that in all respects your imperial will may be done.

Let there, therefore, be between us and our peoples an undivided unity of affection and peace, safe commercial intercourse, so that to you, who are pre-eminent in dignity, may fall the right to command; while we shall not lack the will to obey. And as the generous bestowal of your gifts arouses in us the memory of your serenity, so do we also fondly desire that you may remember us, sending you the most beautiful things we could find, and which were most likely to please you. Consider therefore the affection of the giver, not the gifts, and receive them in the same spirit in which they are given. Regarding the hand of the blessed James,[34] concerning which you have written to us, we have placed our reply on the lips of Master Herbert[35] and William, our clerk.[36]

Witnessed by Thomas the Chancellor[37] at Northampton.

iii. 8. There were present also various embassies of different nations: for instance, from Denmark, Pannonia, Italy, and Burgundy, whose representatives, beholding each other and vying in the bestowal of gifts and petitions, were the cause of mutual amazement and admiration.

In the middle of the month of October [1157] the emperor set out for Burgundy to hold a court at Besançon. Now Besançon is the metropolis of one of the three parts into which the renowned Charles the Great divided his empire for distribution among his three sons, all enjoying the royal title, situated on the river Doubs.[38] In this city practically all the chief men of that land had assembled, and also many men from foreign lands, such as Romans, Apulians, Tuscans, Venetians, Franks, English, and Spaniards, awaited the emperor's arrival, and he was received with the most festive display and solemn acclaim. For the whole world recognized him as the most powerful and most merciful ruler, and undertook, with mingled love and fear, to honour him with new tokens of respect, to extol him with new praises.

But before our pen addresses itself to an account of the affairs of this province and its management, we must speak of the envoys of the Roman pontiff, Adrian— why they came and how they departed—because the authority of this delegation was very great and their errand very serious. No one will complain at the prolixity of this account who considers carefully the importance of the matter and the length of time that this tempest has raged and still rages. The envoys were Roland, cardinal priest of the title of S. Marco and chancellor of the Holy Roman Church, and Bernard, cardinal priest of the title of S. Clemente,[39] both distinguished for their wealth, their maturity of view, and their influence, and surpassing in prestige almost all others in the Roman Church.

Causa vero adventus eorum speciem sinceritatis videbatur habere; sed fermentum et occasionem malorum intus latuisse postmodum evidenter deprehensum est. Principe ergo die quodam a strepitu et populi tumultu declinante, in cuiusdam oratorii privatiore recessu predicti nuncii in conspectum eius deducti ab eoque, ut oportebat, sicut qui *boni* se *nuncii baiolos* assererent benigne et honeste recepti sunt. [40]

Exordium autem sermonis illorum in fronte ipsa notabile comparuit, quod tale fuisse dicitur: 'Salutat vos beatissimus pater noster papa Adrianus et universitas cardinalium sanctae Romanae aecclesiae, ille ut pater, illi ut fratres'. Paucisque interpositis, litteras quas ferebant protulere. Quas et aliarum quae in hac turbulentia hinc inde discurrebant rescripta litterarum idcirco huic operi interserere curavi, ut quivis lector, qui in partem declinare voluerit, non meis verbis vel assertionibus, sed ipsarum partium propriis scriptis tractus et vocatus, libere eligat, utri parti suum velit accommodare favorem. Tenor denique litterarum talis erat:

iii. 9. Adrianus episcopus, servus servorum Dei, dilecto filio Friderico, illustri Romanorum imperatori, salutem et apostolicam benedictionem.

Imperatoriae maiestati paucis retroactis diebus recolimus nos scripsisse, illud horrendum et execrabile facinus et piaculare flagitium tempore nostro commissum, in Teutonicis partibus, sicut credimus, aliquando intemptatum, excellentiae tuae ad memoriam revocantes, nec sine grandi ammiratione ferentes, quod absque digna severitate vindictae usque nunc transire passus sis tam perniciosi sceleris feritatem. Qualiter enim venerabilis frater noster E. Lundenensis archiepiscopus, dum a sede apostolica remearet, a quibusdam impiis et scelestis, quod sine grandi animi merore non dicimus, in partibus illis captus fuerit et adhuc in custodia teneatur; qualiter etiam in ipsa captione predicta viri impietatis, semen nequam, filii scelerati in eum et in suos evaginatis gladiis violenter exarserint et eos, ablatis omnibus, quam turpiter atque inhoneste tractaverint, et tua serenissima celsitudo cognoscit, atque ad longinquas et remotissimas regiones fama tanti sceleris iam pervenit. Ad cuius utique vehementissimi facinoris ultionem, sicut his cui bona placere, mala vero displicere credimus, constantius exurgere debuisti, et gladium, qui tibi ad vindictam malefactorum, laudem vero bonorum est ex divina provisione concessus, in cervicem desevire oportuit impiorum et gravissime conterere presumptores. Tu vero id ipsum ita dissimulasse diceris, seviciam neglexisse, quod eosdem non est quare peniteat commisisse reatum, quia [se] inpunitatem sacrilegii quod gesserunt iamiam sentiunt invenisse.

Cuius quidem dissimulationis et negligentiae causam penitus ignoramus, quoniam nos in aliquo serenitatis tuae gloriam offendisse conscientiae scrupulus nostrum animum non accusat, sed personam tuam sicut karissimi et specialis filii

---

[40]   See above, ch. 7, part iii (d), 'The Besançon incident'.

Now the cause of their coming seemed to have an air of sincerity; but it was afterwards clearly discerned that unrest and an occasion for mischief lay beneath the surface. One day, upon the prince's retiring from the uproar and tumult of the people, the aforesaid messengers were conducted into his presence in the more secluded retreat of a certain oratory and—as was fitting—were received with honour and kindness, as ones who, as they claimed, were 'the bearers of good tidings' [2 Sam. 18: 22].[40]

But the beginning of their speech appeared notable at the very outset. It is said to have been as follows: 'Our most blessed father, Pope Adrian and all the cardinals of the Holy Roman Church salute you, he as father, they as brethren.' After a few words they produced the letter which they bore. Copies of this and other letters which passed back and forth in this time of confusion, I have taken pains to insert in this work so that any reader who may wish to take sides, attracted and summoned not by my words or assertions but by the actual writings of the parties themselves, may choose freely the side to which he desires to lend his favour. Now the content of the letter was as follows:

iii. 9. Bishop Adrian, servant of the servants of God, to his beloved son Frederick, the illustrious emperor of the Romans, greeting and apostolic benediction.

We recollect having written, a few days since, to the imperial majesty, of that dreadful and accursed crime and sacrilegious scandal, committed in our time, and hitherto, we believe, never attempted in the German lands; in recalling it to your excellency, we are greatly amazed that until now you have permitted so pernicious a deed to go unpunished with the severity it deserves. For how our venerable brother E[skil], archbishop of Lund, while returning from the Apostolic See, was taken captive in those parts by certain godless and infamous men—a thing we cannot mention without great and heartfelt sorrow—and is still held in confinement; how in taking him captive, those men of impiety, the seed of evildoers [Isaiah 1: 4.] drew their swords and violently assaulted him and his companions, and how basely and shamefully they treated them, stripping them of all they had, Your Most Serene Highness knows, and the report of so great a crime has already spread abroad to the most distant and remote regions. To avenge this deed of exceptional violence, you, as a man to whom we believe good deeds are pleasing but evil works displeasing, ought with great determination to arise and bring down heavily upon the necks of the wicked the sword which was entrusted by divine providence to you 'for the punishment of evildoers and for the praise of them that do well' [Peter 2: 14], and should most severely punish the presumptuous. But you are reported so to have ignored and indeed been indifferent to this deed, that there is no reason why those men should be repentant at having incurred guilt, because they have long since perceived that they have secured immunity for the sacrilege which they have committed.

Of the reason for this indifference and negligence we are absolutely ignorant, because no scruple of conscience accuses our heart of having in aught offended the glory of your serenity; rather have we always loved, with sincere affection,

nostri et principis christianissimi, quem in apostolicae confessionis petra. non am-
bigimus per Dei gratiam solidatum, sincera semper dileximus karitate et debitae
tractavimus benignitatis affectu.

Debes enim, gloriosissime fili, ante oculos mentis reducere, quam gratanter
et quam iocunde alio anno mater tua sacrosancta Romana aecclesia te susceperit,
quanta cordis affectione tractaverit, quantam tibi dignitatis plenitudinem contulerit
et honoris, et qualiter imperialis insigne coronae libentissime conferens benignis-
simo gremio sue tuae sublimitatis apicem studuerit confovere, nichil prorsus effi-
ciens, quod regiae voluntati vel in minimo cognosceret obviare.

Neque tamen penitet nos tuae desideria voluntatis in omnibus implevisse,
sed, si maiora beneficia[41] excellentia tua de manu nostra suscepisset, si fieri posset, considerantes, quanta aecclesiae Dei et nobis per te incrementa possint et
commoda provenire, non immerito gauderemus.

Nunc autem, quia tam immensum facinus, quod in contumeliam universalis
aecclesiae et imperii tui noscitur etiam commissum, negligere ac dissimulare
videris, suspicamur utique ac veremur, ne forte in hanc dissimulationem et negli-
gentiam propter hoc tuus animus sit inductus, quod suggestione perversi hominis
zizania seminantis adversus clementissimam matrem tuam sacrosanctam Romanam aecclesiam et nos ipsos indignationis, quod absit, aliquam conceperis vel
rancorem.[42]

Ob hoc igitur et ob alia omnia negotia, quae cognoscimus imminere, duos de
melioribus et carioribus quos circa nos habemus, dilectos scilicet filios nostros,
Bernhardum Sancti Clementis presbiterum cardinalem et Rolandum [tituli] Sancti
Marci presbiterum cardinalem et cancellarium nostrum,[43] viros utique religione et
prudentia et honestate conspicuos, serenitati tuae de latere nostro ad presens
duximus destinandos, excellentiam tuam rogantes attentius, quatinus eos tam honorifice quam benigne recipias, honeste tractes et ea, quae ipsi super hoc et super
aliis ad honorem Dei et sacrosanctae Romanae aecclesiae, ad decus etiam et exal-
tationem imperii pertinentia ex parte nostra imperatoriae proposuerint dignitati,
sicut ab ore nostro procedant, absque ulla hesitatione suscipias et ipsorum verbis,
tamquam si ea contingeret nos proferre, fidem non dubites adhibere.

iii. 10. Talibus litteris lectis et per Reinaldum cancellariam[44] fida satis interpretatione diligenter expositis, magna principes qui aderant indignatione commoti sunt,
quia tota litterarum continentia non parum acredinis habere et occasionem futuri
mali iamiam fronte sua preferre videbatur. Precipue tamen universos accenderat,
quod in premissis litteris inter caetera dictum fuisse acceperant dignitatis et honoris plenitudinem sibi a Romano pontifice collatam et insigne imperialis coronae
de manu eius imperatorem suscepisse, nec ipsum penitere, si rnaiora beneficia de

---

[41]   See above, ch. 7, at nn. 114–26.
[42]   Probably an allusion to Adrian's peace with William I of Sicily in 1156: see above,
ch. 7, part i (c), 'The accord of Benevento'.
[43]   For Bernard, cardinal priest of S. Clemente and Roland Bandinelli, see ch. 7, n. 110
and ch. 9, at n. 78.
[44]   Rainald of Dassel, archbishop of Cologne and imperial chancellor.

and treated with an attitude of due kindness, your person as that of our most dear and specially beloved son and most Christian prince, who, we doubt not, is by the grace of God grounded on the rock of the apostolic confession.

For, most glorious son you, should recall before the eyes of your mind how willingly and how gladly your mother, the Holy Roman Church, received you the other year, with what affection of heart she treated you, what great dignity and honour she bestowed upon you, and with how much pleasure she conferred the emblem of the imperial crown, zealous to cherish in her most kindly bosom the height of your sublimity, and doing nothing at all that she knew was in the least at variance with the royal will.

Nor indeed do we regret that we fulfilled in all respects the ardent desires of your heart; but if your excellency had received still greater benefits[41] at our hand (had that been possible), in consideration of the great increase and advantage that might through you accrue to the Church of God and to us, we would have rejoiced, not without reason.

But now, because you seem to ignore and hide so heinous a crime, which is indeed known to have been committed as an affront to the Church universal and to your empire, we both suspect and fear that perhaps your thoughts were directed toward this indifference and neglect on this account: that at the suggestion of an evil man, sowing tares [Matthew 13: 25], you have conceived against your most gracious mother the Holy Roman Church and against ourselves—God forbid!— some displeasure or grievance.[42]

On this account, therefore, and because of all the other matters of business which we know to impend, we have thought best at this time to dispatch from our side to your serenity two of the best and dearest of those whom we have about us, namely, our beloved sons, Bernard, cardinal priest of S. Clemente and Roland, cardinal priest of S. Marco and our chancellor,[43] men very notable for piety and wisdom and honour, very earnestly beseeching your excellency to receive them with as much respect as kindness, treat them with all honour, and accept whatever they themselves set forth before your imperial dignity on our behalf concerning this and other matters, to the honour of God and of the Holy Roman Church, and also to the glory and exaltation of the empire, without any hesitation as though proceeding from our mouth; and you may credence to their words, as if we were uttering them.' [September 20, 1157.]

iii. 10. When this letter had been read and carefully set forth by Chancellor Rainald[44] in a reasonably faithful interpretation, the princes who were present were moved to great indignation, because the entire content of the letter appeared to have no little sharpness and to offer even at the very outset an occasion for future trouble. But what had particularly aroused them all was the fact that in the aforesaid letter it had been stated, among other things, that the fullness of dignity and honour had been bestowed upon the emperor by the Roman pontiff, that the emperor had received from his hand the imperial crown, and that he would not have regretted conferring even greater benefits upon him, in consideration of the great

manu eius suscepisset, habita consideratione, quanta aecclesiae Romanae per ipsam possent incrementa et commoda provenire. Atque ad horum verborum strictam expositionem ac prefatae interpretationis fidem auditores induxerat, quod a nonnullis Romanorum temere affirmari noverant imperium Urbis et regnum Italicum donatione pontificam reges nostros hactenus possedisse, idque non solum dictis, sed et scriptis atque picturis representare et ad posteros transmittere. Unde de imperatore Lothario in palatio Lateranensi super eiusmodi picturam scriptam est:

> Rex venit ante fores, iurans prius Urbis honores,
> Post homo fit papae, sumit quo dante coronam.[45]

Talis pictura talisque superscriptio principi, quando alio anno circa Urbem fuerat, per fideles imperii delata cum vehementer displicuisset, amica prius invectione precedente, laudamentum a papa [Adriano] accepisse memoratur, ut et scriptura pariter atque pictura talis de medii tolleretur, ne tam vana res summis in orbe viris litigandi et discordandi prebere posset materiam.

His omnibus in unum collatis, cum strepitus et turba inter optimates regni de tam insolita legatione magis ac magis invalesceret, quasi gladium igni adderet,[46] dixisse ferunt unum de legatis. 'A quo ergo habet, si a domno papa non habet imperium?' Ob hoc dictum eo processit iracundia, ut unus eorum, videlicet Otto palatinus comes de Baioaria,[47] ut dicebatur, exerto gladio cervici illius mortem intentaret. At Fridericus auctoritate presentiae suae interposita tumultum quidem compescuit, ipsos autem legatos securitate donatos ad habitacula deduci ac primo mane via sua proficisci precepit, addens in mandatis, ne hac vel illac in territoriis episcoporum seu abbatum vagarentur, sed recta via, nec ad dexteram nec ad sinistram declinantes, reverterentur ad Urbem. Ipsis itaque sine efficatia revertentibus, id quod factum fuerat ab imperatore per universum regni ambitum provide litteris declaratur; quarum hic tenor fuit:

> iii. 11. Cum divina potentia, a qua omnis potestas in caelo et in terra, nobis, christo eius, regnum et imperium regendum commiserit et pacem aecclesiarum imperialibus armis conservandam ordinaverit, non sine maximo dolore cordis conqueri cogimur dilectioni vestrae, quod a capite sanctae aecclesiae, cui Christus pacis ac dilectionis suae caracterem impressit, causae dissensionum, seminarium malorum, pestiferi morbi venenum manare videntur; de quibus, nisi Deus avertat, totum corpus aecclesiae commaculari, unitatem scindi, inter regnum et sacerdotium* scisma fieri pertimescimus. Cum enim nuper in curia Bisuncii essemus et de honore imperii et salute aecclesiarum debita sollcitudine tractaremus, venerunt

---

[45]   See above, ch. 7, at n. 129.
[46]   Cf. Horace, *Saturae*, 2. iii. 276.
[47]   Otto of Wittelsbach, count palatine of Bavaria.

gain and advantage that might through him accrue to the Roman Church. And the hearers were led to accept the literal meaning of these words and to put credence in the aforesaid explanation because they knew that the assertion was rashly made by some Romans that our kings had hitherto possessed the imperial power over the City, and the kingdom of Italy, by gift of the popes, and that they made such representations and handed them down to posterity not only orally but also in writing and in pictures. Hence it is written concerning Emperor Lothar, over a picture of this sort in the Lateran palace:

> The king comes before the doors, swearing first to the City's privileges;
> Then, he becomes the man of the pope, by whose grant he assumes the crown.[45]

Since such a picture and such an inscription, reported to him by those faithful to the empire, had greatly displeased the prince when he had been near the City in a previous year [1155], he is said to have received from Pope [Adrian], after a friendly remonstrance, the assurance that both the inscription and the picture would be removed, lest so trifling a matter might afford the greatest men in the world an occasion for dispute and discord.

When all these matters were put together, and a great tumult and uproar was growing more and more heated among princes of the realm at so insolent a message, they said that one of the envoys, as though adding sword to flame,[46] inquired, 'From whom then does he have the empire, if not from the lord pope?' Because of this remark, anger reached such a pitch that one of them, namely, Otto, count palatine of Bavaria[47] (it was said), having unsheathed his sword, aimed a blow at the envoy's neck. But Frederick, using the authority of his presence to quell the tumult, gave the envoys safe-conduct to be led to their lodgings, and ordered them to set out on their way early in the morning, adding the command that they were not to wander here and there through the lands of the bishops and abbots, but return to the City by the direct road, turning neither to the right nor to the left. And so they returned without having accomplished their purpose, and what had been done by the emperor was published throughout the realm in the following letter [October, 1157]:

> iii. 11. Whereas the divine power, from which is derived all dominion in heaven and on earth, has entrusted to us, His anointed, the kingdom and the empire to rule over, and has ordained that the peace of the churches is to be maintained by the imperial arms, not without the greatest distress of heart are we compelled to complain to your benevolence that from the head of the Holy Church, on which Christ has set the imprint of his peace and love, there seem to be emanating the seeds of evils and the poison of an infectious disease, by which, unless God avert it, we fear the body of the Church will be stained, its unity shattered, and a schism created between *regnum* and *sacerdotium** (the royal and papal office). For when we were recently at the court in Besançon and were dealing with the honour of the

---

* These are technical terms for which no entirely satisfactory modern translation is appropriate: see above, ch. 6, n. 134.

legati apostolici, asserentes se talem legationem nostrae afferre maiestati, unde honor imperii non parvum accipere deberet incrementum. Quos cum prima die adventus sui honorifice suscepissemus et secunda, ut mos est, ad audiendam legationem eorum cum principibus nostris consedissemus, ipsi, quasi de mammona iniquitatis inflati, de altitudine superbiae, de fastu arrogantiae, de execrabili tumidi cordis elatione, legationem apostolicis litteris conscriptam nobis presentaverunt, quarum tenor talis erat, quod pre oculis mentis semper deberemus habere, qualiter domnus papa insigne imperialis coronae nobis contulerit neque tamen penitentia moveretur, si maiora excellentia nostra ab eo beneficia suscepisset.

Haec erat illa paternae dulcedinis legatio, quae unitatem aecclesiae et imperii confovere debuit, quae vinculo pacis utrumque colligare studuit, quae ad utriusque concordiam et obedientiam animos audientium allexit. Certe ad vocem illam nefandam et omni veritate vacuam non solum imperialis maiestas debitam indignationem concepit, verum omnes principes qui aderat tanto furore et ira sunt repleti, quod sine dubio illos duos iniquos presbiteros mortis sententia dampnassent, nisi hoc nostra intercepisset presentia.

Porro quia multa paria litterarum apud eos reperta sunt et scedulae sigillatae ad arbitrium eorum adhuc scribendae, quibus, sicut hactenus consuetudinis eorum fuit, per singulas aecclesias Teutonici regni conceptum iniquitatis suae virus respergere, altaria denudare, vasa domus Dei asportare, cruces excoriare nitebantur, ne ultra procedendi facultas eis daretur, eadem qua venerant via ad Urbem eos redire fecimus.

Cumque per electionem principium a solo Deo regnum et imperium nostrum sit, qui in passione Christi filii sui duobus gladiis necessariis regendum orbem subiecit cumque Petrus apostolus hac doctrina mundum informaverit: 'Deum timete, regem honorificate'; quicumque nos imperialem coronam pro beneficio a domno papa suscepisse dixerit divinae institutioni et doctrinae Petri contrarius est et mendacii reus erit. Quia vero hactenus honorem ac libertatem aecclesiarum, quae iam diu indebitae servitutis iugo depressa est, a manu Egyptiorum studuimus eripere et omnia eis dignitatum suarum iura conservare intendimus, universitatem vestram super tanta ignominia nobis et imperio condolere rogamus, sperantes, ne honorem imperii, qui a constitutione Urbis et Christianae religionis institutione ad vestra usque tempora gloriosus et imminutus extitit, fidei vestrae indivisa sinceritas tam inaudita novitate, tam presumptuosa elatione imminui paciatur, sciens, omni ambiguitate remota, quod mortis periculum ante vellemus incurrere, quam nostris temporibus tantae confusionis obprobrium sustinere. [...]

iii. 16. Cum haec agerentur, legati sedis apostolicae Rolandus et Bernhardus reversi quantas iniurias sustinuerint, in quo periculo fuerint, exponunt, gravibus graviora adicientes, ut in ultionem eorum, quae se pertulisse dixerunt, Romanae urbis episcopum provocarent. In hoc negotio clerus Romanus ita inter se divisus

empire and the security of the Church with all due solicitude, apostolic legates arrived asserting that they bore to our majesty such tidings that the honour of the empire should receive no small increase. After we had honourably received them on the first day of their arrival, and on the second, as is customary, had seated ourselves with our princes to hear their message, they, as though inspired by the Mammon of unrighteousness [Luke 16: 9], by lofty pride, by arrogant disdain, by execrable haughtiness, presented the message to us written in letters apostolic, whose content was to the effect that we ought always to remember how the lord pope had bestowed upon us the imperial crown and that he would not regret it if our excellency had received greater benefits from him.

This was the message of fatherly kindness, which was to foster the unity of Church and empire, which was to bind them together in the bonds of peace, which was to bring the hearts of its hearers to harmony with both and obedience to both! Certain it is that at that impious message, devoid of all truth, not only did our imperial majesty conceive a righteous indignation, but all the princes who were present were filled with so great fury and wrath that they would undoubtedly have condemned those two wicked priests to death, had not our presence averted this.

Moreover, because many similar letters were found in their possession, and parchments with seals affixed, still to be written on at their discretion, whereby—as has been their practice hitherto—they were endeavouring to scatter the venom of their iniquity throughout the churches of the German realm, to denude the altars, to carry off the vessels of the house of God [Daniel 1: 2], to strip crosses of their coverings, we obliged them to return to the City by the way they had come, lest an opportunity be afforded them of proceeding further.

And since, through election by the princes, the kingdom and the empire are ours from God alone, Who at the time of the passion of His Son Christ subjected the world to dominion by the two swords, and since the apostle Peter taught the world this doctrine, 'Fear God, honour the king' [1 Peter 2: 17], whosoever says that we received the imperial crown as a benefice from the lord pope contradicts the divine ordinance and the doctrine of Peter and is guilty of a lie. But because we have hitherto striven to snatch from the hand of the Egyptians [Exodus 18: 9] the honour and freedom of the churches, so long oppressed by the yoke of undeserved slavery, and are intent on preserving to them all their rights and dignities, we ask all of you to grieve with us at so great an insult to us and to the empire, hoping that your unwavering loyalty will not permit the honour of the empire, which has stood, glorious and undiminished, from the founding of the City and the establishment of the Christian religion even down to your days, to be disparaged by so unheard-of a novelty, such presumptuous arrogance, knowing that—all ambiguity aside—we would prefer to encounter the risk of death rather than to endure in our time the reproach of so great a disorder. [...]

iii. 16. While this was being done, the legates of the Apostolic See, Roland and Bernard, having returned, and set forth the great insults they had sustained, the great danger they had undergone, adding even more serious charges to what was serious enough, in order to provoke the bishop of the Roman city to seek

est, ut pars eorum partibus faveret imperatoris et eorum qui missi fuerant incuriam seu imperitiam causarentur, quedam vero pars votis sui pontificis adhereret. Unde de hac tempestate dicturi, sicut supra diximus, lectorem non nostris verbis niti volumus, sed ponentes epistolas hinc inde directas, ex eis colligat, quam partem tueatur cuive fidus velit permanere; nobis autem indulgentiam petimus, qui potius utramque personam, sacerdotalem scilicet et regalem, reverentia debita veneramur, quam temere de altera iudicare presumamus. Exemplar itaque litterarum a summo pontifice ad archiepiscopos et episcopos super his directarum tale fuit:

> Quotiens aliquid in aecclesia contra honorem Dei et salutem fidelium attemptatur, fratrum et coepiscoporum nostrorum, et eorum precipue qui spiritu Dei aguntur, cura debet existere, ut ea quae male gesta sunt gratam Deo correctionem debeant invenire.
>
> Hoc autem tempore, quod absque nimio merore non dicimus, karissimus filius noster F[ridericus] Romanorum imperator tale quid egit, quale temporibus antecessorum suorum non legimus perpetratum. Cum enim nos duos de melioribus fratribus nostris, B[ernardum] scilicet tituli Sancti Clementis et R[olandum] cancellarium nostrum tituli Sancti Marci presbiteros cardinales, ad ipsius presentiam misissemus, ipse, cum primum ad eius presentiam pervenerunt, alacriter visus est eos recepisse; sequenti vero die, cum redirent ad eum et litterae nostrae in eius auribus legerentur, accepta occasione cuiusdam verbi, quod ipsarum litterarum series continebat, 'insigne videlicet beneficium coronae tibi contulimus', in tantam animi commotionem exarsit, ut convicia, quae in nos et legatos nostros dicitur coniecisse, et quam inhoneste ipsos a presentia sua recedere ac de terra sua velociter exire compulerit, et audire obprobrium et lamentabile sit referre. Eis autem ab illius presentia excedentibus, facto edicto, ne aliquis de regno vestro ad apostolicam sedem accedat, per omnes fines eiusdem regni custodes dicitur posuisse, qui eos, qui ad apostolicam sedem venire voluerint, violenter debeant revocare.
>
> Super quo facto licet aliquantulum conturbemur, ex hoc tamen in nobis ipsis maiorem consolationem accipimus, quod ad id de vestro et principum consilio non processit. Unde confidimus eum a sui animi motu consilio et persuasione vestra facile revocandum.
>
> Quocirca, fratres, quoniam in hoc facto non solum nostra, sed vestra et omnium aecclesiarum res agi dinoscitur, karitatem vestram monemus et exhortamur in Domino, quatinus opponatis vos murum pro domo Domini et prefatum filium nostrum ad viam rectam quam citius reducere studeatis, attentissimam sollicitudinem adhibentes, ut a Reinaldo cancellario suo et palatino comite, qui magnas blasphemias in prefatos legatos nostros et matrem vestram sacrosanctam Romanam aecclesiam evomere presumpserunt, talem et tam evidentem

vengeance for the things they said they had endured. In this matter the Roman clergy were so divided among themselves, that one section of them favoured the party of the emperor and blamed the thoughtlessness or inexperience of those who had been sent; bur a certain section supported the wishes of their pontiff. For this reason, as we said above when we were about to speak about this period, we desire that the reader should not rely on our words, but as we set down the letters sent back and forth, he may decide from them what side he should favour or to whom he wishes to remain loyal; but we seek indulgence for ourselves, who venerate with due respect both persons, namely, the priestly and the royal, too much to venture to make a rash judgment concerning one of them. And so the following is a copy of a letter sent by the supreme pontiff to the archbishops and bishops concerning these matters:

As often as any attempt is made in the Church against the honour of God and the welfare of the faithful, the solicitude of our brothers and fellow bishops, and in particular of those who are led by the spirit of God, should be aroused, that matters which have been wrongly done may receive the correction that is pleasing to God.

Now at this time, a matter of which we cannot speak without the deepest sorrow, our very dear son F[rederick], emperor of the Romans, has done such a thing as we do not read to have been done in the times of our predecessors. For when we had sent to his presence two of our more honourable brothers, Bernard, of the title of S. Clemente, and Roland, our chancellor, of the title of S. Marco, cardinal priests, he seemed to have received them gladly when first they came into his presence; but on the following day, when they returned to him and our letter was read in his hearing, taking advantage of a certain expression therein employed, namely, 'we have bestowed upon you the favour of the imperial crown,' he blazed forth with such agitation of spirit that it would be disgraceful to hear and painful to repeat the insults that he is said to have hurled at us and our legates, and how dishonourably he compelled them to retire from his presence and with all speed from his land. And as they departed from his presence, he issued an edict that no one from your realm should approach the Apostolic See, and is said to have set guards throughout all the bounds of that same realm who should forcibly call back those who desired to come to the Apostolic See.

Although we are somewhat disturbed by this act, yet at heart we draw very great consolation from the fact that he did not do this on your advice and that of the princes. Hence we are confident that by your counsel and persuasion his wrath may easily be calmed.

Wherefore, brethren, inasmuch as your own interests, and those of all the churches—not our interest only—are clearly at stake in this matter, we admonish and exhort Your Love in the Lord to interpose yourselves as a wall before the house of the Lord [cf. Ezekiel 13: 5], and strive to lead back our aforesaid son to the right way as soon as possible so that he causes his chancellor Rainald and the count palatine, who presumed to spew forth great blasphemies against our aforesaid legates and your very holy mother, the Roman Church, to offer such manifest

satisfactionem faciat exhiberi, ut, sicut multorum aures amaritudo sermonis eorum offendit, ita etiam satisfactio multos ad viam rectam debeat revocare.

Non acquiescat idem filius noster consiliis iniquorum, consideret novissima et antiqua et per illam viam incedat, per quam Iustinianus et alii katholici imperatores incessisse noscuntur. Exemplo siquidem et imitatione illorum et honoremn in terris et felicitatem in caelis sibi poterit cumulare.

Vos etiam, si eum ad rectam semitam reduxeritis, et beato Petro apostolorum principi gratum dependetis obsequium et vobis et aecclesiis vestris suam conservabitis libertatem. Alioquin noverit antedictus filius noster ex ammonitione vestra, noverit ex promissionis ewangelicae veritate quod sacrosancta Romana aecclesia super firmissimam petram, Deo collocante, fundata, quantocumque ventorum turbine quatiatur, in sua firmitate, protegente Domino, in seculum seculi permanebit.

Nec autem, sicut nostis, deceret eum tam arduam viam absque vestro consilio attemptasse; unde credimus, quod auditis ammonitionibus vestris facillime poterit ad frugem sanioris studii, sicut vir discretus et imperator katholicus, revocari.

iii. 17. His litteris talique legatione percepta, presules Alemanniae, communicato in unum assensu et consilio, sedi apostolicae in haec verba rescribunt:

Quamvis sciamus et certii simus, quod aecclesiam Dei fundatam supra firmam petram neque venti neque flumina tempestatum possint deicere, nos tamen infirmiores et pusillanimes, si quando huiusmodi contigerint impetus, concutimur et contremiscimus. Inde nimirum graviter conturbati sumus et conterriti super his, quae inter vestram sanctitatem et filium vestrum devotissimum, dominum nostrum imperatorem, magni mali, nisi Deus avertat, seminarium prebitura videntur. Equidem a verbis illis, quae in litteris vestris continebantur, quas per nuncios vestros prudentissimos et honestissimos, dominum B[ernhardum] et dominum R[olandum] cancellarium,[48] venerabiles presbiteros cardinales, misistis, commota est universa res publica imperii nostri; aures imperialis potentiae ea pacienter audire non potuerunt neque aures principum sustinere; omnes ita continuerunt aures suas, quod nos, salva gratia vestrae sanctissimae paternitatis, ea tueri propter sinistram ambiguitatis interpretationem vel consensu aliquo approbare nec audemus nec possumus, eo quod insolita et inaudita fuerunt usque ad haec tempora. Litteras autem, quas nobis misistis, debita cum reverentia suscipientes et amplectentes commonuimus filium vestrum, dominum nostrum imperatorem, sicut iussistis, et ab eo responsum, Deo gratias, accepimus tale, quale decebat katholicum principem, in hunc modum:

Duo sunt, quibus nostrum regi oportet imperium, leges sanctae imperatorum et usus bonus predecessorum et patrum nostrorum. Istos limites aecclesiae nec volumus preterire nec possumus; quidquid ab his discordat non recipimus. Debitam patri nostro reverentiam libenter exhibemus, liberam

48 Bernard, cardinal priest of S. Clemente and Roland Bandinelli: above, n. 43.

reparation that, just as the bitterness of their speech has offended the ears of many, so also their reparation may recall many to the right way.

Let not our same son give heed to the counsels of the wicked, let him consider what is behind and before [Ps 138 (139): 5], and walk in that way in which Justinian and other Catholic emperors are known to have walked. For by imitating the example of those men he will be able to lay up for himself both honour on earth and blessedness in heaven.

You also, if you lead him back to the right way, will both serve the blessed Peter, prince of apostles, and will preserve your own liberty and that of your churches. Otherwise may our aforesaid son learn from your admonition, may he learn from the truth of the Gospel promise, that the Holy Roman Church founded by God on an immovable rock [cf. Matthew 16: 18] will be steadfast forever, under the Lord's protection, by whatsoever tempests it may be shaken.

Moreover, as you know, it was not seemly for him to have attempted so steep a path without your counsel; hence we believe that upon hearing your admonitions he can the more easily be brought back—like a man of discretion and a Catholic emperor—to a more reasonable frame of mind.

iii. 17. Upon the receipt of this letter and an embassy to the same purport, the bishops of Germany took counsel and replied to the Apostolic See in the following words:

> Although we know and are sure that neither wind nor storm can overthrow the Church of God, founded upon a firm rock, yet we, being weak and faint-hearted, are shaken and tremble whenever blows of this kind befall. Hence we are, of course, gravely disturbed and alarmed at these developments which seem likely to prove—unless God avert it—the source of great evil between your holiness and your most devoted son, our lord, the emperor. Indeed, in consequence of those words which were contained in your letter, which you sent by your messengers, those most prudent and honourable men, the lord B[ernard] and the lord R[oland], the chancellor,[48] venerable cardinal priests, the whole public state of our empire has been thrown into confusion; neither the ears of the imperial power nor those of the princes could endure to hear them; all have so stopped their ears [Acts 7: 57] that—saving your holiness's grace—we dare not and cannot uphold or approve in any way those words, by reason of their unfortunate ambiguity of meaning, because they were hitherto unknown and unheard of. We received and welcomed, however, with due reverence the letter which you sent to us, and have reminded your son, our lord the emperor, as you ordered, and—thanks be to God!—have received from him a reply, worthy of a Catholic prince, in the following form:
>
>> There are two things by which our realm should be governed, the sacred laws of the emperors, and the good customs of our predecessors and our fathers. The limits set by them on the Church we do not wish to overstep, nor can we; whatever is not in accord with them, we reject. We gladly accord to our father the reverence that is his due; the free crown of our empire we

imperii nostri coronam divino tantum beneficio ascribimus, electionis primam vocem Maguntino archiepiscopo, deinde quod superest caeteris secundum ordinem principibus recognoscimus, regalem unctionem Coloniensi,
supremam vero, quae imperialis est, summo pontifici; quidquid preter haec
est, ex habundanti est, a malo est.

Cardinales in contemptum et dilectissimi et reverentissimi patris nostri et
consecratoris a finibus terrae nostrae exire non coegimus. Sed cum his et pro
his quae et scripta et scribenda ferebant in dedecus et scandalum imperii nostri[49] ultra eos prodire pati noluimus. Introitum et exitum Italiae nec clausimus
edicto nec claudere aliquo modo volumus peregrinantibus vel pro suis neces-
sitatibus rationabiliter cum testimonio episcoporum et prelatorum suorum
Romanam sedem adeuntibus; sed illis abusionibus, quibus omnes aecclesiae
regni nostri gravatae et attenuatae sunt et omnes pene claustrales disciplinae
emortuae et sepultae, obviare intendimus. In capite orbis Deus per imperium
exultavit aecclesiam, in capite orbis aecclesia, non per Deum, ut credimus,
nunc demolitur imperium. A pictura cepit, ad scripturam pictura processit,
scriptura in auctoritatem prodire conatur. Non patiemur, non sustinebimus;
coronam ante ponemus, quam imperii coronam una nobiscum sic deponi
consentiamus. Picturae deleantur, scripturae retractentur, ut inter regnum et
sacerdotium* aeterna inimiciciarum monumenta non remaneant.[50]

Haec et alia, utpote de concordia Ro[manorum] et W[illelmi] Siculi[51] et aliis quae
in Italia facta sunt conventionibus, quae ad plenum prosequi non audemus, ab ore
domini nostri imperatoris audivimus. Absente autem palatino comite et in prepa-
ratione expeditionis in Italiam iam premisso, a cancellario ibidem adhuc presente
aliud non audivimus, nisi quod humilitatis erat et pacis, preter quod eis pro periculo vitae, quod a populo imminebat, pro viribus suis astiterit, cunctis qui ibi
aderant huius rei testimonium eis perhibentibus.

De caetero sanctitatem vestram suppliciter rogamus et obsecramus, ut nostrae
parcatis infirmitati, ut magnanimitatem filii vestri sicut bonus pastor leniatis scriptis vestris scripta priora suavitate mellita dulcorantibus, quatinus et aecclesia Dei
tranquilla devotione laetetur et imperium in suae sublimitatis statu glorietur, ipso
mediante et adiuvante, qui mediator Dei et hominum factus est homo Christus Ie-
sus.

iii. 18. Feliciter ergo procinctum movens ac aput Augustam Rhetiae civitatem super ripam Lici fluminis castra ponens confluentem ex diversis partibus militem per
septem dies operitur.

Interea Romanus antistes de adventu principis certior effectus—nam legati
eius, videlicet Reinaldus cancellarius et Otto palatinus comes,[52] quorum supra
meminimus, iam dudum Italiam intraverant—in melius mutato consilio ad

---

49 See above, iii. 11.
50 Above, ch. 7, at n. 129; see also *ibid.*, n. 134.
51 Above, ch. 7, part i (c), 'The accord of Benevento'.
52 Rainald of Dassel and Otto of Wittelsbach.

ascribe solely to divine favour; we recognize the vote of the archbishop of Mainz as first in the election, then those of the other princes, according to their rank; the royal anointing we recognize as the prerogative of the archbishop of Cologne; but the final, that is the imperial, anointing pertains to the supreme pontiff; anything more than these 'comes from what is more, cometh of evil' [Matt. 5: 37].

It is not to show disrespect for our most beloved and reverend father and consecrator that we obliged the cardinals to depart from our land. But we did not wish to permit them to proceed further with the letters which they were carrying, both written and to be written, to the disgrace and shame of our empire.[49] We have not closed the way in and out of Italy by edict, nor do we wish in any way to close it to those going to the Roman see as pilgrims or on their own necessary business, in reasonable fashion, with testimonials from their bishops and prelates; but we intend to resist those abuses by which all the churches of our realm have been burdened and weakened, and almost all the discipline of the cloisters killed and buried. In the chief city of the world God has, through the power of the empire, exalted the Church; in the chief city of the world the Church, not through the power of God, we believe, is now destroying the empire. It began with a picture, the picture became an inscription, the inscription seeks to become an authoritative utterance. We shall not endure it, we shall not submit to it; we shall lay down the crown before we consent to have the crown of the empire and ourselves thus degraded. Let the pictures be destroyed, let the inscriptions be withdrawn, that they may not remain as eternal memorials of enmity between *regnum* and *sacerdotium*.[50]

These and other matters—for instance, concerning the accord with the Ro[mans] and W[illiam] the Sicilian,[51] and other agreements made in Italy—which we do not venture to recount in detail, we heard from the lips of our lord the emperor. In the absence of the count palatine, who has already been sent ahead to make preparations for the expedition into Italy, we have heard nothing from the chancellor, who is still present here, save that he was of humble and peaceful bearing, except when he defended the ambassadors with all his might when their lives were threatened by the people, as everyone there could attest.

As for the rest, we humbly ask and beseech Your Holiness to pardon our weakness and, like a good shepherd, calm the high spirits of your son with a letter more conciliatory than that former one, that the Church of God may rejoice in tranquil devotion and that the empire may glory in its sublimity, with the mediation and aid of Him who is the 'mediator between God and man, the man Christ Jesus [1 Timothy 2: 5].

iii. 18. The emperor began his expedition propitiously, and pitching camp at Augsburg, a city of Rhaetia, on the river Lech, he awaited for seven days the soldiery which poured in from various regions [June, 1158].

Meanwhile the Roman bishop, being made certain of the prince's coming—for his envoys, namely Chancellor Rainald and Count Palatine Otto,[52] whom we

leniendum eius animum nuncios mittit, Heinricum videlicet cardinalem presbiterum tituli Sanctorum Nerei et Achillei et Iacinctum cardinalem diaconem Sanctae Mariae in scola Greca,[53] viros prudentes in secularibus et ad curialia negotia pertractanda prioribus missis multo aptiores. [...]

iii. 20. Itaque in primo suo ingressu in Italiam castrum quod Rivola vocatur, super clausuram Veronensium situm, natura loci inexpugnabile, in deditionem accipiunt, existimantes presidio eiusdem in tam strictis locorum faucibus nostros clementiorem aditum veniendi et redeundi invenire. Excepti cum magna frequentia et honorificentia episcopi civiumque Veronensium tam illic quam in aliis civitatibus [videlicet Mantua, Cremona, Papia] fidelitatem imperatori et amminiculum expeditionis tactis sacrosanctis promitti fecerunt, viamque venturo imperatori preparantes eius adventus fidi et utiles precursores extitere. Sane haec est forma sacramenti, in qua omnes iuraverunt:

> Ego iuro, quod ammodo in antea ero fidelis domino meo Friderico Romanorum imperatori contra omnes homines, sicut iure debeo domino et imperatori et adiuvabo eum retinere coronam imperii et omnem honorem eius in Italia, nominatim et specialiter civitatem N. et quicquid in ea iuris habere debet, vel in omni virtute comitatus vel episcopatos N. Regalia sua ei non auferam ibidem nec alibi, et si fuerint ablata, bona fide recuperare et retinere adiuvabo. Neque in consilio ero nec in facto, quod vitam vel membrum vel honorem suum perdat vel mala captione teneatur. Omne mandatum eius, quod ipse mihi fecerit per se vel per epistolam suam aut per legatum suum de facienda iusticia, fideliter observabo et illud audire vel recipere vel complere nullo male ingenio evitabo. Haec omnia observabo fide bona sine fraude. Sic me Deus adiuvet et haec sancta quatuor ewangelia. [...]

iii. 21. Hisdem diebus Heinricus et Iacinctus supra dicti nuncii Adriani papae, Ferariam venerant, auditoque quod legati imperatoris Mutinam redissent, non sperantes ipsos sibi occurrere, humilitatis formam prebentes, quod insolitam antea fuerat, ad eos pergunt, expositaque causa legationis, quod scilicet ea, quae pacis essent et honor imperio, in mandatis haberent, dimittuntur. Iam vero adventum illorum per omnes partes illas, ubi arta montium transituri erant, fama nunciaverat, multoque mortalium rerum alienarum cupidos id contra eos animaverat, quod pene neminem latebat maiestatem imperialem Romanis infensam existere, quodque vicio aviditatis quisque ardebat, acsi regiae voluntati obsequeretur, temerarius intendebat, sperans in hoc casu latrocinium honestiori nomine posse palliari. A Feraria itaque Veronam, a Verona per vallem Tridentinam iter agunt, habentes secum gratia maioris securitatis venerabilem episopum Tridentinum Albertum. Sed prevaluit auri sacra fames,[54] quae quos arripuit, nil umquam honestum, nil moderatum sentire vel appetere permittit. Nam Fridericus et Heinricus comites,

---

53   Henry of Pisa and Hyacinth of S. Maria in Cosmedin: see ch. 7, n. 126.
54   Vergil, *Aeneid,* iii. 57.

have mentioned above, had entered Italy long before, having changed his attitude for the better, sent envoys to calm Frederick's spirit, namely, Henry, cardinal priest of the title of SS. Nereo e Aquilleo, and Hyacinth, cardinal priest of S. Maria in the Greek School,[53] men of prudence in secular matters, and much better qualified for dealing with matters of state than those previously sent. [...]

iii. 20. And so, on their first entrance into Italy, the [imperial] envoys accepted the capitulation of a stronghold which is called Rivoli, situated above the pass of Verona, impregnable because of its natural setting; for they thought that through the possession of it our men would find the passage easier, both coming and returning, in so narrow a defile. Received by great throngs and with marked respect on the part of the bishop and citizens of Verona, both there and in other cities [namely, Mantua, Cremona, Pavia] they caused [oaths] of fidelity to the emperor and assistance in the expedition to be sworn on the Holy Gospels; and preparing the way for the emperor, they proved themselves trustworthy and valuable precursors of his arrival. Now this is the form of the oath to which all swore:

> I swear that from this time forth I shall be faithful to my lord Frederick, emperor of the Romans, against all men, as I should in law to my lord and emperor, and I shall aid him to retain the crown of the empire and all its *honour* in Italy, namely and specifically the city of N. and whatever right he ought to have in it, or in all his power over the county or bishopric of N. I shall not deprive him of his *regalia* here or elsewhere, and if they have been taken away from him I shall in good faith help him to recover and retain them. I shall be party to no plot or deed to cause him loss of life or limb or honour or to be held in dire captivity. Every command of his, given to me personally, or in writing, or through his representative concerning the doing of justice, I shall faithfully observe, and I shall not by any fraud evade hearing or receiving or complying with it. All these things I shall observe in good faith without deceit. So help me God and these four Holy Gospels. [...]

iii. 21. During this time, Henry and Hyacinth, the aforesaid legates of Pope Adrian, had come to Ferrara, and hearing that the envoys of the emperor had returned to Modena, having no hope of being themselves visited, they made show of humility, hitherto rare, and went directly to them, and, after setting forth the reason for their embassy, namely, what they had in their mandates concerning peace and the honour of the empire, they were dismissed. But by this time throughout all those regions where they had to cross the mountain passes, rumour had reported their coming, and the cupidity of many had been aroused by the fact, of which scarcely a man was unaware, that the imperial majesty was hostile to the Romans, and according as each was inflamed by the vice of greed, he audaciously threatened them as though in compliance with the royal wishes, hoping that in this case brigandage might be extenuated under a more honourable name. And so they proceeded from Ferrara to Verona, from Verona though the valley of the Trent, having with them, for greater security, Albert, the venerable bishop of Trent. But 'the accursed lust for gold'[54] prevailed; once it has possessed a man, it never permits him to contemplate or to seek anything honourable or reasonable. For Counts Frederick and

quorum in illis partibus non parum poterat violentia, tam cardinales quam episcopum obsidem nobilis vir N., germanus Iacincti, episcopum autem evidenter divina potentia liberavit. Hanc tamen inmanitatem nobilissimus dux Baioariae et Saxoniae[55] ob amorem sanctae Romanae aecclesiae et honorem imperii non multo post probe vindicavit. Namque et vadem eripuit et comites multis malis attritos ad deditionem et satisfactionem coegit.

iii. 22. Friderico igitur, ut iam dictum est, castra in campestribus Augustae civitatis metato, ad suam eosdem legatos admittit presentiam, eisque clementer receptis causam adventus exquirit. Illi reverenter ac demisso vultu,[56] voce modesta tale suae legationis assumunt principium: 'Presul sanctae Romanae aecclesiae, vestrae excellentiae devotissimus in Christo pater, salutat vos sicut karissimum et spiritalem sancti Petri filium. Salutant etiam vos venerabiles fratres nostri, clerici autem vestri, universi cardinales, tamquam dominum et imperatorem Urbis et orbis. Quanta dilectione sancta Romana aecclesia amplitudinem et honorem imperii vestri amplectatur, quam sine conscientia peccati vestram satis invita sustinuerit indignationem, et scripta presentia et in ore nostro positae vivae vocis officium declarabit'. Post haec verba litteras efferunt, quae venerabili Ottoni Frisingensi episcopo ad legendum simul et interpretandum datae sunt, viro utique, qui singularem habebat dolorem de controversia inter regnum et sacerdotium.* Exemplar litterarum hoc est:

> iii. 23. Ex quo universalis aecclesiae curam Deo, prout ipsi placuit, disponente suscepimus, ita in cunctis negotiis magnificentiam tuam honorare curavimus, ut de die in diem animus tuus magis ac magis in amore nostro et veneratione sedis apostolicae debuisset accendi. Unde sine grandi ammiratione non ferimus, quod cum, audito ex suggestione quorumdam animum tuum aliquantulum contra nos fuisse conmmotum, duos de melioribus et maioribus fratribus nostris, R[olandum] scilicet cancellarium tituli Sancti Marci et B[ernhardum] tituli Sancti Clementis presbiteros cardinales, qui pro tuae maiestatis honore in Romana aecclesia solliciti semper extiterant, pro voluntatis tuae cognitione ad tuam presentiam direximus, aliter quam imperialem decuerit honorificentiam sunt tractati. Occasione siquidem cuiusdam verbi, quod est *beneficium*, tuus animus, sicut dicitur, est commotus, quod utique nedum tanti viri, sed nec cuiuslibet minoris animum merito commovisset. Licet enim hoc nomen, quod est *beneficium*, apud quosdam in alia significatione, quam ex inpositione habeat, assumatur, tunc tamen in ea significatione accipiendum fuerat, quam nos ipsi posuimus, et quam ex institutione sua noscitur retinere. Hoc enim nomen ex bono et facto est editum, eti dicitur beneficium aput nos non feudum, sed bonum factum; in qua significatione in universo Sacrae Scripturae corpore invenitur, ubi ex beneficio Dei, non tamquam ex feudo, sed velut et benedictione et bono facto ipsius gubernari dicimur et nutriri. Et tua quidem magnificentia liquido recognoscit, quod nos ita bene et honorifice imperialis dignitalis insigne tuo capiti imposuimus, ut bonum factum valeat

---

[55] Henry the Lion.
[56] Cf. Sallust, *Catiline*, xxxi. 7.

Henry [of Eppan, Tyrol], whose deeds of violence in those parts were not a few, taking captive both the cardinals and the bishop, robbed them and kept them in chains until a noble man, N., the brother of Hyacinth, giving himself as a hostage, freed the Romans; but it was evidently divine power that freed the bishop. This outrage, however, was properly avenged not long afterwards, by the most noble duke of Bavaria and Saxony,[55] out of love for the Holy Roman Church and to the honour of the empire. For he both freed the hostage and forced the counts to surrender and make reparation, after inflicting much evil upon them.

iii. 22. Accordingly, when Frederick had pitched his camp in the plains of Augsburg (as has already been said), he admitted to his presence those same legates and, receiving them graciously, asked the cause of their coming. With due reverence and downcast eyes[56] they began their mission in these words, 'The bishop of the Holy Roman Church, Your Excellency's most devoted father in Christ, salutes you as the very dear and spiritual son of St. Peter. Salutations also from our venerable brothers, your clergy, all the cardinals, to you as lord and emperor of the City and of the world. With what great love the Holy Roman Church esteems the dignity and honour of your empire, how she has—though unwillingly enough—endured your anger without consciousness of guilt, both this present writing and the words placed upon our lips shall declare.' They then produced a letter which was given to the venerable Bishop Otto of Freising to read and to interpret—a man who felt a peculiar grief at the controversy between *regnum* and *sacerdotium*.* This is a copy of the letter:

iii. 23. Since we assumed the care of the universal Church by God's will and pleasure, we have been careful so to honour to your magnificence in all matters, that your love of us and veneration for the Apostolic See might daily increase. When we heard that your feelings had been roused against us by certain people, we sent to you, to ascertain your will, two of our best and most distinguished brothers, the Cardinal Priest R[oland], the chancellor, of the title of S. Marco, and Bernard, of the title of S. Clemente, cardinal priests,who had always been solicitous in the Roman Church for the honour of your majesty. Hence, not without great surprise did we learn that they were treated otherwise than became the imperial dignity. For your heart was stirred to anger, it is said, by the use of a certain word, namely *beneficium*, which should not have vexed the heart of even one in lowly station, to say nothing of so great a man. For although this word *beneficium* is by some interpreted in a different significance than it has by derivation, it should nevertheless have been understood in the meaning which we ourselves put upon it, and which it is known to have possessed from the beginning. For this word is formed of *bonus* (good) and *factum* (deed), and among us *bene ficium* means not a fief but a good deed, in which sense it is found in the entire body of Holy Scripture, wherein we are said to be ruled and supported *ex beneficio* Dei, not as by a fief but as by His benediction and His *good deed*. And indeed your magnificence clearly recognizes that we placed the emblem of imperial dignity upon your head in so good and honourable a fashion that merits recognition by all

* See above, ch. 6, n. 134

ab omnibus iudicari. Unde quod quidam verbum hoc et illud, scilicet: *contulimus tibi insigne imperialis coronae*, a sensu suo nisi sunt ad alium retorquere, non ex merito causae, sed de voluntate propria et illorum suggestione, qui pacem regni et aecclesiae nullatenus diligunt, hoc egerunt. Per hoc enim vocabulum *contulimus* nil aliud intelligimus, nisi quod superius dictum est *imposuimus*. Sane quod postmodum personas aecclesiasticas a debita sacrosanctae Romanae aecclesiae visitatione, ut dicitur, revocare iussisti, si ita est, quam inconvenienter actum sit, tua, fili in Christo karissime, discretio, ut credimus, recognoscit. Nam si aput nos aliquid amaritudinis habebas, per nuncios et litteras tuas nobis fuerat intimandum, et nos honori tuo curavissemus, sicut filii karissimi, providere. Nunc igitur quoniam ad commonitionem dilecti filii nostri H[einrici] Baioariae et Saxoniae ducis duos de fratribus nostris, Heinricum tituli Sanctorum Nerei et Achillei [presbiterum] et Iacinctum Sanctae Mariae in Cosmidin diaconem cardinales,[57] prudentes siquidem et honestos viros, ad tuam presentiam destinamus, celsitudinem tuam monentes et hortantes in Domino, quatinus eos honeste ac benigne recipias, et quod ab eis ex parte nostra tuae magnificentiae fuerit intimatum, a sinceritate cordis nostri noverit tua excellentia processisse, ac per hoc cum eisdem filiis nostris, mediante iam dicto filio nostro duce, ita celsitudo tua studeat convenire, ut inter te et matrem tuam sacrosanctam Romanam aecclesiam [ammodo] nullius discordiae seminarium debeat remanere.

iii. 24. Lectis et benigna interpretatione expositis litteris, imperator mitigatus est, clementiorque factus quasdam causas alio loco memorandas[58] quae seminarium discordiae prestarent, si non congrua emendatio interveniret, legatis per capitula distinxit. Quibus ad nutum principis et per omnia bene respondentibus presulemque Romanum in nullo regiae dignitati derogare, sed honorem ac iusticiam imperii semper illibatam conservare pollicentibus, pacem et amiciciam tam summo pontifici quam omni clero Romano reddidit eamque signo pacis et osculo absentibus per presentes destinavit. Sicque hylariores facti legati donatique regalibus muneribus divertunt in civitatem

[...]

iv. 18. Friderico in hibernis agente, Adrianus Romanae urbis antistes quorundam instinctu ea, quae iam inter ipsum et imperatorem aput Augustam sopita fuerant, refricare cepit et denuo meminisse, modo nunciorum suorum iniuriam, modo eorum, qui pro colligendo fodro directi fuerant, insolentiam et castellanorum suorum gravamen incusans: se pro bonis mala recepisse, imperatorem beneficiis suis ingratum existere. Proinde occasionem querens, cum audisset, quod regalia principi tam ab episcopis et abbatibus quam a civitatibus et proceribus recognita fuere, litteras in fronte quidem leniores, diligentius vero consideratae acriori commonitione plenas, super hoc negotio dirigit, easque quidam indignus et vilis nuncius presentans, antequam recitatae fuissent, disparuit. Qua de re commotus caloreque iuvenili, ad vicem rependendam accensus, meditationem concipit, non quidem per

---

[57]   Henry of Pisa and Hyacinth of S. Maria in Cosmedin, above, n. 53.
[58]   See below, iv. 34–6.

as a good deed. Hence when certain people have tried to twist that word and the phrase, *we have conferred upon you the emblem of the imperial crown,* from its own proper meaning to another, they have done this not on the merits of the case, but of their own desire and at the instigation of those who by no means love the concord between the realm and the Church. For by the word[s] *we have conferred* we meant nothing else than when we said before *we have placed.* As for the report that you afterwards ordered the turning back of ecclesiastical persons from due visitation to the Holy Roman Church, if it be so, we believe that your discretion, very dear son in Christ, must realize how unseemly an act that was. For if you harboured any bitterness toward us, it should have been intimated to us by your envoys and letters, and we would have taken care to safeguard your honour, as that of our very dear son. Now therefore, as we have, at the advice of our beloved son H[enry], duke of Bavaria and Saxony, sent into your presence two of our brothers, Henry, cardinal priest of the title of S. Nereo and Aquilleo, and Hyacinth, cardinal deacon of S. Maria in Cosmedin,[57] truly wise and estimable men, we urge and exhort your highness in the Lord to receive them with honour and kindness; and your excellency should also know that what is imparted to your magnificence by them on our behalf has proceeded from the sincerity of our heart; and therefore may your highness so strive to reach an agreement with these our sons, through the mediation of our aforesaid son, the duke, that there may remain no seed of discord between you and your mother, the Holy Roman Church.

iii. 24. When the letter had been read and set forth with favourable interpretation, the emperor was mollified, and becoming more gracious he indicated to the legates certain specific matters to be considered in another place,[58] which might lead to dispute unless properly corrected. When to this they made answer agreeable to the prince and in all respects satisfactory, and promised that the bishop of Rome would do nothing derogatory to the royal dignity, but would always preserve inviolate the honour and the just claims of empire, he restored peace and friendship both to the supreme pontiff and to all the Roman clergy, and sent it to the absent by giving those who were present, a kiss in token of peace. So the envoys, gladdened and enriched with royal gifts, set forth for the City.
[…]

iv. 18. While Frederick was in winter quarters, Adrian, bishop of the city of Rome, prompted by certain people, began to stir up anew and recall the matters between himself and the emperor which had been lulled to rest at Augsburg, now complaining of the insult to his envoys, now of the insolence of those who had been sent to collect the fodrum, and the injury done to his castellans; he had, he claimed, received evil for good, and the emperor was ungrateful for his acts of kindness. As he was looking for an opportunity, when he heard both bishops and abbots and cities and notables had recognized that the *regalia* belonged to the prince, he sent letters concerning the matter, quite mild at first sight, but, when carefully considered, full of sharp criticism; and a certain unworthy messenger—a low fellow—presented it and disappeared before it was read. Aroused by this and moved by youthful ardour to retaliate, Frederick conceived the idea of replying to him

abiectam, sed per honoratam illi respondere personam. Iam antea missus fuerat ad sedem apostolicam episcopus Vercellensis, amicam deferens petitionem, quatinus Gwidonem nobilem iuvenem filium comitis Gwidonis Blanderatensis,[59] cuius supra mentionem fecimus, quem loco Anselmi princeps in Ravennate aecclesia subrogari fecerat, ibidem confirmaret et ordinaret. Nam idem iuvenis infra sacros ordines adhuc existebat, et clericus Romanae aecclesiae pridem factus ac subdiaconum a papa Adriano consecratus, nonnisi eius coniventia et assensu in aliam aecclesiam transferendus putabatur. Cum autem hoc a Romano pontifice, volens in irritum revocare quod factum fuerat, negaretur, mittitur denuo Herimannus Ferdensis episcopus ad id ipsum, eiusque negocium item effectu caruit. Quod si quis plenius scire desiderat, epistolas utrimque directas consulat, quarum talia rescripta inveniuntur.

[...]

iv. 21. Princeps ergo, et ipse accepta occasione, suam hoc modo solatur indignationem. Iubet notario, ut in scribendis cartis nomen suum preferens Romani episcopi subsecundet et dictionibus singularis numeri ipsum alloquatur. Qui mos scribendi cum antiquitus in usu esset communi, a modernis ob quandam personarum reverentiam et honorem putatur immutatus. Aiebat siquidem imperator aut papam debere servare suorum antecessorum ad personam imperialem scribendi consuetudinem, aut seipsum antiquorum principum morem in suis epistolis oportere observare. Haec itaque causa sermonum et nunciorum inter eos simultatis fomitem ministravit, in tantum, ut quaedam litterae deprehensae dicerentur a sede apostolica directae, quae Mediolanenses et quasdam alias civitates rursus ad defectionem hortarentur. Huius negotii veritatem tenor subiectarum epistolarum declarabit, quae a diversis personibus hinc inde missae sunt:

iv. 22. Venerabili patri et fratri et amico karissimo Eberhardo, Dei gratia Babinbergensi episcopo,[60] Heinricus, eadem gratia sanctae Romanae aecclesiae prebiter cardinalis tituli sanctorum Nerei et Achillei,[61] salutem in Domino.

Sicut virtus imperatoria ex eorum, qui sibi assistunt, discretione monstretur, ita et ipsi, quorum munitur consilio, propriae conscientiae et honestati debent attendere, quia et ipsorum honor sic ad dominos spectare videtur, sicut et domini detrimentum in eos procul dubio refunditur et redundant. Eapropter, dilecte pater et venerande frater et amice karissime, vestram non tam docemus quam monemus prudentiam, ut imperialis dignitatis excellentiam, quantum in vobis est, in ea, quae ad pacem sunt et [ad] honestatem spectant, iugiter suadeatis. Subtilius enim et sincerius in his, quae ad Deum pertinent et iusticiae libertatem, ratio et discretio vestra intelligit et cognoscit, quam alii principes, quantumcumque nobiles sint, si tamen sacros canones et ea, quae olim a patribus disposita et ordinata sunt, non noverunt. Interfuistis ipse sicut unus ex nobis fidelissimus mediator eis, quae cum

---

[59] Above, ch. 7, n. 144.
[60] Eberhard II, bishop of Bamberg 1146–72.
[61] Henry of Pisa, above, n. 53.

through honourable rather than through a lowly envoy. The bishop of Vercelli had been sent to the Apostolic See even before this, bearing a friendly request that the pope would confirm and consecrate Guido, a noble youth, the son of Count Guido of Biandrate,[59] of whom we have made mention above, whom the prince had proposed in Anselm's place in the church of Ravenna. For since this young man, not yet in sacred orders, had already been made a clerk in the church at Rome and ordained subdeacon by Pope Adrian, it was thought that only by his permission and assent could he be transferred to another church. When, however, this was done, it was refused; Herman, bishop of Verden, was sent on the same mission, and his effort likewise failed of success. If anyone wishes fuller knowledge about it, let him study the letters sent by both parties. He will find the following copies:

[…]

iv. 21. The prince, thus provoked, relieved his anger in this way. He ordered his notary that in writing documents he should place his name before that of the bishop of Rome and address the later in the singular. This custom of writing, though commonly used in antiquity, is supposed to have been changed by the moderns out of a certain reverence and respect for the persons addressed. For the emperor said that either the pope ought to observe the custom of his predecessors in writing to an imperial personage, or he himself should in his letters follow the style of the emperors of old. This dispute about words and envoys gave rise to such enmity between them that certain letters sent by the Apostolic See were said to have been seized, which urged the people of Milan and certain other cities to revolt again. The tenor of the letters which follow, written by various persons, will reveal the truth of the matter.

iv. 22. To his venerable father and brother, and dearest friend Eberhard, by the grace of God bishop of Bamberg,[60] Henry, by that same grace cardinal priest of the Holy Roman Church of the title of SS. Nereo and Achilleo,[61] greeting in the Lord.

Even as the emperor's character is shown by the conduct of those around him, so also those on whose counsel he depends ought to give heed to their own conscience and sense of honour. For their own honour clearly reflects credit upon their lords, just as their lord's adversity undoubtedly involves and overwhelms them. Therefore, beloved father, venerable brother, and very dear friend, we do not so much instruct as urge your prudence constantly to guide the imperial dignity—as much as you can—along a course of peace and honour. For in matters that pertain to God and the freedom of justice, your reason and good judgment have a more subtle and sincere intelligence than other princes, however noble they may be, if they are ignorant of the sacred canons and those matters which were long ago settled and ordained by the fathers. You yourself were present as a most faithful mediator at the negotiations in Germany with the lord emperor concerning peace between the Church and himself, and at those which, on another occasion,

domino imperatore de pace aecclesiae ad ipsius ordinata sunt in Alemannia, et eis, quae altera die nos secum fidelissime et ipse nobiscum benignissime de eadem pace tractavimus.

Nunc autem ex litteris illis, quas celsitudine suae post reditum meum domino meo placuit destinare, quae videlicet nec stilum nec antiquam consuetudinem imperialiuim litterarum obtinebant, timemus multum, ne sit in diversa mutatus et alia modo sibi sit facies sensusque diversus. Replevit cor meum amaritudine et faciem meam confusione mutatio haec; quidquid honoris et iocunditatis et gloriae adportaveram mecum, ex litteris illis videtur esse sepultum atque obnubilatum.

Ideo, dilectissime frater et amice karissime, episcopalis dignitas et sacerdotii ordo, in quo vos providential divina constituit, moveant discretionem vestram et instruant, ut ad honorem Dei stetis et vestrum pro honestate et liberate aecclesiae, ut in antiques limitibus aecclesiae integritas conservetur, ne temporibus vestris novis consiliis honestas usque modo turbata turbetur.

Satis turbatum est, quidquid secundum consilium vestrum putabamus efficere, et dicimus vobis, quamdiu per homines rerum divinarum ignaros negotia portabuntur, stabiliri pax incepta non poterit. Sed si presentia vestra et domini preposti Magdeburgensis consummandae pacis laborem susceperit, zelus Dei et scientia, qua preminetis uterque, finem pacificum ad honorem Dei et aecclesiae et imperatoris nostri gloriam per industriam vestram et studium vestrum facillime poterit obtinere. Alioquin, si tempore iracundiae repertus non fuerit, qui reconciliationi intendat et in cuius verbis possint ista scandala complanari, res ipsa forsan aliud exiget, et quod hodie integrum est, maior vehementia necessitatis disrumpet....[...]

iv. 34. Preter alios principes, nobiles atque sapientes interfuere huic collatione et negotio sedis apostolicae legati, videlicet Octavianus tituli sanctae Ceciliae presbiter cardinalis, Heinricus tituli sanctorum Nerei et Achillei, Wilhelmus cardinalis diaconus, antea Papiensis archidiaconus, et Gwido Cremensis diaconus cardinalis,[62] missi a papa Adriano. Quorum itineris causas simulque nunciorum senatus populique Romani [necnon et alia quedam] rescriptum litterarum venerabilis viri Eberhardi Babinbergensis episcopi subter annotatum continet; quod tale est:

Reverendissimo patri et domino Eberhardo Salzburgensis aecclesiae archiepiscopo[63] Eberhardus Babinbergensis,[64] gratia Dei si quid est cum oratione qualiscumque servitium devotissimum.

Scio, pater sanctissime, sacrae pietatis affectu vos meis compati laboribus et animae mihi salutem et corpori quietem concupiscere. Ut autem noveritis, quoad compati vos mihi oporteat, dico vobis, quod iam tedet animam meam vitae meae, suo ferens onera in animo meo mihi gravissima, quod et cinctus ducor quo nolo et, quamdiu durare debeat, ignoro, vestris et aliorum fidelium orationibus adiuvari

---

[62] Octavian of S. Cecilia, Henry of SS. Nereo e Achilleo, William of S. Pietro in Vincoli, and Guido of Crema: see ch. 7, n. 148.

[63] Eberhard I, archbishop of Salzburg 1147–64.

[64] Above, n. 59.

we conducted most faithfully with him, and he most graciously with us, with reference to the same peace.

But now because of the letter which it pleased his highness to send my lord after my return, a letter which certainly observed neither the style nor the ancient custom of imperial letters, we greatly fear that he has changed, and that now his countenance and his feelings have altered. This transformation has filled my heart with bitterness and covered my face with confusion; whatever honour and happiness and prestige I had brought back with me seem to have been lost and buried by that letter.

Therefore, most beloved brother and dearest friend, may the dignity of bishop and the order of priesthood in which Divine Providence has placed you so move and instruct your discretion that you will fight for God's honour and your own, and for the liberty of the Church, that the Church may be preserved untouched within its ancient compass, lest in your time its hitherto untarnished honour be tarnished by new devices.

It has been troubled enough, whatever we thought to effect by your counsel, and we assure you that so long as those matters are handled by men who are ignorant of things divine, the peace that has been inaugurated cannot stand firm. But if you and the lord provost of Magdeburg will undertake the task of consolidating the peace, the zeal for God and the knowledge in which you both excell, can very easily obtain a peaceful settlement, to the glory of God and the Church, and the glory of our emperor. Otherwise, if in the time of wrath no one is found who will strive by his words to smooth out the difficulties, this situation may perhaps call forth another, and the greater force of necessity may break what is still intact today.... [...]

iv. 34. Besides other princes, nobles, and wise men there were present at this deliberation envoys of the Apostolic See sent by Pope Adrian, namely, Octavian, cardinal priest of the title of S. Cecilia, Henry, cardinal priest of the title of SS. Nereo e Achilleo, and the cardinal deacons William, previously archdeacon of Pavia, and Guido of Crema.[62] The reasons for their coming, and also for the coming of envoys from the senate and the Roman people, are contained in the subjoined copy of a letter of that venerable man Eberhard, bishop of Bamberg, which is as follows:

To the most reverend father and lord, Eberhard, archbishop of the church of Salzburg,[63] Eberhard, by the grace of God bishop of Bamberg,[64] however unworthy, sends assurance of most loyal devotion, with every prayer.

I know, most holy father, that in your love of holy piety you sympathize with me in my labours and wish me salvation for my soul and peace for my body. But that you may know to what extent you should sympathize with me, I tell you that my soul is now weary of life; I carry in my heart two very heavy burdens, because I am girt and led whither I would not [Jn 21: 18], and I know not how long it must still endure; I desire to be aided by your prayers and those of the faithful, that I

desiderans, ut ab illis separer, quibus iuravit Dominus in ira sua, *Si introibunt in requiem meam*. Super haec tempora periculosa instare videtur, et prope est, ut inter regnum et sacerdotium* moveatur discordia. Et quidem cardinalibus a domno papa ad domnum imperatorem transmissis, domno videlicet Octaviano et domno Wilhelmo quondam Papiensi archidiacono,[65] post lene principium et ingressum quasi pacificum capitula durissima proposita sunt. Verbi gratia: nuncios ad Urbem ignorante apostolico ab imperatore non esse mittendos, cum omnis magistrates inibi beati Petri sit cum universis regalibus. De dominicalibusapostolici fodrum non esse colligendum, nisi tempore suscipiendae coronae. Episcopos Italiae solum sacramentum fidelitatis sine hominio facere debere domno imperatori, neque nuncios imperatoris in palatiis episcoporum recipiendos. De possessionibus aecclesiae Romanae restituendis, Tiburti, Ferrariae, Massae, Ficorolii, totius terrae comitisae Mathildis, totius terrae, quae ab Aquapendente est usque Romam, ducatus Spoletani, insularum Sardiniae, Corsicae.

Domno autem imperatore super his iusticiam vellent facere et recipere, illis vero recipere tantum volentibus et non facere, hac ratione, quod domnum apostolicum [causae] subicere ac iudicio sistere non possent, et e contrario domno imperatore multa proponente de rupta concordia, quae in verbo veritatis sibi compromissa fuerat, de Grecis, de Siculo, de Romanis sine communi consensu non recipiendis, de cardinalibus quoque sine permissione imperiali libere per regnum transeuntibus et regalia episcoporum palatia ingredientibus et aecclesias Dei gravantibus, de iniustis appellationibus et caeteris quam pluribus brevitatem superatibus, cum apostolicus per nuncium et litteras cardinalium predictorum ex consensus imperatoris submonitus, cardinales alios ad haec omnia complananda requisitus his qui aderant nuncios suis et curiae principibus nollet adiungere, unitatis et concordiae verbum diu desideratum peccatis nostris exigentibus evacuatum est

Et dum haec agerentur, nuncii Romanorum supervenientes et ea quae pacis sunt rogantes bene recepti ac dismiss sunt. Rogatu tamen cardinalium domnus imperator nuncios ad domnum papam et ad Urbem missurus est, ut cum apostolico, si ipse voluerit, primo loco pax fiat, sin autem, cum senatu et populo Romano. Domnus imperator in magna est gloria, domnam imperatricem et ducem Baioariae et Saxoniae cum aliis superventuris principibus et copiis exercitus expectans et quosdam ex melioribus de Mediolano et Brexia in vinculis retinens. Valete.

iv. 35. Imperator ad haec verba cardinalium tale dedit responsum:

Quamvis non ignorem ad tanta negotia non ex animi mei sentential, sed ex consilio principum me respondere debere, sine preiudicio tamen sapientum hoc absque consultatione respondeo. Episcoporum Italiae ego quidem non effecto hominium, si tamen et eos de nostris regalibus nichil deletat habere. Qui si

---

[65] Octavian of S. Cecilia and William of S. Pietro in Vincoli: above, n. 62.

may be separated from those to whom the Lord hath sworn in his wrath, 'They shall not enter into my rest' [Ps. 95: 11]. Besides, perilous times seem to be coming [2 Tim. 3: 1.], and the breaking out of conflict between *regnum* and *sacerdotium*[*] is near. And, indeed, when cardinals were sent by the lord pope to the lord emperor, namely, lord Octavian and lord William, formerly archdeacon of Pavia,[65] after a mild beginning and an apparently peaceful introduction, the most severe demands were made. For example: envoys must not be sent by the emperor to the City without the pope's knowledge, since all the magistrates there with all the regalia are under the jurisdiction of blessed Peter. Fodrum is not to be collected from apostolic lands, except at the time of the coronation. The bishops of Italy may render the lord emperor an oath of fealty only, without doing homage, nor are the emperor's envoys to be received in bishops' palaces. Possessions to be restored to the Church of Rome include Tivoli, Ferrara, Massa, Ficarolo, all the land of Countess Matilda, all the land which extends from Aquapendente to Rome, the duchy of Spoleto, the islands of Sardinia and Corsica.

While the lord emperor wished to do and receive justice in these matters, the others wished to receive but not to do justice, on this ground, that they could not subject the lord pope to judgment. On the other hand, the lord emperor said many things concerning the breach of the agreement, which had been entered into in good faith, to make peace with the Greeks, the Sicilian, and the Romans only by common consent; about the cardinals who, without imperial permission, travelled about freely through the realm and entered the regalian palaces of the bishops and burdened the churches of God; about unjust appeals, and many other matters that cannot be briefly set forth, when the aforesaid cardinals, with the approval of the emperor, sent both an envoy and letters to the pope, urging him to send additional cardinals to smooth out these matters with his legates and the princes of the court already present, he refused. So, for our sins, the long-desired word of unity and concord remained unuttered.

And while these things were going on, envoys of the Romans arrived and, desiring conditions of peace, were well received and sent home again. Nevertheless, at the request of the cardinals the lord emperor is about to send envoys to the lord pope and to the City, that peace may first be ratified with the pope, if he wishes it; but if not, with the senate and the Roman people. The lord emperor is in great glory. He awaits the lady empress, and the duke of Bavaria and Saxony, with the other princes and troops expected, and is keeping in chains some of the leading citizens of Milan and Brescia. Farewell.

iv. 35. The emperor made the following reply to these words of the cardinals:

Since I am well aware that I ought to reply to such important matters, not in accordance with my personal feelings but upon the advice of my princes, I give this answer without prejudice to those wise men, not having consulted them. I am not eager for the homage of the bishops of Italy, that is as long as they do not care to hold any of our regalia. If they take pleasure in hearing from the Roman bishop,

---

[*] See above, ch. 6, n. 134.

gratanter audierint a Romano presule, 'Quid tibi et regi?', consequenter quoque eos ab imperatore non pigeat audire, 'Quid tibi et posessioni?' Nuncios nostros non esse recipiendos in palatiis episcoporum asserit. Concedo, si forte aliquis episcoporum habet in suo proprio solo et non in nostrum palatium. Si autem in nostro solo et allodio sunt palatia episcoporum, cum profecto omne quod inedificatur solo cedat, nostra sunt et palatia. Iniuria ergo esset, si quis nuncios nostros a regiis palatiis prohiberet.

Legatis ab imperatore ad Urbem non esse mittendos affirmat, cum omnis magistratus inibi beati Petri sit cum universis regalibus. Haec res, fateor, magna est et gravis graviorque et maturiori egens consilio. Nam cum divina ordinatione ego Romanus imperator et dicar et sim, speciem tantum dominantis effingo et inane utique porto nomen ac sine re, si urbis Romae de manu nostra potestas fuerit excussa.'

iv. 36. Haec augusto et his similia prefatis capitulis argute respondente, consilium initur, ut ex parte summi pontificis cardinales sex et ex parte principis sex episcopi religiosi, prudentes et qui Deum timeant, eligantur, tantorum negotiorum hinc inde cognitionem accepturi tantamque litem congruo fine decisuri. Verum, ut supra taxatum est, ex parte Romanorum etiam hoc consilium dicitur fuisse evacuatum. Super hoc quoque capitulo audi epistolam imperatoris directam Eberhardo Salzburgensi archiepiscopo[66] in hunc modum:

Quoniam quidem fidelitatis tuae constantiam, quam pro consuetudine exhibere soles imperio, frequenter experti sumus, quae aput nos sunt discretioni tuae significemus et prudentiae tuae consilium advocamus.

Venerunt siquidem ad nos duo cardinales a papa missi ad hoc, ut inter nos et illum fieret concordia. Dixerunt igitur, quod papa illam requireret pacem atque concordiam, quae inter papam Eugenium et nos facta fuerat et scripta.[67] Nos respondimus, quod pacem quidem inviolabiliter huc usque tenuissemus, de caetero autem neque eam tenere neque ea teneri vellemus, quoniam ipse prior violasset in Siculo,[68] cui ipse sine nobis reconciliari non debuisset. Adiciemus tamen, quod omnem iusticiam dare et accipere parati essemus sive secundum humana sive secundum scripta divina. Si vero iusticia gravis videretur, consilium principum et religiosorum [virorum] pro amore Dei et aecclesiae libenter nos supponeremus. Placuit verbum nostrum cardinalibus. Dixerunt tamen, nisi prius cognita papae voluntate super hoc se nil posse vel audere. Missis nuncios verbum nostrum cognovit papa mandavitque, sicut prius, aliam se nolle concordiam quam illam, quae inter papam Eugenium et nos facta fuisst. Nos supradicta modo hoc recusavimus et in presentia et sub testimonio omnium Teutonicorum et Longobardorum episcoporum et laicorum principum et baronum et vavassorum omnem iusticiam sive consilium obtulimus, ut et nos acciperemus iusticiam. Presentes ibidem fuere Romanorum civium legati, qui cum indignatione mitabantur super

---

66   Above, n. 63.
67   See ch. 7, part i (a), 'The accord of Constance, 1153'.
68   Above, ch. 7, part i (c), 'The accord of Benevento'.

'What have you to do with the king?' let them consequently not grieve to hear from the emperor, 'What have you to do with estates?' He [the pope] declares that our envoys are not to be received in bishops' palaces. I agree—if perchance any bishop has a palace which stands on his own land, and not on ours. But if the bishops' palaces are on our land and alod, then, since certainly everything that is built upon it goes with the land, the palaces are also ours. Therefore, it would be an injustice to debar our envoys from royal palaces.

He states that envoys are not to be sent by the emperor to the City, since all the magistrates there, together with all their regalia, are under the jurisdiction of the blessed Peter. This is, I admit, a great and serious matter, which requires more serious and more mature consideration. For since, by divine ordinance, I am emperor of Rome and am so styled, I have merely the appearance of ruling and bear an utterly empty name, lacking in meaning, if authority over the city of Rome should be torn from our grasp.

iv. 36. When the emperor had made these and other subtle replies to the aforesaid articles, it was determined that six cardinals should be chosen for the pope, and for the emperor, six bishops—pious, wise, and God-fearing—to obtain from all possible sources full information about matters of such importance, and to find for so great a dispute a satisfactory solution. But, as has been set out above, this plan, too, is said to have been rendered vain by the Romans. On this point hear the letter of the emperor addressed to Eberhard, archbishop of Salzburg,[66] in this form:

As we have often had proof of the constant fidelity you have always displayed towards the empire, we make known to your discretion the state of our affairs and ask the advice of your prudence.

Well then, there have come to us two cardinals, sent by the pope for the purpose of creating harmony between us and him. They said that the pope desired that peace and harmony which had been made and written between Pope Eugenius and ourselves.[67] We replied that we had in fact kept that peace inviolate until now; as for the future, however, we desired neither to keep it nor to be bound by it, because he himself had been the first to violate it in respect of the Sicilian,[68] with whom he should not have been reconciled without our agreement. We added, however, that we were ready to render or to receive full justice according either to human or to divine law. And if judicial procedure appeared to him too stern, we would gladly submit to the judgment of the priests and men of religion, out of love for God and the Church. Our words pleased the cardinals. But they said that they could not and dared not take any action in the matter without first knowing the pope's will. The pope learned of our proposal through messengers and declared, as before, that he desired no other harmony than that which had existed between Pope Eugenius and us. We refused this, in the aforesaid fashion, and, in the presence of all the German and Lombard bishops and lay princes and barons and vavasors, bearing witness thereto, we offered full justice or arbitration, so that we should ourselves receive justice. There were present on that occasion the envoys of the citizens of Rome, who were amazed and indignant at what they heard. For

his quae audierunt. Mandavit enim papa nova et gravia et numquam prius audita, quae sine consilio tuo et aliorum fidelium imperii pertractari non possunt. Haec disretioni tuae communicavimus, ut, si qua tibi super his occurrerint, nosse veritatem non sit inutile. Rogamus etiam, ut, si necesse fuerit et nos tibi mandaverimus, ad nos pro tanto negotio venire non differas.

3
William of Newburgh, *Historia rerum Anglicarum,* ii. 6

Chronicles of the Reigns of Stephen, Henry II, and Richard I, ed. R. G. Howlett, RS 82/i–ii (1884–5), i, 109–12.

William was a life-long member of the Augustinian priory of Newburgh in Yorkshire ,which had close connexions not only with Bridlington from which its own first members came in 1142–3 (when they were settled at Hood) but also with the great Cistercian monastery of Byland, and with the Mowbray family, who supported both.

Quomodo Nicholaus Anglicus factus est papa Romanus

Sane anno primo Regis Henrici secundi obiit Anastasius papa,[69] successor Eugenii, cum fuisset pontifex anni unius. Cui successit Nicholaus Albanensis episcopus, mutans nomen cum omine, dictusque est Adrianus. De quo dicendum est quomodo tanquam de pulvere elevatus sit, ut sederet in medio principum, et Apostolicae teneret solium gloriae. Is enim, natione Anglicus, patrem habuit clericum quondam non multae facultatis, qui, relicto cum seculo impubere filio, apud Sanctam Albanum factus est monachus. Ille vero adolescentiam ingressus, cum propter inopiam scholis vacare non posset, idem monasterium quotidianae stipis gratia frequentabat. Unde pater erubuit, verbisque mordacibus socordiam eius increpitans, omni solatio destitutum cum gravi indignatione abegit. Ille vero sibi relictus, et forte necessitate aliquid audere coactus, Gallicanas adiit regiones, ingenue erubescens in Anglia vel fodere vel mendicare. Cumque in Francia minus prosperaretur, ad remotiora progrediens, trans Rhodanum peregrinatus est in regione quae Provincia dicitur. Est autem in illa regione monasterium nobile regularum clericorum, quod dicitur, Sancti Rufi, ad quem locum ille veniens, et subsistendi occasionem ibidem inveniens, quibus potuit obsequiis eisdem se fratribus commendare curavit. Et quoniam erat corpore elegans, vultu iocundus, prudens in verbis, ad iniuncta impiger, placuit omnibus: rogatusque canonici ordinis suscipere habitum, annis plurimis ibidem resedit, regularis inter primos disciplinae aemulator. Cumque esset acris ingenii et linguae expeditae, frequenti et studiosa lectione ad scientiam atque eloquentiam multum profecit.[70] Unde factum est ut abbate defuncto fratres eum

[69] 1153–4.
[70] See Christoph Egger, above, ch. 2, at nn. 2–3.

the pope made new and serious and hitherto unheard-of demands, which cannot be discussed without your counsel and that of the others loyal to the empire. These we have communicated to your discretion, so that you may know the facts—which may be of value in case reports of these matters should reach you. We ask also that, if it should be necessary, and if we summon you on so grave a matter, you will come to us without delay.

3
William of Newburgh, *History of English Affairs,* ii. 6

Indeed, William dedicated his History of English Affairs *to Ernald, abbot of Rievaulx, another great Cistercian monastery in Yorkshire. Although composed in the last years of the twelfth century (c. 1196–8), its importance for the story of the English pope lies in the possibility that as a member of the same canonical order (Saint-Ruf was a congregation of Augustinian canons regular) its author may have had access to information not generally known in England.*

How Nicholas the Englishman was made Roman Pontiff

In the first year of the reign of King Henry II, Pope Anastasius,[69] successor of Eugenius, died when he had been pope for one year. Nicholas, bishop of Albano, succeeded him, and, changing his name with his fortune, he was called Adrian. It should be explained that he was raised as if from the dust to sit in the midst of princes and to occupy the throne of apostolic glory. For, English by race, he had a certain clerk of no great skill as his father, who, after abandoning his young son, together with the world, was made a monk at St Albans. Since he [Nicholas], on the threshold of adolescence, was not able to attend the schools because of poverty, he haunted the same monastery for the sake of daily handouts. His father was embarrassed because of this, reproaching his sloth with biting words; denied all solace, he went away very indignantly. But, left to his own devices and forced by necessity to take a risk, he went to the regions of Gaul, being embarrassed, as a freeborn man, either to dig or to beg in England. And when he failed to prosper in France, going into remoter regions, he travelled across the Rhone to the region called Provence. There is in that area a noble monastery of canons regular called Saint-Ruf, to which place he came and, finding there an opportunity of subsistence, he took care to commend himself to the brethren there by whatever services he could. And because he was handsome of body, smiling of face, prudent in words, and swift to carry out instructions, he pleased everyone; and having been asked to accept the habit of the canonical order, he remained there for many years, among the leading followers of the regular discipline. And since he was of quick mind and ready tongue, he made great strides in learning and eloquence by regular and careful study.[70] Thus it happened that when the abbot died, the brethren

concorditer atque sollemniter in patrem eligerent. Quibus cum aliquamdiu praefuisset, poenitentia ducti atque indignati quod hominem peregrinum levassent super capita sua, facti sunt ei de cetero infidi atque infesti. Odiis itaque paulatim
crudescentibus, ut iam graviter aspicerent in quo sibi paulo ante tam bene complacuerat, tandem confectis et propositis contra eum capitulis ad sedem Apostolicam
provocarunt. Piae autem memoriae Eugenius,[71] qui tunc arcem pontificii tenebat,
cum rebellium filiorum contra patrem querelas audisset, et eius pro se allegantis
prudentiam modestiamque adverteret, paci inter eos reformandae efficacem operam dedit, multumque improperans et saepius inculcans utrique parti, ut partes
esse desinerent et unitatem spiritus in vinculo pacis servarent, reconciliatos ad
propria remisit. At non diu quievit nescia quietis malitia, grandiusque intonuit
rediviva tempestas. Interpellatus est iterum idem venerabilis pontifex, cuius iam
aures fratrum illorum querelis et susurriis tinnebant. Utrique ergo parti pie et prudenter prospiciens: 'Scio', inquit, 'fratres, ubi sit sedes sit Sathanae: scio quid in
vobis suscitet procellam istam. Ite, eligite vobis patrem, cum quo pacem habere
possitis, vel potius velitis; iste enim non erit vobis ulterius oneri.' Itaque dimissis
fratribus abbatem in beati Petri obsequio retinens, Albanensem ordinavit episcopum, ac non multo post, sumptis industriae eius experimentis, in gentes ferocissimas Dacorum et Norrensium cum plentitudine potestatis direxit legatum. Quo
ille officio in barbaris nationibus per annos aliquot sapienter et strenue adminis-
trato, Romam cum salute et gaudio remeavit; susceptusque a summo pontifice et
cardinalibus cum honore et gloria, evolutis diebus non multis, Anastasio qui
Eugenio successerat decedente, omnium in eum votis concurrentibus, Romanae
urbis pontificatum suscepit, ex Nicholao Adrianus. Qui nimirum suorum non immemor rudimentorum, ob paternam maxime memoriam, beati martyris Albani
ecclesiam et donariis honoravit, et perpetuis insignivit privilegiis.

---

[71] 1145–53.

unanimously and solemnly elected him as their father. When he had ruled them for some time, they became regretful and angry that they had raised a wayfarer over their heads, and they became thenceforth disloyal and rebellious. And so, as the hatred slowly grew, they looked askance at the man with whom slightly before they had been so pleased; finally, having constructed and drawn up complaints against him, they appealed him to the Apostolic See. But when Eugenius of pious memory,[71] who was then holding the pinnacle of the pontifical office, heard the complaints of the rebellious sons against their father, and observed the prudence and restraint of his arguments in defence, he strove to establish true peace between them, and often reproaching and more often impressing on both sides that they should cease to be divided and maintain a unified spirit in the bond of peace, he sent them back reconciled to their own place. But ignorant malice was not peaceful for long and the storm rekindled thundered forth more loudly. The same venerable pontiff was again approached and his ears were soon ringing with the whisperings and complaints of those brethren. Therefore, gazing piously and wisely at both parties, he said, 'I know, brothers, where Satan has his seat; I know what is raising up this storm among you. Go, elect yourselves a father with whom you will be able to have peace, or one who is more pleasing to you; for this man will no longer be a burden to you.' And so, having dismissed the brethren, retaining the abbot in the service of St Peter, he ordained him bishop of Albano, and not long afterwards, having had experience of his hard work, he sent him as legate with full power to the wild people of Denmark and Norway. Having wisely and effectively carried out his office for some years among the barbarous peoples, he returned to Rome safely and joyfully; and having been received by the supreme pontiff and cardinals with honour and glory, after not many days, when Anastasius who had succeeded Eugenius died, he received the pontificate of the Roman City by unanimous vote, from Nicholas becoming Adrian. Not unmindful of his origins, he honoured the church of the blessed martyr Alban with grants, especially in memory of his father, and distinguished it with perpetual privileges.

4
Godfrey of Viterbo, *Gesta Friderici I*

From *Gotifredi Viterbiensis Gesta Friderici I. et Heinrici VI. imperatorum metrice scripta*, ed. G. H. Pertz, *MGH SRG* 30 (Hanover, 1870), 10–11, cc. 10–12

Godfrey of Viterbo, born in the city from which he took his name, was a life-long member of the imperial court. Recruited by Lothar III in 1133, he had been educated at Bamberg and served as notary and priest-chaplain until the reign of Frederick's son, Henry VI. His name appears among the witnesses of Frederick I's ratification of the Accord of Constance (1153), for example, and he travelled extensively with the imperial court, especially in Italy.

10. *De initio discordie inter papam Adrianum et imperatorem Fridericum.*

> Cesar ut in patriam vexilla retorsit ab Urbe,
> Grandis et orribilis discordia crevit in orbe;
> > Pax perit aecclesiae: scismatis error adest.
> Federe connexus fuerat cum cesare papa:
> Si foret interdum pars altera forte gravata,
> > Altera subveniat: stent ea pacta rata.
> Absque pari voto cui consensisset uterque,
> Nullum pacis opus Grecis pars altera prestet;
> > Sic neque cum Siculis pax agitanda fuit.
> Federe corrupto, quo fertur papa teneri,
> Migrat in Apuliam; vult cesaris hostis habeni.
> > Pactio nostra perit, Grecus amicus erit.
> Hostibus imperii presul Romanus adhesit;
> Federa dat Siculis, paniter dat federa Grecis:
> > Fit modo materies mortis et hora necis.

11. *De discordia et divisione omnium cardinalium*
    ubi pars erat cum papa, pars erat cum imperatore.

> Scinditur aecciesia: pars altera pacta recusat,
> Munera despiciunt, et federa Greca refutat;
> > Cesaris auxilia pars retinere putat.
> Hac in parte manus misit prior Octavianus,
> Guidoque Cremanusi, vir nobilis et veterannus,
> > Et reliqui secum scismata longa petunt.
> Pars monocratorem pleno fovet ista favore.
> Papa suo more werram movet in regione;
> > Sic et aput Ligures pacta nociva movet.
> Pactio qualis erat, satis hic describere possem.
> Parco tamen dictis, ne forte pericla reportent.
> > Sit satis asserere, pacta nociva fore.

4
Godfrey of Viterbo, *Deeds of the Emperor Frederick I*

Although Godfrey's account of papal-imperial affairs was dependent on Otto of Freising and Rahewin (no. 2, above), and clearly reflects the imperial bias of the author and his sources, the poem was revised c. 1181—that is, after Frederick's reconciliation with Alexander III and the ending of the papal schism (peace of Venice, 1177). Godfrey's condemnation of Pope Adrian thus reflects the radically changed political circumstances of the early 1180s. Since Alexander III and the emperor are now friends, Adrian is made the scapegoat for the schism, and the rebellion of the Lombard League is soft-pedalled.

10. *The beginning of discord between Pope Adrian and Emperor Frederick.*

As Caesar withdrew his banner from the City to his homeland,
Great and terrible discord erupted throughout the world;
     The Church's peace perishes; the uncertainty of schism is at hand.
The pope had bound himself to Caesar with a bond:
If in the meanwhile either should be oppressed,
     Each is to assist the other: the pact confirmed stands.
Without an equal desire to which each should consent,
The other makes no undertaking of peace with the Greeks;
     Nor was peace to be discussed with the Sicilians.
Breaking the peace by which the pope was held to be bound,
He goes into Apulia; he wishes to be regarded as an enemy of Caesar.
     Our agreement collapses, he will be the Greeks' friend.
To the enemies of the empire the Roman bishop clings;
He offers treaties to the Sicilians, and equally grants compacts to the Greeks:
     Now is the cause of death and the hour of slaughter.

11. *Discord and division of all the cardinals,*
     where one part was with the pope, and one with the emperor.

The Church is divided; one part rejects the pacts,
They despise the gifts, and reject the Greek treaties;
     It considers retaining the emperor's support.
Octavian was the first to support this party,
And Guido of Crema, a noble and mature man,
     And the rest with him seek a protracted schism.
One part supports the tyrant with full favour.
The pope in his usual fashion provokes war in the area;
     And so he inspires harmful agreements with the Ligurians.
What kind of pact it was, I should be able to describe enough here.
But I pass over the words lest they bring danger.
     Suffice it to say that the pacts will be harmful.

12. *De morte pape Adriani in Campania.*

   Ad sua Campana dum predia papa rediret
   Et gelidos fontes modicum spatiatus adiret,
      Impenio varias intulit ore minas.
   Qua iacet astricta nullo medicamine victa,
   Colla tument, moritur, werra pro pace relicta;
      Nam caput orribilis scismatis ipse fuit.

12. *The Death of Pope Adrian in the Campagna.*

    As the pope returns to his estate of Campagna
    And grandly comes to cool springs,
        He uttered various threats against the empire.
    Wherefore he lies constricted, overthrown, without medicine,
    His neck swells, he dies, having left war in place of peace;
        For he himself was the grizzly head of schism.

5a
Giraldus Cambrensis, *Speculum ecclesiae*, li. 30

From *Giraldi Cambrensis Opera*, i–iv, ed. J. S. Brewer, RS 21/iv (1873), 94–6.

Gerald de Barri, 'of Wales' (1146–1223), archdeacon of Brecon, a highly educated clerk of mixed Norman and Welsh descent (through his mother Angharad he was a grandson of Gerald of Windsor and Nest, daughter of Rhys ap Tewdwr) was a prolific writer and indefatigable traveller. In 1185 he accompanied John, Henry II's son to Ireland; he travelled in 1188 to Wales with Archbishop Baldwin of Canterbury in support of the Third Crusade, and made several journeys to Rome.

De monasterio S. Albani per superbiam opulentiae filiam nostris diebus exempto, et duobus aliis in Anglia similiter prius exemptis.

Adiiciendum hic quoque de monasteriis egregiis, S. Albani scilicet et S. Edmundi, et de Westmonasterio Londoniis S. Petri, quae quidem inter Anglicana coenobia, quodammodo principalia praecipuaque loca tenere videntur. Haec etenim tria, superabundantis filia, se prorsus eximere et matribus suis, Lincolniensi scilicet et Norwicensi et Londoniensi ecclesiis, debitam [per] filias reverentiam et obedientiam, superciliose se subtrahere fecit. Verum quod apud Sanctum Albanum nostris diebus accidit hic explicare praeter rem non putavi.

Cum itaque venerabilis sanctaeque recordationis Hugo Lincolniae episcopus, de carcere Carthusiensi feliciter assumptus, post consecrationem suam Londoniis factam, versus ecclesiam suam veniens, in ecclesia S. Albani per quam rediit divina celebrare vellet, prohibitus a monachis loci eiusdem fuit et non admissus. Quoniam enimvero exempti fuerant more monachorum scrupulosi nimis existentes, et ubi metus non erat meticulosi, praeiudicium iuri suo fieri, si Lincolniae episcopus in ecclesia sua divina celebraret vel audiret, minus discrete suspiciari praesumpserunt. Episcopus autem accepta post consecrationem suam ea injuria prima, ad ecclesiam suam veniens, postquam ibidem cum honore debito susceptus a clero et populo et incathedratus fuit, habita cum fratribus et maioribus ac maturioribus ecclesiae suae super hoc dedecore deliberatione, statuit ut nusquam dicti monasterii monachi per episcopatum suum totum, qui magnus est et amplus valde, vii. scilicet comitatus et dimidium tenens, in quibus etiam ecclesias plurimas et terras habent, ad divina celebrandum vel audiendum admitterentur. Statuit etiam ut in tanto totius dioecesis suae spatio nusquam per loca transeuntes hospitio susciperentur; nec in emptione, venditione, seu permutione, aliove contractu quolibet, quisquam eis sub anathematis interminatione communicare praesumeret. Audientes haec autem abbas et monachi praedicti videntes etiam et animis anxie ferentes quod tanquam ethnici et publicani dictis in locis omnibus sunt habiti et fidelium communione vitati, scientes quoque quod neque scandalum hoc tantum, neque rei familiaris damnum diu sustinere valebant, poenitentia ducti ad dictum episcopum quam citius poterant accelerarunt, et ad pedes ipsius humiliter prostrati culpamque suam confessi, ad nutum eiusdem satisfacientes, veniam pariter et

Gerald of Wales, *Mirror of the Church*, li. 30

Gerald's contacts at the royal court, in Paris, Lincoln (where he stayed in the 1190s), and Rome, are all reflected in his extensive writings, to all of which he brought considerable erudition and powerfully-held opinions. The Speculum Ecclesiae *or* Mirror of the Church, *composed just after 1216, is a general satirical attack on monks, but the particular venom of his attack on papal privileges of exemption for monasteries reflects his friendship with Bishop Hugh of Lincoln.*

Concerning the monastery of St Albans exempted in our days as a result of pride in its wealth and two others in England, similarly exempted before.

We should add something here about the distinguished monasteries of St Albans, St Edmund's, and St Peter's at Westminster in London, which seem to hold the principal and most distinguished place among the English monasteries. For these three, by pride, by love of excessive wealth, have freed themselves and arrogantly withdrawn from their mothers, the churches of Lincoln, Norwich, and London, the reverence and obedience owed by daughters to their mothers. Indeed I have not considered it irrelevant to describe here what happened in our time at St Albans.

When the venerable bishop Hugh of Lincoln, of holy memory, happily raised from the prison of Chartreuse, was coming to his own church after his consecration at London and wished to celebrate divine office in the church of St Albans, by way of which he returned, he was prevented by the monks of the place and not admitted. Because they had indeed been exempted, as is the way with monks, they were excessively fussy, and, fearful where there was no need to fear, with lack of judgment they presumed to suspect that their rights would be prejudiced if the bishop of Lincoln celebrated or heard divine office in their church. The bishop, however, having accepted that first injury after his consecration, coming to his own church, after he had been received there with due honour by the clergy and people and enthroned, after discussing this dishonour with his brethren and with the older and more important members of his church, he decreed that no monks from the said monastery were to be admitted to celebrate or hear divine office throughout his whole bishopric, which is very large and extensive, comprising seven and a half counties, in which they have many churches and estates. He also decreed that none of them throughout the whole area of his diocese should receive hospitality as they travelled through it; nor in buying or selling or exchanging, or any other kind of contract, should anyone presume under threat of anathema to communicate with them. Hearing and seeing these things, however, and troubled in mind that in all these places they were regarded as heathens and Publicans and shut out from the communion of the faithful, knowing also that they could not long sustain either so great a scandal or injury to their own affairs, the aforesaid abbot and monks hurried as quickly as they could under the impulse of repentance to the said bishop; humbly prostrate at his feet, confessing their fault and making

misericordiam impetrarunt. Et sic quoniam frangit Deus omnem superbum, et quoniam superbis resistit Deus humilibus autem dat gratiam, communionis gratiam quam per elationis tumorem amiserunt, per humilitatis antidotum et mitis animi medicinale remedium, recuperarunt.

Notandum hic autem quod nostris diebus, Adriano papa, qui proximus ante Alexandrum III erat, papatum regente, qui Anglicus fuit et apud S. Albanum originem duxit, abbas et monachi loci eiusdem exemptionem ab ipso confidentius impetrarunt. Et quoniam papam, causa localis originis favorabilem magisque propitium in cunctis agendis suis, cunctisque petendis aut etiam non petendis invenerunt, ut etiam de monachis suis tam archidiaconos facerent, quos et sic nuncuparent, qui clericis terrarum suarum praeessent, capitulaque tenerent, et litibus ac causis ventilandis et decidendis operam darent, quam senescallos quoque ad laicalia negotia tractandum et saeculares causas audiendum et dirimendum, obtinuerunt; cum tamen clamat apostolus quia nemo militans Domino saecularibus negotiis se debeat implicare.

[There follows a diatribe about monks in general and St Albans in particular.]

satisfaction according to his will, they obtained pardon and mercy. And thus does God shatter every proud man, and because God opposes the proud and gives grace to the humble, they recovered the grace of communion, which they had lost through the tumour of pride by the antidote of humility and the healing remedy of a gentle soul.

At this point it should be noted, however, that in our days, while Pope Adrian, who was English and originated from St Albans, was presiding over the papacy last before Alexander III, the abbot and monks of that place very confidently received exemption from him. And since they found the pope, on account of his place of origin, favourable and particularly generous towards all their actions and all their petitions, or even what they did not ask, they obtained the right to appoint monks both as archdeacons, with that title, who preside over the clergy of their estates, and hold chapters and engage in law suits and in the presentation and deciding of cases, and also as stewards to handle secular business and to hear and decide secular cases, although the Apostle declares that no one fighting for the Lord should involve himself in secular affairs.

[There follows a diatribe about monks in general and St Albans in particular.]

5b
Giraldus Cambrensis, *Expugnatio Hibernica*, ii. 5

From *Expugnatio Hibernica. The Conquest of Ireland by Giraldus Cambrensis*, ed. and trans. A. B. Scott and F. X. Martin, Irish Medieval Texts, 1 (Dublin, 1978), 142–9.

The Expugnatio Hibernica (Conquest of Ireland), *written in the last year of Henry II's life (1188–9) equally reflected his particular outlook. Gerald was closely related to the Geraldines, who played a significant rôle in the invasion; and the theme of his work is the prophetic and providential nature of the Angevin/Cambro-Norman acquisition of Ireland. . Both his assertion that Henry II was acting on the authority of a bull issued by Adrian IV (*Laudabiliter*) *and his text are highly suspect, and the Alexandrine bull is a fake. See above, ch. 6, part iv.*

Privilegiorum impetratio.

Interea quamquam marciis plurimum intentus et detentus exerciciis, Anglorum rex, sue tamen inter agendum Hibernie non immemor, cum prenotatis spurciciarum litteris in sinodo Cassiliensi per indusrtiam quesitis directis ad curiam Romanam nunciis, ab Alexandro tercio tunc presidente privilegium impetravit, eiusdem auctoritate simul et assensu, Hibernico populo tam dominandi quam ipsum, in fidei rudimentis incultissimum, ecclesiasticis normis et disciplinis iuxta Anglicane ecclesie mores informandi. In Hiberniam itaque transmissio per Nicolaum Gualingefordensem tunc priorem, Malmesburiensem quoque postmodum abbatem tam positum quam depositum, necnon et Guillelmum Aldelini filium, convocata statim apud Guaterfordiam episcoporum sinodo, in publica audiencia eiusdem privilegii cum universitatis assensu sollemnis recitacio facta fuit; necnon et alterius privilegii per eosdem transmissi, quod idem rex ab Adriano papa Alexandri decessore antea perquisierat per Iohannem Salesberiensem, postmodum episcopum Karnotensem, Romam ad hoc destinatum. Per quem etiam idem papa Anglorum regi annulum aureum in investiture signum presentavit, qui statim cum privilegia in archivis Guintonie repositus fuerat. Unde et utriusque privilegii tenorem hic interserere non superflum reputavi. Erat itaque primi et primo impetrati tenor hic.

Privilegium Adriani Pape.

Adrianus episcopus, seruus servorum Dei, carissimo in Christo filio illustri Anglorum regi, salutem et apostolicam benedictionem.

Laudabiliter satis et fructuose de glorioso nomine propagando in terris et eterne felicitatis premio cumulando in celis tua magnificencia cogitat, dum ad dilatandos ecclesie terminos, ad declarandam indoctis et rudibus populis Christiane fidei veritatem et viciorum plantaria de agro Dominico extirpanda, sicut

5b
Gerald of Wales, *The Conquest of Ireland*, ii. 5

His account of the impetration of papal privileges is followed immediately by a chapter, ii. 6, on the fivefold right of English kings in Ireland, which culminates 'As well as all this there is the added weight of the authority of the supreme pontiffs....' Laudabiliter and its supposititious confirmation by Alexander III (Quoniam ea) were thus crucial to Gerald's presentation of the Irish conquest as a noble and just undertaking.

The Procuring of the Privileges.

Meanwhile, although the English king was very much preoccupied and his attention was detained by military matters, yet even in the midst of all this essential business he did not forget his realm of Ireland. Accordingly he sent messengers to the Roman *curia* with the aforesaid letters giving an account of abuses, letters which he had been careful to ask for at the synod of Cashel. He thereupon obtained from the then Pope Alexander III a privilege empowering him, with the pope's full authority and consent, to rule over the Irish people and, as it was very ignorant of the rudiments of the faith, to instruct it in the laws and disciplines of the church according to the usage of the church in England. So the privilege was conveyed to Ireland by William FitzAldelin and Nicholas, then prior of Wallingford, who later became abbot of Malmesbury and was deposed from that office. An episcopal synod was immediately convened at Waterford, and the privilege was formally read in public session and received with approval by the assembled company. They also read out the other privilege which had been conveyed by the aforesaid, and which the king had formerly procured from Alexander's predecessor Adrian through the offices of John of Salisbury, afterwards bishop of Chartres, who had been sent to Rome for this purpose. By John's hand the aforesaid Pope Adrian also sent the king of England the present of a gold ring as a sign of his investiture, and this had been immediately deposited along with the privilege in the archives at Winchester. I have therefore considered it not irrelevant to include at this point the contents of both these privileges. The first of these, being the first to be procured, ran as follows:

Privilege of Pope Adrian.

Adrian, bishop, servant of the servants of God, to his dearest son in Christ the illustrious king of the English, greeting and apostolic blessing.

In right praiseworthy fashion, and to good purpose, your magnificence is considering how to spread abroad the glorious name of Christ[*] on earth, and thus store up for yourself in heaven the reward of eternal bliss, while striving as a true

---

[*] So translated in *Expugnatio*, ed. Scott and Martin, but the word 'Christ' is not found in the Latin text.

catholicus princeps intendis; et ad id conveniencius exequendum consilium apostolice sedis exigis et favorem. In quo facto quanto altiori consilio et maiori discrecione procedis tanto in eo feliciorem progressum te, prestante Domino, confidimus habiturum, eo quod ad bonum exitum semper et finem soleant attingere que de ardore fidei et religionis amore principium acceperunt. Sane Hiberniam et omnes insulas quibus sol iusticie Christus illuxit, et que documenta fidei Christiane ceperunt, ad ius beati Petri et sacrosancte Romane ecclesie, quod tua etiam nobilitas recognoscit, non est dubium pertinere. Unde tanto in eis libencius plantacionem fidelem et germen gratum Deo inserimus quanto id a nobis interno examine districtius prospicimus exigendum. Significasti siquidem nobis, fili in Christo carissime, te Hibernie insulam ad subdendum illum populum legibus et uiciorum plantaria inde extirpanda velle intrare, et de singulis domibus annuam unius denarii beato Petro velle solvere pensionem, et iura ecclesiarum illius terre illibata et integra conservare. Nos itaque pium et laudabile desiderium tuum cum favore congruo prosequentes, et peticioni tue benignum impendentes assensum, gratum et acceptum habemus ut pro dilatandis ecclesie terminis, pro viciorum restringendo decursu, pro corrigendis moribus et virtutibus inserendis, pro Christiane religionis augmento, insulam illam ingrediaris et que ad honorem Dei et salutem illius terre spectaverint exequaris, et illius terre populus honorifice te recipiat et sicut dominum veneretur; iure nimirum ecclesiarum illibato et integro permanente, et salva beato Petro et sacrosancte Romane ecclesie de singulis domibus annua unius denarii pensione. Si ergo quod concepisti animo effectu duxeris prosequente complendum, stude gentem illam bonis moribus informare, et agas tam per te quam per illos quos ad hoc fide, verbo et vita idoneos esse prospexeris, ut decoretur ibi ecclesia, plantetur et crescat fidei Christiane religio, et que ad honorem Dei et salutem pertinent animarum per te taliter ordinentur ut a Deo sempiterne mercedis cumulum consequi merearis, et in terris gloriosum nomen valeas in seculis obtinere.

Catholic prince should, to enlarge the boundaries of the Church, to reveal the truth of the Christian faith to peoples still untaught and barbarous, and to root out the weeds of vice from the Lord's field; and the more expeditiously to achieve this end, you seek the counsel and favour of the Apostolic See. We are confident that in this matter, with God's help, you will attain that degree of success which is in proportion to the loftiness of your aims and the amount of discretion you display as you proceed with them. For enterprises which have their starting point in burning faith and love of religion are always ultimately successful in achieving their goal. That Ireland, and indeed all islands on which Christ, the sun of justice, has shed His rays, and which have received the teaching of the Christian faith, belong to the jurisdiction of blessed Peter and the holy Roman church is a fact beyond doubt, and one which your nobility recognizes. So we are all the more eager to implant in those islands the offshoot of faith, an offshoot pleasing to God, as we realize that an examination of our own heart sternly requires of us that we should take this action. You have indeed indicated to us, dearly beloved son in Christ, that you wish to enter this island of Ireland, to make that people obedient to the laws, and to root out from there the weeds of vices, that you are willing to pay St Peter the annual tax of one penny from each household, and to preserve the rights of the churches of that land intact and unimpaired. We therefore support your pious and praiseworthy intention with the favour which it deserves and, granting our benevolent consent, we consider it pleasing and acceptable that you should enter that island for the purpose of enlarging the boundaries of the church, checking the descent into wickedness, correcting morals and implanting virtues, and encouraging the growth of the faith of Christ; that you pursue policies directed towards the honour of God and the well-being of that land, and that the people of that land receive you honourably and respect you as their lord, all this being on condition that the rights of the churches remain intact and unimpaired, and without prejudice to the payment to St Peter and the holy Roman church of an annual tax of one penny from every household. Therefore if you wish to bring to a successful conclusion the design which you have thus conceived, take particular care to instruct that people in right behaviour and, both in person, and acting through those whom you consider well-suited for this purpose by reason of their strong faith, eloquence and pure lives, take action to ensure that the church there may be enhanced, that the Christian religion may be planted and grow, and that everything pertaining to the honour of God and the salvation of men's souls may be so ordered that you may be deemed worthy to win from God that crowning reward of everlasting life, and may obtain on earth a glorious name for all ages.

6a
Matthew Paris, *Historia Anglorum*

From *Matthaei Parisiensis, monachi sancti Albani, Historia Anglorum*, ed. F. Madden, 3 vols, RS 44 (London, 1866–69), i (1866), 299, 304, 310.

*One of the most prolific, entertaining, and controversial chroniclers of thirteenth-century England, Matthew Paris (c. 1200–59) inherited and continued the historiographical tradition of St Albans.**

1. *De papa Adriano nato apud Sanctum Albanum*

1154. Anno quoque sub eodem, defuncto papa Anastasio, successit ei Nicholaus, Albanensis episcopus, et creatus in papam vocatus est Adrianus; vir quidem religious et natione Anglicus, de territorio quidem Sancti Albani procreatus. Qui postea ecclesiae Sancti Albani, licet antea multis privilegiis insigniretur, multa contulit libertatum insignia et exeniorum beneficia. [cf. Roger of Wendover, ii, 272]

2. *1155. Papa Adrianus insulam Hybernie regi Anglorum Henrico dedit*

Per idem tempus rex Anglorum Henricus nuncios sollempnes Roman mittens, rogavit papam Adrianum, ut sibi liceret, sine scandalo laesionis fidei Christianae, Hiberniae insulam intrare, et terram illam, locum videlicet horroris et vastae solitudinis, utpote limbum mundi, sibi et Dei cultui subjugare; atque homines illos bestiales ad fidem et viam reducere veritatis et obedientiam ecclesiae Romanae. Quod papa regi gratanter annuens, hoc ei privilegium destinavit. [A version of *Laudabiliter* follows, for which see above, no. 5b] [cf. Roger of Wendover, ii, 281]

3. *1159. Scisma ortum est inter duos papas*

Eodem anno defuncto papa Adriano, qui Anglicus fuit natione, et de Sancto Albano oriundus, scisma oritur inter duos, Alexandrum et Octovianum. Nam imperator cum clero suo receperat Octovianum, sed a regibus Francorum et Anglorum consensum est in Alexandrum. Imperator autem ad dictos reges literas direxit, ut Octovianum reciperent, sed ipsis contradicentibus, Alexander papatum optinuit.

---

* Vaughan, *Matthew Paris*, 78–91, 182–9.

6a
Matthew Paris, *History of the English*

His History of the English *was abridged from his much more extensive* Chronica majora *c. 1256–9, but the* Chronica *was itself much dependent on the* Flores historiarum *of his predecessor Roger of Wendover For the complex inter-relationship between his various works and their sources, see Richard Vaughan,* Matthew Paris *Cambridge Studies in Medieval Life and Thought, 2nd ser. 6 (Cambridge, 1958; reiss. 1979), esp. 107, 123.*

1. *Concerning Pope Adrian who was born at St Albans*

1154. In the same year, when Pope Anastasius died, Nicholas, bishop of Albano succeeded to him and was called Adrian after his appointment as pope; he was a religious of English race, born on an estate of St Albans. Although it had already been distinguished by many privileges, he bestowed many conspicuous marks of liberty and the favour of many gifts.

2. *1155. Pope Adrian gave the island of Ireland to the king of the English*

At about the same time, Henry king of the English, sending special envoys to Rome, asked Pope Adrian to allow him to enter the island of Ireland, without the scandal of damaging the Christian faith, and subject that land—a place of dread and desolate deprivation, on the very edge of the world—to himself and to the cult of God; and to bring those bestial men back to the faith and lead them to the path of truth and obedience to the Roman church. Graciously allowing this to the king, the pope sent this privilege to him. [The text of *Laudabiliter* follows, for which see above, no. 5b.]

3. *1159. A schism arose between two popes*

In the same year, on the death of Pope Adrian, who was English by race and risen from St Albans, a schism arose between Alexander and Octavian. For the emperor and his clergy had received Octavian, but the English and French kings agreed on Alexander. The emperor, however, sent letters to the said kings to receive Octavian, but when they refused, Alexander secured the papacy.

6b
Matthew Paris, *Gesta abbatum S. Albani*

The most easily accessible text of the Gesta abbatum, *compiled by Matthew Paris in the 1240s and 1250s, is the revised and extended version made by Thomas Walsingham in* c. *1394 (London, BL, Cotton MS, Claudius E. iv, fols 98–171v), from which derives the Rolls Series edn,* Gesta abbatum...a Thoma Walsingham ...compilata, *3 vols, in* Chronica monasterii S. Albani, *ed. H. T. Riley, 12 vols in 7, RS 28 (London, 1863–76), 4/i–iii (1867–9); but the better text, based on Matthew's autograph (London, BL, Cotton MS, Nero D. i, fols 30–68v), is still the seventeenth-century printing,* Vitae Viginti Trium Abbatum S. Albani *in* Matthaei Paris Monachi Albanensis Angli, Historia Major, *ed. William Wats (A. Mearne, T. Dring, B. Tooke, G. Sawbridge, G. Wells: London, 1639, repr. 1683), 989–1074.[72] This edition is used here, with cross-references to the* Gesta abbatum.

1. *De origine Adriani papae*

Hujus quoque tempore, quidam clericus, nomine Nicholaus, de quodam viculo Abbatis, scilicet, Langele, oriundus, cognomento 'Brekespere', in arte clericali satis supinus, aetate adolescens, corpore elegans, venit ad Abbatem Robertum, postulans humiliter habitum sibi concedi religionis. Qui cum examinatus et insufficiens inveniretur, dixit ei abbas satis civiliter, 'Expecta, fili, et adhuc scholam mmmexerce, ut aptior habearis.' Unde ipse clericus, verecundus, reputans talem dilationem repulsam, abiit, et Parisius adiens, ubi scholaris vigilantissimus effectus, omnes socios discendo superavit. Tandem canonicus factus, apud Sanctum Rufum, non procul a Valentia, Romam pro quibusdam agendis destinatus, strenue negotium consummavit, et iterum melius; et tertio missus, electus est in cardinalem, et postea in papam (ed. Wats, 1016; ed. Riley, i, 112–13).

2. *Adrianus Papa*

Paucos post hos dies, obiit papa Anastasius, cui Nicholaus, tunc episcopus Albanensis, successit, vocatus deinde 'Adrianus Quartus'. Vir quidem religiosus, et natione Anglicus, qui fuerat prius abbas canonicorum Sancti Rufi in Provincia. Et quia non videtur penitus alienum a materia mea, de serie vitae eius summam opusculo huic duximus interserere (ed. Wats, 1019; ed. Riley, i, 124).

3. *De papa Adriano*

Hic Nicholaus, de quo praelibavimus paucula, filius fuit cuiusdam Roberti de Camera** qui, honeste vivens in saeculo, litteratus aliquantulum, habitum religionis in domo Sancti Albani suscepit, et filium suum, memoratum Nicholaum, clericum et scholarem in claustrum attrahere volens, interpellavit abbatem pro

---

[72]   R. M. Thomson, *Manuscripts from St Albans Abbey 1066–1235*, 2 vols (Tasmania/Woodbridge, 1982), i, 3.

6b
Matthew Paris, *Deeds of the Abbots of St Albans*

Although compiled in the mid-thirteenth century, Matthew Paris's Gesta abbatum
sancti Albani *drew on earlier St Albans' tradition and records. His principal
source was the lost* rotulus *of Adam the Cellarer, perhaps written by his clerk Bartholomew, contained information about the abbey's history down to the death of
Robert de Gorron in 1166, the abbot who secured so many privileges from Pope
Adrian. But Matthew also had access to the monastery's impressive muniments, to
which he referred as occasion demanded, as well as to the active oral tradition of
the monastic community. At the same time, of course, Matthew was a lively raconteur; and it is not easy to differentiate between solid tradition, whether oral or
written, and the elaborations of a well informed but opinionated story-teller.*[*]

1. *Concerning the origins of Pope Adrian*

At this time, a certain clerk called Nicholas, from a certain hamlet of the abbot,
that is, Langley, with the surname Brekespere, a handsome youth, fairly backward
in clerical skills, came to Abbot Robert humbly asking for the religious habit to be
conferred upon him. When he was found upon examination to be inadequate, the
abbot said to him courteously enough, 'Wait, my son, and work further at school,
so that you may be better prepared.' Therefore the clerk, ashamed, considering
such delay to be rejection, went away and, going to Paris, he became a most assiduous student and surpassed all his associates in learning. At length, having been
made a canon at Saint-Ruf, not far from Valence; sent to Rome for certain business, he briskly completed the commission; sent again, he did even better; dispatched a third time, he was appointed cardinal and afterwards as pope.

2. *Pope Adrian*

After these few days, Pope Anastasius died, to whom Nicholas, then bishop of
Albano, succeeded, and was thenceforward called 'Adrian IV'. A man of religion
and English by race, he had first been abbot of the canons of Saint-Ruf in
Provence. And since it does not seem to be wholly irrelevant to my theme, we
have decided to insert a summary of the course his life in this little work.

3. *About Pope Adrian*

This Nicholas, about whom we have had a little taste before, was the son of a certain Robert de Camera[**] who, living honourably in the world, moderately educated, received the habit of religion in the house of St Alban, and, wishing to draw
his son, the aforesaid Nicholas, clerk and student, into the cloister, he appealed to

---

[**] *Recte* Richard: see above ch. 1, at n. 13.

ipso, ut eundem in monachum susciperet. Abbas autem concessit, si idoneus idem Nicholaus inveniretur. Sed examinatus, insufficiens repertus est. Recessit igitur confusus Nicholaus, et abiens in Provinciam, in domo Sancti Rufi canonicus effectus est, qui postea meritis exigentibus, in eadem domo sortitus abbatis est dignitatem. Et postea cum bene per aliquot annos vixisset, et negotia domus prudenter pertractaret Romam adiit, pro quibusdam arduis suae domus negotiis expe-diendis. Et cum ipsa in curia romana efficaciter et prudenter consummasset, famosus effectus est, et cum vacasset sedes Albanensis, electus, ipsam sortitus est. Qui hic de magno maior effectus, diatim felix in omni virtute suscipiens incrementum; demum papali sede vacante, papa, post Anastasium, ut dictum est, feliciter est sublimatus.

Hic in tantum ecclesiam beati Albani dilexit, ut quicquid eiusdem ecclesiae fratres ab eo petiissent, sine difficultate consequerentur. Illius namque pater, ut praetactum est, monachus Sancti Albani quinquaginta annis, et amplius, vitam laudabiliter continuavit, et felici fine terminavit. Unde in capitulo, tum propriis, tum filii sui domini papae meritis exigentibus, meruit sepeliri, non procul a tumulo Richardi abbatis, qui postea tegulis pavimentalibus est coopertus. (*ibid.*).

4. *Abbas ad papam accedit*

Audita igitur apud nos promotione domini papae Adriani, exultans Robertus abbas ad reparandus huius ecclesiae antiquas dignitates, ad iter transalpinum accingitur, equos praeparat, impensas perquiret, exenia congregat, quae ad pretium septies viginti marcarum, praeter cyphos quinque, et mitras tres pretiosissimas, et sandalia et desirabilia, sunt aestimata. Die igitur Sancti Dionysii iter arripuit, Romam peti-turus; illius comitatui adhaerentibus tribus episcopis, Cenomannensi, Luxoviensi, et Ebroicensi. Dederat namque in mandatis rex Henricus secundus, noviter inunctus, ipsis episcopis et eidem abbati Roberto, quatenus quaedam ardua negotia regalia, de quibus non pertinet ut enarremus ad praesens, Romae expedirent. Constituit etiam rex ipsum abbatem sui negotii suum procuratorem praecipuum et summum, et confecit eis inde literas, regio sigillo signatas. In quibus humiliter et devote dominum papam deprecatus est, ut se favorabilem tam negotiis ecclesiae Sancti Albani, quam suis propriis, exhiberet, utpote patrocinatui ipsius specialiter subiacentis. Recedentes igitur ab Anglia, naves conscendunt. Intumescente autem mari, imminet periculum iam demersionis. Abbas autem, specialiter invocans auxilium beatae Margaretae, Virginis et Martyris, repentinum, et contra omnium opinionem, sensit in naufragio suffragium. Unde vovit, quod in ecclesia nomen eius in Litania poneretur propensius honorandum. Prospere igitur applicantes, et postea itinerantes, et multas latronum insidias evadentes, tandem Beneventum ubi dominum papam inveniunt, pervenerunt. Qui eos sereno vultu et animo gaudenti suscepit, et insolitum honorem exhibuit. Expediunt regalia pro libitu negotia. Remanente igitur abbate, recedunt episcopi, regi favorem papalem et diligentiam abbatis

the abbot on his behalf, to receive him as a monk. The abbot agreed, if Nicholas should be found suitable. But upon examination, he was found to be inadequate. Therefore, Nicholas withdrew in confusion and, going to Provence, he became a canon in the house of Saint-Ruf; afterwards by reason of his merits, he was elected to the dignity of abbot in the same house. And afterwards, when he had lived well for some years and had prudently discharged the business of the house, he went to Rome to expedite certain difficult matters relating to his house. And since he had effectively and prudently brought these affairs to a conclusion in the Roman Curia, he became famous; and when the see of Albano became vacant, he was elected and chosen for it. Here, from a high position he was raised higher, receiving daily increase in all the virtues; finally when the papal see was vacant, he was auspiciously raised up as pope after Anastasius, as said above.

He so loved the church of St Albans that whatever the brethren of that church petitioned from him was achieved without difficulty. For his father, as touched on above, lived his life laudably as a monk at St Albans for fifty years and more and brought it to a happy end. For this reason, on account both of his own merits and those of his son, the lord pope, he deserved to be buried in the Chapter House, not far from the tomb of Abbot Richard, which was later covered with pavement tiles.

4. *The Abbot goes to the Pope*

When the promotion of the lord pope Adrian was heard among us, Abbot Robert, rejoicing, made preparations to cross the Alps in order to restore the ancient dignities of this church; he prepared horses, gathered supplies, collected gifts to the value of 140 marks, apart from five goblets and three very valuable mitres, and sandals, and other desirable items. On the day of St Denis, therefore, he set out on his journey to go to Rome, accompanied by three bishops, of Le Mans, Lisieux and Évreux. For King Henry II, newly anointed, had sent those bishops and Abbot Robert to conduct at Rome certain difficult royal business, which it is not appropriate for us to narrate at the moment. Furthermore, the king had appointed the abbot as his primary and chief proctor and made for them letters sealed with the royal seal, in which he humbly and devoutly begged the lord pope to show himself as favourable to the business of the church of St Albans as to his own, as being specially subject to his own patronage. Leaving England, they boarded ship. But as the sea swelled up they were soon at risk of submersion. The abbot, however, particularly invoking the aid of blessed Margaret, virgin and martyr, contrary to the expectation of all, experienced her protection in the shipwreck. He vowed, therefore, that her name should be inserted in the church's litanies to be honoured more readily. Landing safely, therefore, and afterwards travelling and avoiding many robbers' ambushes, they came finally to Benevento where they found the lord pope. He received them with a smiling countenance and joyful heart and showed them unusual honour. They settled the king's business at their pleasure. Consequently the bishops withdrew, reporting to the king the papal favour and the abbot's diligence, while the abbot remained behind. For the lord pope amicably

renunciantes. Dominus enim papa amicabiliter coegit abbatem remanere, ut propensius cum ipso colloquium continuaret, et eiusdem moram, versus regem per episcopos excusavit (ed. Wats, 1019; ed. Riley, i, 125–6).

5. *Mutua collocutio papae et abbatis*

Obtulit igitur abbas domino papae, aurum et argentum non minimi ponderis, et alia munera pretiosa; mitras etiam tres, et sandalia operis mirifici, quae domina Christina, priorissa de Markyate, diligentissime fecerat. Et cum omnia serenissimo vultu intuitus est dominus papa, omnia acceptavit, sed non accepit, praeter mitras et sandalia, quia admirabilis operis. Multum autem devotionem et urbanitatem ipsius commendavit, et iocose ait, 'Abnuo recipere munera tua, quia me aliquando ad alas religionis domus tuae confugientem, et habitum monasticum caritative postulantem, recipere renuisti.' Cui abbas, 'Domine, vos nequaquam potuimus recipere, voluntas enim domini repugnavit, cuius prudentia [providentia] vitam vestram direxit ad altiora'. Et respondit dominus papa, 'Eleganter et civiliter respondisti;' et complacuit ei responsionis verbum, et addidit, 'Abbas carissime, audacter pete quod vis, non poterit Beato Albano deesse suus Albanensis.' Tunc abbas in bonam spem erectus, circumspectus et prudens, de licentia domini papae, omnia illa auri et argenti munera, quae fere ad ducentas marcas aestimabantur, cardinalibus et familiaribus domini papae, iocundos amiscendo sermones, et sociles, liberaliter distribuit. Et praeter [Wats: propter] haec, jocalia desiderabilia, quae Londoniis et Parisius comparaverat, munificentissime donavit: sciens ipsos Romanos esse insatiabiles sanguisugae filios pecuniae sitibundos. Quid plura? Extollitur nomen eius ad sidera, omnium adepto favore Romanorum (ed. Wats, 1020; ed. Riley, i, 127).

6. *Privilegium Adriani Papae*

Cum igitur una dierum familiariter, et secreto colloquerentur dominus papa et abbas, intimavit abbas, quasi abortis lacrymis et singultibus sermonem prorumpentibus, varias oppressiones Lincolniensis episcopi, insidias, irruptiones, preces imperiosas, repulsas damnosas, episcopalium, etiam vilium personarum superbiam, intolerabilem. Dominus igitur papa, misertus et miseratus, concessit ecclesiae Sancti Albani insigne privilegium, sic incipiens, '*Incomprehensibilis*, et caetera',[73] in quo nos ab omni episcoporum subjectione, tam in corpore monasterii degentes, quam in cellis seu in custodiis villarum habitantes, ita liberos effecit, ut nullum episcopum, praeter Romanum pontificem, in posterum habeamus. Et praeter hoc, privilegia nobilia alia plura, adeo ut non sit aliud coenobium in Anglia, ipsi ecclesiae Sancti Albani in privilegiis comparabile. Et cum aliquandiu in curia cum domino papa moram protraxisset abbas, et familiare colloquium saepe commiscerent, retulit abbas. quasdam consuetudines hospitalis caritatis ceonobii Sancti Albani: et quomodo per unam dietam competentem, ita ut omnibus tam pedes, quam eques itinerantibus, nec minima nec magna indicetur; distet a Londoniis, ubi totius regni

---

[73]   See below, Part II/ii, no. 1.

compelled the abbot to remain so that he could more easily to talk to him, and he excused the abbot's delay to the king through the bishops.

5. *Discussion between the Pope and the Abbot*

Then the abbot offered the lord pope not insubstantial amounts of gold and silver and other precious gifts; also three mitres and sandals of astonishing workmanship which the Lady Christina, prioress of Markyate, had most carefully made. And when the lord pope had considered everything with a smiling countenance, he approved everything but accepted only the mitres and the sandals, because of their admirable workmanship. He greatly commended the devotion and urbanity of the abbot, and said, jokingly, 'I refuse to receive your gifts because you refused to receive me when I once sought refuge under the wings of your church and asked in charity for the monastic habit.' To which the abbot replied, 'My Lord, we were never able to receive you; for the will of God, whose providence directed your life to higher things, opposed it.' And the lord pope replied, 'You have replied elegantly and courteously,' and he was pleased by the form of the response and added, 'Dear abbot, courageously you can ask whatever you wish; his Albano cannot fail St Alban.' Then the abbot, raised to good hope, circumspect and prudent, by licence of the lord pope, liberally distributed all those gold and silver gifts which were estimated at about 200 marks to the cardinals and familiars of the lord pope, together with happy and friendly words; and apart from these desirable trinkets, which he had bought in London and Paris, he gave most generously; knowing that those Romans are insatiable sons of bloodsuckers, thirsting for money. What more need I say? His name was extolled to the stars, having earned the favour of all the Romans.

6. *The Privilege of Pope Adrian*

When, therefore, one day the lord pope and the abbot were speaking privately and familiarly together, the abbot brought into the conversation, as if holding back his tears and uttering sobs, the various oppressions of the bishop of Lincoln, the plots, attacks, imperious demands, injurious rebuttals and the intolerable pride of episcopal and even common people. Therefore, the lord pope, taking pity and with compassion, granted to the church of St Alban, the special privilege which thus begins, '*Incomprehensibilis etc.*,'[73] in which he made us, both those who live in the monastery and those in the cells or in watch houses in the villages, so free from all subjection to bishops that we should have no bishop for the future except the Roman pontiff; and apart from this, many other noble privileges, so much so that there is not another monastery in England which is comparable to the church of St Albans in its privileges. And when the abbot had extended his stay in the Curia with the lord pope for some time and they had often joined in friendly discourse, the abbot referred to certain customs of charitable hospitality in the monastery of St Albans, and how neither a maximum nor a minimum is indicated as a suitable daily allowance for all, whether travelling by foot or on horseback: [the monastery] is not far from London, where the people of the whole kingdom converge; and there

concursus est populorum. Et illac omnium aquilonarium meantium et remeantium, frequens hospitatio. Interseruit quoque, quasi occasionaliter abbas, qui ipse et episcopi praedicti Romam tendentes, cum ad monasterium Sancti Benedicti super Ligerim gratia hospitandi declinassent, abbas eis tam procurationem quam tectum, procaciter denegavit. Unde papa commotus, scripsit eiusdem ecclesiae abbati, epistolam acrem, comminationem et paternam correptionem continentem, sic incipientem: *Si religiosae professionis*, et caetera.[74] Unde abbas memoratus confusus, correptus et correctus, statuta hospitalitatis coenobii sui salubriter ampliavit, papalem metuens severitatem (ed. Wats, 1020; ed. Riley, i, 128–9).

7. *Abbas redit a Curia*

Expeditis quidem negotiis, pro quibus abbas Robertus Romam adierat, literisque acceptis a domino papa specialibus regi, atque legato, pro se et ecclesia sua directis, cum benedictione apostolica, et omnium peccatorun suorum absolutione, omniumque fratrum benevolentia, remeavit. Iamque consumptis expensis omnibus, insuper LXXX marcis, quas more Romano a quodam mercatore mutuo acceperat, domum sanus et incolumis octavo die Ascensionis Dominicae pervenit; et cum solemni processione susceptus, singulos fratres deosculatus est, et obtulit ad altare maius pallium optimum, duodecim marcis comparatum. Et intrans capitulum, eventus varios itineris et periculorum in mari et in terra, seriatim conventui enarravit; deinde clausulam laborum explanavit, quomodo, scilicet, propositum suum ad plenum in omnibus feliciter consummavit. Laetati sunt audientes, Deo sanctoque martyri gratias persolventes (ed. Wats, 1020; ed. Riley, i, 129).

8. *Synodus Londini*

Paucis itaque post hac evolutis diebus, congregantur apud Londonium archiepiscopi, episcopi, abbates, multarumque ecclesiarum praelati, cum comitibus et baronibus totius regni, ut negotia regni et ecclesiae pertractarent; cum Theobaldo Cantuariensi archiepiscopo, apostolicae sedis legato, eidem consilio praesidente. Episcopus vero Lincolniensis Robertus, cognomento 'de Querceto', id est, 'de Chesnei', audiens Robertum abbatem cum specialibus quibusdam et singularibus privilegiorum libertatibus a Roma redisse, noluit illuc venire, sed missis nunciis, suam allegavit impotentiam; timens ne in illo concilio, privilegiis huius ecclesiae ostensis et auditis, aut clericorum suorum iram eis assensum praebendo incurreret, (et sic libertati suae et ecclesiae suae derogaret) aut eis [*Wats*: suis] contradicendo, domini papae offensam subiret.

Adest tamen Robertus abbas, suis stipatus amicis, qui quadam die episcopis congregatis literas apostolicas porrexit, in quibus eidem episcopis dominus papa praecipiebat, quatenus festivitatem Sancti Albani per singulas ecclesias earum devotissime celebrandam denunciarent. Hiis auditis, omnes unanimiter Apostolico praecepto parere se velle, cum summo honore, fatentur. Hiis siquidem responsis abbas exhilaratus, alias litteras Domini papae de solemni processione clericorum et

---

[74]   *PUE*, iii, 254, no. 113; see ch. 6, at n. 153 above.

is constant hospitality for all Northerners, whether coming or going. The abbot also slipped in, as if by chance, that when he and the aforesaid bishops, as they were travelling to Rome, went to the monastery of Saint Benoît-sur-Loire for hospitality, the abbot insolently denied them both assistance and a roof. Wherefore the pope, annoyed, wrote a sharp letter to the abbot of that church, containing a threat and paternal correction, thus beginning, '*Si religiosae professionis, etc.*'[74] Consequently, the aforesaid abbot, confused, chastised and corrected, increased in salutary fashion the established hospitality of his monastery, in fear of the papal severity.

7. *The Abbot returns from the Curia*

Having completed the business for which he had gone to Rome, and having received from the lord pope special letters to the king and the legate on behalf of himself and his church, with apostolic blessing and absolution of all his sins and the goodwill of all the brethren, Abbot Robert returned. Having spent all the money, as well as 80 marks which in the Roman fashion he had borrowed from a certain merchant, he came to his house, healthy and safe on the octave of the Lord's Ascension; and, having been received in solemn procession, he kissed every brother and offered at the High Altar a fine cloth worth 12 marks. And entering the chapter, he related the various events of his journey and the perils by sea and by land one by one; then he expounded the conclusion of his labours, namely how he had achieved his purpose fully and fortunately in all things. Happy were the listeners, giving thanks to God and the holy martyr.

8. *The Synod of London*

A few days after these events, the archbishops, bishops, abbots and many prelates of churches assembled in London together with the earls and barons of the whole realm to discuss the affairs of kingdom and church, under the presidency of Archbishop Theobald of Canterbury, legate of the Apostolic See. Hearing that Abbot Robert had returned from Rome with certain special and remarkable liberties and privileges, Bishop Robert of Lincoln, called 'de Querceto', that is, 'de Chesney', refused to go there, but sent messengers to excuse his incapacity, fearing that when the privileges of this church were presented and heard in that council, he would either suffer the displeasure of his clergy by giving his assent to them (and thus derogating from his own and his church's liberty), or by opposing them suffer the lord pope's displeasure.

Abbot Robert was present, nevertheless, accompanied by his friends who on a certain day put forward before the assembled bishops the apostolic letters, in which the lord pope ordered the bishops to command the devout celebration of the Feast of St Alban in each of their churches. When this had been heard everyone unanimously declared that they wished to obey the apostolic mandate with the utmost respect. The abbot was very happy at these responses and caused other letters of the lord pope regarding the solemn procession of the clergy and laity of the

laicorum Hertifordensis provinciae, per singulos annos huic ecclesiae exhibendo, Lincolniensis clericis astantibus, perlegi fecit (ed. Wats, 1020; ed.Riley, i, 129–30).

9. *Appellatio Lincolniensium*

Quibus auditis, indignati ipsum abbatem et capitulum suum, ad audientiam Apostolicam appellaverunt, praefigentes diem appellationi, diem Dominicam qua cantatur *Gaudete in Domino*, sumentes occasionem de hoc, quod dominus papa in eisdem litteris interdicebat, ne clerici vel laici inter Hertifordensem provinciam constituti, iteratam processionem ad Lincolniensem civitatem facere, a quolibet compellarentur (ed. Wats, 1021; ed. Riley, i, 130).

10. *Compositio*

Robertus abbas domum revertitur; haec conventui nuncians. Quo prosequi volente, venit Hugo Dunelmensis episcopus, utriusque ecclesiae tunc fidelis amicus, partes suas interponens, ut utraque ecclesia inter se amicabiliter componerent. Locus et dies ab utraque ecclesia, fide interposita, constituitur, quo res de reformatione pacis die apostolorum Simonis et Judae apud Sanctum Neotum actitaretur. Adest episcopus Lincolniensis, cum Ricardo Londoniensi et Gileberto Herefordensi,[75] cum copiosa clericorum multitudine. Adest et Robertus [abbas] cum suis. Illis vero hac de re altercantibus tandem dictis episcopis, cum episcopo Dunelmensi mediantibus, inter utramque ecclesiam compositio formata est. Huius vero compositionis forma a praedicto episcopo Gileberto Herefordensi cognomento 'Foliott', dictata est: utriusque ecclesiae sigillis concessa et confirmata est. Nam duobus ex fratribus nostris cum medietate chyrographi, huius ecclesiae sigillo sigillati, Lincolniensem ecclesiam [episcopum] adeuntibus, medietatem alteram Lincolniensis ecclesiae sigillo signatam, ab eis absque reclamatione, vel morae etiam dispendio, receperunt (ed. Wats, 1021; ed. Riley, i, 131).

11. *De candelabris missis*

His itaque peractis, abbas Robertus Romam mittere disposuit, non quia supradictam appellationem, quae iam expiraverat, prosequi vellet, sed ut quae domino papae hoc petenti, cum adhuc Beneventi esset, de duobus candelabris promissum, effectui maniparet [manciparet]. Igitur initio Martii, unum ex fratribus nostris Robertum de Gorham, Romam ad pedes domini papae, cum praedictis candelabris, ex auro et argento artificiosissime fabrifactis, et aliis desiderabilibus muneribus et denariis ad viatica copiosis destinavit: adjuncto eidem alio fratre pro socio Gaufrido de Gorham. Qui Romam venientes a domino papa benigne ac honorifice suscepti sunt: cuius illico pedibus, ut moris est, provoluti, memorata candelabra proferentes ei, ex parte domini Roberti abbatis et conventus sui, civiliter obtulerunt. Quibus visis et singulariter ac mirifice laudatis, papa immensas gratias

---

[75] Hugh du Puiset of Durham, Richard Belmeis of London, and Gilbert Foliot of Hereford.

county of Hertfordshire to be made every year to this church to be read in the presence of the Lincoln clerks.

9. *Appeal of the Lincoln Clergy*

When they heard these things, they were indignant and appealed the abbot himself and his chapter to the Apostolic audience, setting the Sunday on which is chanted *Gaudete in Domino* as the day of their appeal, on the grounds that in the same letters the lord pope forbade clergy and laity in the county of Hertfordshire to be compelled by anyone to make a second procession to the city of Lincoln.

10. *Agreement*

Abbot Robert returned to his house and reported these things to the convent. Wishing to pursue this matter, Bishop Hugh of Durham, a faithful friend of both churches came, acting as mediator, so that both churches should make an amicable agreement between themselves. Under oath, both churches agreed a day and a place—the feast of the Apostles Simon and Jude and St Neots—when the restoration of peace should be debated. The bishop of Lincoln was present, with Richard of London and Gilbert of Hereford[75] and a large number of clergy. Also present was [Abbot] Robert with his supporters. When these had debated the question, an agreement was finally made between the two churches through the mediation of the said bishops, with the bishop of Durham. The form of this agreement was dictated by bishop Gilbert of Hereford, surnamed 'Folioth', and it was granted and confirmed by the seals of both churches. For when two of our brethren went to the church of Lincoln with one half of the chirograph, sealed with this church's seal, they received the other half from them, sealed with the seal of the church of Lincoln, without any challenge or delay.

11. *The Sending of Candlesticks*

When these things had been done, Abbot Robert arranged to send to Rome, not because he wished to pursue the above appeal which had already expired, but to give effect to the promise of two candlesticks, which he had made at the lord pope's request, when he was in Benevento. At the beginning of May, therefore, he sent one of our brothers, Robert de Gorham, to Rome to the feet of the lord pope, with the aforesaid candlesticks, most skilfully made from gold and silver, and other desirable gifts, and a great deal of money for the journeys, with Geoffrey de Gorham, another brother, as his companion. When they reached Rome, they were most kindly and honourably received by the lord pope, at whose feet, kneeling in the customary manner, they courteously presented the said candlesticks to him on behalf of lord Robert the abbot and his convent. When he had seen them and

eidem abbati et fratribus pro talibus exeniis multiplicavit. Quae statim, ob honorem et reverentiam beati Albani Anglorum protomartyris, cuius se ministrum, immo servum palam professus est, beato Petro, apostolorum principi, solemniter ac de vote obtulit; ut essent in eius ecclesia dicti martyris perpetuum memoriale (ed. Wats, 1021; ed. Riley, i, 131–2).

12. *Nota: de pontificalibus ornamentis. Munera missa per Adrianum papam*

Expositis itaque negotiis, quicquid postulabant celeri consequebantur effectu. Duo namque maxima privilegia adepti sunt. Primum, de pontificalibus ornamentis; secundum de huius ecclesiae libertatibus, et alia plura nobilia ac necessaria. Quibus impetratis, a domino papa licentia repatriandi postulatur; et cum benedictione apostolica et omnium fratrum conceditur. Dominus autem papa, ut ipsius memoria semper haberetur in ecclesia beati Albani, per eosdem fratres eidem ecclesiae misit reliquias de Legione Thebaea, propter quod postea statutum est in dicta ecclesia, ut eorum festivitas ampliaretur et duodecim lectiones propriaque legenda legeretur; et insigne pallium, quod dominus imperator ipsi miserat, et sandalia pretiosa, et annulum pretiosissimum; et alia, quae longum esset enarrare. Repatriantes igitur, die Passionis beati Albani, non sine nutu Dei, domum veniunt, ut sicut ipsa die anima beati protomartyris ante Deum coronanda ab angelis fuerat presentata, ita et in terra ab hominibus instrumenta honoris [sui] terreni, loco martyrii sui solemniter praesentarentur. Exhilarantur, visis tot exeniis insignibus, abbas et conventus vehementer, grates et gratiae martyri ampliatur devotio, honor augetur, solemnitas dilatatur, et completur festivitas cum jubilo incomparabili (ed. Wats, 1021; ed. Riley, i, 132–3). [...]

13. *Dissentio inter Abbatem et Lincolniensem Episcopum*

Audientes itaque Lincolnienses tanta a papa Adriano, quem 'Albanensem' nominarunt, indignabantur, minas congerentes, potentesque viros ad nostram perniciem excitabant, iramque regiam adversus nos accendebant. Iamiamque universa privilegia quae a papa Adriano adepti fueramus, sollicita inquisitione cognoverunt, ideoque magis inflammabantur. Proinde memoratus Hugo Dunelmensis episcopus tristis effectus; iterum sicut prius, diligenter partes suas interposuit: atque ab utraque ecclesia, quatenus sub die certo et loco denominato, inter se amicabiliter componerent, ut vir eloquens et nobilis exegit. Adveniente igitur die, affuit Robertus Lincolniensis episcopus cum Hilario [Cicestrensi] et Gileberto Herefordiensi, coepiscopis; et copiosa clericorum nobilium multitudine. Adest et Robertus abbas cum episcopo Dunelmense, et aliis potentibus et discretis quamplurimis: initoque conflictu, diutius hinc et inde decertatum est. Tandem mediante dicto Hugone Donelmensi, cum coepiscopis suis, et aliis jurisperitis, formam pacis inter ecclesias dictas componere studuerunt; quae tamen utriusque ecclesiae sigillis nullatenus est

greatly praised each one in turn, the pope greatly thanked the abbot and brethren for such gifts. Then he forthwith offered them solemnly and devotedly to blessed Peter, prince of the apostles, in honour and reverence for St Alban, whose minister and servant he publicly professed himself to be, so that they should be a perpetual memorial of the said Martyr in his church.

12. *Note: concerning the pontifical ornaments. Gifts sent by Pope Adrian*

And so, having explained the commission, they were able to achieve quickly whatever they requested. Two great privileges were obtained. The first, concerning pontifical regalia; the second, concerning the liberties of this church; and many other notable and necessary things. When these were secured, they asked the lord pope's permission to return to their own country, and this was granted, with the apostolic blessing and that of all the brethren. The lord pope, however, sent relics of the Theban Legion to the said church by the hands of those brethren so that his memory would remain forever in the church of St Albans, following which it was later laid down in the said church that their feast should be extended, and twelve lections and their proper readings should be read; and a splendid pallium, which the lord emperor had sent to him, and precious sandals, and a very expensive ring, and other things which it would be tedious to describe. Returning, therefore, on the day of the Passion of blessed Alban, not without divine providence, they came to the house so that, just as the soul of the blessed Protomartyr had been presented by the angels before God on that day to be crowned, so on earth the symbols of his earthly honour might be solemnly presented by men in the place of his martyrdom. When they saw so many splendid gifts, the abbot and convent were greatly delighted; they poured out thanks to the martyr, devotion was increased, honour augmented, celebration extended and the feast was completed with jubilation beyond compare. [...]

13. *Disagreement between the Abbot and the Bishop of Lincoln*

Thus, when the people of Lincoln heard that so much [had been granted] by Pope Adrian, whom they called 'of St Albans', they were very angry and rained down threats and stirred up powerful men to our disadvantage, and inflamed the royal anger against us. By careful investigation, they learned at this very moment about all the privileges we had received from Pope Adrian, and so they were even more incensed. Accordingly, the said Bishop Hugh of Durham, greatly saddened for a second time, intervened again, as before; and as an eloquent and noble man, he required both churches to make an amicable agreement on a certain day and at a pre-arranged place. When that day came, Bishop Robert of Lincoln was present with his fellow bishops, Hilary of Chichester and Gilbert of Hereford, and an ample gathering of noble clerks. There was also present Abbot Robert, with the bishop of Durham and many other powerful and discreet men; and at the beginning of the dispute there was a long debate backwards and forwards. Finally, through the mediation of the said Hugh of Durham, with his fellow bishops and other men learned in the law, they strove to devise a form of peace between the two churches,

roborata. Nam mediante Dei gratia, utrisque partibus domum remeantibus, Lincolnienses, quam se in posterum servare inviolabiliter promiserant, infirmantes refuta-
runt, et initam pactionem pro nihilo duxerunt. Iterum vero aliam utrinque inierunt,
quae similiter cassata est: et tertiam simili modo. Porro quoad usque dominus papa
Adrianus vixit, non est ausus episcopus Lincolniensis vexare vel niti trahere ad
suam subjectionem, monasterium Sancti Albani, quod a primis suae fundationis
initiis, et iam magis, privilegiatum fuisse dinoscitur (ed. Wats, 1022; ed. Riley, i,
135–6).

14. *Mors Adriani Papae*

Post hos autem paucos dies, idem papa Adrianus, quia cuiusdam potentis civis
Romani filium indignum, in episcopum, timore repressus divino, creare et conse-
crare noluit, praeventus insidiis, potionatus, veneno infectus, et interfectus est. Qui
Kalendis Septembris, scilicet die Sancti Egidii martyr Dei et confessor egregius, ab
hoc mundi exilio migravit ad coeli patriam, cui successit venerabilis Rollandus
domini papae Adriani cancellarius: cui adjectum est nomen Alexandri Tertii, vir
iustus et prudens. Adversus quem insurrexit Octavianus schismaticus anti-papa, se
'Victorem' cognominans, binario fultus cardinalium numero; unde versus:

> Guido de Crema, Io et hannes sunt anathema:
> Nunquid peccavi, nunquid male grammaticavi;
> Schismatici pravi si nomen schismaticavi.

Idem tamen Octavianus, paulo post miserabiliter defunctus, haeredem habuit
eiusdem vesaniae Guidonem Cremensem. Quos fovit Fredericus Imperator, qui vir
martius et victoriosus, Mediolanum septenni obsidione fatigatam, tandem subvertit
(ed. Wats, 1022; ed. Riley, i, 136).

which was confirmed by the seals of both churches. For, through God's grace, when both parties returned home, the men of Lincoln rejected what they had promised to observe inviolably for the future and deemed that the agreement had no value. A second and a third time they entered into an agreement, which was similarly quashed. But as long as the lord pope Adrian lived, the bishop of Lincoln did not dare to annoy or attempt to draw to his subjection the monastery of St Albans; which is known to have been privileged from the earliest moment of its foundation and now even more.

14. *Death of Pope Adrian*

A few days later, because the same Pope Adrian refused to create and consecrate as bishop the unworthy son of a certain powerful Roman citizen, he was ambushed, held, poisoned, and killed. On 1 September, that is, on the feast of St Giles, God's martyr and renowned confessor, he passed from the exile of this world to his fatherland of heaven, and was succeeded by the venerable Roland, chancellor of the lord pope Adrian, a just and prudent man, given the name of Alexander III. Against him there rose the schismatic anti-pope Octavian, calling himself 'Victor', supported by two cardinals, whence the verse,

> Guido of Crema, Jo and Hannes are anathema.
> Have I ever sinned, have I ever badly conjugated,
> If I have broken the name of a wicked schismatic in two?

The same Octavian, however, who miserably died soon afterwards, had as heir to the same madness Guido of Crema. The emperor Frederick, warlike and victorious, who wore down Milan with a seven-year siege and finally overwhelmed it, supported both of them.

7

Bernardus Guidonis, *Vita Adriani Papae IV*

From Bernard Gui, *Flores chronicorum seu catalogus pontificum Romanorum*, in Muratori, Rer. Ital. SS, 3/i, 440b–441a.

Despite its late date (early fourteenth century), this short memorial on the life of Pope Adrian from Bernard Gui's synopsis of papal history has a significance far outweighing its brevity, for it throws important light on the most obscure phase of Nicholas Breakspear's career.

Adrianus IV natione Anglicus coepit anno Domini MCLIV. Sedit annis IV, mensibus IX, diebus XVIII. Vacavit sedes dies XVIII.

Hic prius dictus est Nicholaus, fuitque primo ut pauper clericus, siue clericus pauperculus in ecclesia beati Jacobi in Melgorio Magolonensis dyocesis enutritus; tandem sic frater et post abbas sancti Ruffi prope Valentiam. Indeque de abbate factus est cardinalis episcopus Albanensis, et missus legatus in Norvegiam pro praedicatione verbi Dei gentem barbaram in lege Divina diligenter instruxit. Post reditum vero a legatione sua, defuncto Anastasio, in papam est electus.

Hic Guillelmum Regem Siciliae tanquam rebellem sibi excommunicavit. Qui postmodum absolutus homagium Domno Papae faciens terram ab ipso Papa suscepit.

Hic primus Papa dicitur fuisse, qui in Urbe veteri cum curia sua moram traxit. Hic castrum, et multas possessions, circa locum Sanctae Cristinae a comitibus comparavit.

Hic Fredericum primum Romae in ecclesia Sancti Petri imperiali diademate coronavit

[...]

Adrianus papa obiit pridie Kalendas Septembris sepultusque est in Vaticano Sancti Petri, iuxta sepulchrum Eugenii Papae Anno Domini MCLIX. Quo mortuo facta est in Ecclesia Romana turbatio magna. Cardinales namque ad invicem divisi duos sibi Pontifices elegerunt Ricardum Cancellarium, qui Papa Alexander dictus est, et Octavianum gravi schismate Dei Ecclesiam disrumpentes; unde proceres regionum turbati, quidam uni, quidam alteri adhaeserunt. Imperator siquidem Romanorum Fredericus cum episcopis Octaviano, qui a sibi faventibus Papa Victor acclamatus est. Cessit. Rex vero Francorum Ludovicus et Rex Angliae Henricus cum suis Alexandrum in Papam et in Dominium susceperunt. Fredericus autem primus Imperator XIX annis in tali Schismate perseveravit.

7
Bernard Gui, O.P., *Life of Pope Adrian IV*

Bernard Gui is best known as an historian of the Dominican Order,which he had entered in 1279, but his extensive knowledge of Toulouse and Provence (he was prior of the Dominican house in Carcassonne from 1297 to 1301, for example) and his historical interests in the region *meant that he was well placed to uncover sound local traditions about the young Englishman's sojourn Provence.*

Adrian IV, English by race, began his reign in the year of the Lord 1154. He reigned for 4 years, 9 months, 18 days. The see was vacant for 18 days.

He was formerly called Nicholas, and at first he was maintained as a poor or very poor clerk in the church of St James in Melgueil in the diocese of Maguelonne; then as brother, and afterwards as abbot of Saint-Ruf near Valence. And from abbot he was made cardinal bishop of Albano, and sent as legate to Norway to preach God's word, and he diligently instructed that barbarous race in the divine law. After his return from his legation, he was elected pope on the death of Anastasius.

He excommunicated William, king of Sicily, for rebelling against him. When he was later absolved, [King William] paid homage to the lord pope and received his land from him.

He was said to have been the first to have spent time with his Curia in Orvieto. Here he bought the *castrum* and many estates near Santa Cristina from the counts.

He crowned Frederick I with the imperial diadem in the church of St Peter at Rome.

[…]

Pope Adrian died on 31 August and was buried in the Vatican of St Peter, near the tomb of Pope Eugenius, in the year of the Lord 1159. Following his death there was great disturbance in the Roman church. For the cardinals were divided and elected two popes, Richard [*recte* Roland] the chancellor, who was called Alexander III, and Octavian, rending God's church with a serious schism, so that the leaders of the regions were thrown into disorder, some supporting the one, some the other. The Roman emperor Frederick, however, with his bishops [supported] Octavian, who was acclaimed by his supporters as Pope Victor. He failed. For Louis king of the French and King Henry of England and their people, accepted Alexander as pope and lord. The emperor Frederick I, however, held out in this schism for 19 years.

---

* He compiled the history of the establishment and priors of Dominican houses in Toulouse and Provence: *Bernardus Guidonis, de fundatione et prioribus conventuum provinciarum Tolosanae et Provinciae ordinis predicatorum*, ed. P. A. Amargier, O.P., Monumenta Ordinis Fratrum Praedicatorum Historica, 24 (Rome, 1961). For his life and writings, see *ibid.*, xi–xvi.

8
Bartolomeo Platina (1421–81), *Hadrianus IIII*

Latin text from *Platynae Historici, Liber de vita Christi ac omnium pontificum*, ed. Giacincto Gaida, in Muratori, *Rer. Ital. SS*, 3/i, 215–17.

Bartolomeo Sacchi, from Piadena, known as 'La Platina', a leading humanist at the papal court under Pius II (1458–64), Paul II (1464–71), and Sixtus IV (1471–84), who crowned his career with the office of Prefect of the newly-founded Vatican Library from 1475 to 1481.

Hadrianus Quartus, natione Anglicus, Albanus episcopus et cardinalis ab Eugenio creatur, quod in Norvegian missus, praedicando et bene monendo provinciam illam ad Christi redegerat. Mortuo deinde Anastasio pontifex creatus, tentatusque a Romanis tum precibus, tum minis, ut consulibus liberam Urbis administrationem relinqueret, id se facturum constantissime renuit. Instabat Romanus clerus ut in Lateranum profisceretur faciendae consecrationis causa, quod etiam facere recusavit, nisi prius Arnoldus Brixianus haereticus, ab Eugenio antea damnatus, ex Urbe pelleretur. Hoc autem aegre ferens populus, cardinalem Sanctae Pudentianae ad pontificem via Sacra proficiscentem, uno atque altero vulnere afficiunt. Hanc ob rem iratus pontifex, eos acerba etiam execratione persecutus est, quoad mutata sententia, et Arnoldum ab Urbe pepulere, et consules abdicare se magistratu coegere, relicta pontifici administrandae urbis libera facultate. Interim vero Gulielmus Siciliae rex qui mortuo Rogerio successerat, Beneventana suburbia, Ceperanum Baucumque in Hernici de ecclesia occupat. Ob quam rem indignatus pontifex, regem gravi anathenmate notat, eiusque ditioni subiectos omni sacramento liberat, quo facilius a rege deficerent, nullo iure iurando astricti. Federicus autem primus hoc tempore ex gente Sveva imperator creatus, Cisalpineam Galliam cum exercitu ingressus, cum Dertonam haud satis imperio obtemperantem aliquandiu obsessam, vi tandem cepisset, magnaque celeritate Romam versus iter statim fecit. Pontifex autem Viterbii, tum agens confirmaturus in fide ecclesiasticas civitates circumquaque positas, Orvetum et Civitatem Castellanam adiit. Verum cum postremo se imparem tanto exercitui cerneret, pace per internuncios composita, in agro Sutrino imperatori fit obviam; qui ex equo descendens, eum ut verum Christi vicarium salutat. Cum vero ad Urbem venissent, et pontifex in basilica Petri Federicum imperii corona donaret, populus Romanus clausis tum portis ne quid tumultus excitaretur, per Hadriani pontem vi erumpens, Teutonicos cum pontifice praeter eorum voluntatem sentientes, passim caedit. Excitus quidem tanto

8
Bartolomeo Platina (1421–81), *Adrian IIII*

This summation of the life of Pope Adrian comes from what was his major and most popular work, The Life of Christ and all the popes, *following the format and in large part derived from the* Liber pontificalis. *Dependence on Boso's* Vita Adriani *(above, no. 1) is clearly evident; but Platina's Humanist credentials commended his work to Protestant and Catholic alike and so brought the story of the English pope to a much wider audience than ever before.*[*]

Adrian IV, English by race, was created cardinal and bishop of Albano by Eugenius, so that, sent to Norway, he should bring back that province to Christ by preaching and good advice. Then, made pontiff on Anastasius's death, pressed by the Romans by prayers and threats to relinquish the free administration of the City to the consuls, he insistently refused to do it. The Roman clergy arranged that he should go to the Lateran for his consecration, but he refused to do so unless the heretic, Arnold of Brescia, formerly condemned by Eugenius, was expelled from the City. The people, however, taking this very badly, inflicted one or two blows on the cardinal of S. Pudenziana as he was on his way along the Via Sacra to visit the pontiff. Angered by this action, the pontiff pursued them with a stinging curse, so that, having changed their opinion, they would compel Arnold to leave the City and the consuls to give up the magistracy, leaving to the pontiff the faculty of freely administering the City. Meanwhile, however, King William of Sicily, who had succeeded on the death of Roger, seized from the Church the suburbs of Benevento, Ceprano, and Boville Ernica. Indignant at this, the pontiff branded the king with heavy anathema, and freed his subjects from every oath of subjection, so that they might more easily defect from him, since they were no longer bound by oath. Moreover, Frederick I, the Swabian, made emperor at this time, entered Cisalpine Gaul with an army, and when he had finally taken Tortona by force, after besieging the city for a long time because it was not sufficiently obedient to the empire, he immediately made his way with the greatest speed towards Rome. But the pontiff, seeking to strengthen the fidelity of the ecclesiastical cities round about, went from Viterbo to Orvieto and Civita Castellana. But when he later realized that he was unequal to so great an army, having made peace through intermediaries, he met the emperor in a field at Sutri; dismounting from his horse, the emperor saluted him as the true Vicar of Christ. And when they came to the City, and the pontiff was conferring on Frederick the crown of the empire in the Basilica of Peter, after the gates had been closed to avoid tumult, the Roman people, realizing that the Germans were with the pontiff against their will, bursting in by force across Adrian's bridge, killed indiscriminately. The emperor, however, stirred up by so great a tumult, having brought in the army, which had been encamped in

[*] Denys Hay, *Annalists & Historians. Western Historiography from the Eighth to the Eighteenth Centuries* (London, 1977), 105–9.

tumultu imperator intromisso exercitu, qui in pratis Neronianis[76] consederat, Romanos ex Vaticano in Urbem retrudit, multis caesis captisque, pontificis tamen precibus imperator lenitus, captivos incolumes dimittit. Verum cum postea, ut mos est, ituri simul ad Lateranum pontifex et imperator essent, fierique id nequaquam tuto viderent, Romanis ad arma spectantibus, Mallianam simul profiscuntur: ubi transmisso flumine, per Sabinos et pontem Lucanum ad Lateranum pervenientes solennia persolvere. Dum haec autem Romae agerentur, Tiburtini ad imperatorem venientes, se ac omnia ei sponte dedunt. Verum cum imperator intellexisset urbem illam ad pontificatum pertinere, eandem Hadriano statim restituit, neque ita diu immoratus, in Germaniam rediit. At Pontifix a proceribus Apuliae rogatus: Beneventum se contulit, maioremque regni partem sua tantum praesentia Gulielmo abstulit. Interea vero, Paleologus, vir quidem nobilitate insignis, Hemanuleis Secundi imperatoris Constantinopolitani nuncios et orator, Anconam primo navigio delatus, terra deinde Beneventum petiit, pontificique imperatoris nomine sponte obtulit auri libras quinque milia, fugaturumque se ex Italia Gulielmum, si tres maritimae in Apulia urbes, ei ex foedere rebus bene gestis darentur. Quod ubi Gulielmus rescivisset, pontificem ad misericordiam cohortatus, pollicetur non modo se restituturum quae de Ecclesia abstulerat, verum ultro quaedam alia condonaturum, Romanosque Ecclesiae rebelles in officio retenturum, si utriusque regni titulis tam citra quam ultra Pharum positi insignior fieret. Facere id quidem pontifici nequaquam licuit, adversantibus quibusdam cardinalibus. Hanc ob rem Gulielmus instructo exercitu Apuliam hostili animo ingressus, cum omnia ferro ac flamma consumpsisset, in Graecos et Apulos movens, qui apud Brundusium castra posuerant, eos facile superat; unde Salentini Apulique omnes deditionem statim fecere. Pontifex autem cardinalibus infensus, qui obstiterant quo minus pax componeretur, Gulielmum in gratiam recipit, eidemque utriusque regni titulos ascripsit, adhibito prius sacramento, se nil deinceps moliturum, quod Ecclesiam Romanam offenderet. Rebus autem ex sententia compositis, pontifex per Cassinates, Marsos, Reatinos, Narnienses, Tudertinos iter faciens, ad Orvetum tandem pervenit, primus pontificum Romanorum, a quo ea urbs et inhabitata et cultior reddita est. Cum vero instantibus Romanis ad Urbem rediisset, vexareturque a consulibus libertatem Romanam restituere conantibus, Arignanum petiit: ubi non ita multo post moritur, pontificatus sui anno quarto mense x., relicta magno in precio Ecclesiae Romanae ditione. Nam et circa lacum Sanctae Christinae multae castella munivit, et Rhadicophanum, quod nunc Seneses obtinent, muro et arce prope inexpugnabile reddidit. Horum autem temporum historiam scripsit satis eleganti stylo et oratione Richardus Cluniacensis monachus, quem alii scriptores non parum laudant. Corpus autem Hardriani Romam delatum, in basilica Petri sepellitur non longe a sepulcro Eugenii pontificis.

---

[76]   Formerly the Circus of Nero (on the western side of St Peter's).

the Neronian fields,[76] thrust back the Romans from the Vatican into the City, capturing and killing many, but at the prayers of the pontiff the emperor, mollified, let the prisoners go without injury. But when later, as was the custom, the pontiff and the emperor were about to go to the Lateran together, they saw that it was in no way safe; while the Romans looked on with their weapons, they set out together for Magliano, where having crossed the river by way of the Sabines and Ponte Lucano, they arrived at the Lateran to conduct the solemnities. While these things were happening in Rome, the people of Tivoli came to the emperor and freely gave themselves and everything they had to him. But when the emperor learned that that town belonged to the pontifical office, he immediately restored it to Adrian, and, not staying there very long, he returned to Germany. But the pontiff, requested by the nobles of Apulia, took himself to Benevento, and by his mere presence took away the greater part of his kingdom from William. Meanwhile, however, Paleologus, a man of the most distinguished nobility, emissary and spokesman of Manuel II, emperor of Constantinople, was first brought to Ancona by ship, then travelled to Benevento and willingly offered the pontiff five thousand pounds of gold in the name of the emperor, and that he would himself drive William out of Italy, if three maritime towns in Apulia were given to him on the successful completion of the treaty. But when William learned this, having exhorted the pontiff to mercy, he promised not only that he would restore what he had taken from the Church, but grant other things in addition; and that he would firmly restrain the Romans who had rebelled against the Church, if he were to be more honoured with the titles of the two kingdoms situated on either side of the Lighthouse. But the pontiff was not allowed to do this because of the opposition of some of the cardinals. For this reason, when William, having raised an army and entered Apulia in hostile spirit and had consumed everything with fire and sword, moving against the Greeks and Apulians who had placed their camp at Brindisi, he easily overcame them; wherefore all the Salentines and Apulians immediately surrendered. The pontiff, however, angry with the cardinals who had resisted the making of peace, received William into his grace and gave him the titles of both kingdoms, having first imposed the oath that he would not in the future attempt anything which would offend the Roman Church. When these things had been arranged to the best of his judgment, the pontiff, making his way through the regions of Cassino, Marsi, Rieti, Narni, and Todi, came at length to Orvieto, the first of the Roman pontiffs to repopulate the city and make it more civilized. And when, at the insistence of the Romans, he had returned to the City, and was harassed by the consuls who were trying to restore the Roman liberty, he went to Anagni, where not long afterwards he died, in the fourth year and tenth month of his pontificate, leaving the Roman Church greatly enriched. For he strengthened many fortifications around the lake of Santa Cristina, and he made Radicofani, which the Siennese have now obtained, almost impregnable by a wall and an arch. Richard, monk of Cluny, whom other writers praise as without equal, wrote the history of these times in an elegant style and language. The body of Adrian was taken to Rome and buried in the basilica of Peter, not far from the tomb of Pope Eugenius.

ii. Privileges and Charters

1

Incomprehensibilis: Adrianus IV Roberto abbati monasterii sancti Albani eiusque fratribus

Benevento, 5 February, 1156.

Latin text from *PUE*, iii, 234–8 no. 100.

Adrianus episcopus seruus seruorum Dei. Dilectis filiis Roberto abbati monasterii sancti Albani eiusque fratribus tam presentibus quam futuris regularem vitam professis in perpetuum.

Incomprehensibilis et ineffabilis diuine miseratio maiestatis nos hac providentie ratione in apostolice sedis administratione constituit, ut paternam de omnibus ecclesiis sollicitudinem gerere debeamus. Sacrosancta siquidem Romana ecclesia, quae a Deo sibi concessum omnium ecclesiarum obtinet principatum, tanquam diligens mater singulis ecclesiis instanti cogitur uigilantia prouidere. Ad ipsam enim quasi ad caput atque principium est ab omnibus concurrendum, ut eius defendantur auctoritate, uberibus nutriantur et a suis oppressionibus releuentur. Expedit igitur, ut religiosa monasteria et venerabilia loca specialioris prerogatiue sortiantur honorem et apostolice auctoritatis munimine roborentur.

Eapropter, dilecti in domino filii, ob reuerentiam beati Albani gloriosi Anglorum prothomartiris, cuius sacratissimum corpus in loco uestro requiescere dinoscitur, predecessorum nostrorum felicis memorie Calixti, Celestini, Eugenii et Anastasii Romanorum pontificum uestigiis inherentes uestris iustis postulationibus annuimus et monasterium ipsius, in quo diuino uacatis obsequio, cum adiacentibus ecclesiis ot omnibus eidem monasterio pertinentibus sub beati Petri et nostra protectione suscipimus et presentis scripti priuilegio communimus.

Statuentes et uniuersa, que illustris memoriae Offa uidelicet et filius eius Egifridus, Adelredus, Willelmus et Henricus Anglorum reges aut alii fideles de suo iure uestro monasterio contulerunt, quecumque etiam ipsum monasterium in presentiarum iuste et canonice possidet aut in futurum concessione pontificum, largitione regum uel principum, oblatione fidelium seu aliis iustis modis prestante domino poterit adipisci, firma uobis uestrisque successoribus et illibata permaneant. In quibus haec propriis duximus exprimenda uocabulis: uidelicet monasterium ipsum beati Albani cum uilla tota et ecclesia sancti Petri, ecclesia quoque sancti Stephani et ecclesias de Kingesberia, de Watford, de Richemareswrtha, de Langelega, de Redburna, de Cudecote, de Waldena, de Hecstunestuna, de Nortuna, de Newenham, de Wineslawe, de Estuna, de Barnet, de Brantesfeld, de Sepehale, de Tingeherst cum eisdem uillis et omnibus omnium earum pertinentiis, ecclesiam de Lutonia cum ecclesia de Hohtuna et cum tota terra, quam Willelmus camerarius tenuit de feudo comitis do Glocestre in soca Lutonie et in uilla de Hohtuna et in Hertewella et in Badelesduna et in Potesgraua cum omnibus terris et decimis et quibuscumque rebus ad eas pertinentibus, sicut regis Henrici et Willelmi comitis Glocestrie charte contestantur; ad sustentationem pauperum ecclesiam de

1

Incomprehensibilis: Adrian IV to Abbot Robert of St Albans and his brethren

Benevento, 5 February, 1156.

Adrian, bishop, servant of the servants of God, to his dear sons, Robert, abbot of the monastery of St Albans, and his brethren, both present and future, who profess the regular life, for ever.

The incomprehensible and ineffable mercy of the Divine Majesty has established us in the apostolic see for this providential reason, that we should exercise paternal care for all the churches. For the Holy Roman Church, which holds the primacy of all churches granted to her by God, like a careful mother is obliged to exercise constant vigilance over every church. For to her, as if to the head and foundation, all should hasten, so that they may be defended by her authority, nourished at her breasts, and relieved from their oppressions. It is, therefore, expedient that religious monasteries and venerable places should be assigned the honour of a more special privilege and strengthened by the defence of apostolic authority.

Therefore, dear sons in the Lord, out of reverence for the blessed Alban, glorious proto-martyr of the English, whose most holy body is known to rest in your place, following in the footsteps of our predecessors of happy memory, Calixtus, Celestine, Eugenius, and Anastasius, Roman pontiffs, we approve your just requests and receive that monastery, in which you devote yourself to divine service, together with the adjacent churches and everything pertaining to that monastery under the protection of blessed Peter and ourselves, and confirm by the privilege of this present document.

We declare that everything which Offa of illustrious memory and Egfrith, his son, Aethelred, William, and Henry, kings of the English, or other faithful, have conferred upon your monastery from their right, whatever that monastery rightly and canonically possesses now or can in the future obtain by the grant of pontiffs, the generosity of kings and princes, the offering of the faithful, or by any other just means, by the Lord's action, shall remain firm and unimpaired for you and your successors. Among which we have chosen to express in their proper names: namely, the monastery of St Albans itself with the whole vill and the church of St Peter, the church of St Stephen and the churches of Kingsbury, Watford, Rickmansworth, [Abbots] Langley, Redbourn, Codicote, Walden, Hexton, Norton, Newnham, Winslow, Aston [Abbots], Barnet, Bramfield, Shephall, Fingest, with their vills and all their appurtenances, the church of Luton with the church of Houghton and with all the land which William the Chamberlain held from the fee of the earl of Gloucester in the soke of Luton and in the vill of Houghton and in Hartwell and in Biddlesden and in Potsgrove, with all the lands and tithes and all other things pertaining to them, as is witnessed in the charter of King Henry and Earl William of Gloucester; for the support of the poor, the church of Elfresduna,

Efresduna, decimam de Estwella et de Ringetuna, decimam de Roinges, ecclesiam de Kenebella cum adiacente terra, terram quoque, quam Willelmus filius Gaufridi dedit, scilicet unam hidam in uilla de Eselberga de sartis de Widhhala et unam uirgatam de nemore eiusdem Widehale, sicut donatoris charta confirmat; ad sacristariam ex dono Hannonis in uilla de Chalfhunte unam uirgatam terre et dimidiam et unum essartum cum libera pastura pecudum et porcorum; in Eboraciscira, ecclesiam, de Appeltuna cum ecclesia de Aimundebi et omnibus earum pertinentiis; preterea cellam de Tinemutha, cellam de Binneham, cellam de Wimundeham, cellam de Walengeford, cellam de Hertford, cellam de Beluedir, cellam de Hehtfeld, cellam de Bello loco cum omnibus omnium earum pertinentiis, dignitatibus ac liberis consuetudinibus necnon et alias ecclesias, decimas, uillas, terras, aquas, prata, pascua, siluas, redditus etiam et omnia eidem monasteno uel cellis eius pertinentia, sicut in priulegiis pontificum, regum uel aliorum fidelium scriptis continetur.

Quicquid preterea dignitatis, libertatis et competentis ecclesie ac monasterio consuetudinis per regum uel aliorum fidelium scripta loco sidem collatum est, nos quoque huius scripti nostri robore confirmamus, ut uidelicet ecclesia sancti Albani et omnia ad eam pertinentia libera sint ab omni tributo siue regis siue episcopi siue comitis, uicecomitis, ducis nel iudicis et exactoris et omnibus operibus, quae indici solent, uel emendatione pontium, castellorum, parcorum. Omnia etiam pontificalia iura ecclesiarum sancti Albani sub eiusdem abbatis dispositione atque arbitrio pendeant, sicut per iamdictorum predecessorum nostrorum siue regum Anglie Offe scilicet, Egifridi, Adelredi successorumque eorum priuilegia statutum esse dinoscitur. Crisma uero, oleum sanctum, consecrationes altarium seu basilicarum benedictionem abbatis, monachorum seu clericorum ordinationes a quocumque malueritis catholico suscipiatis antistite, qui nimirum nostra fultus auctoritate, quod postulatus fuerit, indulgeat nec negare, quod petieritis, audeat. Obeunte uero te nunc eiusdem loci abbate uel tuorum quolibet successorum nullus ibi qualibet surreptionis astutia seu uiolentia preponatur, sed liceat uobis communi consilio uel partis consilii sanioris secundum Dei timorem et beati Benedicti regulam absque ullius contradictione abbatem eligere. Monachos preterea sancti Albani ubilibet habitantes nulla omnino persona preter Romanum pontificem et legatum, qui ad hoc missus fuerit, excommunicet aut interdicat.

Prohibemus quoque, ut nullus episcopus in eodem cenobio uel adiacentibus ecclesiis, in quibus eiusdem monasterii abbas ius pontificale habere dinoscitur, missas publicas uel conuentum siue synodum celebrare uel cathedram collocare presumat, uniuersaliter statuentes, ne quicumque episcopi uel eorum clerici aut ministri super ipsum monasterium uel super predictas parochiales ecclesias ullam aliquatenus potestatem habeant nec earum presbiteros uel clericos quosque siue laicos sed nec abbatem uel monachos ad synodum suam uel capitulum conuocare uel ab officio diuino suspendere seu aliquid in eos uel minimum ius exercere presumant, sed omnia, quaecumque ecclesiae sancti martyris Albani fuerint, abbatis solummodo eiusdem monasterii potestati tractanda libere subiaceant. Ecclesiae autem, in quibus iura pontificalia non habetis, seu capelle uestre et cimiteria libera

the tithe of Eastwell and Ringetuna, the tithe of Roinges, the church of Kimble with its adjacent land and the land which William, son of Geoffrey gave, that is, one hide in the vill of Ellesborough/Edlesborough from the assarts of Widehale, and one virgate from the wood of the same Widehale as the charter of the donor confirms; for the sacristy from the gift of Hanno in the vill of Chalfont one and a half virgates of land and one assart with free pasture for cattle and pigs; in Yorkshire, the church of Appleton with the church of Almundeby and all their appurtenances; moreover, the cell of Tynemouth, the cell of Binham, the cell of Wymondham, the cell of Wallingford, the cell of Hertford, the cell of Belvoir, the cell of Hatfield, the cell of Beaulieu with all their appurtenances, dignities, and free customs and also other churches, tithes, vills, lands, water courses, meadows, pasturages, woods, rents, and everything pertaining to the monastery or its cells as contained in the written privileges of pontiffs, kings, and other faithful.

Moreover, we confirm by the authority of this our document whatever dignity, liberty, and custom, appropriate for church and monastery, has been conferred on that place in writing by kings and other faithful, so that the church of St Alban and everything pertaining to it shall be free from all tribute to king, bishop, earl, viscount, duke or judge or tax collector and all works which are usually assigned, whether building bridges, castles, or parks. Furthermore, all pontifical rights over the churches of St Albans shall depend on the disposition and judgment of the abbot, as is known to have been established by the privileges of our said predecessors or the kings of England, namely Offa, Egfrith, Aethelred, and their successors. You may receive the chrism, holy oil, consecration of altars or basilicas, the blessing of abbots, the ordination of monks or clerics from whichever Catholic bishop you prefer, who supported by our authority may boldly grant what is requested and not deny what you have asked for. When you, the present abbot of the place or your successors die no one shall be promoted there by any cunning ploy or violence, but you may without any contradiction elect an abbot by common counsel or by the wiser part of the counsel in the fear of God according to the rule of St Benedict. Moreover no person whatever, apart from the Roman pontiff or his legate sent for that purpose may excommunicate or interdict the monks of St Albans, wherever they are living.

And we forbid any bishop to presume to celebrate masses in public or to hold a meeting or synod or set up a cathedral in that monastery or in the adjacent churches in which the abbot of that monastery is known to exercise pontifical rights, and we declare by universal decree that no bishops whatsoever or their clergy or ministers may have any power at all over the monastery itself or the aforesaid parish churches nor may they summon any of their priests, clerics, or laity, or the abbot and monks to their synods or chapters or suspend them from divine office or presume to exercise even the smallest right over them, but all churches belonging to the church of St Alban the Martyr shall be subject only to the power of the abbot of the said monastery to be freely managed. Moreover, the churches in which you do not have pontifical rights, or your chapels and cemeteries shall be free and immune from all exaction apart from the customary right and

sint et ab omni exactione immunia preter consuetam episcopi paratam et iustitiam in presbyteros, si aduersum sui ordinis dignitatem offenderint. In quibus uidelicet ecclesiis uel capellis liceat uobis seu fratribus uestris presbyteros eligere, ita tamen, ut ab episcopis nel episcoporum vicariis animarum curam absque uenalitate suscipiant, quam si committere illi, quod absit, ex prauitate noluerint, tunc presbyteri ex conscientia primatis uel apostolicae sedis legati diuina celebrandi officia licentiam consequantur. Precipimus etiam, ut monachi sancti Albani, sine in cellis siue in custodiis uillarum uel ubicumque constituti fuerint, nec a diuinis suspendantur officiis nec pro qualibet culpa discutiantur aut puniantur nisi ab abbate suo, sed ita per omnia liberi sint ab episcoporum subiectione, ac si in corpore monasterii morarentur, adeo ut tam de monachis quam deuotis et famulis uestris ab abbate pro iustitia requiratur nec cellarum uestrarum ubilibet positarum fratres pro qualibet interdictione uel excommunicatione diuinorum officiorum suspensionem' patiantur, sed tam monachi ipsi quam et famuli eorum et qui se monastice professioni denuouerint, clausis ecclesiarum ianuis, non admissis excommunicatis et interdictis, non pulsatis tintinnabulis humiliori uoce diuina officia celebrent et sepulture eis debita peragant. In ponendis etiam uel remouendis prioribus uel monachis nullus omnino clericus siue laicus se obiciat, sed abbas, qui pro tempore fuerit, ponendi uel remouendi eos, ubi opportunum fuerit, absque alicuius contradictione liberam habeat facultatem, quatinus monachi semper in abbatum suorum potestate permaneant. Preterea si qui fidelium aliquam possessionem monasterio uestro pietatis intuitu conferre uoluerint, nullus audeat impedire. Ad haec sancimus, ne quis fratres uestros post factam in monasterio uestro professionem absque abbatis licentia suscipere audeat uel retinere.

Decernimus ergo, ut nulli omnino hominum liceat supradictum monasterium temere perturbare aut eius possessiones auferre uel ablatas retinere, minuere seu quibuslibet temerariis uexationibus fatigare, sed illibata omnia et integra conseru entur eorum, pro quorum gubernatione et sustentatione concessa sunt, usibus omnimodis profutura, salua nimirum apostolice sedis auctoritate. Ad indicium autem huius a sede apostolica percepte libertatis nobis nostrisque successoribus auri unciam annis singulis persoluetis. Si qua igitur in futurum ecclesiastica secularisue persona hanc nostre constitutionis paginam sciens contra earn temere uenire temptauerit, secundo tertioue commonita, nisi presumptionem suam congrua satisfactione correxerit, potestatis honorisque sui dignitate careat reamque se diuino iudicio existere de perpetrata iniquitate cognoscat et a sacratissimo corpore ac sanguine Dei et domini redemptoris nostri Iesu Christi aliena fiat atque in extremo examine districte ultioni subiaceat. Cunctis autem eidem loco sua iura seruantibus sit pax domini nostri Iesu Christi, quatinus et hic fructum bone actionis percipiant et apud districtum iudicem premia aeterne pacis inueniant. Amen. Amen. Amen.

Ego Adrianus catholicae ecclesiae episcopus ss. BV.
† Ego Imarus Tusculanus episcopus ss.
† Ego Cencius Portuensis et sancte Rufine episcopus ss.

justice of bishops over priests who offend against the dignity of their order. In these churches or chapels, you or your brethren may appoint priests, in such a way that they shall receive from the bishops or from the bishops' vicars the cure of souls without any payment, and if they out of malice shall refuse to commit them to them, then the priests may acquire the right of celebrating divine office from the primate or the legate of the apostolic see. Furthermore, we command that monks of St Albans, whether in the cells or within the vills or wherever they may be, may not be suspended from divine office nor examined or punished for any fault except by their abbot, but they should be as free in all matters from subjection to the bishops as if they were staying within the body of the monastery, so much so that justice in regard to both monks and your faithful and devoted servants should be sought from the abbot, nor should the brethren placed in any of your cells suffer suspension from divine office on account of any interdict or excommunication, but both the monks themselves and their servants and those who have dedicated themselves to the monastic life, may celebrate divine office with closed doors, without admitting excommunicates and those interdicted, without ringing bells and with low voices and they may carry out necessary burials. Furthermore, in the appointment and removal of priors and monks, no cleric or lay person whatsoever may interpose himself, but the abbot who is there for the time being, shall have free power to place or remove them whenever it is appropriate, without the contradiction of anyone, so that the monks shall always remain in the power of their abbot. In addition, if any of the faithful wish out of piety to grant any possession to your monastery, no one may prevent it. To this end we decree that no one may dare to receive or retain your brethren after they have made profession in your monastery without the abbot's licence.

We declare, therefore, that no man whatsoever may rashly disturb the aforesaid monastery or take away its possessions or retain what it has taken or reduce by any kind of rash persecution burden them, but everything shall be conserved whole and unimpaired for the use of those for whose governance and sustenance they had been granted, saving the authority of the apostolic see. As a mark of this liberty received from the apostolic see, you shall pay to us and to our successors, one ounce of gold every year. If any person clerical or lay shall in the future knowingly attempt rashly to contravene this text of our constitution, let him lose the dignity of his power and honour, unless he makes condign satisfaction for his presumption on the second or third warning, and let him know that he will be found guilty in the divine judgment for the wickedness he has committed, and let him be cut off from the most holy Body and Blood of our redeemer Jesus Christ, our Lord and God, and let him undergo severe punishment in the Last Judgment. May all those, however, who preserve the rights of the monastery, have the peace of our lord Jesus Christ, that they may receive the fruits of their good actions in this life and find the reward of eternal peace before the strict Judge. Amen, amen, amen.

I, Adrian, bishop of the Catholic church, have subscribed. B[ene] V[alete]
† I, Imar, bishop of Tusculum, have subscribed
† I, Cencio, bishop of Porto and S. Rufina, have subscribed

† Ego Guido presb. card. tit. sancti Chrisogoni ss.

† Ego Humbaldus presb. card. tit. sancte Praxedis ss.

† Ego Manfredus presb. card. tit. sancte Sauine ss.

† Ego Iulius presb. card. tit. sancti Marcelli ss.

† Ego Bernardus presb. card. sancti Clementis ss.

† Ego Humbaldus presb. card. tit. S. Crucis in Ierusalem ss.

† Ego Octauianus presb. card. tit sancte Cecilie ss.

† Ego Astaldus presb. card. tit. S. Prisce ss.

† Ego Girardus presb. card. tit. sancti Stephani ss.

† Ego Henricus presb. card. tit. sanctorum Nerei et Achillei ss.

     † Ego Ioannes presb. card. tit. sanctorum Siluestri et Martini ss.

     † Ego Oddo diac. card. sancti Georgii ad uelum aureum ss.

     † Ego Guido diac. card. sancte Marie in porticu ss.

     † Ego Iacinctus diac. card. sancte Marie in Cosmydyn ss.

     † Ego Ioannes diac. card. sanctorum Sergii et Bachi ss.

     † Ego Odo diac. card. sancti Nicholai in carcere Tulliano ss.

Datum Beneuenti per manus Rollandi sanctae Romane ecclesie presbyteri cardinalis et cancellarii non. Febru(arii), indictione quarta, incarnationis dominice anno M°. C°. L°. V, pontificatus uero domni Adriani pape IIII anno secundo.

2

Effectum iusta: Adrian IV Rogero abbati ecclesie beati Marie de Bellalanda eiusque fratribus

Lateran, 23 November, 1156.

Latin text from *PUE*, iii, 256–8 no. 116.

Adrianus episcopus seruus seruorum Dei. Dilectis filiis Rogero abbati ecclesie beati Marie de Bellalanda eiusque fratribus tam presentibus quam futuris regularem vitam professis in perpetuum.

Effectum iusta postulantibus indulgere et uigor equitatis et ordo exigit rationis, presertim quando petentium uoluntatem et pietas adiuuat et pietas non relinquit. Quocirca, dilecti in domino filii, uestris iustis postulationibus clementer annuimus et ecclesiam, in qua diuino mancipati estis obsequio, sub beati Petri et nostra protectione suscipimus et presentis scripti priuilegio communimus.

Statuentes ut quascumque possessiones, quecumque bona eadem ecclesia in presentiarum iuste et canonice possidet aut in futurum concessione pontificum, largitione regum uel principum, oblatione fidelium seu aliis iustis modis prestante domino poterit adipisci, firma uobis uestrisque successoribus et illibata permaneant. In quibus hec propriis duximus exprimenda uocabulis: locum illum in quo abbatia ista sita est, que in carta Rogeri de Molbray habentur, Beghlandem, Mortoniam, Wildoniam, Skakedenam, Spaldingtonam, Balastagham, Cambe, Suyleswath et omnia terris istis adiacentia in terras et aqua, in plano et bosco. Libertates

† I, Guido, cardinal priest of the title of S. Crisogono, have subscribed

† I, Humbald, cardinal priest of the title of S. Prassede, have subscribed

† I, Manfredo, cardinal priest of the title of S. Sabina, have subscribed

† I, Bernardo, cardinal priest of the title of S. Clemente, have subscribed

† I, Humbald, cardinal priest of the title of S. Cruce in Gerusalemme, have subscribed

† I, Ottaviano, cardinal priest of the title of S. Cecilia, have subscribed

† I, Astaldo, cardinal priest of the title of S. Prisca, have subscribed

† I, Giraldo, cardinal priest of the title of S. Stefano, have subscribed

† I, Enrico, cardinal priest of the title of SS. Nereo e Achilleo, have subscribed

† I, Giovanni, cardinal priest of the title of SS. Silvestro e Martino, have subscribed

> † I, Odo, cardinal deacon of S. Giorgio in Velabro, have subscribed

> † I, Guido, cardinal deacon of S. Maria in Porticu, have subscribed

> † I, Iacincto, cardinal deacon of S. Maria in Cosmedin, have subscribed

> † I, Giovanni, cardinal priest of the title of SS. Sergio e Baccho, have subscribed

> † I, Odo, cardinal deacon of S. Nicola in carcere Tulliano, have subscribed.

Given at Benevento by the hands of Roland, cardinal priest and chancellor of the holy Roman church, on 5 February, in the fourth indiction, in the year of the Lord's incarnation 1155, in the second year of the pontificate of the lord pope Adrian IV.

2
Effectum iusta: Adrian IV to Abbot Roger of the church of St Mary of Byland and his brethren

Lateran, 23 November, 1156.

Bishop Adrian, servant of the servants of God, to his dear sons Roger, abbot of the church of St Mary of Byland and his brethren, present and future, who profess the regular life, for ever.

The force of equity and the order of reason require that those who ask for what is right should be granted the accomplishment of their desires, especially when the petitioners' wish is supported, and not deserted, by piety. Therefore, dear sons in the Lord, we have compassionately approved your just petitions and we receive the church in which you are bound to the service of God into the protection of St Peter and of ourselves and confirm it to you by the authority of the present letter.

We ordain that whatever possessions or goods that church now possesses canonically and justly or shall in the future with the Lord's help acquire through the gift of pontiffs, the generosity of kings or princes, the offering of the faithful, or by any other lawful means, shall remain fixed and undiminished to you and to your successors. From these we have selected the following to be listed by their proper names: the place in which the abbey is sited, according to the boundaries contained in the charter of Roger de Mowbray, Byland, Morton, Wildoniam, Skakedenam, Spaldingtonam, Balastagham, Cambe, Suyleswath, and everything adjacent to them, in lands and water, plain, and wood. We confirm also by apostolic authority

etiam seu immunitates ac regias consuetudines a carissimo filio nostro Henrico Anglorum rege rationabiliter uobis et ecclesie uestre indultas et scripti sui pagina roboratas auctoritate apostolica confirmamus et illibatas perpetuis temporibus statuimus permanere. Sane laborum noualium uestrorum, que propriis manibus autsumptibus colitis, siue de nutrimentis animalium uestrorum, nullus omnino clericus uel laicus a uobis decimas exigere presumat. Adicientes preterea constituimus, ut si super decimis inter uos et aliquam personam ecclesiasticam cum consensu archidiaconi episcopi sui compositio rationabiliter facta est, rata perpetuis temporibus et inconcussa persistat. Si qua uero libera et absoluta persona pro redemptione anime sue uestro monasterio se conferre uoluerit, suscipiendi eam liberam facultatem habeatis. Addentes etiam auctoritate apostolica interdicimus, ne quis fratres uestros clericos siue laicos post factam in uestro monasterio professionem absque uestra liuentia suscipere audeat uel retinere.

Presenti quoque decreto sancimus, ut episcopus, in cuius episcopatu eccesia uestra consistit, nec regularem electionem abbatis uestri umquam impediat nec de remouendo aut depionendo eo, qui pro tempore fuerit, contra statuta Cisterciensis ordinis et auctoritatem priuilegiorum suorum se ullatenus intromittat. Sancimus autem, ne quis archiepiscopus uel episcopus siue cuiuslibet ordinis locum uestrum a diuinis interdicat officiis, sed liceat uobis omni tempore clausis ianuis et exclusis excommunicatis et interdictis diuina officia celebrare, nisi abbatis uel fratrum ipsius loci euidens et manifesta culpa extiterit. Paci quoque et tranquillitati uestre paterna sollicitudine prouidentes auctoritate apostolica prohibemus, ut infra clausarum locorum siue grangiarum uestrarum nullus uiolentiam uel rapinam siue furtum facere uel hominem capere audeat, et si quis hoc temerario ausu presumpserit, tamquam sacrilegus iudicetur et excommunicationis ultione plectetur.

Decernimus ergo, ut nulli omnino hominum liceat prefatam ecclesiam temere perturbare aut eius possessiones auferre uel ablatas retinere, minuere seu quibuslibet temerariis uexationibus fatigare, sed illibata omnia et integra conseruentur eorum, pro quorum gubernatione et sustentatione concessa sunt, usibus omnimodis profutura, salua nimirum sedis apostolice auctoritate et diocesani episcopi canonica reuerentia. Si qua igitur in futurum ecclesiastica secularisue persona hanc nostre constitutionis paginam sciens contra earn temere uenire temptauerit, secundo tertioue commonita, nisi presumptionem suam congrua satisfactione correxerit, potestatis honorisque sui dignitate careat reamque se diuino iudicio existere de perpetrata iniquitate cognoscat et a sacratissimo corpore ac sanguine Dei et domini redemptoris nostri Iesu Christi aliena fiat atque in extremo examine districte ultioni subiaceat. Cunctis autem eidem loco sua iura seruantibus sit pax domini nostri Iesu Christi, quatinus et hic fructum bone actionis percipiant et apud districtum iudicem premia eterne pacis inueniant. Amen.

Dat. Lat. per manum Rolandi sancte Romane ecclesie presbiteri cardinalis et cancellarii IX kal. decembris, indictione [V], incarnationis dominice anno M^{o}. C^{o}. LVI^{to}, pontificatus uero domni Adriani pape quarti anno secundo.

the liberties and immunities or royal customs reasonably conferred on your church by our dearest son in Christ, Henry, King of the English, and confirmed by the written authority of his charter and ordain that they shall remain inviolate for all time. Let no-one whatsoever, whether cleric or lay, presume to exact tithes from you from the new lands which you cultivate with your own hands or from the fodder of your animals. Additionally, we have established that any agreement concerning tithe, which you have reasonably made with an ecclesiastical person with the assent of his bishop's archdeacon shall remain valid and firm for all time. You may have full liberty to receive any free and unattached person who wishes to give himself to your monastery for the redemption of his soul, and we forbid by apostolic authority anyone to dare to receive or retain any of your brethren, whether clerical or lay, after they have made profession in your monastery.

By the present decree we forbid the bishop in whose diocese your monastery is established to impede the regular election of your abbot or to participate in the removal or deposition of any abbot, contrary to the statutes of the Cistercian Order and the authority of this privilege. Moreover, we forbid archbishops and bishops to interdict the celebration of divine office in any place belonging to you, and you are permitted to celebrate divine office at all times, with closed doors and excommunicates and interdicts excluded, unless the manifest fault of the abbots or brethren of the place shall be evident. As we make provision for your peace and tranquillity with paternal solicitude, we forbid by apostolic authority that anyone shall commit violence or plunder or theft within the boundaries of your estates or granges or dare to seize a man there, and let anyone who rashly presumes so to do be judged to have committed sacrilege and be struck with the penalty of excommunication.

Therefore we declare that no man whatever may rashly disturb the forenamed church or carry off its property or keep what has been taken away, or reduce or harass it by any kind of hardship, but everything shall be preserved whole and inviolate to those for whose governance and sustenance they were granted, to be used for their advantage in any manner, saving the authority of the apostolic see and the canonical respect due to the diocesan bishop. If any person clerical or lay shall in the future knowingly attempt rashly to contravene this text of our constitution, let him lose the dignity of his power and honour, unless he makes condign satisfaction for his presumption on the second or third warning, and let him know that he will be found guilty in the divine judgment for the wickedness he has committed, and let him be cut off from the most holy Body and Blood of our redeemer Jesus Christ, our Lord and God, and let him undergo severe punishment in the Last Judgment. May all those, however, who preserve the rights of the monastery, have the peace of our lord Jesus Christ, that they may receive the fruits of their good actions in this life and find the reward of eternal peace before the strict Judge. Amen.

Given at the Lateran by the hand of Roland, cardinal priest and chancellor of the holy Roman Church, on the 11th kalends of December, in the [fifth] indiction, in the year of the Lord's Incarnation 1156, and the second year of the pontificate of the lord pope Adrian IV.

3
Religiosam uitam: Adrianus Roberto abbati monasterii sancti Albani eiusque fratribus

Lateran, 14 May, 1157.

Latin text from *PUE*, iii, 258–61 no. 118.

Adrianus episcopus servus servorum Dei. Dilectis filiis Roberto abbati monasterii sancti Albani eiusque fratribus tam presentibus quam futuris regularem vitam professis in perpetuum.

Religiosam uitam eligentibus apostolicum conuenit adesse presidium, ne forte cuiuslibet temeritatis incursus aut eos a proposito reuocet aut robur quod absit sacre religionis infringat. Eapropter, dilecti in domino filii, uestris iustis postulationibus clementer annuimus et prefatum monasterium, quod ad ius beati Petri proprie spectare dinoscitur, sub beati Petri et nostra protectione suscipimus et presentis scripti priuilegio communimus.

Statuentes ut quascumque possessiones, quecumque bona idem monasterium in presentiarum iuste et canonice possidet aut in futurum concessione pontificum, largitione regum uel principum, oblatione fidelium seu aliis iustis modis prestante domino poterit adipisci, firma uobis uestrisque successoribus et illibata permaneant. In quibus hec propriis duximus exprimenda uocabulis: ecclesiam beati Petri in uilla sancti Albani, ecclesiam sancti Stephani, ecclesias de Kingesberia, de Watford, de Richemarewrtha de Langeliga, de Redburna, de Cudicota, de Waldena, de Hecstanestuna, de Nortuna, de Newenham, de Wineslawe, de Estuna, de Barnet. Statuimus autem, ut predicte ecclesie cum capellis suis et parrochiarum finibus ab omni episcoporum subiectione libere penitus habeantur nec alicui episcoporum liceat presbiteros aut clerios sius laicos sed nec abbatem uel monachos ad synodum suam uel capitulum conuocare uel ab officio diuino suspendere seu aliquod in eos uel minimum ius nullatenus exercere, sed omnia pontificalia earum iura abbatis solummodo monasterii beati Albani potestati libere subiaceant disponenda.

Nolumus enim, ut alicui nisi tantum Romano pontifici debeant in aliqno respondere. Cui etiam abbati licitum sit, sicut et mos hactenus inoleuit, personam quam uoluerit de suis constituere, que curam animarum sub eo gerat et archidiaconi officium in omnibus impleat. Verum ne per huius dignitatis prerogatiuam abbatis predicti monastorium aliquo tempore faciliorom fortassis habeat ad episcopatum accessum, auctoritate apostolica interdicimus, ne umquam in monasterio beati Albani sedes episcopalis constituatur, ne occasione ista monachi quandoque dispositioni subiaceant clericorum et claustralis quies turbetur nec non et regularis obseruantie disciplina simul cum substantia monastorii minuatur, sed cunctis in posterum temporibus ecclesia sancti Albani non episcopum, sed abbatem, a quo regatur, habeat, qui ob reuerentiam eiusdem preciosi martyris pontificalis dignitatis honorern, in quantum abbati concedi fas est, debeat optinere. Videlicet ut, sicut ei per antiqua priuilegia concessum est habere omnia pontificalia iura, ita et pontifi-

3
Religiosam uitam: Adrian IV
to Abbot Robert of St Albans and his brethren

Lateran, 14 May, 1157.

Bishop Adrian, servant of the servants of God, to his dear sons Robert, abbot of the monastery of St Alban and his brethren present and future who profess the regular life, for ever.

It is appropriate that Apostolic protection should be given to those who choose the regular life, lest any rash assault should either call them back from their purpose or, which God forbid, weaken the vigour of holy religion. For this reason, dear sons in the Lord, we have compassionately approved your just petitions, and we receive the foresaid monastery, which is known to belong to the right of St Peter, into the protection of St Peter and ourselves, and we confirm this to you by the privilege of this present letter.

We declare that whatever possessions, whatever goods that same monastery now possesses canonically and justly or shall in the future obtain with the Lord's help through the gift of pontiffs, the generosity of kings or princes, the offering of the faithful, or by any other lawful means, shall remain fixed and undiminished to you and your successors. From these we have selected the following to be listed by their proper names: the church of St Peter in the town of St Albans, the church of St Stephen, the churches of Kingsbury, Watford, Rickmansworth, Langley, Redbourn, Codicote, Walden, Hecstanestuna, Norton, Newnham, Wimslow, Easton, Barnet. We have moreover ordained that the forenamed churches together with their chapels and the confines of their parishes shall be held entirely free from subjection to any bishop, nor shall any bishop be permitted to summon priests, clergy, laymen, neither the abbot nor the monks to his synod or summon a chapter or suspend divine office or exercise even the smallest right over them, but let all pontifical rights be freely subject to the disposition of the abbot of the monastery of St Alban.

For we do not desire that they should be compelled to answer for anything except to the Roman Pontiff. It shall be lawful for the abbot to appoint whichever of his subjects he wishes to exercise the cure of souls under his authority and fulfil the office of archdeacon in all respects, as has hitherto been the custom. Lest the prerogative of this dignity of the abbot of this monastery should any time provide an easier avenue for the setting up of a bishopric, by apostolic authority we forbid any episcopal see ever to be set up in the monastery of St Alban, lest on that account the monks should ever be subject to clerics and the quiet of the cloister be disturbed or the discipline of regular observance together with the substance of the monastery be diminished, but let the church of St Albans be ruled in all future times not by a bishop but by an abbot, who should enjoy the honour of pontifical dignity, so far as it is lawful to concede it to an abbot, out of respect for the precious martyr: namely, since he has every episcopal right, as granted to him by

calia habeat ornamenta, mitram scilicet, cyrothecas, anulum et sandalia, ita tamen ut numquam hac occasione intra claustra monasterii uel in loco, ubi regularis obseruantia debet custodiri, abbas ipse presumat uti uel cappa clericali uel seculari aliquo indumento, sed monastici habitus reuerentiam in omnibus diligenter obseruet et formam religionis pretendere intuentium oculis comprobetur, ut, sicut beatus Albanus prothomartyr esse dinoscitur, ita et abbas monasterii ipsius inter abbates Anglie primus omni tempore dignitatis ordine habeatur et in susceptione benedictionis sue cunctis in posterum diebus soli Romane ecclesie professionem obediencie debeat exhibere. Interdicimus etiam, ne quilibet episcopus in ecclesia sancti Albani uel intra fines parrochie eius aliquod sibi ius uendicare presumat uel sollempnem processionem exigendi uel regem coronandi aut aliquod episcopale officium exercendi.

Prohibemus insuper, ne abbati quecumque persona qualibet occasione in uestro monasteno preponatur. Decernimus ergo, ut nulli omnino hominum liceat supradictum monasterium temere pertubare aut eius possessiones auferre uel ablatas retinere, minuere seu quibuslibet uexationibus fatigare, sed illibata omnia et integra conseruentur eorum, pro quorum gubernatione et sustentatione concessa sunt usibus omnimodis profutura, salua nimirum apostolice sedis auctoritate. Ad indicium autem huius a sede apostolica percepte libertatis unam unciam auri nobis nostrisque successoribus annis singulis persoluetis. Si qua igitur in futurum ecclesiastica secularisue persona hanc nostre constitutionis paginam sciens contra eam temere uenire temptauerit, secundo tertioue commonita, nisi presumptionem suam congrua satisfactione correxerit, potestatis honorisque uel dignitate careat reamque se diuino iudicio existere de perpetrata iniquitate cognoscat et a sacratissimo corpore ac sanguine Dei et domini redemptoris nostri Iesu Christi aliena fiat atque in extremo examine districte ultioni subiaceat. Cunctis autem eidem loco sua iura seruantibus sit pax domini nostri Iesu Christi, quatinus et hic fructum bone actionis percipiant et apud districtum iudicem premia eterne pacis inueniant. Amen.

Ego Adrianus catholice ecclesie episcopus ss.
† Ego Gregorius Sabinensis episcopus ss.
† Ego Manfredus presb. card. tit. [sancte Sabine] ss.
† Ego Iulius presb. card. tit. sancti Marcelli ss.
† Ego Humbaldus presb. card. tit. sancte Crucis in Ierusalem ss.
† Ego Octauianus presb. card. tit. sancte Cecilie ss.
† Ego Gerardus presb. card. tit. sancti Stephani in Celio monte ss.
† Ego Ioannes presb. card. sanctorum Ioannis et Pauli tit. Pammachii ss.
    † Ego Odo diac. card. sancti Georgii ad nelum aureum ss.
    † Ego Rodulfus diac. card. sancti Lucie in Septa solis ss.

Dat. Lat. per manum Rolandi sancte Romane ecclesie presbyteri cardinalis et cancellarii II. idus maii, indictione V., incarnationis dominice anno M°CL°VII., pontificatus uero domni Adriani pape anno tercio.

ancient privileges, so should he have episcopal ornaments, namely the mitre, gloves, ring and sandals, but in such a way that he may never by reason of this presume to wear either the clerical cloak or any secular dress within the monastic cloister or in any other place where regular observance should be maintained, but he should diligently observe the reverence of the monastic habit in all things and be acknowledged to set a model of religion before the eyes of onlookers so that, like the blessed protomartyr Alban, the abbot of his monastery should for ever be first in rank and dignity among the abbots of England, and for all future time should profess obedience only to the Roman Church, when he receives his blessing. Moreover we forbid that any bishop should presume to claim any right for himself in the church of St Alban or within the confines of its parish in holding processions, crowning kings, or exercising any kind of episcopal office.

Finally we forbid that any person whatever be placed before the abbot in your monastery for whatever reason. Therefore we declare that no man whatever may rashly disturb the above-named monastery or carry off its property or keep what has been taken away, or reduce or harass it by any kind of hardship, but everything shall be preserved whole and inviolate to those for whose governance and sustenance they were granted, to be used for their advantage in any manner, saving the authority of the Apostolic See. As a mark of the reception of this freedom from the Apostolic See, you are to pay one ounce of gold to us and to our successors every year. If any person clerical or lay shall in the future knowingly attempt rashly to contravene this text of our constitution, let him lose the dignity of his power and honour, unless he makes condign satisfaction for his presumption on the second or third warning, and let him know that he will be found guilty in the divine judgment for the wickedness he has committed, and let him be cut off from the most holy Body and Blood of our redeemer Jesus Christ, our Lord and God, and let him undergo severe punishment in the Last Judgment. May all those, however, who preserve the rights of the monastery, have the peace of our lord Jesus Christ, that they may receive the fruits of their good actions in this life and find the reward of eternal peace before the strict Judge. Amen.

I Adrian, bishop of the Catholic church, have subscribed.

† I Gregory, bishop of Sabina, have subscribed.

† I Manfred, cardinal priest of the title [of S. Sabina], have subscribed.

† I Julius, cardinal priest of the title of S. Marcello, have subscribed.

† I Humbald, cardinal priest of the title of S. Croce in Gerusalemme, have subscribed.

† I Octavian, cardinal priest of S. Cecilia, have subscribed.

† I Gerard, cardinal priest of the title of S. Stefano in Monte Celio, have subscribed.

† I John, cardinal priest of SS. Giovanni e Paolo of the title of the Pammachii, have subscribed.

† I Odo, cardinal deacon of S. Giorgio ad Velum Aureum, have subscribed.

† I Rodolfo, cardinal deacon of S. Luca in Septa Solis, have subscribed.

Given at the Lateran by the hand of Roland, cardinal priest and chancellor of the holy Roman Church, on the 2nd Ides of May, in the fifth indiction, in the year of the Lord's Incarnation 1157, and the third year of the pontificate of the lord pope Adrian.

4
Carta Oddonis de Poli

Latin text from *Liber censuum*, 387–8 no. 101.

Transcriptum cartule Oddonis de Poli de tota terra sua, quam beato Petro et sancte Romane Ecclesie in proprietatem donavit in perpetuum.

In nomine Domini, Anno dominice incarnationis MCLVII, anno vero tertio pontificatus Domni Adriani IIII Pape, indictione v, mense Januario, die xvii. Quoniam exemplo veterum sapientum usque ad nos multis auctoritatibus significat[o] protractum est, ut memoria gestarum rerum litteris commendetur, quatenus earum inspectione, omni oblivionis nube amota, veritas apud homines clarescere possit: idcirco ego quidem Oddo, qui vocor de Poli, hac die, propria spontaneaque voluntate mea et inter vivos non causa mortis investiens, ad propriam perpetuamque hereditatem trado, dono, et offero Deo et beato Petro apostolo et tibi predicto domino, patri, et totius christianitatis capiti, Adriano IIII Pape, tuisque successoribus in perpetuo et cui largiri et concedere volueris; id est totam et integram meam terram, videlicet Poli, et Fustuano et Anticuli et rocha, que vocatur de Nibli (Rocca di Nibli), et monte qui dicitur Manno (Monte Manno) et Gadabiolo, et Sarracenisco, et rocha, quae vocatur de Muri (Rocca di Muri), et Castellus novus; et ubicumque mihi in aliis locis et vocabulis quolibet modo pertinet, una cum omnibus suis edificiis, munitionibus, turribus, domibus, ortis, canapinis et vineis, terris, sementis, villis, silvis et pantanis, pratis et arnariis, fontibus, rivis, aque, aquarumque discursibus, aquimolis et lacora, montibus, collibus, plagis et planitiis, vacuum et plenum et cum omnibus suis usibus et utilitatibus vel pertinentiis; sicut mihi predicta omnia quocumque modo competunt, taliter ea tibi, tuisque successoribus concedo, et inter vivos, noncausa mortis, irrevocabiliter dono et offero, et investiens ad perpetuam hereditatem trado: ita ut amodo in antea licentiam et potestatem habetis ibidem introeundi, videlicet fruendi, possidendi, et quidquid volueritis faciendi sine mea meorum heredum contrarietate. Quod si contra hec, que dicta sunt, quodam modo venire, et si opus aut necesse fuerit, si eam defendere noluere aut non potuero, tam ego quam mei heredes simus tibi tuisque successoribus composituri pro pena centum libras obrizi auri: et soluta pena hec perpetua donationis cartula firma nichilominus et stabilis permaneat. Quam scribendam rogavi Astaldum sancte Romane Ecclesie scriniarium, in mense et indictione suprascripta v:

† Signum manus predicti Oddonis huius cartule ad confirmandum quod superius dicere rogavit.

Testes, Oddo scilicet [filius quondam?] Petri Benedicti de Bona de Insula, Petrus filius quondam Alexandri Cirici Domne Bone, Berardus de Rigofrigidu, Alexius Scrinarius de Albano, Petrus Ritius, Petrus buticularius.

Ego Astaldus Domini gratia sancte Romane Ecclesie scrinarius, sicut rogatus fui et vidi et audivi, scripsi, complevi et absolvi.

4
Charter of Odo di Poli

Transcription of the deed of Odo di Poli touching all his land which he granted in proprietary right to Blessed Peter and the Holy Roman Church in perpetuity.

In the name of our Lord. In the year of the Lord's Incarnation 1157, and in the third year of the pontificate of the lord pope Adrian IV, in the fifth indiction, in the month of January on the seventeenth day. Since by the example of the wise men of old indicated by many authorities down to our own day, the practice has continued that the record of history should be entrusted to writing, so that by the inspection of it, with all the cloud of doubt removed, truth can shine forth among men. Therefore, I, Odo, who am called 'of Poli', on this day, by my own spontaneous will and investing it amongst the living and not for the sake of death, deliver, present and offer for individual and perpetual inheritance to God and to the blessed Peter, the Apostle, and to you, Pope Adrian IV, the aforesaid lord, father and head of all Christendom, and to your successors in perpetuity and to whomsoever you may wish to grant and yield it; my land, whole and complete, namely, Poli and Giustiniano and Anticoli Corrado, and the rock which is called 'de Nibli' and the mountain which is called Manno and Guadagnolo and Saracinesco and the rock which is called 'de Muri' and Castel Nuovo; and wheresoever belongs to me in any way or in other places and under other names, together with all their buildings, fortifications, towers, houses, gardens, wine cellars and vineyards, lands, crops, farmsteads, woods and new plantations, meadows and sheep pastures, springs, streams of water and rivulets, aqueducts, water courses, watermills and mill-ponds, mountains, hills, tracts and plains, empty and full, and with all their uses and utilities or appurtenances; as all the aforesaid belong to me in whatsoever way, so I yield them to you and to your successors, and I give and offer them irrevocably among the living and not for the sake of death, and I deliver them, investing them for an everlasting inheritance, so that you may have licence and power henceforth, of entering there, enjoying, possessing and doing with them whatsoever you wish without opposition from me and my heirs. But if circumstances occur contrary in any way to these which have been described, and, if needful or necessary, if I am unwilling or unable to defend it, then let both I and my heirs be liable to pay one hundred pounds in pure gold to you and your successors as compensation and when the compensation is paid, let this perpetual deed of gift nevertheless remain firm and steadfast. For the writing of which I have asked Astaldo, archivist of the Holy Roman Church, in the month and fifth indiction written above:

† Sign manual of the said Odo confirming what he asked to be said above.

Witnesses, Odo, that is [son of the late] Pietro Benedetto de Bona de Insula, Pietro, son of the late Alessandro Cirici Domne Bonae, Berardo de Rigofrigido, Alessio, archivist of Albano, Pietro Ritio, Pietro the Butler.

I, Astaldo, by the Lord's grace, archivist of the Holy Roman Church have written, completed and fulfilled just as I was asked and saw and heard.

5
Carta pro Oddoni de Poli

From *Liber censuum*, 388, no. 102.

Exemplum alterius cartule super eadem re.

In nomine Domini. Anno dominice incarnationis et cetera usque idcirco. Nos quidem Rollandus presbyter cardinalis tituli sancti Marci domni pape cancellarius et Boso diaconus sancti Cosme et Damiani domni pape camerarius, ex mandato et voluntate predicti domni Adriani IIII pape, hac die propria spontaneaque nostra voluntate sicut ipse nobis commisit et potestatem dedit, concedimus et investimus, tradimus et in feudum damus tibi Oddo de Poli et heredibus tuis legitimis quos sibi in testamento constituerit in perpetuum, id est Poli et Sustiniano et Anticuli et rocca que vocatur de Nibli et cetera ut supra, cum omnibus suis pertinentiis, sicut ecclesie beati Petri apostoli et predicto domno Adriano quocumque modo competit, taliter eas tibi concedimus, tradimus et in feodo damus, sub hac conditione quod tu et supradicti heredes tui et heredes heredum tuorum in perpetuum predicto domno pape et successoribus suis facies et facient in perpetuum fidelitatem sine alio feudo. Et hoc feudum jam dictus domnus papa et successoribus sui tibi et supradictis heredibus in perpetuum auferre pro nulla re potestatem habeant, nisi tu et heredes tui in nobis vel contra nos aliquid tale quod absit feceritis, quod juste et juditio tuorum bonorum parium amittere debeatis qui in te inimicitiam non habeant, et insuper licenciam habeas pro tua anima centum libras luccenses vel valens centum libras reliquere, ita ut amodo in antea ut predictum est licentiam et potestatem habeas ibidem introeundi, tenendi, possidendi, lucrandi, et ut superius dicit faciendi. Quod si contra hec que dicta sunt quodam modo venire temptaverimus et, si opus aut necesse fuerit, si eam defendere nolumus aut non poterimus, tam nos quam nostri successors simus tibi tuisque heredibus composituri pro pena centum libras auri et soluta pena hec cartula firma permaneat. Quam scribendam rogavi Astaldum scrinarium in mense et indictione suprascripta v.

Signum manus † supradicti Orlandi presbyteri cardinalis cancellarii et Bosonis diaconi cardinalis camerarii hujus cartule rogatoris ad confirmandum quod superius legitur. Odo filius quondam Petri Benedicti de Bona de Insula testis, Berardus de Rigofrigido testis, Alexius scrinarius de Albano testis, Petrus Ricius testis, Petrus buttilierius testis.

Ego Astaldus Domini gratis, etc. ut supra.

5
Charter for Odo di Poli

Copy of a second charter relating to the same matter.

In the name of the Lord. In the year of the Lord's incarnation etc. as far as 'id-circo'. We, Rolandus, cardinal priest of the title of San Marco, chancellor of the Lord pope, and Boso, cardinal deacon of SS Cosma e Damiano, chamberlain of the Lord pope, according to the will and mandate of the aforesaid Lord pope, Adrian IV, on this day by our own spontaneous will as he has entrusted to us and given us the power, yield and invest, deliver and give in fee to you, Oddo de Poli and your lawful heirs whom he has appointed for himself in his will for ever, that is, Poli and Giustiniano and Anticoli and the rock which is called 'de Nibli' and the rest as above, with all their appurtenances, as belongs to the church of the blessed Peter the apostle and the aforesaid Lord Adrian in whatever way, so we yield them to you, deliver and give in fee, under the condition that you and your aforesaid heirs and the heirs of your heirs forever will do fealty to the Lord pope and his successors without other fee. And let the aforesaid Lord pope and his successors have power to remove this fee from you and your aforesaid heirs for ever for no reason unless you and your heirs do in connection with us or (may it not be so) against us something which justly and by the judgement of your good equals who have no enmity against you, you ought not to pay for, and in addition may you have the licence for your soul to relinquish a hundred pounds in money of Lucca or the value of a hundred pounds so that in future you may have licence and power of entering there, holding, possessing, making profit and doing as is stated above. But if we try to go in some way contrary to what has been said, and, if it is needful and necessary, we are unwilling or unable to defend it, let us and our successors be ready to agree with you and your heirs for a penalty of a hundred pounds of gold and when this penalty is paid let this deed remain firm.

I have asked Astaldo, the notary, to write it in the month and indiction written above. Sign manual † of the above-mentioned Orlando (Rolandus), cardinal priest and chancellor, and of Boso, cardinal deacon, proposer of this charter, to confirm what is read above. Odo son of the late Pietro Benedetto de Bona de Insula, witness; Bernardo de Rigofrigido, witness; Alessio, archivist of Albano, witness; Pietro Ritio, witness; Pietro the Butler, witness.

I Astaldo, by the Lord's grace, etc., as above.

Index